BINGE-WORTHY

PIZZA

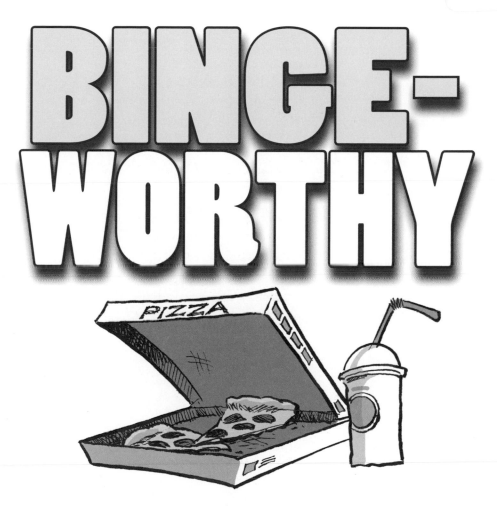

ALSO BY JERRY SCOTT AND JIM BORGMAN

Zits: Sketchbook 1
Growth Spurt: Zits Sketchbook 2
Don't Roll Your Eyes at Me, Young Man!: Zits Sketchbook 3
Are We an "Us"?: Zits Sketchbook 4
Zits Unzipped: Zits Sketchbook 5
Busted!: Zits Sketchbook 6
Road Trip: Zits Sketchbook 7
Teenage Tales: Zits Sketchbook No. 8
Thrashed: Zits Sketchbook No. 9
Pimp My Lunch: Zits Sketchbook No. 10
Are We Out of the Driveway Yet?: Zits Sketchbook No. 11
Rude, Crude, and Tattooed: Zits Sketchbook No. 12
Jeremy and Mom
Pierced
Lust and Other Uses for Spare Hormones
Jeremy & Dad
You're Making That Face Again
Drive!
Triple Shot, Double Pump, No Whip Zits
Zits en Concert
Peace, Love, and Wi-Fi
Zits Apocalypse
Extra Cheesy Zits
What Was That All About?: 20 Years of Strips and Stories
Dance Like Everybody's Watching!
Not Sparking Joy
Screentime
Undivided Inattention

TREASURIES

Humongous Zits
Big Honkin' Zits
Zits: Supersized
Random Zits
Crack of Noon
Alternative Zits
My Bad
Sunday Brunch

GIFT BOOK

A Zits Guide to Living with Your Teenager

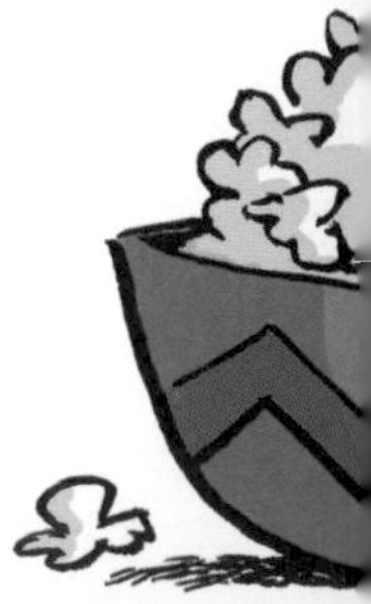

BINGE-WORTHY ZITS®

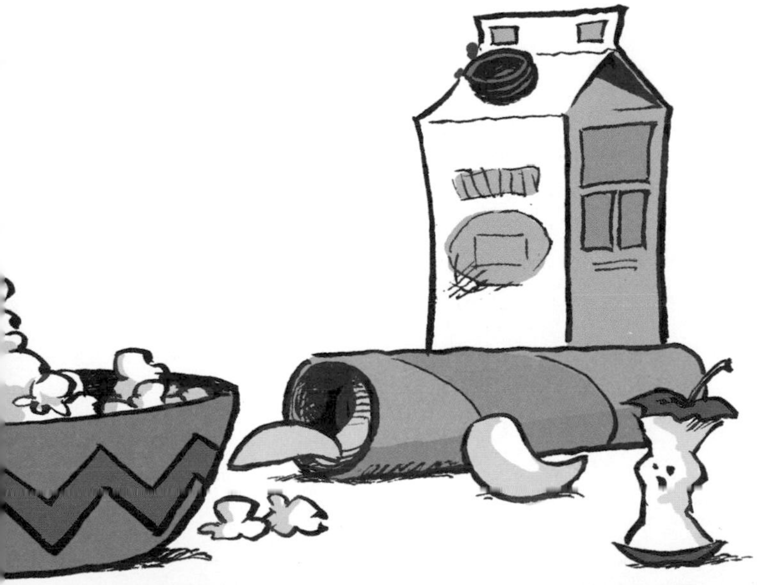

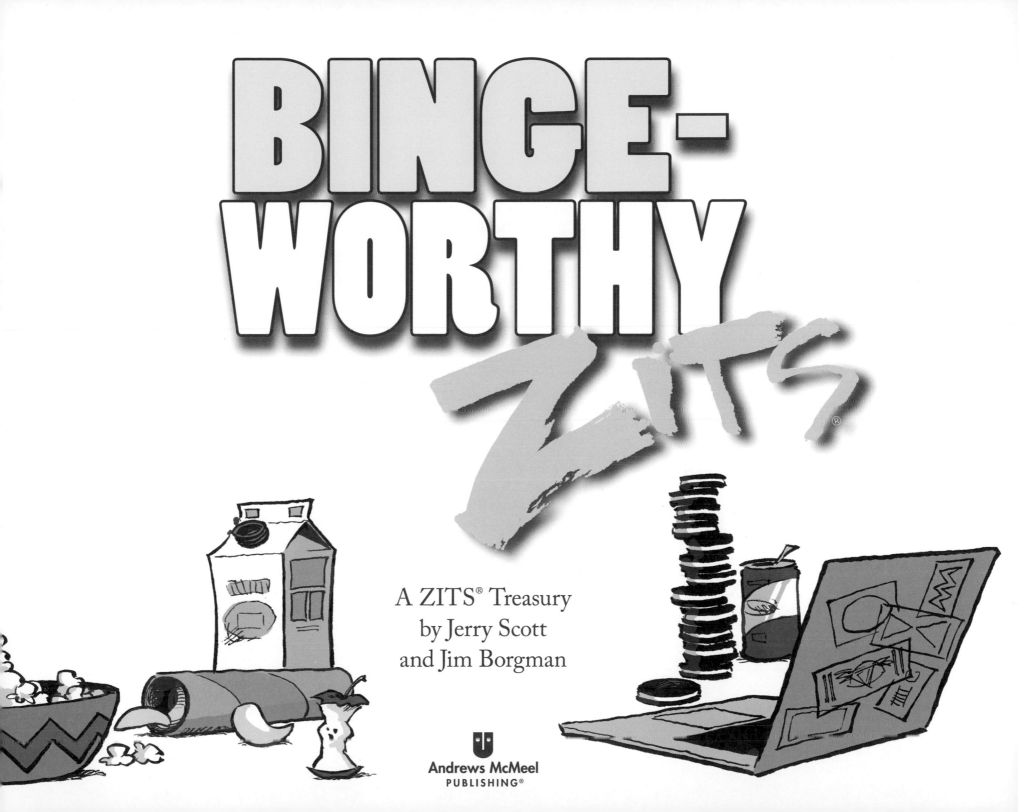

A ZITS® Treasury
by Jerry Scott
and Jim Borgman

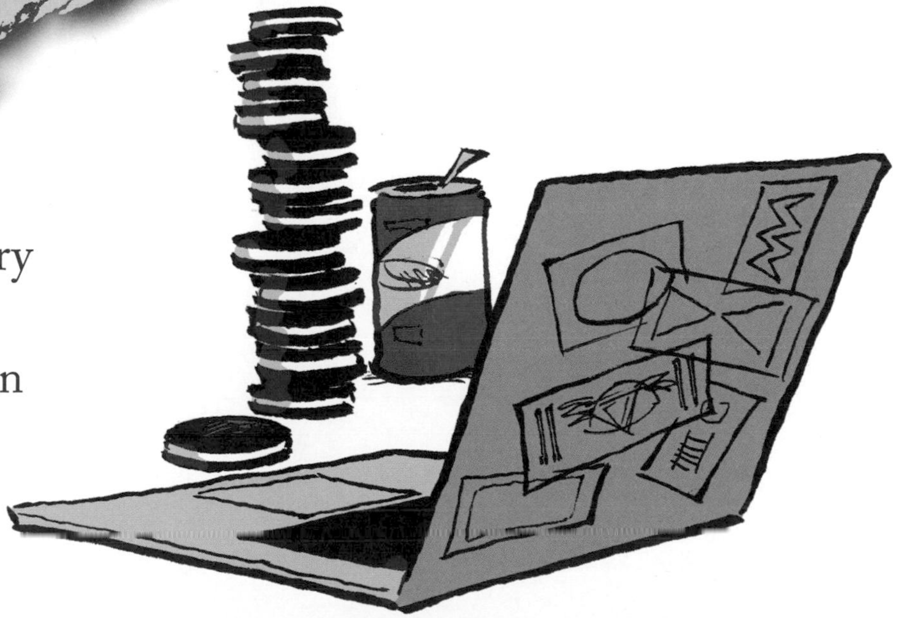

Andrews McMeel
PUBLISHING®

For the musicians, podcasters, webmasters, streamers, filmmakers, writers, online museum guides, audiobook readers, cartoonists, and comedians, who kept our heads above water during these crazy times.

—JS and JB

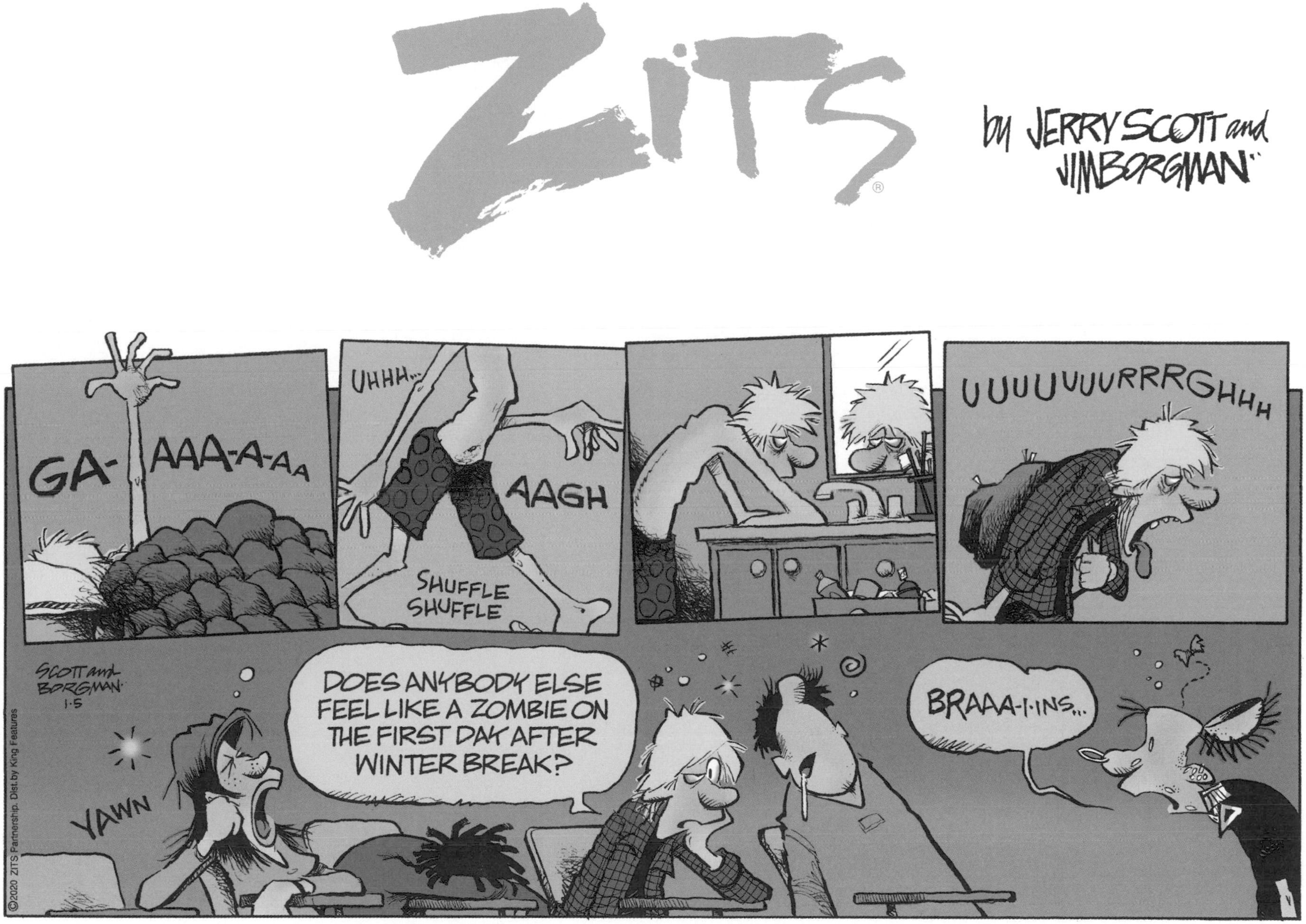
ZITS
by JERRY SCOTT and JIM BORGMAN
GA- AAA-A-AA
UHHH...
AAGH
SHUFFLE SHUFFLE
UUUUUUURRRGHHH
SCOTT and BORGMAN 1·5
©2020 ZITS Partnership. Dist. by King Features
YAWN
DOES ANYBODY ELSE FEEL LIKE A ZOMBIE ON THE FIRST DAY AFTER WINTER BREAK?
BRAAA-I-INS...

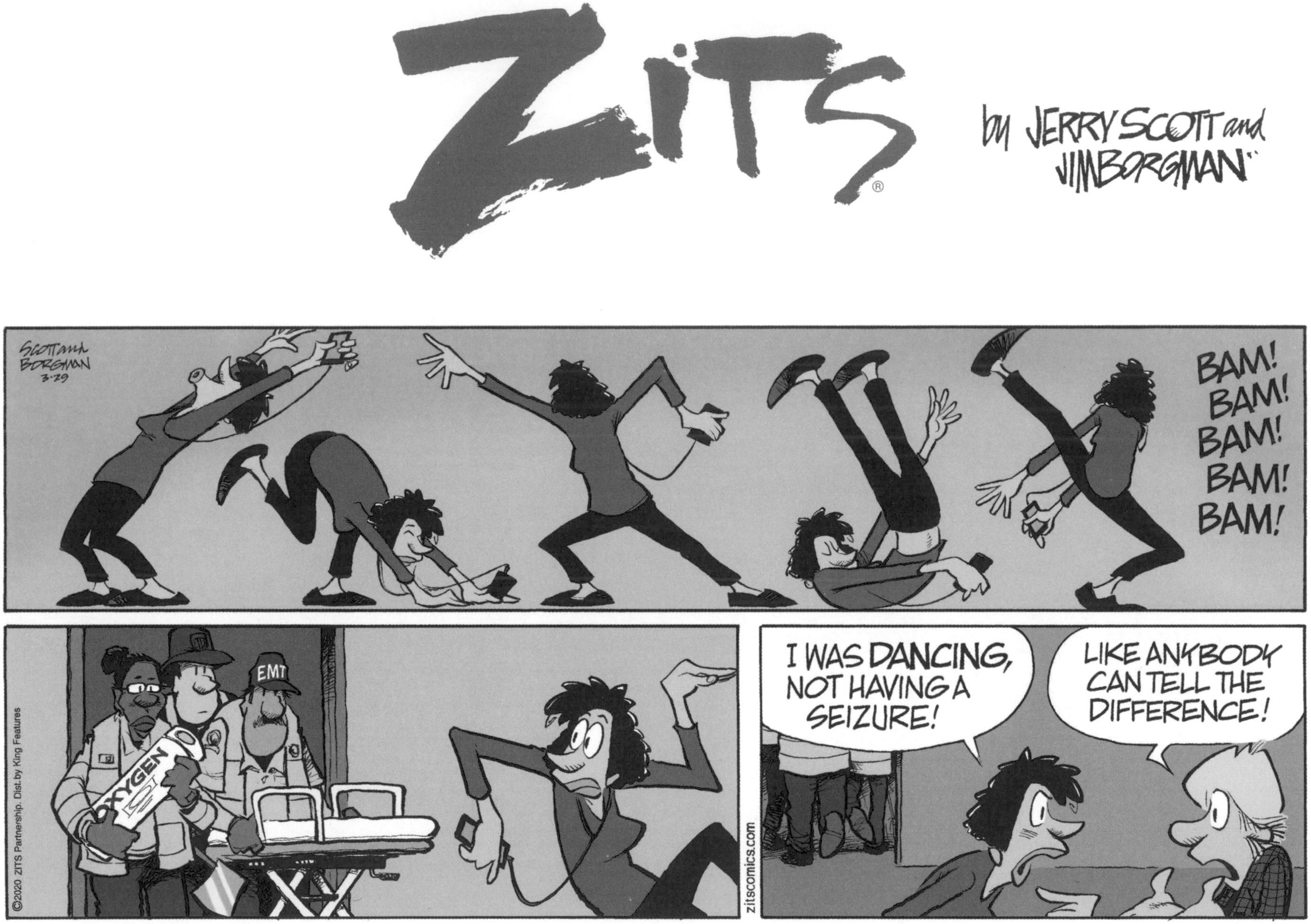
ZITS®
by JERRY SCOTT and JIM BORGMAN
SCOTT and BORGMAN 3·29
BAM! BAM! BAM! BAM! BAM!
©2020 ZITS Partnership. Dist. by King Features
EMT
OXYGEN
zitscomics.com
I WAS DANCING, NOT HAVING A SEIZURE!
LIKE ANYBODY CAN TELL THE DIFFERENCE!

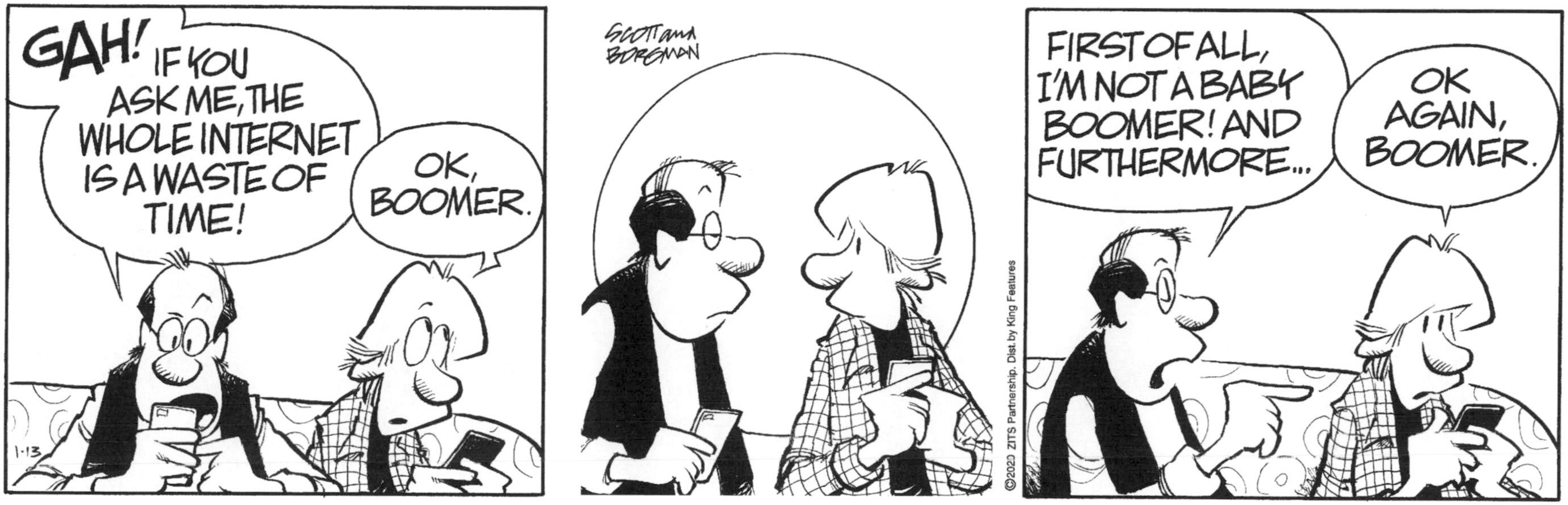
GAH! IF YOU ASK ME, THE WHOLE INTERNET IS A WASTE OF TIME!
OK, BOOMER.
1·13
SCOTT AND BORGMAN
FIRST OF ALL, I'M NOT A BABY BOOMER! AND FURTHERMORE...
OK AGAIN, BOOMER.
©2020 ZITS Partnership. Dist. by King Features

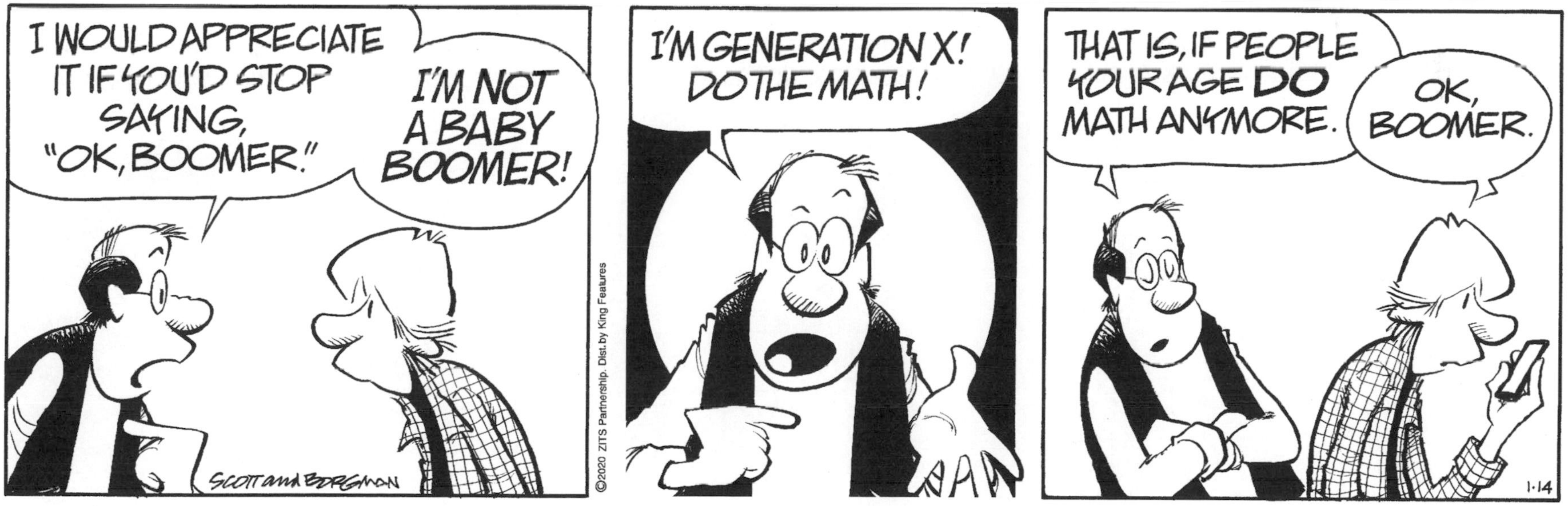
I WOULD APPRECIATE IT IF YOU'D STOP SAYING, "OK, BOOMER."
I'M NOT A BABY BOOMER!
SCOTT AND BORGMAN
©2020 ZITS Partnership. Dist. by King Features
I'M GENERATION X! DO THE MATH!
THAT IS, IF PEOPLE YOUR AGE DO MATH ANYMORE.
OK, BOOMER.
1·14

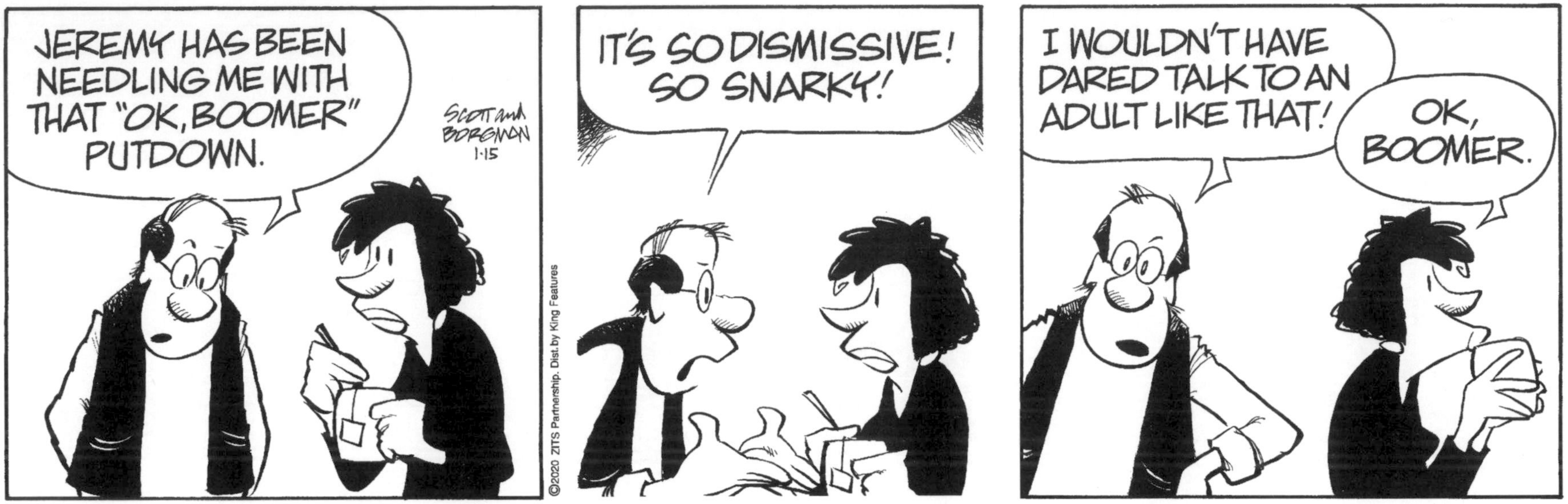
JEREMY HAS BEEN NEEDLING ME WITH THAT "OK, BOOMER" PUTDOWN.
SCOTT AND BORGMAN 1·15
IT'S SO DISMISSIVE! SO SNARKY!
©2020 ZITS Partnership. Dist. by King Features
I WOULDN'T HAVE DARED TALK TO AN ADULT LIKE THAT!
OK, BOOMER.

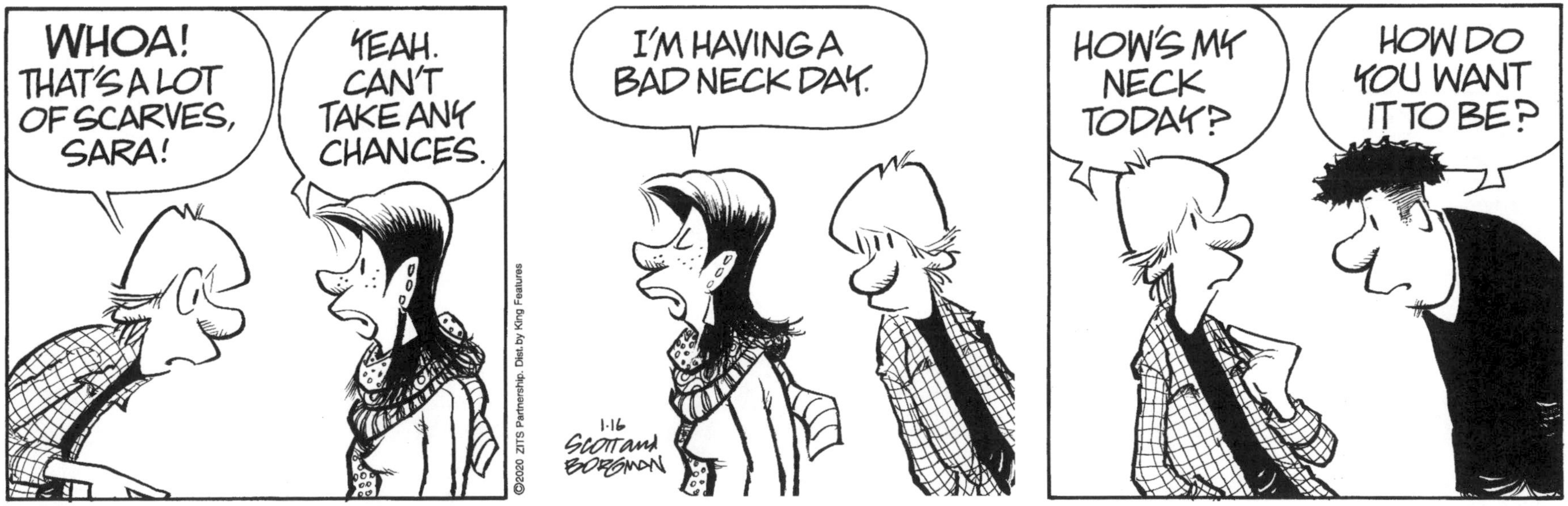
WHOA! THAT'S A LOT OF SCARVES, SARA!
YEAH. CAN'T TAKE ANY CHANCES.
©2020 ZITS Partnership. Dist. by King Features
I'M HAVING A BAD NECK DAY.
1·16 SCOTT AND BORGMAN
HOW'S MY NECK TODAY?
HOW DO YOU WANT IT TO BE?

ZITS®

by JERRY SCOTT and JIM BORGMAN

BUM!
THUM!
TIK-A-TA-TIK-A-TA
TIK-
TIK-A-TA-TIK-A-TA-
WHAM!
KUH-WOMP
MOM! YOU SHOULD COME UP AND HEAR PIERCE'S NEW DRUM KIT!
©2020 ZITS Partnership. Dist. by King Features
1-12 SCOTT and BORGMAN

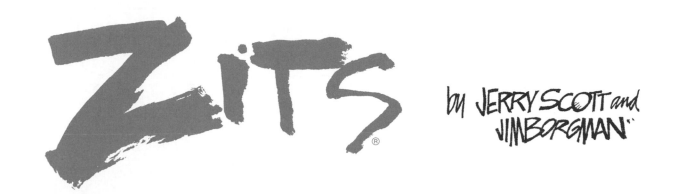

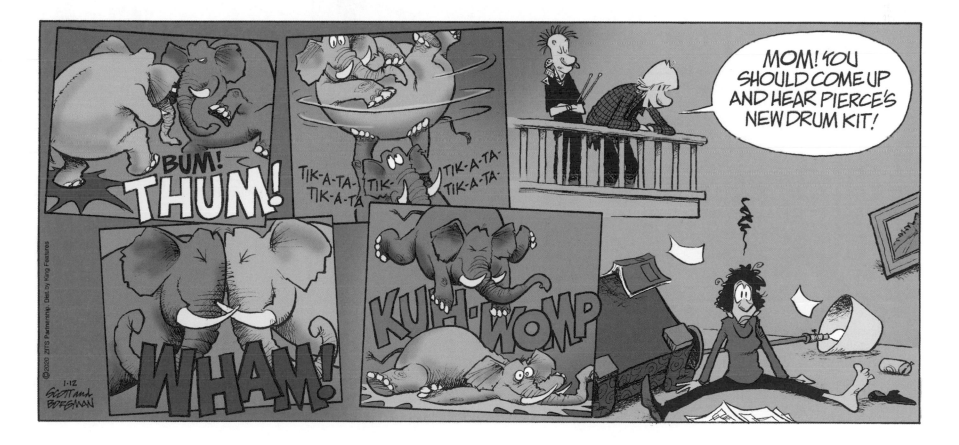

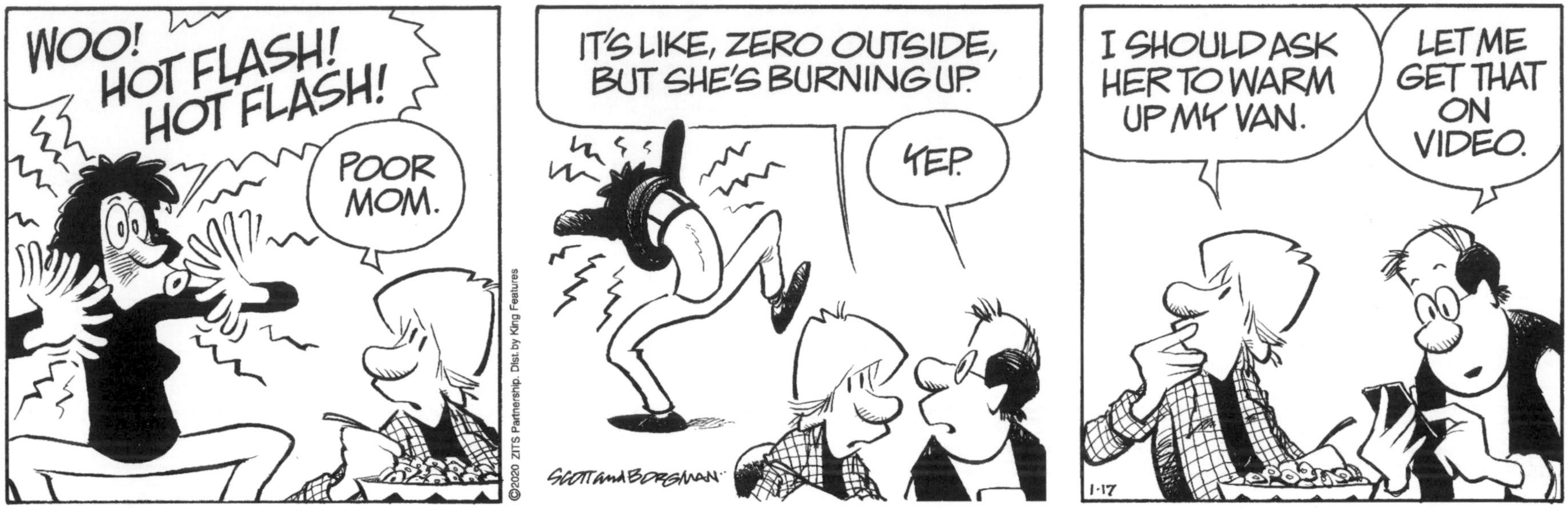
WOO! HOT FLASH! HOT FLASH!
POOR MOM.
©2020 ZITS Partnership. Dist. by King Features
IT'S LIKE, ZERO OUTSIDE, BUT SHE'S BURNING UP.
YEP.
SCOTT AND BORGMAN
I SHOULD ASK HER TO WARM UP MY VAN.
LET ME GET THAT ON VIDEO.
1·17

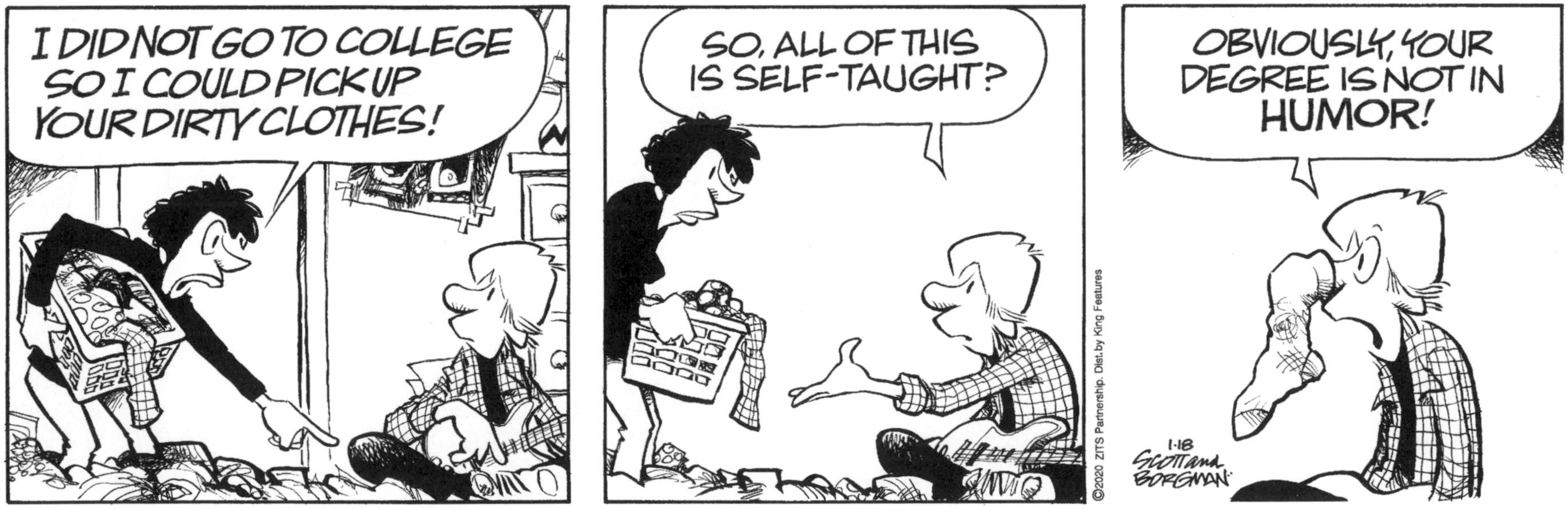
I DID NOT GO TO COLLEGE SO I COULD PICK UP YOUR DIRTY CLOTHES!
SO, ALL OF THIS IS SELF-TAUGHT?
©2020 ZITS Partnership. Dist. by King Features
OBVIOUSLY, YOUR DEGREE IS NOT IN HUMOR!
1·18 SCOTT AND BORGMAN

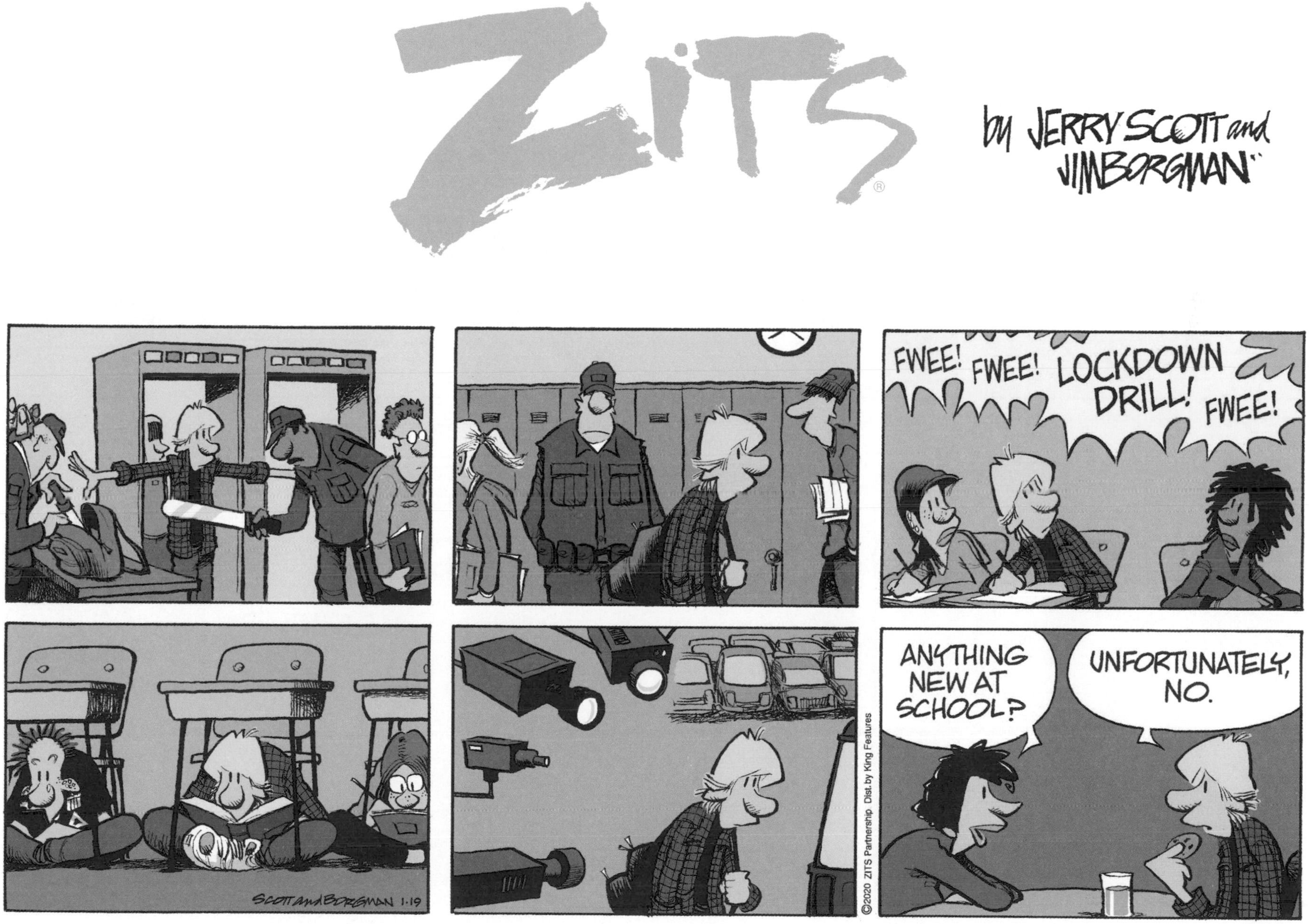
ZITS®
by JERRY SCOTT and JIM BORGMAN
FWEE! FWEE! LOCKDOWN DRILL! FWEE!
SCOTT and BORGMAN 1.19
©2020 ZITS Partnership Dist. by King Features
ANYTHING NEW AT SCHOOL?
UNFORTUNATELY, NO.

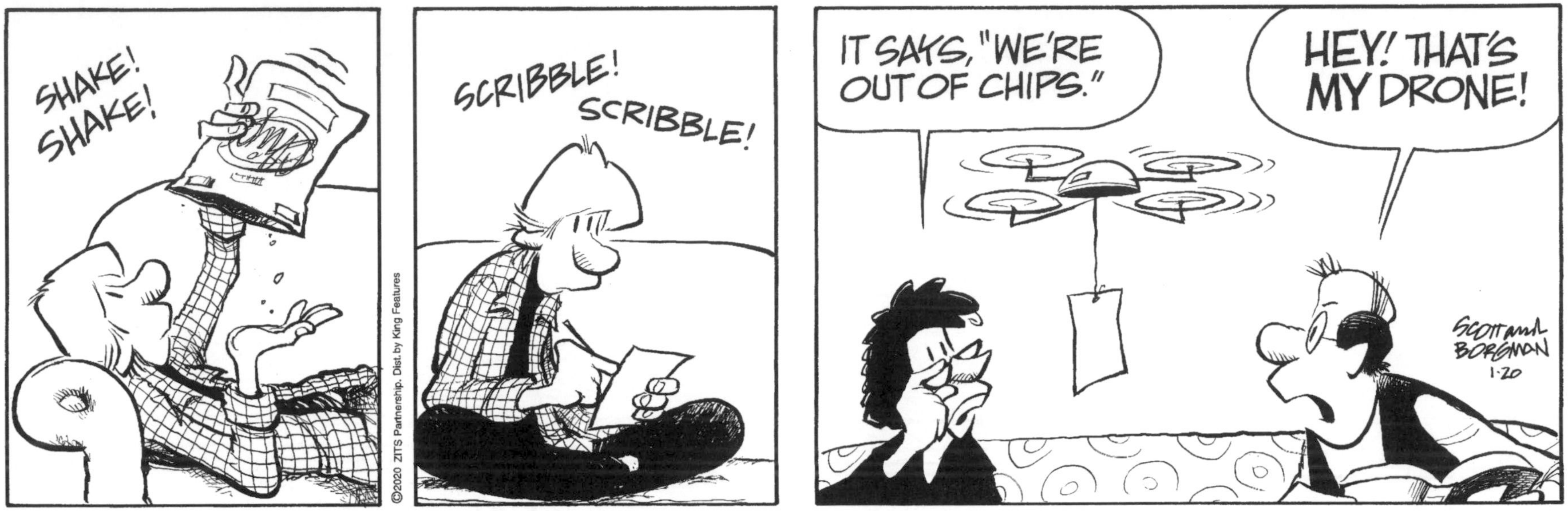
SHAKE! SHAKE!
SCRIBBLE! SCRIBBLE!
IT SAYS, "WE'RE OUT OF CHIPS."
HEY! THAT'S MY DRONE!
SCOTT and BORGMAN 1·20

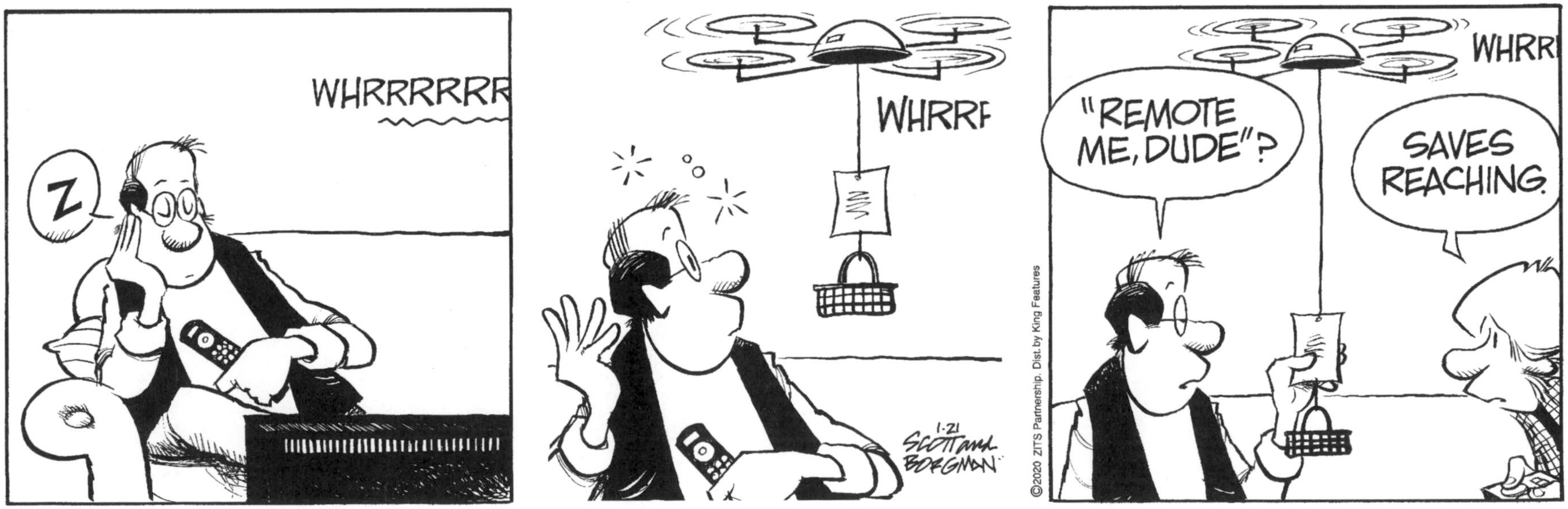
WHRRRRRR
Z
WHRR
1·21 SCOTT and BORGMAN
WHRR
"REMOTE ME, DUDE"?
SAVES REACHING.

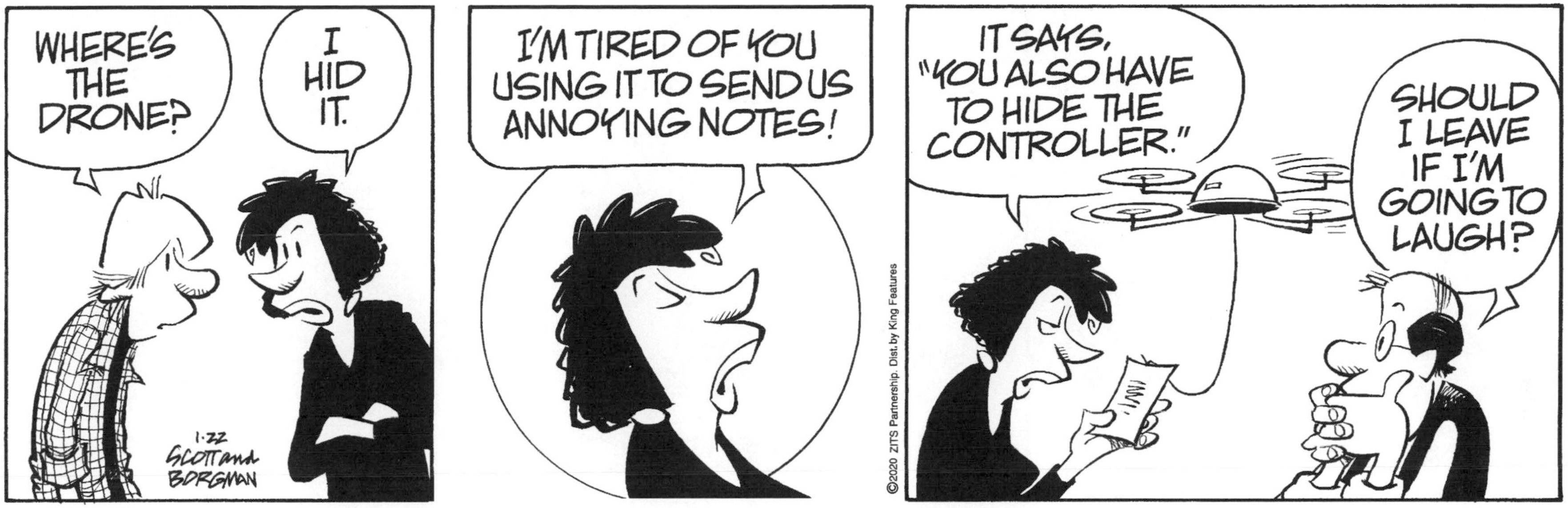
WHERE'S THE DRONE?
I HID IT.
1·22 SCOTT and BORGMAN
I'M TIRED OF YOU USING IT TO SEND US ANNOYING NOTES!
©2020 ZITS Partnership. Dist. by King Features
IT SAYS, "YOU ALSO HAVE TO HIDE THE CONTROLLER."
SHOULD I LEAVE IF I'M GOING TO LAUGH?

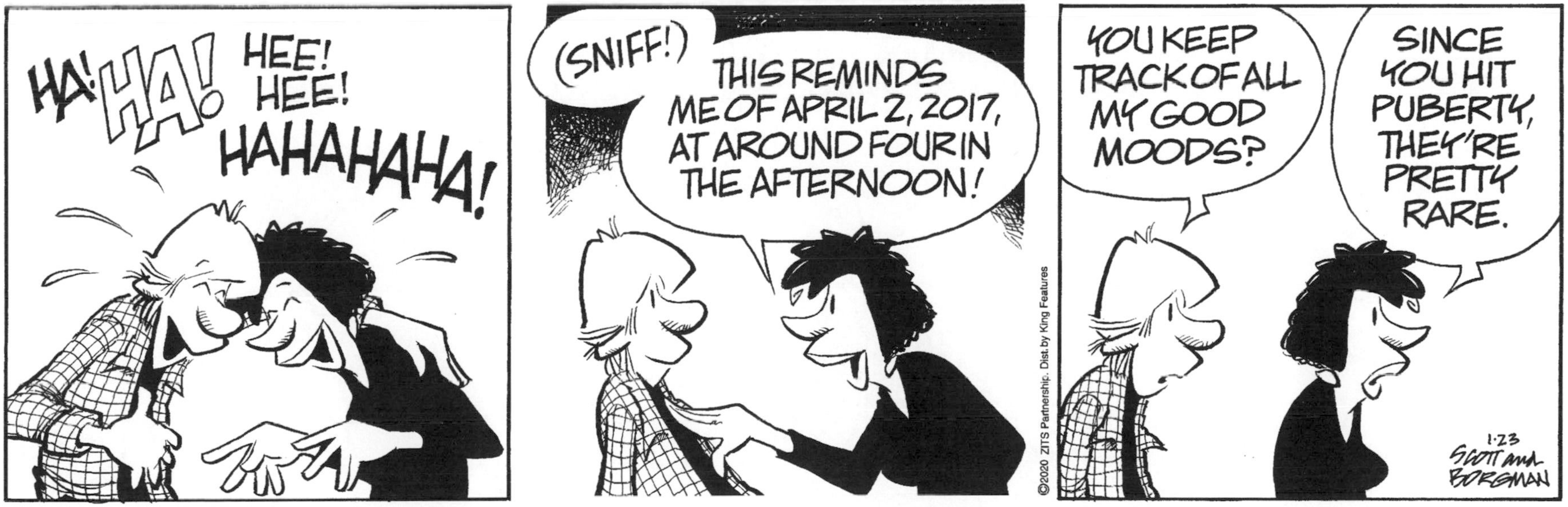
HA! HA!
HEE! HEE!
HAHAHAHA!
(SNIFF!)
THIS REMINDS ME OF APRIL 2, 2017, AT AROUND FOUR IN THE AFTERNOON!
©2020 ZITS Partnership. Dist. by King Features
YOU KEEP TRACK OF ALL MY GOOD MOODS?
SINCE YOU HIT PUBERTY, THEY'RE PRETTY RARE.
1·23 SCOTT and BORGMAN

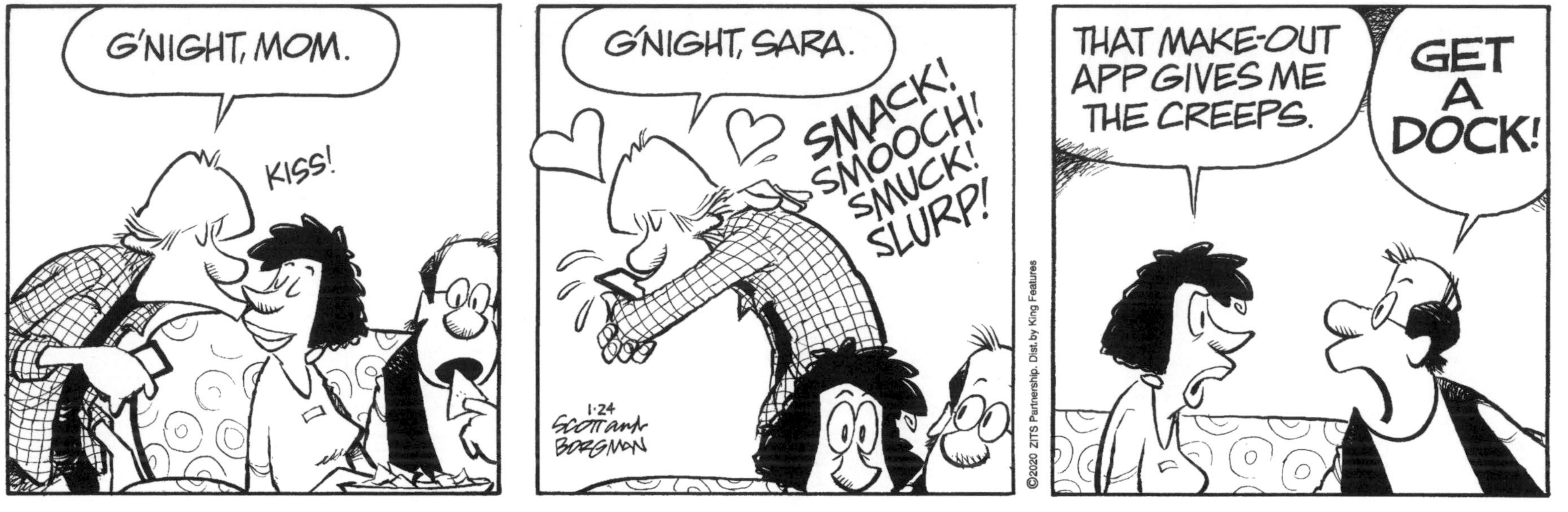
G'NIGHT, MOM.
KISS!
G'NIGHT, SARA.
SMACK! SMOOCH! SMUCK! SLURP!
1·24
SCOTT and BORGMAN
©2020 ZITS Partnership. Dist. by King Features
THAT MAKE-OUT APP GIVES ME THE CREEPS.
GET A DOCK!

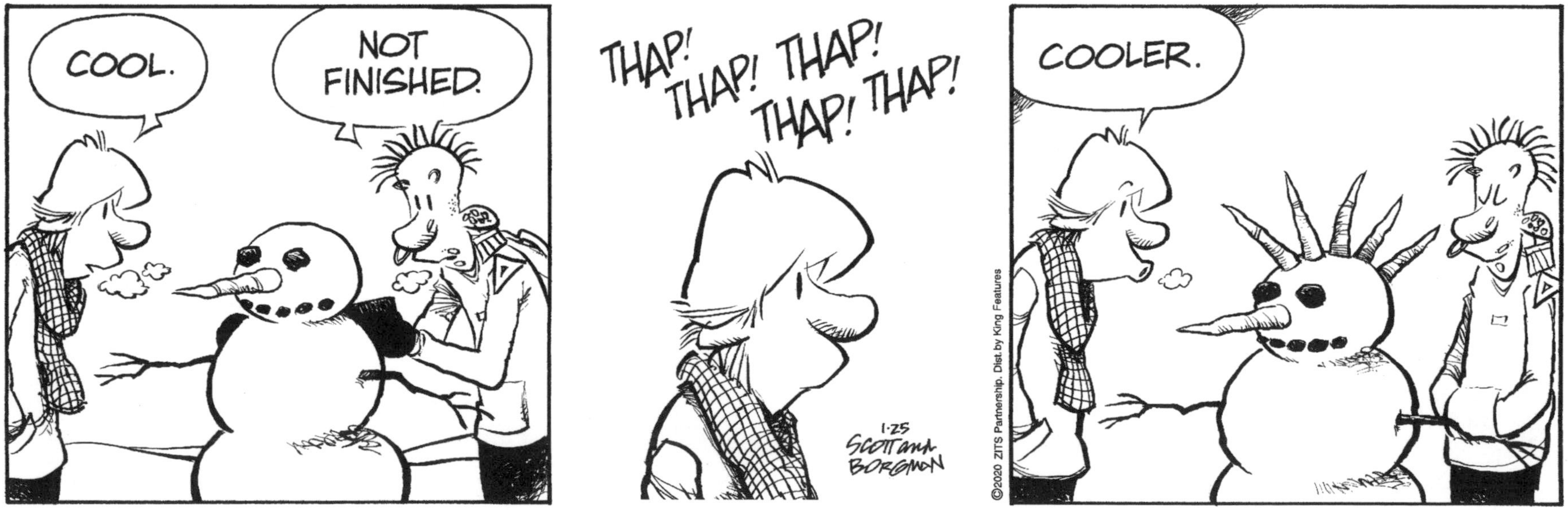
COOL.
NOT FINISHED.
THAP! THAP! THAP! THAP! THAP!
1·25
SCOTT and BORGMAN
©2020 ZITS Partnership. Dist. by King Features
COOLER.

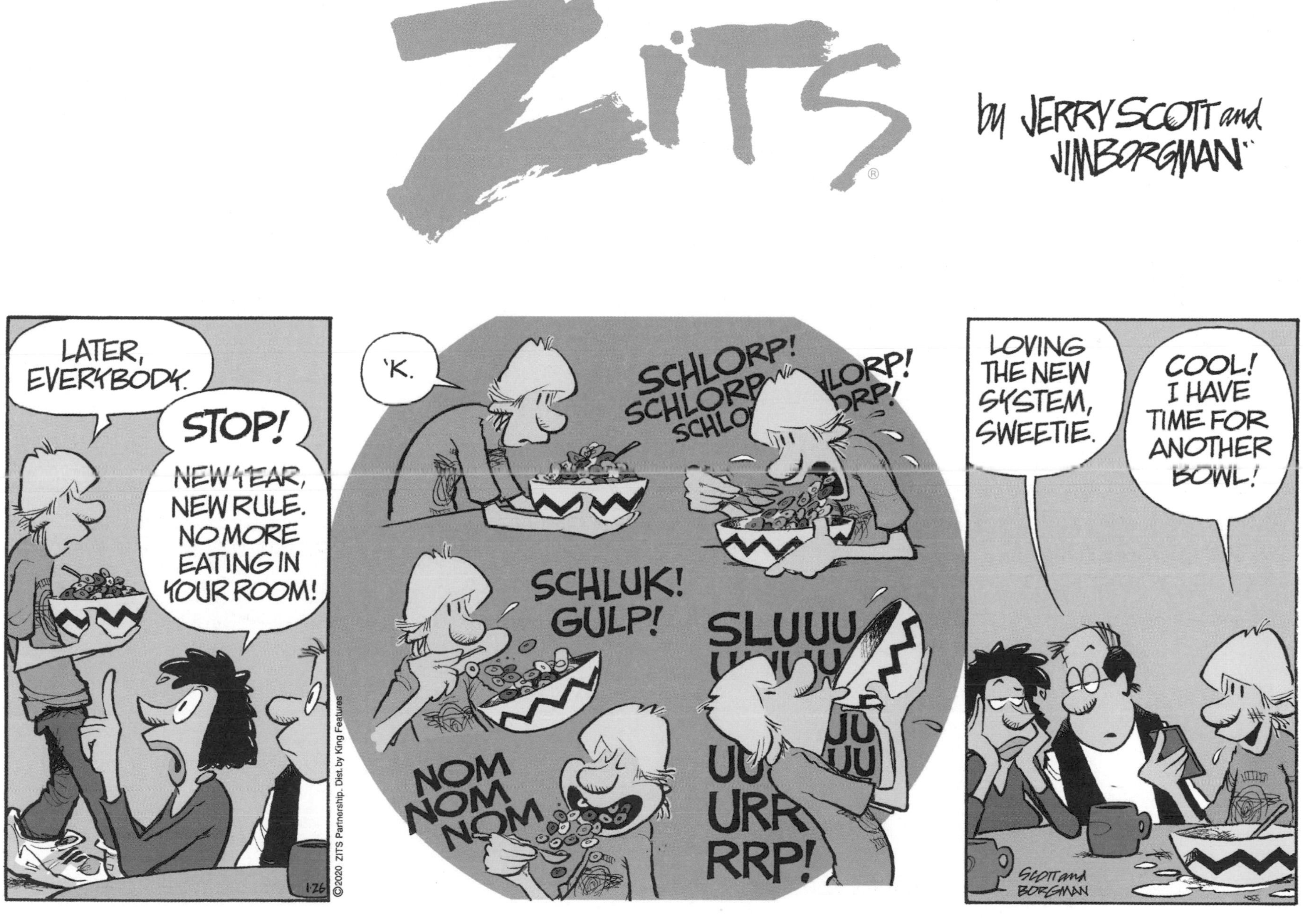
ZITS
by JERRY SCOTT and JIM BORGMAN
LATER, EVERYBODY.
STOP!
NEW YEAR, NEW RULE. NO MORE EATING IN YOUR ROOM!
©2020 ZITS Partnership. Dist. by King Features
1·26
'K.
SCHLORP! SCHLORP! SCHLORP!
SCHLUK! GULP!
SLUUUUUUUUUUUUUUUURRRRP!
NOM NOM NOM
LOVING THE NEW SYSTEM, SWEETIE.
COOL! I HAVE TIME FOR ANOTHER BOWL!
SCOTT and BORGMAN

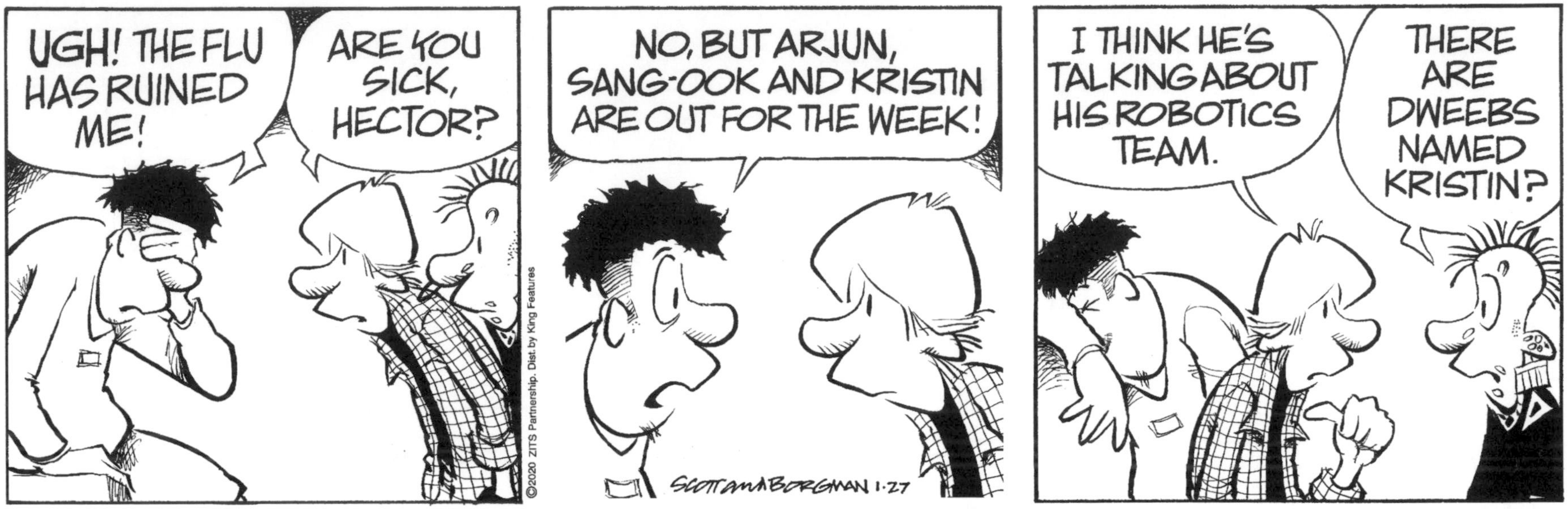
UGH! THE FLU HAS RUINED ME!
ARE YOU SICK, HECTOR?
©2020 ZITS Partnership. Dist. by King Features
NO, BUT ARJUN, SANG-OOK AND KRISTIN ARE OUT FOR THE WEEK!
SCOTT AND BORGMAN 1·27
I THINK HE'S TALKING ABOUT HIS ROBOTICS TEAM.
THERE ARE DWEEBS NAMED KRISTIN?

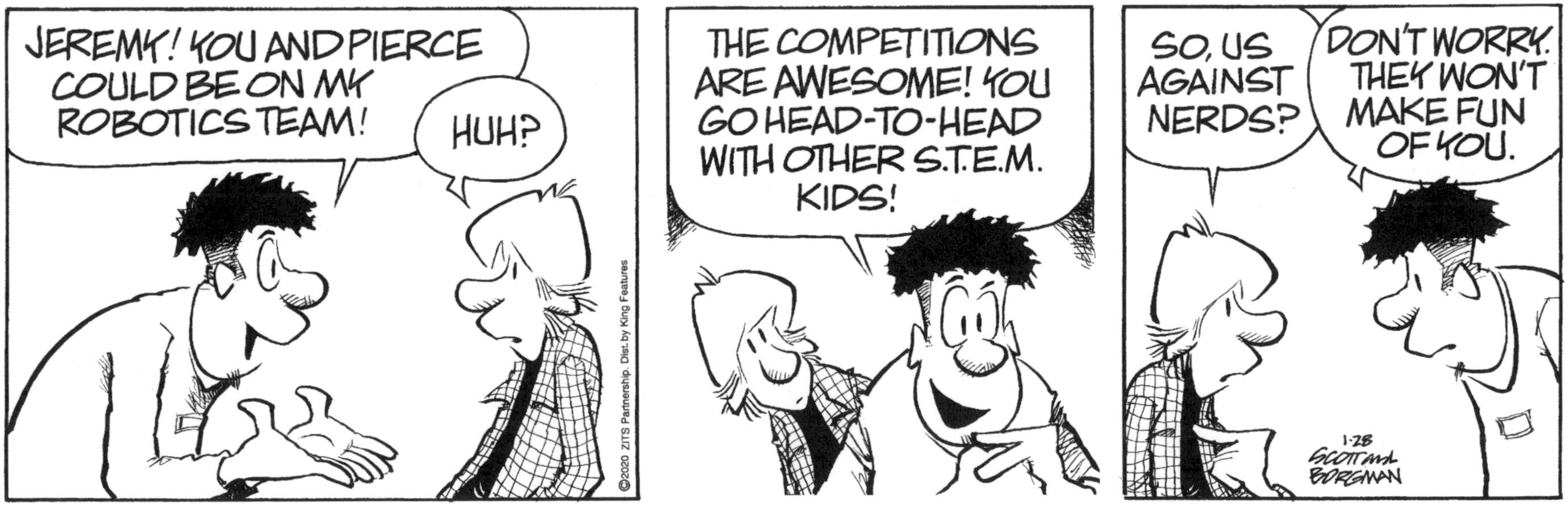
JEREMY! YOU AND PIERCE COULD BE ON MY ROBOTICS TEAM!
HUH?
©2020 ZITS Partnership. Dist. by King Features
THE COMPETITIONS ARE AWESOME! YOU GO HEAD-TO-HEAD WITH OTHER S.T.E.M. KIDS!
SO, US AGAINST NERDS?
DON'T WORRY. THEY WON'T MAKE FUN OF YOU.
1·28 SCOTT AND BORGMAN

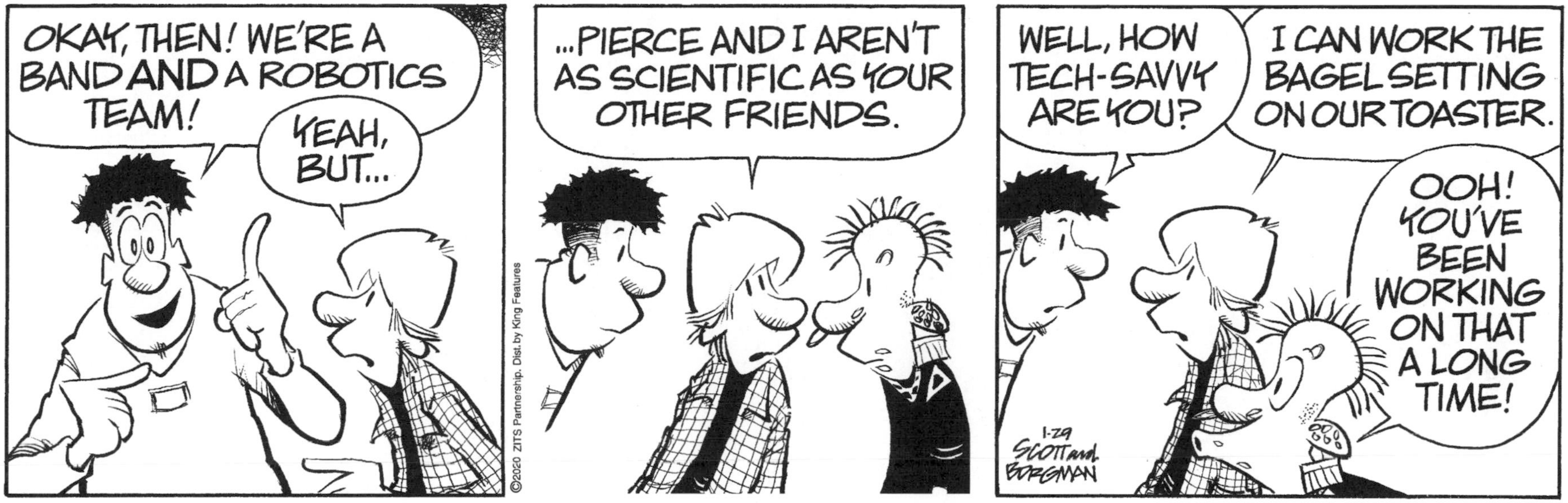
OKAY, THEN! WE'RE A BAND AND A ROBOTICS TEAM!
YEAH, BUT...
...PIERCE AND I AREN'T AS SCIENTIFIC AS YOUR OTHER FRIENDS.
©2020 ZITS Partnership. Dist. by King Features
WELL, HOW TECH-SAVVY ARE YOU?
I CAN WORK THE BAGEL SETTING ON OUR TOASTER.
OOH! YOU'VE BEEN WORKING ON THAT A LONG TIME!
1-29 SCOTT and BORGMAN

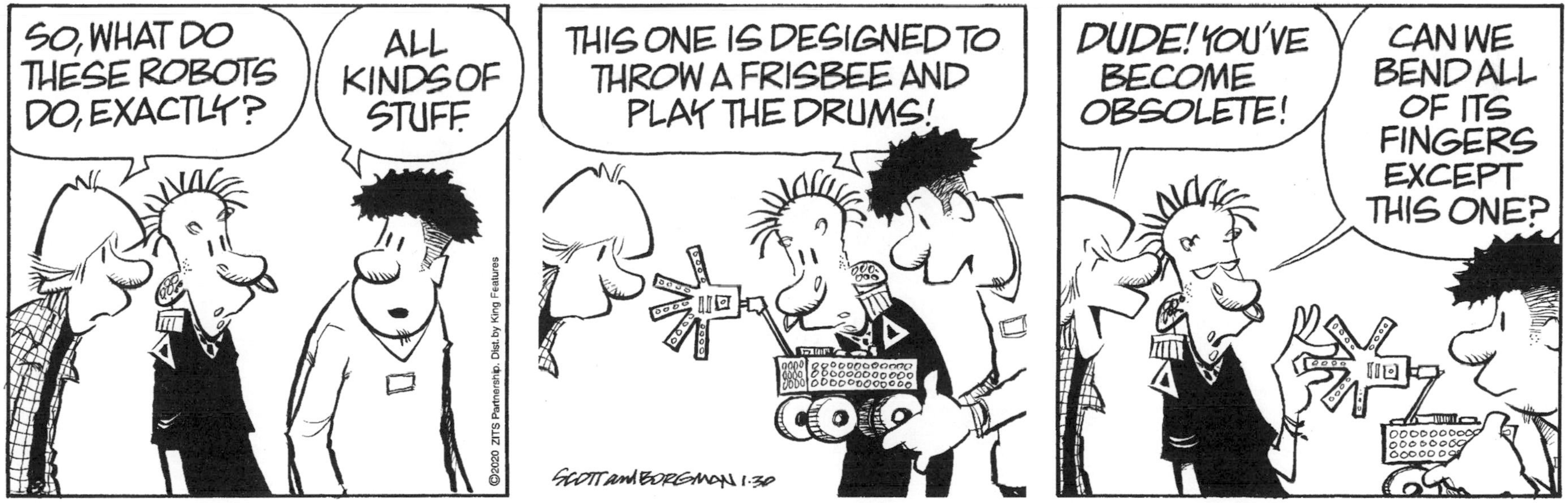
SO, WHAT DO THESE ROBOTS DO, EXACTLY?
ALL KINDS OF STUFF.
©2020 ZITS Partnership. Dist. by King Features
THIS ONE IS DESIGNED TO THROW A FRISBEE AND PLAY THE DRUMS!
SCOTT and BORGMAN 1-30
DUDE! YOU'VE BECOME OBSOLETE!
CAN WE BEND ALL OF ITS FINGERS EXCEPT THIS ONE?

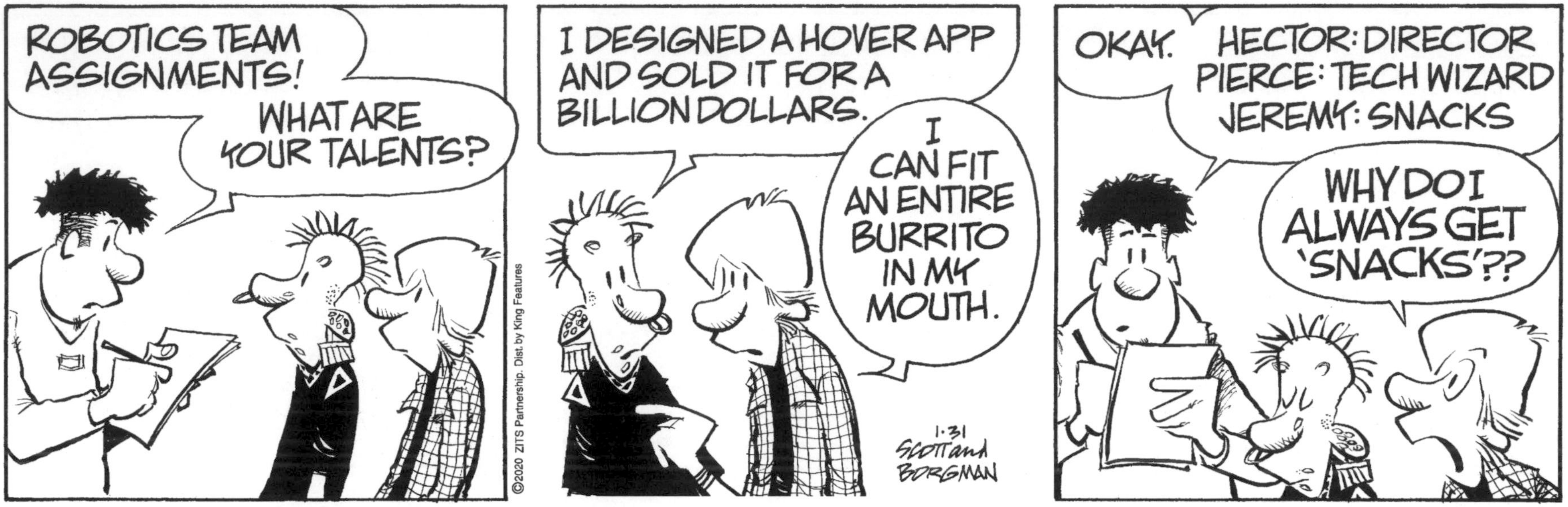
ROBOTICS TEAM ASSIGNMENTS!
WHAT ARE YOUR TALENTS?
©2020 ZITS Partnership. Dist. by King Features
I DESIGNED A HOVER APP AND SOLD IT FOR A BILLION DOLLARS.
I CAN FIT AN ENTIRE BURRITO IN MY MOUTH.
1·31 SCOTT and BORGMAN
OKAY.
HECTOR: DIRECTOR
PIERCE: TECH WIZARD
JEREMY: SNACKS
WHY DO I ALWAYS GET 'SNACKS'??

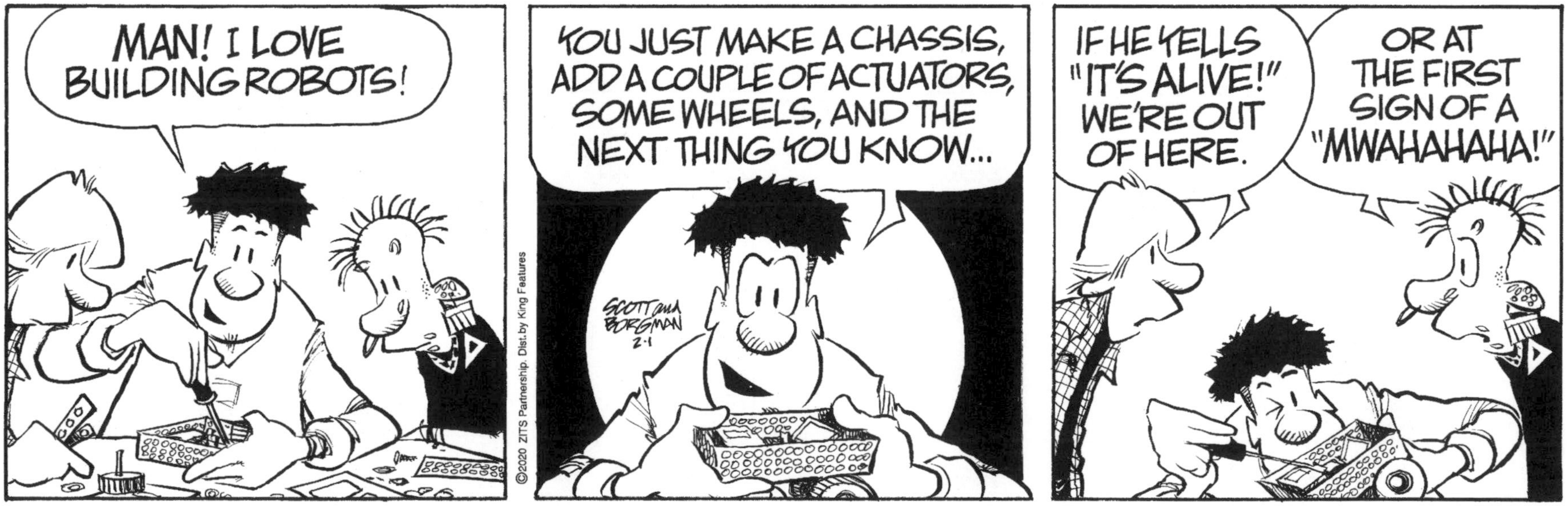
MAN! I LOVE BUILDING ROBOTS!
©2020 ZITS Partnership. Dist. by King Features
YOU JUST MAKE A CHASSIS, ADD A COUPLE OF ACTUATORS, SOME WHEELS, AND THE NEXT THING YOU KNOW...
SCOTT and BORGMAN 2·1
IF HE YELLS "IT'S ALIVE!" WE'RE OUT OF HERE.
OR AT THE FIRST SIGN OF A "MWAHAHAHA!"

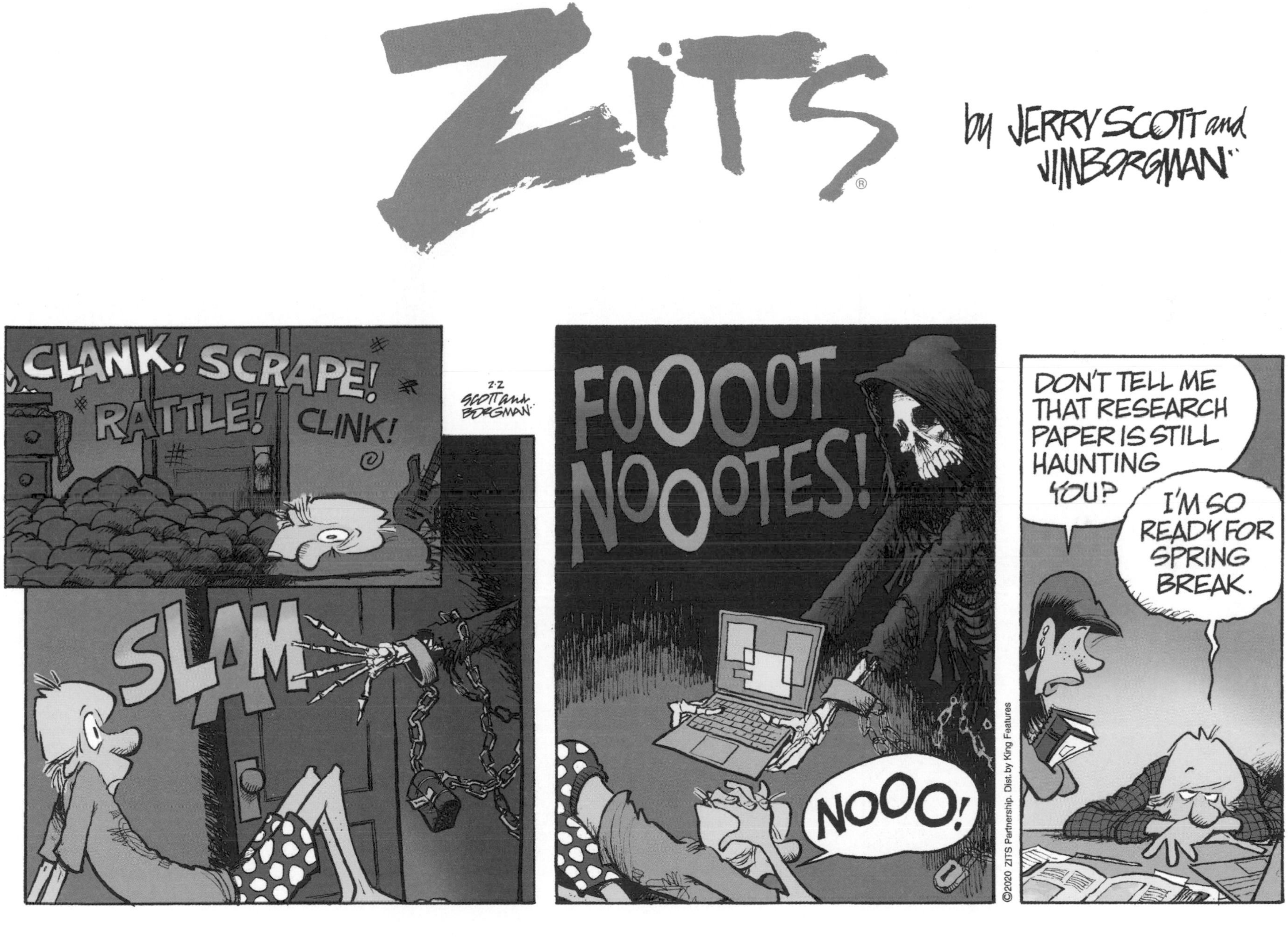
ZITS®
by JERRY SCOTT and JIM BORGMAN
CLANK! SCRAPE! RATTLE! CLINK!
2·2 SCOTT and BORGMAN
SLAM
FOOOOT NOOOTES!
NOOO!
©2020 ZITS Partnership. Dist. by King Features
DON'T TELL ME THAT RESEARCH PAPER IS STILL HAUNTING YOU?
I'M SO READY FOR SPRING BREAK.

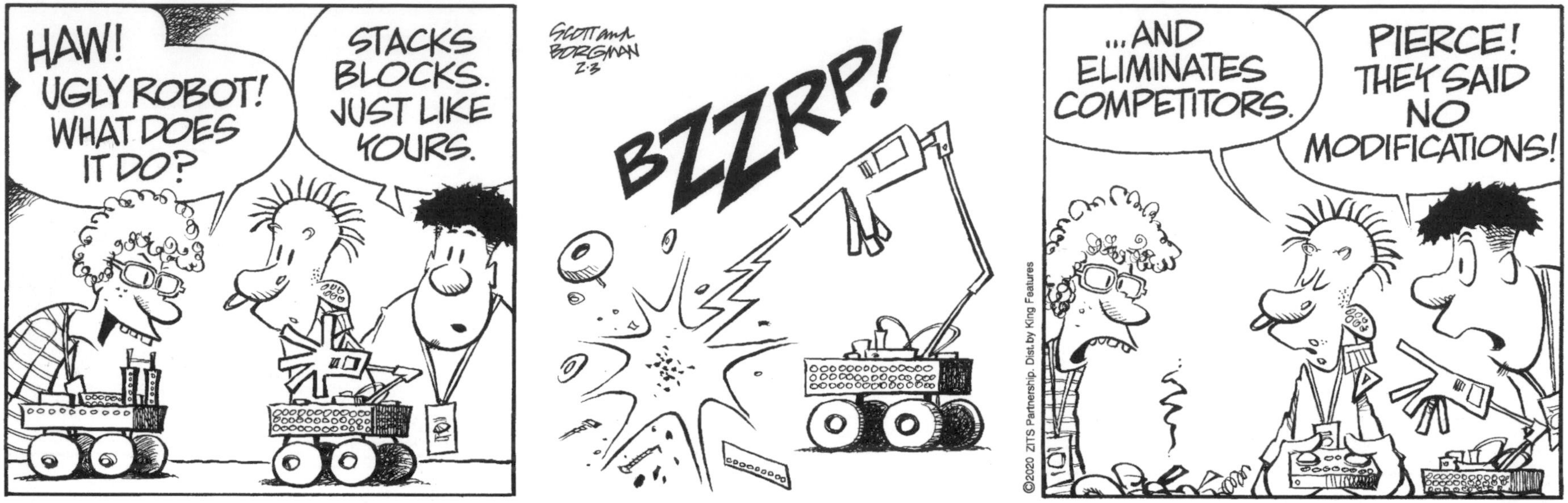
HAW! UGLY ROBOT! WHAT DOES IT DO?
STACKS BLOCKS. JUST LIKE YOURS.
SCOTT AND BORGMAN 2·3
BZZRP!
...AND ELIMINATES COMPETITORS.
PIERCE! THEY SAID NO MODIFICATIONS!
©2020 ZITS Partnership. Dist. by King Features

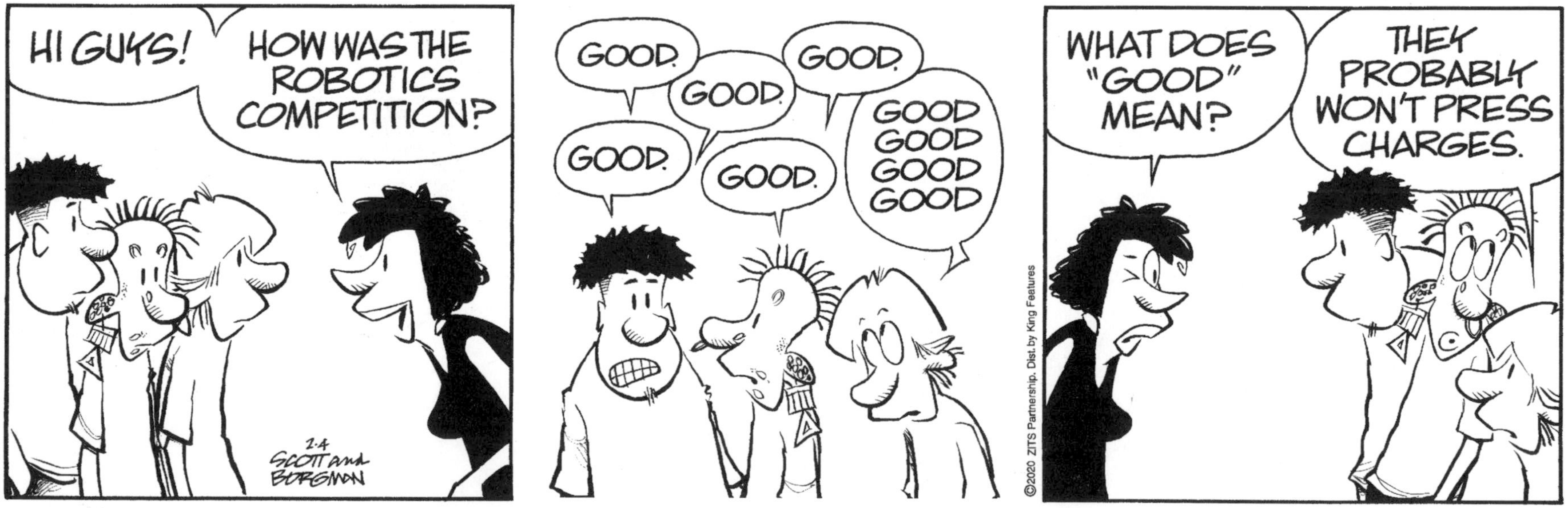
HI GUYS!
HOW WAS THE ROBOTICS COMPETITION?
2·4 SCOTT AND BORGMAN
GOOD.
GOOD.
GOOD.
GOOD.
GOOD.
GOOD GOOD GOOD GOOD
WHAT DOES "GOOD" MEAN?
THEY PROBABLY WON'T PRESS CHARGES.
©2020 ZITS Partnership. Dist. by King Features

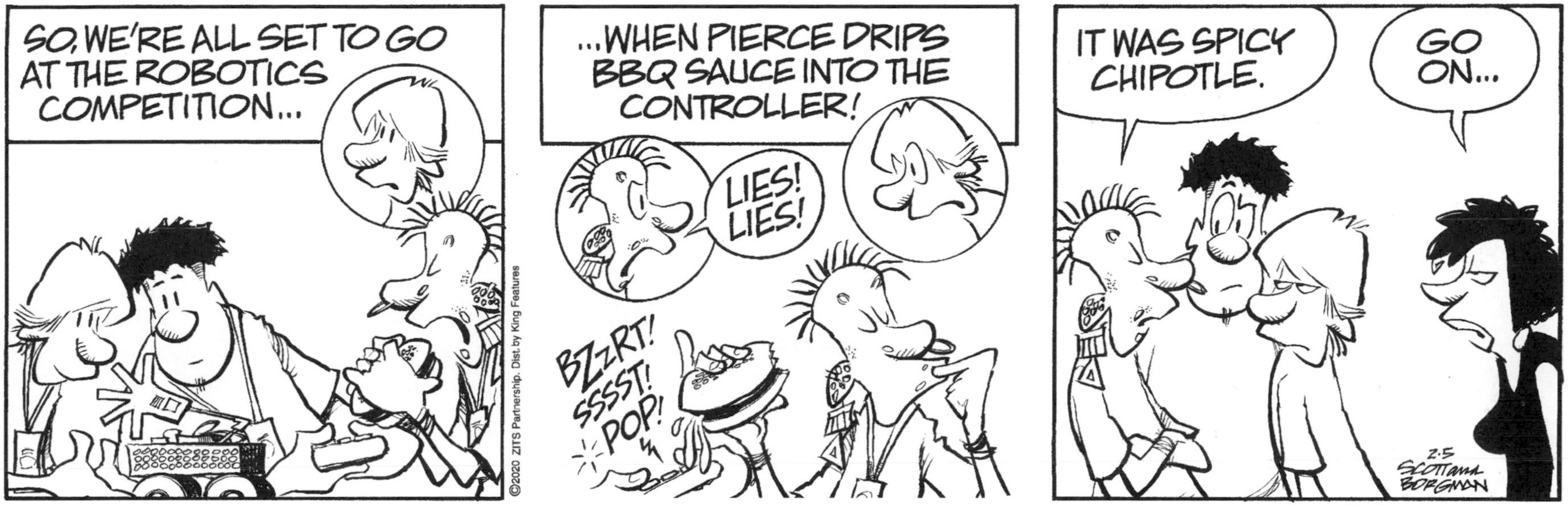
SO, WE'RE ALL SET TO GO AT THE ROBOTICS COMPETITION...
©2020 ZITS Partnership. Dist. by King Features
...WHEN PIERCE DRIPS BBQ SAUCE INTO THE CONTROLLER!
LIES! LIES!
BZZRT! SSSST! POP!
IT WAS SPICY CHIPOTLE.
GO ON...
2·5
SCOTT AND BORGMAN

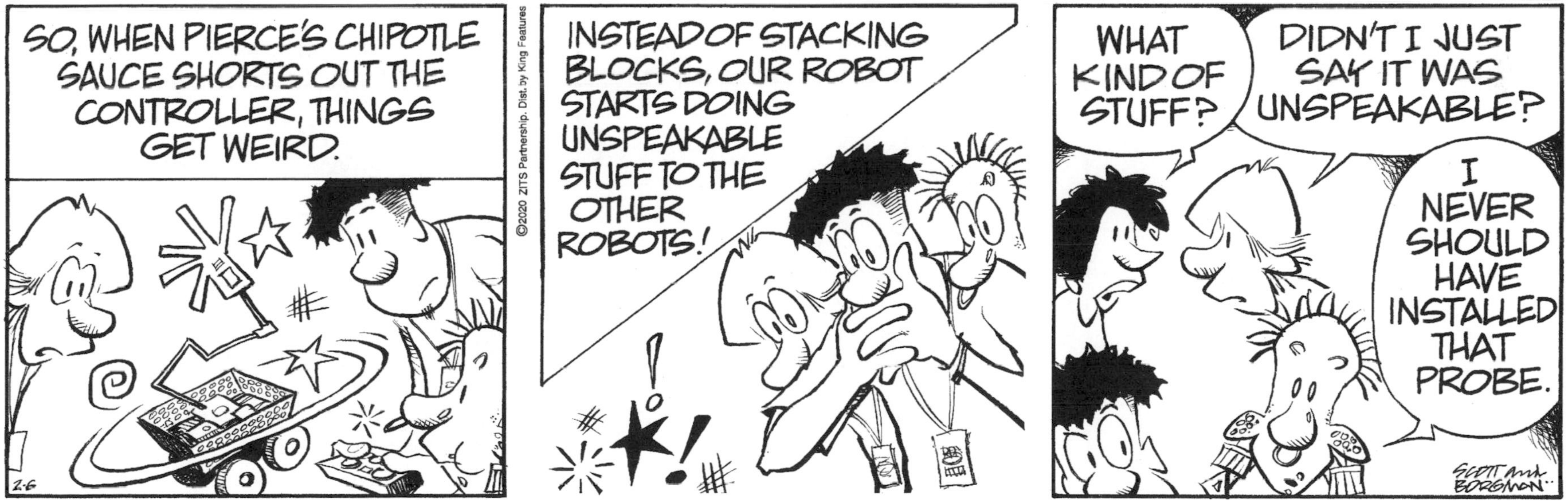
SO, WHEN PIERCE'S CHIPOTLE SAUCE SHORTS OUT THE CONTROLLER, THINGS GET WEIRD.
2·6
©2020 ZITS Partnership. Dist. by King Features
INSTEAD OF STACKING BLOCKS, OUR ROBOT STARTS DOING UNSPEAKABLE STUFF TO THE OTHER ROBOTS!
WHAT KIND OF STUFF?
DIDN'T I JUST SAY IT WAS UNSPEAKABLE?
I NEVER SHOULD HAVE INSTALLED THAT PROBE.
SCOTT AND BORGMAN

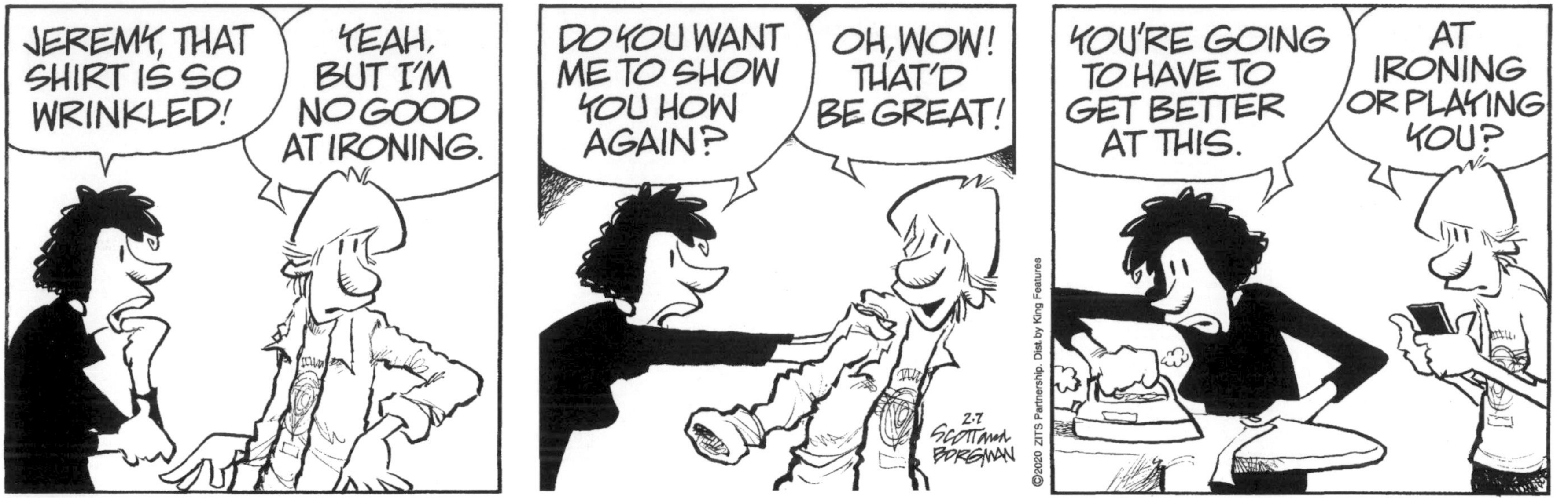
JEREMY, THAT SHIRT IS SO WRINKLED!
YEAH, BUT I'M NO GOOD AT IRONING.
DO YOU WANT ME TO SHOW YOU HOW AGAIN?
OH, WOW! THAT'D BE GREAT!
2.7 SCOTT and BORGMAN
©2020 ZITS Partnership. Dist. by King Features
YOU'RE GOING TO HAVE TO GET BETTER AT THIS.
AT IRONING OR PLAYING YOU?

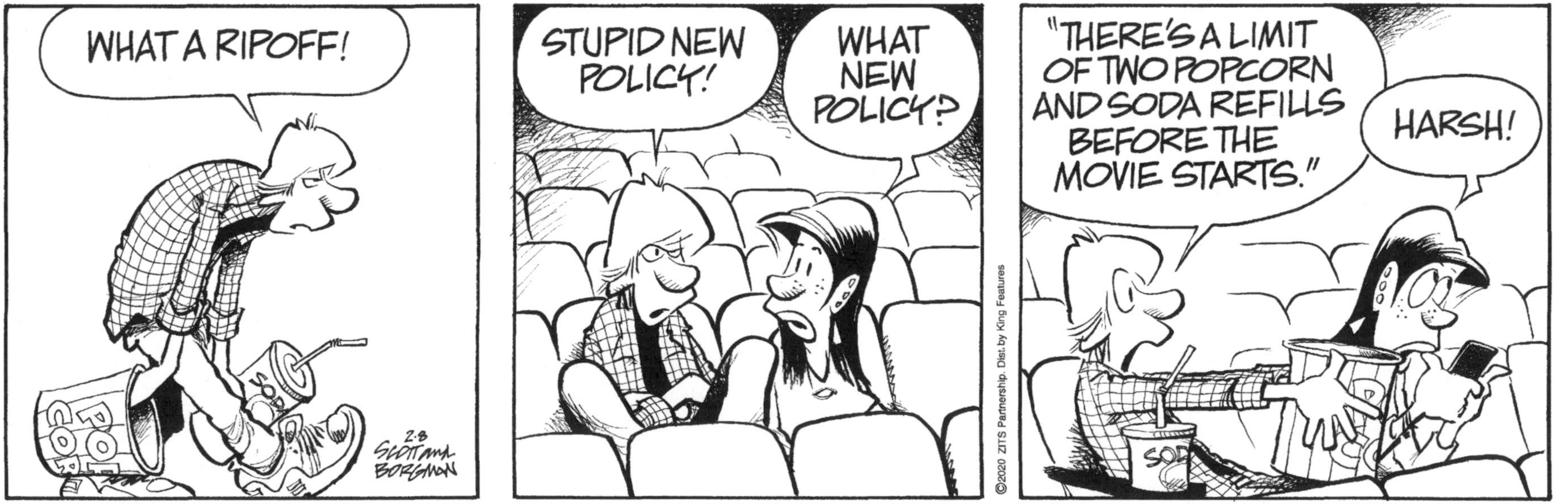
WHAT A RIPOFF!
2.8 SCOTT and BORGMAN
STUPID NEW POLICY!
WHAT NEW POLICY?
©2020 ZITS Partnership. Dist. by King Features
"THERE'S A LIMIT OF TWO POPCORN AND SODA REFILLS BEFORE THE MOVIE STARTS."
HARSH!

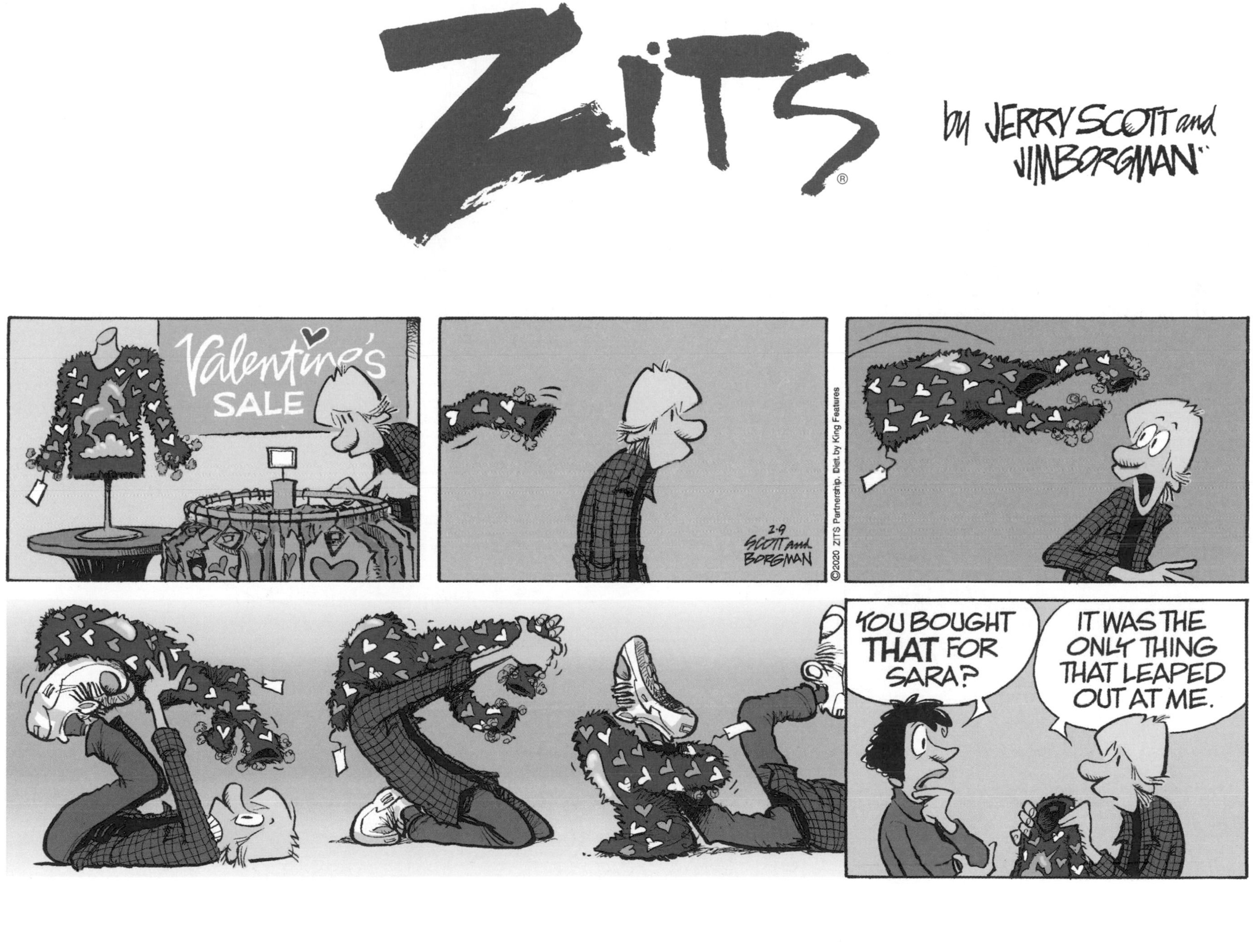
ZITS®
by JERRY SCOTT and JIM BORGMAN
Valentine's SALE
2-9 SCOTT and BORGMAN
©2020 ZITS Partnership. Dist. by King Features
YOU BOUGHT THAT FOR SARA?
IT WAS THE ONLY THING THAT LEAPED OUT AT ME.

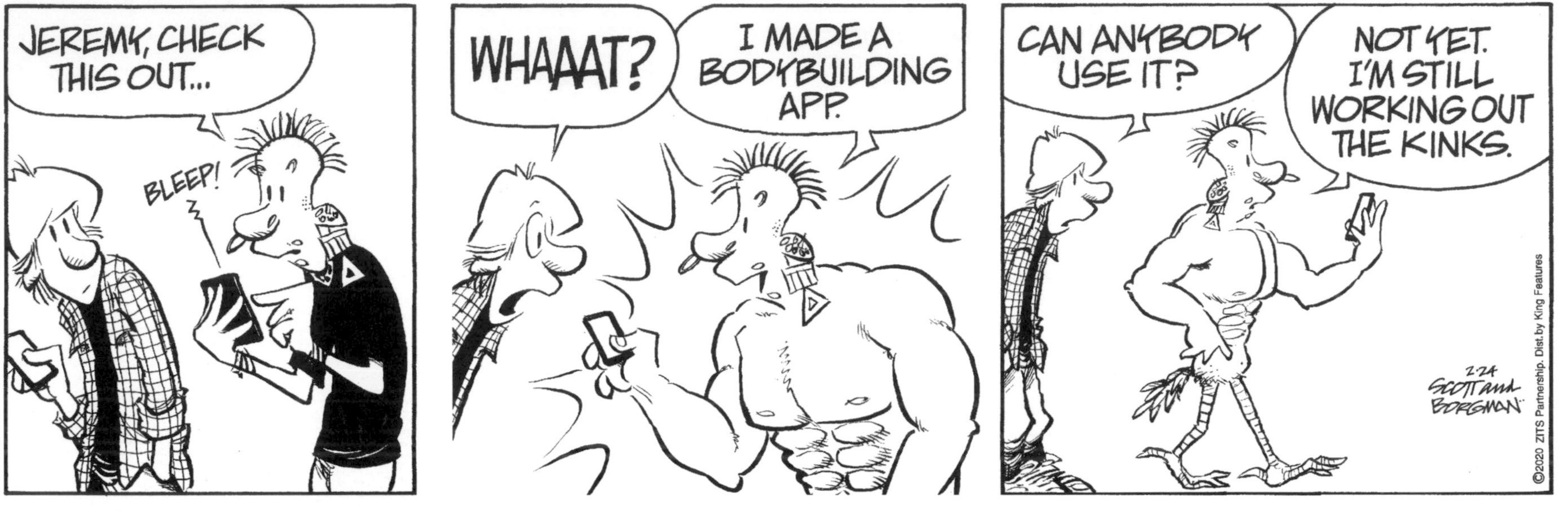
JEREMY, CHECK THIS OUT...
BLEEP!
WHAAAT?
I MADE A BODYBUILDING APP.
CAN ANYBODY USE IT?
NOT YET. I'M STILL WORKING OUT THE KINKS.
2·24
©2020 ZITS Partnership. Dist.by King Features

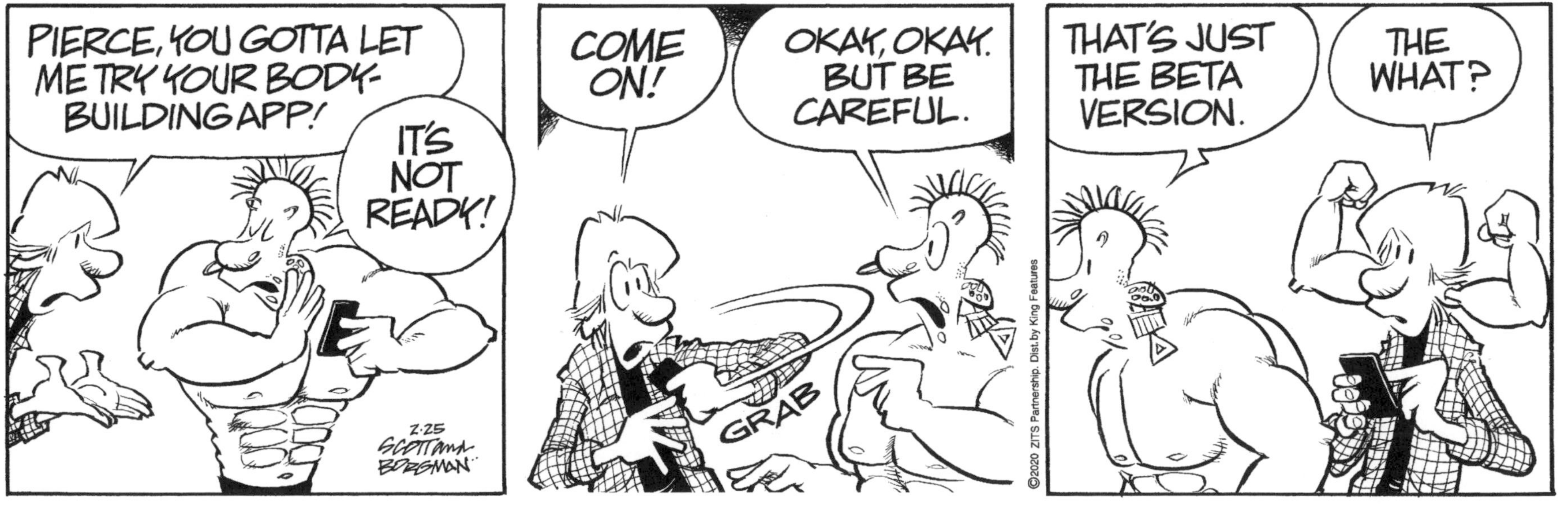
PIERCE, YOU GOTTA LET ME TRY YOUR BODY-BUILDING APP!
IT'S NOT READY!
2·25
COME ON!
OKAY, OKAY. BUT BE CAREFUL.
GRAB
©2020 ZITS Partnership. Dist.by King Features
THAT'S JUST THE BETA VERSION.
THE WHAT?

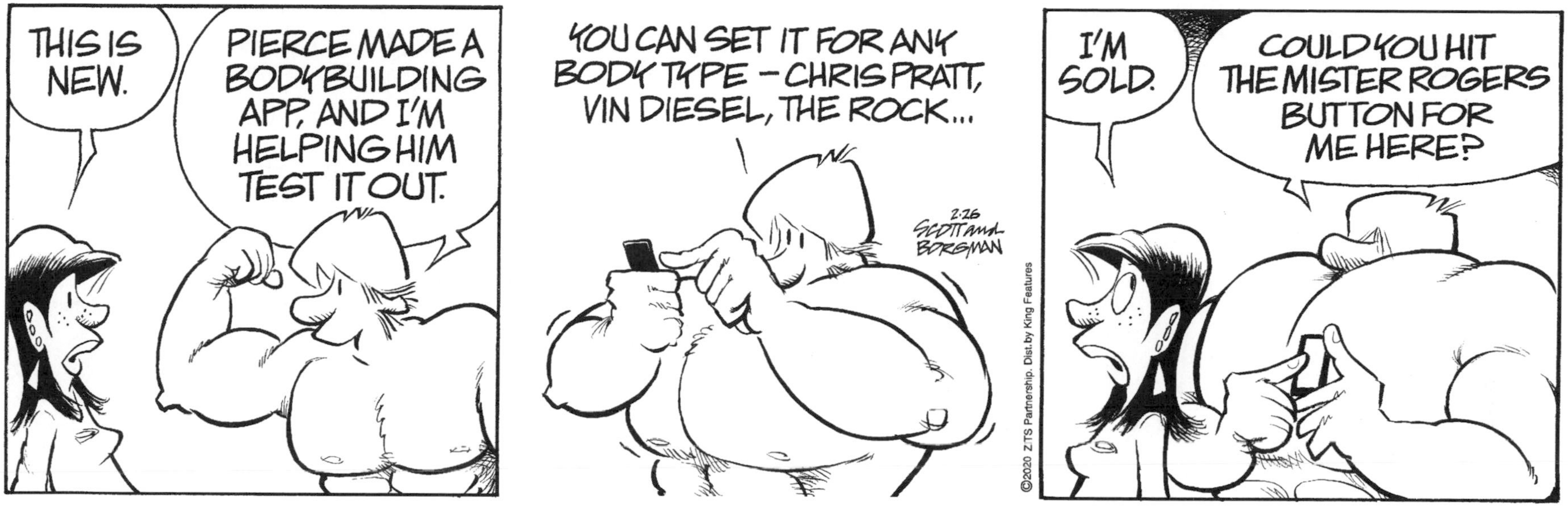
THIS IS NEW.
PIERCE MADE A BODYBUILDING APP, AND I'M HELPING HIM TEST IT OUT.
YOU CAN SET IT FOR ANY BODY TYPE – CHRIS PRATT, VIN DIESEL, THE ROCK...
2·26 SCOTT and BORGMAN
©2020 ZITS Partnership. Dist.by King Features
I'M SOLD.
COULD YOU HIT THE MISTER ROGERS BUTTON FOR ME HERE?

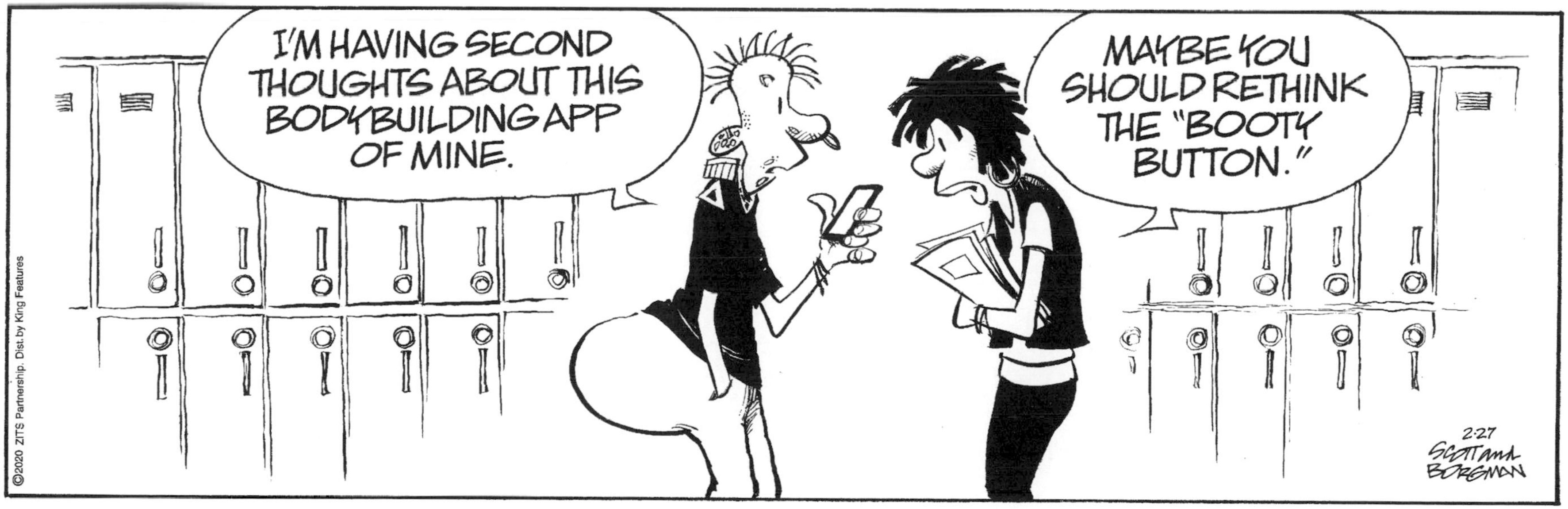
©2020 ZITS Partnership. Dist.by King Features
I'M HAVING SECOND THOUGHTS ABOUT THIS BODYBUILDING APP OF MINE.
MAYBE YOU SHOULD RETHINK THE "BOOTY BUTTON."
2·27 SCOTT and BORGMAN

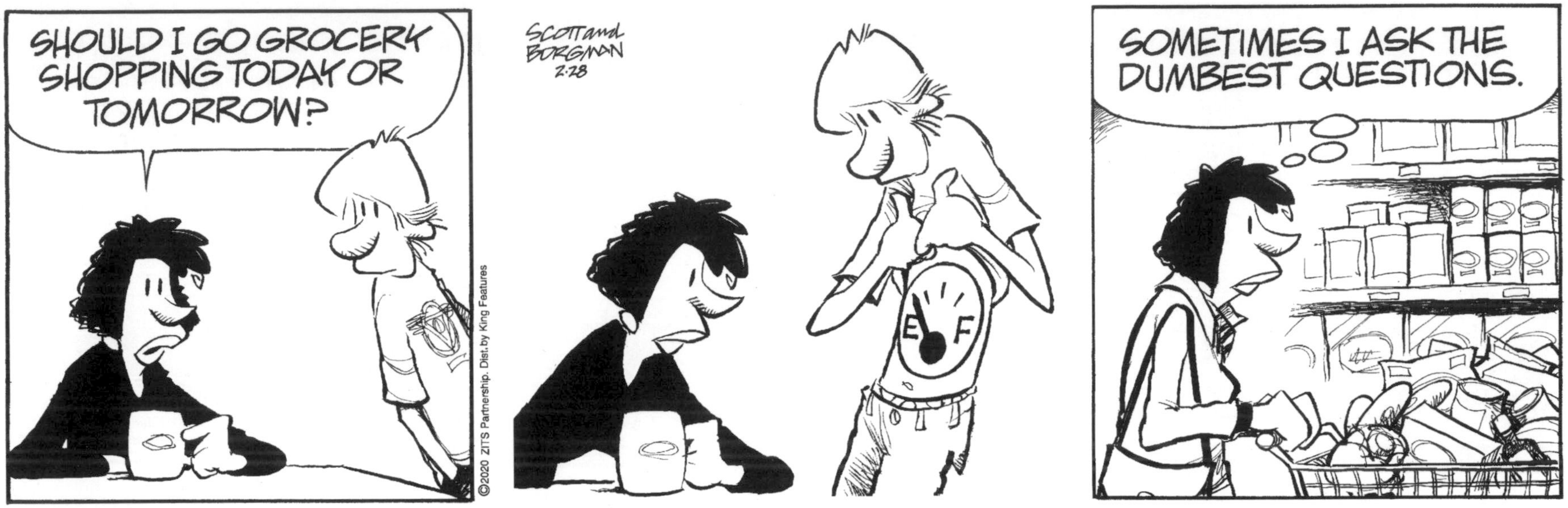
SHOULD I GO GROCERY SHOPPING TODAY OR TOMORROW?
SCOTT and BORGMAN 2·28
©2020 ZITS Partnership. Dist. by King Features
E F
SOMETIMES I ASK THE DUMBEST QUESTIONS.

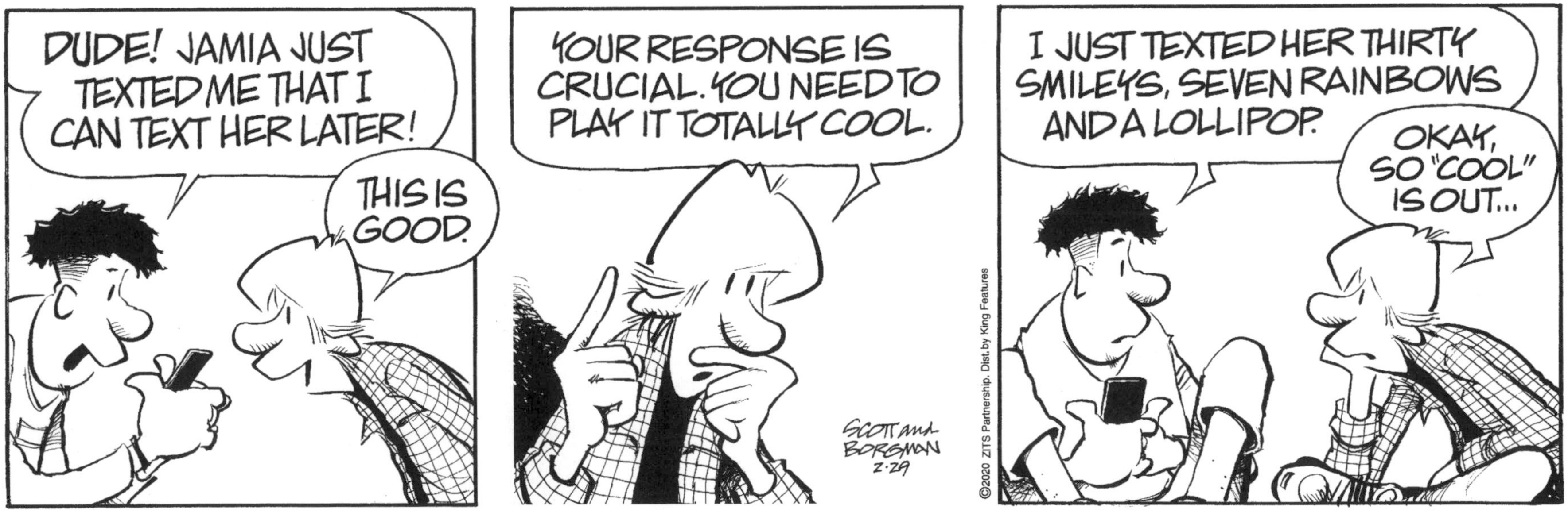
DUDE! JAMIA JUST TEXTED ME THAT I CAN TEXT HER LATER!
THIS IS GOOD.
YOUR RESPONSE IS CRUCIAL. YOU NEED TO PLAY IT TOTALLY COOL.
SCOTT and BORGMAN 2·29
©2020 ZITS Partnership. Dist. by King Features
I JUST TEXTED HER THIRTY SMILEYS, SEVEN RAINBOWS AND A LOLLIPOP.
OKAY, SO "COOL" IS OUT...

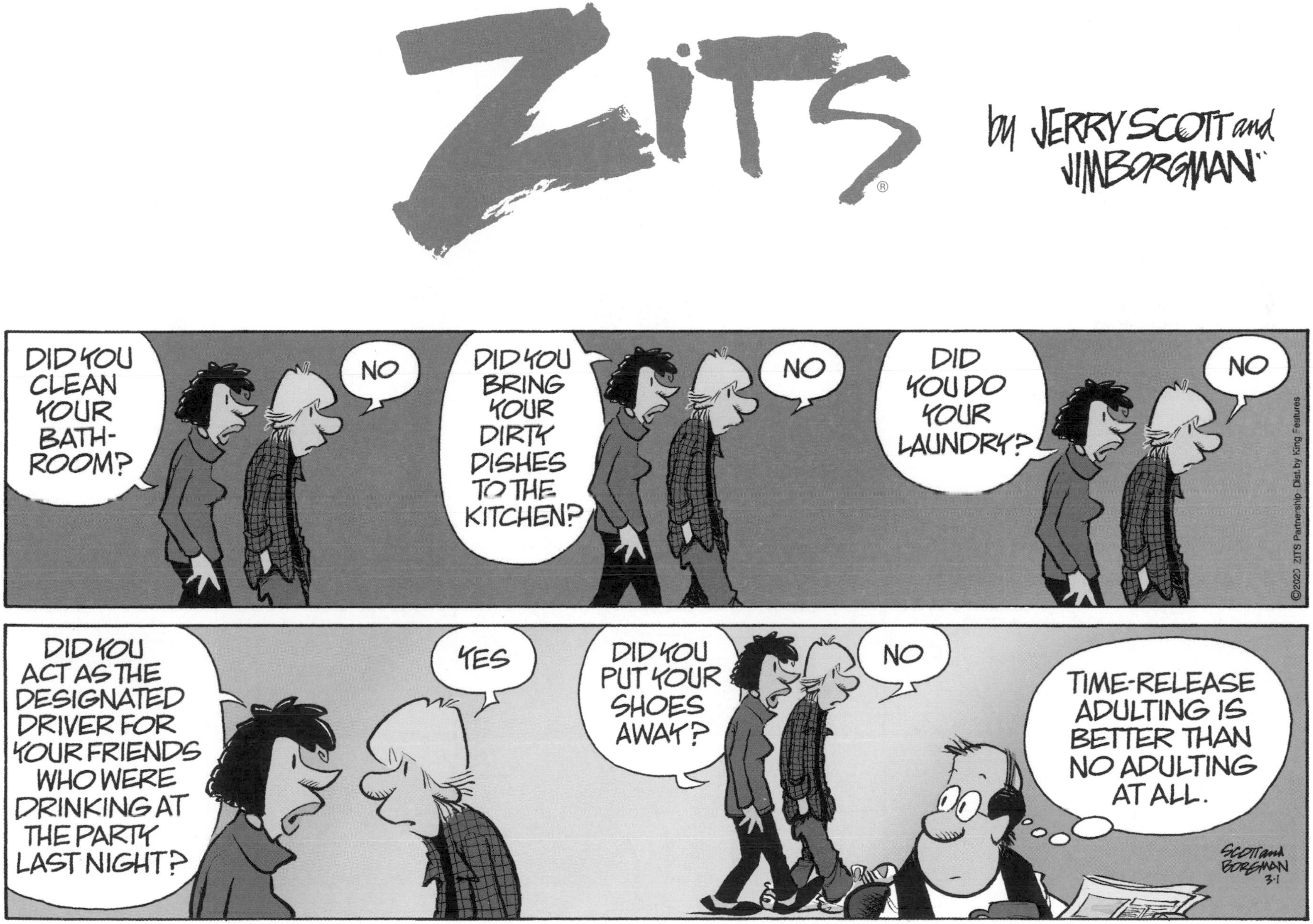
ZITS®
by JERRY SCOTT and JIM BORGMAN
DID YOU CLEAN YOUR BATH-ROOM?
NO
DID YOU BRING YOUR DIRTY DISHES TO THE KITCHEN?
NO
DID YOU DO YOUR LAUNDRY?
NO
©2020 ZITS Partnership Dist.by King Features
DID YOU ACT AS THE DESIGNATED DRIVER FOR YOUR FRIENDS WHO WERE DRINKING AT THE PARTY LAST NIGHT?
YES
DID YOU PUT YOUR SHOES AWAY?
NO
TIME-RELEASE ADULTING IS BETTER THAN NO ADULTING AT ALL.
SCOTT and BORGMAN 3·1

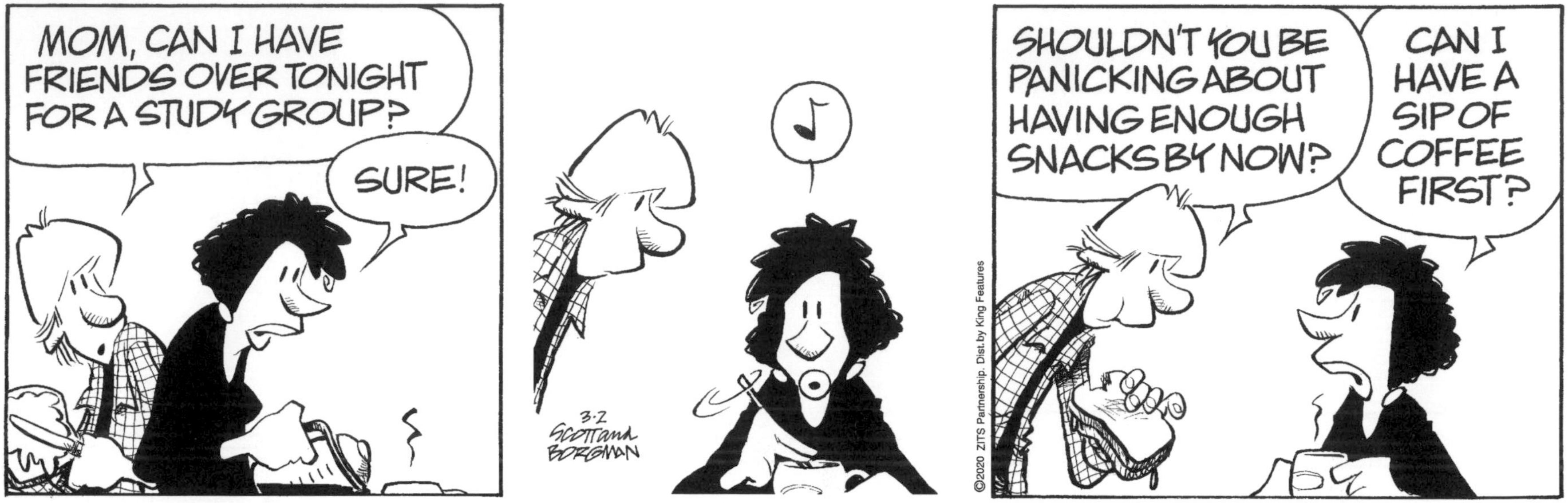
MOM, CAN I HAVE FRIENDS OVER TONIGHT FOR A STUDY GROUP?
SURE!
♩
3·2 SCOTT and BORGMAN
SHOULDN'T YOU BE PANICKING ABOUT HAVING ENOUGH SNACKS BY NOW?
CAN I HAVE A SIP OF COFFEE FIRST?
©2020 ZITS Partnership. Dist. by King Features

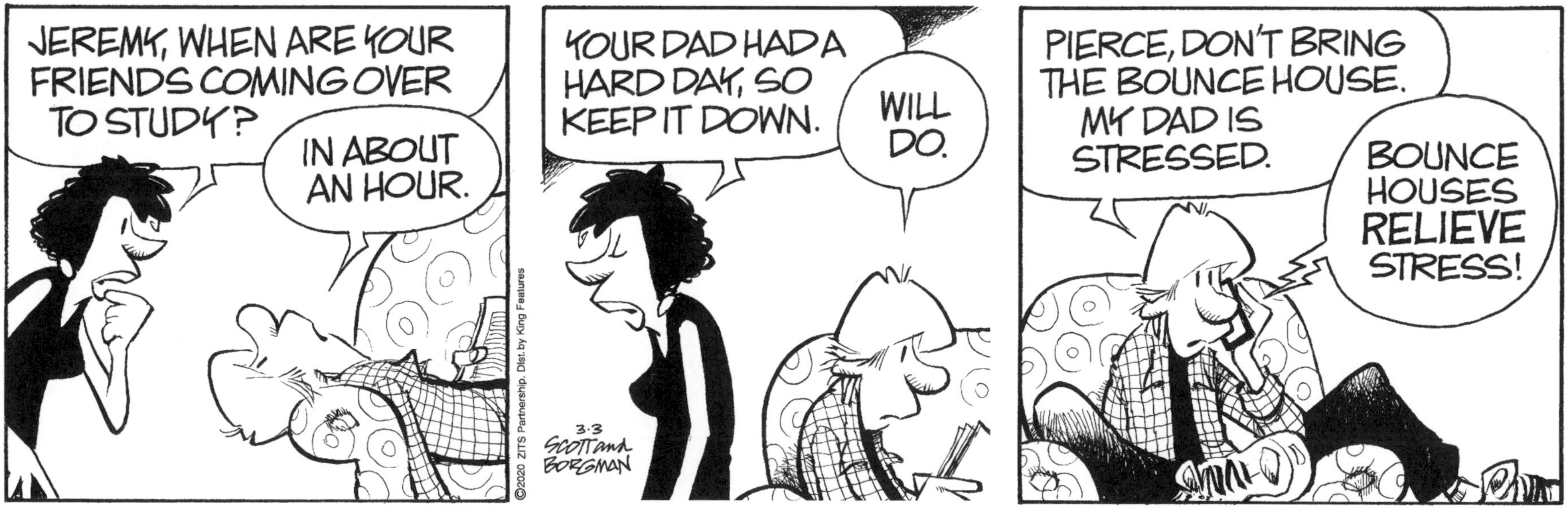
JEREMY, WHEN ARE YOUR FRIENDS COMING OVER TO STUDY?
IN ABOUT AN HOUR.
©2020 ZITS Partnership. Dist. by King Features
YOUR DAD HAD A HARD DAY, SO KEEP IT DOWN.
WILL DO.
3·3 SCOTT and BORGMAN
PIERCE, DON'T BRING THE BOUNCE HOUSE. MY DAD IS STRESSED.
BOUNCE HOUSES RELIEVE STRESS!

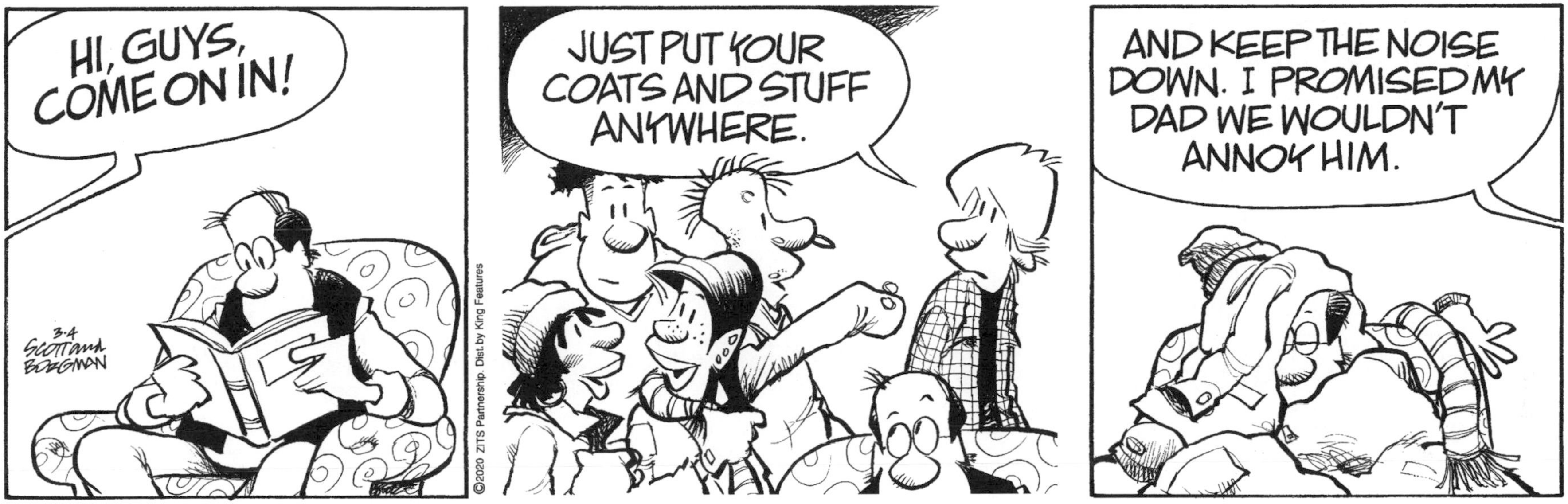
HI, GUYS, COME ON IN!
3·4 SCOTT and BORGMAN
©2020 ZITS Partnership. Dist. by King Features
JUST PUT YOUR COATS AND STUFF ANYWHERE.
AND KEEP THE NOISE DOWN. I PROMISED MY DAD WE WOULDN'T ANNOY HIM.

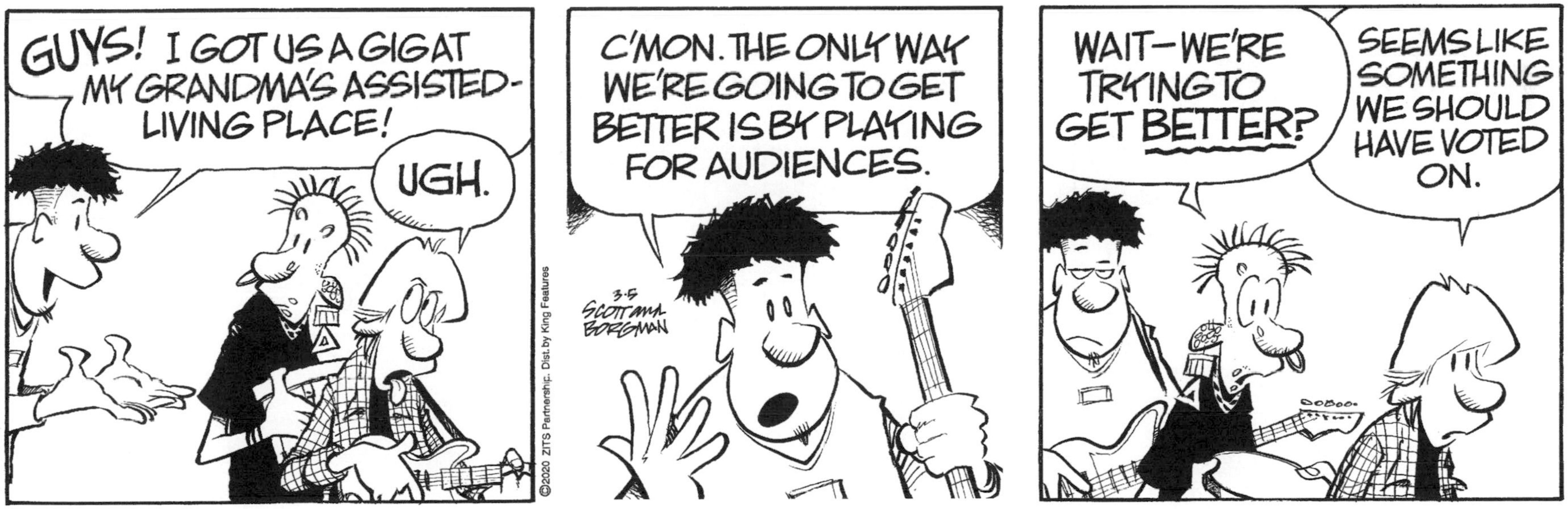
GUYS! I GOT US A GIG AT MY GRANDMA'S ASSISTED-LIVING PLACE!
UGH.
©2020 ZITS Partnership. Dist. by King Features
C'MON. THE ONLY WAY WE'RE GOING TO GET BETTER IS BY PLAYING FOR AUDIENCES.
3·5 SCOTT and BORGMAN
WAIT—WE'RE TRYING TO GET BETTER?
SEEMS LIKE SOMETHING WE SHOULD HAVE VOTED ON.

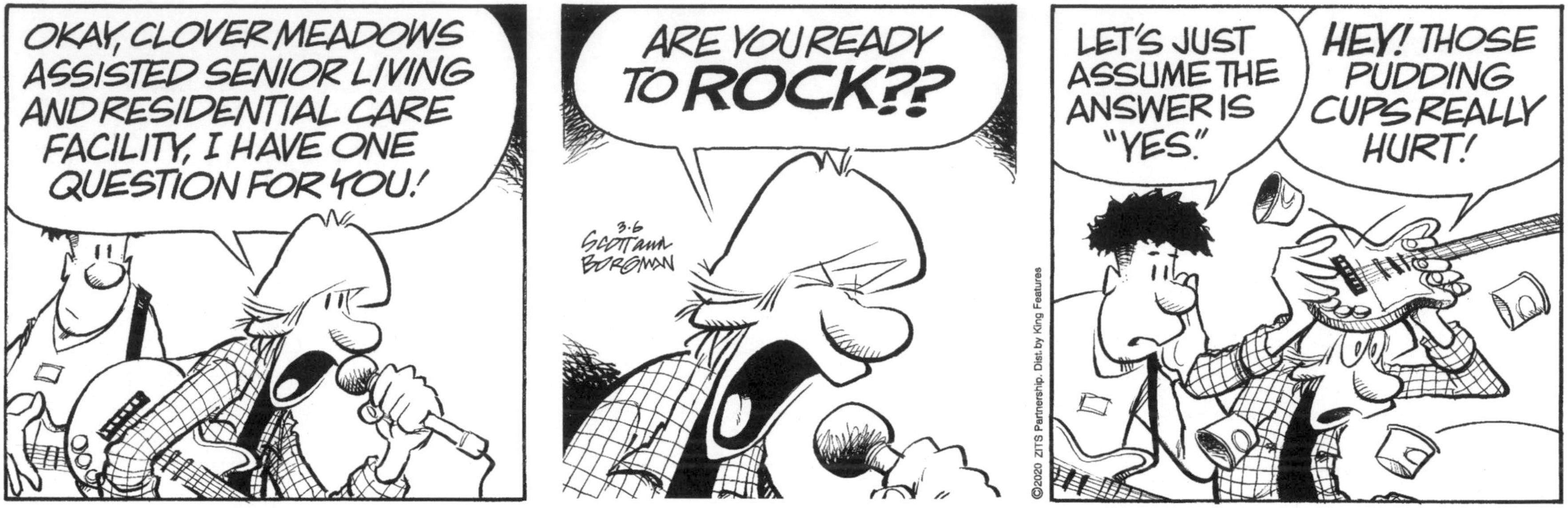
OKAY, CLOVER MEADOWS ASSISTED SENIOR LIVING AND RESIDENTIAL CARE FACILITY, I HAVE ONE QUESTION FOR YOU!
ARE YOU READY TO **ROCK??**
3-6 SCOTT and BORGMAN
LET'S JUST ASSUME THE ANSWER IS "YES."
HEY! THOSE PUDDING CUPS REALLY HURT!
©2020 ZITS Partnership. Dist. by King Features

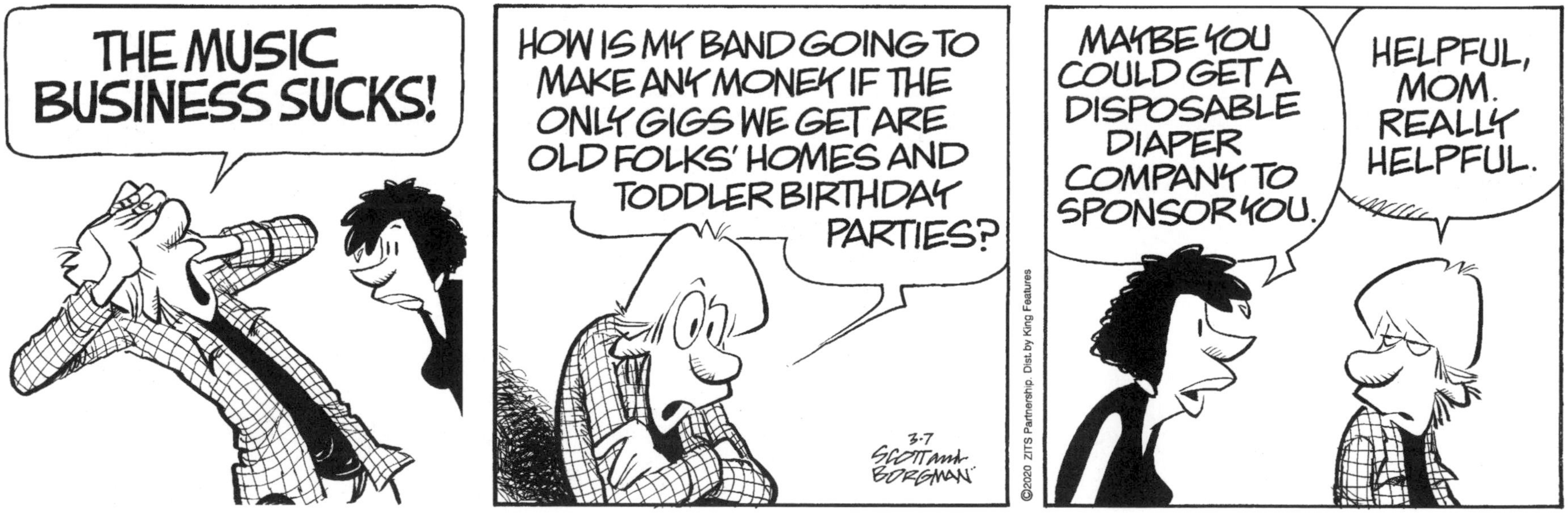
THE MUSIC BUSINESS SUCKS!
HOW IS MY BAND GOING TO MAKE ANY MONEY IF THE ONLY GIGS WE GET ARE OLD FOLKS' HOMES AND TODDLER BIRTHDAY PARTIES?
3-7 SCOTT and BORGMAN
©2020 ZITS Partnership. Dist. by King Features
MAYBE YOU COULD GET A DISPOSABLE DIAPER COMPANY TO SPONSOR YOU.
HELPFUL, MOM. REALLY HELPFUL.

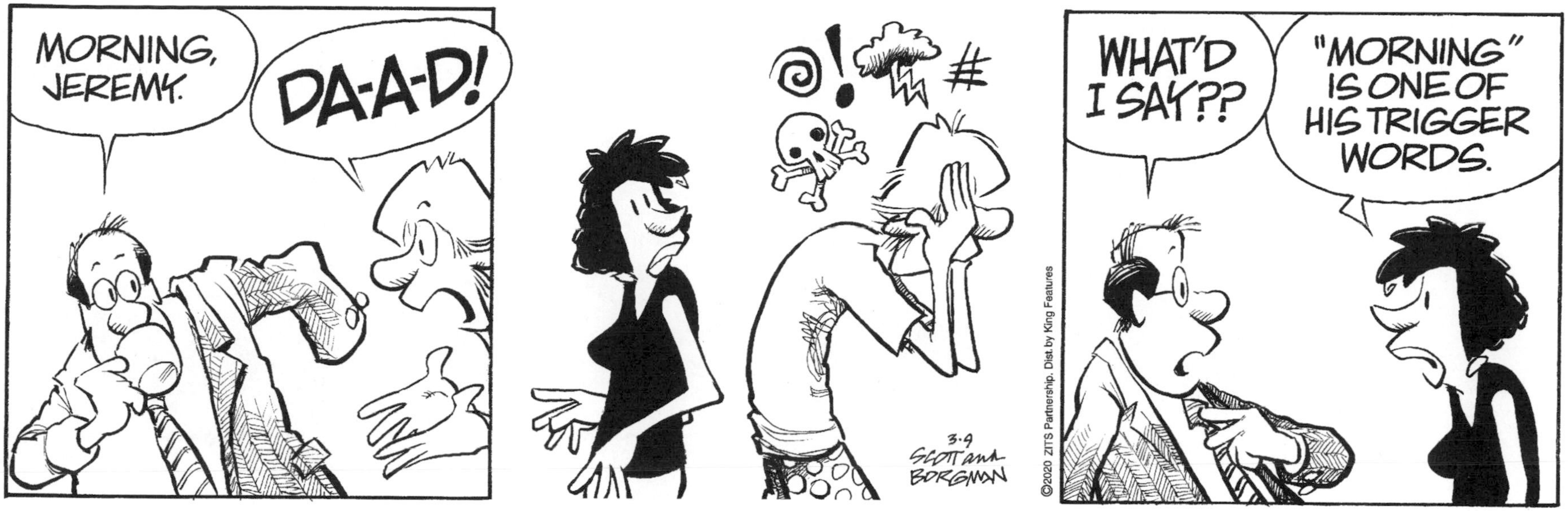
MORNING, JEREMY.
DA-A-D!
3-9 SCOTT and BORGMAN
WHAT'D I SAY??
"MORNING" IS ONE OF HIS TRIGGER WORDS.
©2020 ZITS Partnership. Dist. by King Features

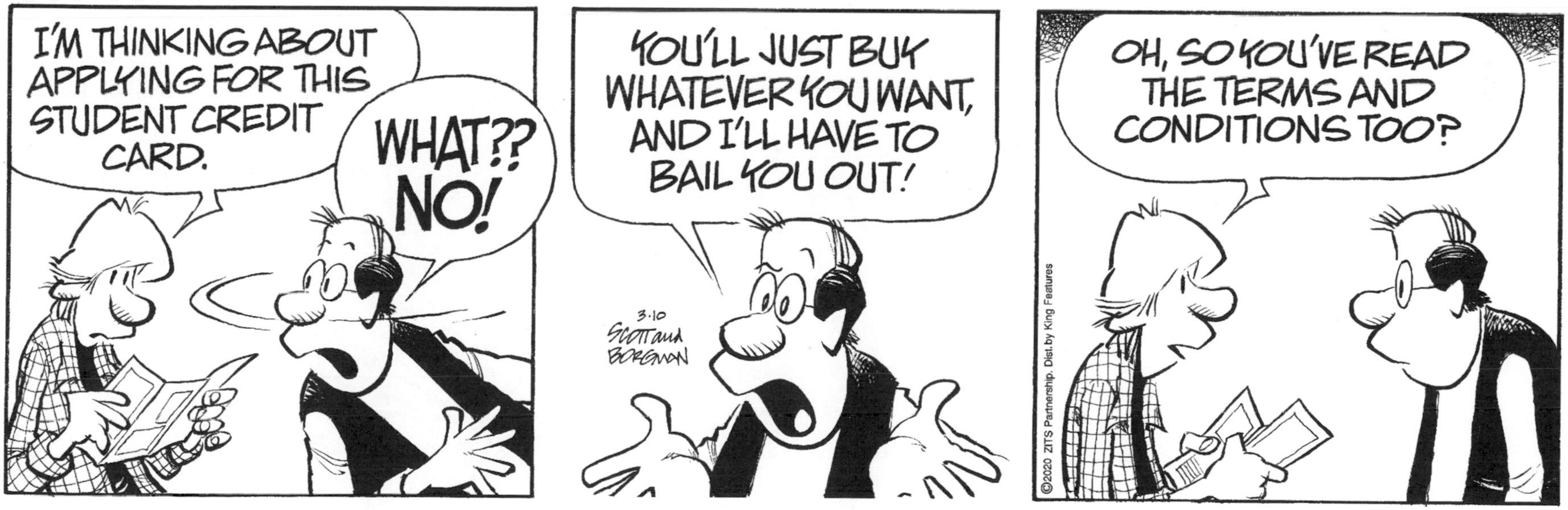
I'M THINKING ABOUT APPLYING FOR THIS STUDENT CREDIT CARD.
WHAT?? NO!
YOU'LL JUST BUY WHATEVER YOU WANT, AND I'LL HAVE TO BAIL YOU OUT!
3-10 SCOTT and BORGMAN
OH, SO YOU'VE READ THE TERMS AND CONDITIONS TOO?
©2020 ZITS Partnership. Dist. by King Features

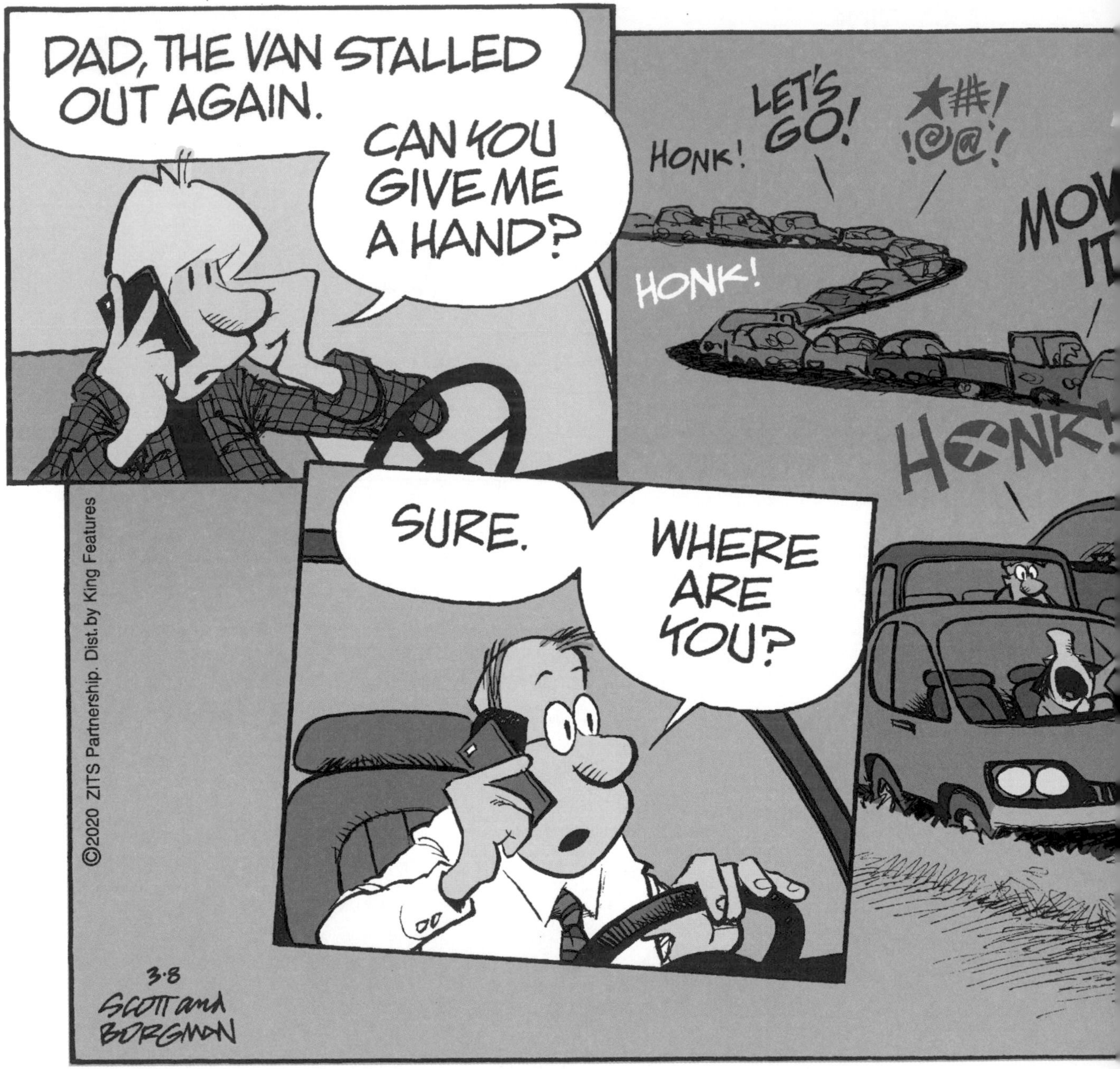
DAD, THE VAN STALLED OUT AGAIN.
CAN YOU GIVE ME A HAND?
HONK!
LET'S GO!
HONK!
HONK!
SURE.
WHERE ARE YOU?
3·8
SCOTT and BORGMAN

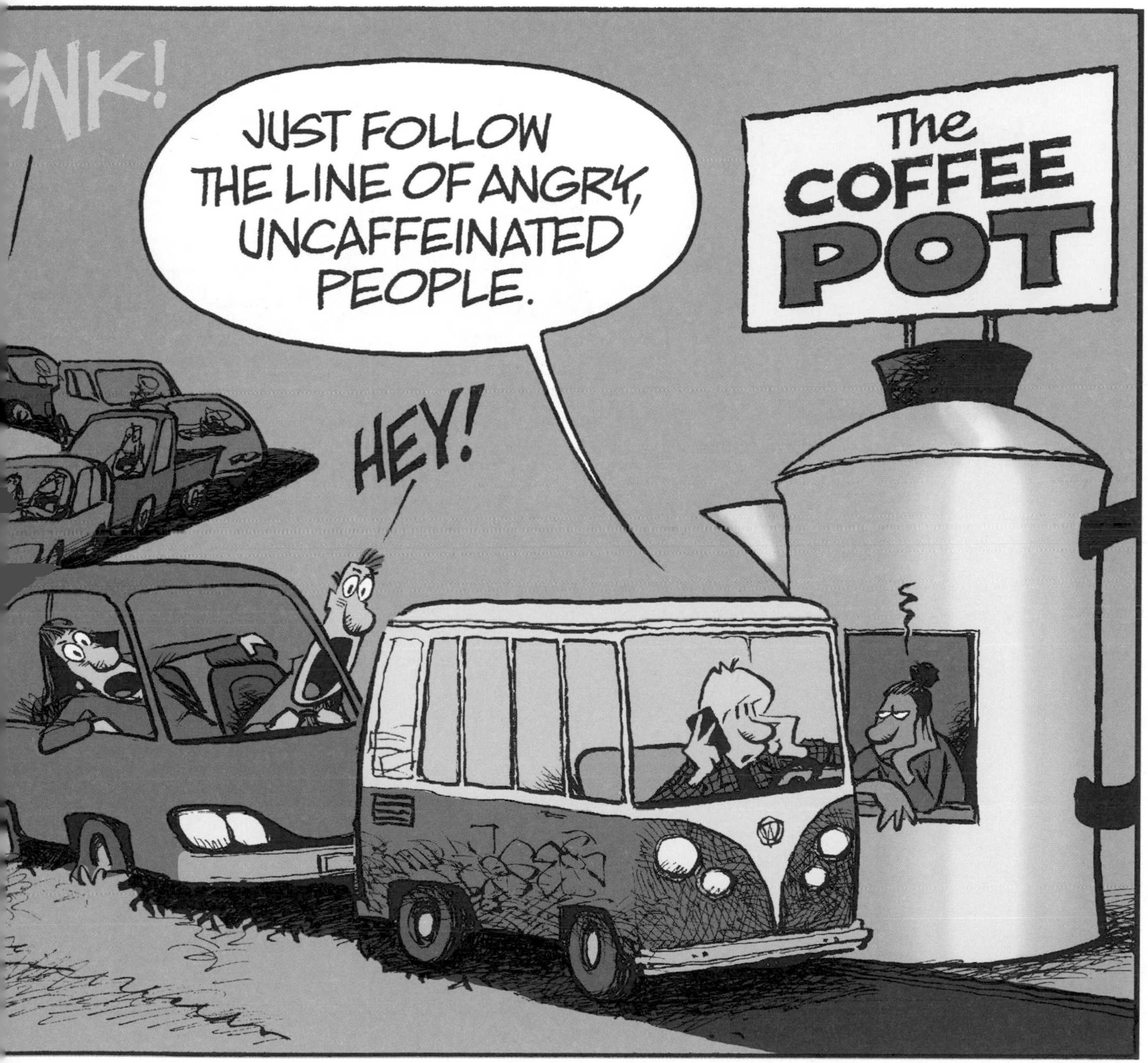
JUST FOLLOW THE LINE OF ANGRY, UNCAFFEINATED PEOPLE.
HEY!
The COFFEE POT

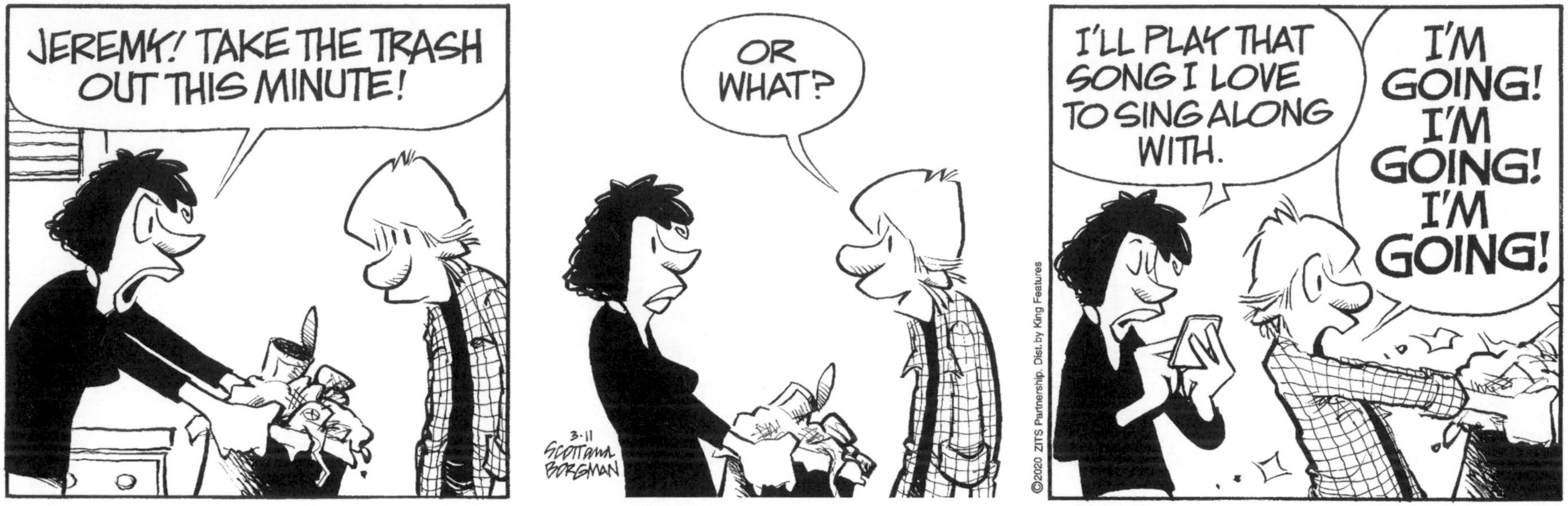
JEREMY! TAKE THE TRASH OUT THIS MINUTE!
OR WHAT?
3-11 SCOTT and BORGMAN
I'LL PLAY THAT SONG I LOVE TO SING ALONG WITH.
I'M GOING! I'M GOING! I'M GOING!
©2020 ZITS Partnership. Dist. by King Features

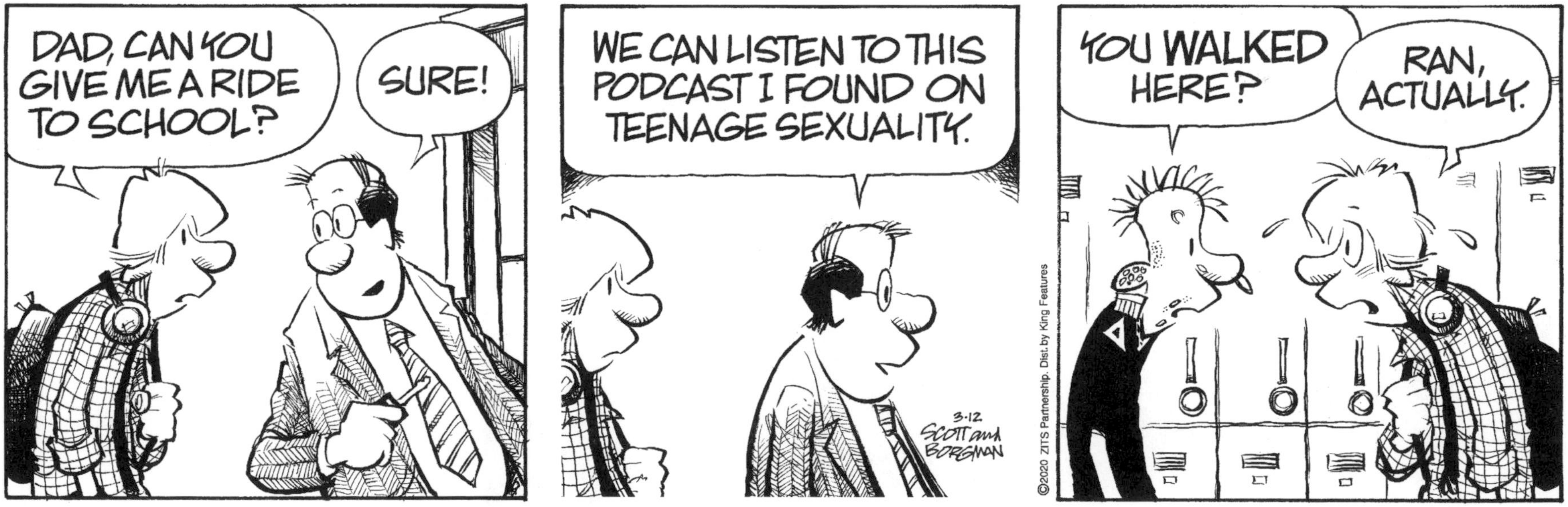
DAD, CAN YOU GIVE ME A RIDE TO SCHOOL?
SURE!
WE CAN LISTEN TO THIS PODCAST I FOUND ON TEENAGE SEXUALITY.
3-12 SCOTT and BORGMAN
YOU WALKED HERE?
RAN, ACTUALLY.
©2020 ZITS Partnership. Dist. by King Features

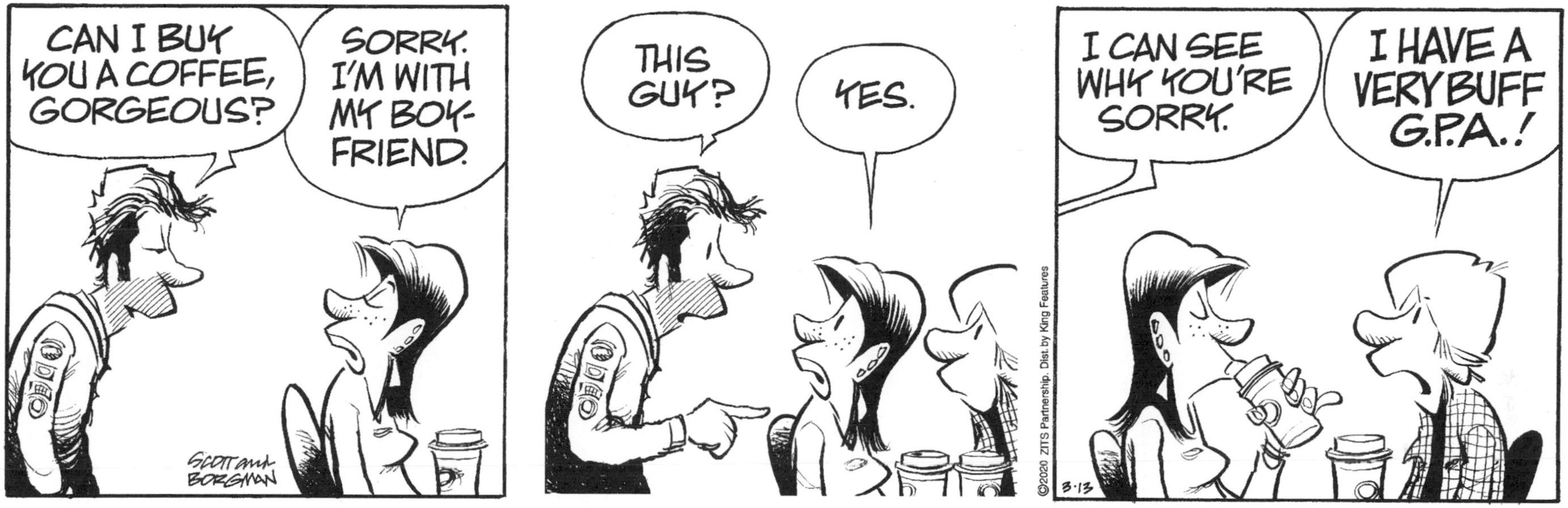
CAN I BUY YOU A COFFEE, GORGEOUS?
SORRY. I'M WITH MY BOY-FRIEND.
THIS GUY?
YES.
I CAN SEE WHY YOU'RE SORRY.
I HAVE A VERY BUFF G.P.A.!
SCOTT and BORGMAN
3·13
©2020 ZITS Partnership. Dist. by King Features

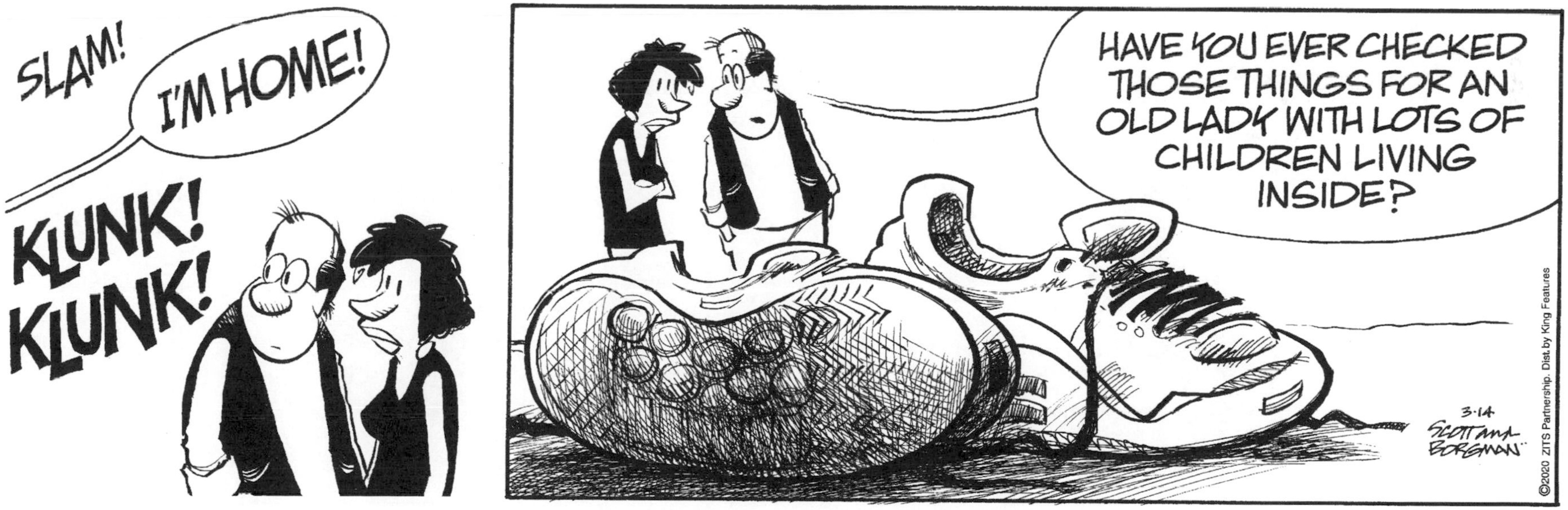
SLAM!
I'M HOME!
KLUNK! KLUNK!
HAVE YOU EVER CHECKED THOSE THINGS FOR AN OLD LADY WITH LOTS OF CHILDREN LIVING INSIDE?
3·14
SCOTT and BORGMAN
©2020 ZITS Partnership. Dist. by King Features

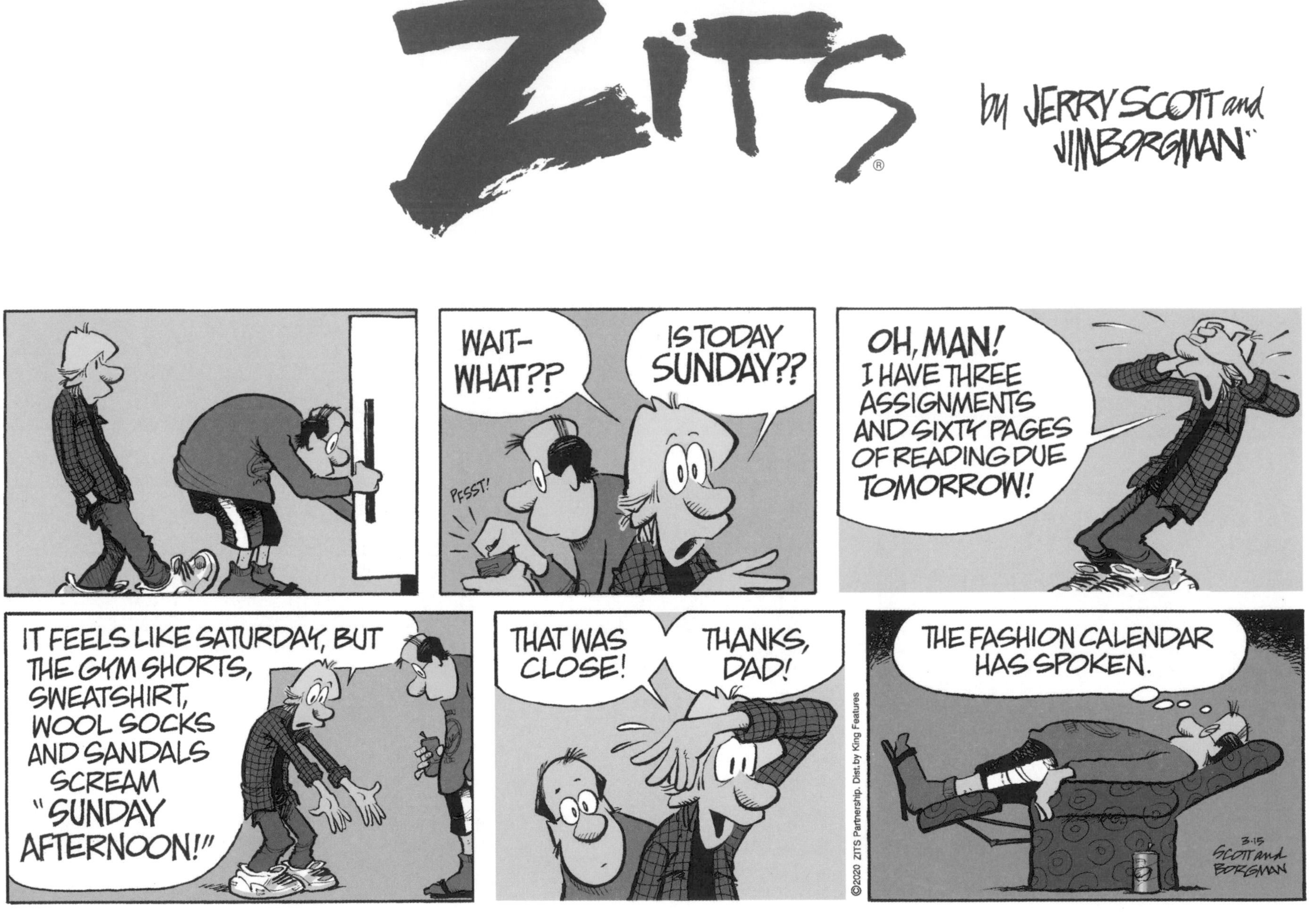
ZITS®
by JERRY SCOTT and JIM BORGMAN
WAIT- WHAT??
IS TODAY SUNDAY??
PFSST!
OH, MAN! I HAVE THREE ASSIGNMENTS AND SIXTY PAGES OF READING DUE TOMORROW!
IT FEELS LIKE SATURDAY, BUT THE GYM SHORTS, SWEATSHIRT, WOOL SOCKS AND SANDALS SCREAM "SUNDAY AFTERNOON!"
THAT WAS CLOSE!
THANKS, DAD!
©2020 ZITS Partnership. Dist. by King Features
THE FASHION CALENDAR HAS SPOKEN.
3-15 SCOTT and BORGMAN

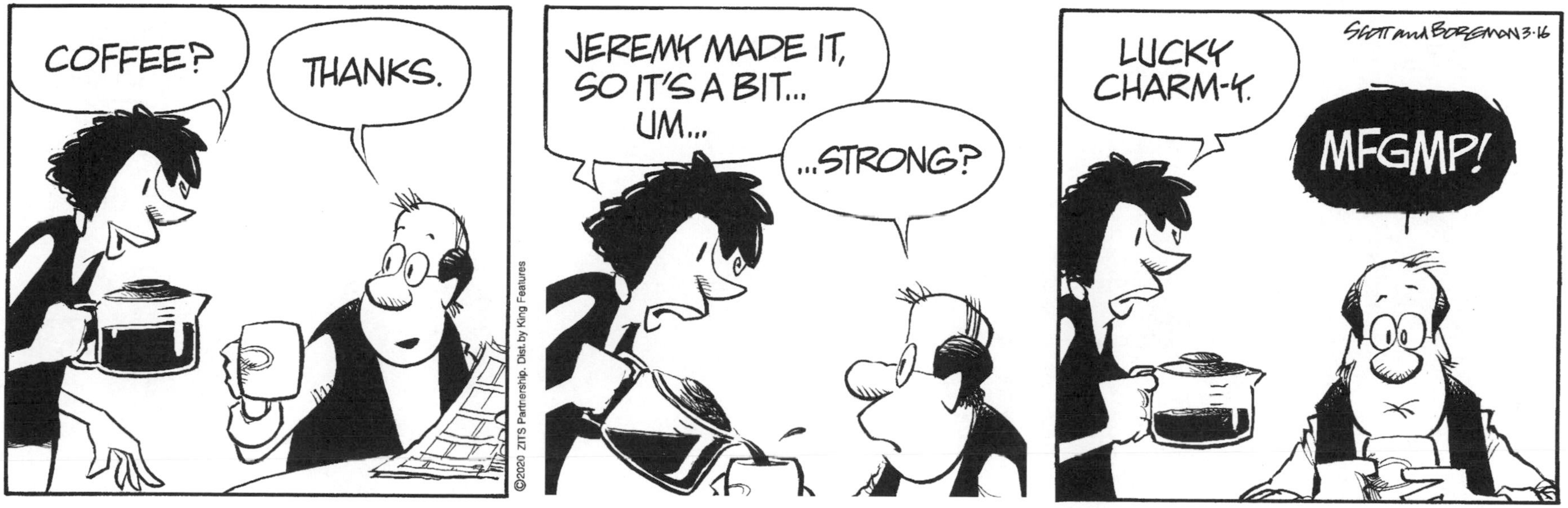
COFFEE?
THANKS.
©2020 ZITS Partnership. Dist. by King Features
JEREMY MADE IT, SO IT'S A BIT... UM...
...STRONG?
SCOTT and BORGMAN 3·16
LUCKY CHARM-Y.
MFGMP!

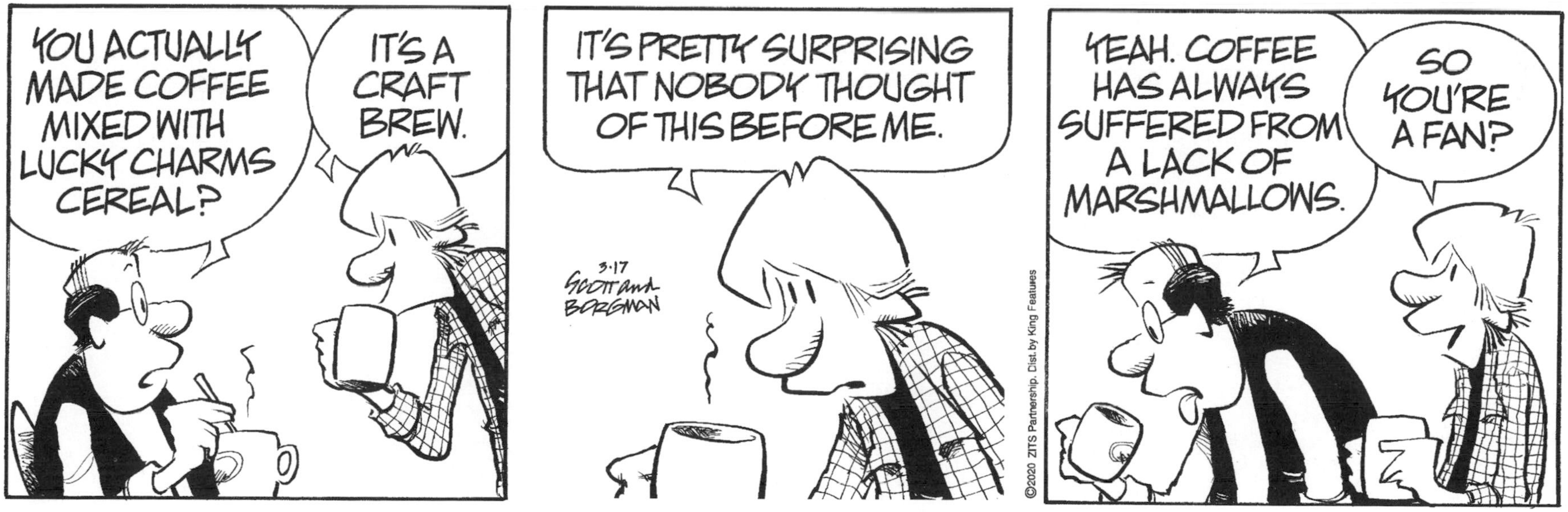
YOU ACTUALLY MADE COFFEE MIXED WITH LUCKY CHARMS CEREAL?
IT'S A CRAFT BREW.
3·17 SCOTT and BORGMAN
IT'S PRETTY SURPRISING THAT NOBODY THOUGHT OF THIS BEFORE ME.
©2020 ZITS Partnership. Dist. by King Features
YEAH. COFFEE HAS ALWAYS SUFFERED FROM A LACK OF MARSHMALLOWS.
SO YOU'RE A FAN?

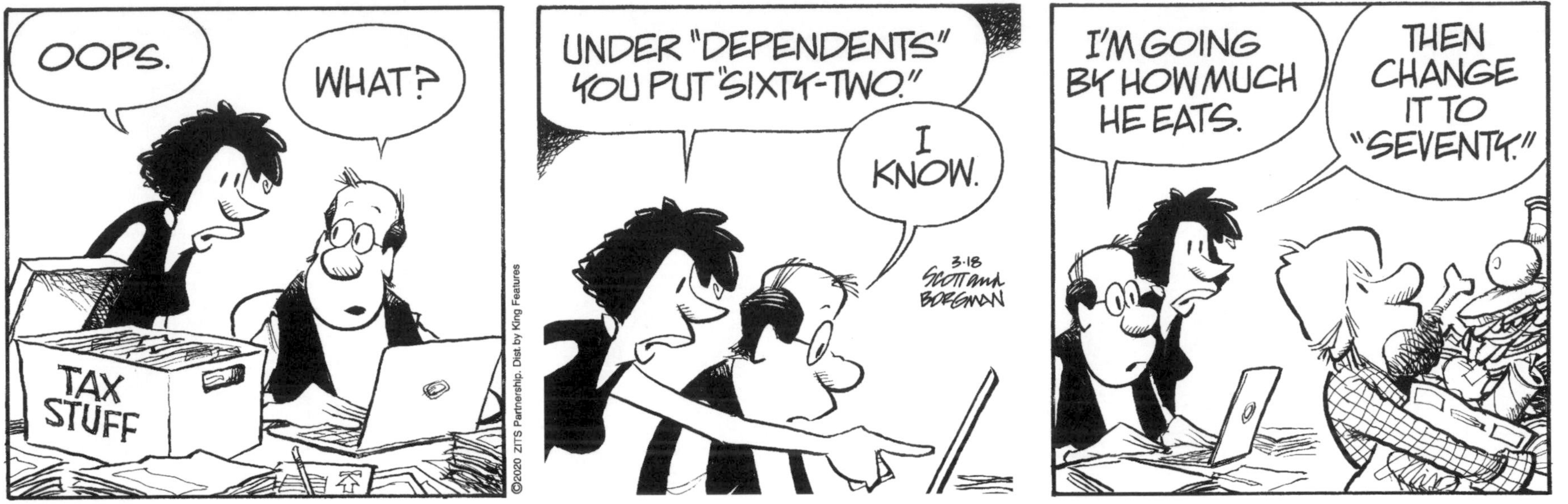
OOPS.
WHAT?
TAX STUFF
©2020 ZITS Partnership. Dist. by King Features
UNDER "DEPENDENTS" YOU PUT "SIXTY-TWO."
I KNOW.
3.18 SCOTT and BORGMAN
I'M GOING BY HOW MUCH HE EATS.
THEN CHANGE IT TO "SEVENTY."

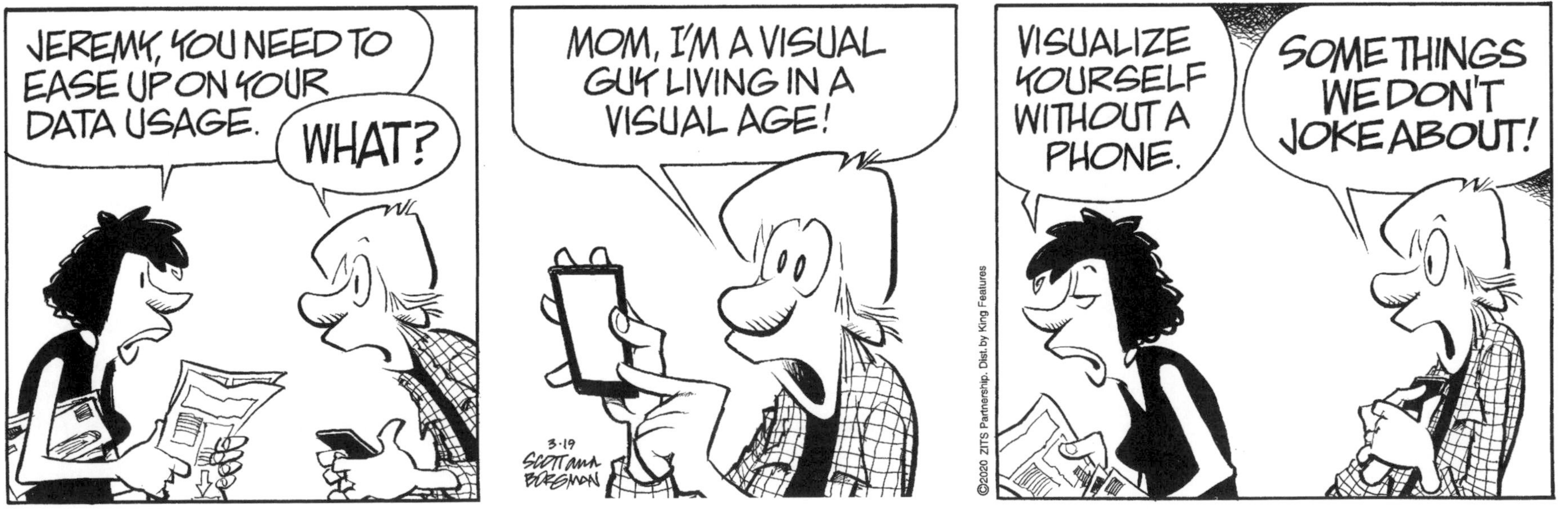
JEREMY, YOU NEED TO EASE UP ON YOUR DATA USAGE.
WHAT?
MOM, I'M A VISUAL GUY LIVING IN A VISUAL AGE!
3.19 SCOTT and BORGMAN
©2020 ZITS Partnership. Dist. by King Features
VISUALIZE YOURSELF WITHOUT A PHONE.
SOME THINGS WE DON'T JOKE ABOUT!

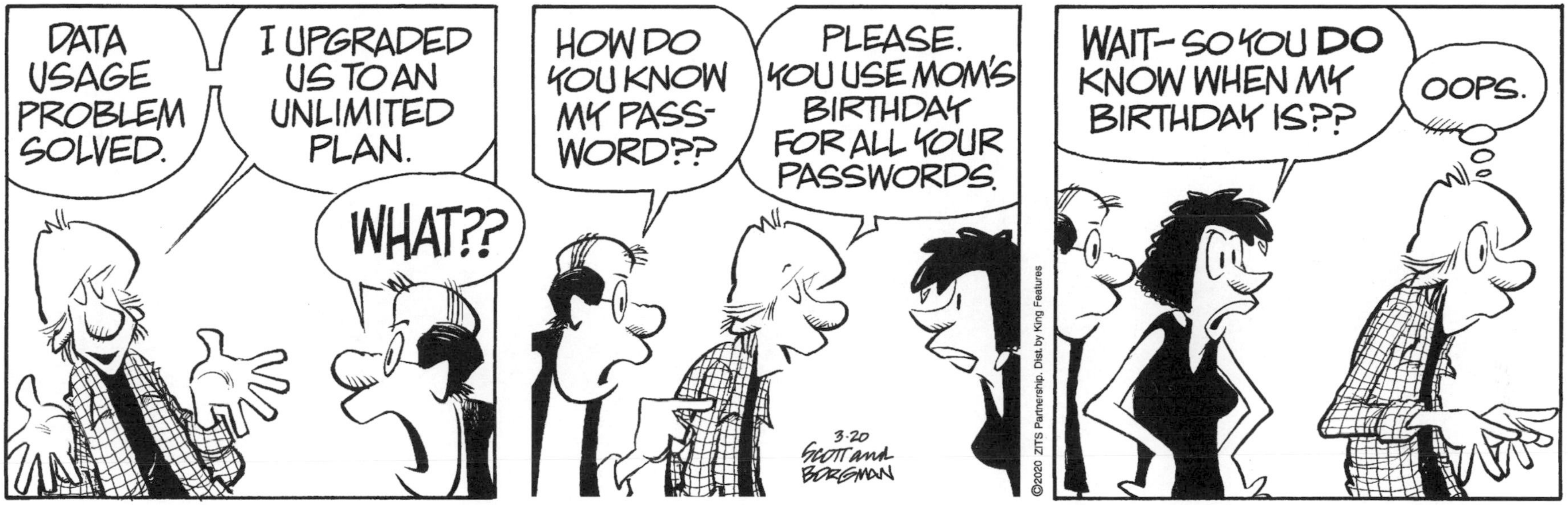
DATA USAGE PROBLEM SOLVED.
I UPGRADED US TO AN UNLIMITED PLAN.
WHAT??
HOW DO YOU KNOW MY PASS-WORD??
PLEASE. YOU USE MOM'S BIRTHDAY FOR ALL YOUR PASSWORDS.
3-20 SCOTT AND BORGMAN
©2020 ZITS Partnership. Dist. by King Features
WAIT– SO YOU **DO** KNOW WHEN MY BIRTHDAY IS??
OOPS.

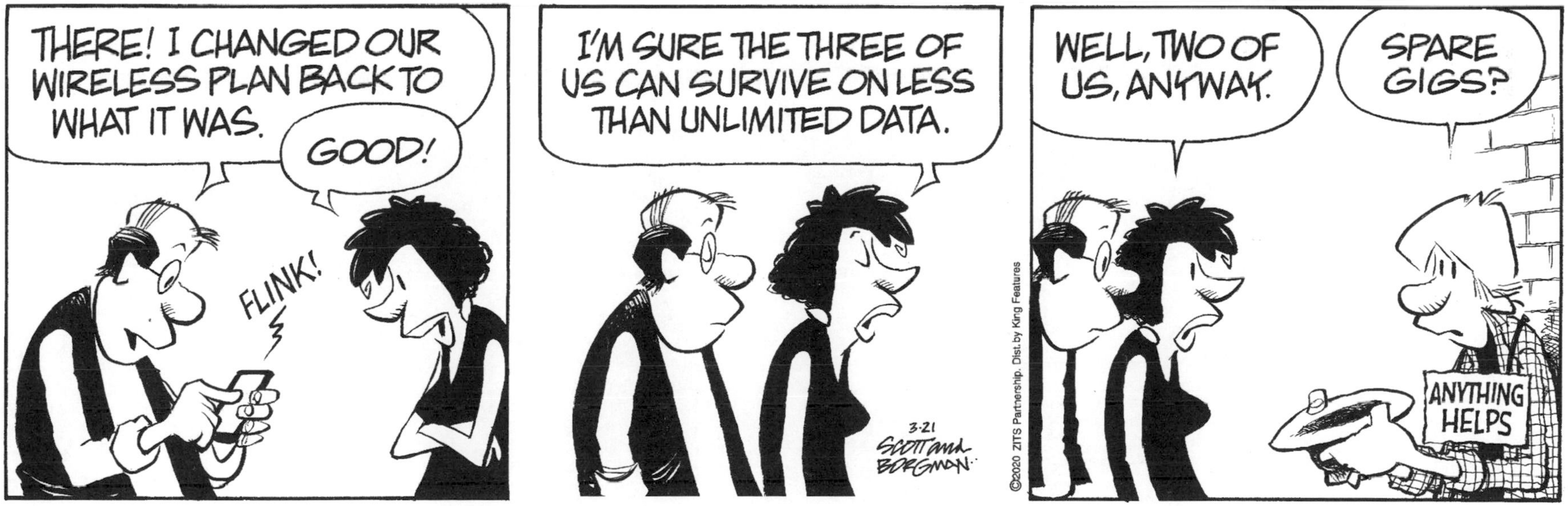
THERE! I CHANGED OUR WIRELESS PLAN BACK TO WHAT IT WAS.
GOOD!
FLINK!
I'M SURE THE THREE OF US CAN SURVIVE ON LESS THAN UNLIMITED DATA.
3-21 SCOTT AND BORGMAN
©2020 ZITS Partnership. Dist. by King Features
WELL, TWO OF US, ANYWAY.
SPARE GIGS?
ANYTHING HELPS

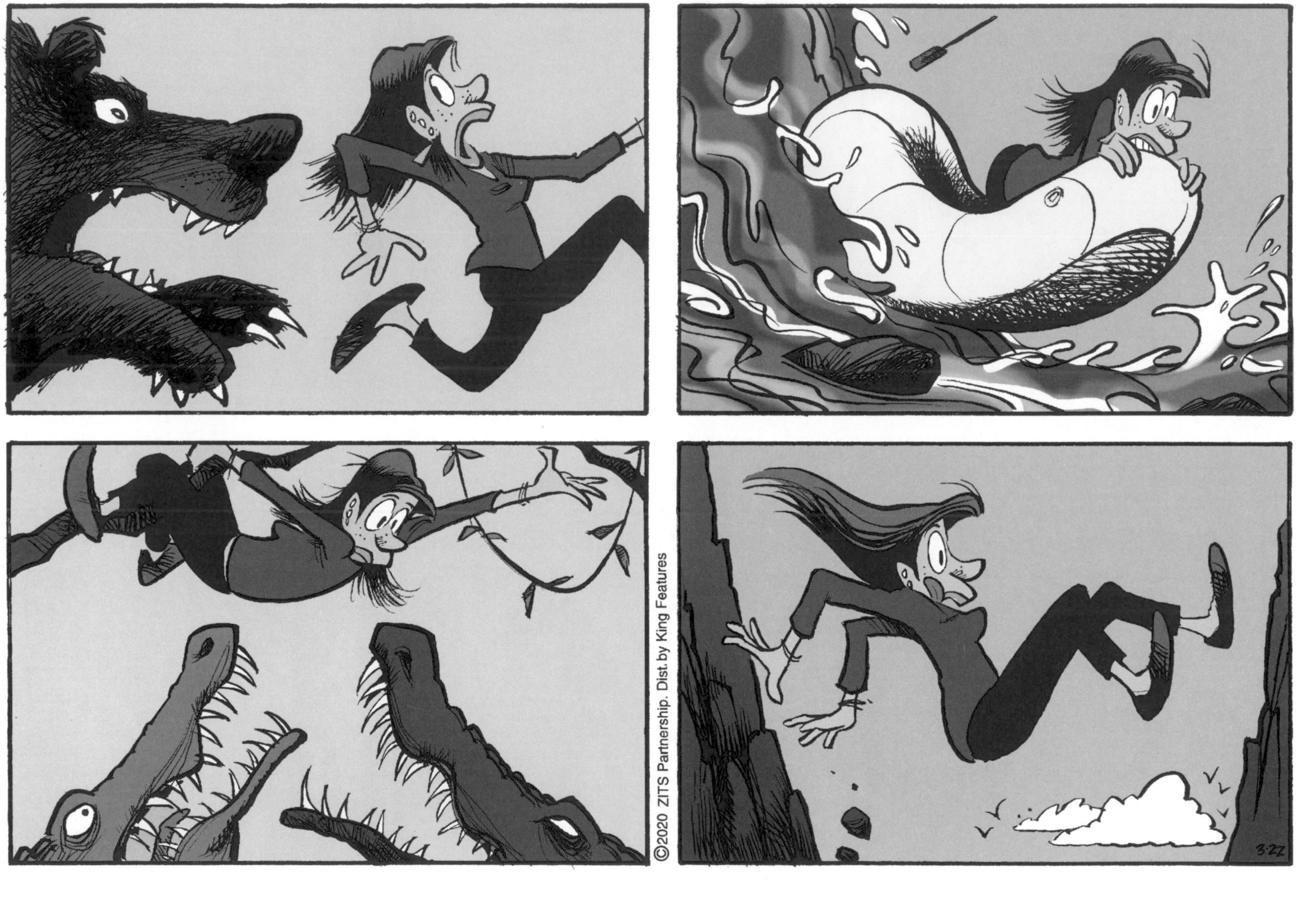
©2020 ZITS Partnership. Dist. by King Features
3-27

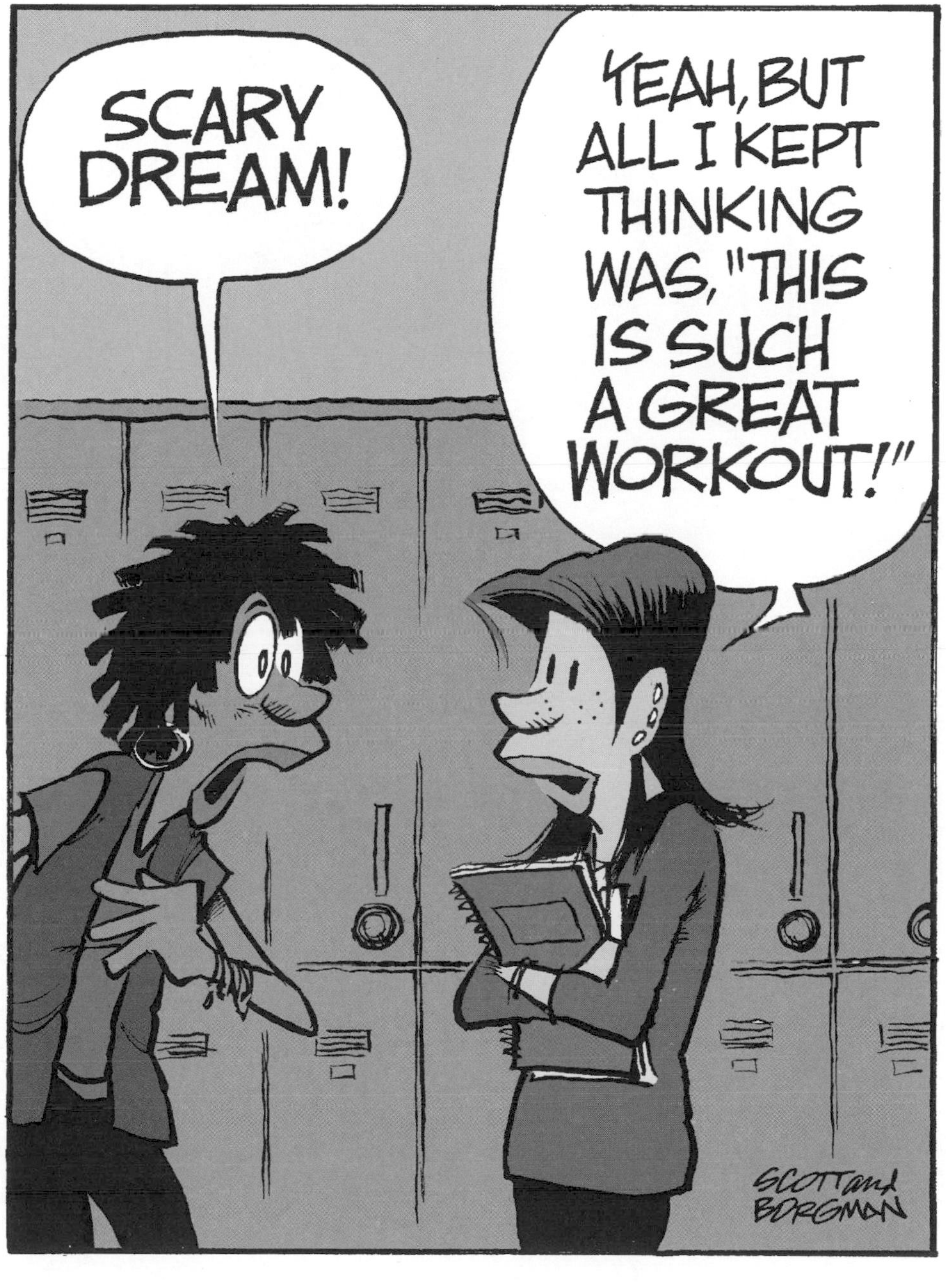
SCARY DREAM!
YEAH, BUT ALL I KEPT THINKING WAS, "THIS IS SUCH A GREAT WORKOUT!"
SCOTT and BORGMAN

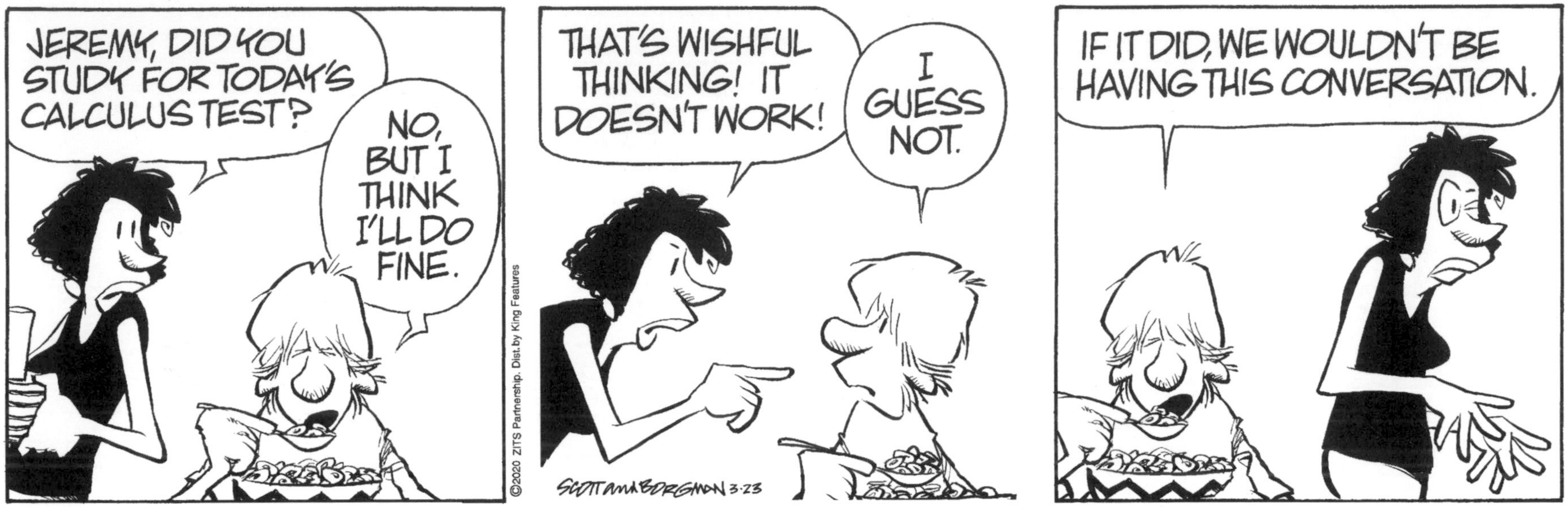
JEREMY, DID YOU STUDY FOR TODAY'S CALCULUS TEST?
NO, BUT I THINK I'LL DO FINE.
©2020 ZITS Partnership. Dist. by King Features
THAT'S WISHFUL THINKING! IT DOESN'T WORK!
I GUESS NOT.
SCOTT AND BORGMAN 3-23
IF IT DID, WE WOULDN'T BE HAVING THIS CONVERSATION.

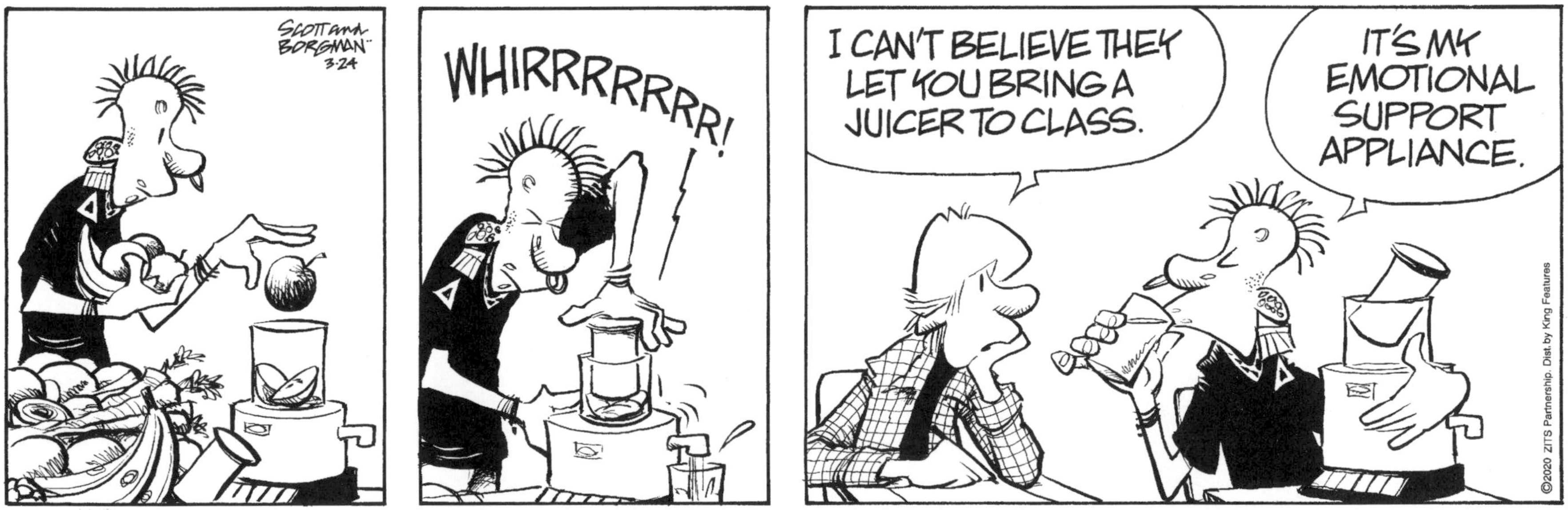
SCOTT AND BORGMAN 3-24
WHIRRRRRRRR!
I CAN'T BELIEVE THEY LET YOU BRING A JUICER TO CLASS.
IT'S MY EMOTIONAL SUPPORT APPLIANCE.
©2020 ZITS Partnership. Dist. by King Features

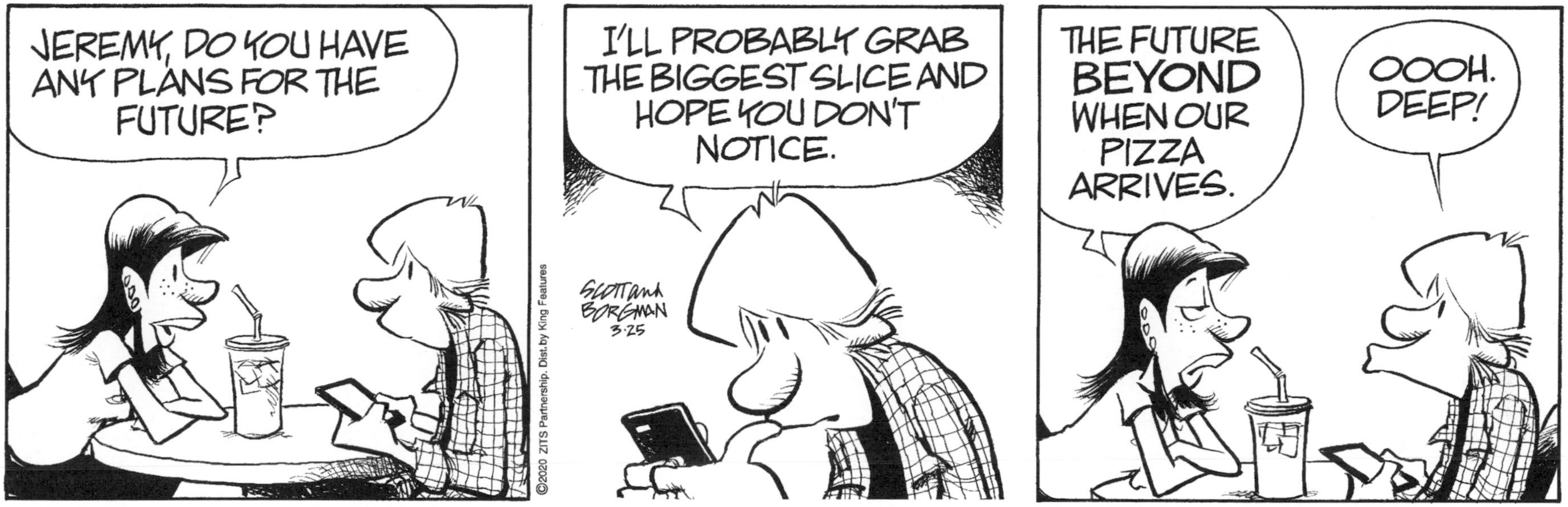
JEREMY, DO YOU HAVE ANY PLANS FOR THE FUTURE?
I'LL PROBABLY GRAB THE BIGGEST SLICE AND HOPE YOU DON'T NOTICE.
SCOTT and BORGMAN 3.25
©2020 ZITS Partnership. Dist. by King Features
THE FUTURE BEYOND WHEN OUR PIZZA ARRIVES.
OOOH. DEEP!

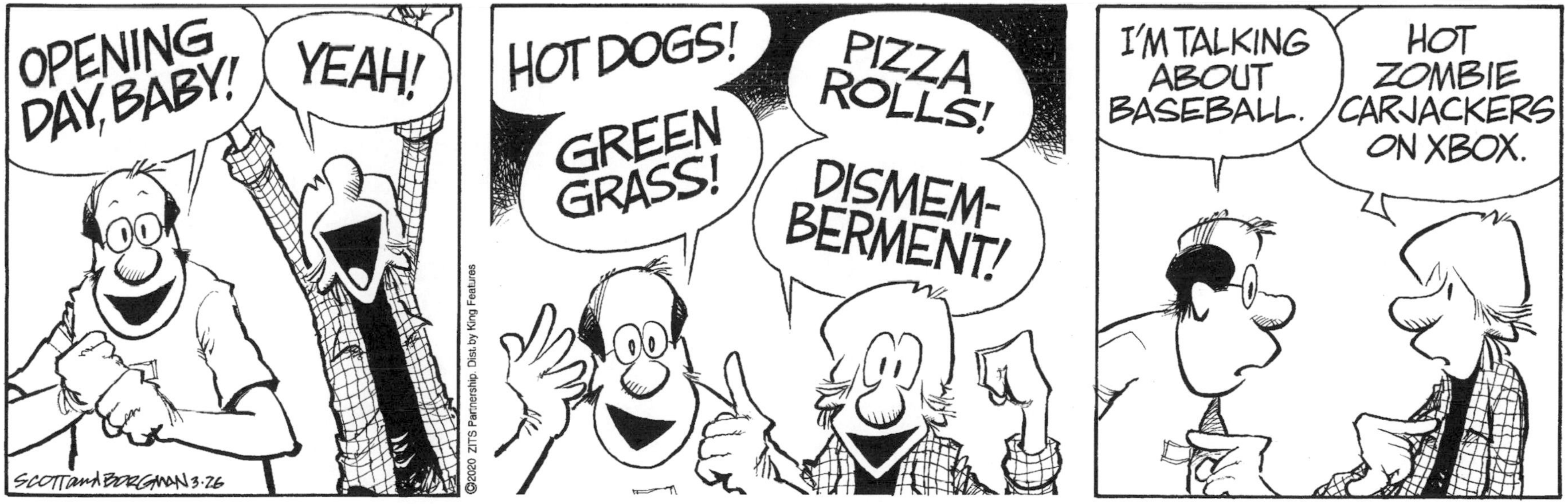
OPENING DAY, BABY!
YEAH!
SCOTT and BORGMAN 3.26
©2020 ZITS Partnership. Dist. by King Features
HOT DOGS!
PIZZA ROLLS!
GREEN GRASS!
DISMEMBERMENT!
I'M TALKING ABOUT BASEBALL.
HOT ZOMBIE CARJACKERS ON XBOX.

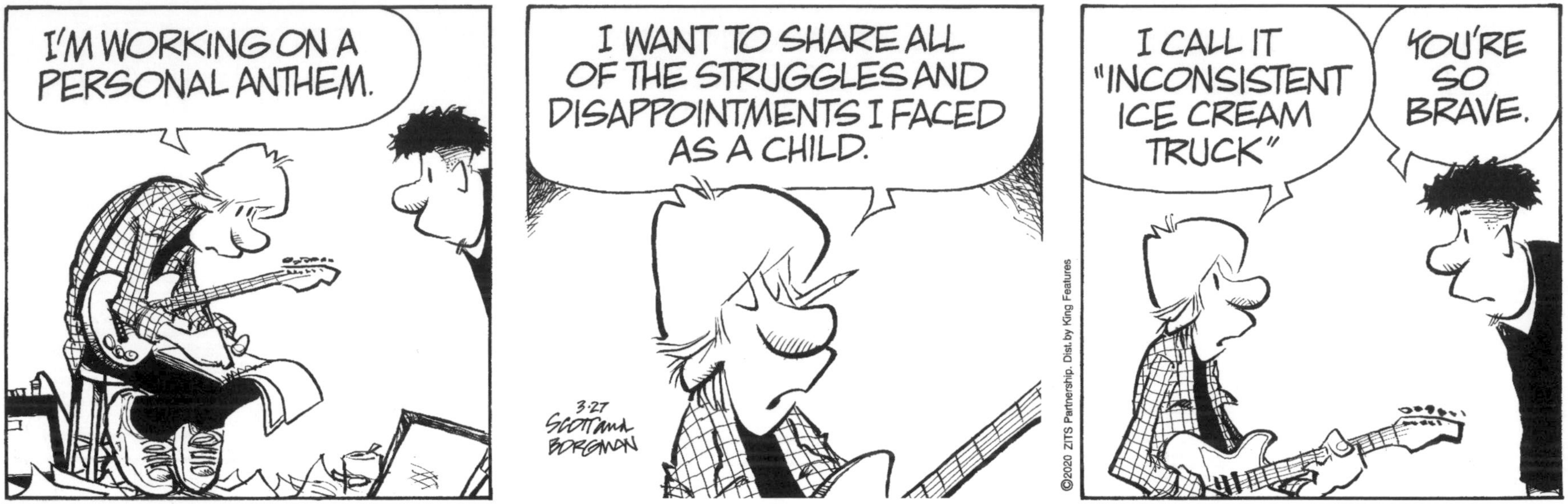
I'M WORKING ON A PERSONAL ANTHEM.
I WANT TO SHARE ALL OF THE STRUGGLES AND DISAPPOINTMENTS I FACED AS A CHILD.
3-27 SCOTT and BORGMAN
©2020 ZITS Partnership. Dist. by King Features
I CALL IT "INCONSISTENT ICE CREAM TRUCK"
YOU'RE SO BRAVE.

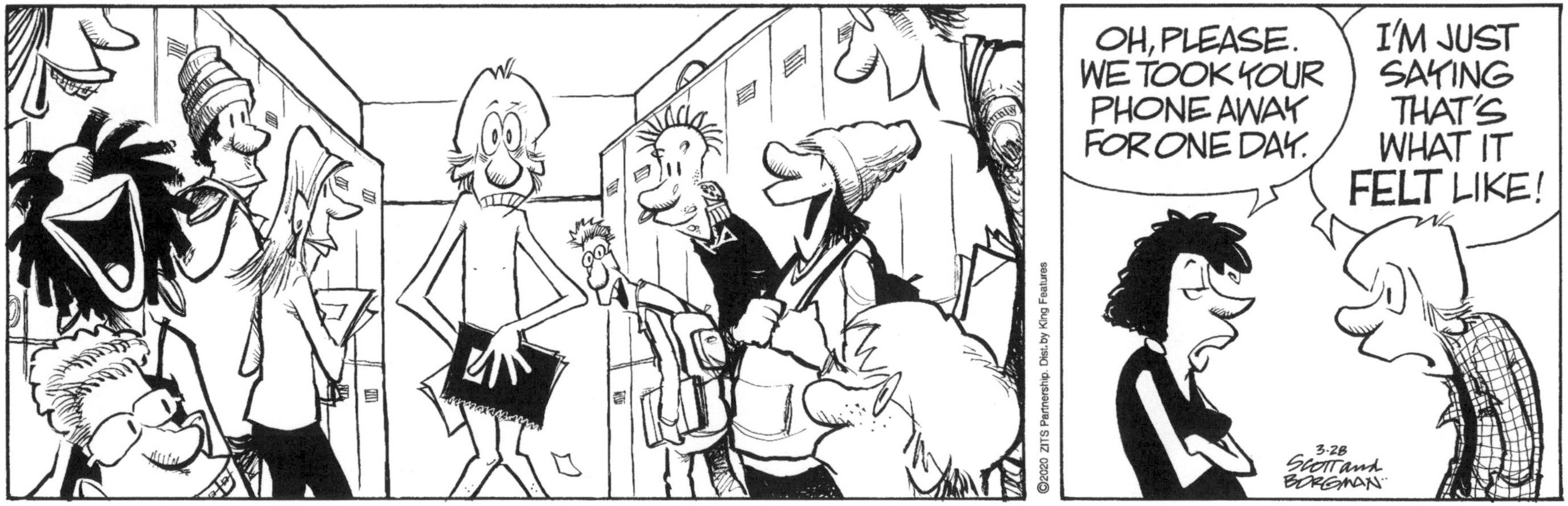
©2020 ZITS Partnership. Dist. by King Features
OH, PLEASE. WE TOOK YOUR PHONE AWAY FOR ONE DAY.
I'M JUST SAYING THAT'S WHAT IT **FELT** LIKE!
3-28 SCOTT and BORGMAN

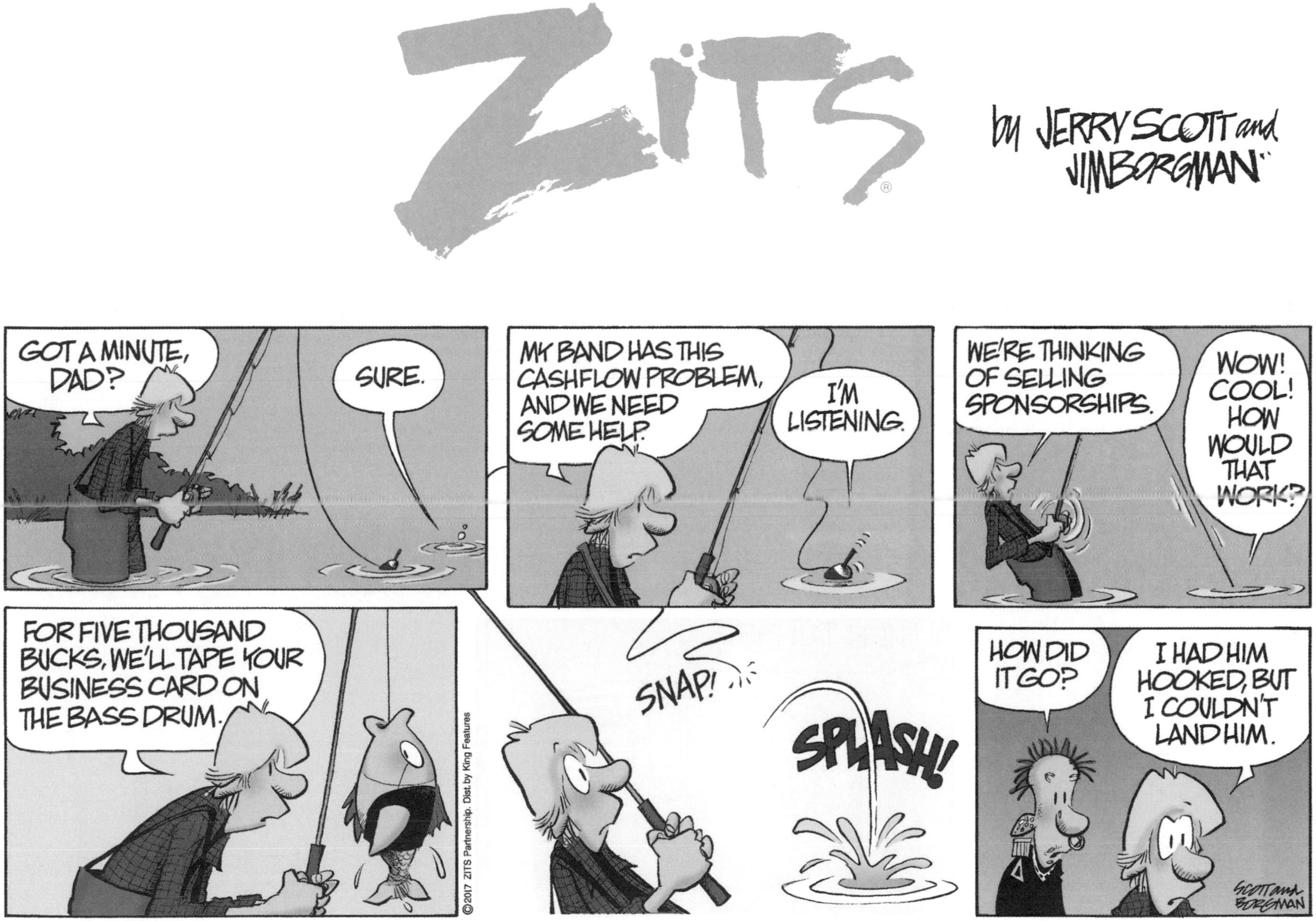
ZITS
by JERRY SCOTT and JIM BORGMAN
GOT A MINUTE, DAD?
SURE.
MY BAND HAS THIS CASHFLOW PROBLEM, AND WE NEED SOME HELP.
I'M LISTENING.
WE'RE THINKING OF SELLING SPONSORSHIPS.
WOW! COOL! HOW WOULD THAT WORK?
FOR FIVE THOUSAND BUCKS, WE'LL TAPE YOUR BUSINESS CARD ON THE BASS DRUM.
©2017 ZITS Partnership. Dist. by King Features
SNAP!
SPLASH!
HOW DID IT GO?
I HAD HIM HOOKED, BUT I COULDN'T LAND HIM.
SCOTT and BORGMAN

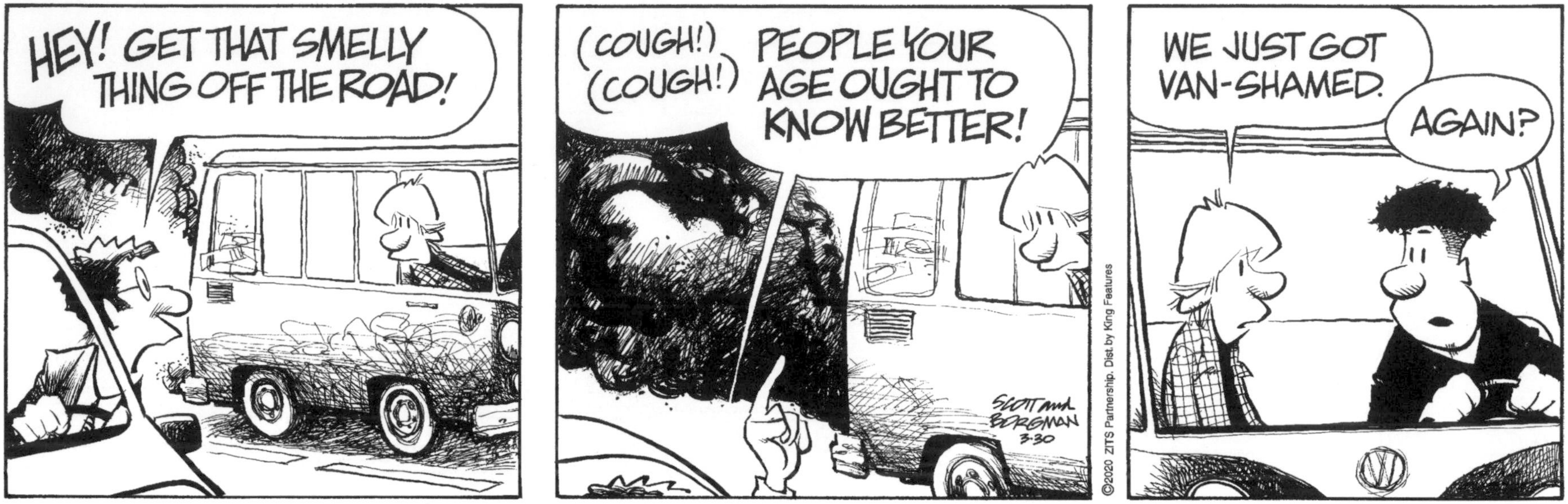
HEY! GET THAT SMELLY THING OFF THE ROAD!
(COUGH!) (COUGH!)
PEOPLE YOUR AGE OUGHT TO KNOW BETTER!
SCOTT and BORGMAN 3-30
©2020 ZITS Partnership. Dist. by King Features
WE JUST GOT VAN-SHAMED.
AGAIN?

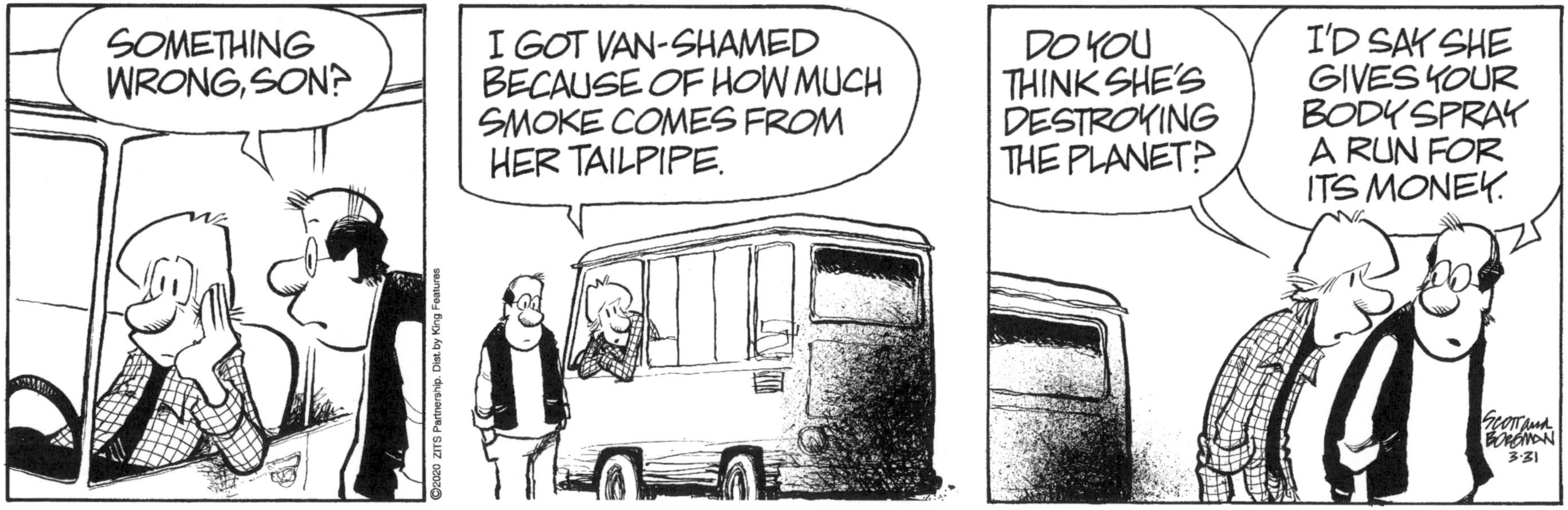
SOMETHING WRONG, SON?
©2020 ZITS Partnership. Dist. by King Features
I GOT VAN-SHAMED BECAUSE OF HOW MUCH SMOKE COMES FROM HER TAILPIPE.
DO YOU THINK SHE'S DESTROYING THE PLANET?
I'D SAY SHE GIVES YOUR BODY SPRAY A RUN FOR ITS MONEY.
SCOTT and BORGMAN 3-31

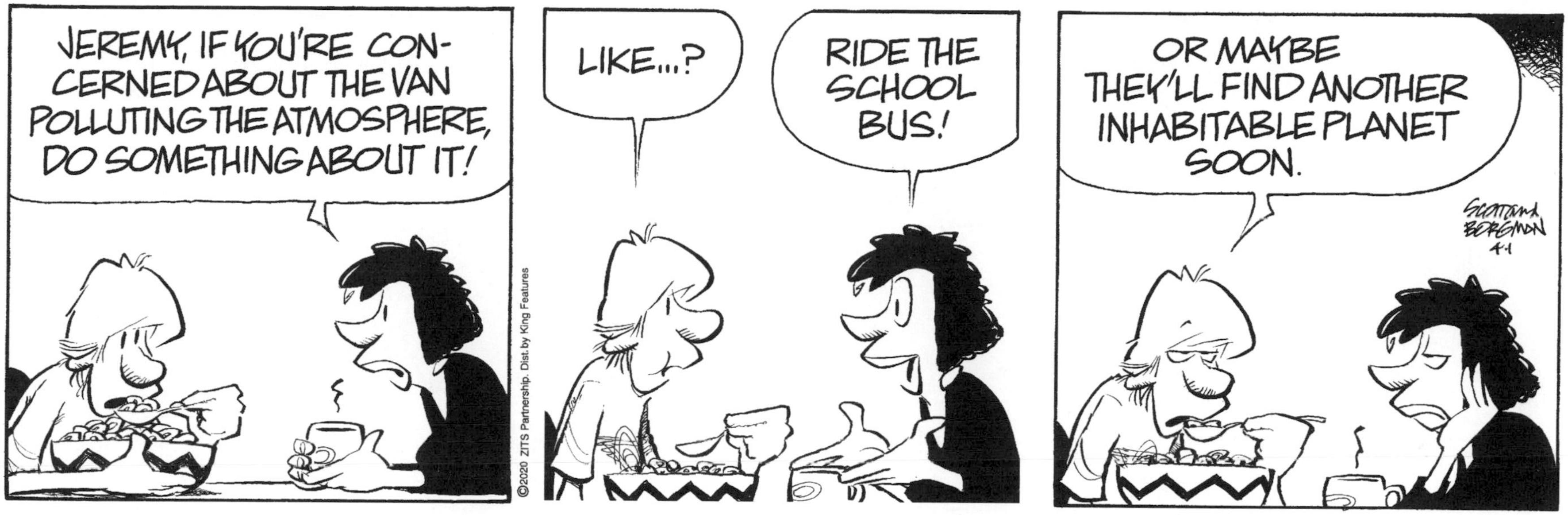
JEREMY, IF YOU'RE CONCERNED ABOUT THE VAN POLLUTING THE ATMOSPHERE, DO SOMETHING ABOUT IT!
©2020 ZITS Partnership. Dist. by King Features
LIKE...?
RIDE THE SCHOOL BUS!
OR MAYBE THEY'LL FIND ANOTHER INHABITABLE PLANET SOON.
SCOTT and BORGMAN 4-1

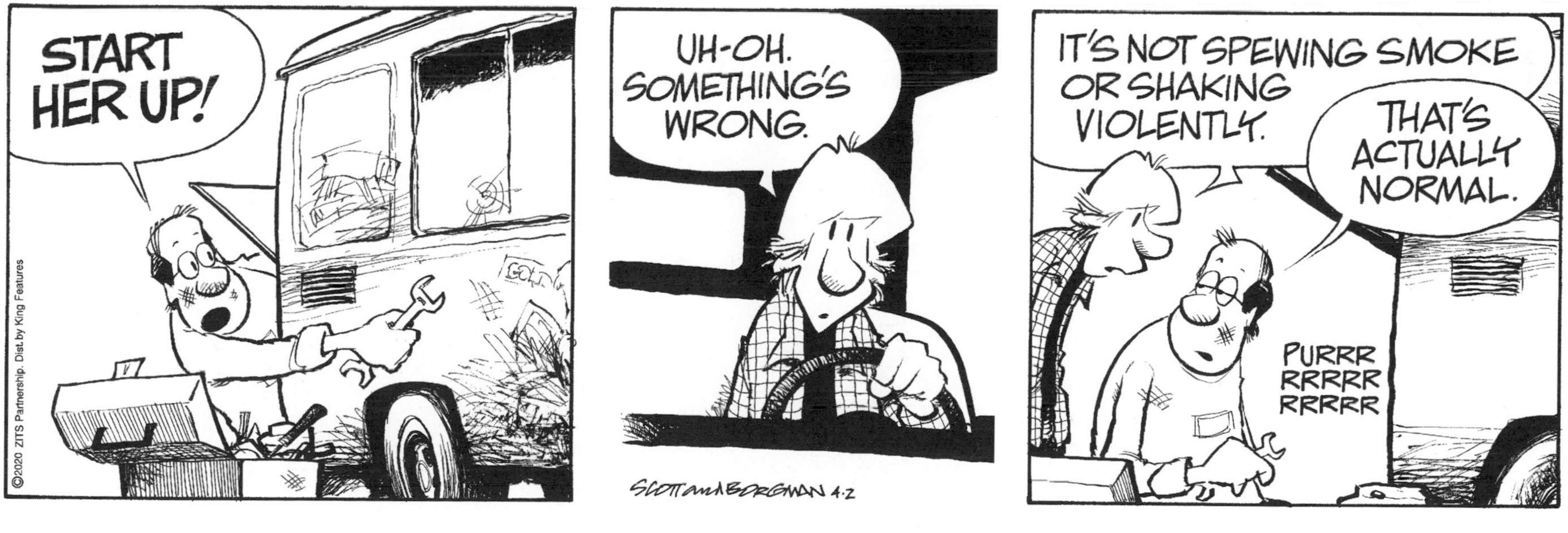
START HER UP!
©2020 ZITS Partnership. Dist. by King Features
UH-OH. SOMETHING'S WRONG.
SCOTT and BORGMAN 4-2
IT'S NOT SPEWING SMOKE OR SHAKING VIOLENTLY.
THAT'S ACTUALLY NORMAL.
PURRR RRRRR RRRRR

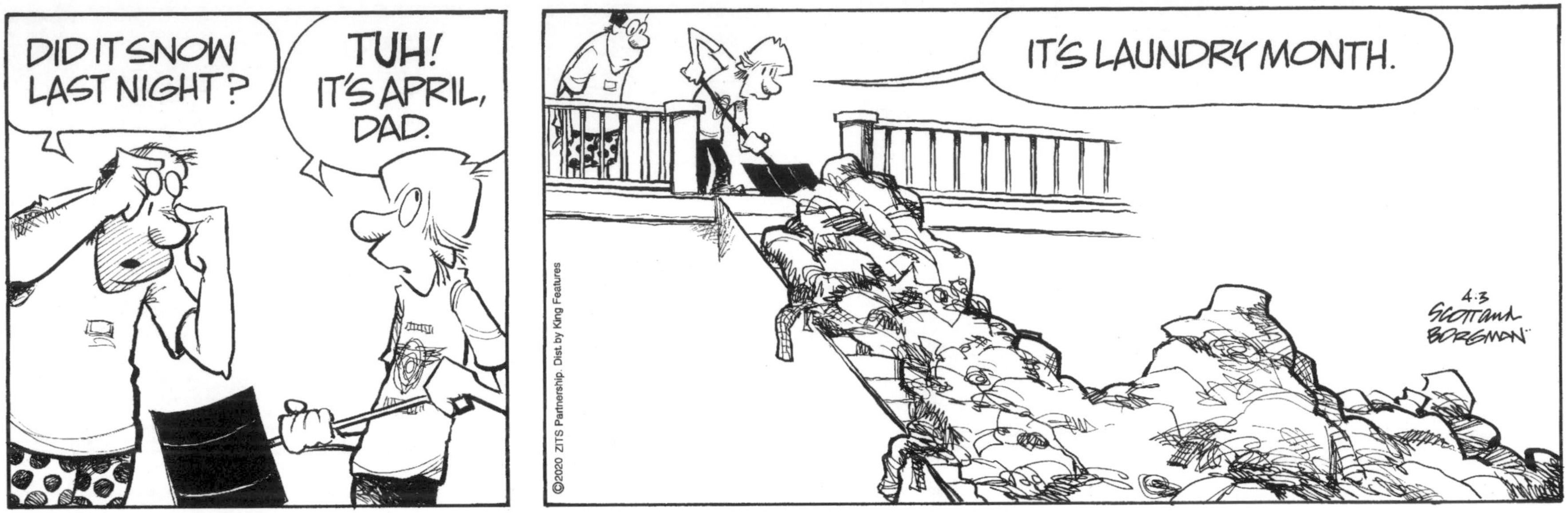
DID IT SNOW LAST NIGHT?
TUH! IT'S APRIL, DAD.
IT'S LAUNDRY MONTH.
©2020 ZITS Partnership. Dist. by King Features
4.3
SCOTT and BORGMAN

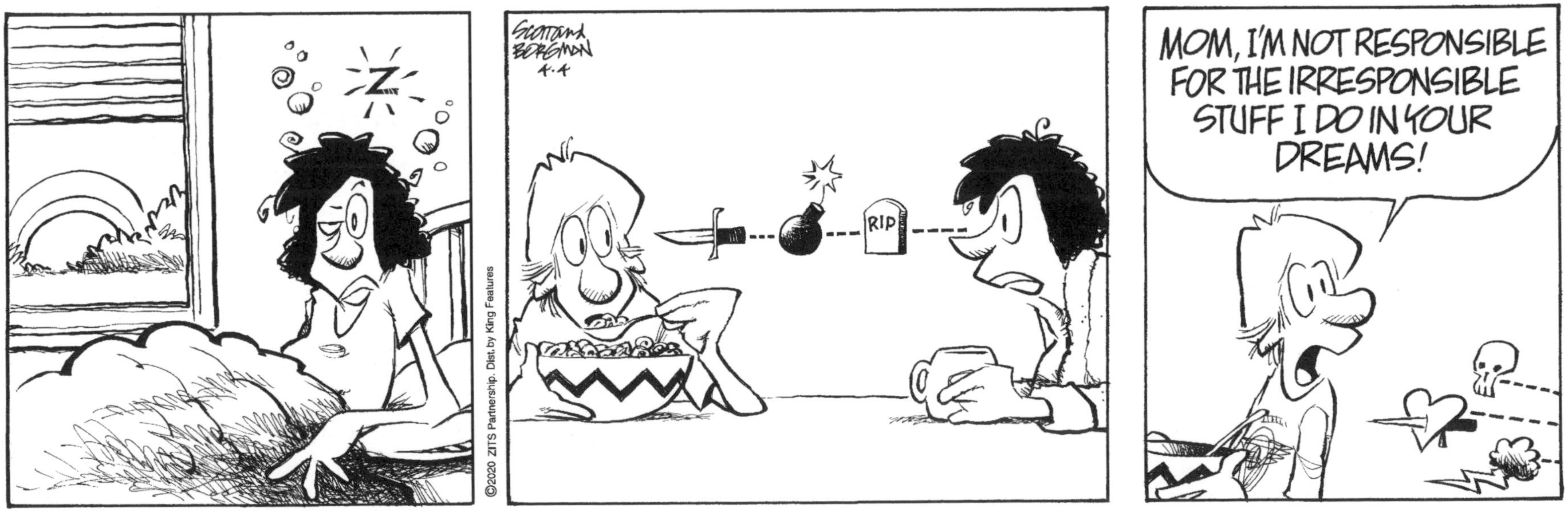
Z
©2020 ZITS Partnership. Dist. by King Features
SCOTT and BORGMAN
4.4
RIP
MOM, I'M NOT RESPONSIBLE FOR THE IRRESPONSIBLE STUFF I DO IN YOUR DREAMS!

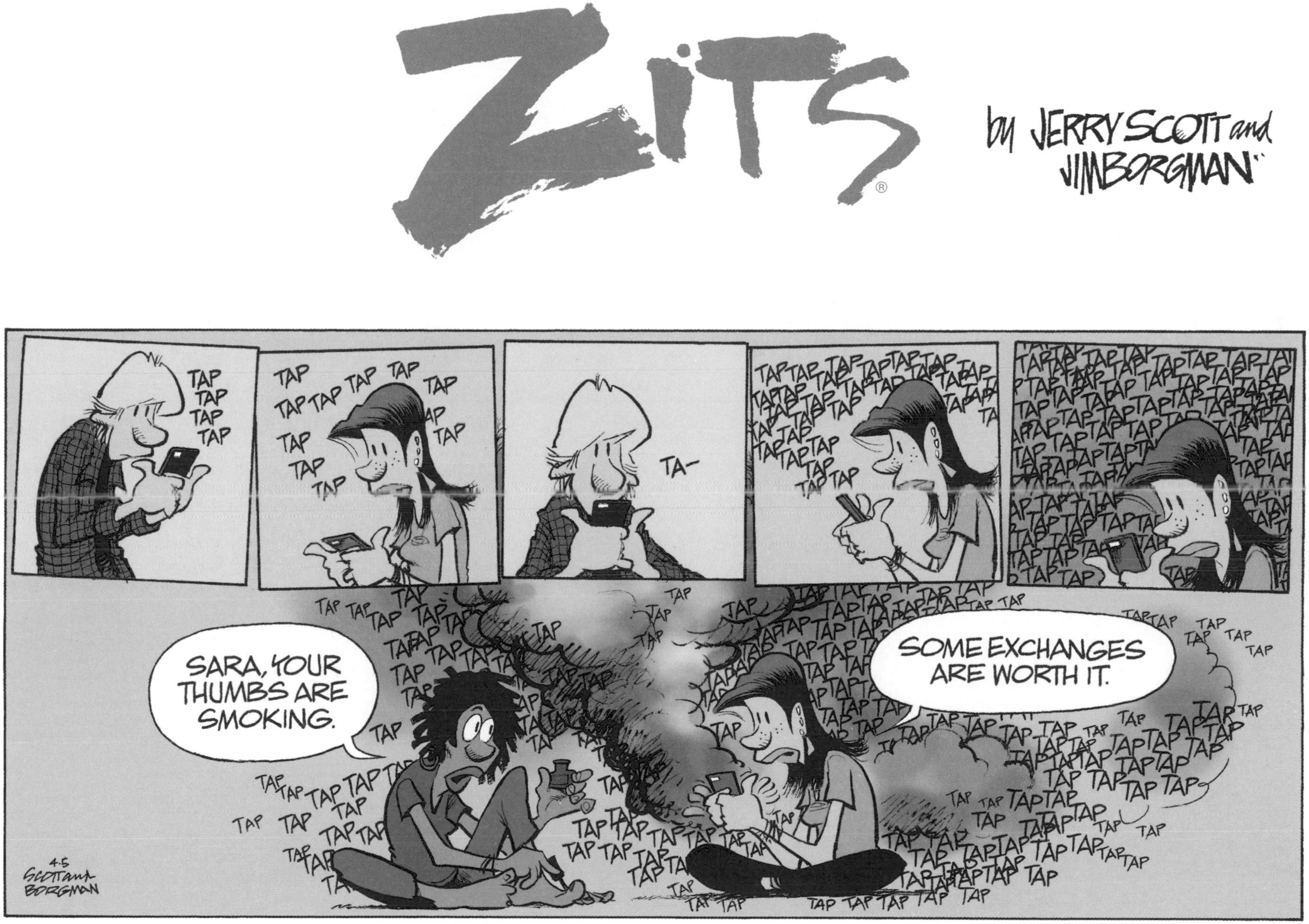
ZITS
by JERRY SCOTT and JIM BORGMAN
TAP TAP TAP TAP
TA-
SARA, YOUR THUMBS ARE SMOKING.
SOME EXCHANGES ARE WORTH IT.
4-5 SCOTT and BORGMAN

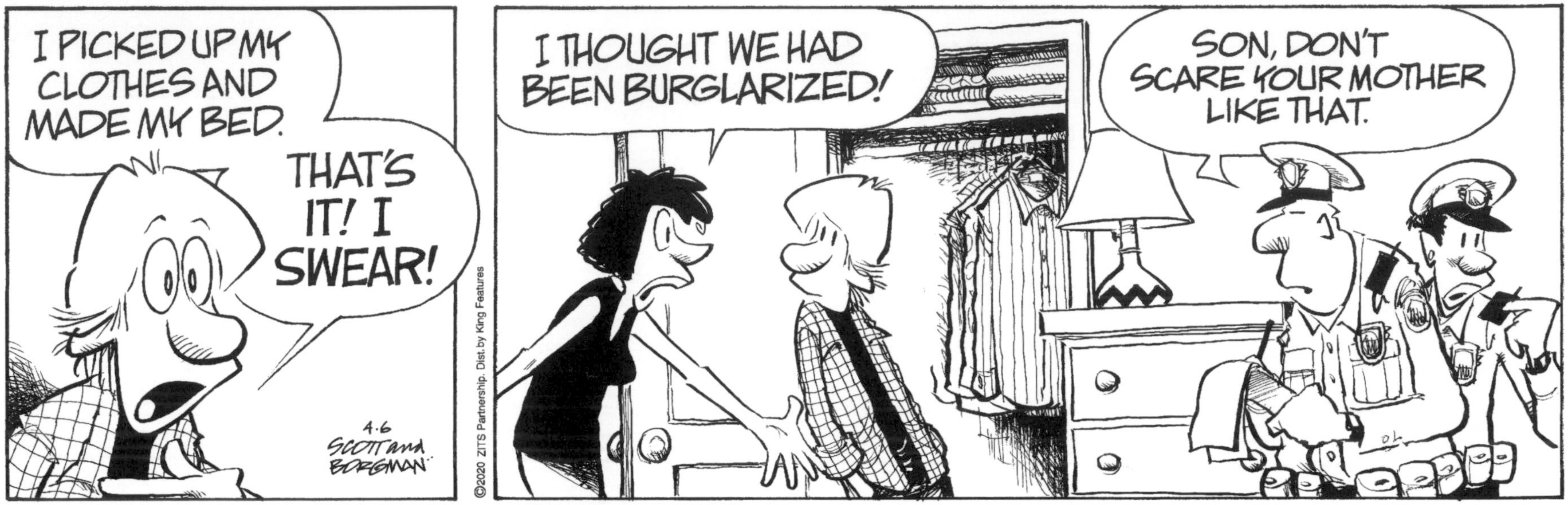
I PICKED UP MY CLOTHES AND MADE MY BED.
THAT'S IT! I SWEAR!
4·6 SCOTT AND BORGMAN
©2020 ZITS Partnership. Dist. by King Features
I THOUGHT WE HAD BEEN BURGLARIZED!
SON, DON'T SCARE YOUR MOTHER LIKE THAT.

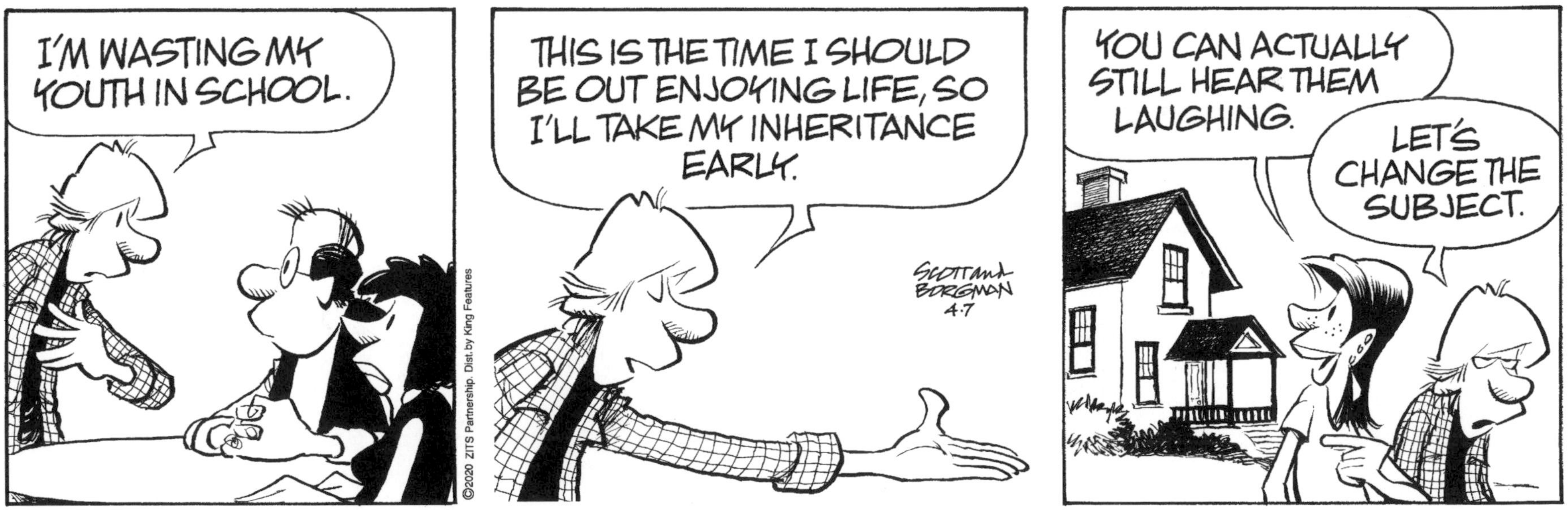
I'M WASTING MY YOUTH IN SCHOOL.
©2020 ZITS Partnership. Dist. by King Features
THIS IS THE TIME I SHOULD BE OUT ENJOYING LIFE, SO I'LL TAKE MY INHERITANCE EARLY.
SCOTT AND BORGMAN 4·7
YOU CAN ACTUALLY STILL HEAR THEM LAUGHING.
LET'S CHANGE THE SUBJECT.

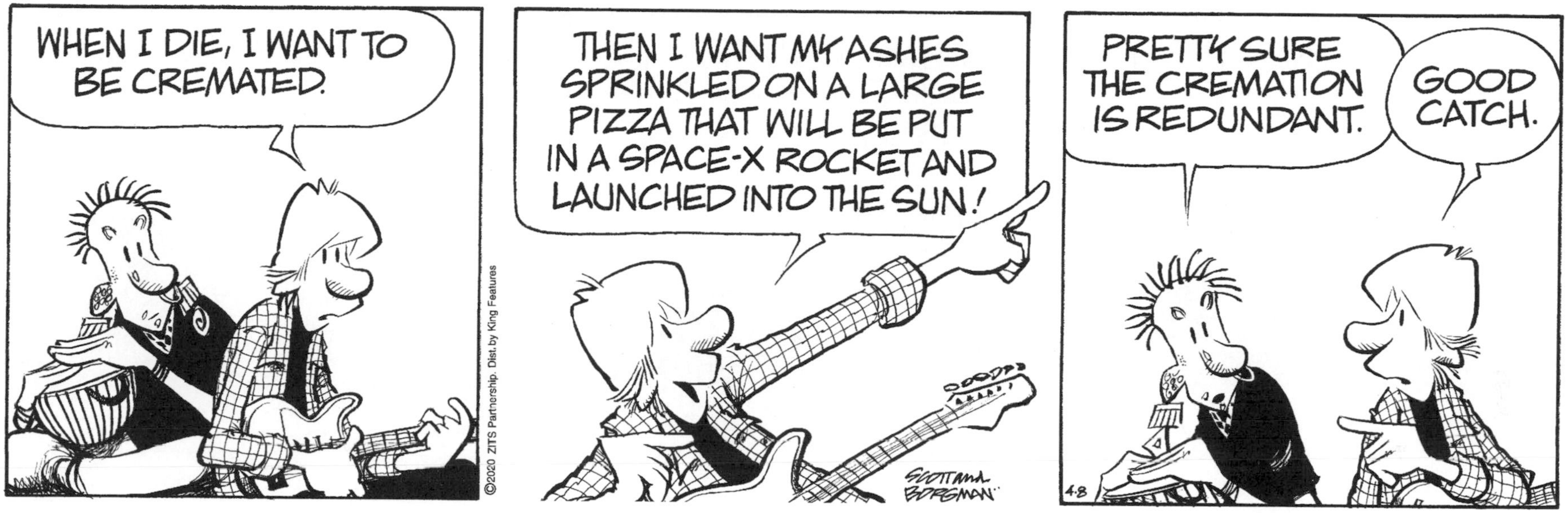
WHEN I DIE, I WANT TO BE CREMATED.
©2020 ZITS Partnership. Dist. by King Features
THEN I WANT MY ASHES SPRINKLED ON A LARGE PIZZA THAT WILL BE PUT IN A SPACE-X ROCKET AND LAUNCHED INTO THE SUN!
SCOTT AND BORGMAN
4·8
PRETTY SURE THE CREMATION IS REDUNDANT.
GOOD CATCH.

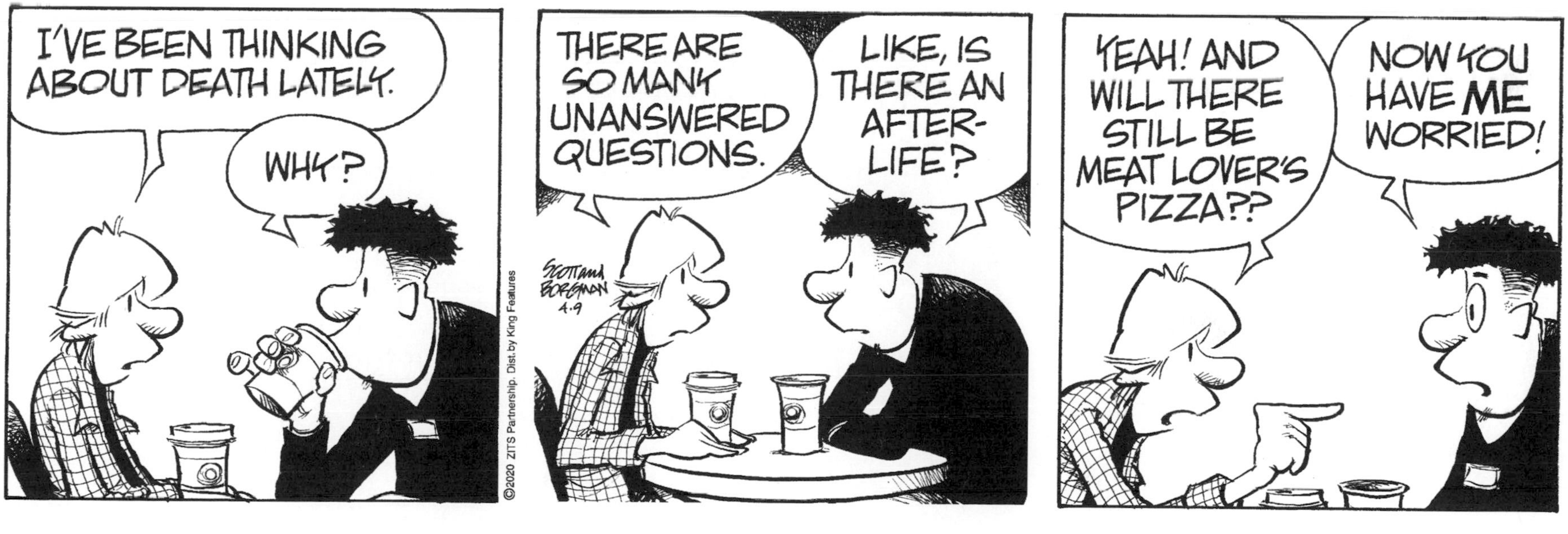
I'VE BEEN THINKING ABOUT DEATH LATELY.
WHY?
©2020 ZITS Partnership. Dist. by King Features
THERE ARE SO MANY UNANSWERED QUESTIONS.
LIKE, IS THERE AN AFTER-LIFE?
SCOTT AND BORGMAN
4·9
YEAH! AND WILL THERE STILL BE MEAT LOVER'S PIZZA??
NOW YOU HAVE **ME** WORRIED!

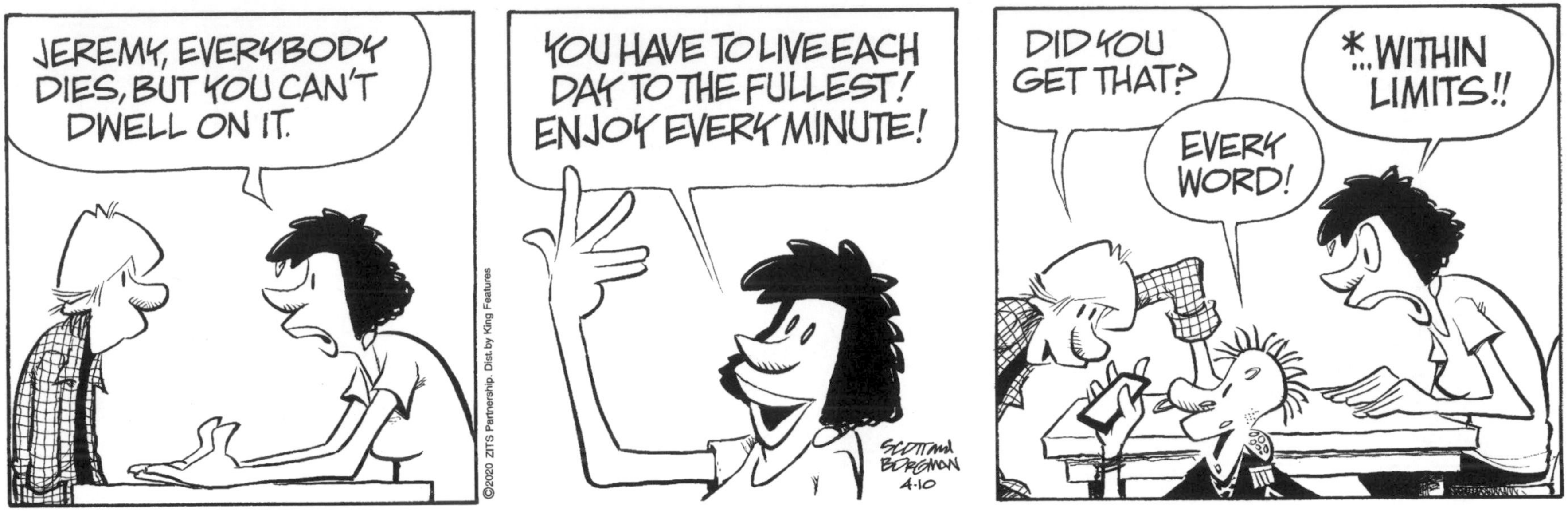
JEREMY, EVERYBODY DIES, BUT YOU CAN'T DWELL ON IT.
©2020 ZITS Partnership. Dist. by King Features
YOU HAVE TO LIVE EACH DAY TO THE FULLEST! ENJOY EVERY MINUTE!
SCOTT AND BORGMAN 4·10
DID YOU GET THAT?
EVERY WORD!
*...WITHIN LIMITS!!

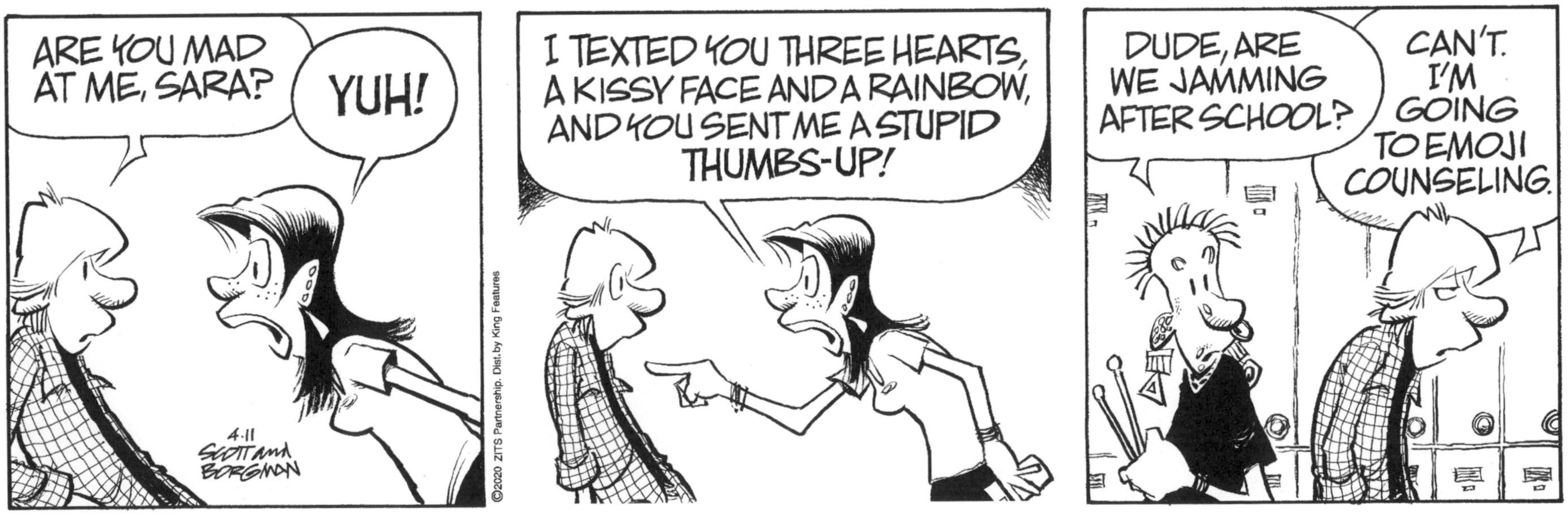
ARE YOU MAD AT ME, SARA?
YUH!
4·11 SCOTT AND BORGMAN
©2020 ZITS Partnership. Dist. by King Features
I TEXTED YOU THREE HEARTS, A KISSY FACE AND A RAINBOW, AND YOU SENT ME A STUPID THUMBS-UP!
DUDE, ARE WE JAMMING AFTER SCHOOL?
CAN'T. I'M GOING TO EMOJI COUNSELING.

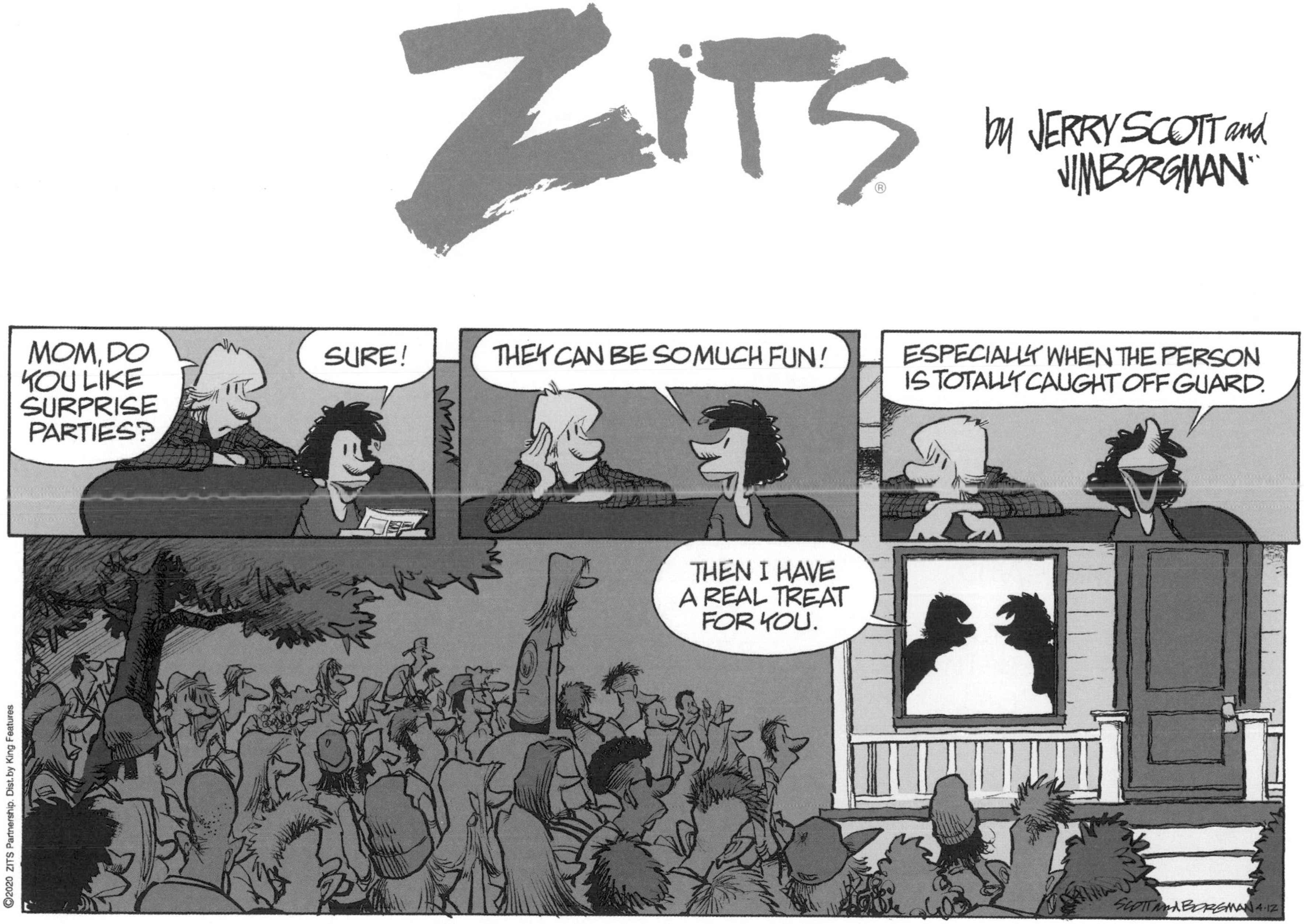
ZITS
by JERRY SCOTT and JIM BORGMAN
MOM, DO YOU LIKE SURPRISE PARTIES?
SURE!
THEY CAN BE SO MUCH FUN!
ESPECIALLY WHEN THE PERSON IS TOTALLY CAUGHT OFF GUARD.
THEN I HAVE A REAL TREAT FOR YOU.
SCOTT and BORGMAN 4-12

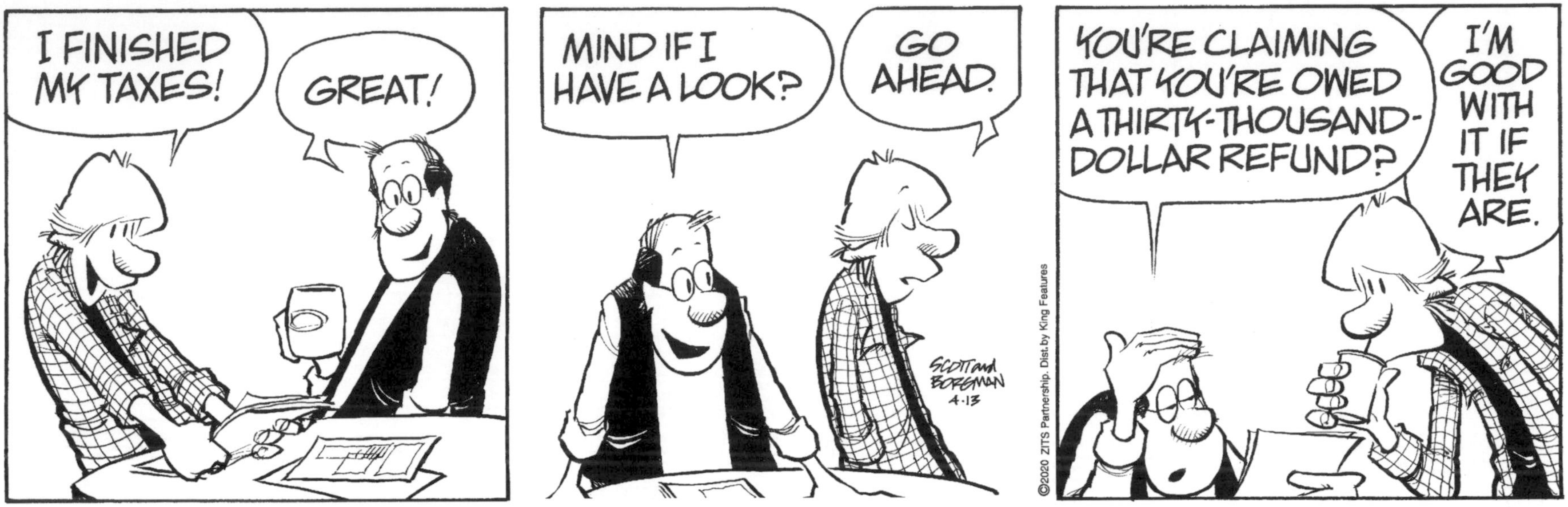
I FINISHED MY TAXES!
GREAT!
MIND IF I HAVE A LOOK?
GO AHEAD.
SCOTT and BORGMAN 4·13
YOU'RE CLAIMING THAT YOU'RE OWED A THIRTY-THOUSAND-DOLLAR REFUND?
I'M GOOD WITH IT IF THEY ARE.
©2020 ZITS Partnership. Dist. by King Features

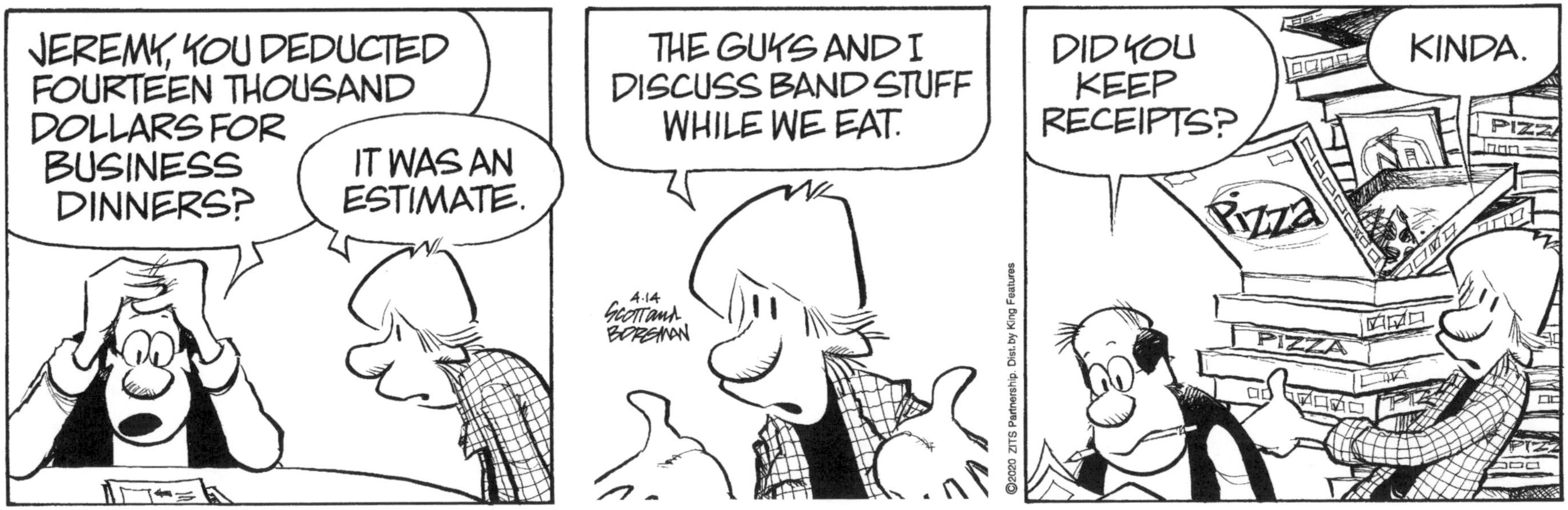
JEREMY, YOU DEDUCTED FOURTEEN THOUSAND DOLLARS FOR BUSINESS DINNERS?
IT WAS AN ESTIMATE.
THE GUYS AND I DISCUSS BAND STUFF WHILE WE EAT.
4·14 SCOTT and BORGMAN
DID YOU KEEP RECEIPTS?
KINDA.
PIZZA
©2020 ZITS Partnership. Dist. by King Features

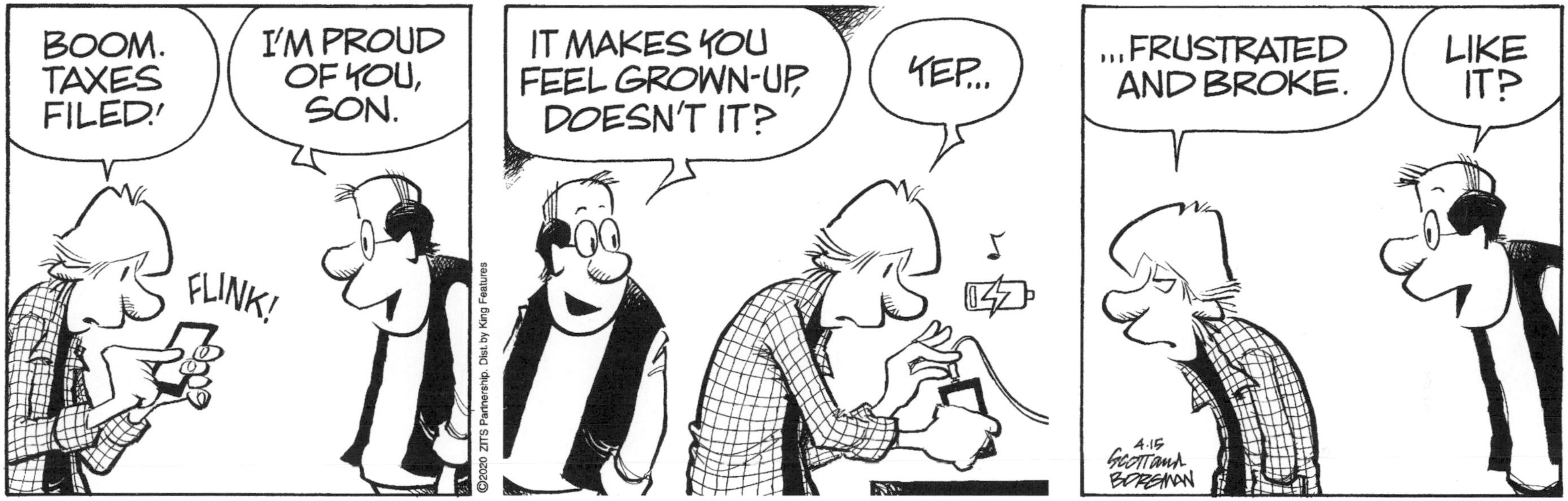
BOOM. TAXES FILED!
I'M PROUD OF YOU, SON.
FLINK!
©2020 ZITS Partnership. Dist. by King Features
IT MAKES YOU FEEL GROWN-UP, DOESN'T IT?
YEP...
...FRUSTRATED AND BROKE.
LIKE IT?
4.15 SCOTT and BORGMAN

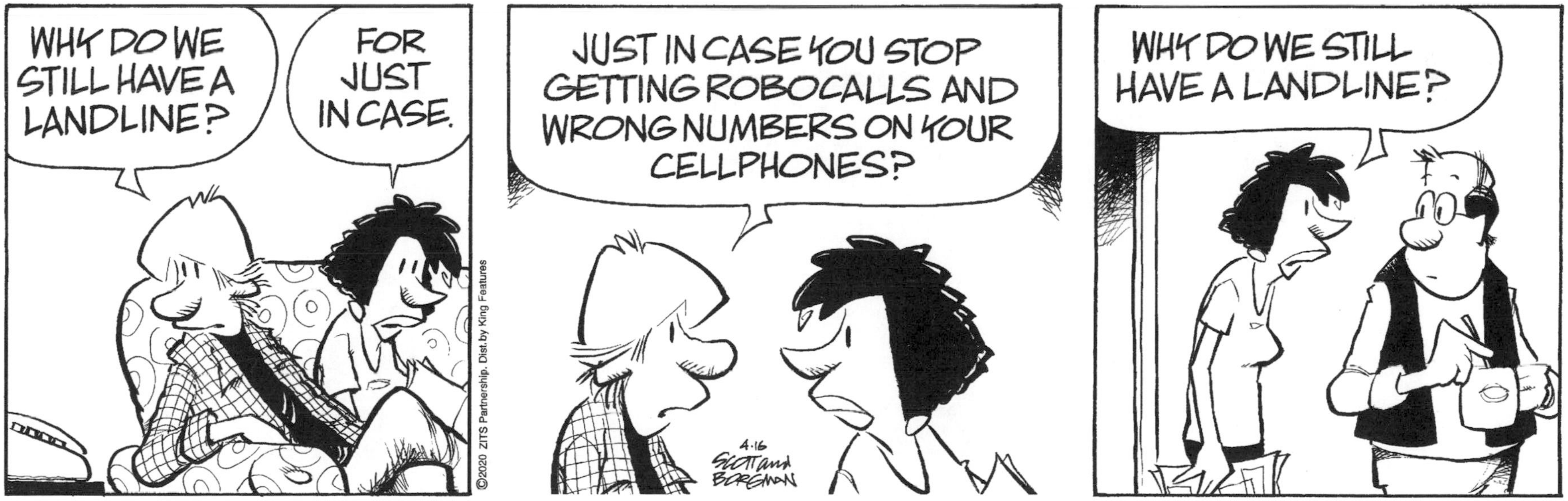
WHY DO WE STILL HAVE A LANDLINE?
FOR JUST IN CASE.
©2020 ZITS Partnership. Dist. by King Features
JUST IN CASE YOU STOP GETTING ROBOCALLS AND WRONG NUMBERS ON YOUR CELLPHONES?
4.16 SCOTT and BORGMAN
WHY DO WE STILL HAVE A LANDLINE?

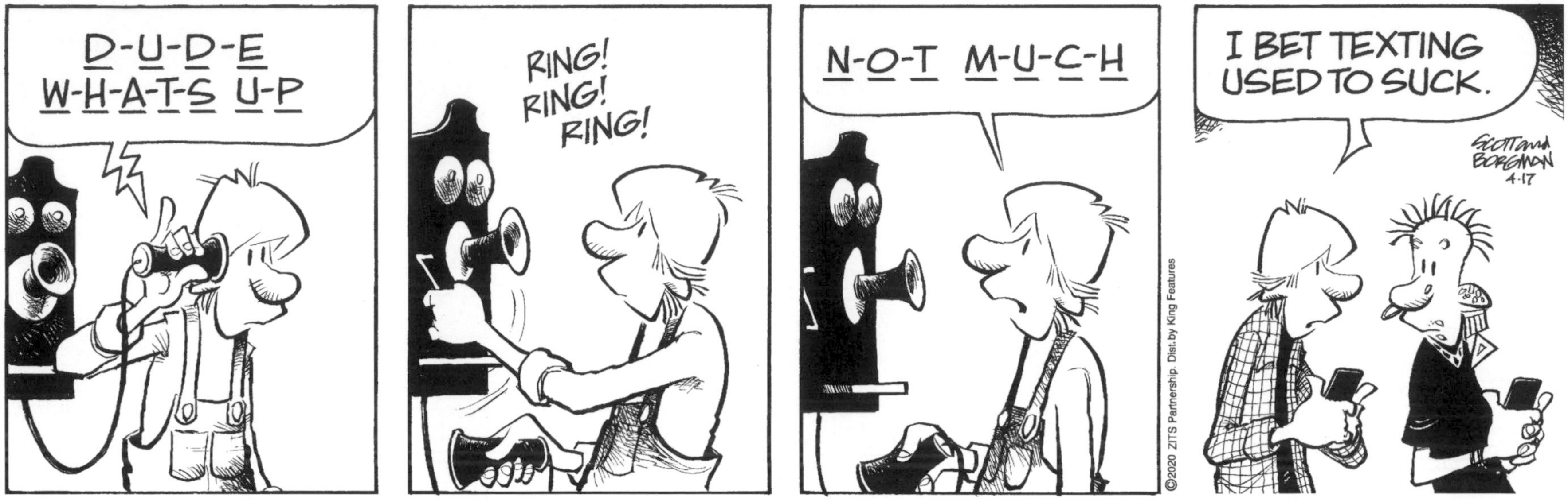
D-U-D-E W-H-A-T-S U-P
RING! RING! RING!
N-O-T M-U-C-H
©2020 ZITS Partnership. Dist. by King Features
I BET TEXTING USED TO SUCK.
SCOTT and BORGMAN 4·17

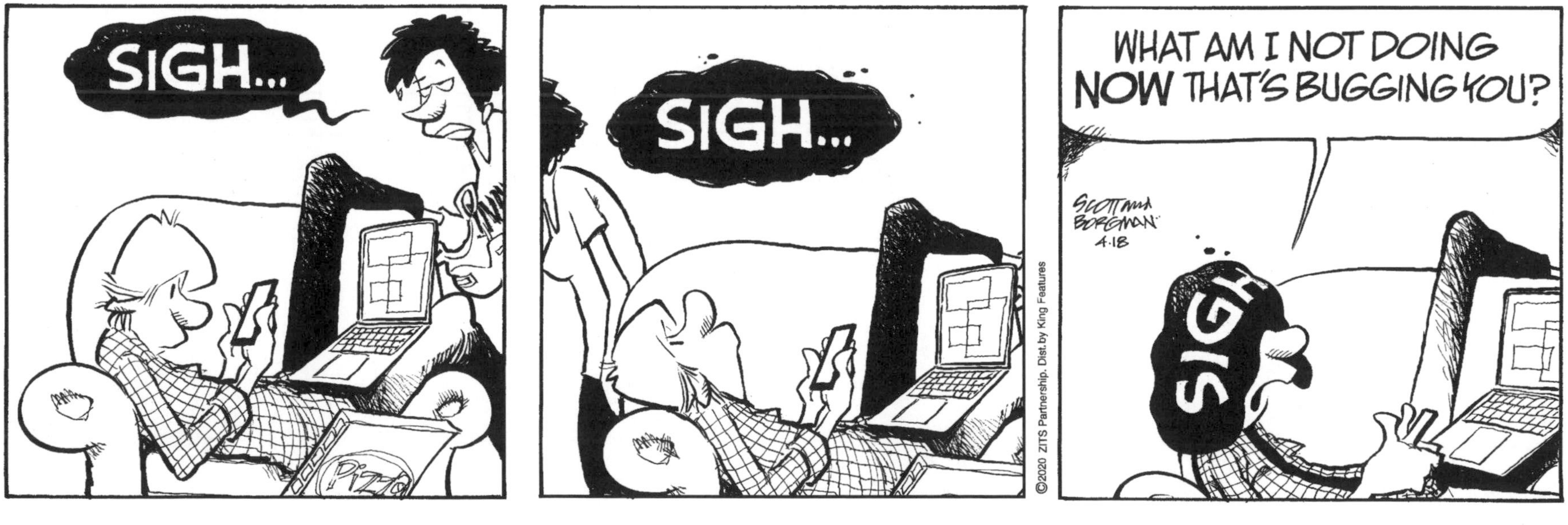
SIGH...
SIGH...
©2020 ZITS Partnership. Dist. by King Features
WHAT AM I NOT DOING NOW THAT'S BUGGING YOU?
SCOTT and BORGMAN 4·18
SIGH

ZITS®

by JERRY SCOTT and JIM BORGMAN

HAPPY BIRTHDAY, MOM.
THANK YOU, JEREMY!
4.19
SCOTT and BORGMAN
DO YOU REMEMBER WHEN YOU DROPPED YOUR FAVORITE EARRING DOWN THE SEWER GRATE?
UGH. YES.
!!!
WELL, I WENT TO THE WATER & POWER COMPANY AND ASKED THEM TO SHUT EVERYTHING OFF AND SEARCH THE PIPES UNTIL THEY FOUND YOUR EARRING.
AND THIS IS...?
©2020 ZITS Partnership. Dist. by King Feat.
...A STARBUCKS GIFT CARD.
WATER & POWER TOLD ME TO GET LOST.

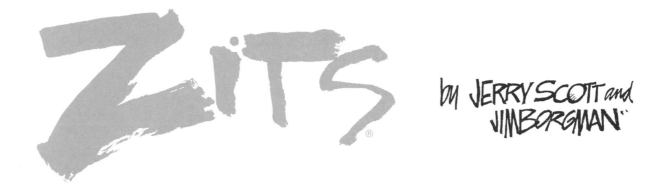

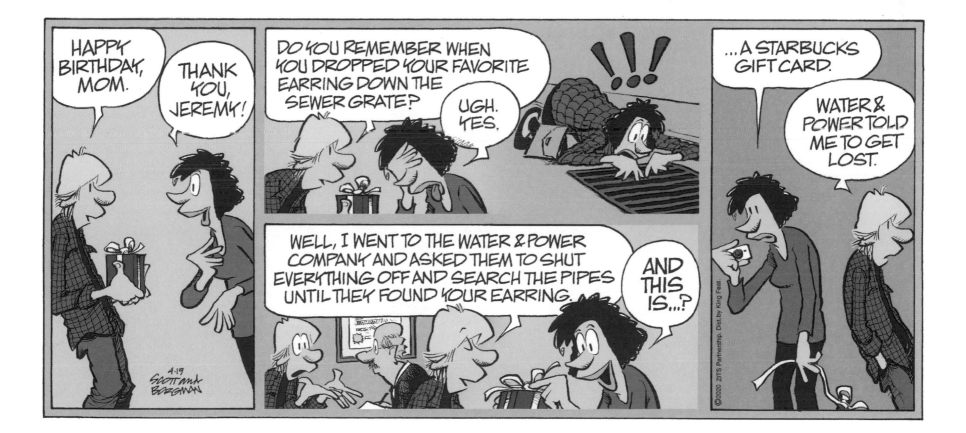

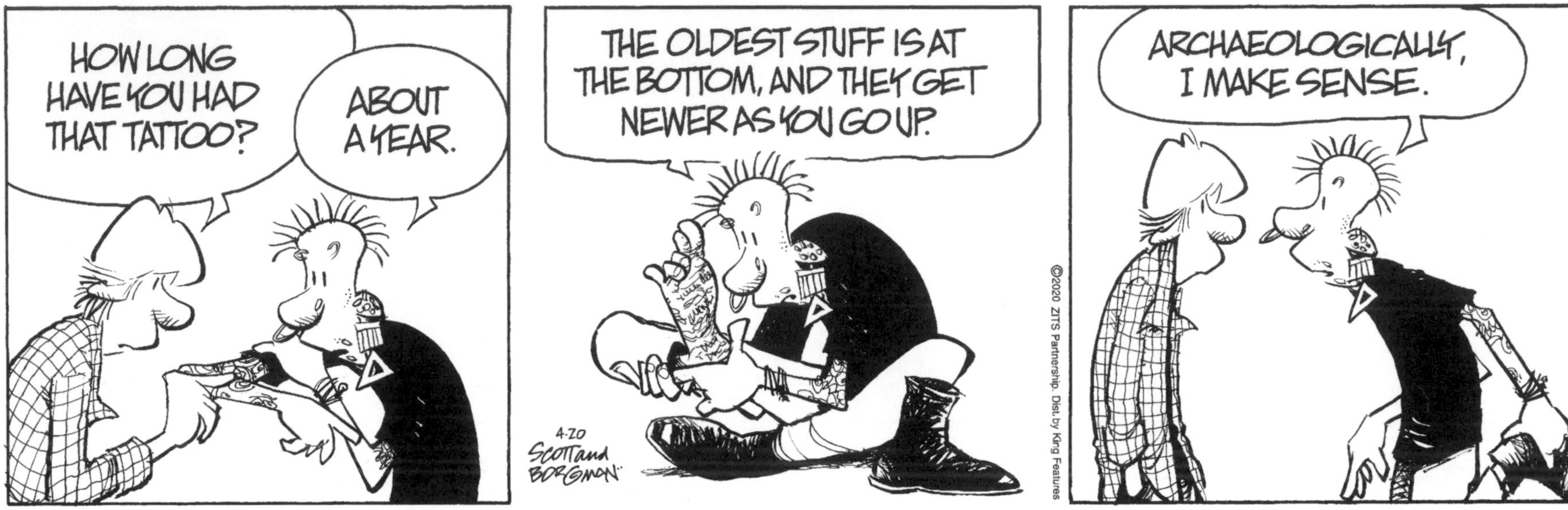
HOW LONG HAVE YOU HAD THAT TATTOO?
ABOUT A YEAR.
THE OLDEST STUFF IS AT THE BOTTOM, AND THEY GET NEWER AS YOU GO UP.
4-20
SCOTT and BORGMAN
©2020 ZITS Partnership. Dist. by King Features
ARCHAEOLOGICALLY, I MAKE SENSE.

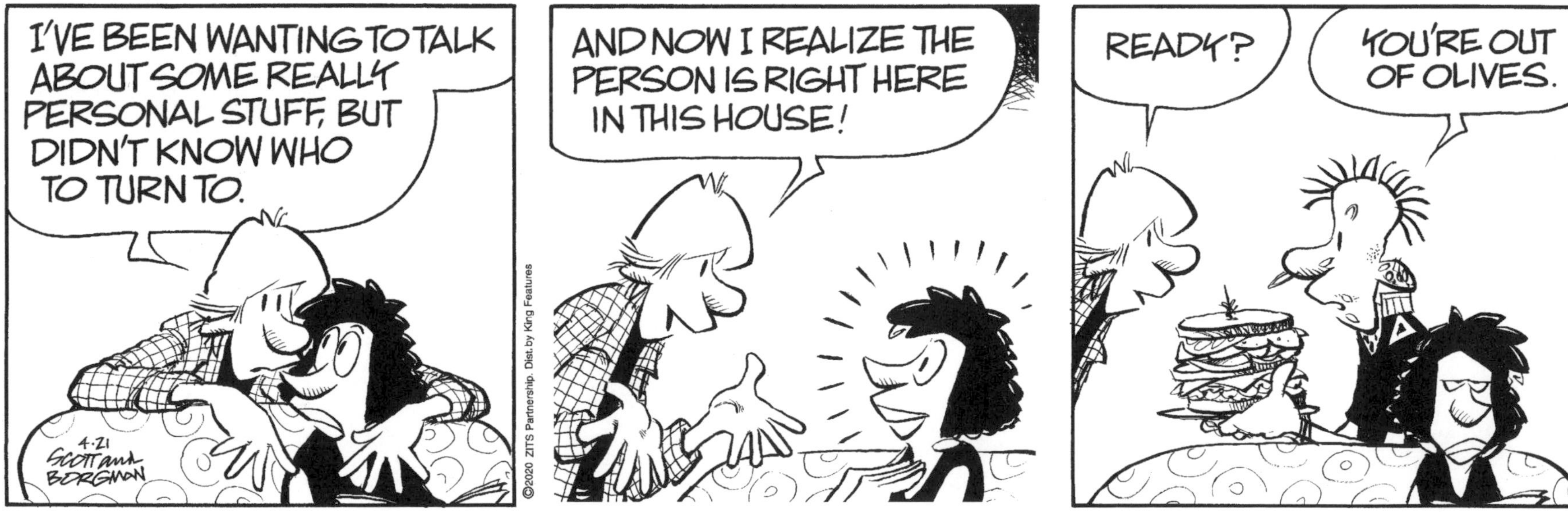
I'VE BEEN WANTING TO TALK ABOUT SOME REALLY PERSONAL STUFF, BUT DIDN'T KNOW WHO TO TURN TO.
4-21
SCOTT and BORGMAN
©2020 ZITS Partnership. Dist. by King Features
AND NOW I REALIZE THE PERSON IS RIGHT HERE IN THIS HOUSE!
READY?
YOU'RE OUT OF OLIVES.

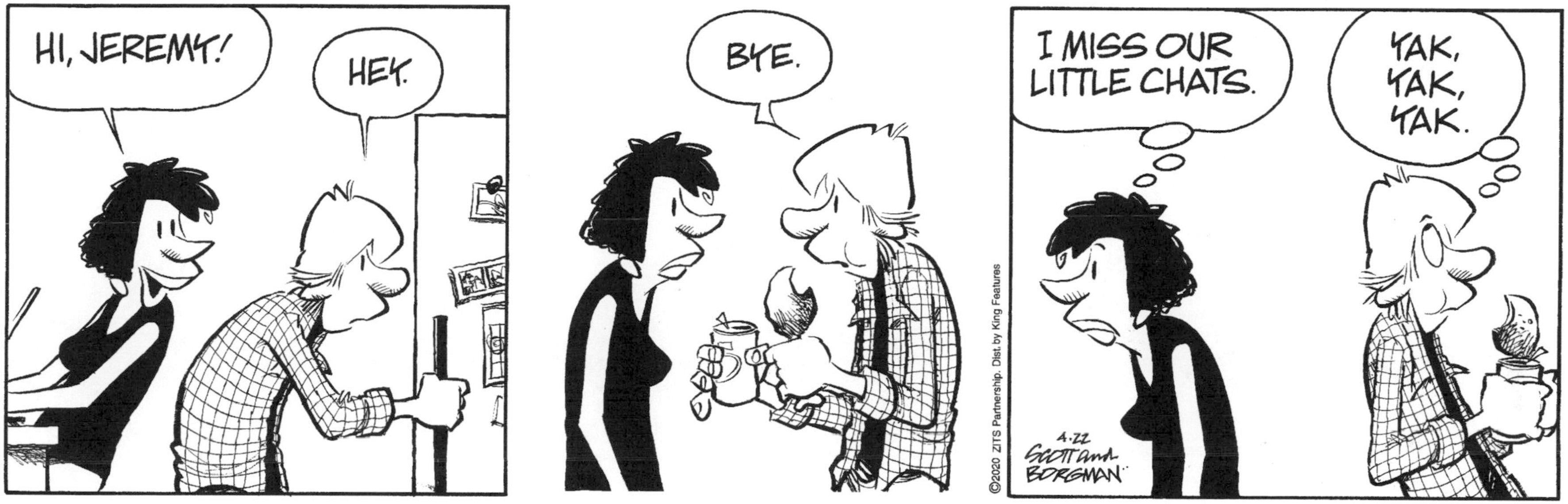

HI, JEREMY!
HEY.
BYE.
I MISS OUR LITTLE CHATS.
YAK, YAK, YAK.
4·22
SCOTT and BORGMAN
©2020 ZITS Partnership. Dist. by King Features

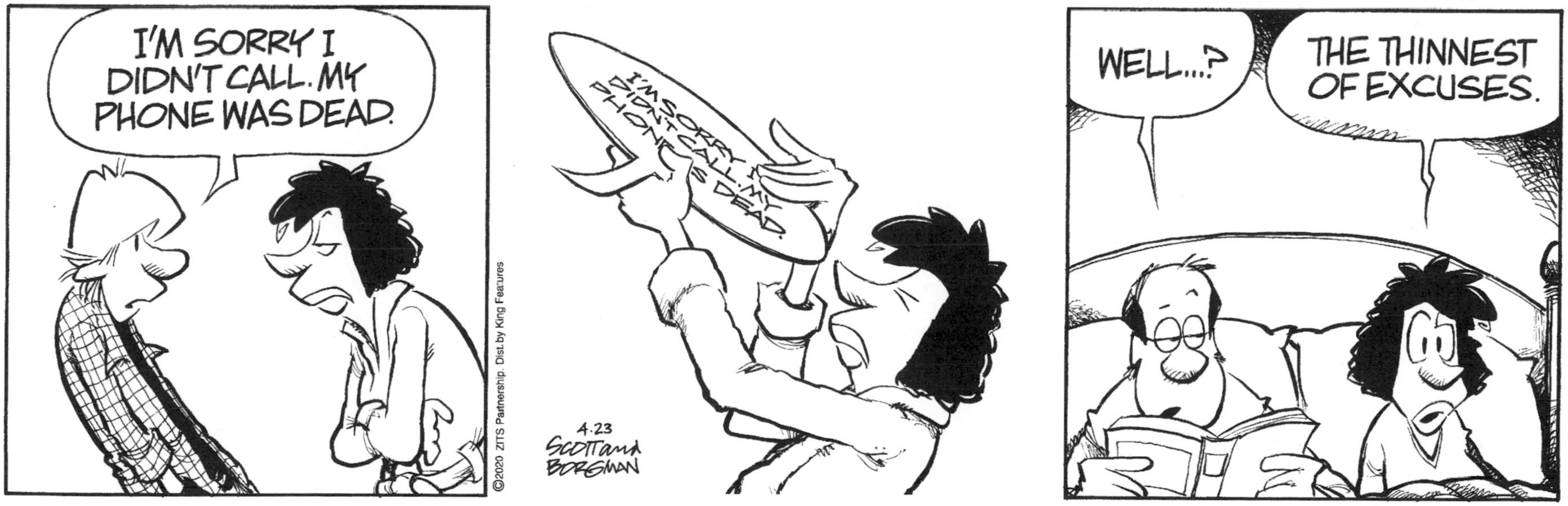

I'M SORRY I DIDN'T CALL. MY PHONE WAS DEAD.
©2020 ZITS Partnership. Dist. by King Features
4·23
SCOTT and BORGMAN
WELL...?
THE THINNEST OF EXCUSES.

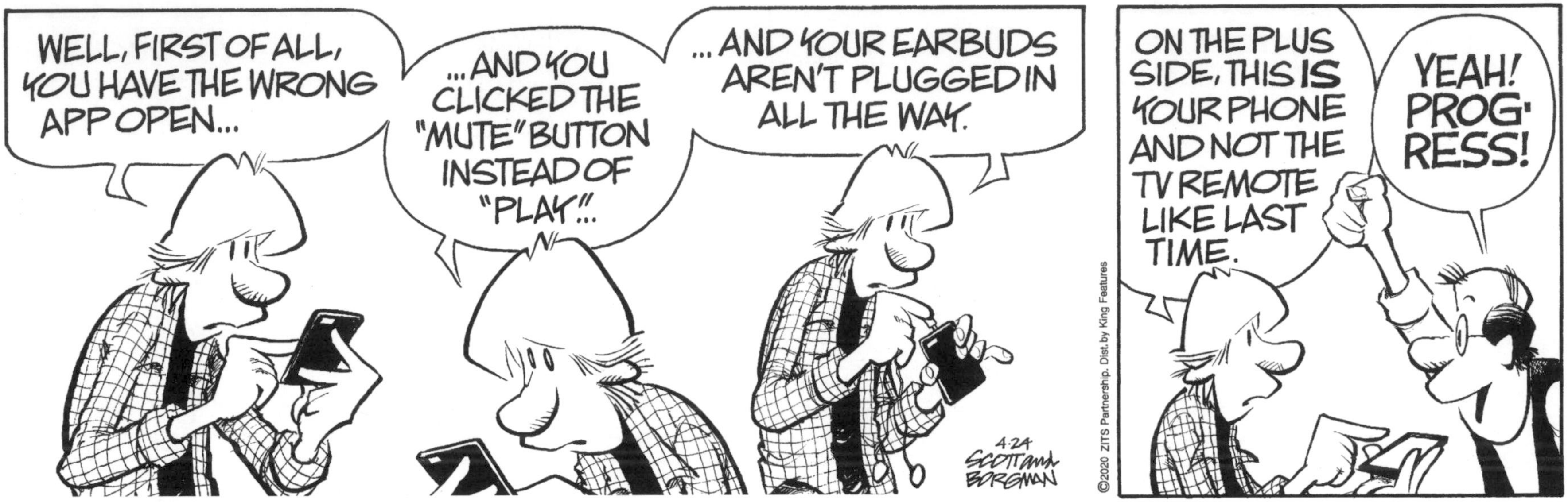
WELL, FIRST OF ALL, YOU HAVE THE WRONG APP OPEN...
...AND YOU CLICKED THE "MUTE" BUTTON INSTEAD OF "PLAY"!...
...AND YOUR EARBUDS AREN'T PLUGGED IN ALL THE WAY.
4·24 SCOTT AND BORGMAN
©2020 ZITS Partnership. Dist. by King Features
ON THE PLUS SIDE, THIS IS YOUR PHONE AND NOT THE TV REMOTE LIKE LAST TIME.
YEAH! PROG-RESS!

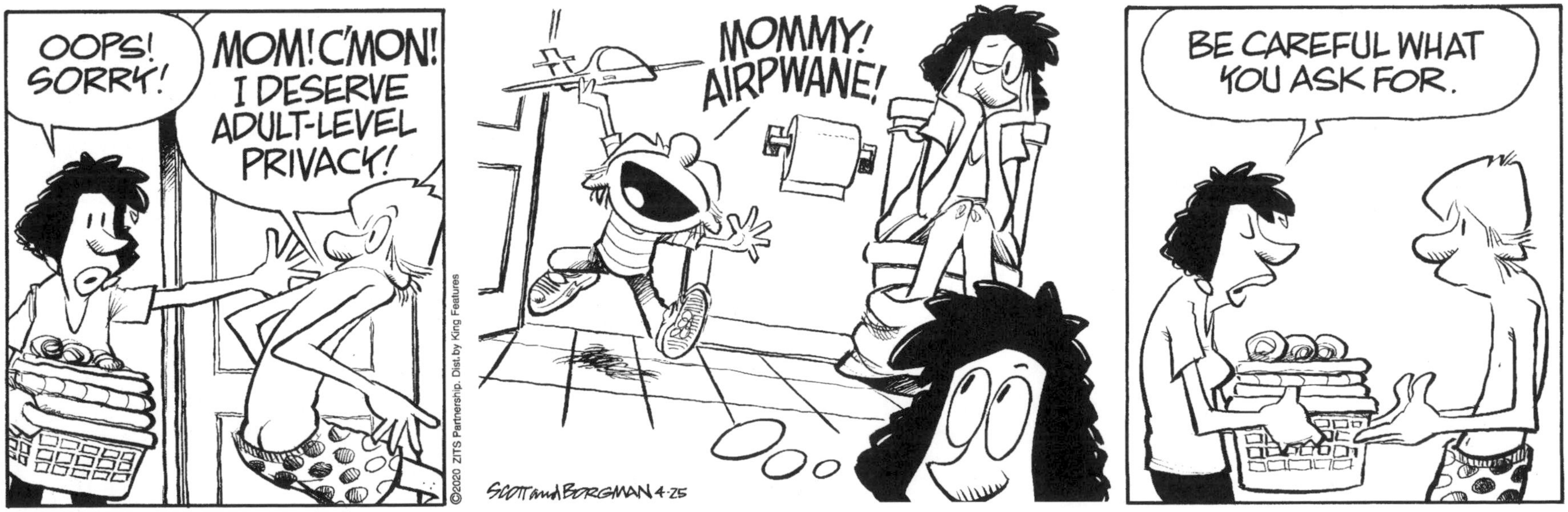
OOPS! SORRY!
MOM! C'MON! I DESERVE ADULT-LEVEL PRIVACY!
©2020 ZITS Partnership. Dist. by King Features
MOMMY! AIRPWANE!
SCOTT AND BORGMAN 4·25
BE CAREFUL WHAT YOU ASK FOR.

ZITS®

by JERRY SCOTT and JIM BORGMAN

UM, THANKS, DAD.
THAT WAS A COMPLIMENT, RIGHT?
4-26 SCOTT and BORGMAN

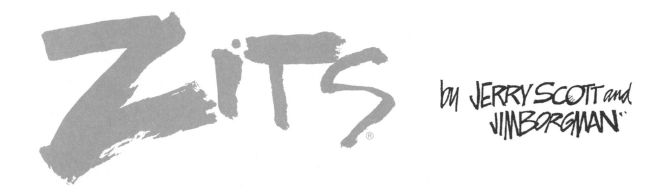

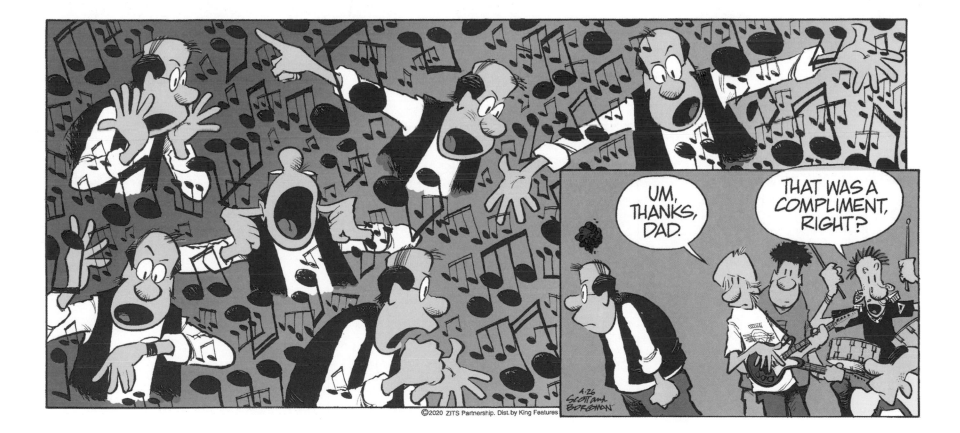

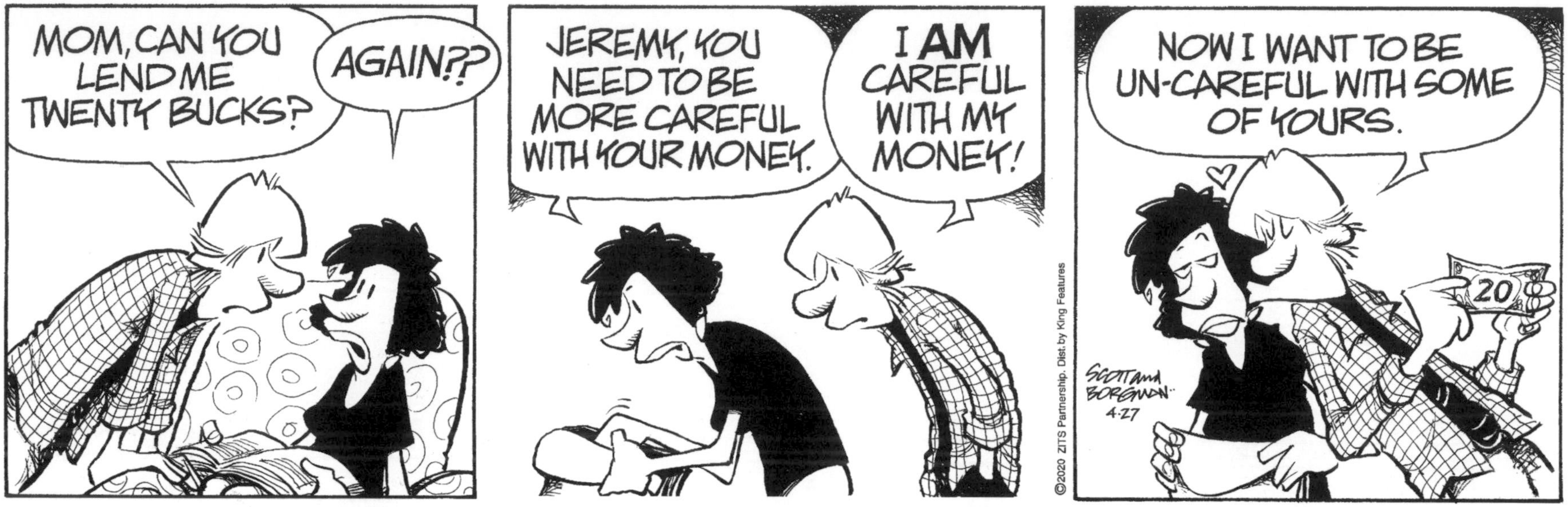
MOM, CAN YOU LEND ME TWENTY BUCKS?
AGAIN??
JEREMY, YOU NEED TO BE MORE CAREFUL WITH YOUR MONEY.
I AM CAREFUL WITH MY MONEY!
©2020 ZITS Partnership. Dist. by King Features
NOW I WANT TO BE UN-CAREFUL WITH SOME OF YOURS.
SCOTT AND BORGMAN 4·27
20

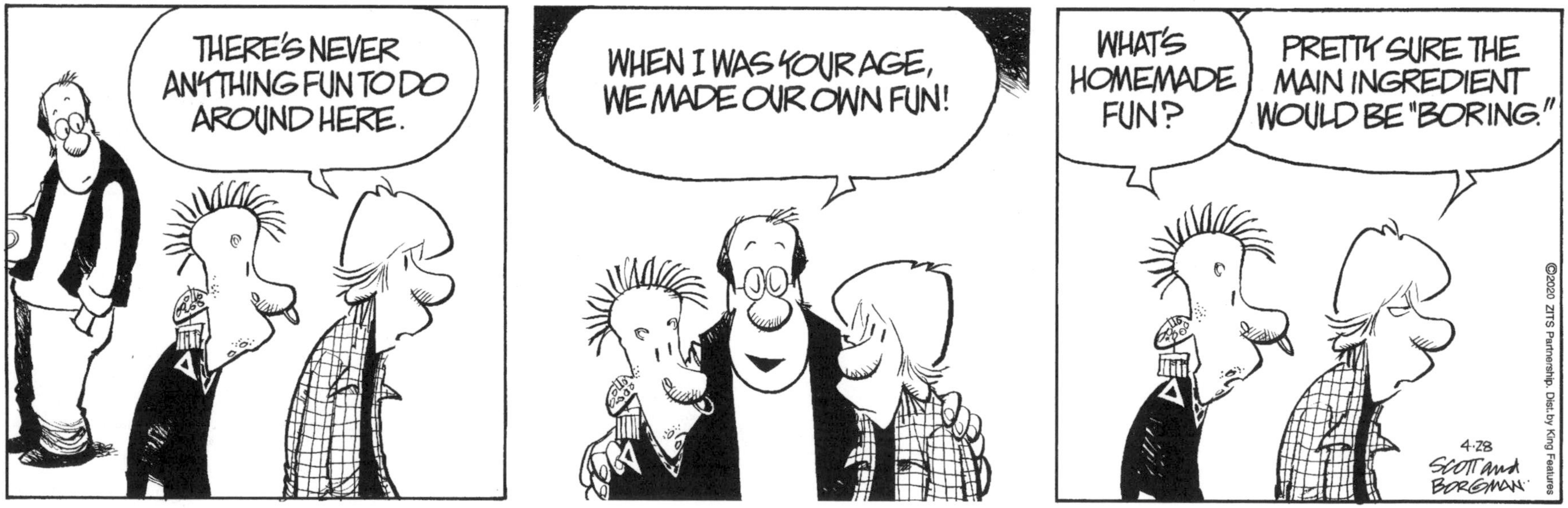
THERE'S NEVER ANYTHING FUN TO DO AROUND HERE.
WHEN I WAS YOUR AGE, WE MADE OUR OWN FUN!
WHAT'S HOMEMADE FUN?
PRETTY SURE THE MAIN INGREDIENT WOULD BE "BORING."
4·28 SCOTT AND BORGMAN
©2020 ZITS Partnership. Dist. by King Features

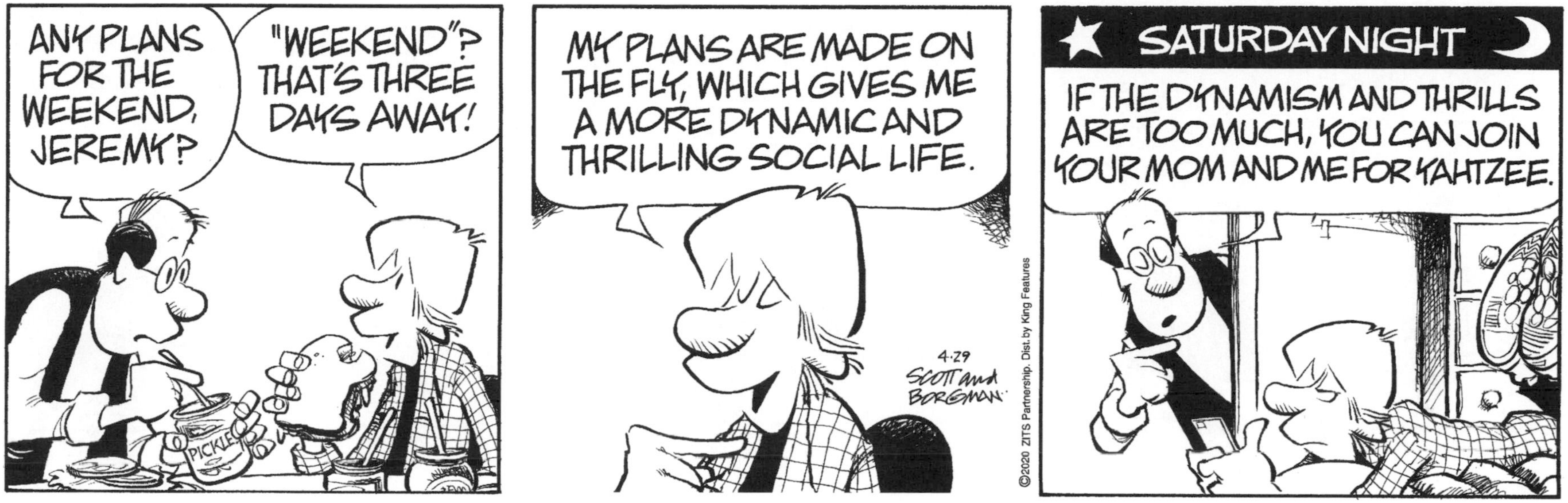
ANY PLANS FOR THE WEEKEND, JEREMY?
"WEEKEND"? THAT'S THREE DAYS AWAY!
PICKLE
MY PLANS ARE MADE ON THE FLY, WHICH GIVES ME A MORE DYNAMIC AND THRILLING SOCIAL LIFE.
4·29
SCOTT and BORGMAN
©2020 ZITS Partnership. Dist. by King Features
SATURDAY NIGHT
IF THE DYNAMISM AND THRILLS ARE TOO MUCH, YOU CAN JOIN YOUR MOM AND ME FOR YAHTZEE.

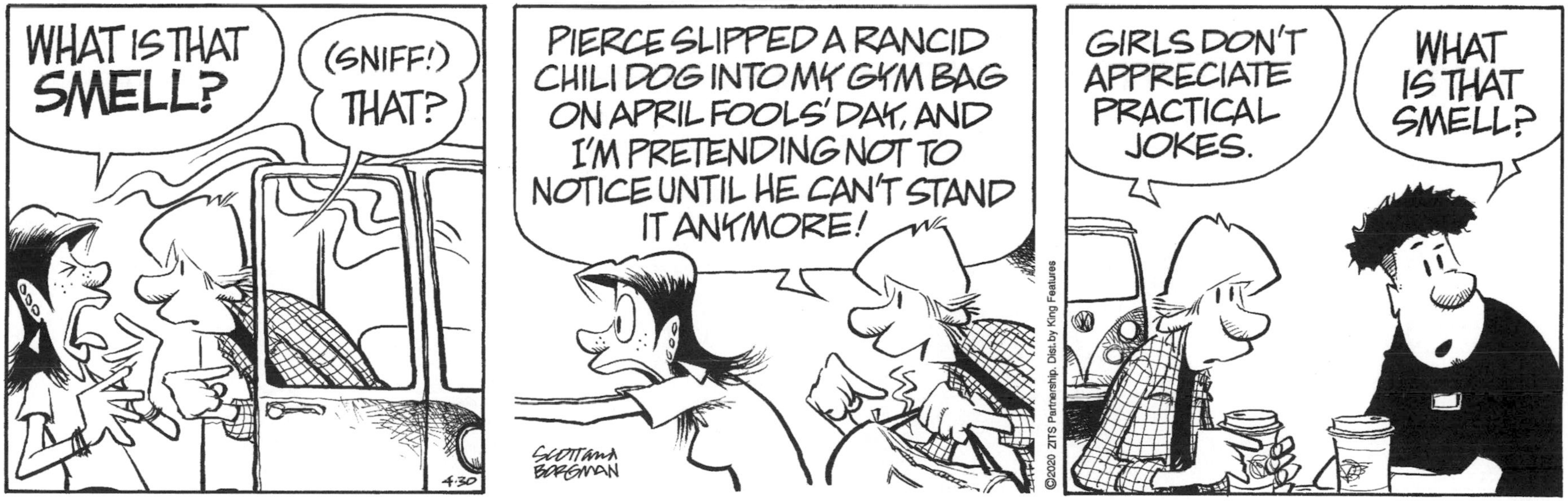
WHAT IS THAT SMELL?
(SNIFF!) THAT?
4·30
PIERCE SLIPPED A RANCID CHILI DOG INTO MY GYM BAG ON APRIL FOOLS' DAY, AND I'M PRETENDING NOT TO NOTICE UNTIL HE CAN'T STAND IT ANYMORE!
SCOTT and BORGMAN
©2020 ZITS Partnership. Dist. by King Features
GIRLS DON'T APPRECIATE PRACTICAL JOKES.
WHAT IS THAT SMELL?

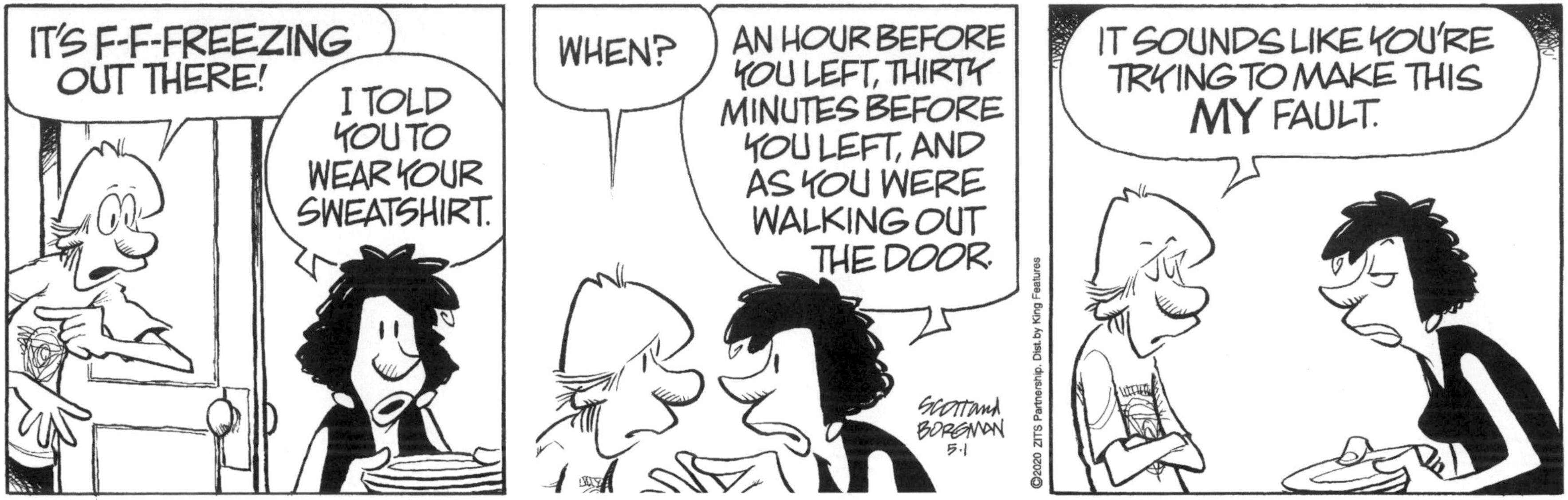
IT'S F-F-FREEZING OUT THERE!
I TOLD YOU TO WEAR YOUR SWEATSHIRT.
WHEN?
AN HOUR BEFORE YOU LEFT, THIRTY MINUTES BEFORE YOU LEFT, AND AS YOU WERE WALKING OUT THE DOOR.
SCOTT and BORGMAN 5·1
©2020 ZITS Partnership. Dist. by King Features
IT SOUNDS LIKE YOU'RE TRYING TO MAKE THIS MY FAULT.

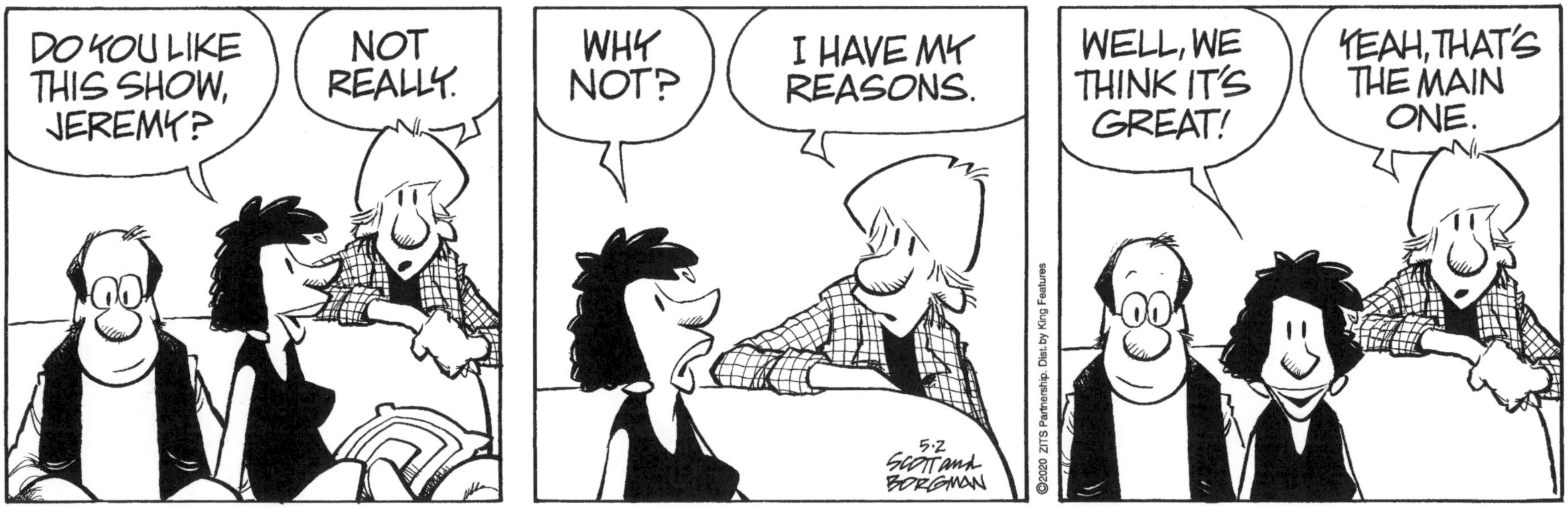
DO YOU LIKE THIS SHOW, JEREMY?
NOT REALLY.
WHY NOT?
I HAVE MY REASONS.
5·2 SCOTT and BORGMAN
©2020 ZITS Partnership. Dist. by King Features
WELL, WE THINK IT'S GREAT!
YEAH, THAT'S THE MAIN ONE.

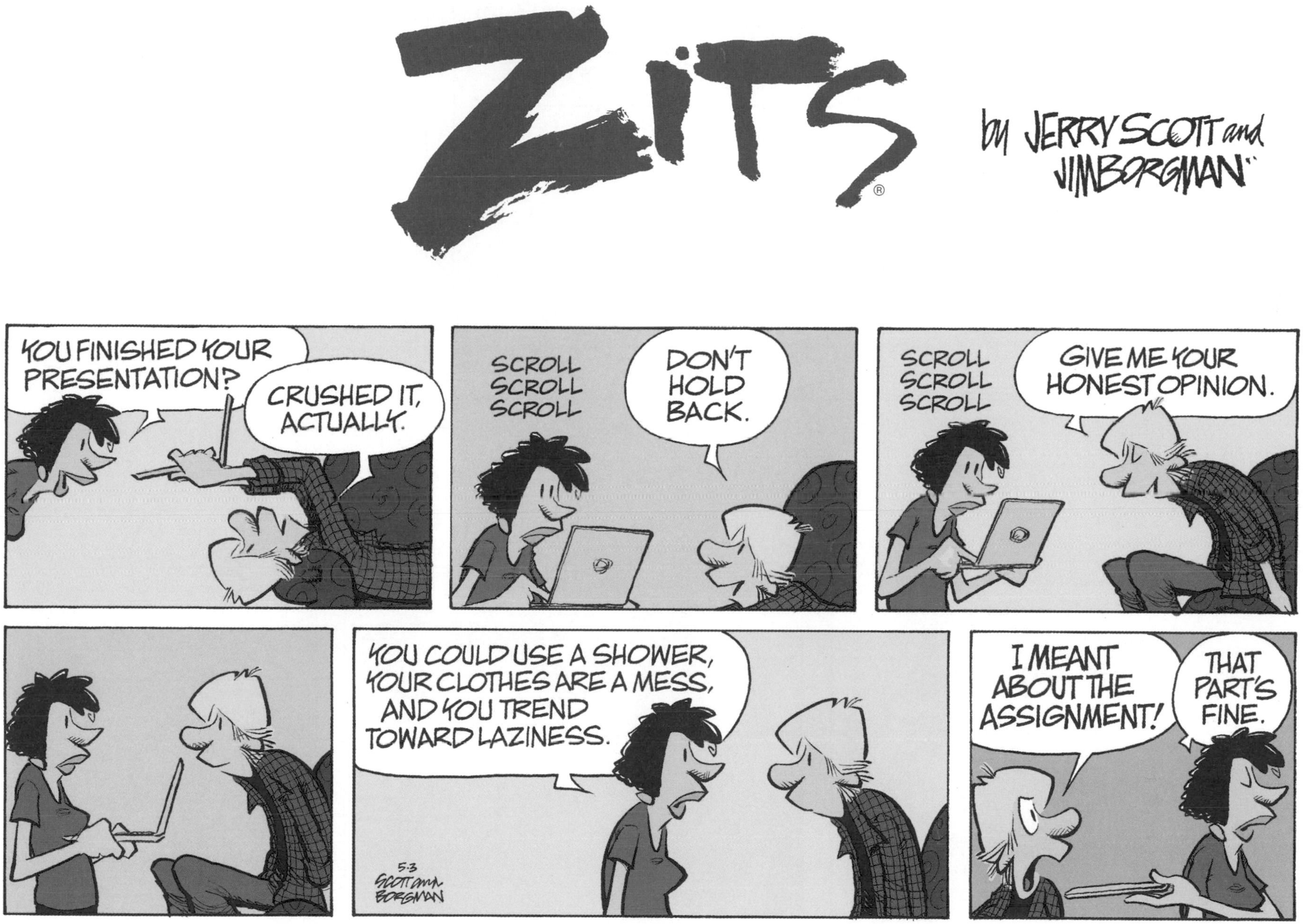
ZITS
by JERRY SCOTT and JIM BORGMAN
YOU FINISHED YOUR PRESENTATION?
CRUSHED IT, ACTUALLY.
SCROLL SCROLL SCROLL
DON'T HOLD BACK.
SCROLL SCROLL SCROLL
GIVE ME YOUR HONEST OPINION.
YOU COULD USE A SHOWER, YOUR CLOTHES ARE A MESS, AND YOU TREND TOWARD LAZINESS.
5-3 SCOTT and BORGMAN
I MEANT ABOUT THE ASSIGNMENT!
THAT PART'S FINE.

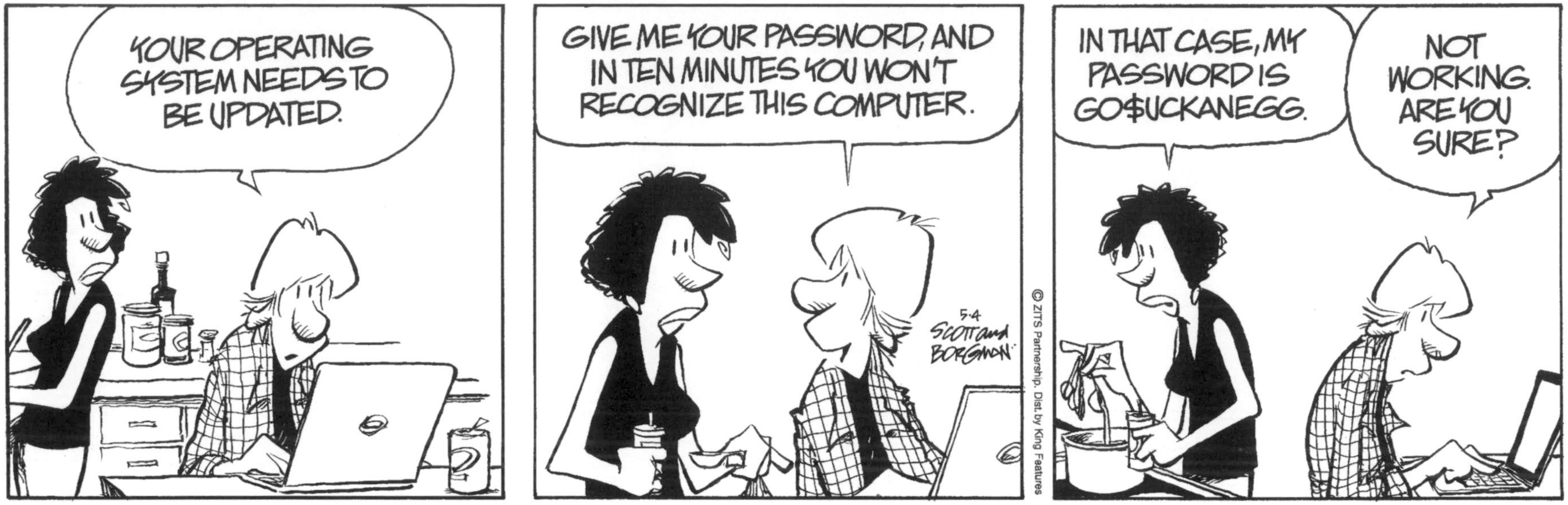
YOUR OPERATING SYSTEM NEEDS TO BE UPDATED.
GIVE ME YOUR PASSWORD, AND IN TEN MINUTES YOU WON'T RECOGNIZE THIS COMPUTER.
5·4 SCOTT and BORGMAN
© ZITS Partnership. Dist. by King Features
IN THAT CASE, MY PASSWORD IS GO$UCKANEGG.
NOT WORKING. ARE YOU SURE?

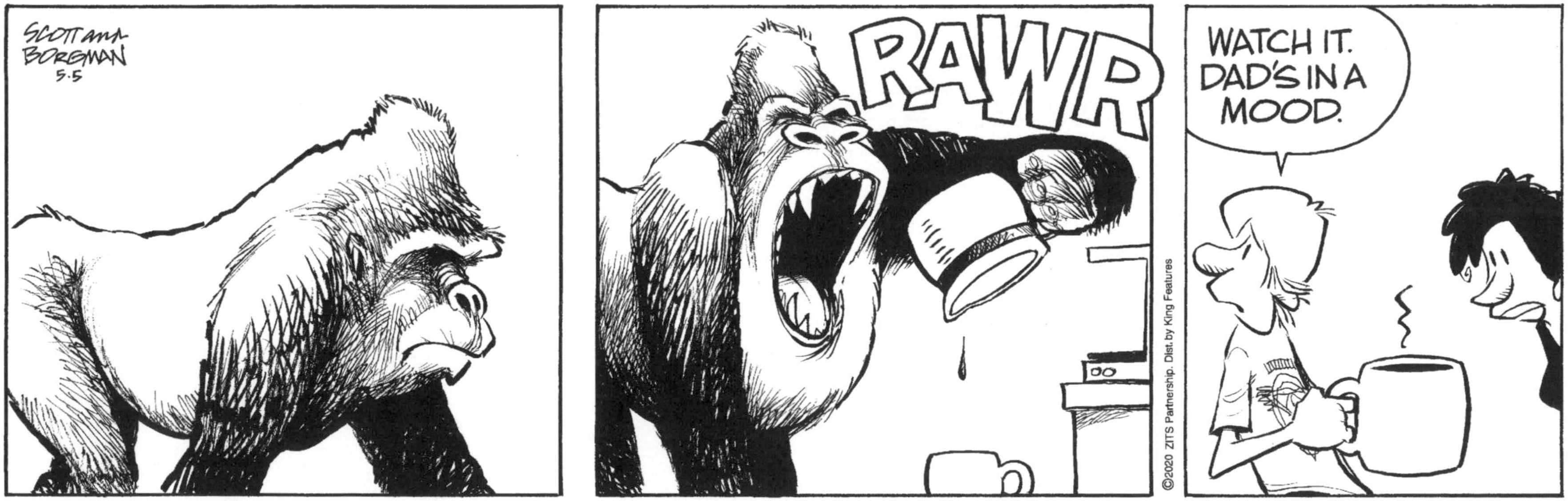
SCOTT and BORGMAN 5·5
RAWR
©2020 ZITS Partnership. Dist. by King Features
WATCH IT. DAD'S IN A MOOD.

WHAT ARE YOU SO HAPPY ABOUT, MOM?
LOOK!
I WORE THIS SKIRT FIFTEEN YEARS AGO, AND IT STILL FITS!
5-6 SCOTT and BORGMAN
IF THAT HAPPENED TO ME, I'D BE SO BUMMED.
AND SHORT!
©2020 ZITS Partnership. Dist. by King Features

JEREMY, DO YOU HAVE ANY OLD GIRLFRIENDS IN YOUR CONTACTS?
WHAT?
NO!
5-7 SCOTT and BORGMAN
©2020 ZITS Partnership. Dist. by King Features
ALL MY GIRLFRIENDS HAVE BEEN MY AGE.

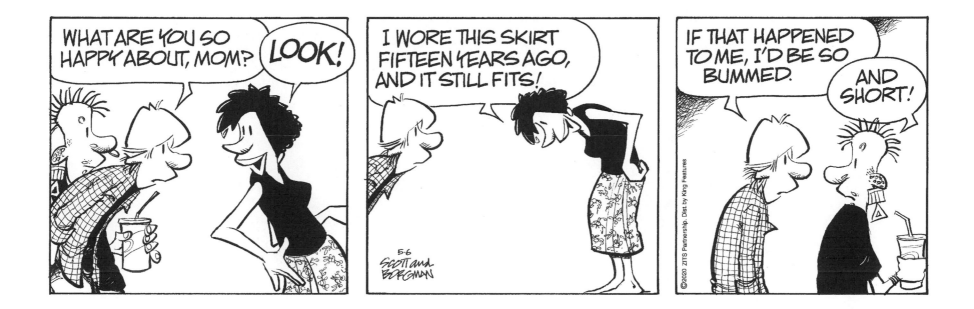

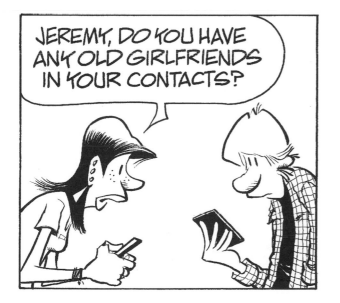

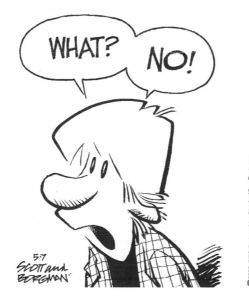

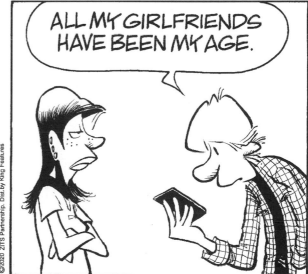

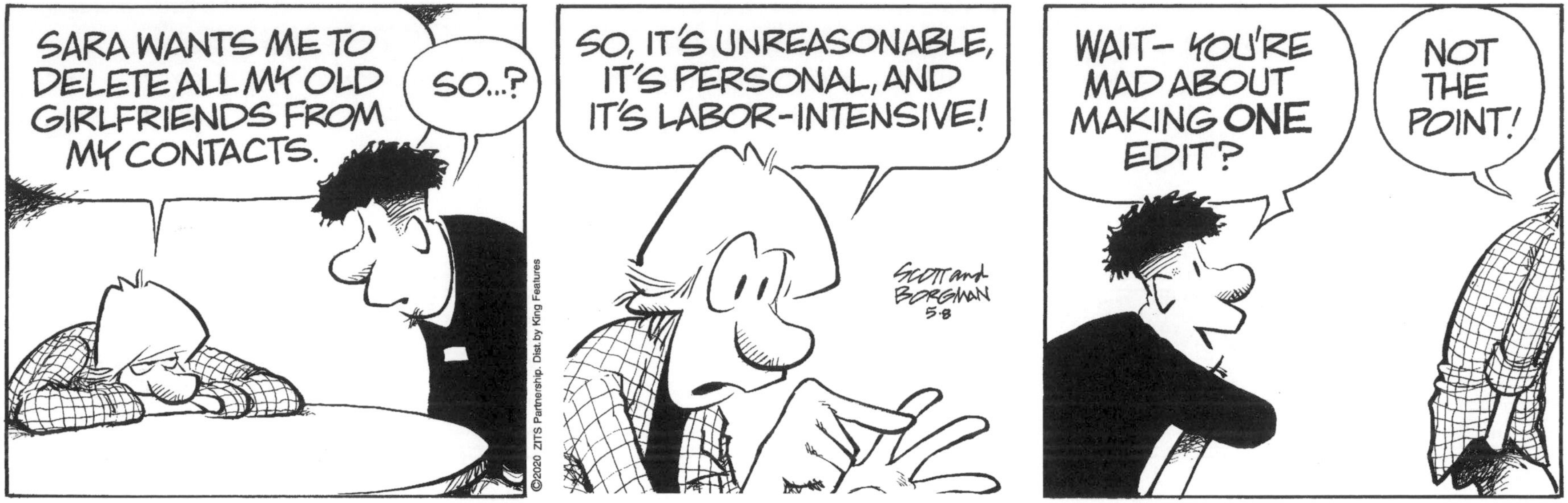
SARA WANTS ME TO DELETE ALL MY OLD GIRLFRIENDS FROM MY CONTACTS.
SO...?
©2020 ZITS Partnership. Dist. by King Features
SO, IT'S UNREASONABLE, IT'S PERSONAL, AND IT'S LABOR-INTENSIVE!
SCOTT and BORGMAN 5·8
WAIT- YOU'RE MAD ABOUT MAKING **ONE** EDIT?
NOT THE POINT!

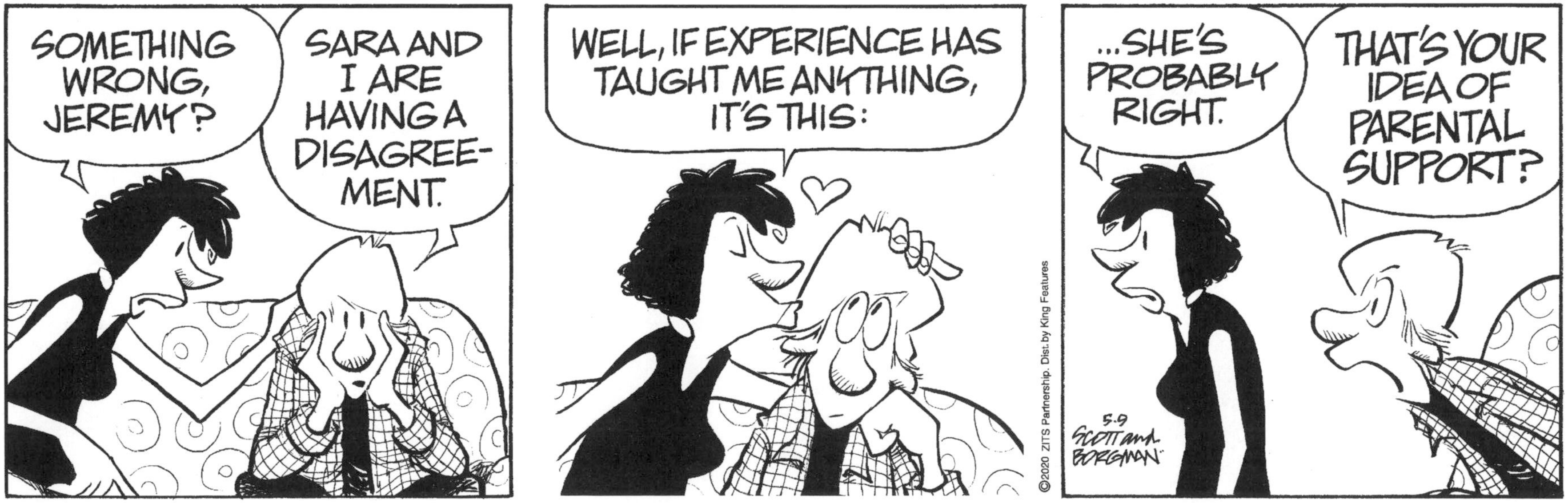
SOMETHING WRONG, JEREMY?
SARA AND I ARE HAVING A DISAGREE-MENT.
WELL, IF EXPERIENCE HAS TAUGHT ME ANYTHING, IT'S THIS:
©2020 ZITS Partnership. Dist. by King Features
...SHE'S PROBABLY RIGHT.
THAT'S YOUR IDEA OF PARENTAL SUPPORT?
5·9 SCOTT and BORGMAN

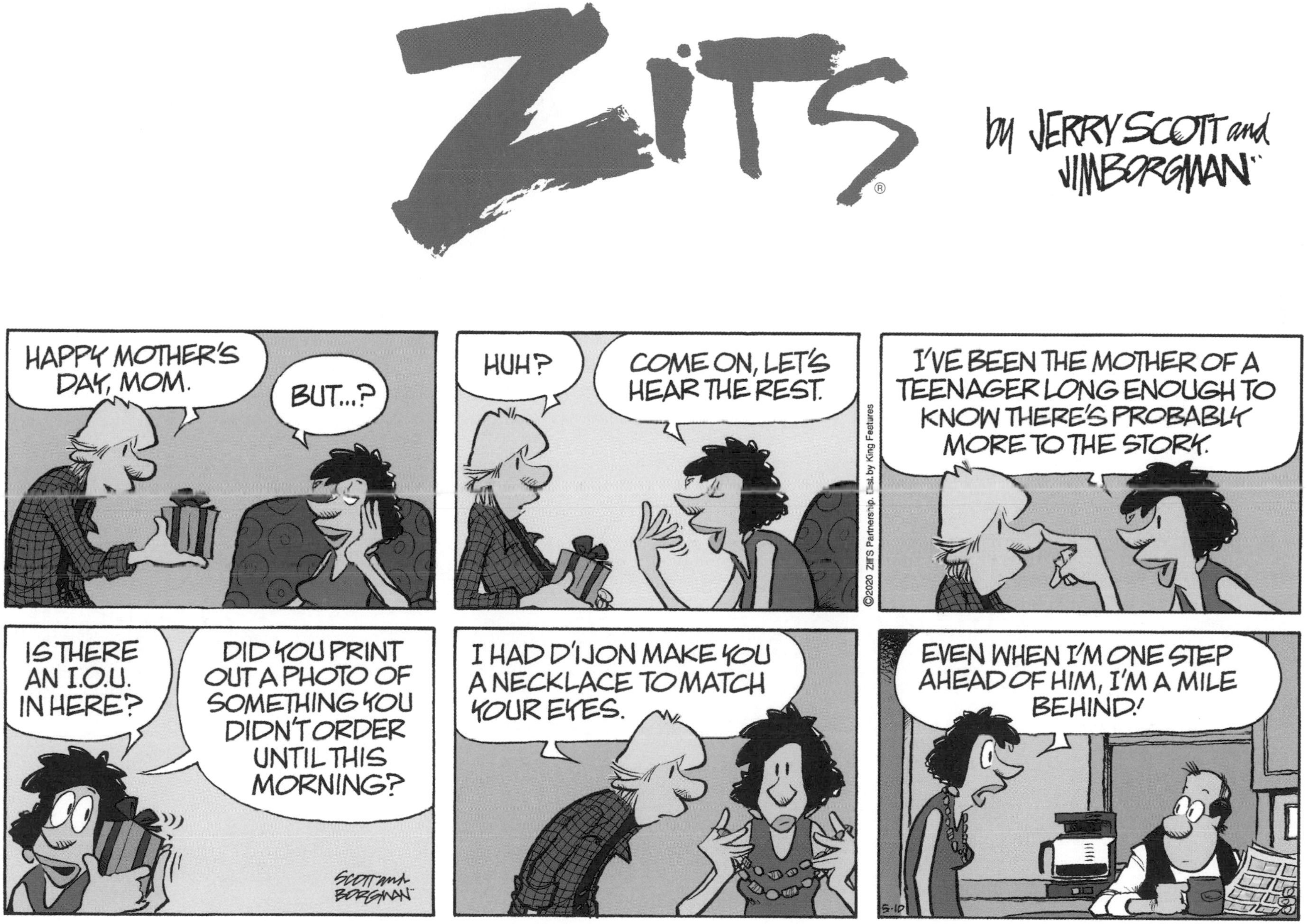
ZITS®
by JERRY SCOTT and JIM BORGMAN
HAPPY MOTHER'S DAY, MOM.
BUT...?
HUH?
COME ON, LET'S HEAR THE REST.
©2020 ZITS Partnership. Dist. by King Features
I'VE BEEN THE MOTHER OF A TEENAGER LONG ENOUGH TO KNOW THERE'S PROBABLY MORE TO THE STORY.
IS THERE AN I.O.U. IN HERE?
DID YOU PRINT OUT A PHOTO OF SOMETHING YOU DIDN'T ORDER UNTIL THIS MORNING?
SCOTT and BORGMAN
I HAD D'IJON MAKE YOU A NECKLACE TO MATCH YOUR EYES.
EVEN WHEN I'M ONE STEP AHEAD OF HIM, I'M A MILE BEHIND!
5-10

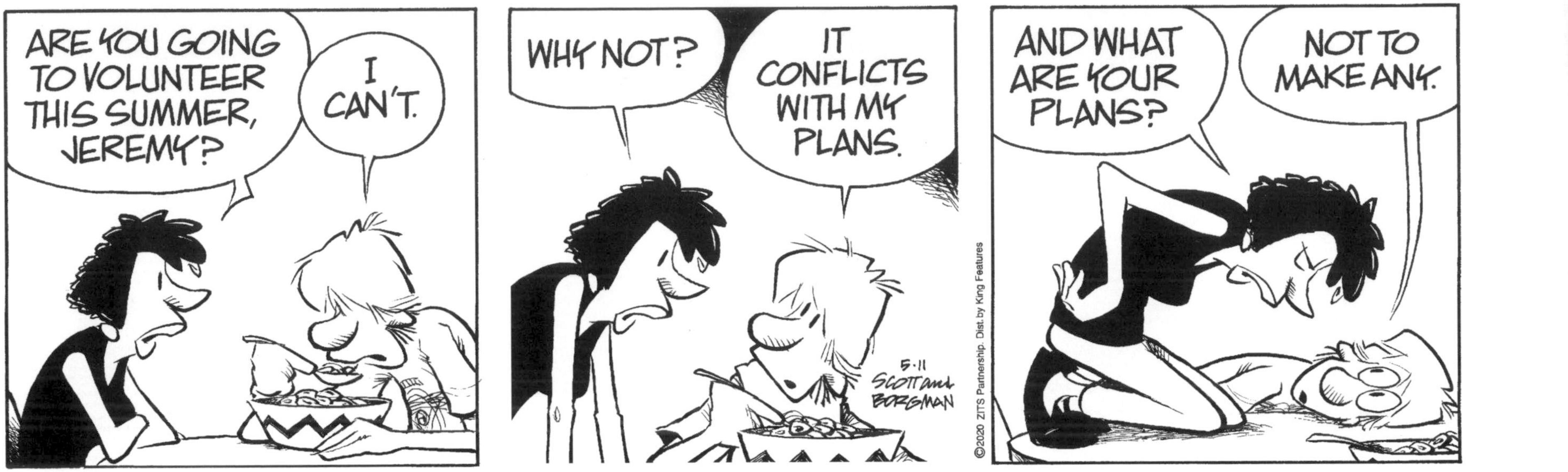
ARE YOU GOING TO VOLUNTEER THIS SUMMER, JEREMY?
I CAN'T.
WHY NOT?
IT CONFLICTS WITH MY PLANS.
5·11
SCOTT and BORGMAN
©2020 ZITS Partnership. Dist. by King Features
AND WHAT ARE YOUR PLANS?
NOT TO MAKE ANY.

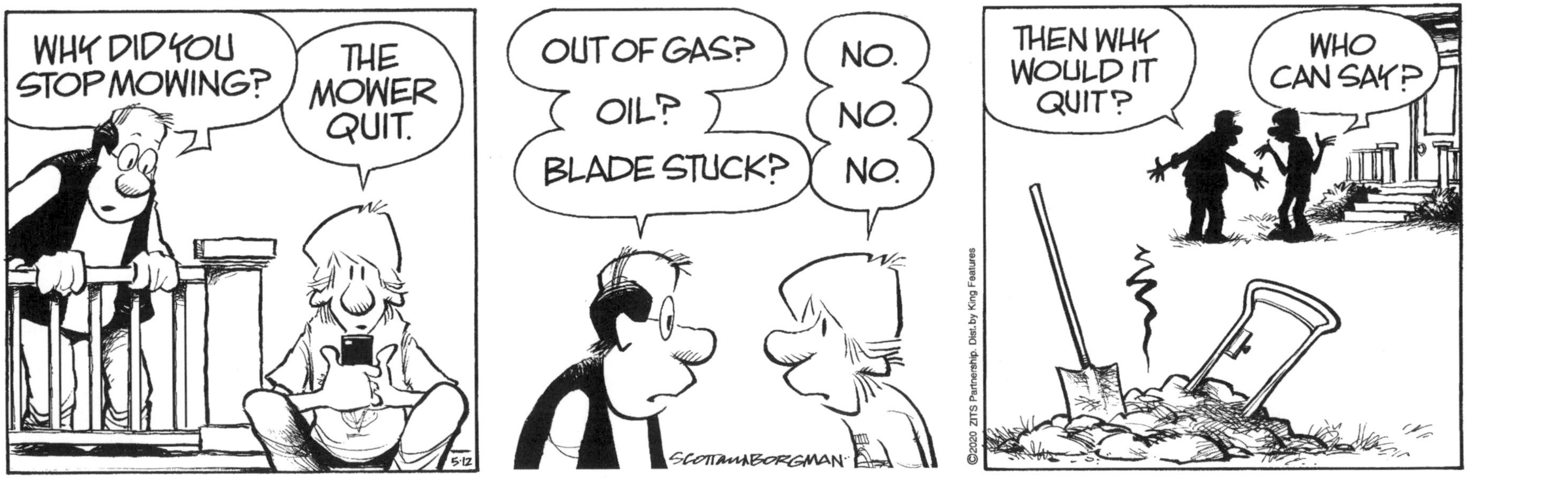
WHY DID YOU STOP MOWING?
THE MOWER QUIT.
5·12
OUT OF GAS?
OIL?
BLADE STUCK?
NO.
NO.
NO.
SCOTT and BORGMAN
©2020 ZITS Partnership. Dist. by King Features
THEN WHY WOULD IT QUIT?
WHO CAN SAY?

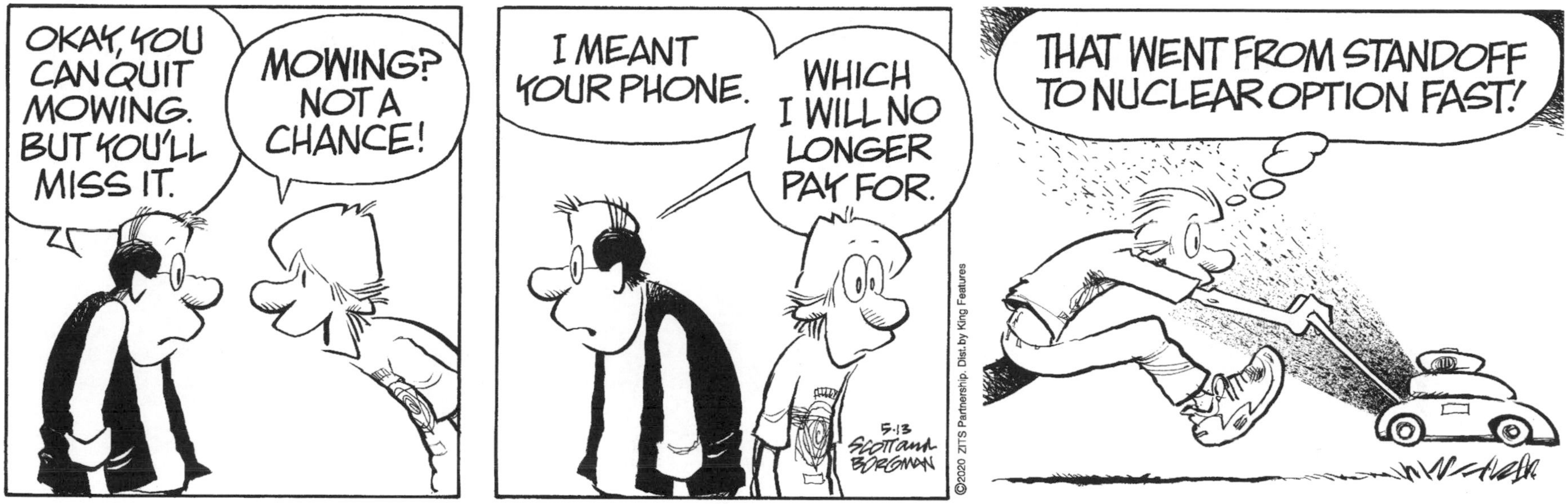
OKAY, YOU CAN QUIT MOWING. BUT YOU'LL MISS IT.
MOWING? NOT A CHANCE!
I MEANT YOUR PHONE.
WHICH I WILL NO LONGER PAY FOR.
5·13
SCOTT and BORGMAN
©2020 ZITS Partnership. Dist. by King Features
THAT WENT FROM STANDOFF TO NUCLEAR OPTION FAST!

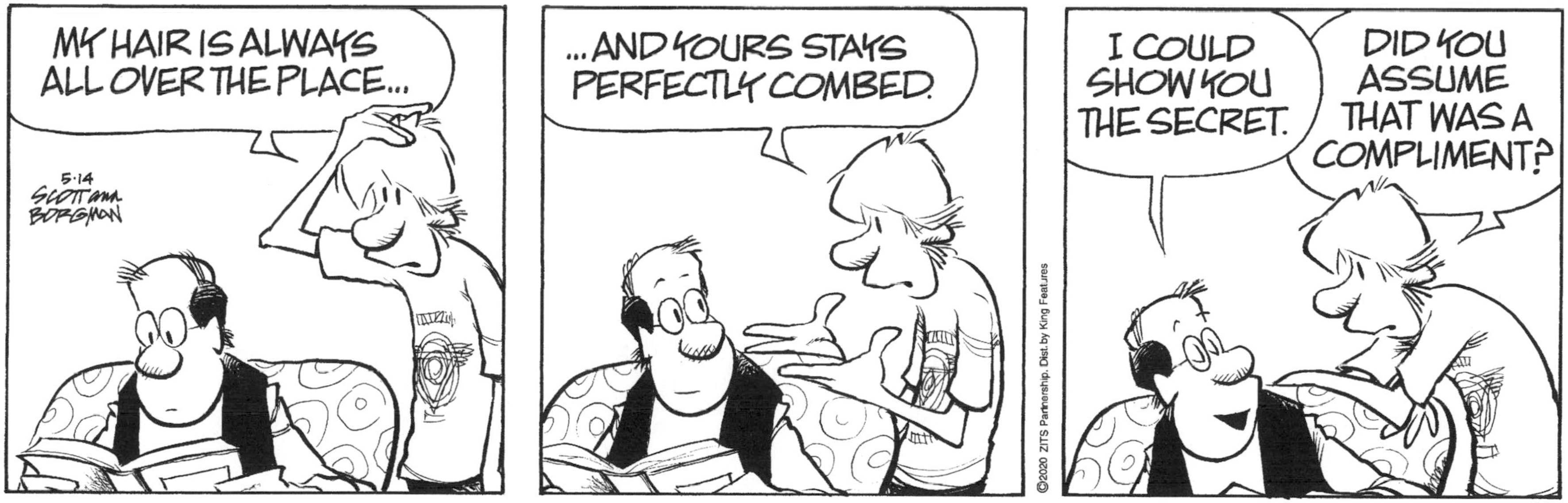
MY HAIR IS ALWAYS ALL OVER THE PLACE...
5·14
SCOTT and BORGMAN
...AND YOURS STAYS PERFECTLY COMBED.
©2020 ZITS Partnership. Dist. by King Features
I COULD SHOW YOU THE SECRET.
DID YOU ASSUME THAT WAS A COMPLIMENT?

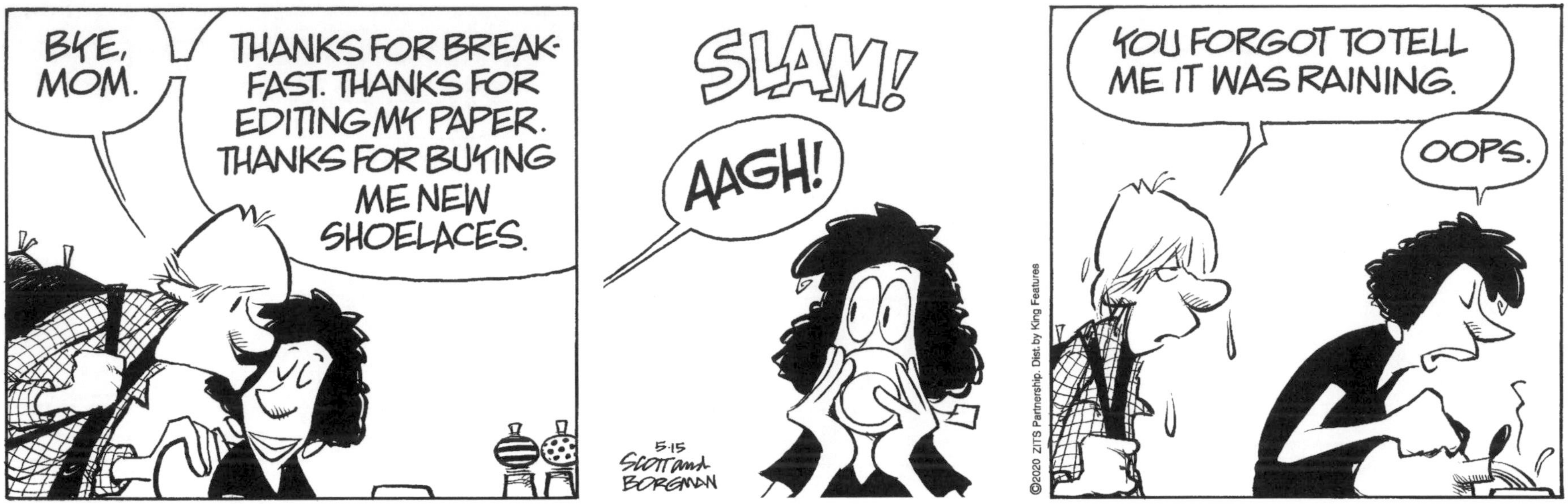
BYE, MOM.
THANKS FOR BREAKFAST. THANKS FOR EDITING MY PAPER. THANKS FOR BUYING ME NEW SHOELACES.
SLAM!
AAGH!
5.15 SCOTT and BORGMAN
YOU FORGOT TO TELL ME IT WAS RAINING.
OOPS.
©2020 ZITS Partnership. Dist. by King Features

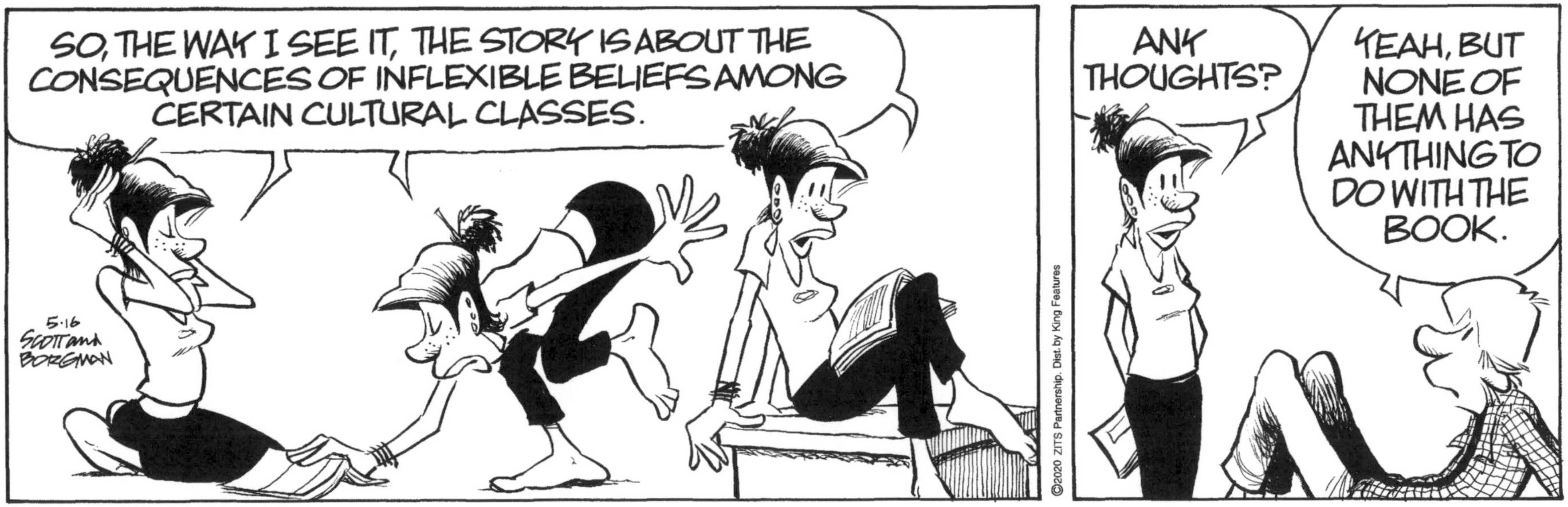
SO, THE WAY I SEE IT, THE STORY IS ABOUT THE CONSEQUENCES OF INFLEXIBLE BELIEFS AMONG CERTAIN CULTURAL CLASSES.
5.16 SCOTT and BORGMAN
©2020 ZITS Partnership. Dist. by King Features
ANY THOUGHTS?
YEAH, BUT NONE OF THEM HAS ANYTHING TO DO WITH THE BOOK.

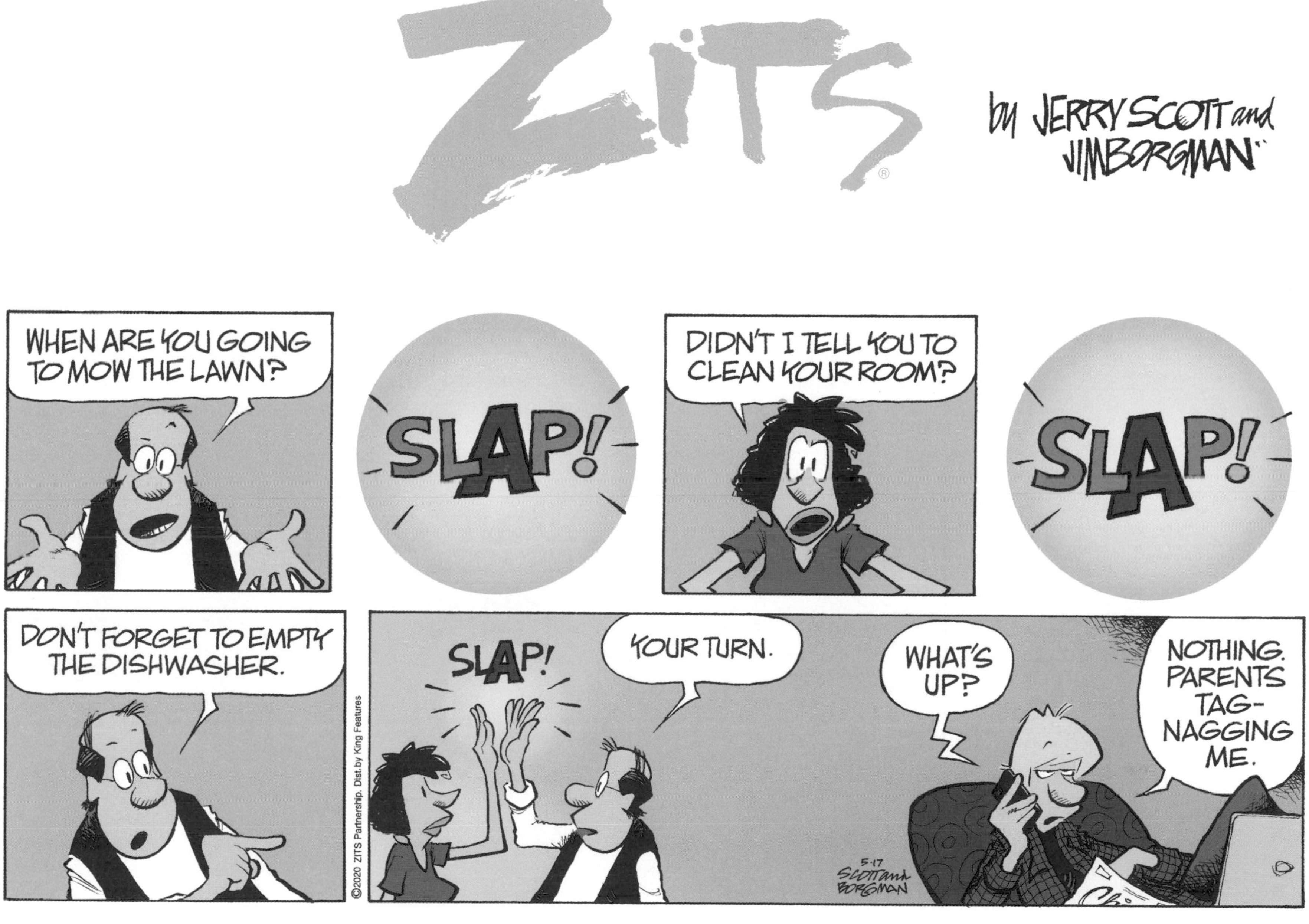
ZITS
by JERRY SCOTT and JIM BORGMAN
WHEN ARE YOU GOING TO MOW THE LAWN?
SLAP!
DIDN'T I TELL YOU TO CLEAN YOUR ROOM?
SLAP!
DON'T FORGET TO EMPTY THE DISHWASHER.
©2020 ZITS Partnership. Dist.by King Features
SLAP!
YOUR TURN.
WHAT'S UP?
NOTHING. PARENTS TAG-NAGGING ME.
5-17 SCOTT and BORGMAN

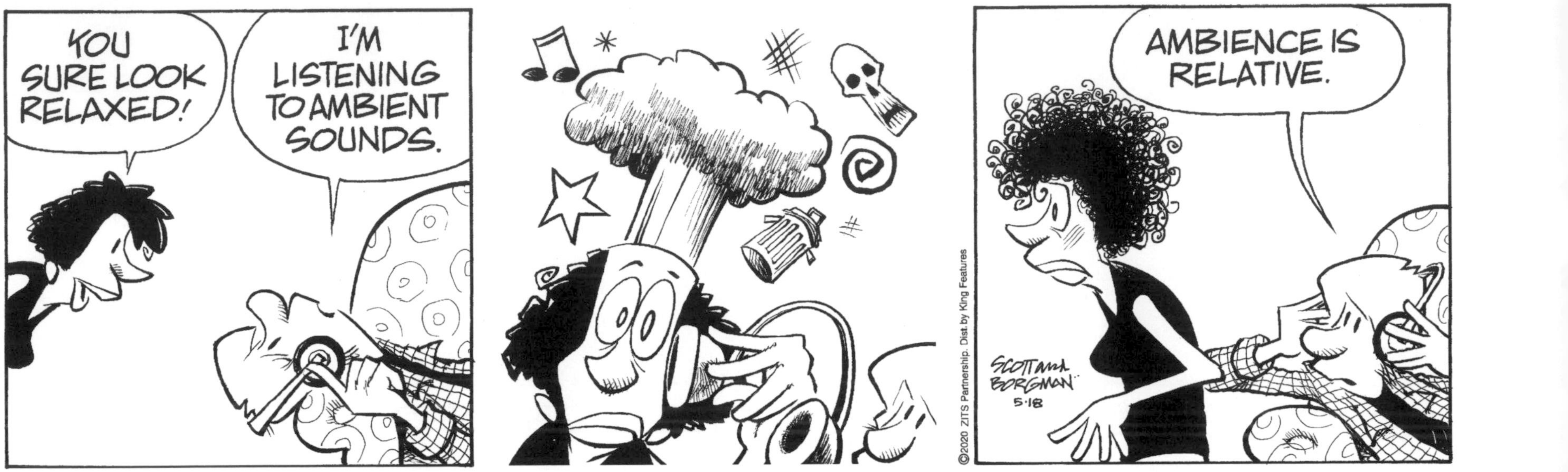

YOU SURE LOOK RELAXED!
I'M LISTENING TO AMBIENT SOUNDS.
AMBIENCE IS RELATIVE.
©2020 ZITS Partnership. Dist by King Features
SCOTT AND BORGMAN 5·18

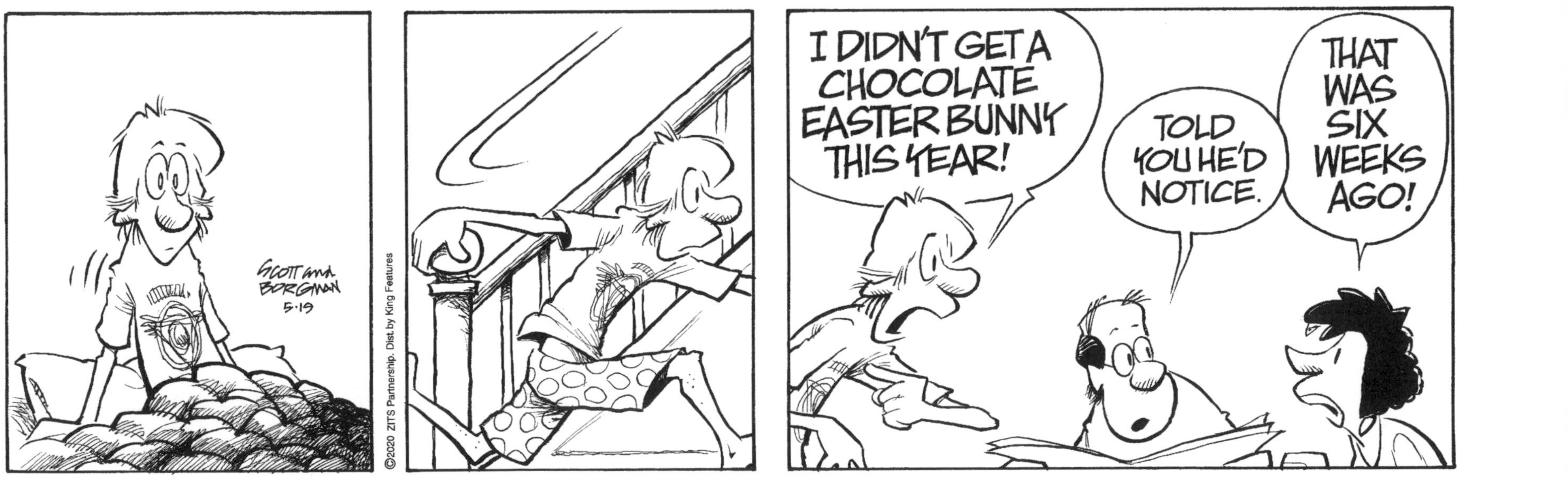

SCOTT AND BORGMAN 5·19
©2020 ZITS Partnership. Dist by King Features
I DIDN'T GET A CHOCOLATE EASTER BUNNY THIS YEAR!
TOLD YOU HE'D NOTICE.
THAT WAS SIX WEEKS AGO!

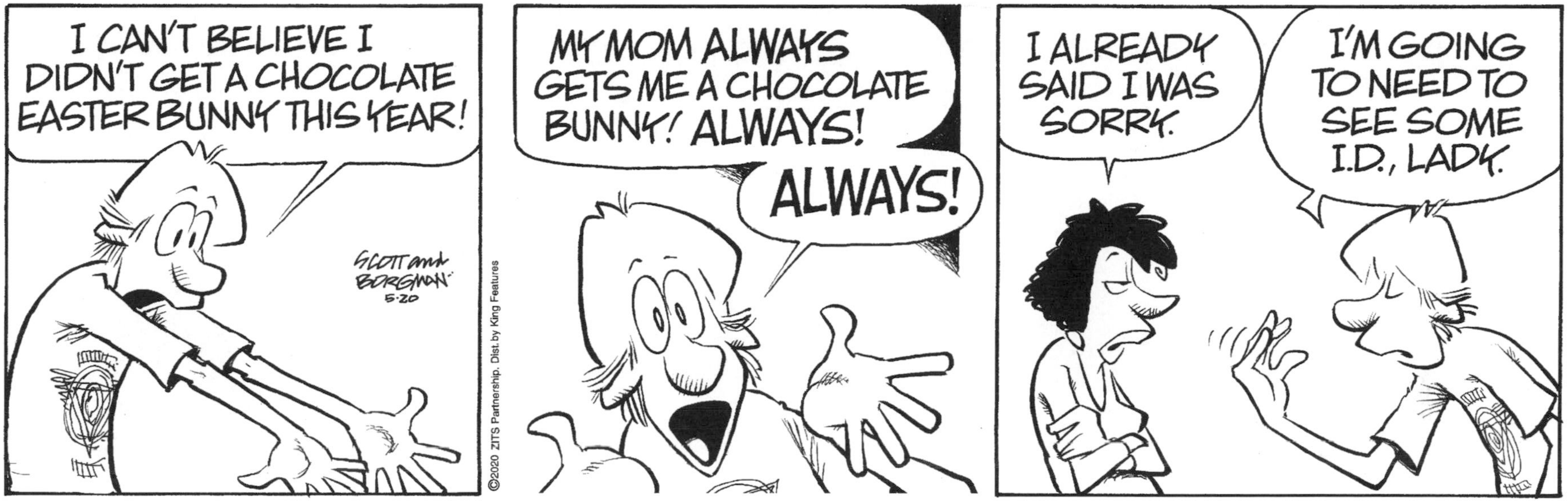
I CAN'T BELIEVE I DIDN'T GET A CHOCOLATE EASTER BUNNY THIS YEAR!
SCOTT AND BORGMAN 5·20
MY MOM ALWAYS GETS ME A CHOCOLATE BUNNY! ALWAYS!
ALWAYS!
©2020 ZITS Partnership. Dist. by King Features
I ALREADY SAID I WAS SORRY.
I'M GOING TO NEED TO SEE SOME I.D., LADY.

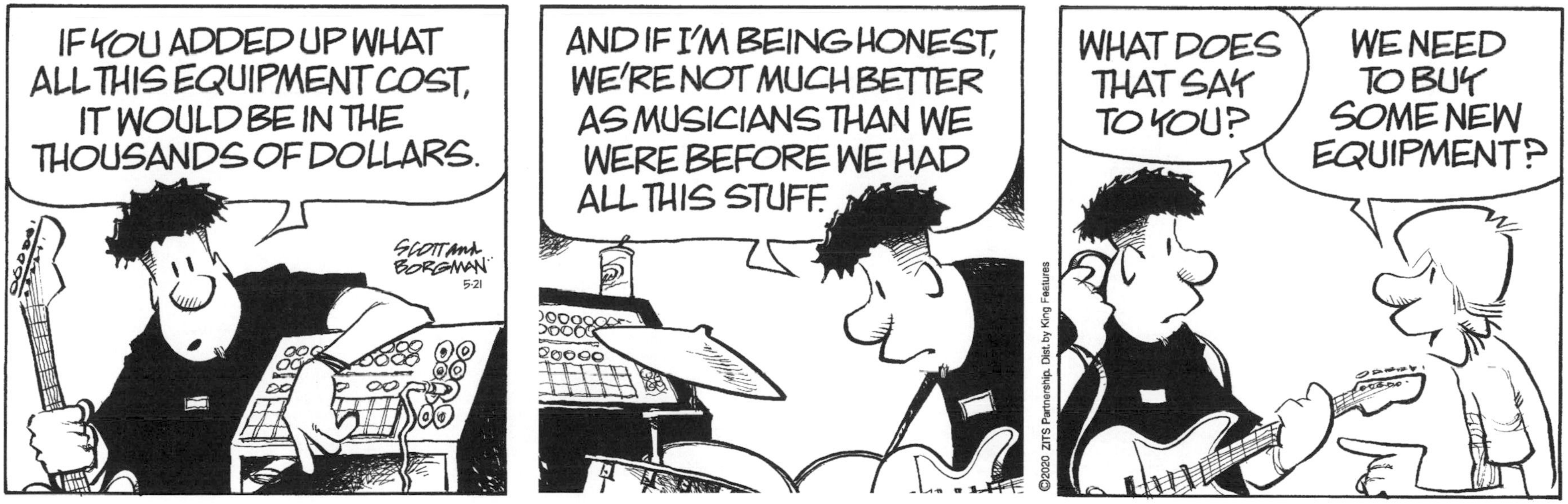
IF YOU ADDED UP WHAT ALL THIS EQUIPMENT COST, IT WOULD BE IN THE THOUSANDS OF DOLLARS.
SCOTT AND BORGMAN 5·21
AND IF I'M BEING HONEST, WE'RE NOT MUCH BETTER AS MUSICIANS THAN WE WERE BEFORE WE HAD ALL THIS STUFF.
©2020 ZITS Partnership. Dist. by King Features
WHAT DOES THAT SAY TO YOU?
WE NEED TO BUY SOME NEW EQUIPMENT?

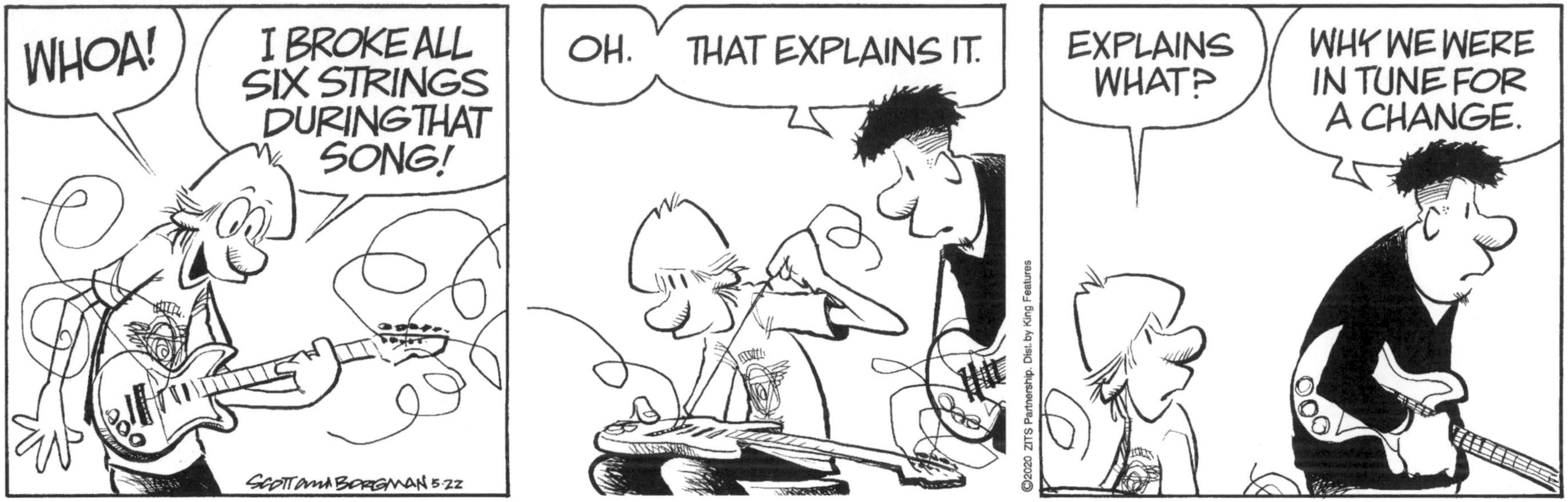
WHOA!
I BROKE ALL SIX STRINGS DURING THAT SONG!
SCOTT and BORGMAN 5-22
OH.
THAT EXPLAINS IT.
©2020 ZITS Partnership. Dist. by King Features
EXPLAINS WHAT?
WHY WE WERE IN TUNE FOR A CHANGE.

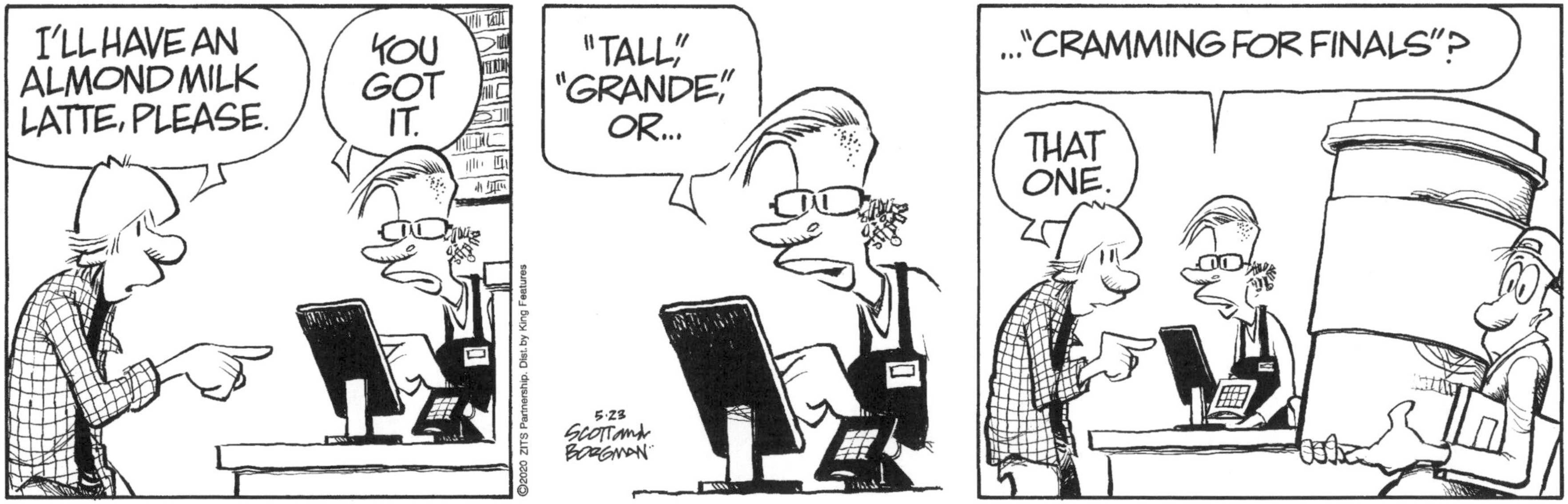
I'LL HAVE AN ALMOND MILK LATTE, PLEASE.
YOU GOT IT.
©2020 ZITS Partnership. Dist. by King Features
"TALL," "GRANDE," OR...
5-23 SCOTT and BORGMAN
..."CRAMMING FOR FINALS"?
THAT ONE.

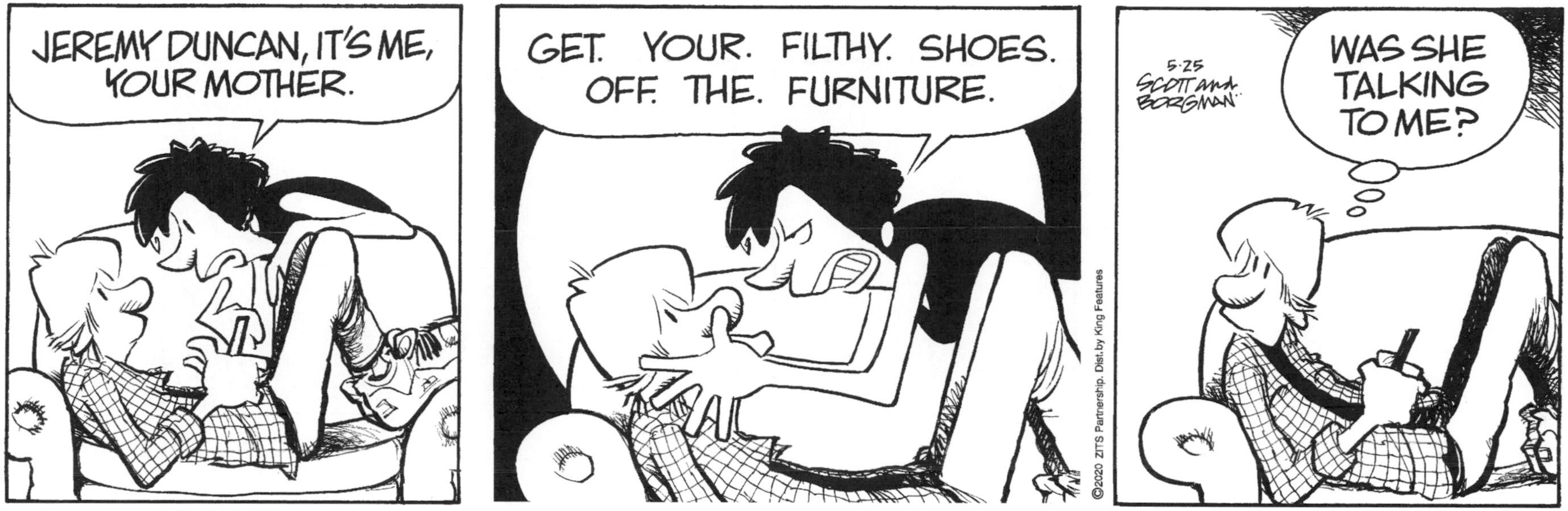
JEREMY DUNCAN, IT'S ME, YOUR MOTHER.
GET. YOUR. FILTHY. SHOES. OFF. THE. FURNITURE.
©2020 ZITS Partnership. Dist. by King Features
5·25 SCOTT and BORGMAN
WAS SHE TALKING TO ME?

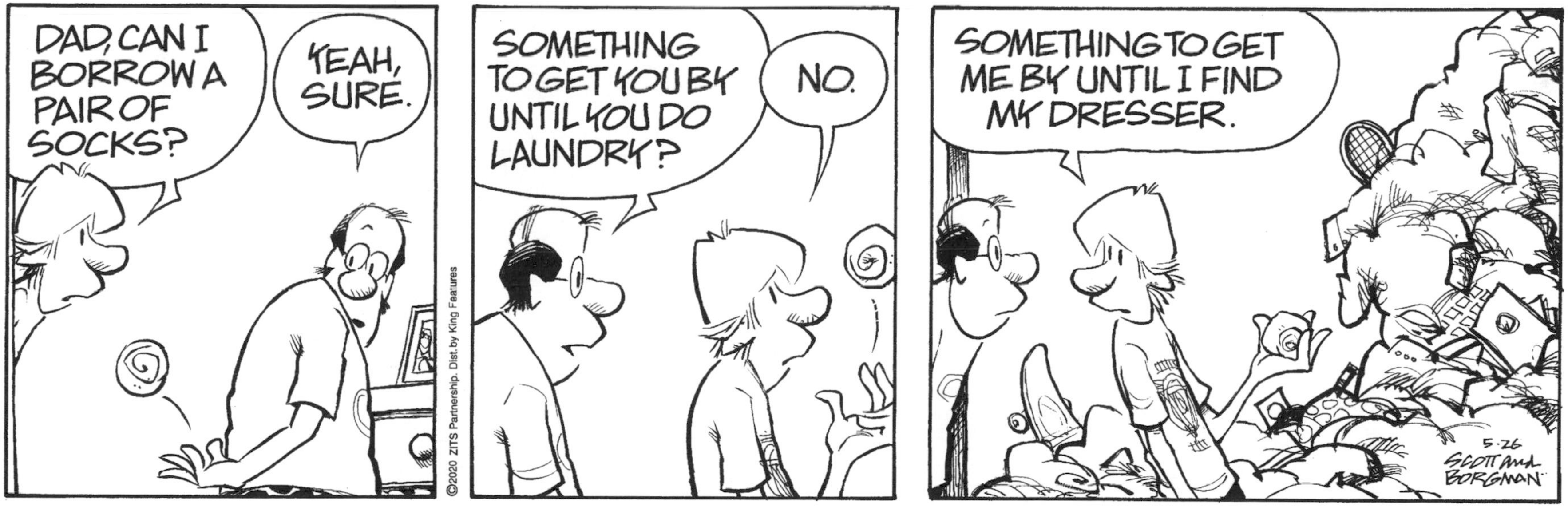
DAD, CAN I BORROW A PAIR OF SOCKS?
YEAH, SURE.
©2020 ZITS Partnership. Dist. by King Features
SOMETHING TO GET YOU BY UNTIL YOU DO LAUNDRY?
NO.
SOMETHING TO GET ME BY UNTIL I FIND MY DRESSER.
5·26 SCOTT and BORGMAN

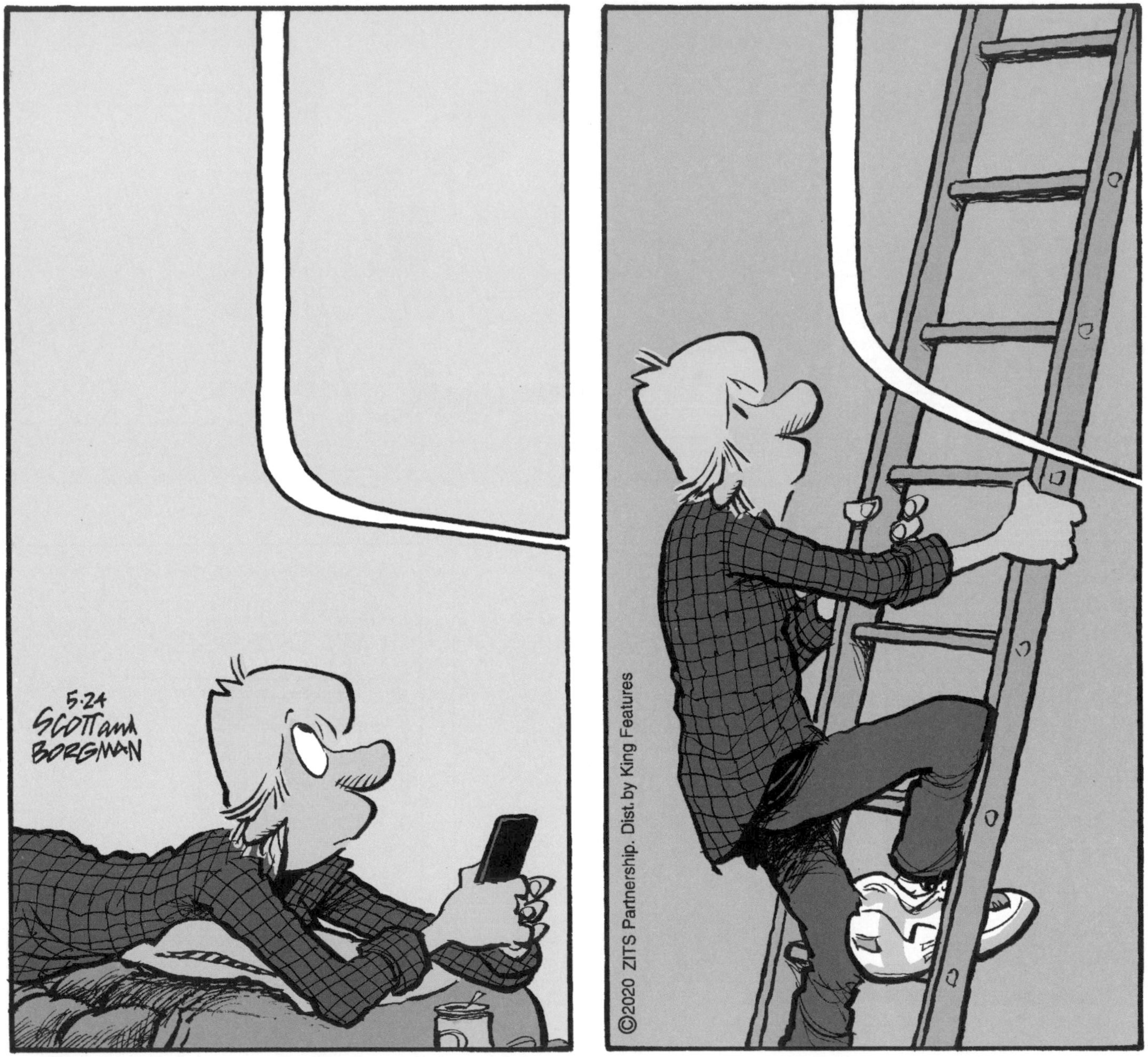
5·24
SCOTT and
BORGMAN
©2020 ZITS Partnership. Dist. by King Features

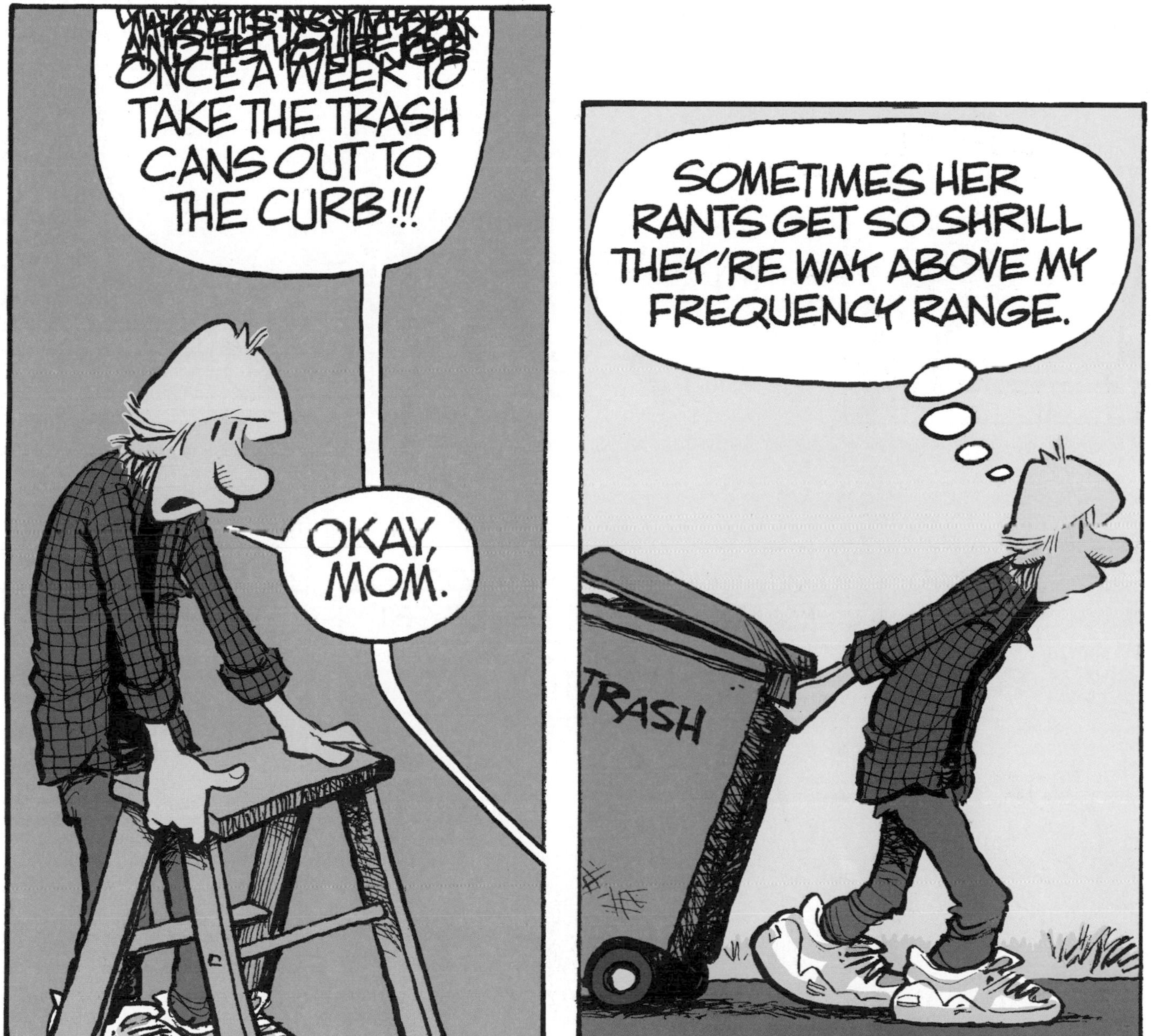
ONCE A WEEK TO TAKE THE TRASH CANS OUT TO THE CURB!!!
OKAY, MOM.
SOMETIMES HER RANTS GET SO SHRILL THEY'RE WAY ABOVE MY FREQUENCY RANGE.
TRASH

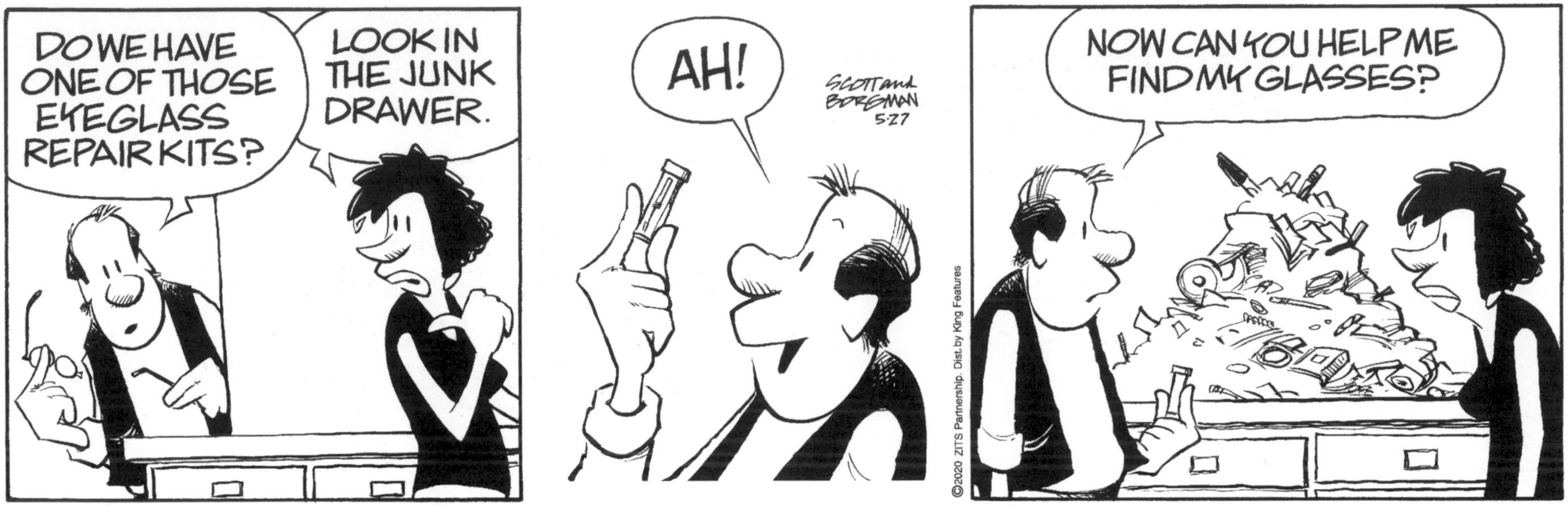
DO WE HAVE ONE OF THOSE EYEGLASS REPAIR KITS?
LOOK IN THE JUNK DRAWER.
AH!
SCOTT AND BORGMAN 5·27
©2020 ZITS Partnership. Dist. by King Features
NOW CAN YOU HELP ME FIND MY GLASSES?

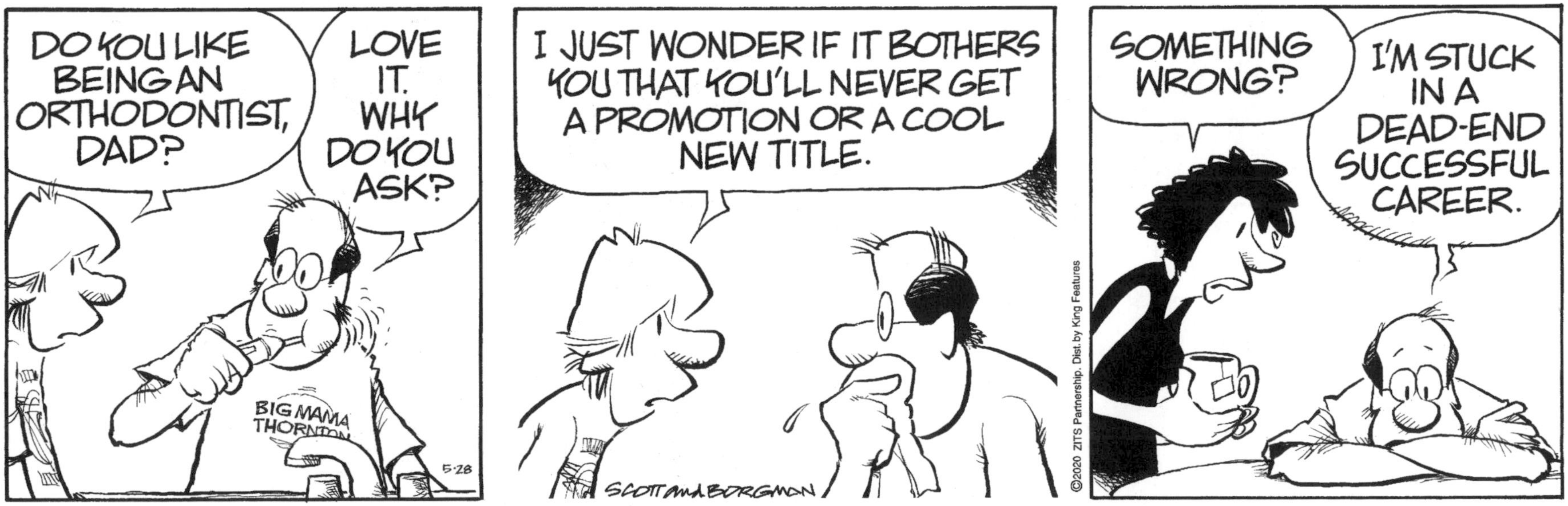
DO YOU LIKE BEING AN ORTHODONTIST, DAD?
LOVE IT. WHY DO YOU ASK?
BIG MAMA THORNTON
5·28
I JUST WONDER IF IT BOTHERS YOU THAT YOU'LL NEVER GET A PROMOTION OR A COOL NEW TITLE.
SCOTT AND BORGMAN
©2020 ZITS Partnership. Dist. by King Features
SOMETHING WRONG?
I'M STUCK IN A DEAD-END SUCCESSFUL CAREER.

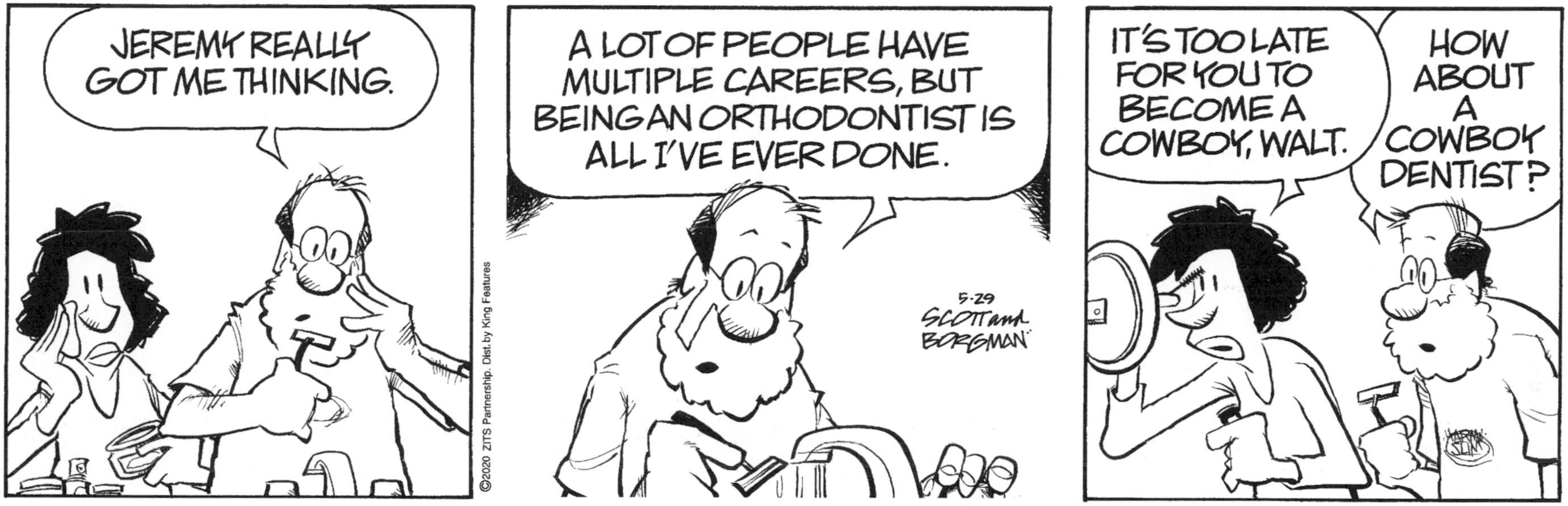

JEREMY REALLY GOT ME THINKING.
©2020 ZITS Partnership. Dist. by King Features
A LOT OF PEOPLE HAVE MULTIPLE CAREERS, BUT BEING AN ORTHODONTIST IS ALL I'VE EVER DONE.
5-29 SCOTT and BORGMAN
IT'S TOO LATE FOR YOU TO BECOME A COWBOY, WALT.
HOW ABOUT A COWBOY DENTIST?

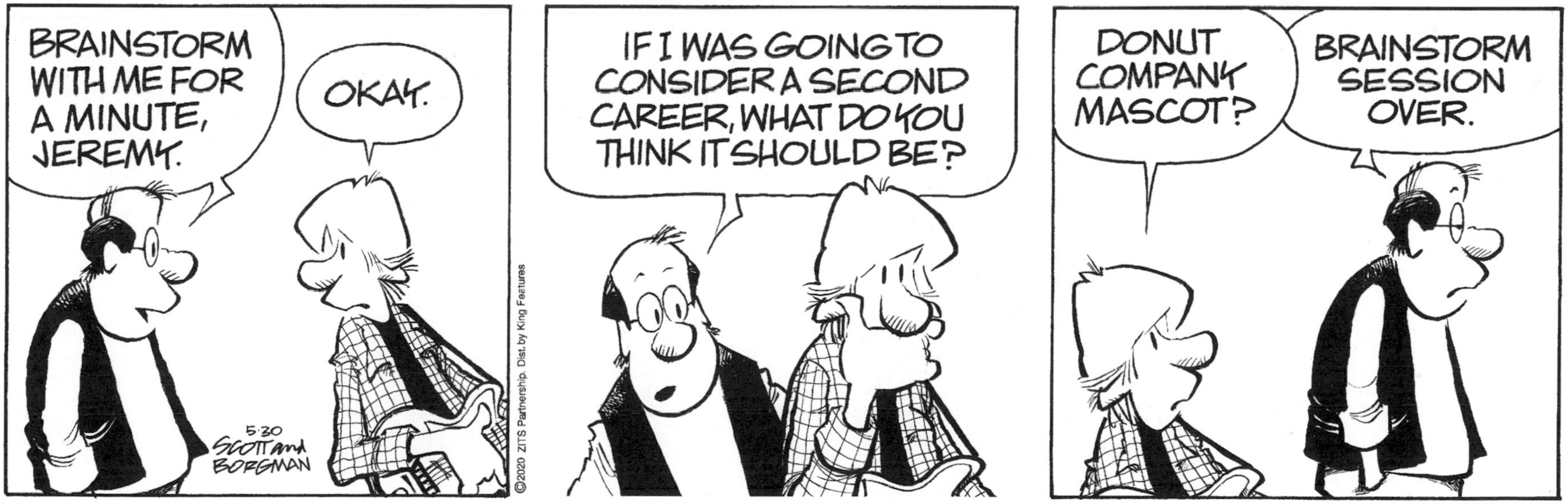

BRAINSTORM WITH ME FOR A MINUTE, JEREMY.
OKAY.
5-30 SCOTT and BORGMAN
©2020 ZITS Partnership. Dist. by King Features
IF I WAS GOING TO CONSIDER A SECOND CAREER, WHAT DO YOU THINK IT SHOULD BE?
DONUT COMPANY MASCOT?
BRAINSTORM SESSION OVER.

ZITS®

by JERRY SCOTT and JIM BORGMAN

IS IT GOING TO RAIN?
NO...
...JUST A PASSING CLOUD.
GRUMBLE GRIPE
WHINE GLOOM
5-31 SCOTT and BORGMAN
©2020 ZITS Partnership. Dist. by King Features

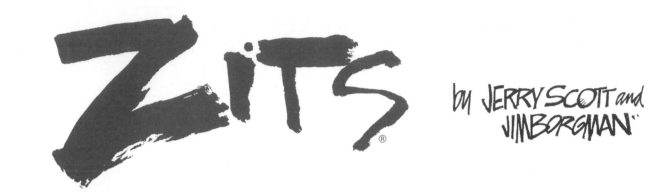

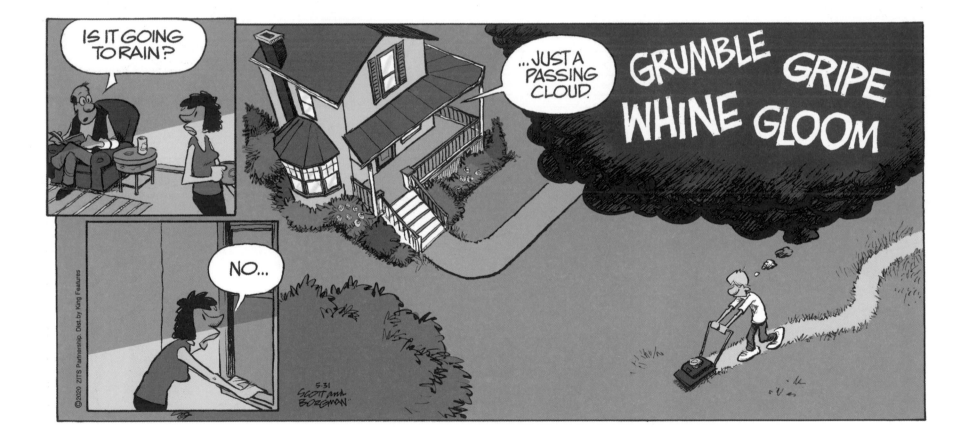

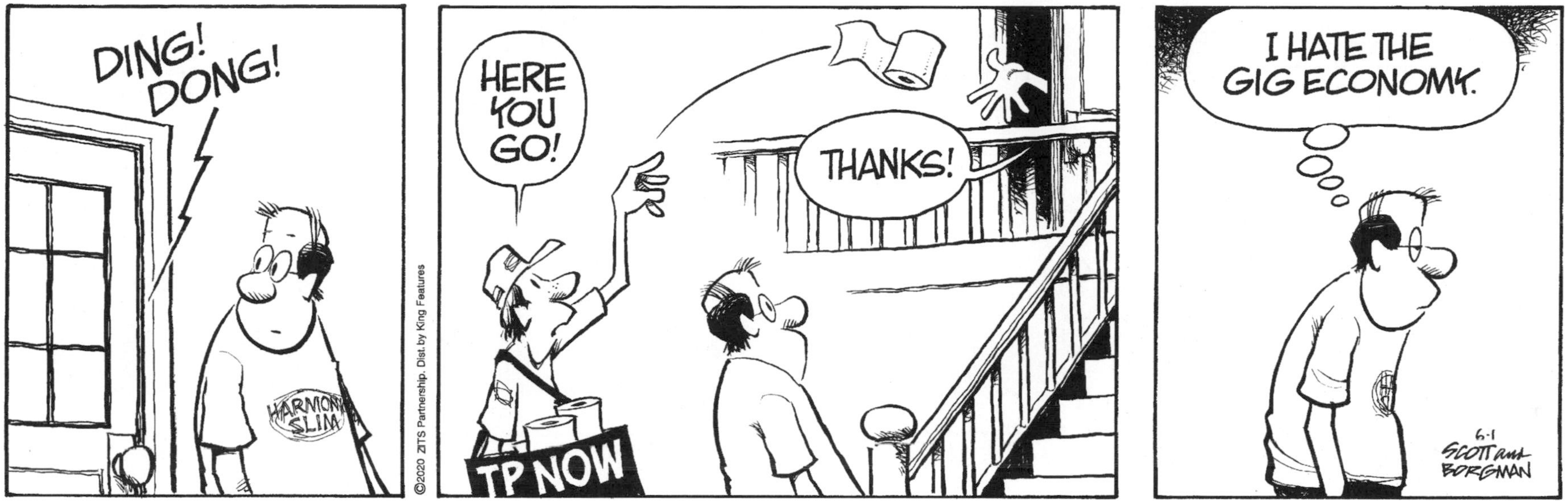
DING! DONG!
©2020 ZITS Partnership. Dist. by King Features
HERE YOU GO!
THANKS!
TP NOW
I HATE THE GIG ECONOMY.
6·1 SCOTT and BORGMAN

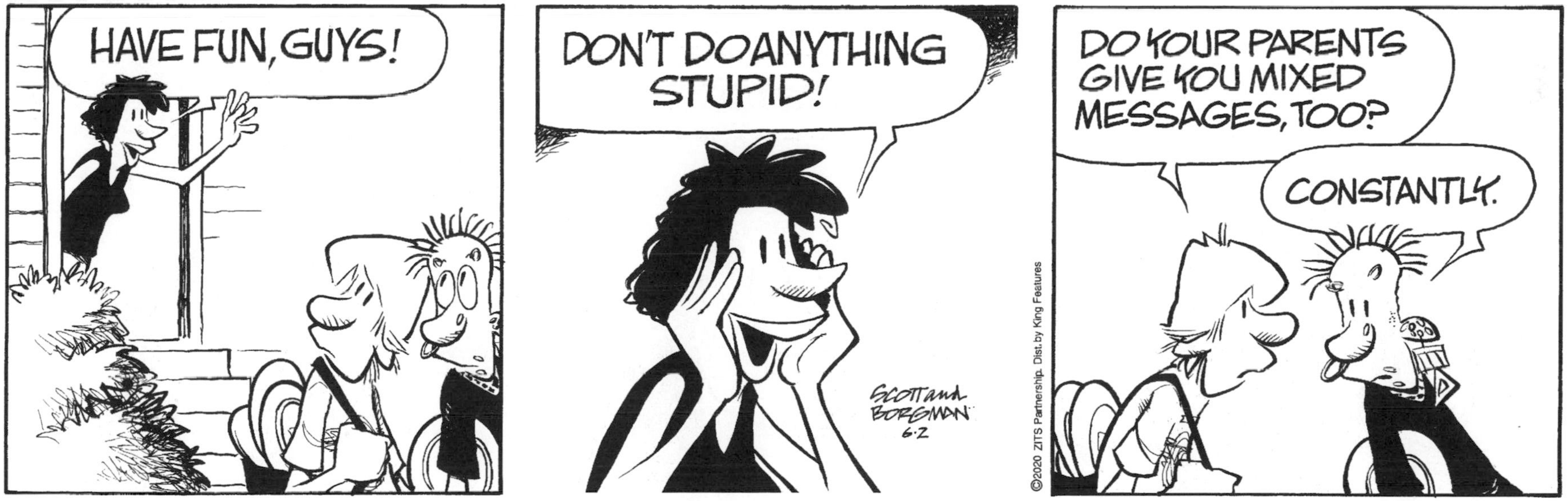
HAVE FUN, GUYS!
DON'T DO ANYTHING STUPID!
SCOTT and BORGMAN 6·2
©2020 ZITS Partnership. Dist. by King Features
DO YOUR PARENTS GIVE YOU MIXED MESSAGES, TOO?
CONSTANTLY.

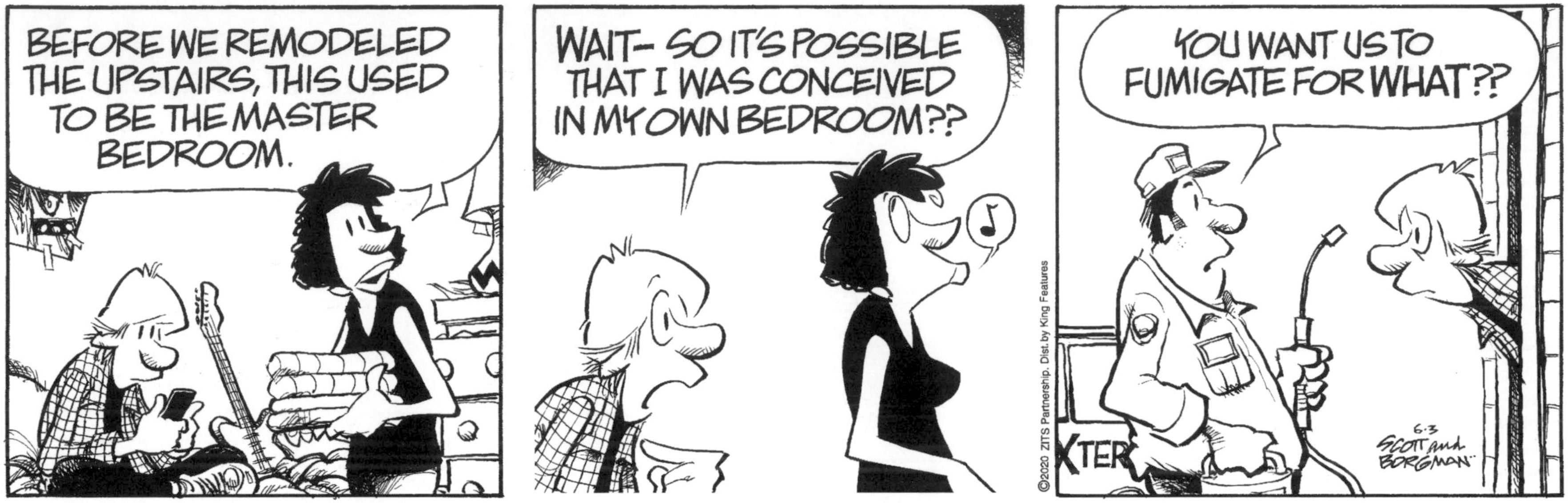
BEFORE WE REMODELED THE UPSTAIRS, THIS USED TO BE THE MASTER BEDROOM.
WAIT- SO IT'S POSSIBLE THAT I WAS CONCEIVED IN MY OWN BEDROOM??
©2020 ZITS Partnership. Dist. by King Features
YOU WANT US TO FUMIGATE FOR WHAT??
XTER
6·3
SCOTT and BORGMAN

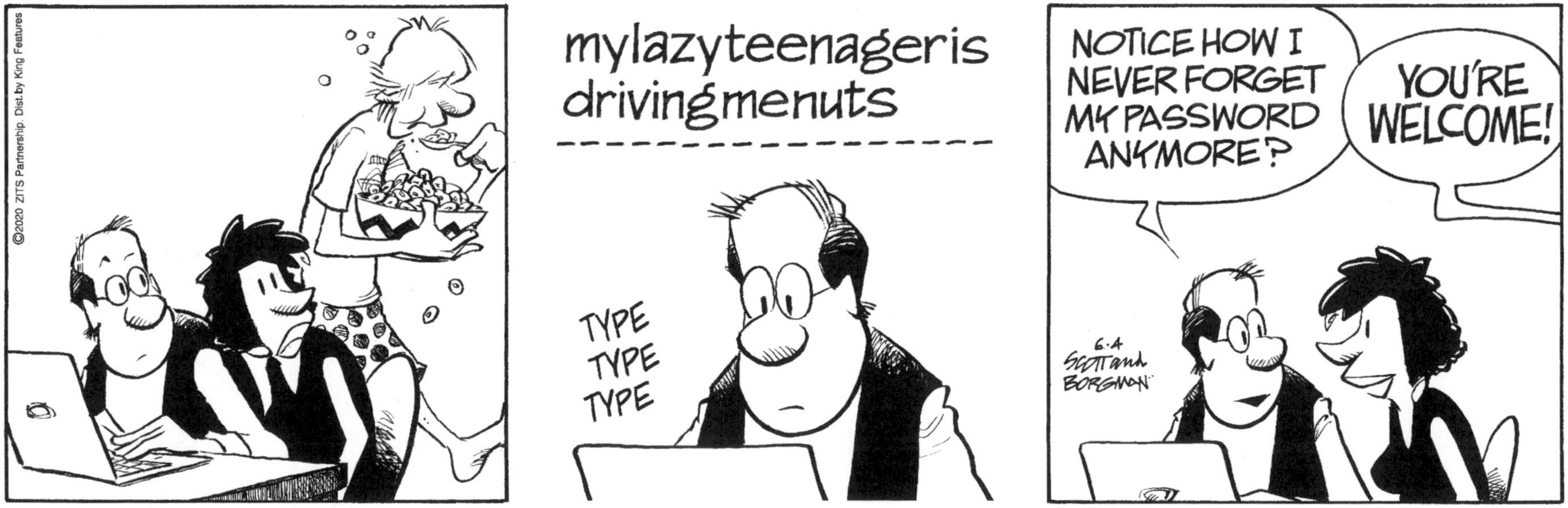
©2020 ZITS Partnership. Dist. by King Features
mylazyteenageris drivingmenuts
TYPE TYPE TYPE
NOTICE HOW I NEVER FORGET MY PASSWORD ANYMORE?
YOU'RE WELCOME!
6·4
SCOTT and BORGMAN

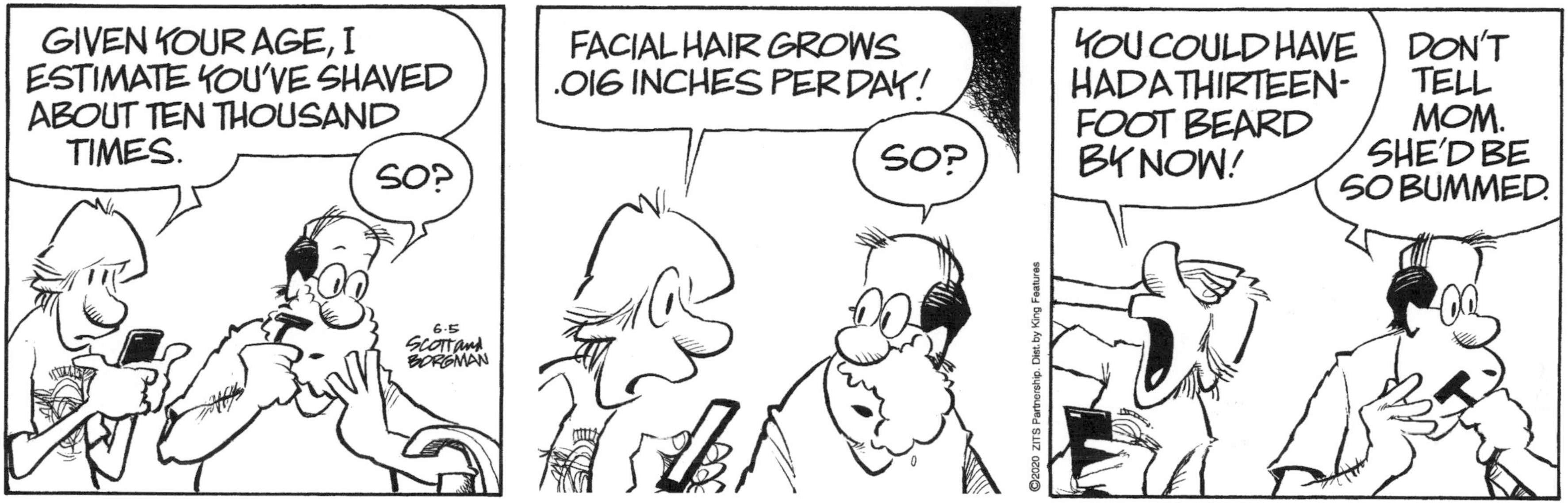
GIVEN YOUR AGE, I ESTIMATE YOU'VE SHAVED ABOUT TEN THOUSAND TIMES.
SO?
6-5 SCOTT AND BORGMAN
FACIAL HAIR GROWS .016 INCHES PER DAY!
SO?
©2020 ZITS Partnership. Dist. by King Features
YOU COULD HAVE HAD A THIRTEEN-FOOT BEARD BY NOW!
DON'T TELL MOM. SHE'D BE SO BUMMED.

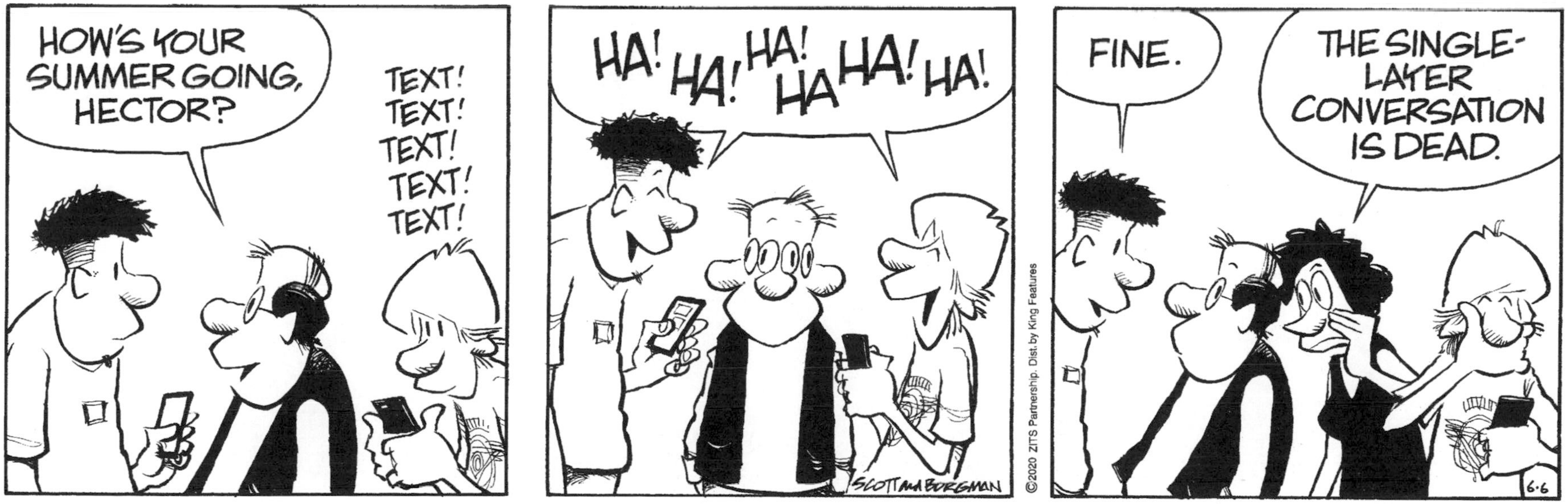
HOW'S YOUR SUMMER GOING, HECTOR?
TEXT! TEXT! TEXT! TEXT! TEXT!
HA! HA! HA! HA HA! HA!
SCOTT AND BORGMAN
©2020 ZITS Partnership. Dist. by King Features
FINE.
THE SINGLE-LAYER CONVERSATION IS DEAD.
6-6

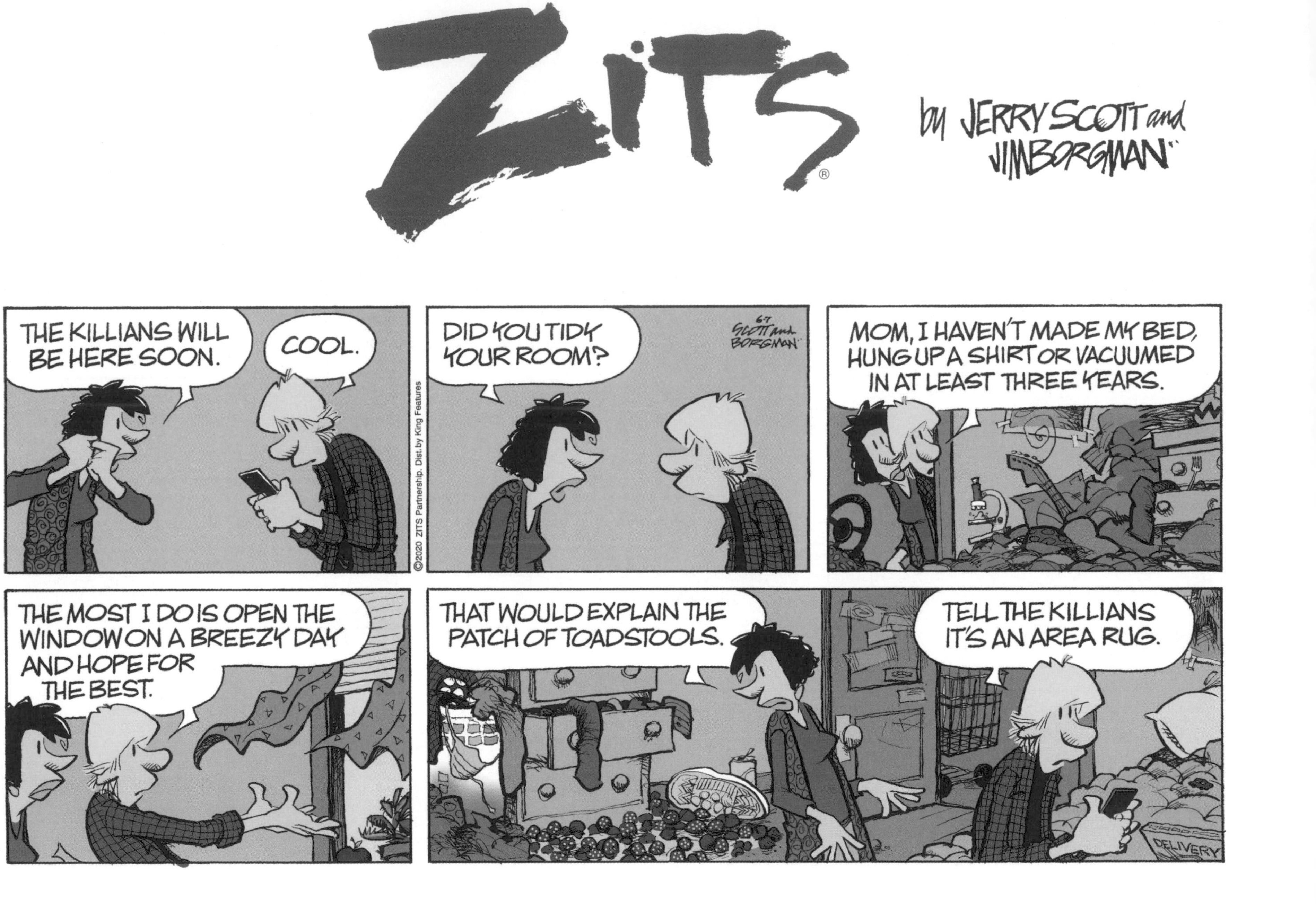
ZITS®
by JERRY SCOTT and JIM BORGMAN
THE KILLIANS WILL BE HERE SOON.
COOL.
©2020 ZITS Partnership. Dist. by King Features
DID YOU TIDY YOUR ROOM?
SCOTT and BORGMAN
MOM, I HAVEN'T MADE MY BED, HUNG UP A SHIRT OR VACUUMED IN AT LEAST THREE YEARS.
THE MOST I DO IS OPEN THE WINDOW ON A BREEZY DAY AND HOPE FOR THE BEST.
THAT WOULD EXPLAIN THE PATCH OF TOADSTOOLS.
TELL THE KILLIANS IT'S AN AREA RUG.
DELIVERY

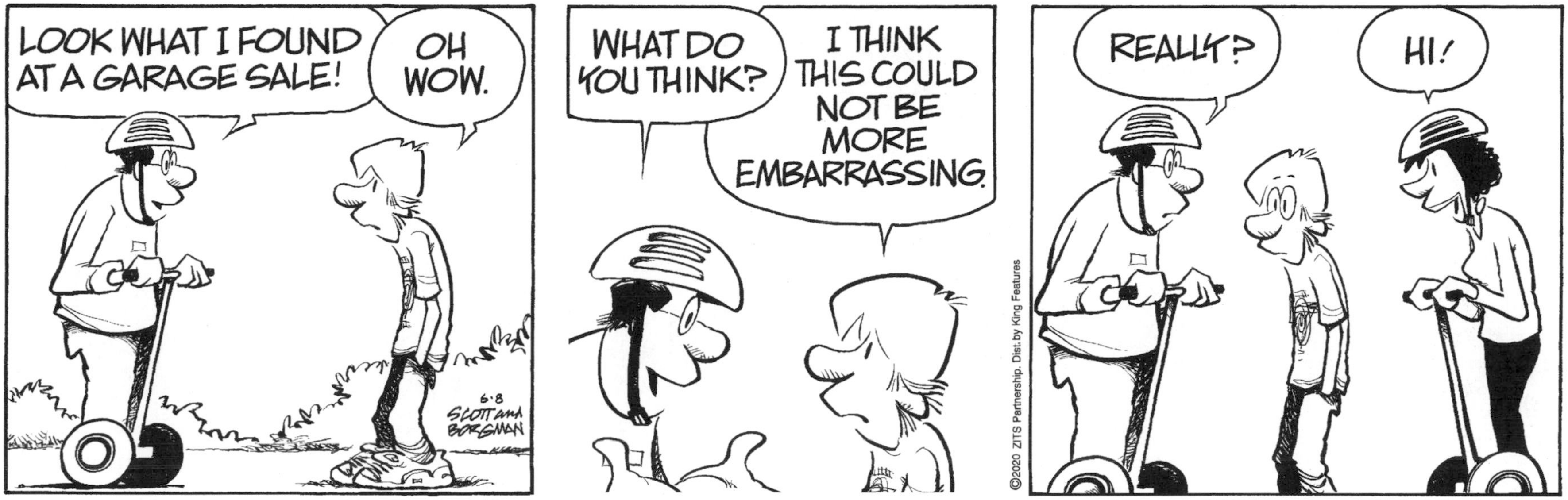
LOOK WHAT I FOUND AT A GARAGE SALE!
OH WOW.
WHAT DO YOU THINK?
I THINK THIS COULD NOT BE MORE EMBARRASSING.
REALLY?
HI!
©2020 ZITS Partnership. Dist. by King Features

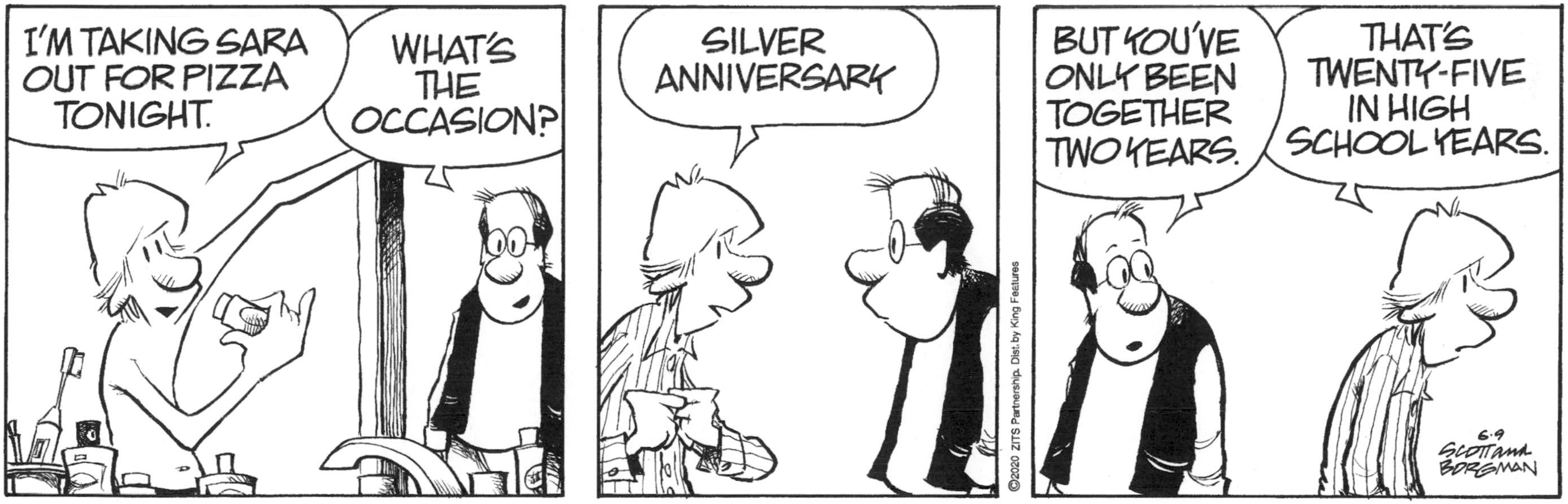
I'M TAKING SARA OUT FOR PIZZA TONIGHT.
WHAT'S THE OCCASION?
SILVER ANNIVERSARY
BUT YOU'VE ONLY BEEN TOGETHER TWO YEARS.
THAT'S TWENTY-FIVE IN HIGH SCHOOL YEARS.
©2020 ZITS Partnership. Dist. by King Features

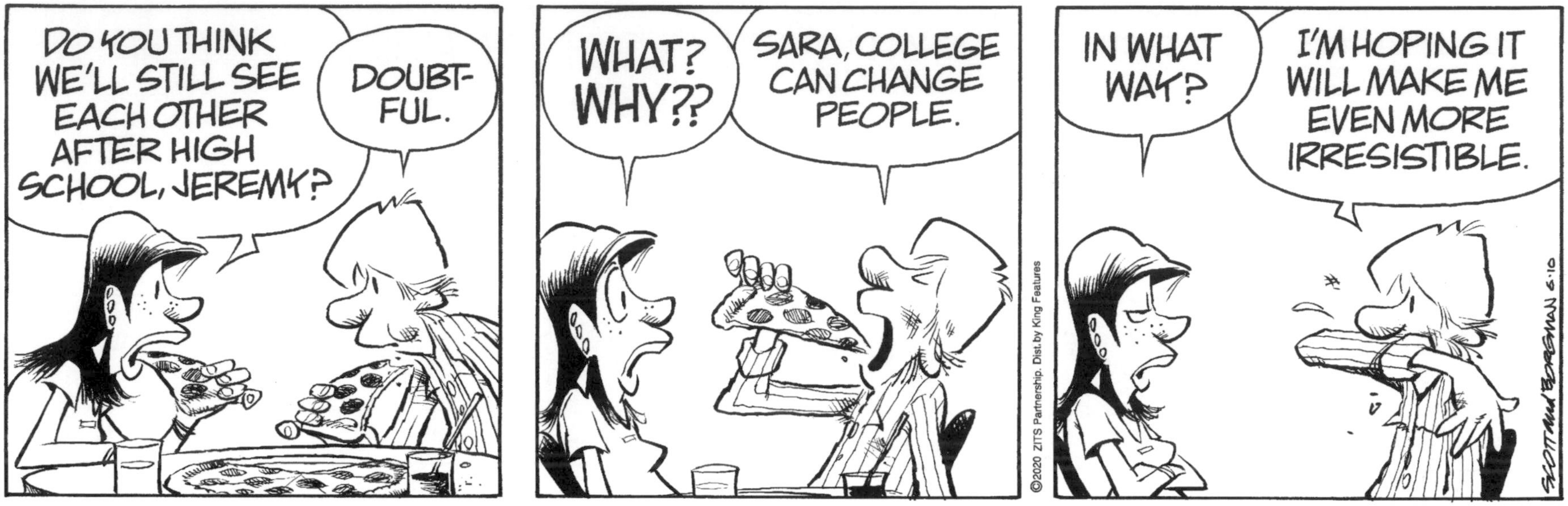
DO YOU THINK WE'LL STILL SEE EACH OTHER AFTER HIGH SCHOOL, JEREMY?
DOUBT-FUL.
WHAT? WHY??
SARA, COLLEGE CAN CHANGE PEOPLE.
©2020 ZITS Partnership. Dist. by King Features
IN WHAT WAY?
I'M HOPING IT WILL MAKE ME EVEN MORE IRRESISTIBLE.
SCOTT AND BORGMAN 6·10

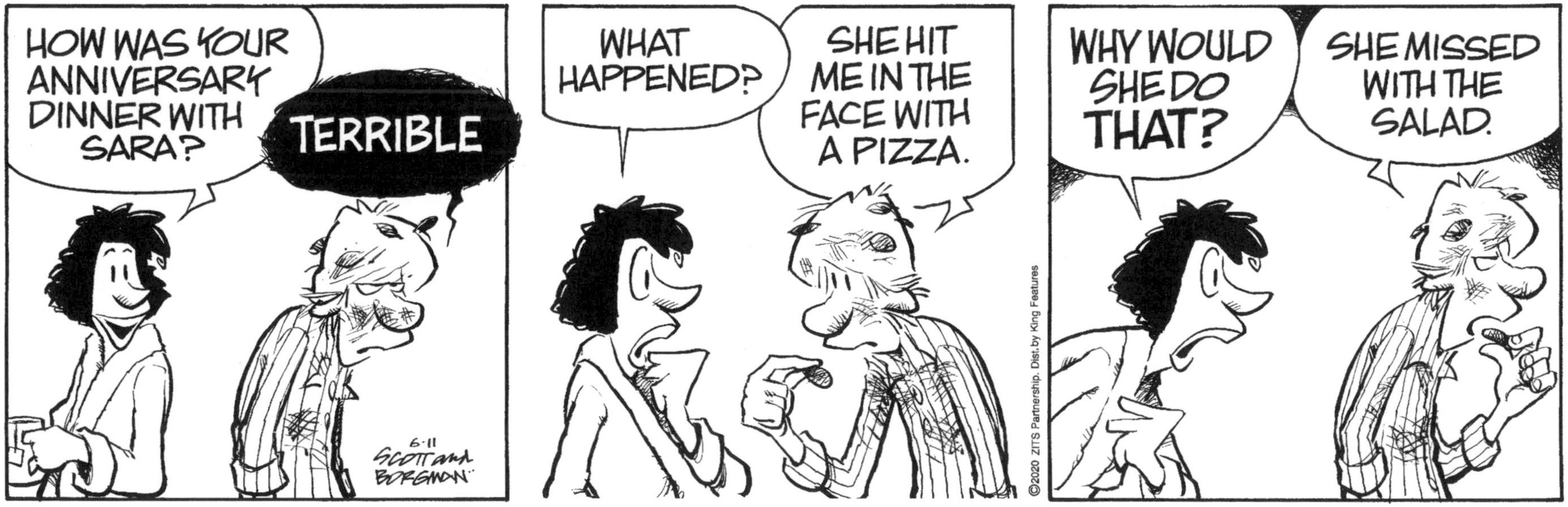
HOW WAS YOUR ANNIVERSARY DINNER WITH SARA?
TERRIBLE
6·11 SCOTT AND BORGMAN
WHAT HAPPENED?
SHE HIT ME IN THE FACE WITH A PIZZA.
©2020 ZITS Partnership. Dist. by King Features
WHY WOULD SHE DO THAT?
SHE MISSED WITH THE SALAD.

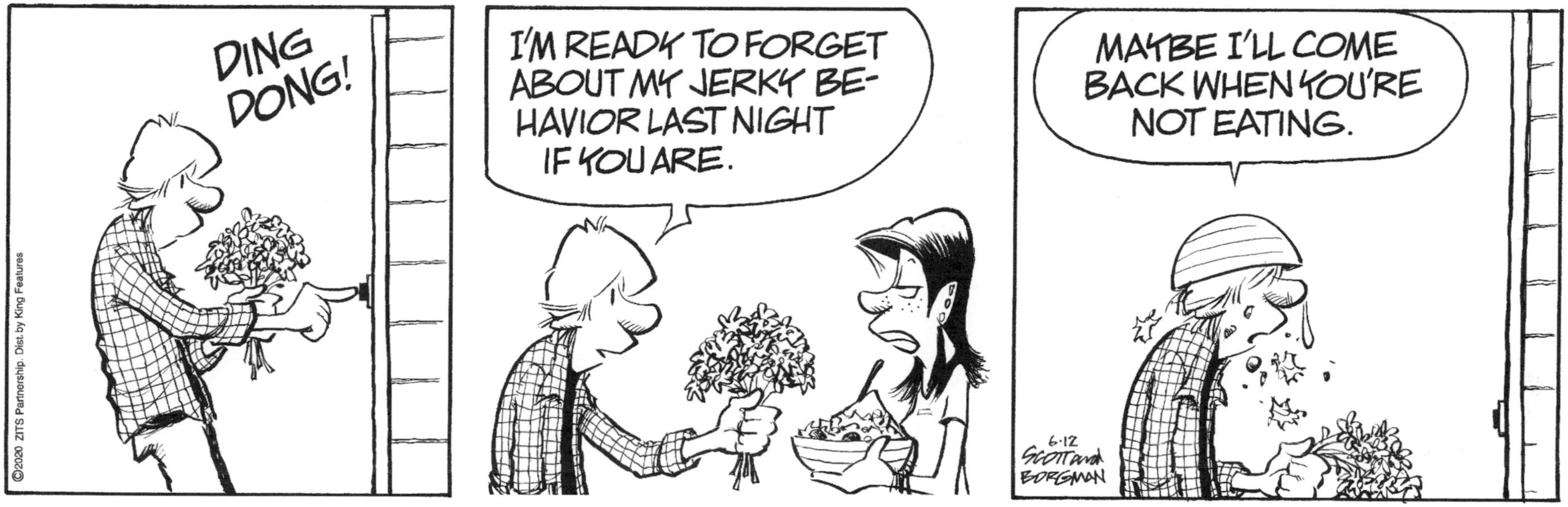
DING DONG!
I'M READY TO FORGET ABOUT MY JERKY BE-HAVIOR LAST NIGHT IF YOU ARE.
MAYBE I'LL COME BACK WHEN YOU'RE NOT EATING.
6-12 SCOTT and BORGMAN
©2020 ZITS Partnership. Dist by King Features

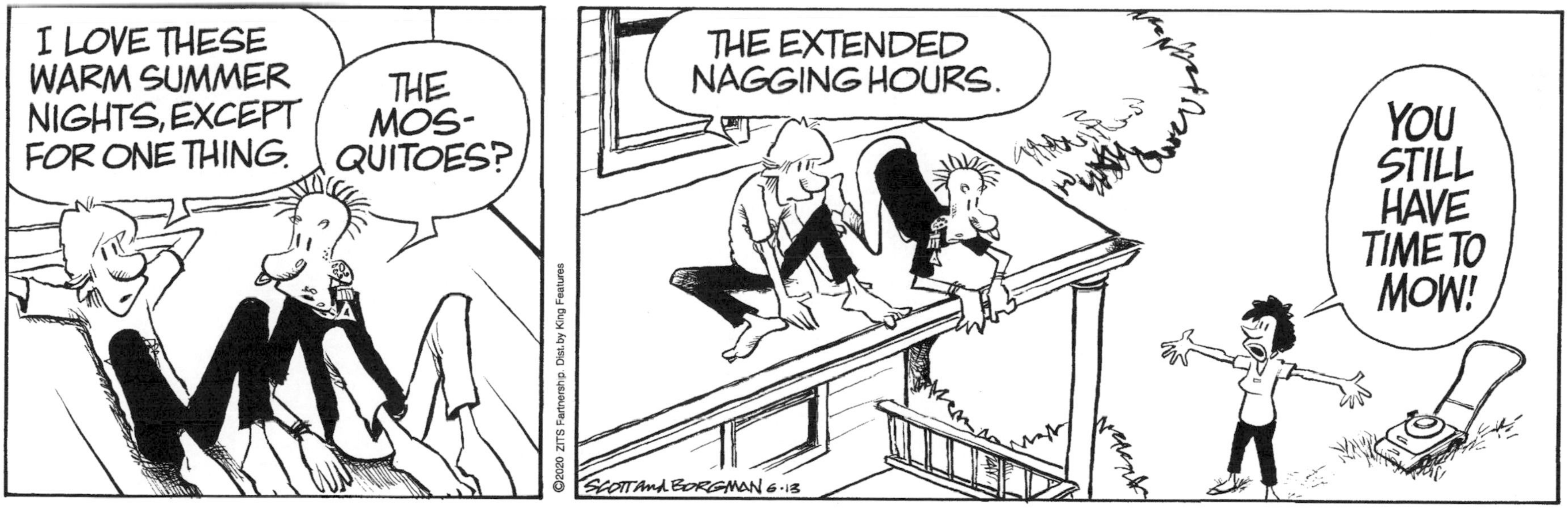
I LOVE THESE WARM SUMMER NIGHTS, EXCEPT FOR ONE THING.
THE MOS-QUITOES?
THE EXTENDED NAGGING HOURS.
YOU STILL HAVE TIME TO MOW!
SCOTT and BORGMAN 6-13
©2020 ZITS Partnership. Dist by King Features

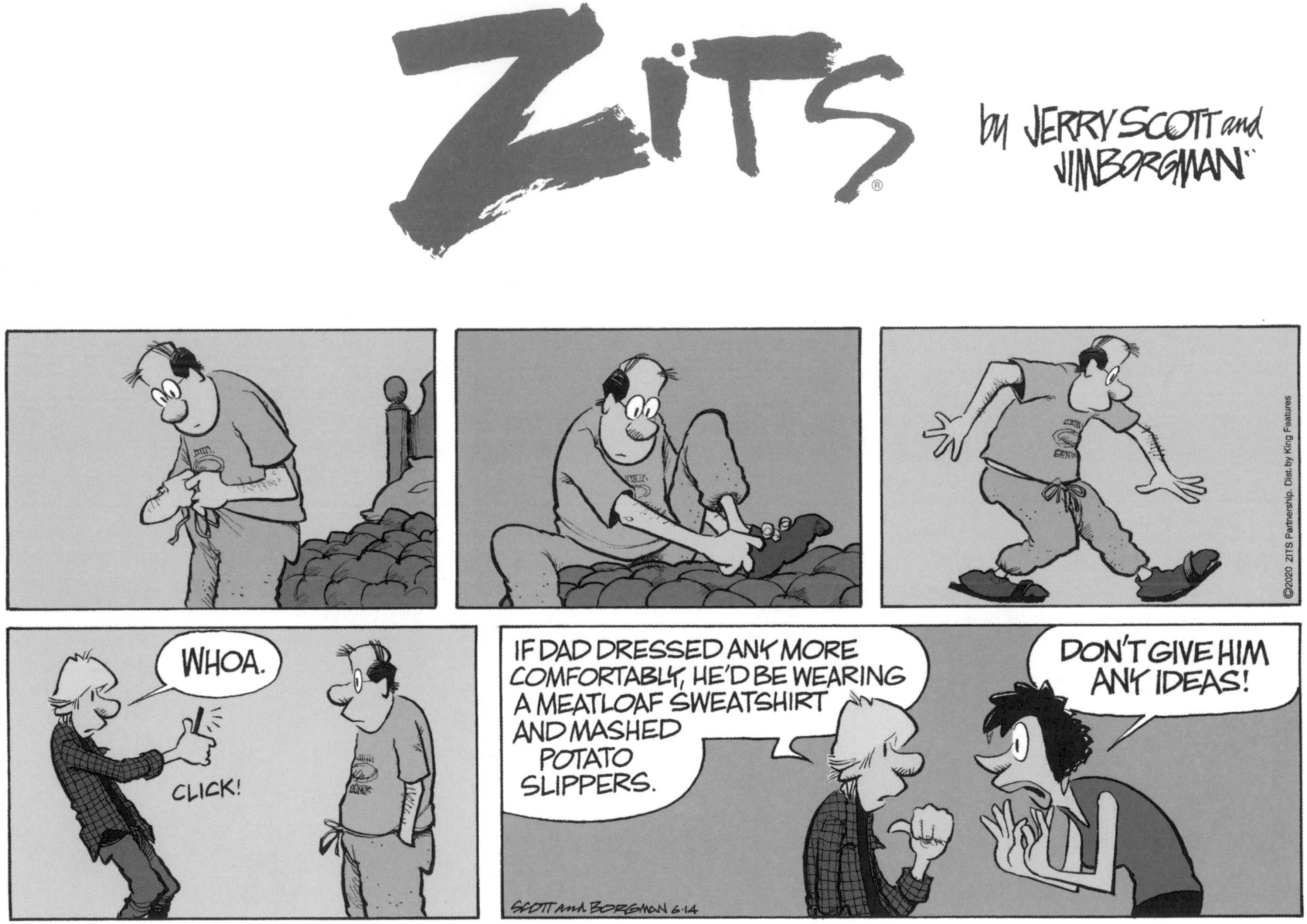
ZITS®
by JERRY SCOTT and JIM BORGMAN
©2020 ZITS Partnership. Dist. by King Features
WHOA.
CLICK!
IF DAD DRESSED ANY MORE COMFORTABLY, HE'D BE WEARING A MEATLOAF SWEATSHIRT AND MASHED POTATO SLIPPERS.
DON'T GIVE HIM ANY IDEAS!
SCOTT and BORGMAN 6.14

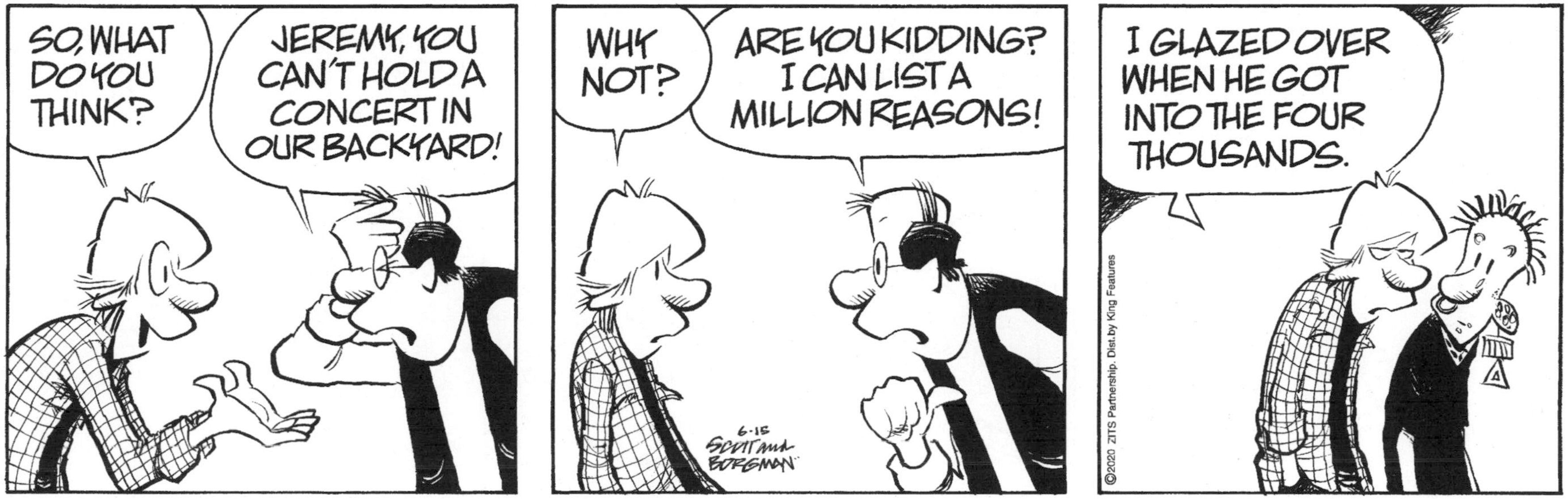
SO, WHAT DO YOU THINK?
JEREMY, YOU CAN'T HOLD A CONCERT IN OUR BACKYARD!
WHY NOT?
ARE YOU KIDDING? I CAN LIST A MILLION REASONS!
I GLAZED OVER WHEN HE GOT INTO THE FOUR THOUSANDS.
©2020 ZITS Partnership. Dist. by King Features

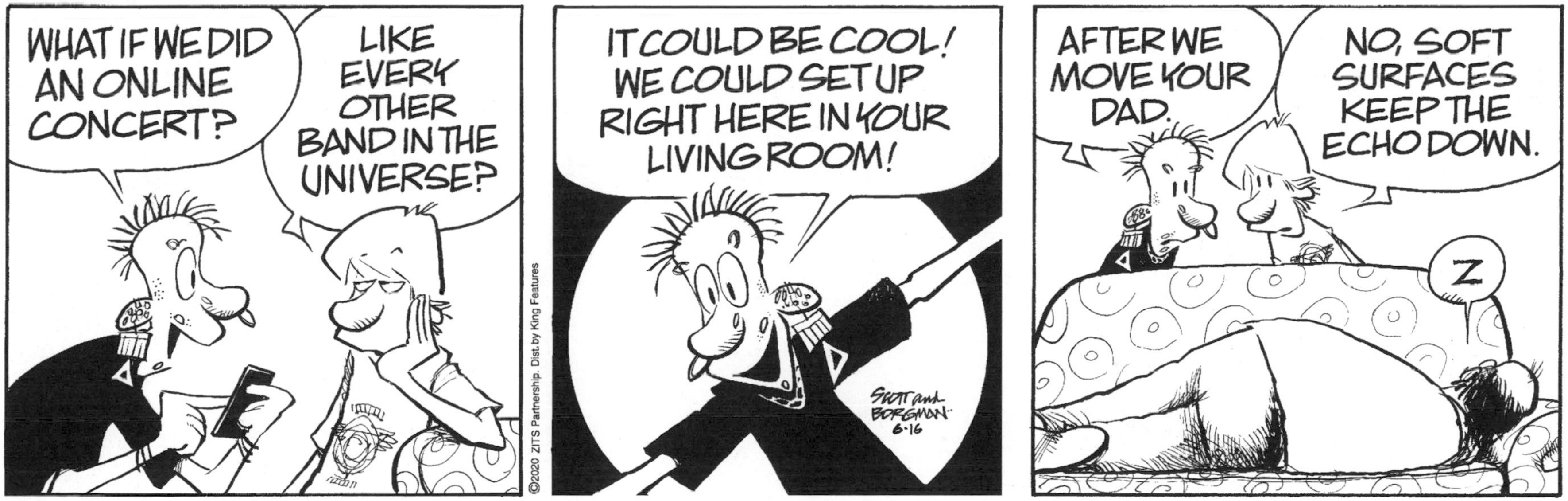
WHAT IF WE DID AN ONLINE CONCERT?
LIKE EVERY OTHER BAND IN THE UNIVERSE?
IT COULD BE COOL! WE COULD SET UP RIGHT HERE IN YOUR LIVING ROOM!
AFTER WE MOVE YOUR DAD.
NO, SOFT SURFACES KEEP THE ECHO DOWN.
Z
©2020 ZITS Partnership. Dist. by King Features

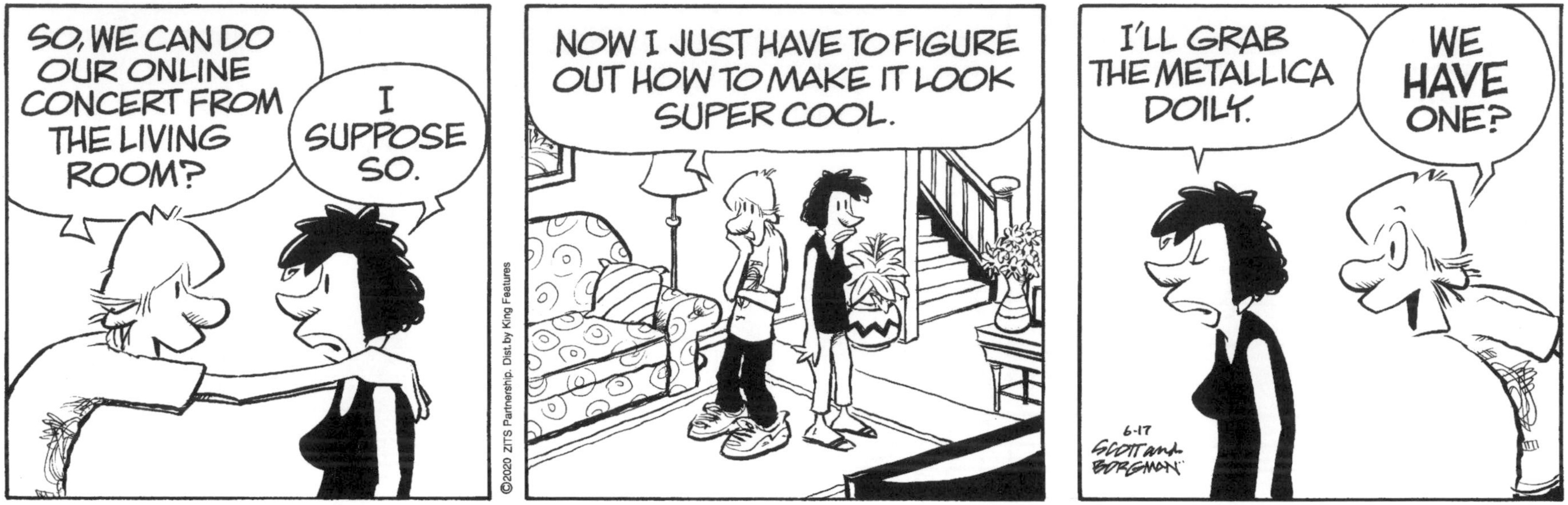
SO, WE CAN DO OUR ONLINE CONCERT FROM THE LIVING ROOM?
I SUPPOSE SO.
©2020 ZITS Partnership. Dist. by King Features
NOW I JUST HAVE TO FIGURE OUT HOW TO MAKE IT LOOK SUPER COOL.
I'LL GRAB THE METALLICA DOILY.
WE **HAVE** ONE?
6-17
SCOTT and BORGMAN

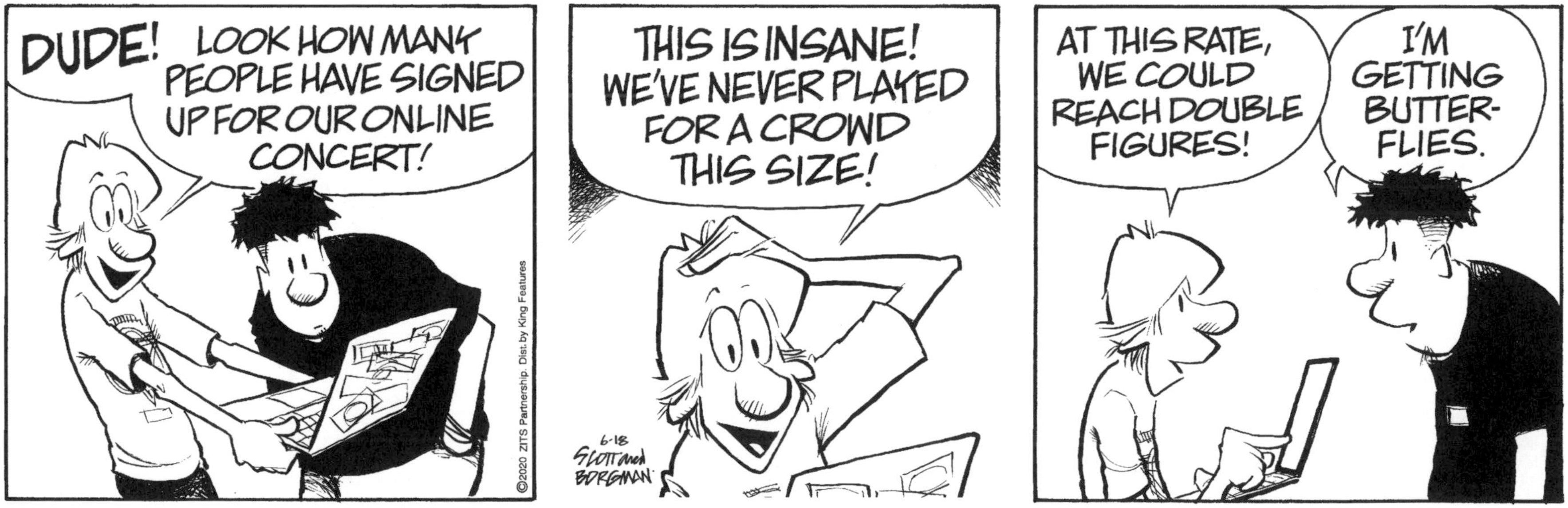
DUDE!
LOOK HOW MANY PEOPLE HAVE SIGNED UP FOR OUR ONLINE CONCERT!
©2020 ZITS Partnership. Dist. by King Features
THIS IS INSANE! WE'VE NEVER PLAYED FOR A CROWD THIS SIZE!
6-18
SCOTT and BORGMAN
AT THIS RATE, WE COULD REACH DOUBLE FIGURES!
I'M GETTING BUTTER-FLIES.

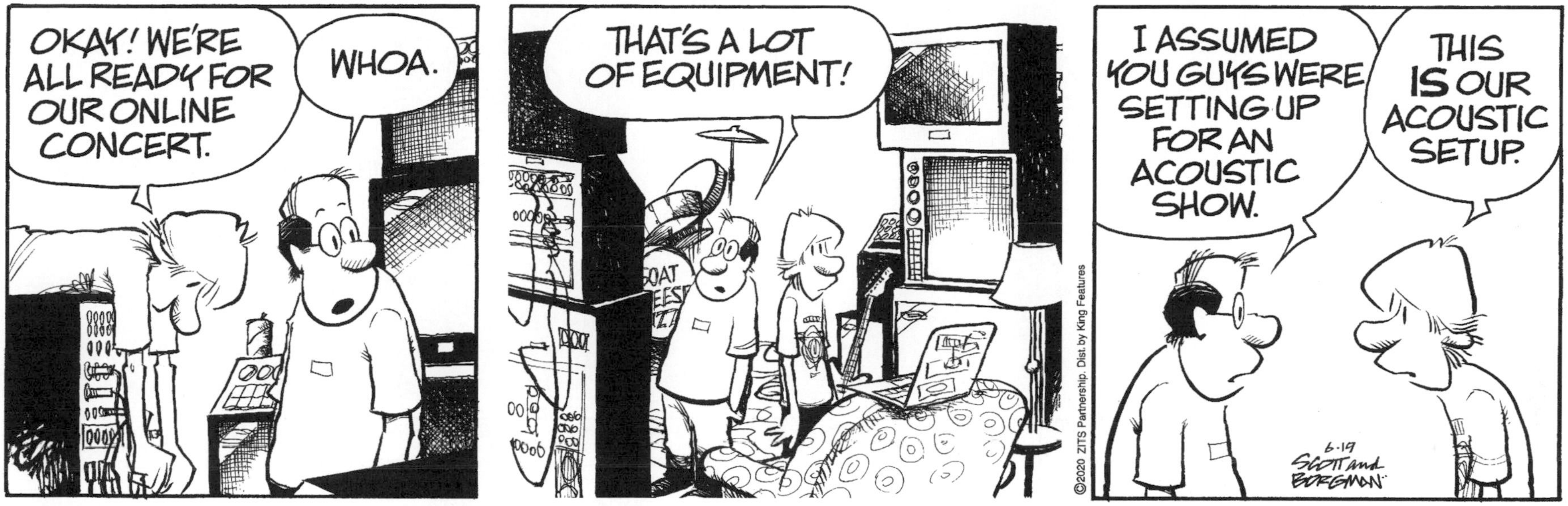
OKAY! WE'RE ALL READY FOR OUR ONLINE CONCERT.
WHOA.
THAT'S A LOT OF EQUIPMENT!
©2020 ZITS Partnership. Dist. by King Features
I ASSUMED YOU GUYS WERE SETTING UP FOR AN ACOUSTIC SHOW.
THIS **IS** OUR ACOUSTIC SETUP.
6-19
SCOTT and BORGMAN

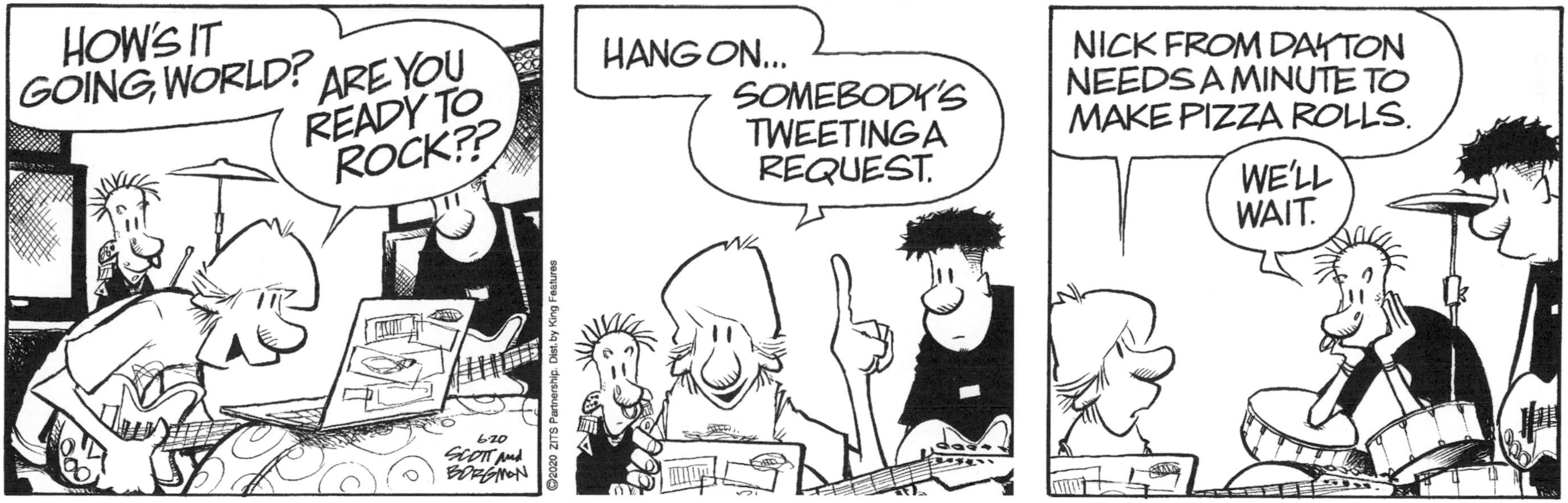
HOW'S IT GOING, WORLD?
ARE YOU READY TO ROCK??
6-20
SCOTT and BORGMAN
©2020 ZITS Partnership. Dist. by King Features
HANG ON...
SOMEBODY'S TWEETING A REQUEST.
NICK FROM DAYTON NEEDS A MINUTE TO MAKE PIZZA ROLLS.
WE'LL WAIT.

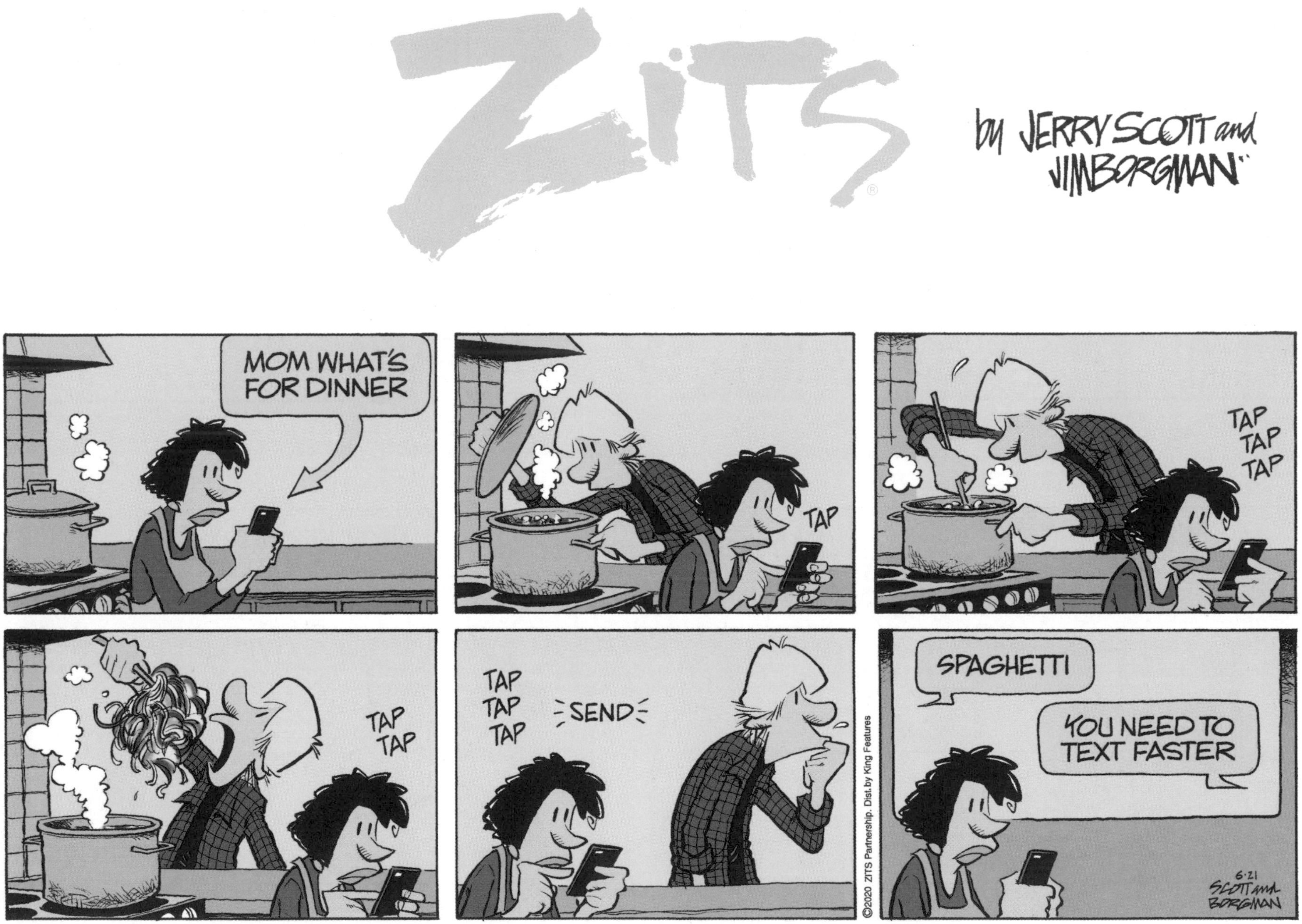
ZITS
by JERRY SCOTT and JIM BORGMAN
MOM WHAT'S FOR DINNER
TAP
TAP TAP TAP
TAP TAP
TAP TAP TAP
SEND
©2020 ZITS Partnership. Dist. by King Features
SPAGHETTI
YOU NEED TO TEXT FASTER
6·21
SCOTT and BORGMAN

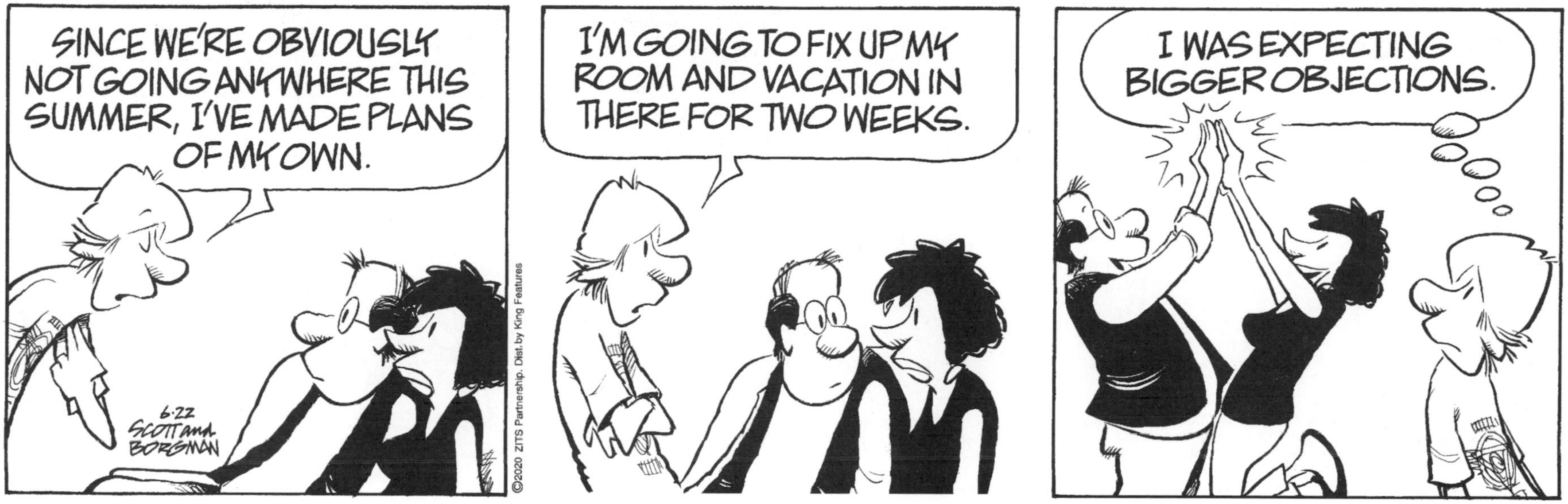
SINCE WE'RE OBVIOUSLY NOT GOING ANYWHERE THIS SUMMER, I'VE MADE PLANS OF MY OWN.
6·22 SCOTT and BORGMAN
©2020 ZITS Partnership. Dist. by King Features
I'M GOING TO FIX UP MY ROOM AND VACATION IN THERE FOR TWO WEEKS.
I WAS EXPECTING BIGGER OBJECTIONS.

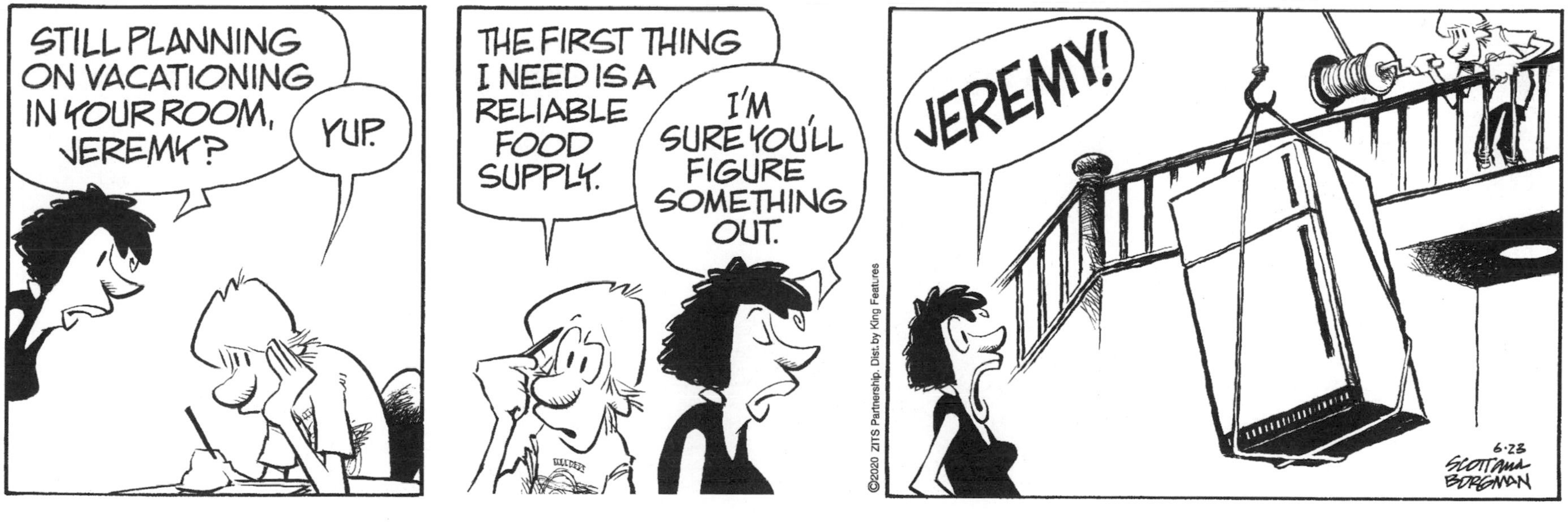
STILL PLANNING ON VACATIONING IN YOUR ROOM, JEREMY?
YUP.
THE FIRST THING I NEED IS A RELIABLE FOOD SUPPLY.
I'M SURE YOU'LL FIGURE SOMETHING OUT.
©2020 ZITS Partnership. Dist. by King Features
JEREMY!
6·23 SCOTT and BORGMAN

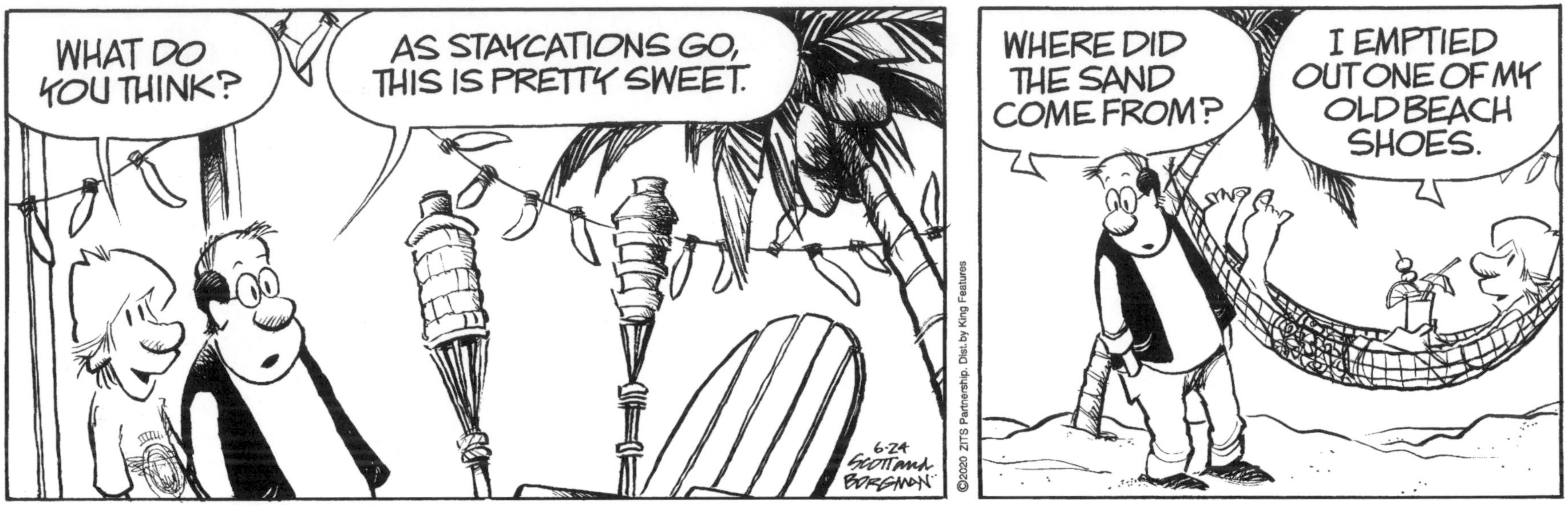
WHAT DO YOU THINK?
AS STAYCATIONS GO, THIS IS PRETTY SWEET.
6·24 SCOTT and BORGMAN
©2020 ZITS Partnership. Dist. by King Features
WHERE DID THE SAND COME FROM?
I EMPTIED OUT ONE OF MY OLD BEACH SHOES.

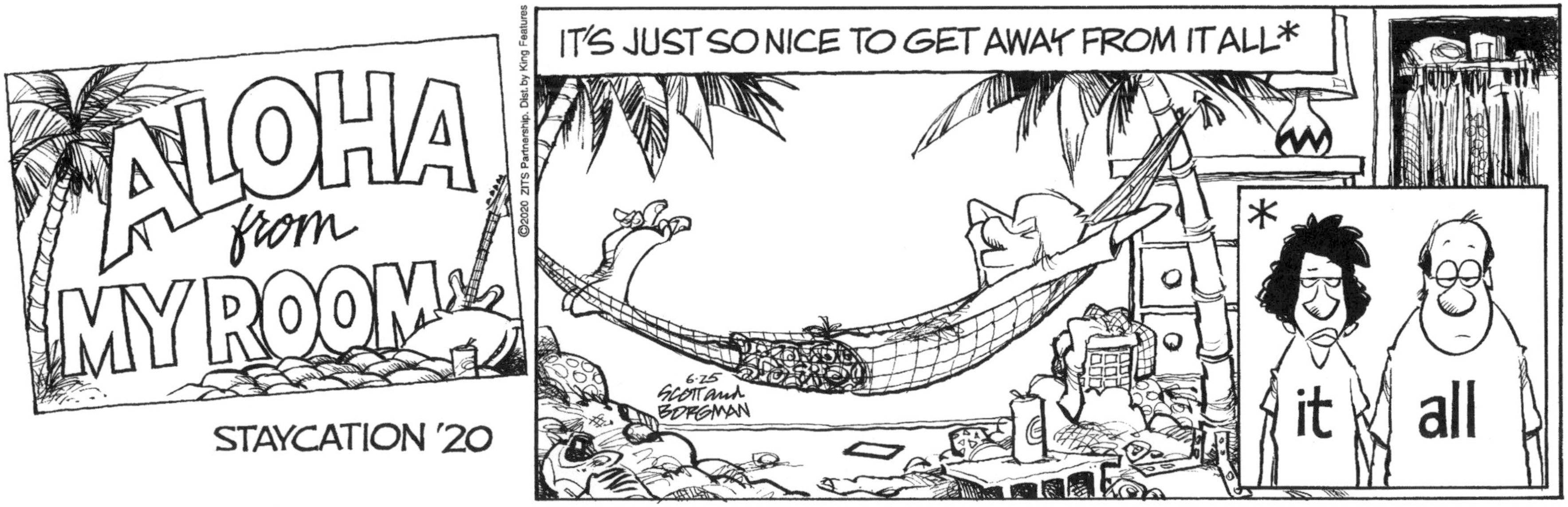
ALOHA from MY ROOM
STAYCATION '20
©2020 ZITS Partnership. Dist. by King Features
IT'S JUST SO NICE TO GET AWAY FROM IT ALL*
6·25 SCOTT and BORGMAN
*
it
all

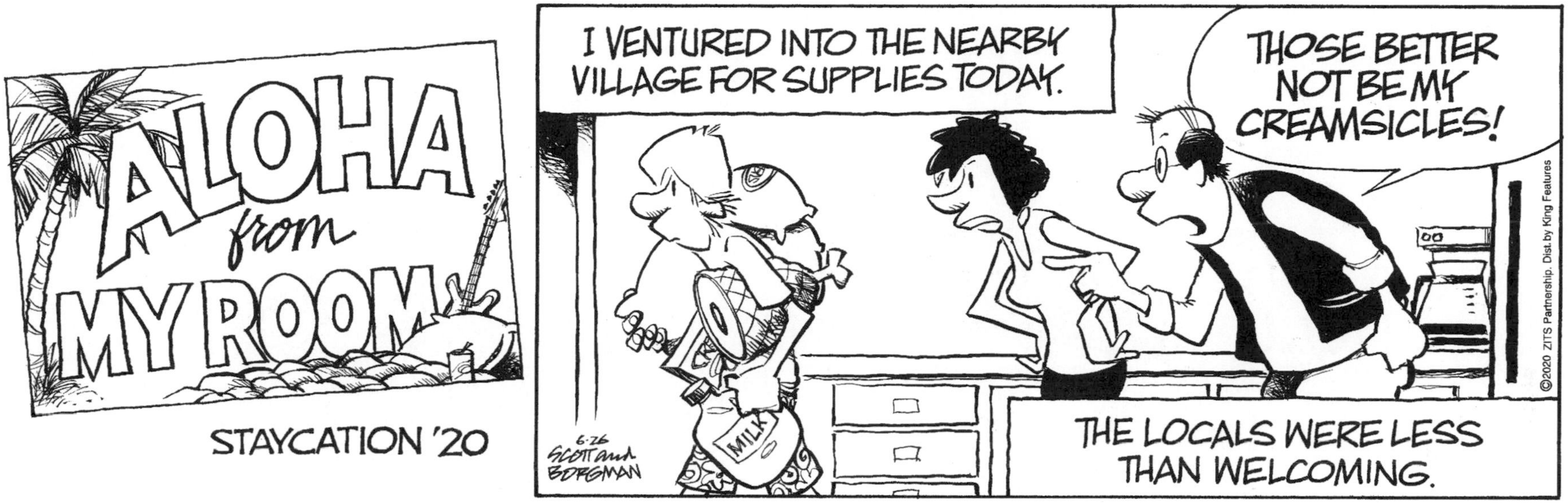
ALOHA from MY ROOM
STAYCATION '20
I VENTURED INTO THE NEARBY VILLAGE FOR SUPPLIES TODAY.
THOSE BETTER NOT BE MY CREAMSICLES!
THE LOCALS WERE LESS THAN WELCOMING.
MILK
6·26 SCOTT and BORGMAN
©2020 ZITS Partnership. Dist. by King Features

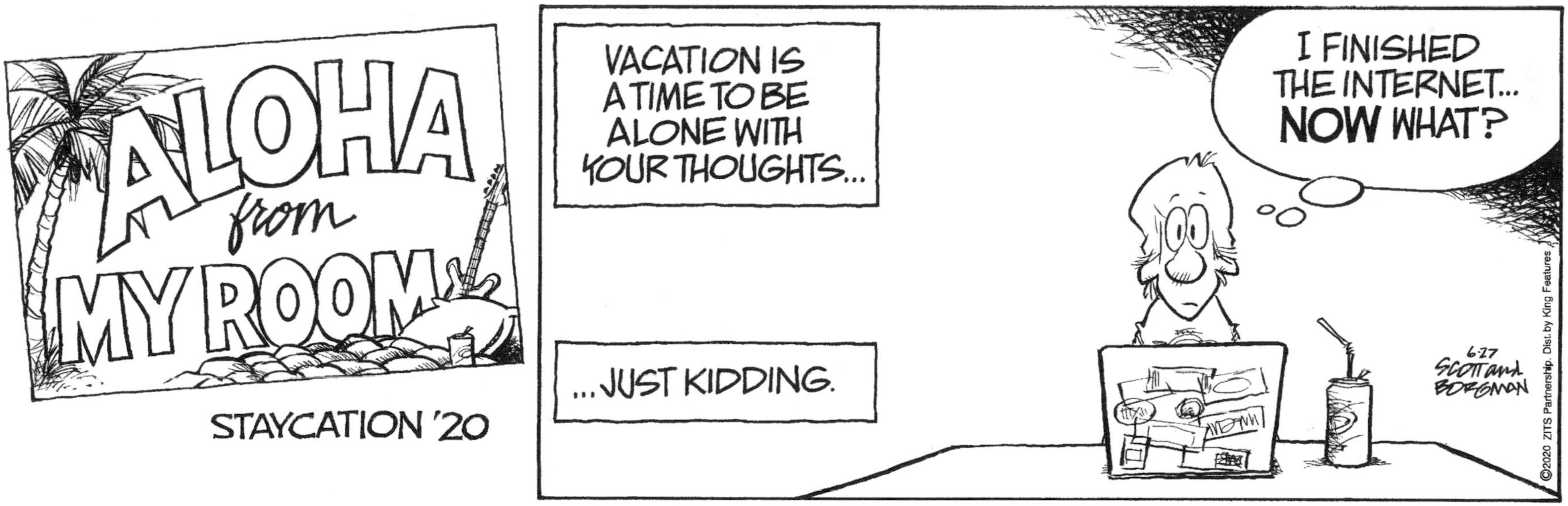
ALOHA from MY ROOM
STAYCATION '20
VACATION IS A TIME TO BE ALONE WITH YOUR THOUGHTS...
I FINISHED THE INTERNET... NOW WHAT?
...JUST KIDDING.
6·27 SCOTT and BORGMAN
©2020 ZITS Partnership. Dist. by King Features

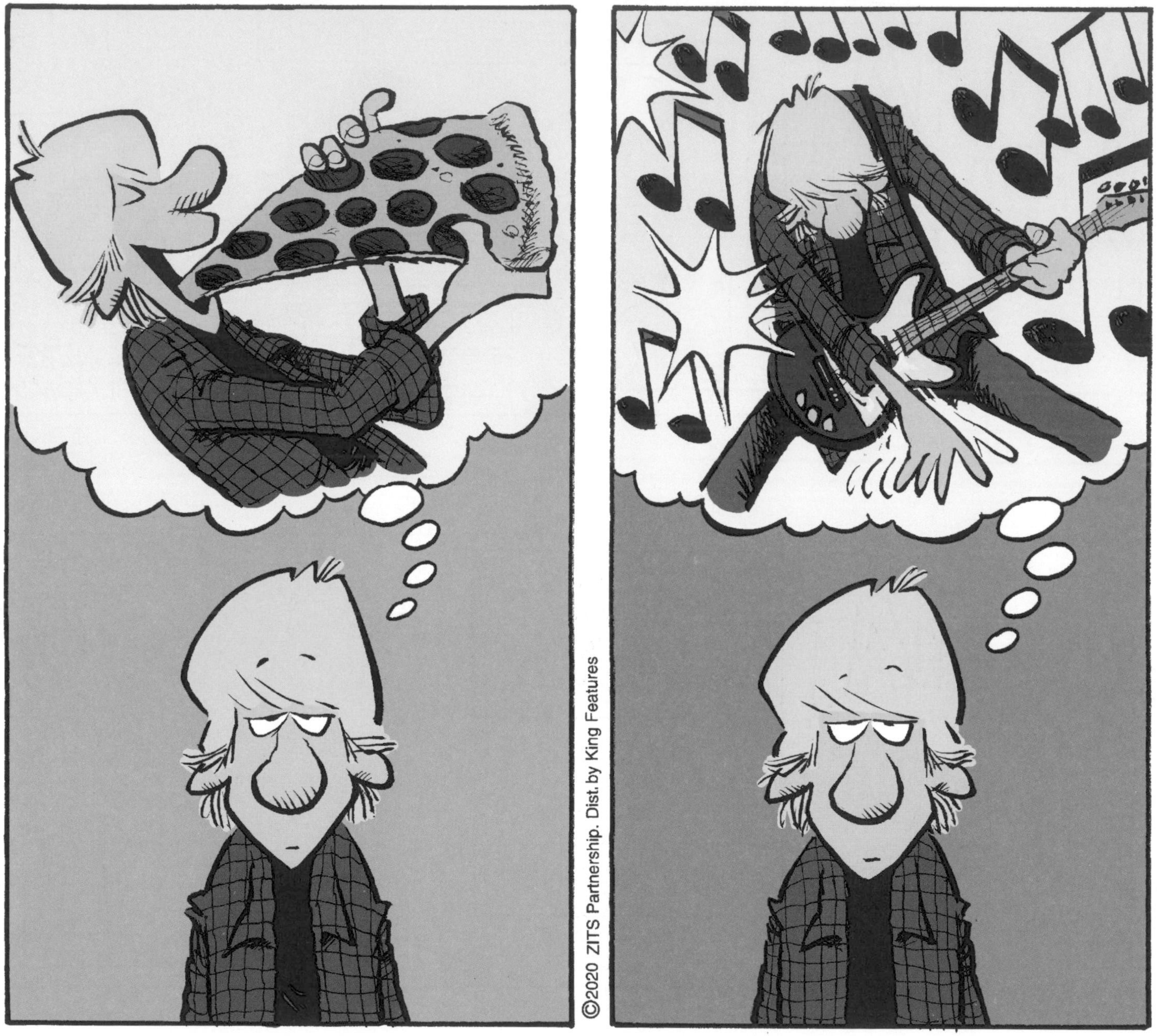
©2020 ZITS Partnership. Dist. by King Features

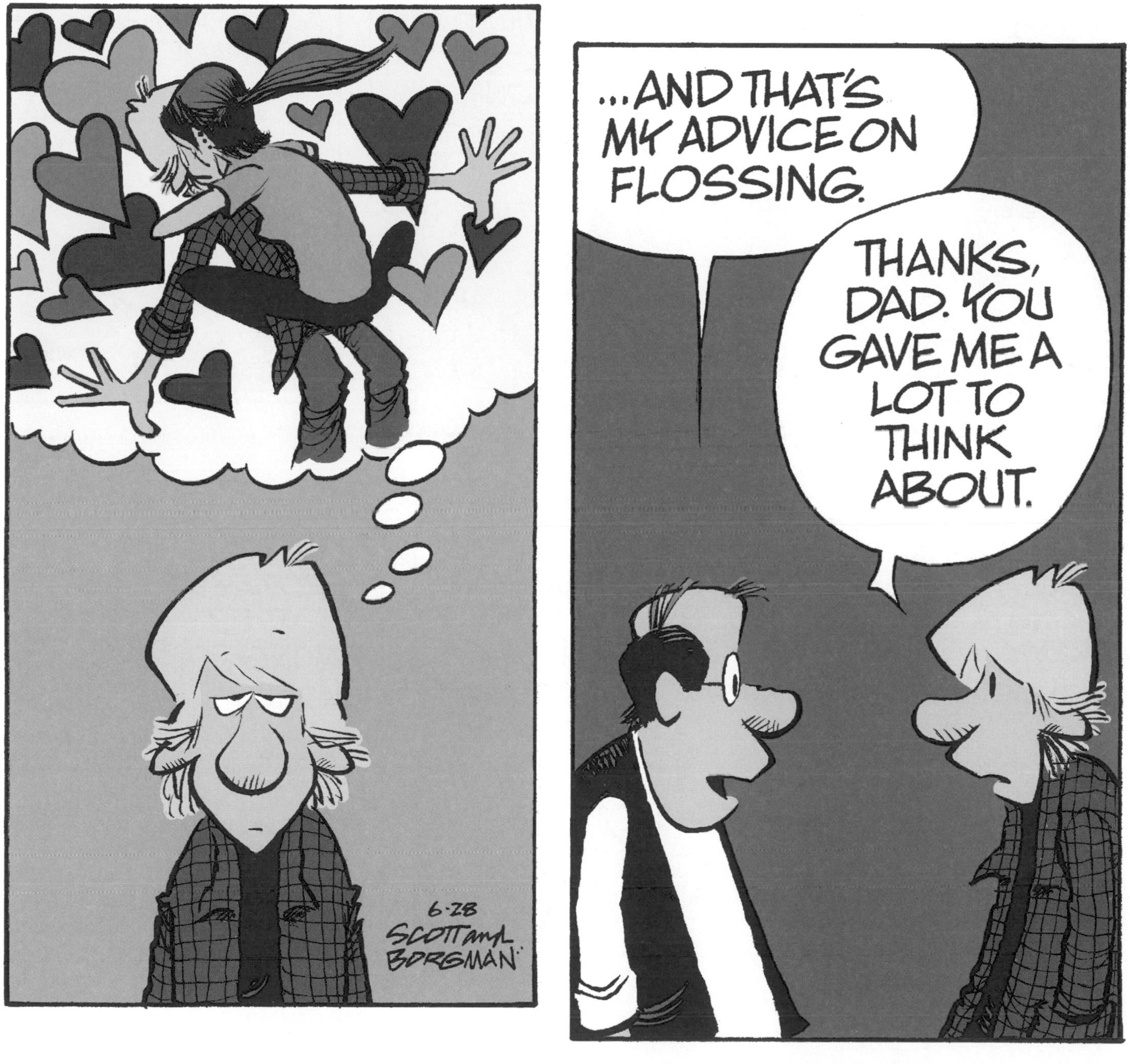
...AND THAT'S MY ADVICE ON FLOSSING.
THANKS, DAD. YOU GAVE ME A LOT TO THINK ABOUT.

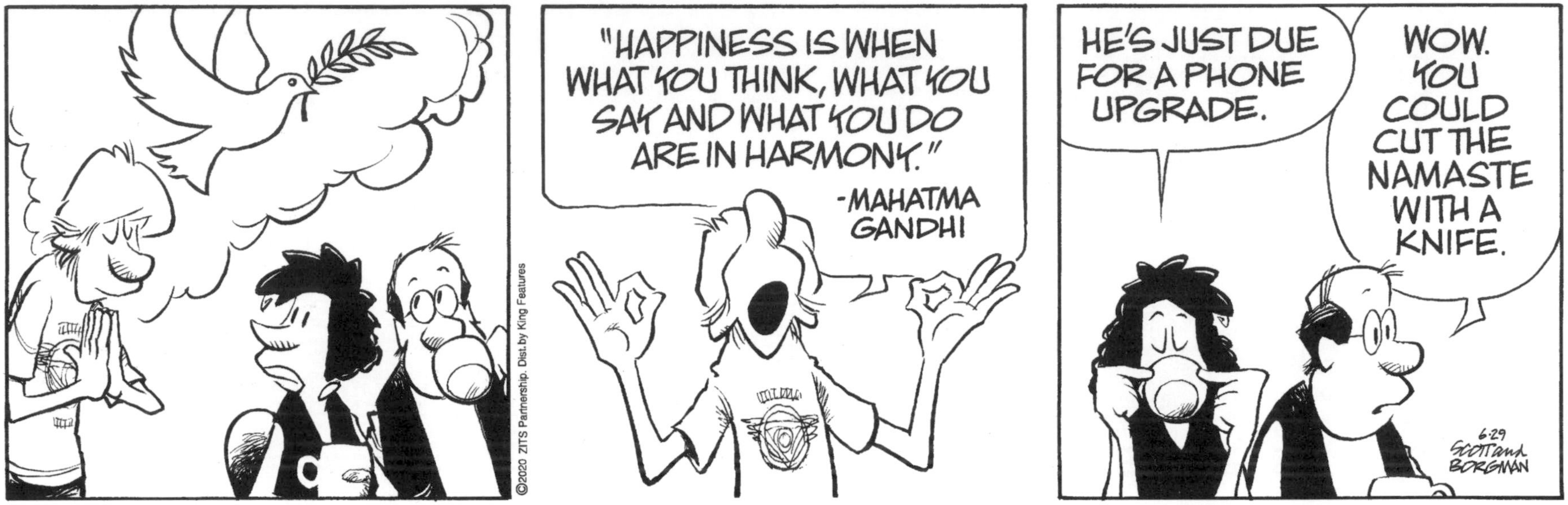
©2020 ZITS Partnership. Dist. by King Features
"HAPPINESS IS WHEN WHAT YOU THINK, WHAT YOU SAY AND WHAT YOU DO ARE IN HARMONY." -MAHATMA GANDHI
HE'S JUST DUE FOR A PHONE UPGRADE.
WOW. YOU COULD CUT THE NAMASTE WITH A KNIFE.
6·29 SCOTT and BORGMAN

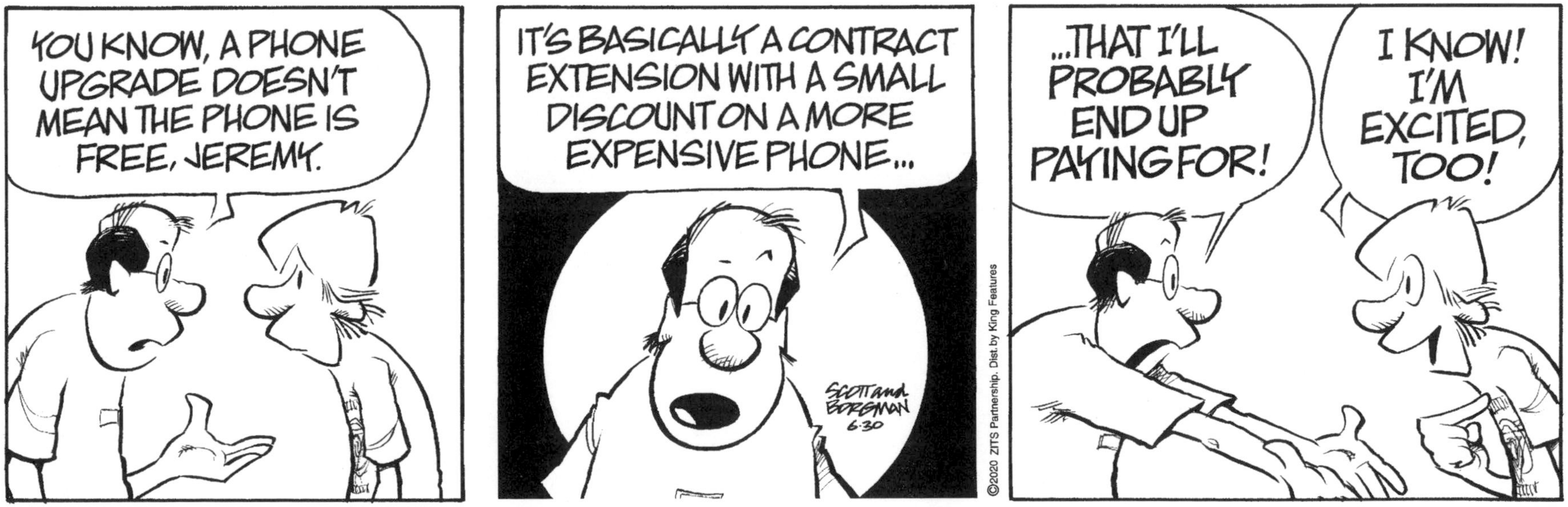
YOU KNOW, A PHONE UPGRADE DOESN'T MEAN THE PHONE IS FREE, JEREMY.
IT'S BASICALLY A CONTRACT EXTENSION WITH A SMALL DISCOUNT ON A MORE EXPENSIVE PHONE...
SCOTT and BORGMAN 6·30
©2020 ZITS Partnership. Dist. by King Features
...THAT I'LL PROBABLY END UP PAYING FOR!
I KNOW! I'M EXCITED, TOO!

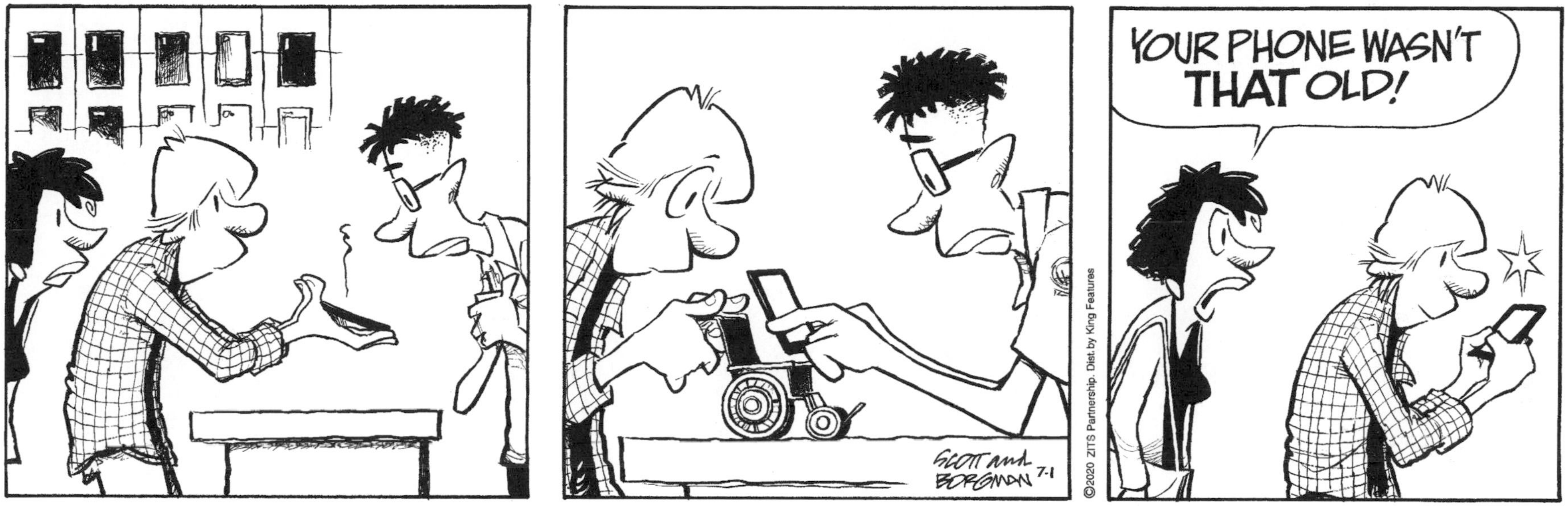
YOUR PHONE WASN'T THAT OLD!
©2020 ZITS Partnership. Dist. by King Features

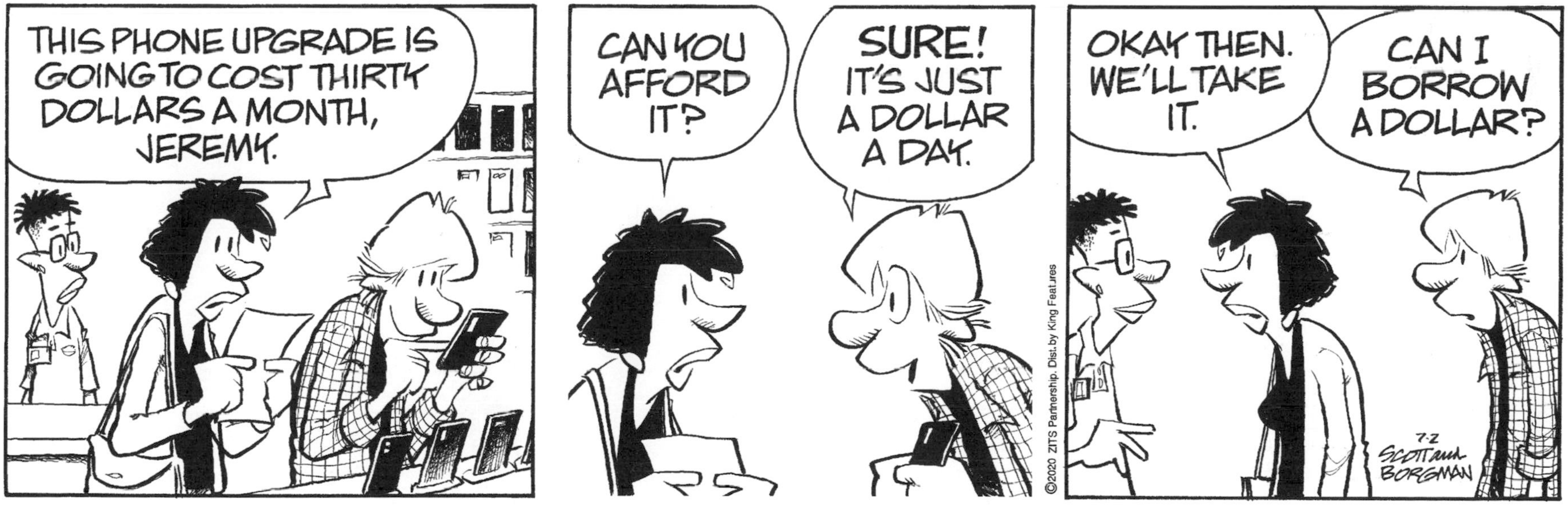
THIS PHONE UPGRADE IS GOING TO COST THIRTY DOLLARS A MONTH, JEREMY.
CAN YOU AFFORD IT?
SURE! IT'S JUST A DOLLAR A DAY.
OKAY THEN. WE'LL TAKE IT.
CAN I BORROW A DOLLAR?
©2020 ZITS Partnership. Dist. by King Features

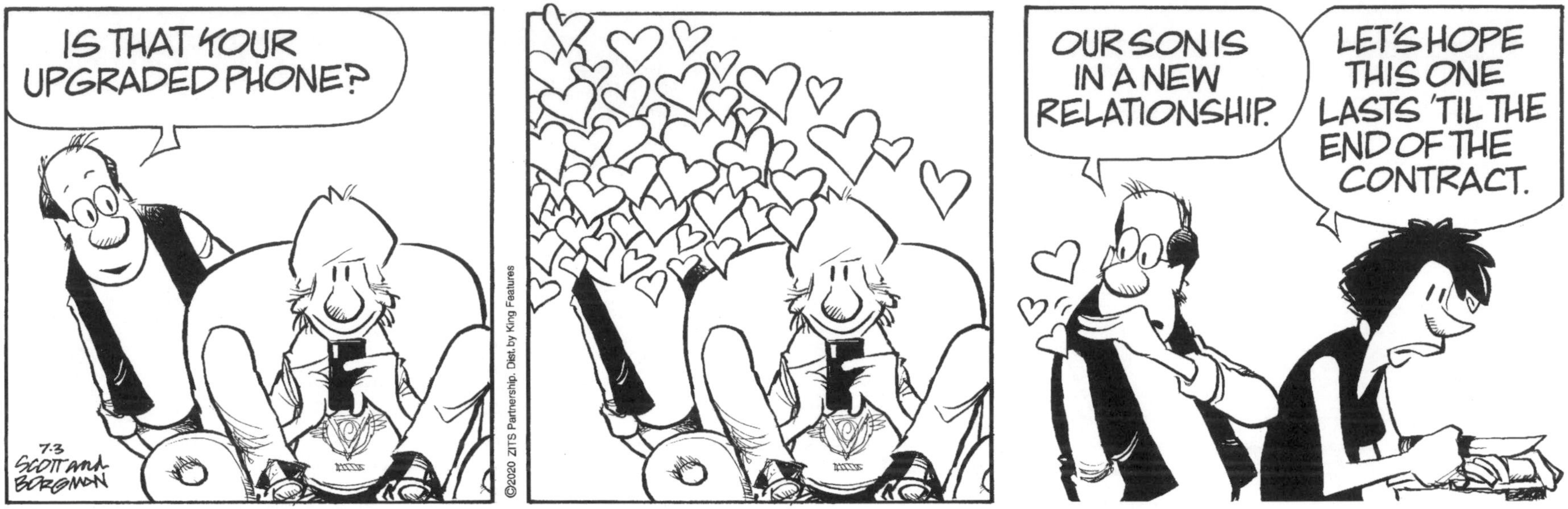
IS THAT YOUR UPGRADED PHONE?
7-3 SCOTT AND BORGMAN
©2020 ZITS Partnership. Dist. by King Features
OUR SON IS IN A NEW RELATIONSHIP.
LET'S HOPE THIS ONE LASTS 'TIL THE END OF THE CONTRACT.

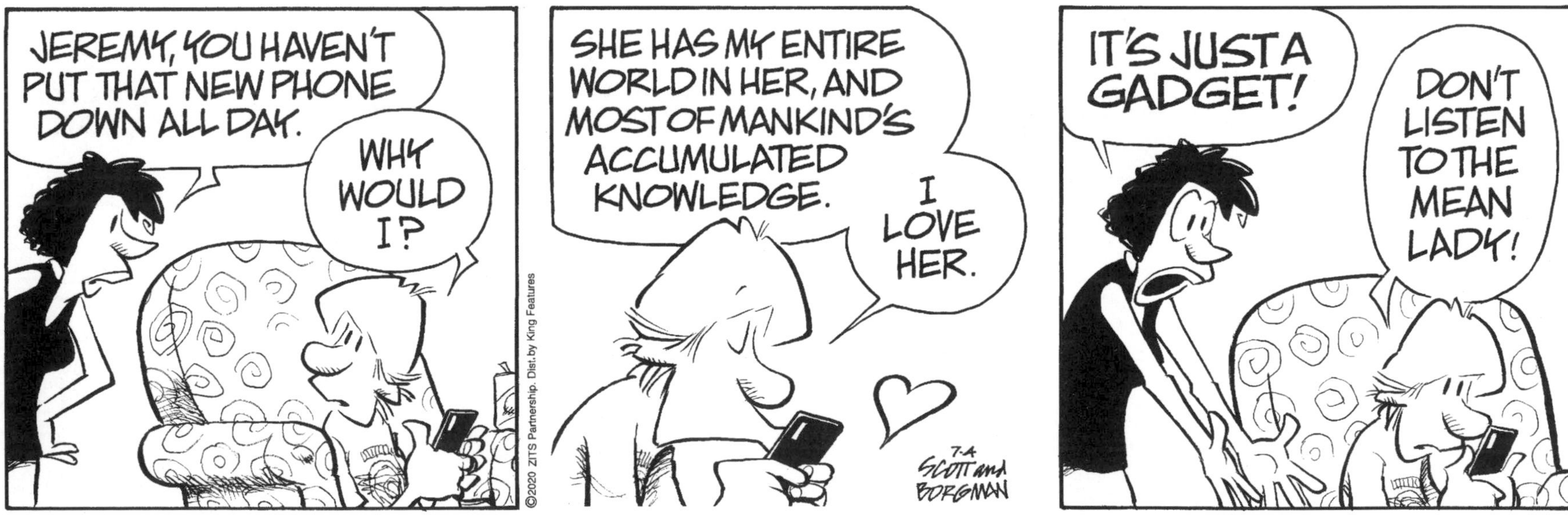
JEREMY, YOU HAVEN'T PUT THAT NEW PHONE DOWN ALL DAY.
WHY WOULD I?
©2020 ZITS Partnership. Dist. by King Features
SHE HAS MY ENTIRE WORLD IN HER, AND MOST OF MANKIND'S ACCUMULATED KNOWLEDGE.
I LOVE HER.
7-4 SCOTT AND BORGMAN
IT'S JUST A GADGET!
DON'T LISTEN TO THE MEAN LADY!

ZITS

by JERRY SCOTT and JIM BORGMAN

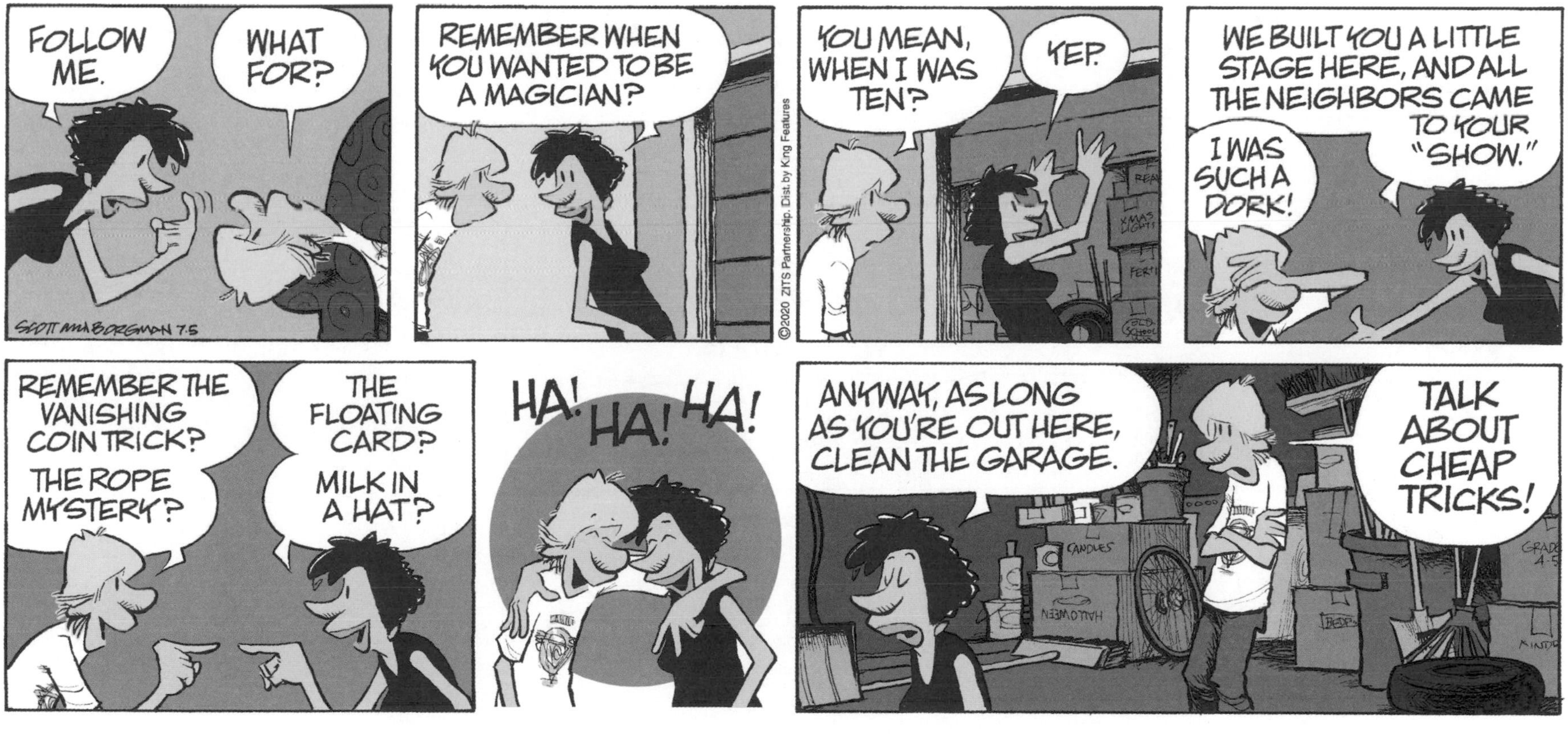
FOLLOW ME.
WHAT FOR?
SCOTT AND BORGMAN 7.5
REMEMBER WHEN YOU WANTED TO BE A MAGICIAN?
©2020 ZITS Partnership. Dist. by King Features
YOU MEAN, WHEN I WAS TEN?
YEP.
WE BUILT YOU A LITTLE STAGE HERE, AND ALL THE NEIGHBORS CAME TO YOUR "SHOW."
I WAS SUCH A DORK!
REMEMBER THE VANISHING COIN TRICK?
THE ROPE MYSTERY?
THE FLOATING CARD?
MILK IN A HAT?
HA! HA! HA!
ANYWAY, AS LONG AS YOU'RE OUT HERE, CLEAN THE GARAGE.
TALK ABOUT CHEAP TRICKS!

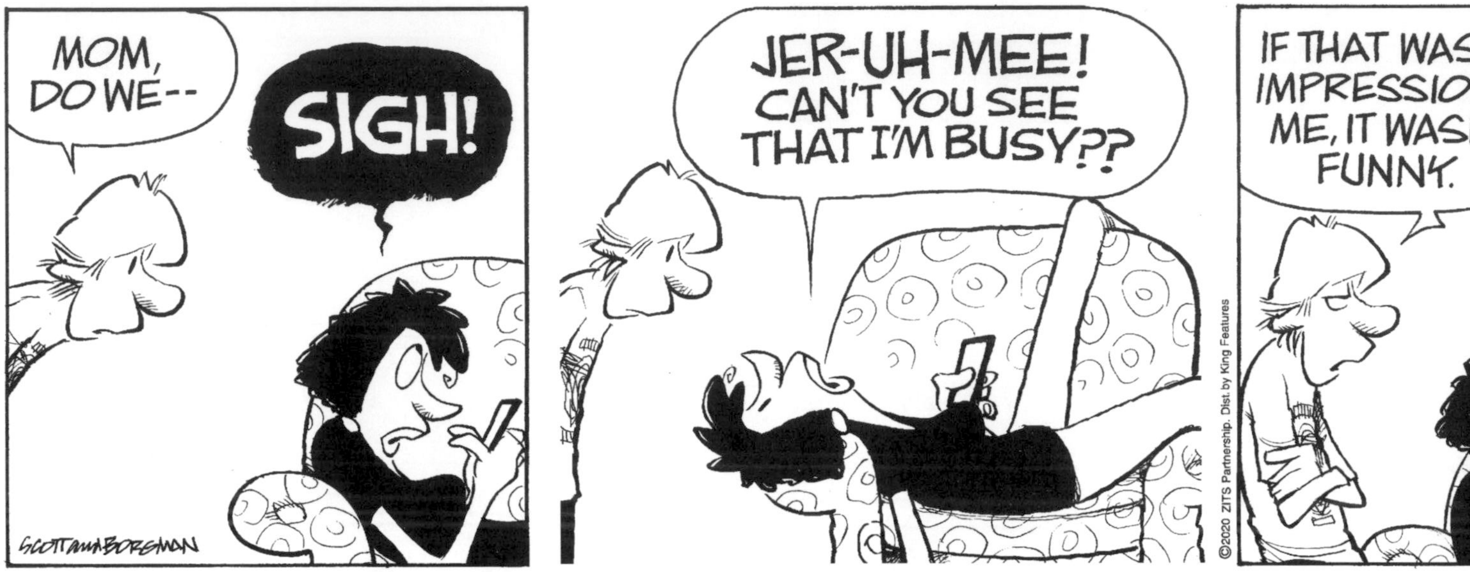
MOM, DO WE--
SIGH!
SCOTT AND BORGMAN
JER-UH-MEE! CAN'T YOU SEE THAT I'M BUSY??
©2020 ZITS Partnership. Dist. by King Features
IF THAT WAS AN IMPRESSION OF ME, IT WASN'T FUNNY.
HA! HA! DO IT AGAIN!
7-6

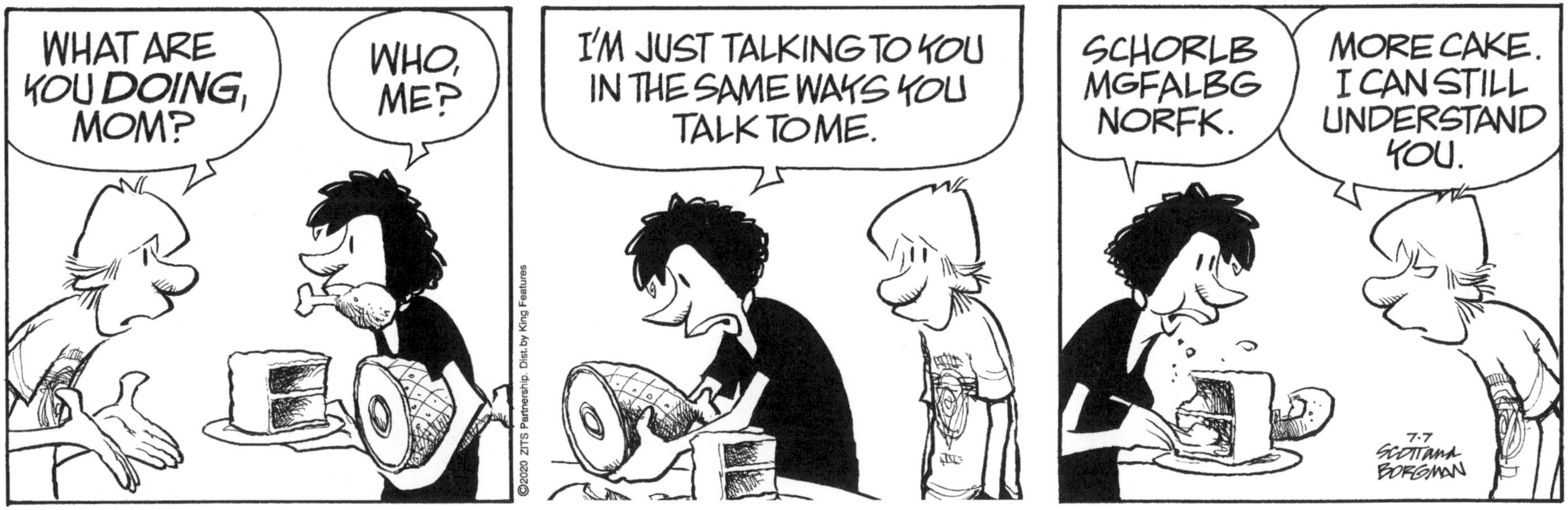
WHAT ARE YOU DOING, MOM?
WHO, ME?
©2020 ZITS Partnership. Dist. by King Features
I'M JUST TALKING TO YOU IN THE SAME WAYS YOU TALK TO ME.
SCHORLB MGFALBG NORFK.
MORE CAKE. I CAN STILL UNDERSTAND YOU.
7-7
SCOTT AND BORGMAN

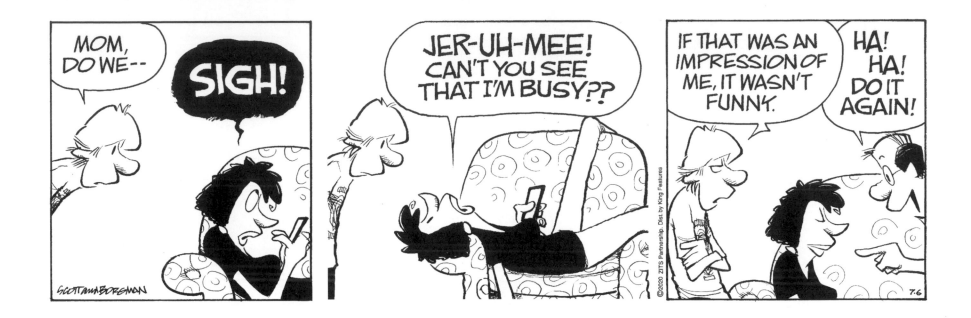

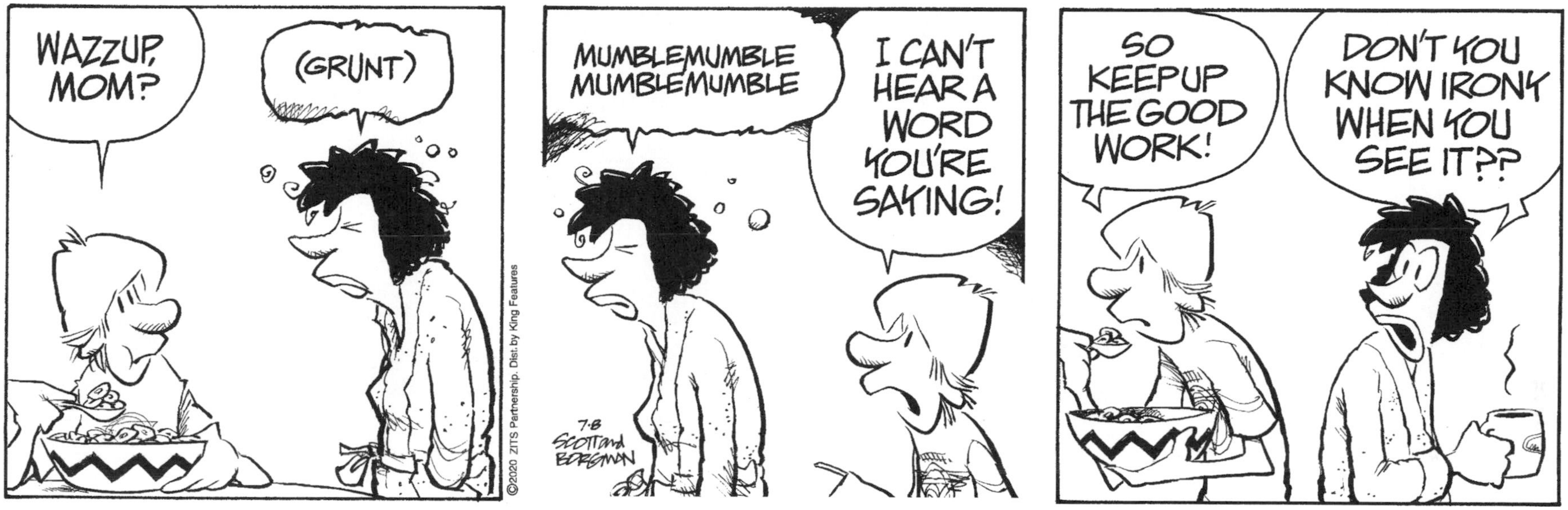
WAZZUP, MOM?
(GRUNT)
©2020 ZITS Partnership. Dist. by King Features
MUMBLEMUMBLE MUMBLEMUMBLE
I CAN'T HEAR A WORD YOU'RE SAYING!
7-8
SCOTT and BORGMAN
SO KEEP UP THE GOOD WORK!
DON'T YOU KNOW IRONY WHEN YOU SEE IT??

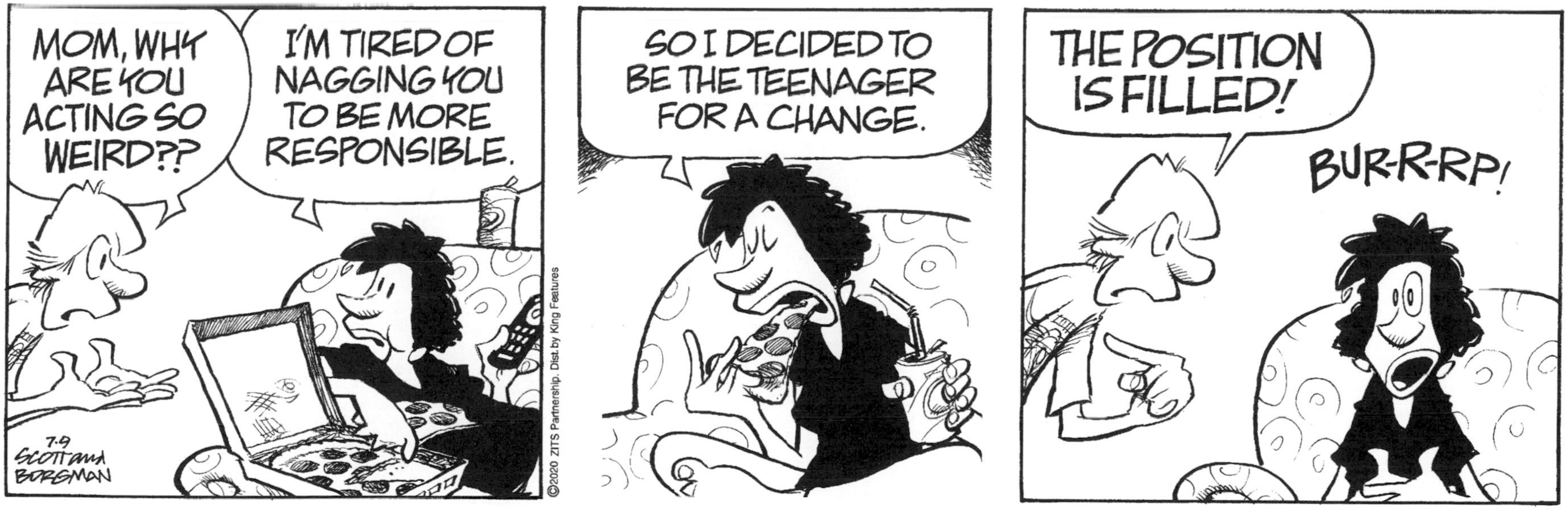
MOM, WHY ARE YOU ACTING SO WEIRD??
I'M TIRED OF NAGGING YOU TO BE MORE RESPONSIBLE.
7-9
SCOTT and BORGMAN
©2020 ZITS Partnership. Dist. by King Features
SO I DECIDED TO BE THE TEENAGER FOR A CHANGE.
THE POSITION IS FILLED!
BUR-R-RP!

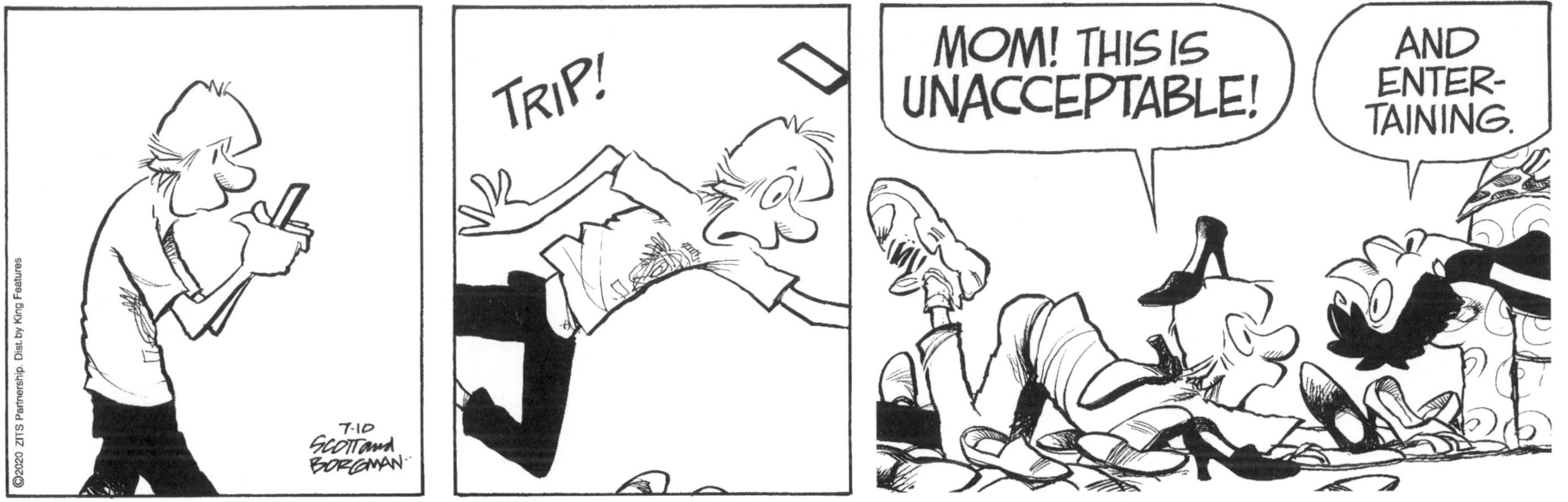
©2020 ZITS Partnership. Dist. by King Features
7-10
SCOTT and BORGMAN
TRIP!
MOM! THIS IS UNACCEPTABLE!
AND ENTER-TAINING.

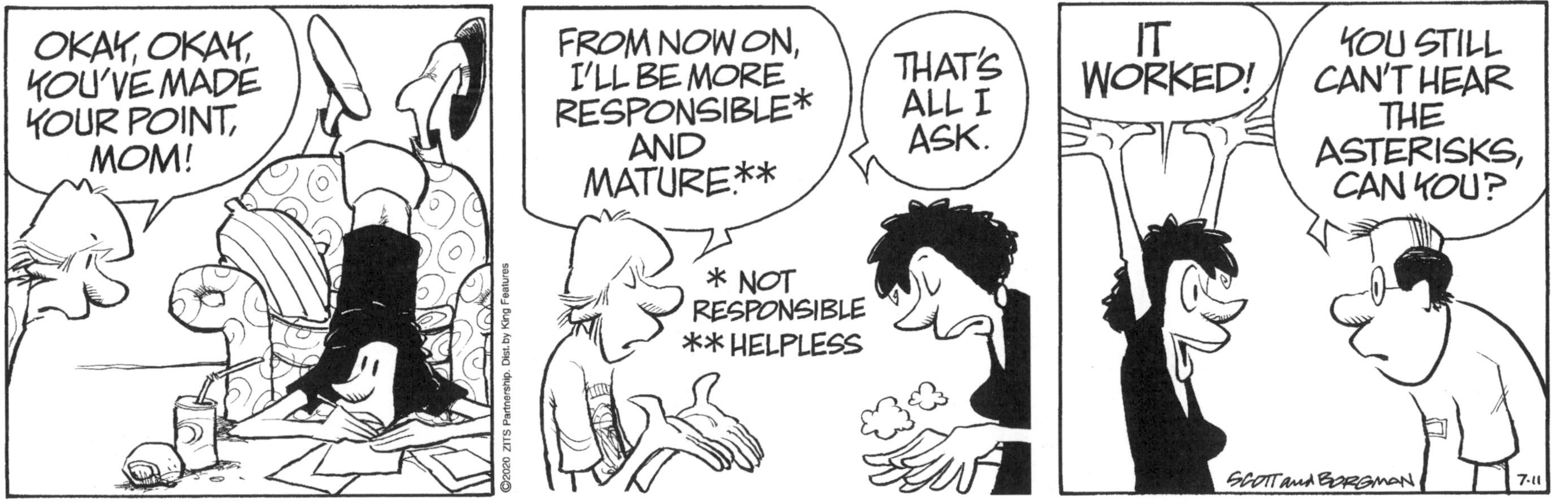
OKAY, OKAY, YOU'VE MADE YOUR POINT, MOM!
©2020 ZITS Partnership. Dist. by King Features
FROM NOW ON, I'LL BE MORE RESPONSIBLE* AND MATURE.**
* NOT RESPONSIBLE
** HELPLESS
THAT'S ALL I ASK.
IT WORKED!
YOU STILL CAN'T HEAR THE ASTERISKS, CAN YOU?
SCOTT and BORGMAN
7-11

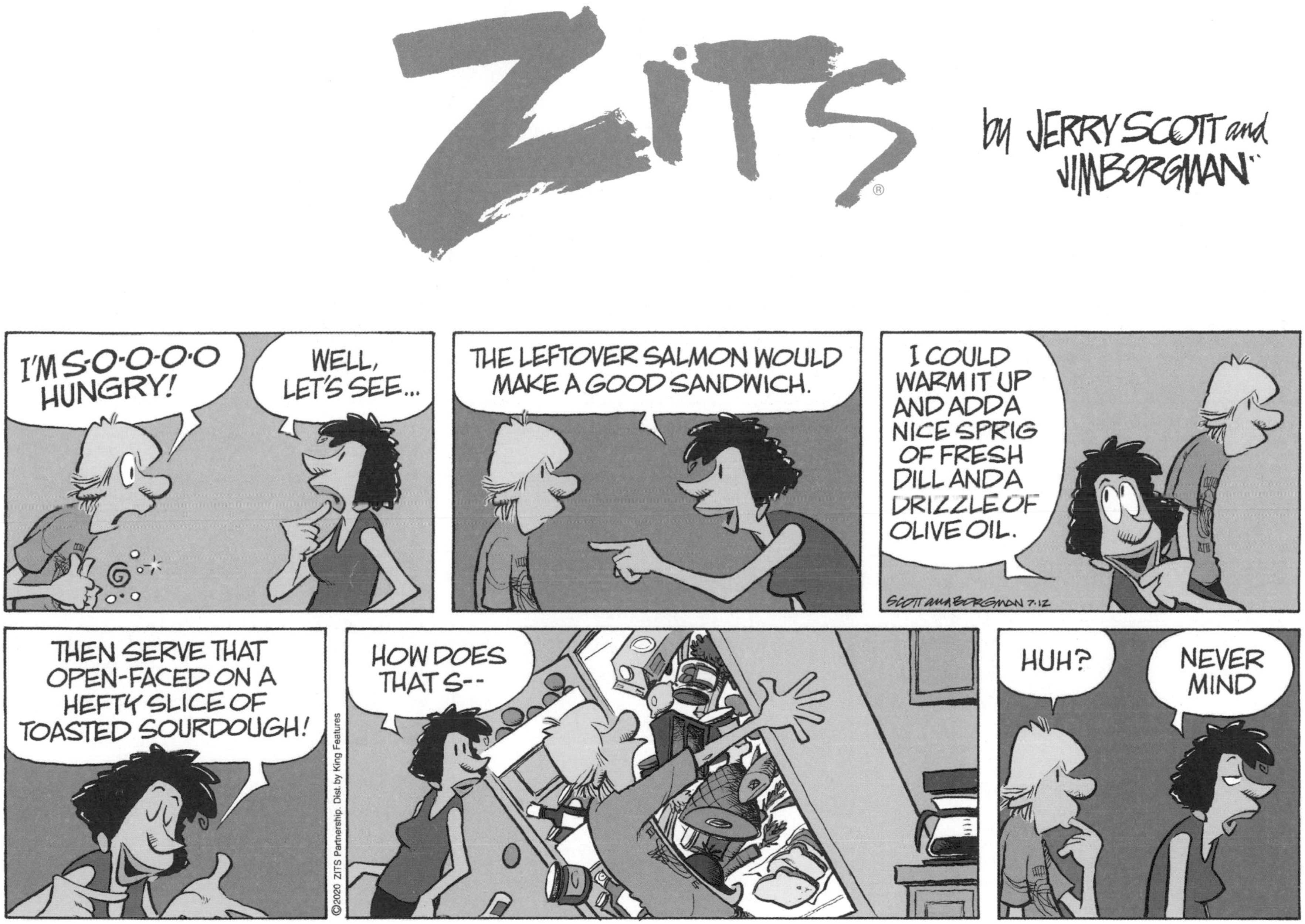

ZITS
by JERRY SCOTT and JIM BORGMAN
I'M S-O-O-O-O HUNGRY!
WELL, LET'S SEE...
THE LEFTOVER SALMON WOULD MAKE A GOOD SANDWICH.
I COULD WARM IT UP AND ADD A NICE SPRIG OF FRESH DILL AND A DRIZZLE OF OLIVE OIL.
SCOTT and BORGMAN 7.12
THEN SERVE THAT OPEN-FACED ON A HEFTY SLICE OF TOASTED SOURDOUGH!
©2020 ZITS Partnership. Dist. by King Features
HOW DOES THAT S--
HUH?
NEVER MIND

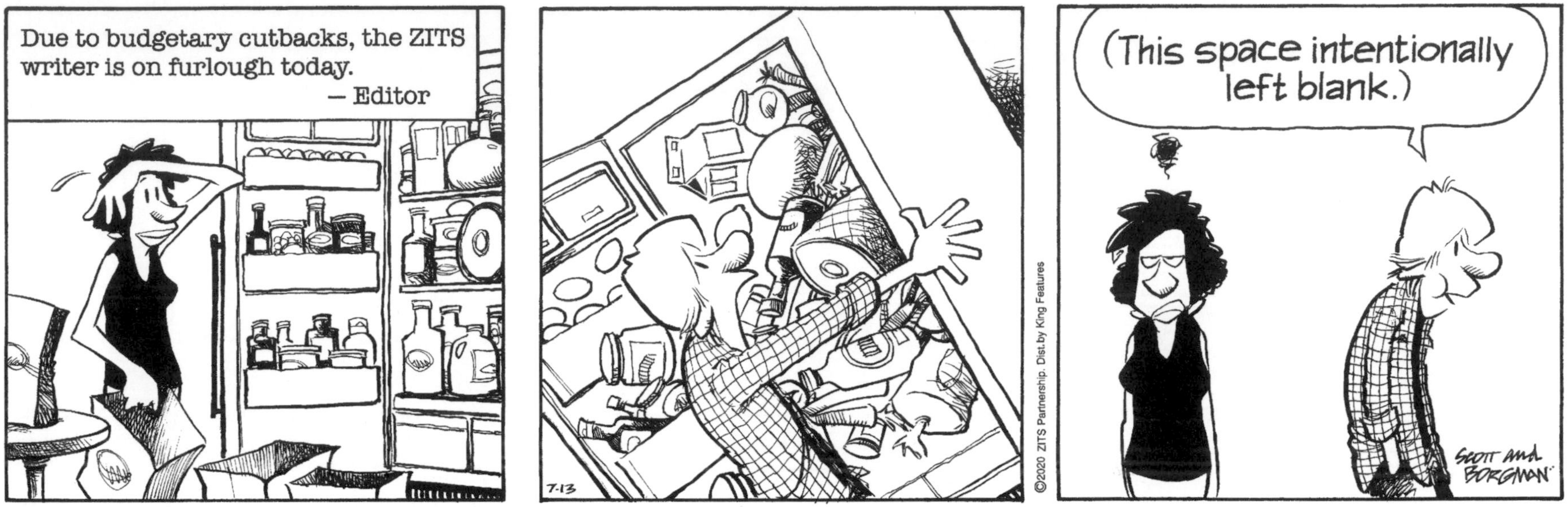
Due to budgetary cutbacks, the ZITS writer is on furlough today.
— Editor
7-13
©2020 ZITS Partnership. Dist.by King Features
(This space intentionally left blank.)
SCOTT AND BORGMAN

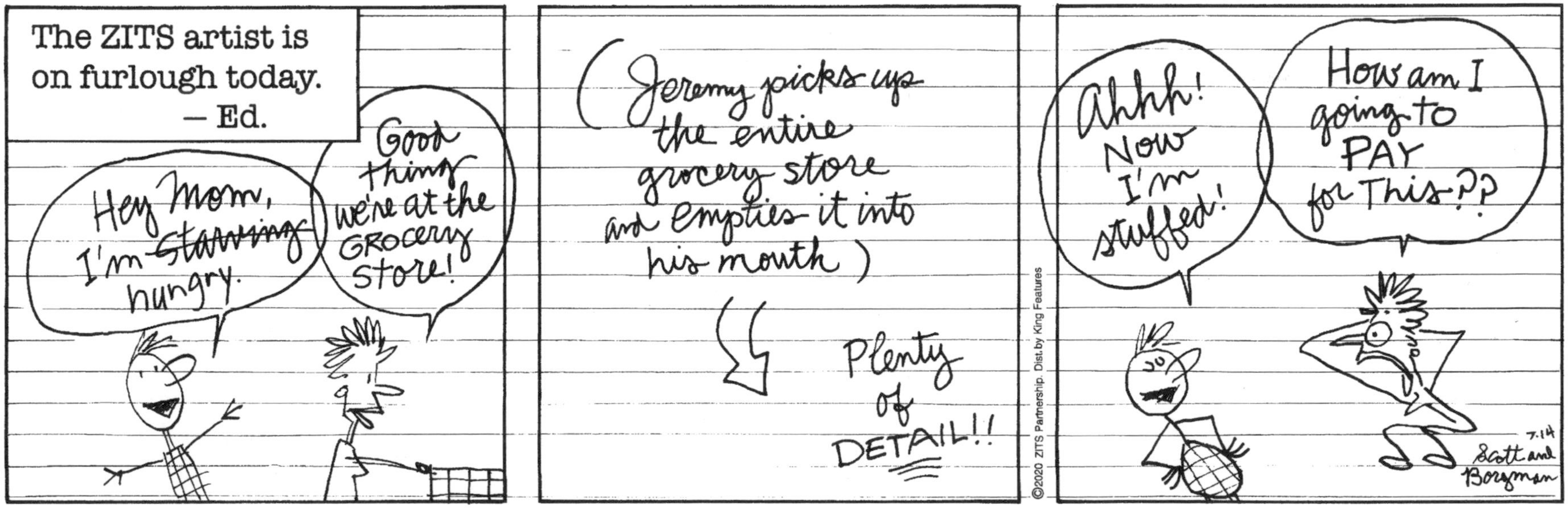
The ZITS artist is on furlough today.
— Ed.
Hey Mom, I'm ~~starving~~ hungry.
Good thing we're at the GROCERY STORE!
(Jeremy picks up the entire grocery store and empties it into his mouth)
Plenty of DETAIL!!
©2020 ZITS Partnership. Dist.by King Features
Ahhh! Now I'm stuffed!
How am I going to PAY for This??
7-14
Scott and Borgman

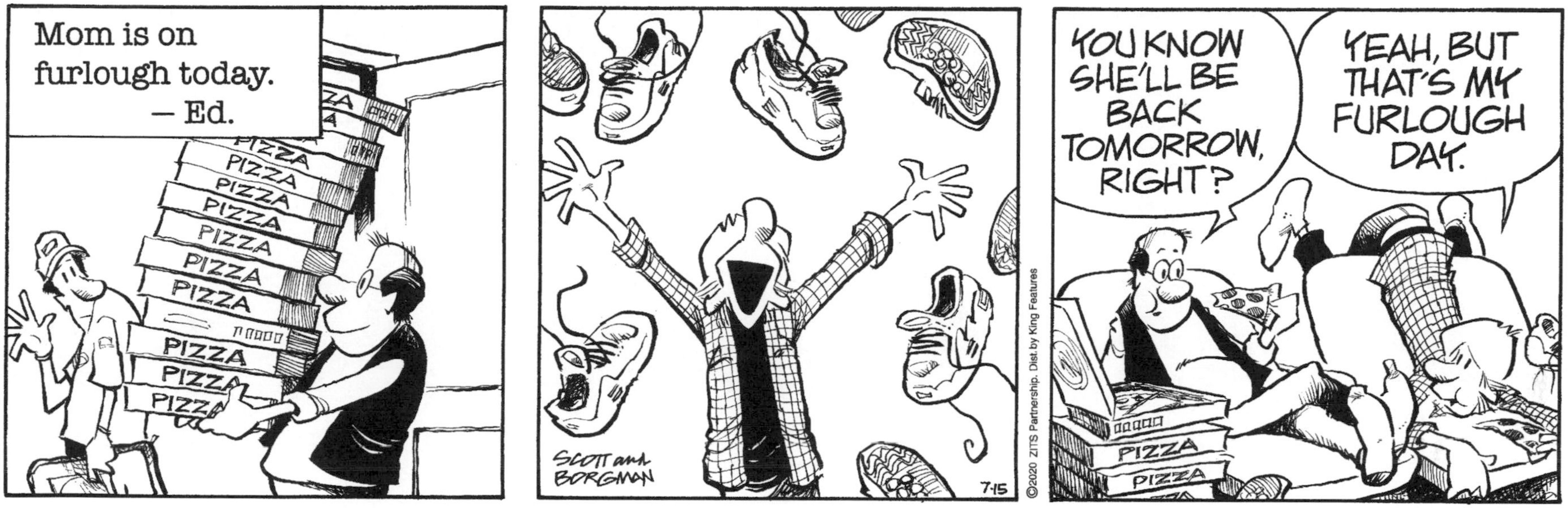
Mom is on furlough today. — Ed.
PIZZA
SCOTT and BORGMAN
7-15
YOU KNOW SHE'LL BE BACK TOMORROW, RIGHT?
YEAH, BUT THAT'S MY FURLOUGH DAY.
©2020 ZITS Partnership. Dist. by King Features

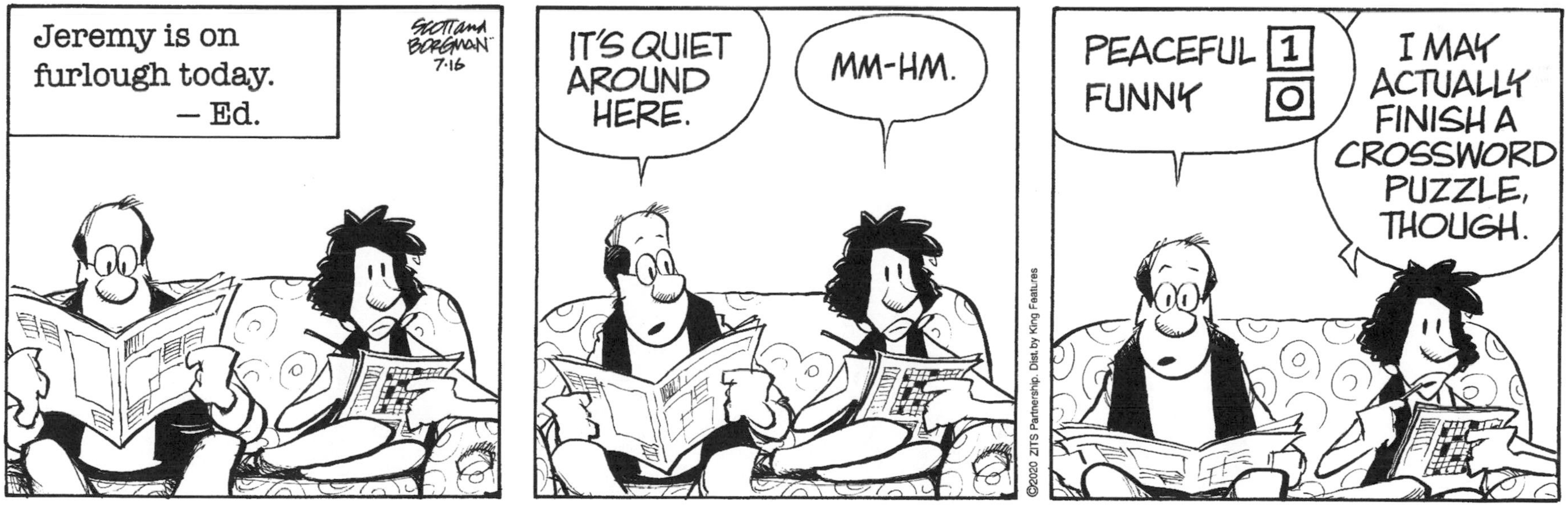
Jeremy is on furlough today. — Ed.
SCOTT and BORGMAN
7-16
IT'S QUIET AROUND HERE.
MM-HM.
PEACEFUL 1
FUNNY 0
I MAY ACTUALLY FINISH A CROSSWORD PUZZLE, THOUGH.
©2020 ZITS Partnership. Dist. by King Features

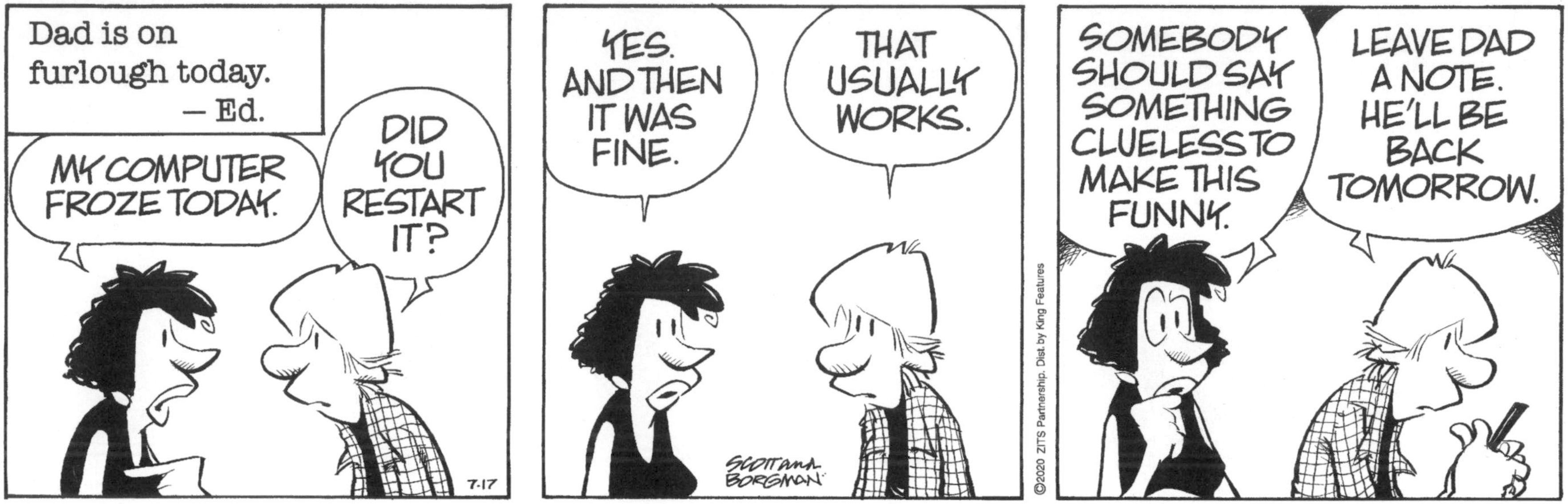

Dad is on furlough today. — Ed.
MY COMPUTER FROZE TODAY.
DID YOU RESTART IT?
7-17
YES. AND THEN IT WAS FINE.
THAT USUALLY WORKS.
SCOTT and BORGMAN
©2020 ZITS Partnership. Dist. by King Features
SOMEBODY SHOULD SAY SOMETHING CLUELESS TO MAKE THIS FUNNY.
LEAVE DAD A NOTE. HE'LL BE BACK TOMORROW.

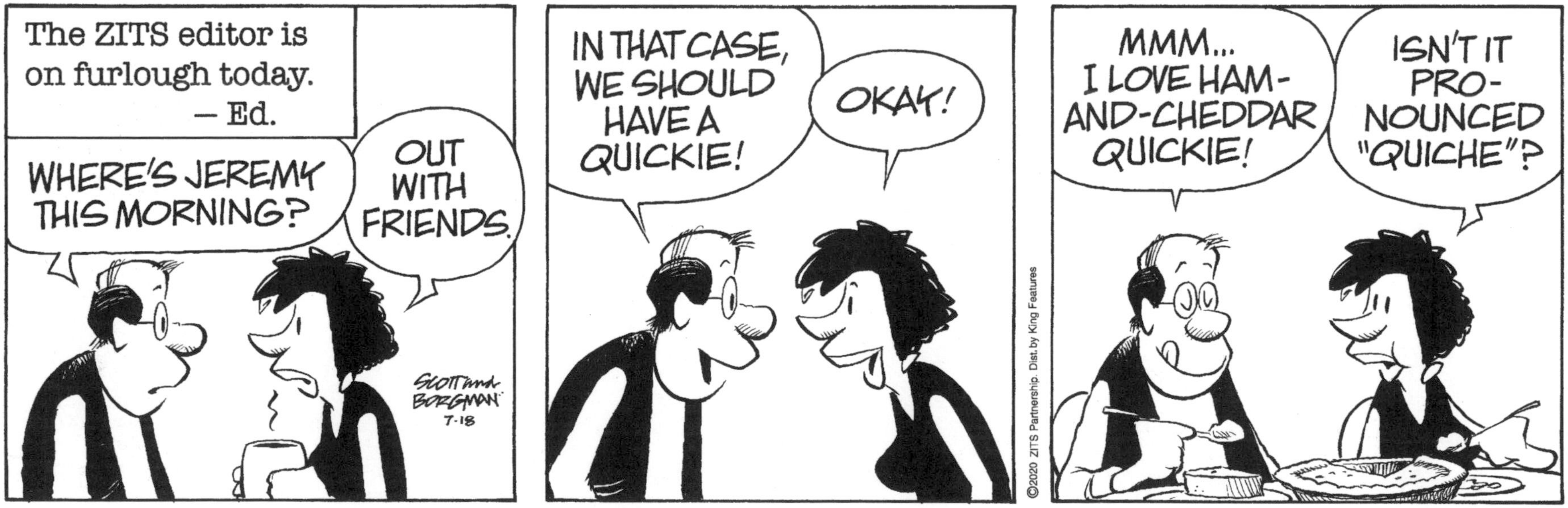

The ZITS editor is on furlough today. — Ed.
WHERE'S JEREMY THIS MORNING?
OUT WITH FRIENDS.
SCOTT and BORGMAN
7-18
IN THAT CASE, WE SHOULD HAVE A QUICKIE!
OKAY!
©2020 ZITS Partnership. Dist. by King Features
MMM... I LOVE HAM-AND-CHEDDAR QUICKIE!
ISN'T IT PRO-NOUNCED "QUICHE"?

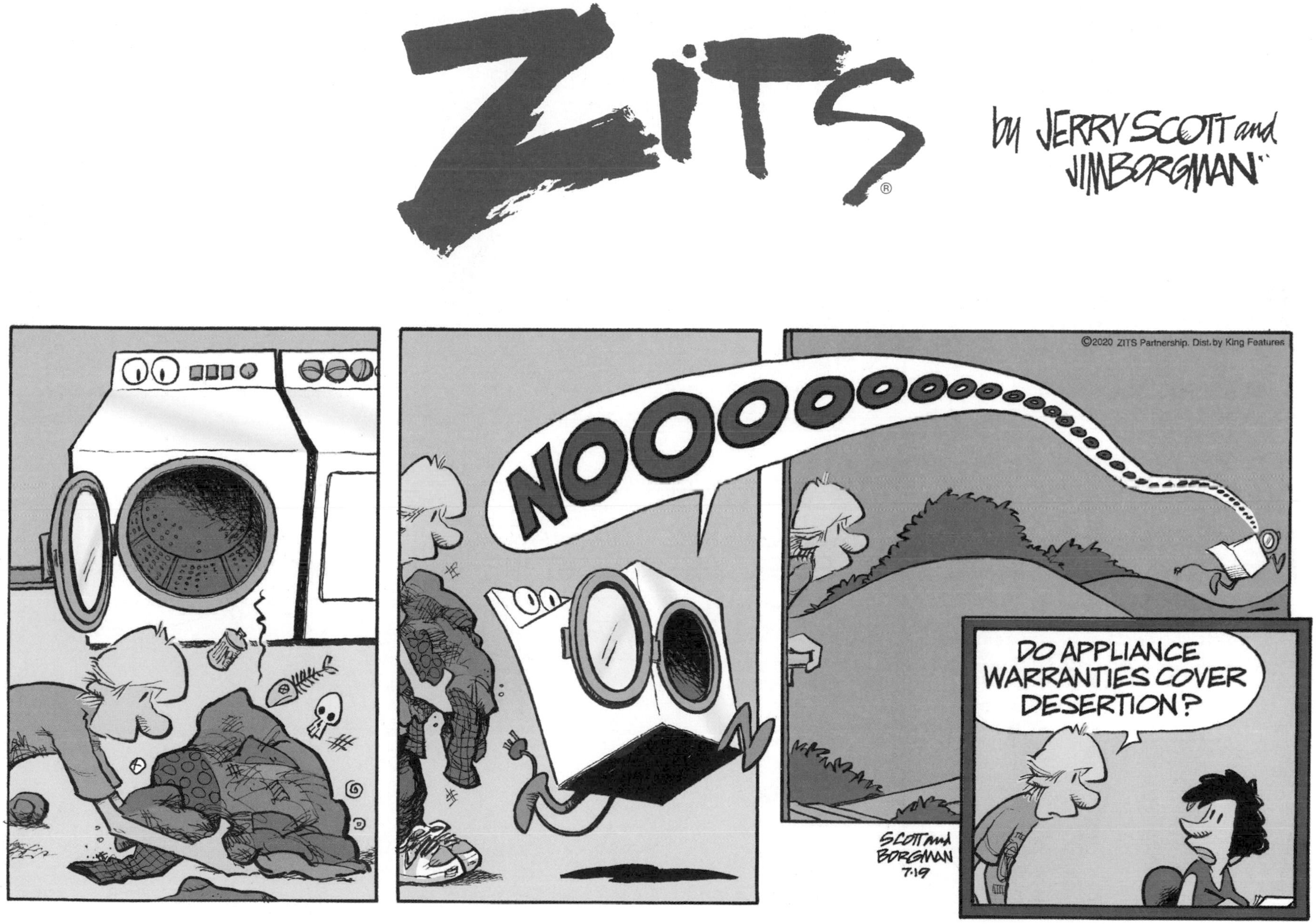
ZITS®
by JERRY SCOTT and JIM BORGMAN
©2020 ZITS Partnership. Dist. by King Features
NOOOOOOOOOOOOOOOOOOOOOOOOOOOOO
DO APPLIANCE WARRANTIES COVER DESERTION?
SCOTT and BORGMAN 7·19

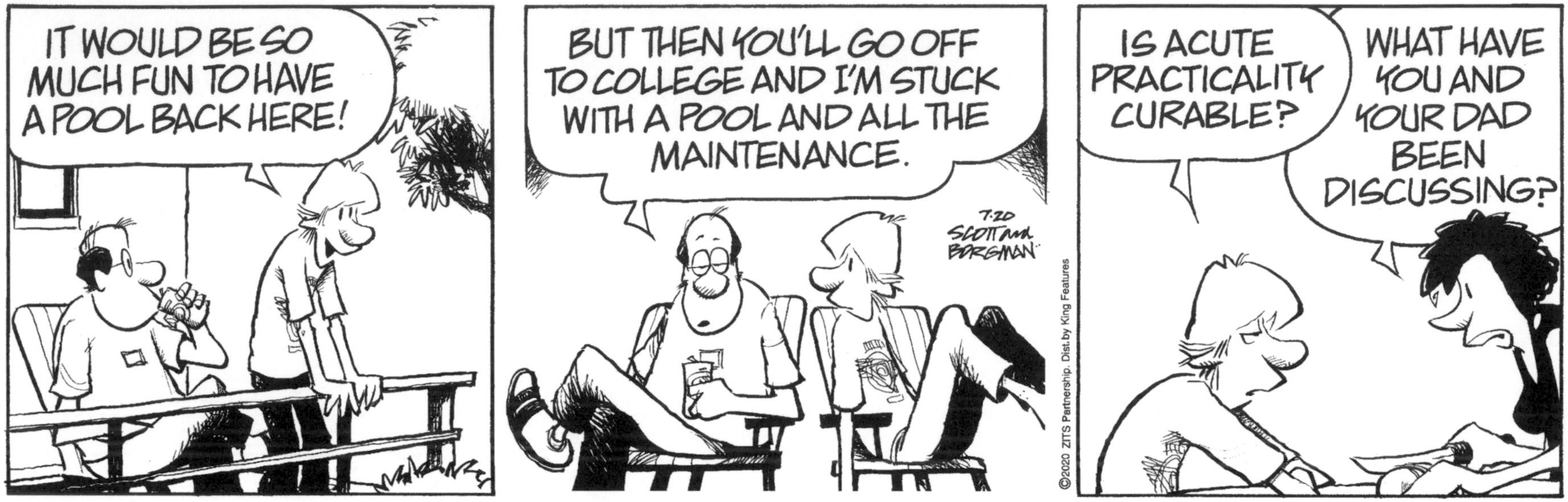
IT WOULD BE SO MUCH FUN TO HAVE A POOL BACK HERE!
BUT THEN YOU'LL GO OFF TO COLLEGE AND I'M STUCK WITH A POOL AND ALL THE MAINTENANCE.
7·20 SCOTT and BORGMAN
©2020 ZITS Partnership. Dist. by King Features
IS ACUTE PRACTICALITY CURABLE?
WHAT HAVE YOU AND YOUR DAD BEEN DISCUSSING?

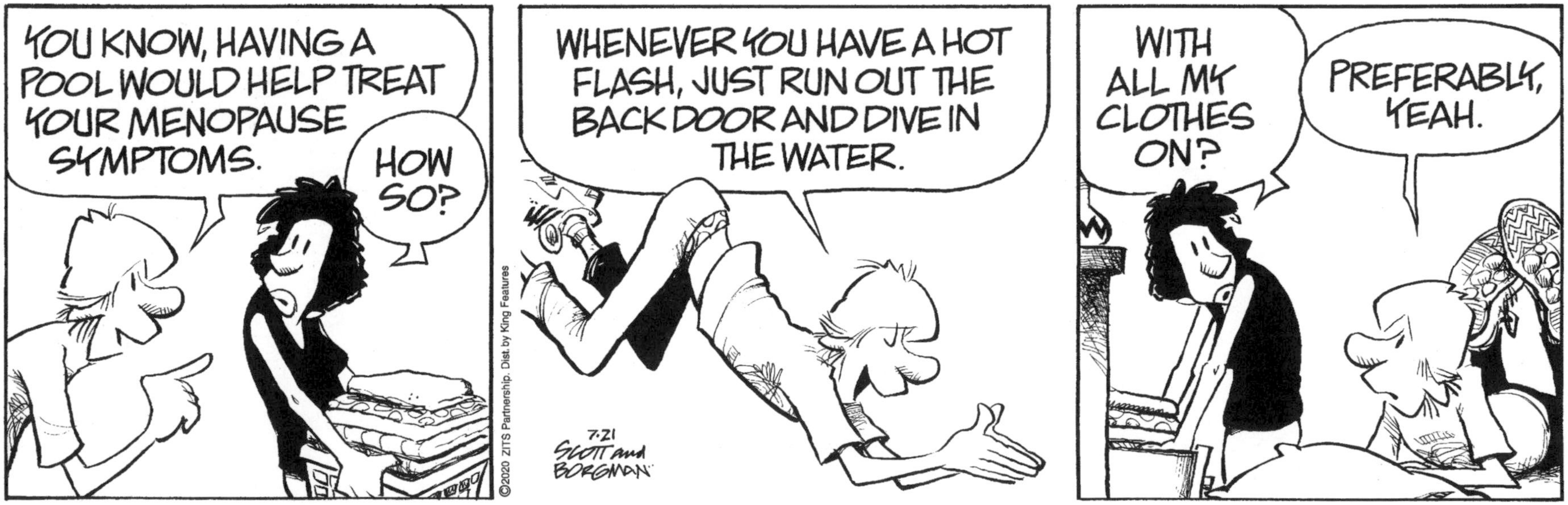
YOU KNOW, HAVING A POOL WOULD HELP TREAT YOUR MENOPAUSE SYMPTOMS.
HOW SO?
©2020 ZITS Partnership. Dist. by King Features
WHENEVER YOU HAVE A HOT FLASH, JUST RUN OUT THE BACK DOOR AND DIVE IN THE WATER.
7·21 SCOTT and BORGMAN
WITH ALL MY CLOTHES ON?
PREFERABLY, YEAH.

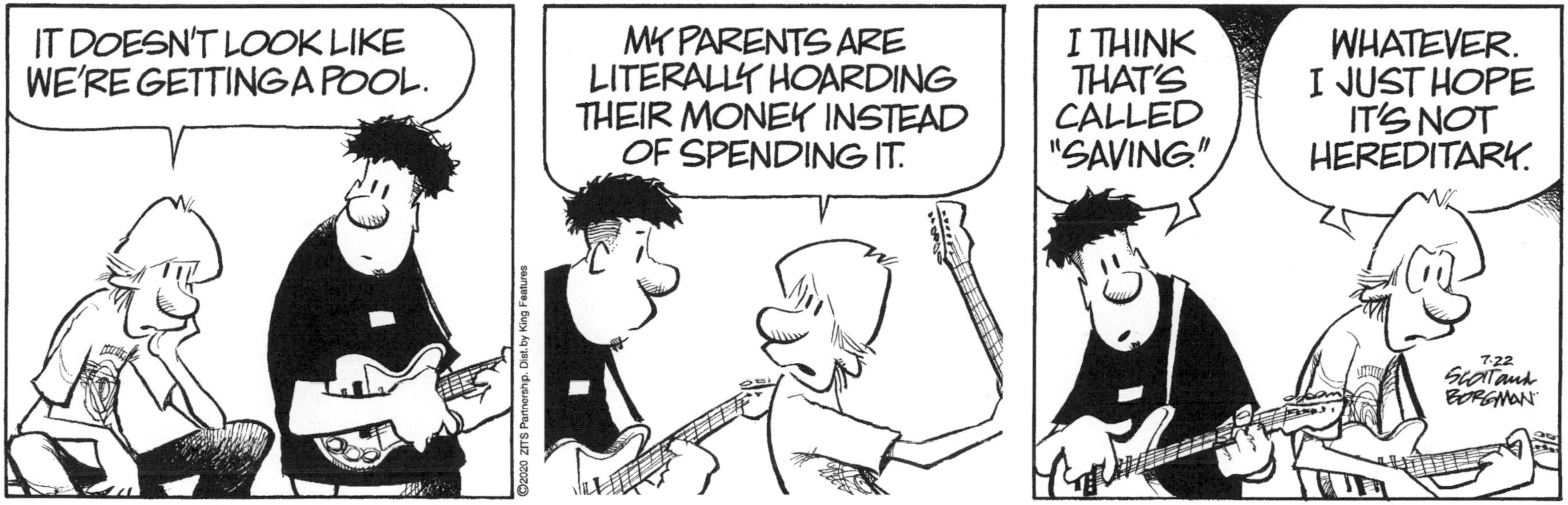
IT DOESN'T LOOK LIKE WE'RE GETTING A POOL.
MY PARENTS ARE LITERALLY HOARDING THEIR MONEY INSTEAD OF SPENDING IT.
I THINK THAT'S CALLED "SAVING."
WHATEVER. I JUST HOPE IT'S NOT HEREDITARY.
©2020 ZITS Partnership. Dist. by King Features
7·22 SCOTT and BORGMAN

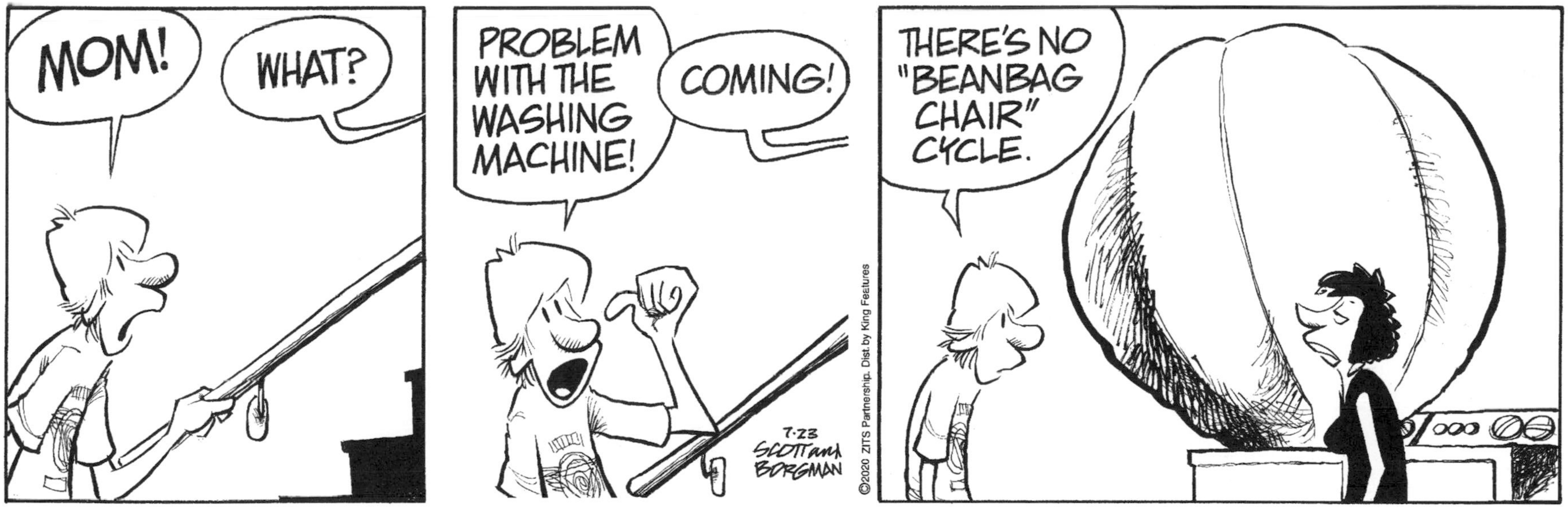
MOM!
WHAT?
PROBLEM WITH THE WASHING MACHINE!
COMING!
7·23 SCOTT and BORGMAN
©2020 ZITS Partnership. Dist. by King Features
THERE'S NO "BEANBAG CHAIR" CYCLE.

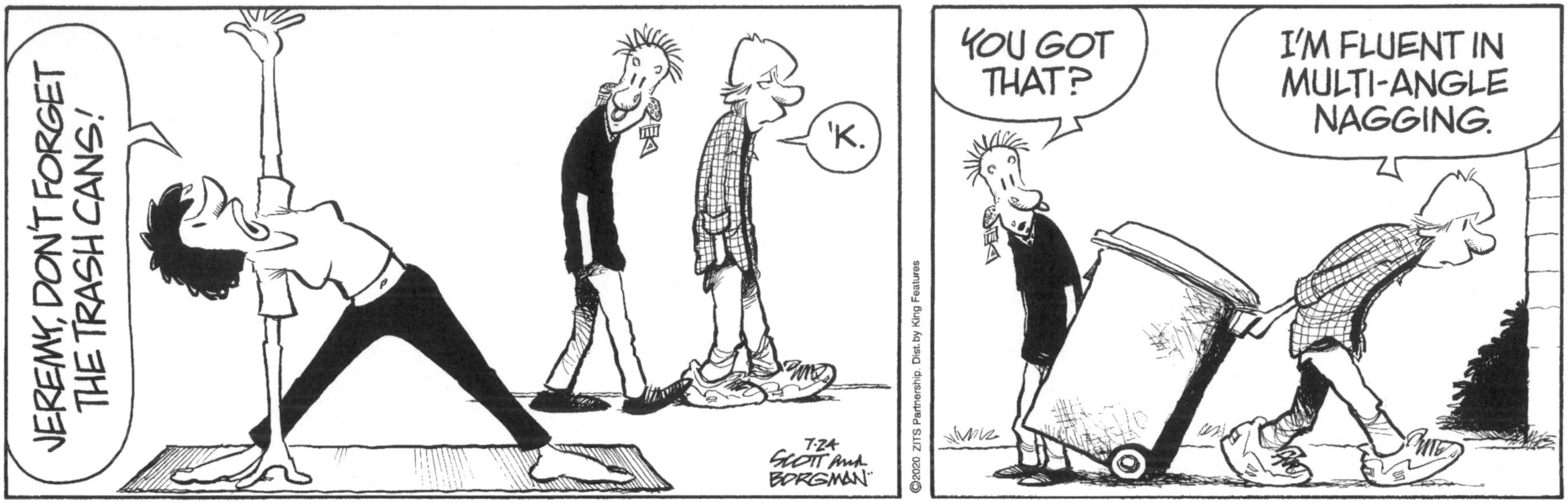
JEREMY, DON'T FORGET THE TRASH CANS!
'K.
7·24
SCOTT AND BORGMAN
YOU GOT THAT?
I'M FLUENT IN MULTI-ANGLE NAGGING.

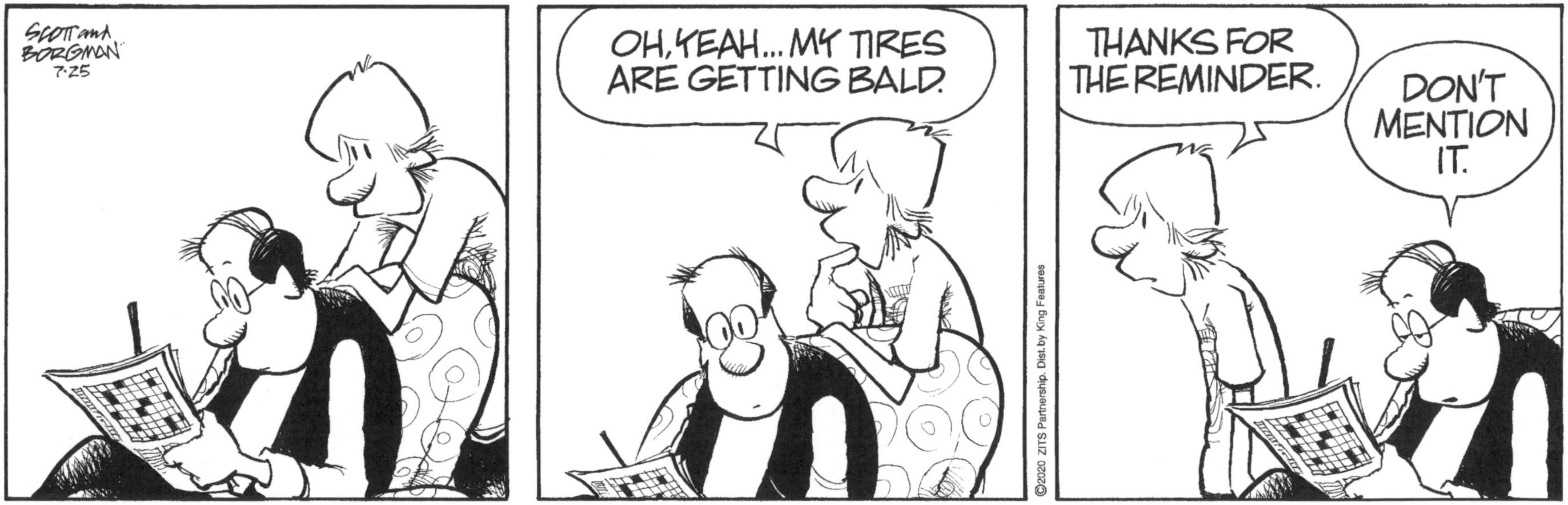
SCOTT AND BORGMAN
7·25
OH, YEAH... MY TIRES ARE GETTING BALD.
THANKS FOR THE REMINDER.
DON'T MENTION IT.

ZITS

by JERRY SCOTT and JIM BORGMAN

EMILY BAKES THE BEST CAKES!
SHE MIGHT RUN FOR MAYOR!
I SHOULD FERTILIZE THE PEONIES.
DO YOU LIKE EGGPLANT?
WE SHOULD GET NEW TIRES.
COULD WE DEDUCT A HOT TUB?
I SMELL BACON!
SCOTT and BORGMAN 7-26
©2020 ZITS Partnership. Dist. by King Features
MONKEY MIND?
I CALL THEM "MOM SEQUITURS."
I THINK BEIGE IS MY FAVORITE COLOR!

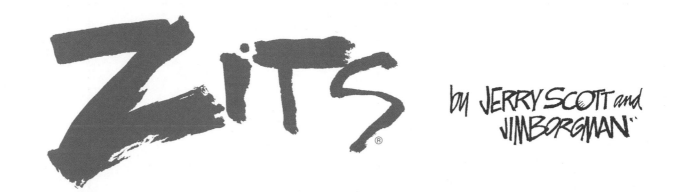

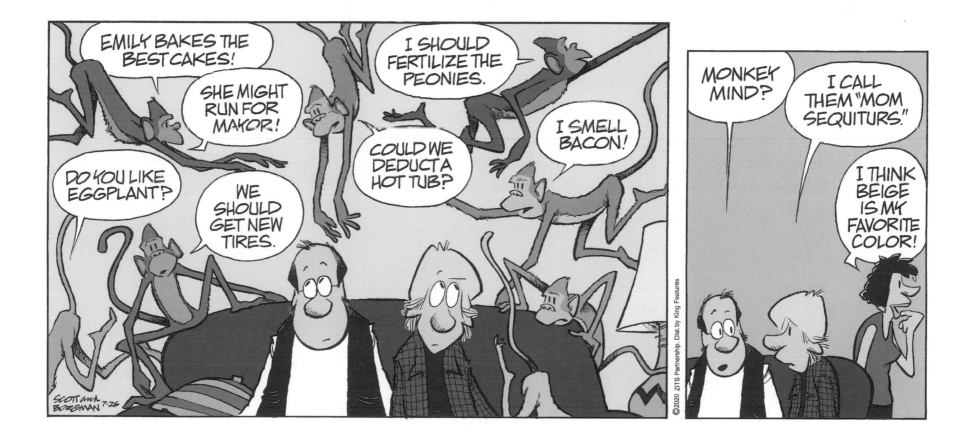

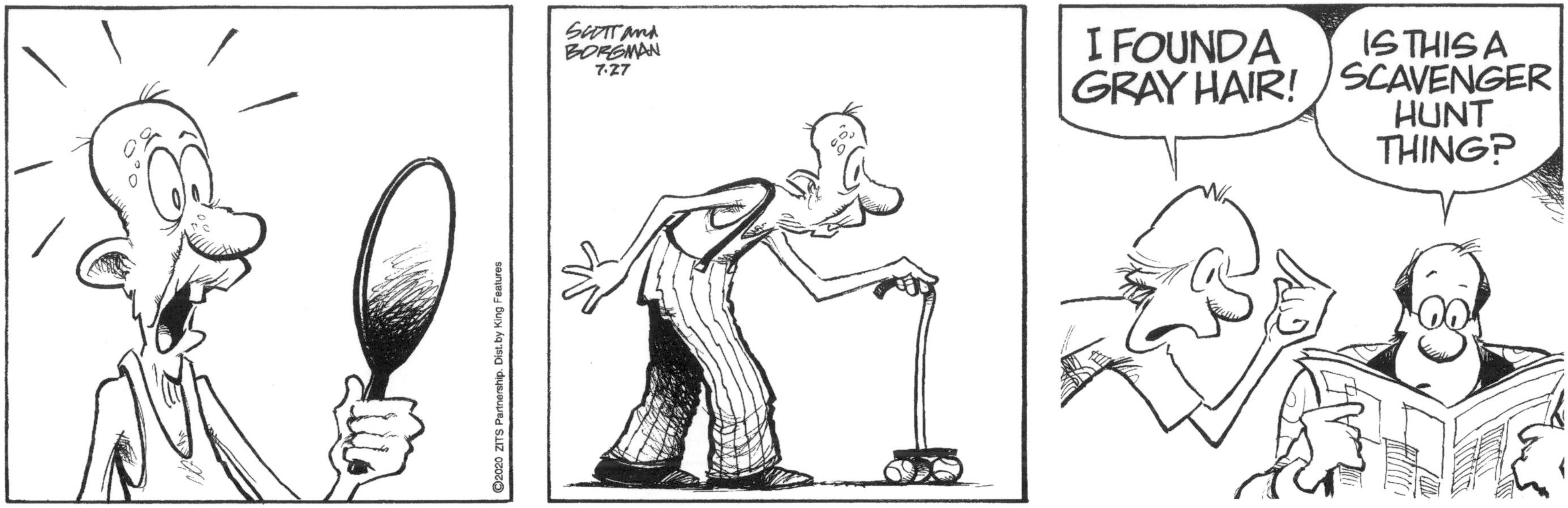
©2020 ZITS Partnership. Dist. by King Features
SCOTT AND BORGMAN 7-27
I FOUND A GRAY HAIR!
IS THIS A SCAVENGER HUNT THING?

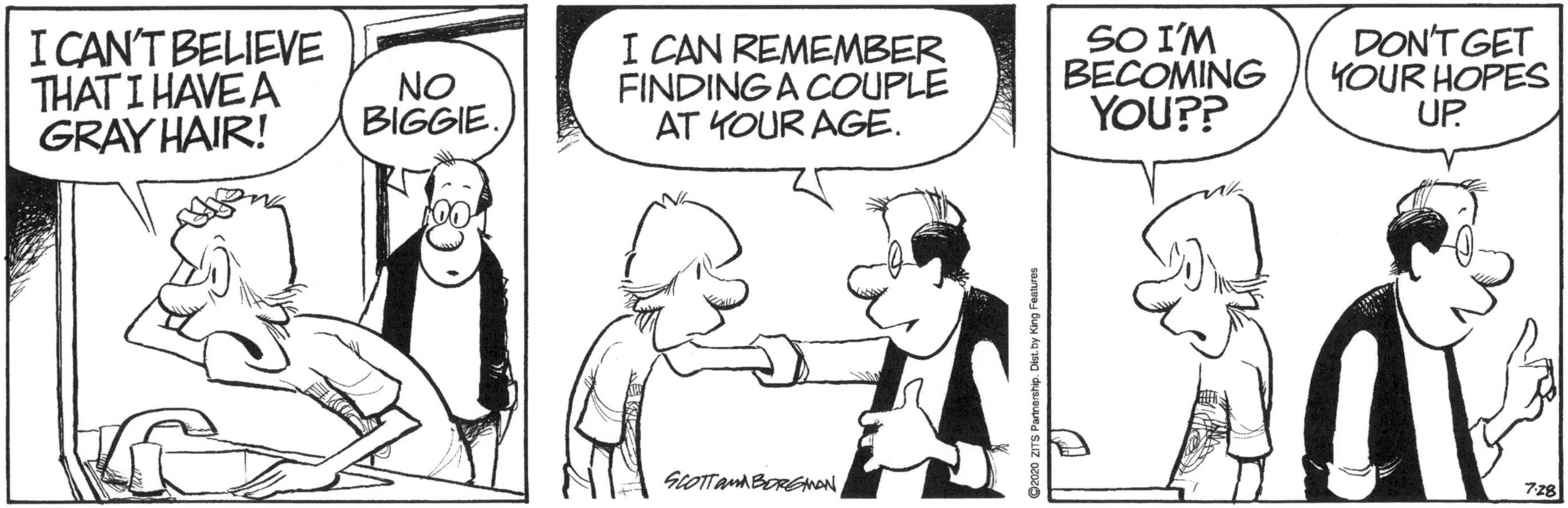
I CAN'T BELIEVE THAT I HAVE A GRAY HAIR!
NO BIGGIE.
I CAN REMEMBER FINDING A COUPLE AT YOUR AGE.
SCOTT AND BORGMAN
©2020 ZITS Partnership. Dist. by King Features
SO I'M BECOMING YOU??
DON'T GET YOUR HOPES UP.
7-28

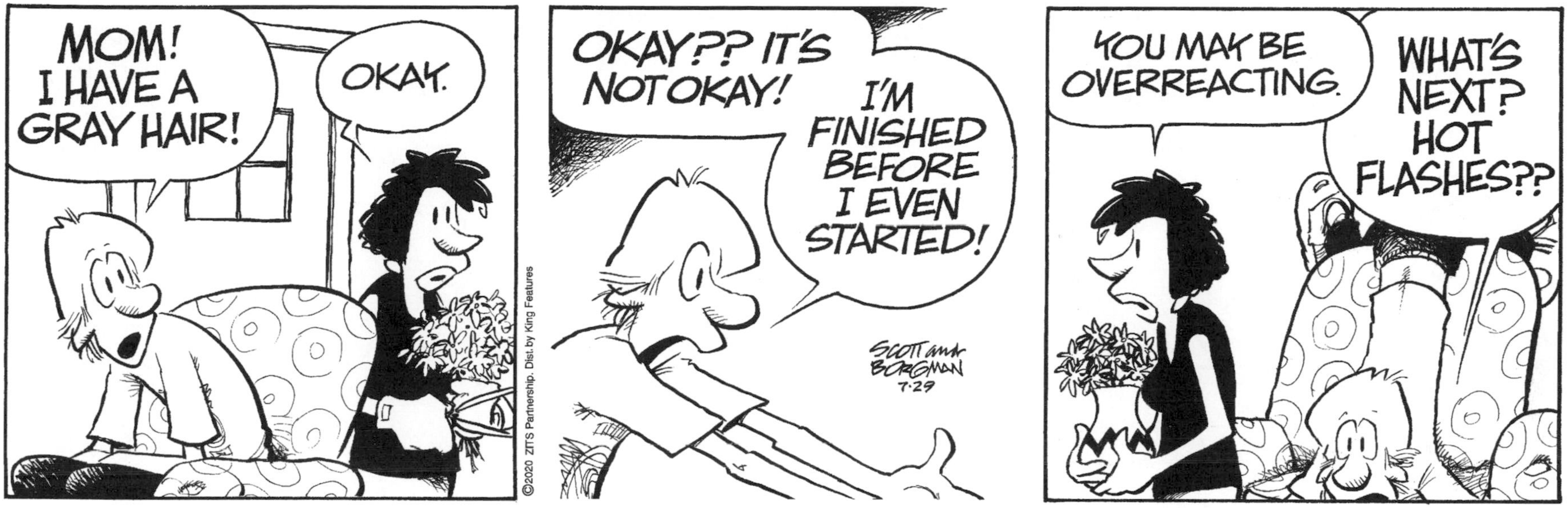
MOM! I HAVE A GRAY HAIR!
OKAY.
©2020 ZITS Partnership. Dist. by King Features
OKAY?? IT'S NOT OKAY!
I'M FINISHED BEFORE I EVEN STARTED!
SCOTT and BORGMAN 7-29
YOU MAY BE OVERREACTING.
WHAT'S NEXT? HOT FLASHES??

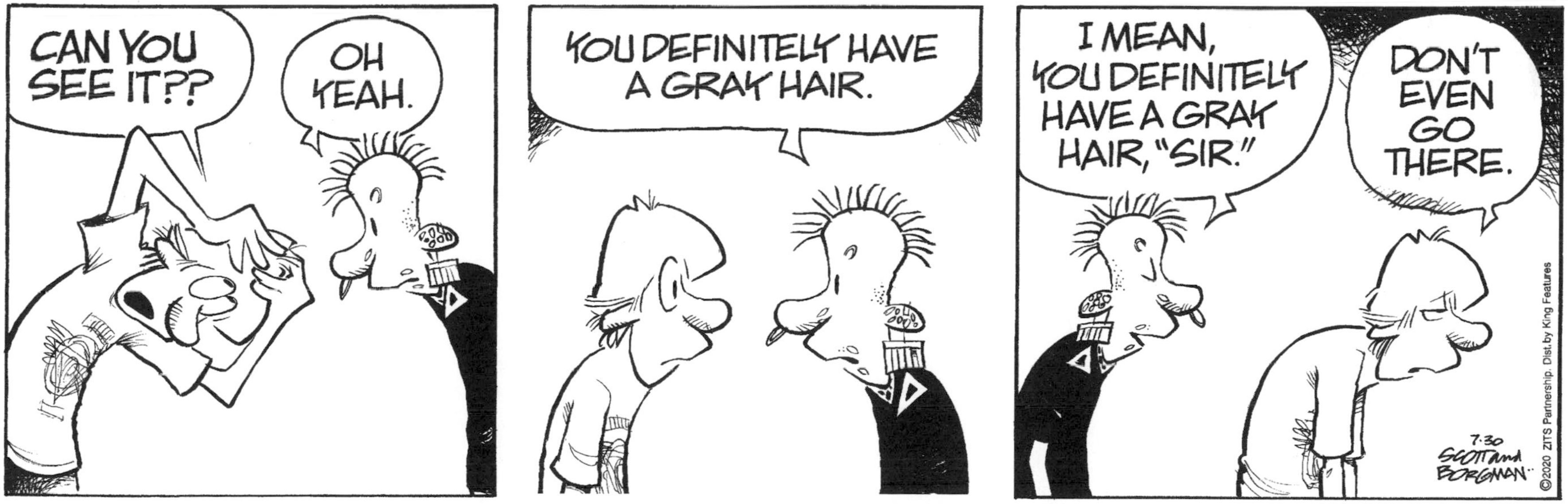
CAN YOU SEE IT??
OH YEAH.
YOU DEFINITELY HAVE A GRAY HAIR.
I MEAN, YOU DEFINITELY HAVE A GRAY HAIR, "SIR."
DON'T EVEN GO THERE.
7-30 SCOTT and BORGMAN
©2020 ZITS Partnership. Dist. by King Features

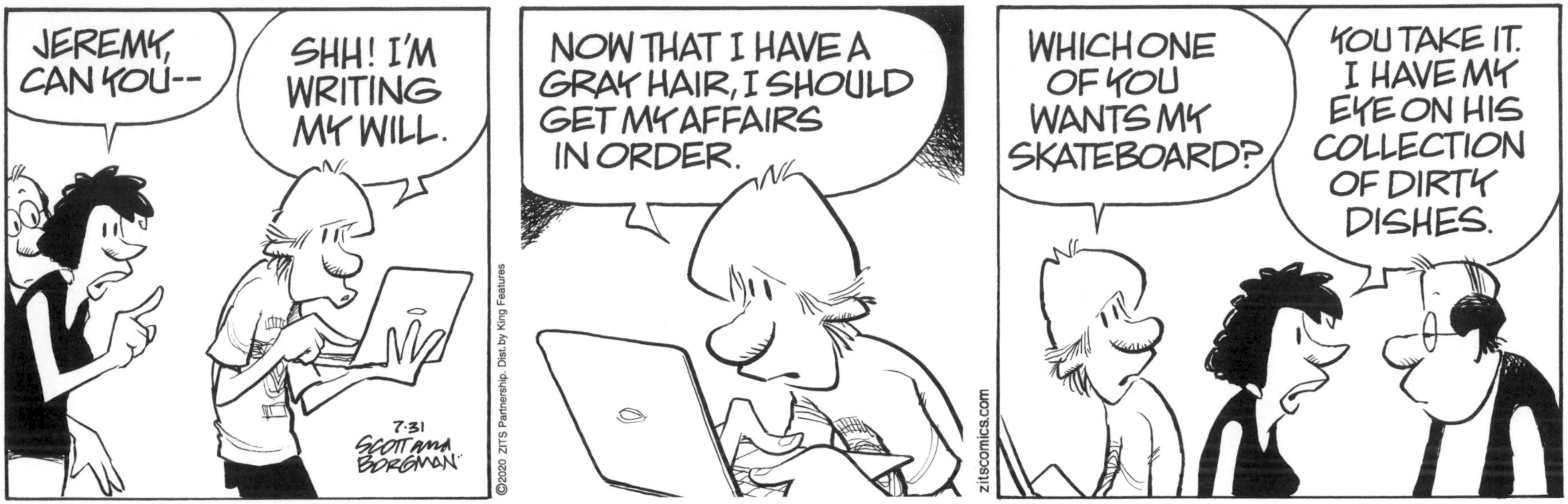
JEREMY, CAN YOU--
SHH! I'M WRITING MY WILL.
7·31
SCOTT and BORGMAN
©2020 ZITS Partnership. Dist. by King Features
NOW THAT I HAVE A GRAY HAIR, I SHOULD GET MY AFFAIRS IN ORDER.
zitscomics.com
WHICH ONE OF YOU WANTS MY SKATEBOARD?
YOU TAKE IT. I HAVE MY EYE ON HIS COLLECTION OF DIRTY DISHES.

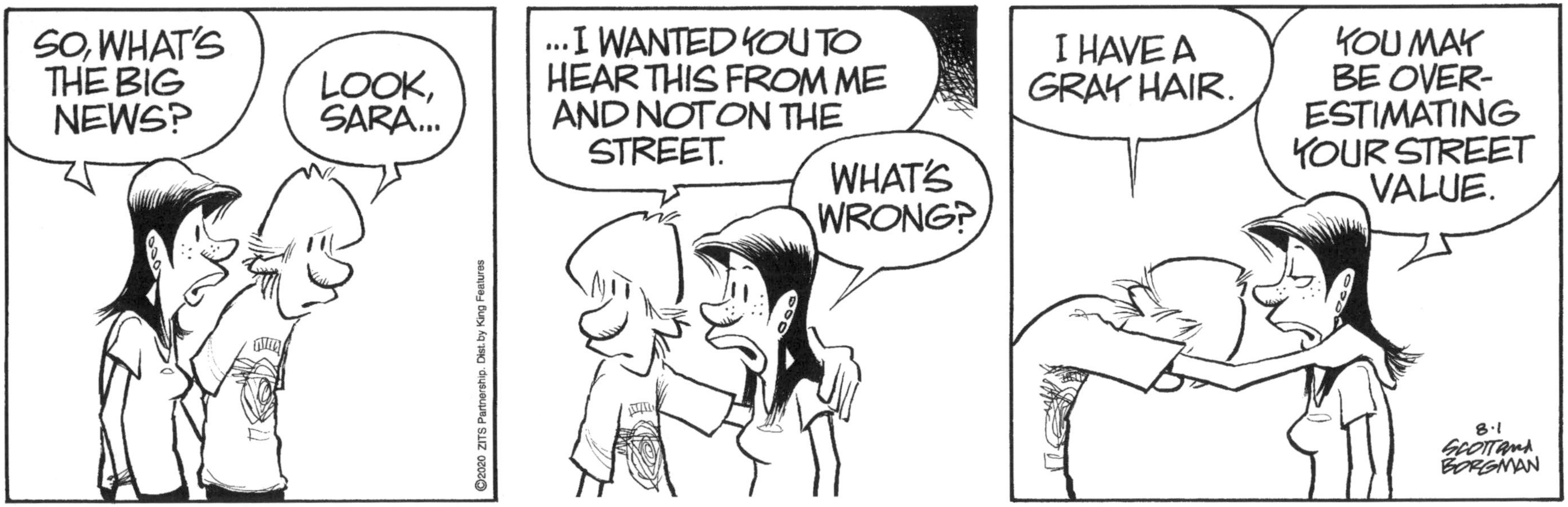
SO, WHAT'S THE BIG NEWS?
LOOK, SARA....
©2020 ZITS Partnership. Dist. by King Features
...I WANTED YOU TO HEAR THIS FROM ME AND NOT ON THE STREET.
WHAT'S WRONG?
I HAVE A GRAY HAIR.
YOU MAY BE OVER-ESTIMATING YOUR STREET VALUE.
8·1
SCOTT and BORGMAN

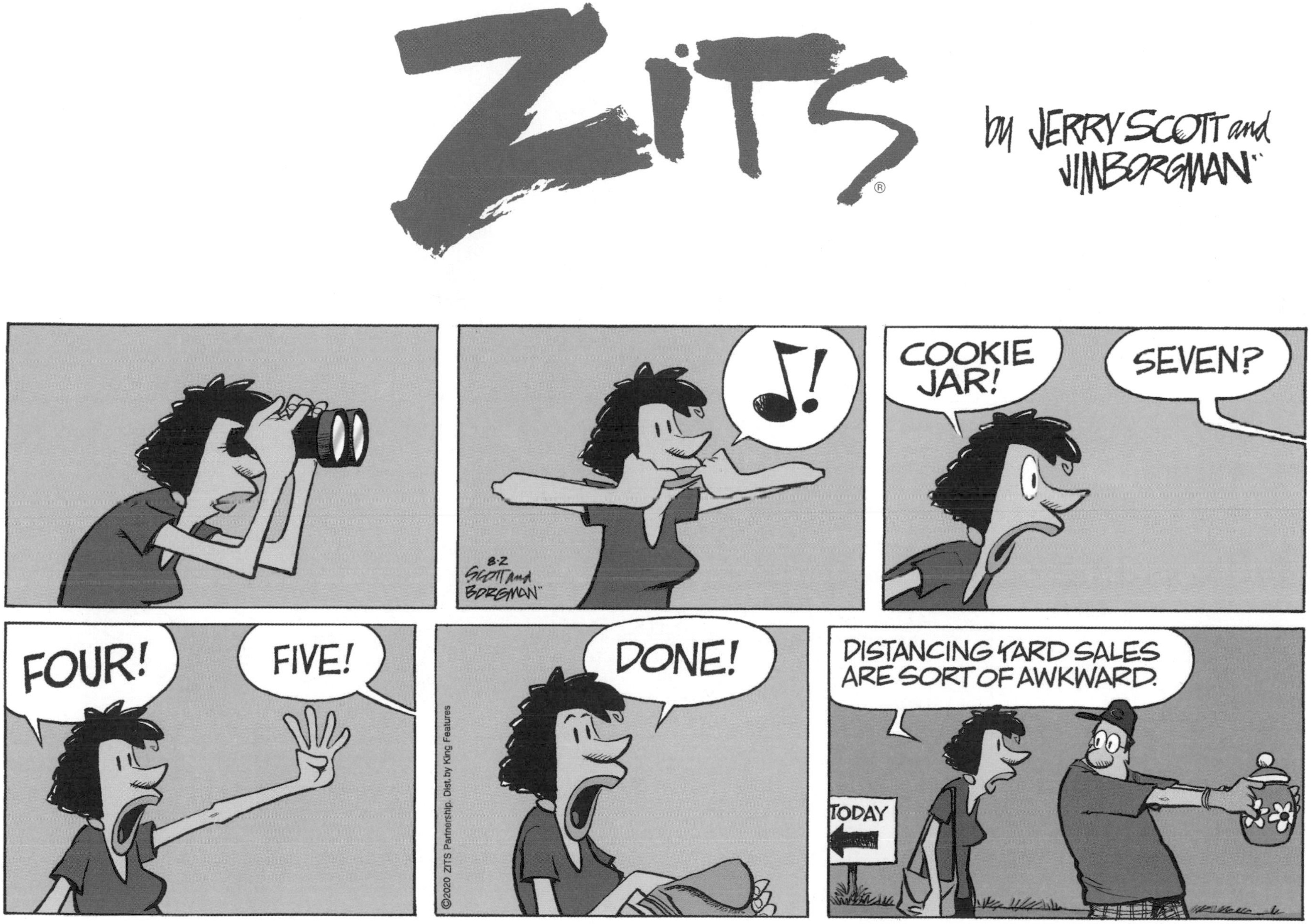
ZITS®
by JERRY SCOTT and JIM BORGMAN
♪!
8-2 SCOTT and BORGMAN
COOKIE JAR!
SEVEN?
FOUR!
FIVE!
©2020 ZITS Partnership. Dist. by King Features
DONE!
DISTANCING YARD SALES ARE SORT OF AWKWARD.
TODAY

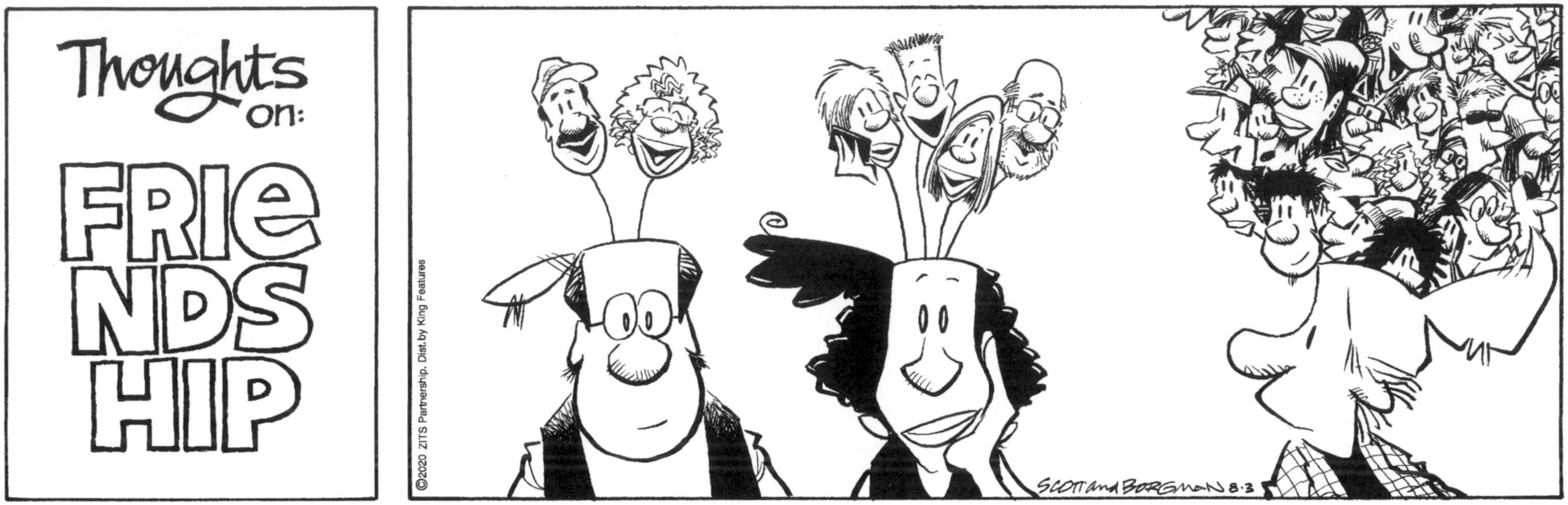
Thoughts on:
FRIE
NDS
HIP
©2020 ZITS Partnership. Dist. by King Features
SCOTT and BORGMAN 8·3

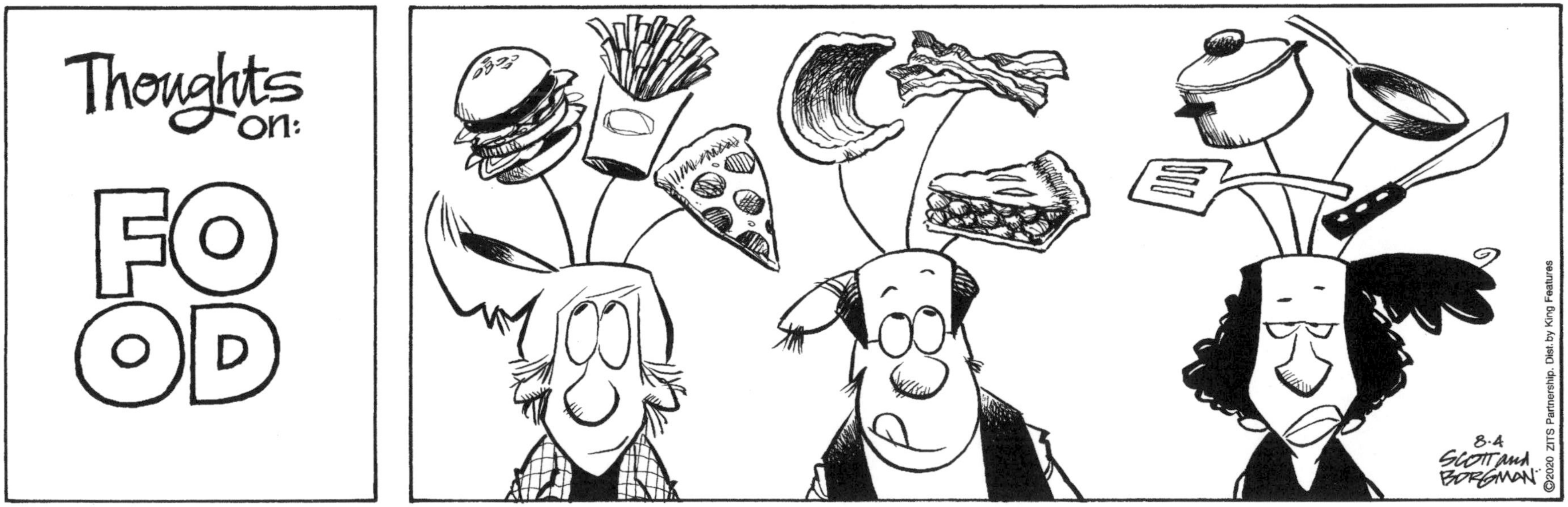
Thoughts on:
FO
OD
8·4
SCOTT and BORGMAN
©2020 ZITS Partnership. Dist. by King Features

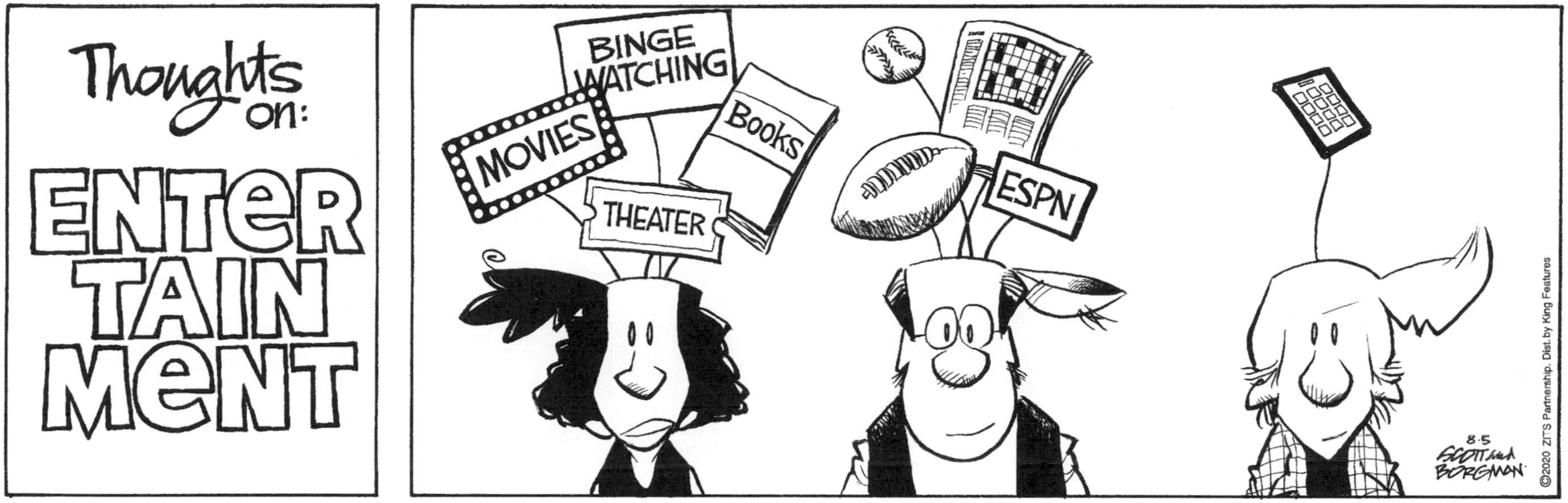

Thoughts on:
ENTERTAINMENT
BINGE WATCHING
MOVIES
THEATER
Books
ESPN
8·5
SCOTT and BORGMAN
©2020 ZITS Partnership. Dist. by King Features

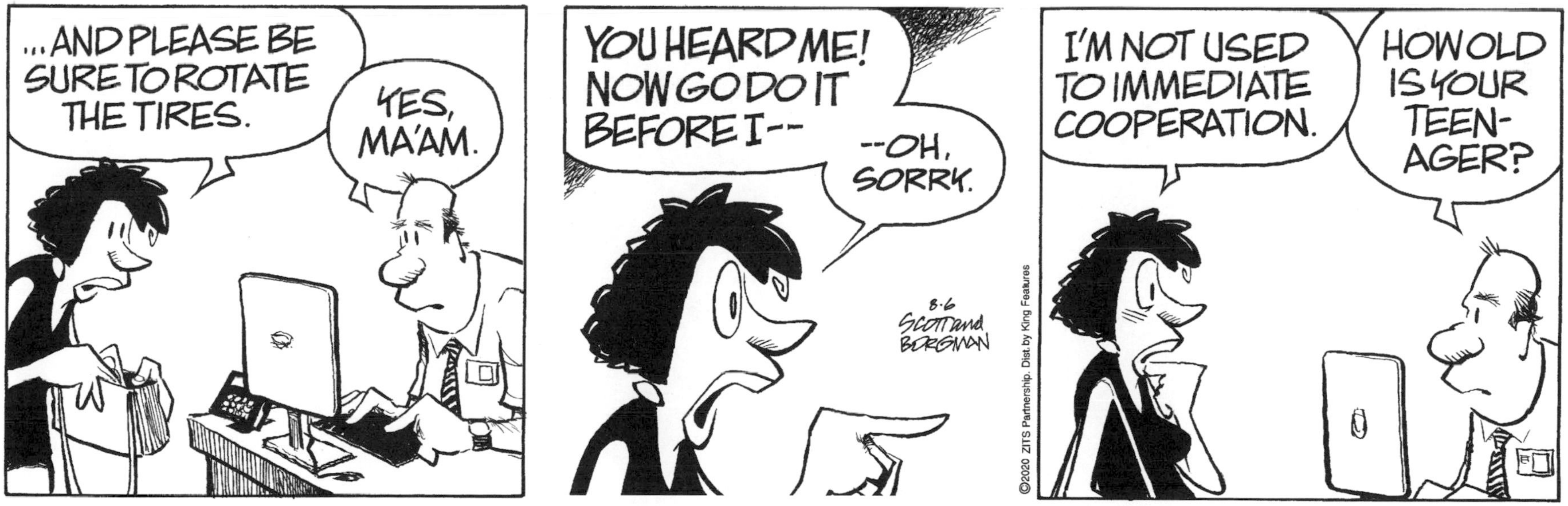

...AND PLEASE BE SURE TO ROTATE THE TIRES.
YES, MA'AM.
YOU HEARD ME! NOW GO DO IT BEFORE I--
--OH, SORRY.
8·6
SCOTT and BORGMAN
©2020 ZITS Partnership. Dist. by King Features
I'M NOT USED TO IMMEDIATE COOPERATION.
HOW OLD IS YOUR TEEN-AGER?

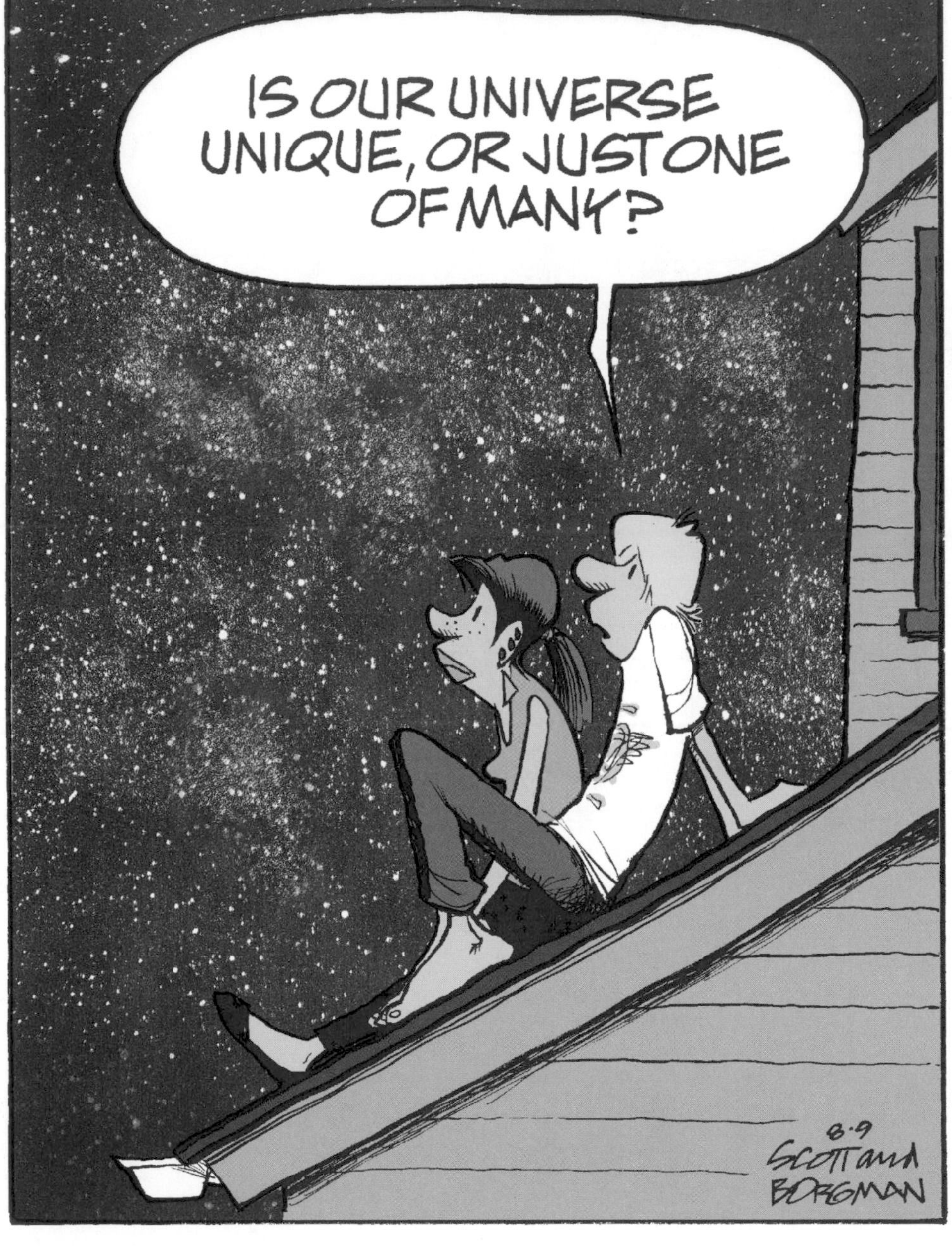
IS OUR UNIVERSE UNIQUE, OR JUST ONE OF MANY?
8·9
SCOTT and BORGMAN

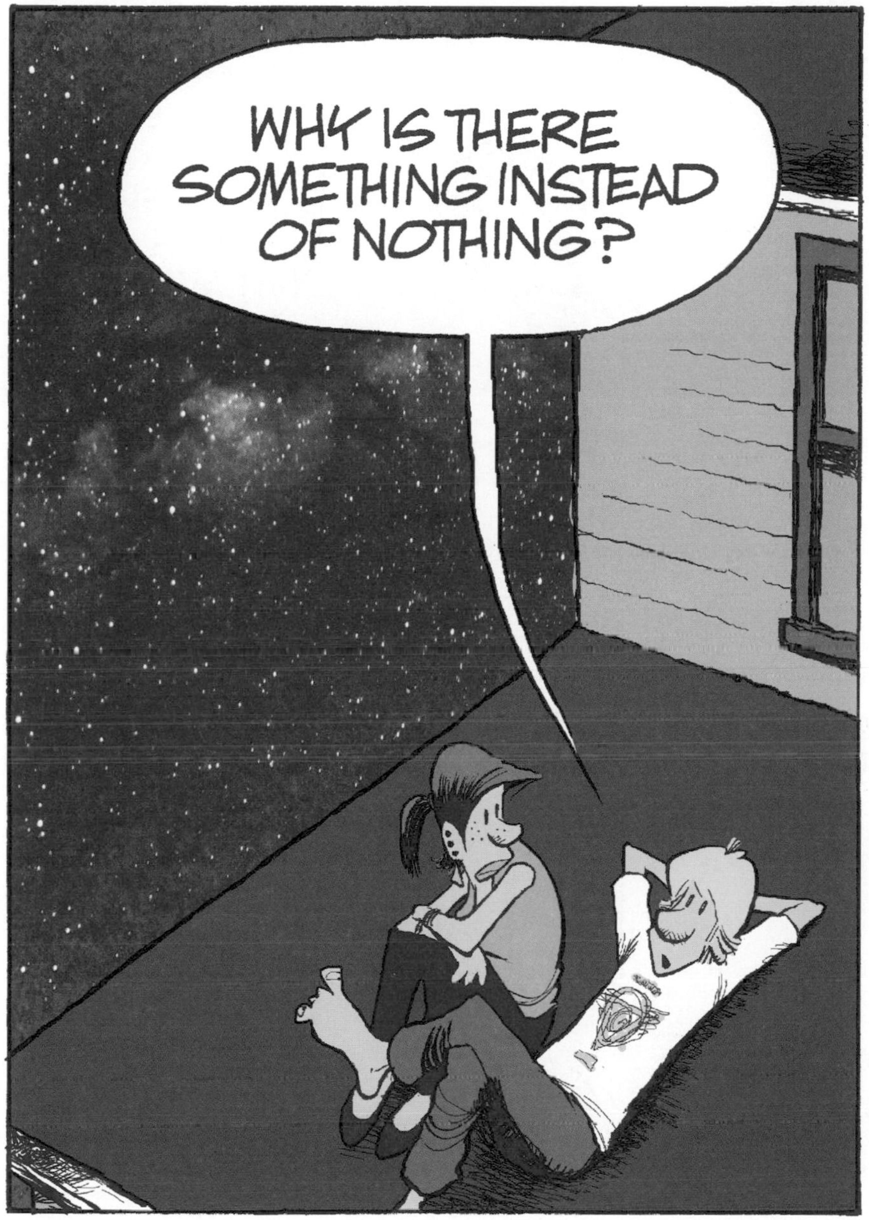
WHY IS THERE SOMETHING INSTEAD OF NOTHING?

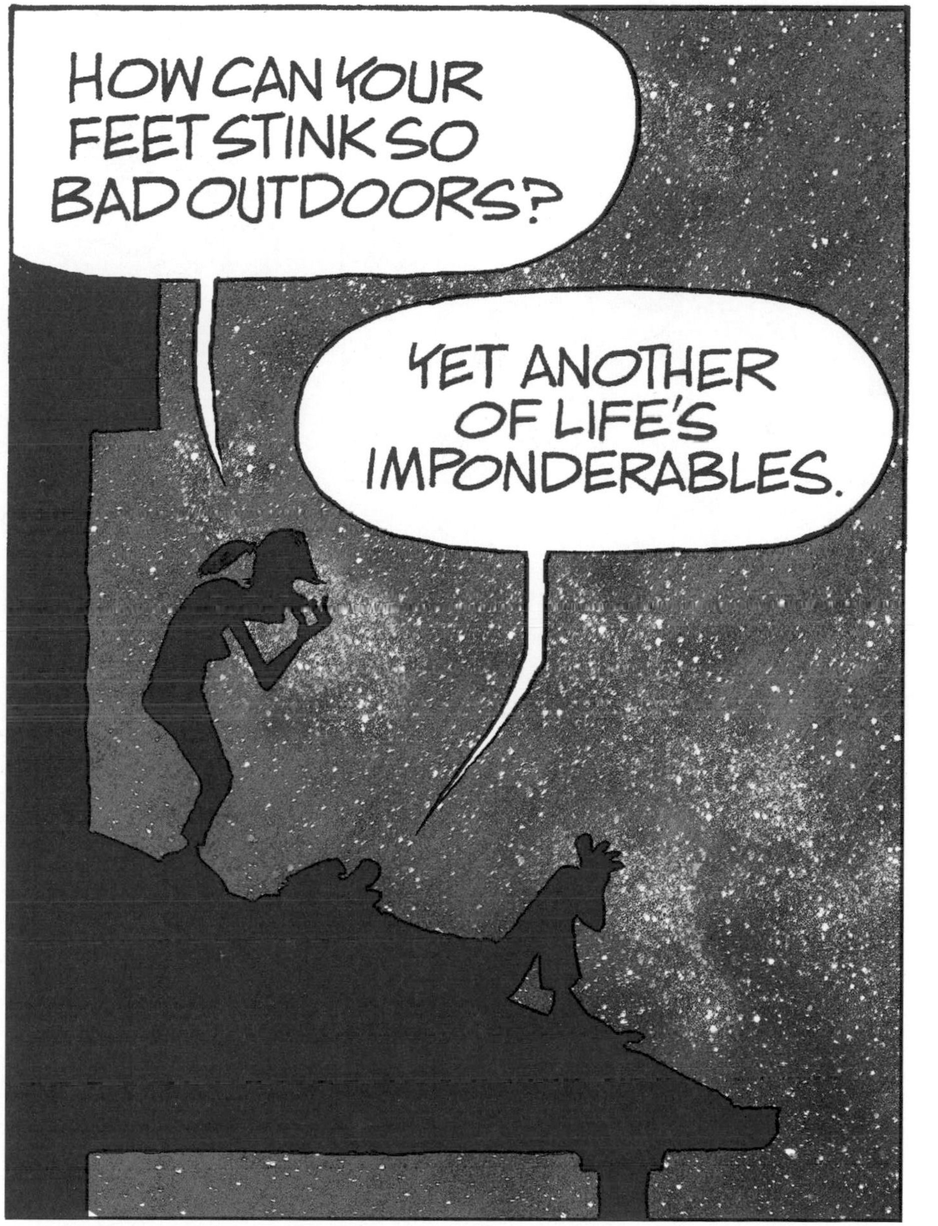
HOW CAN YOUR FEET STINK SO BAD OUTDOORS?
YET ANOTHER OF LIFE'S IMPONDERABLES.

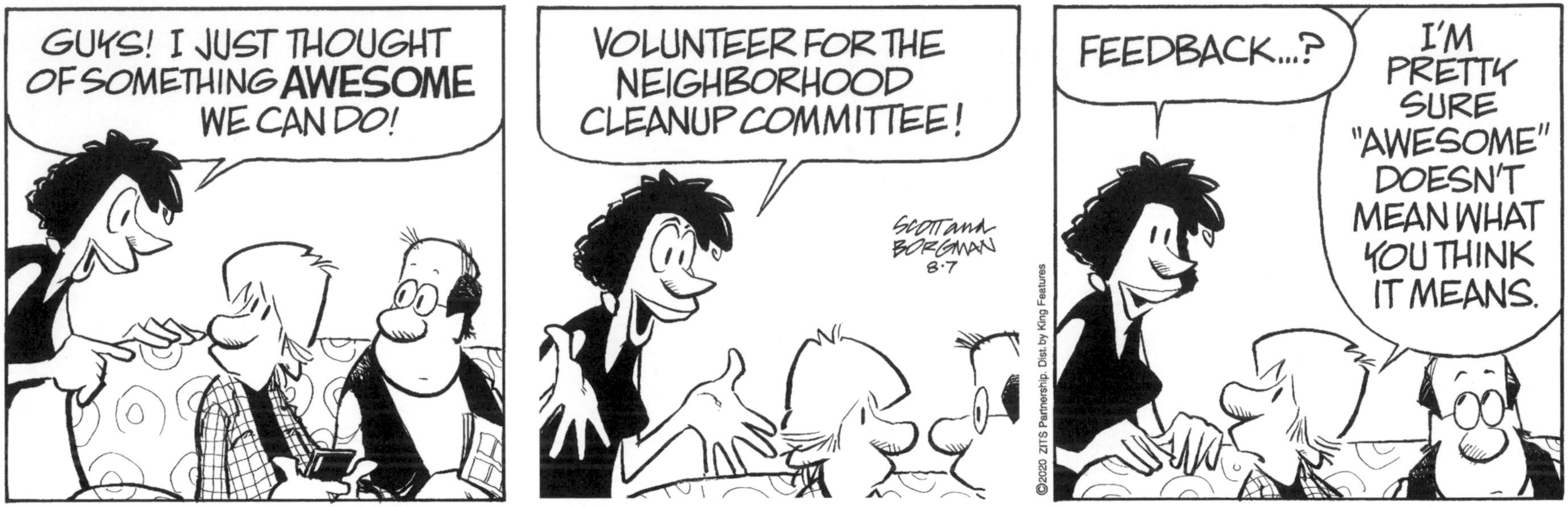
GUYS! I JUST THOUGHT OF SOMETHING **AWESOME** WE CAN DO!
VOLUNTEER FOR THE NEIGHBORHOOD CLEANUP COMMITTEE!
SCOTT and BORGMAN 8·7
©2020 ZITS Partnership. Dist. by King Features
FEEDBACK...?
I'M PRETTY SURE "AWESOME" DOESN'T MEAN WHAT YOU THINK IT MEANS.

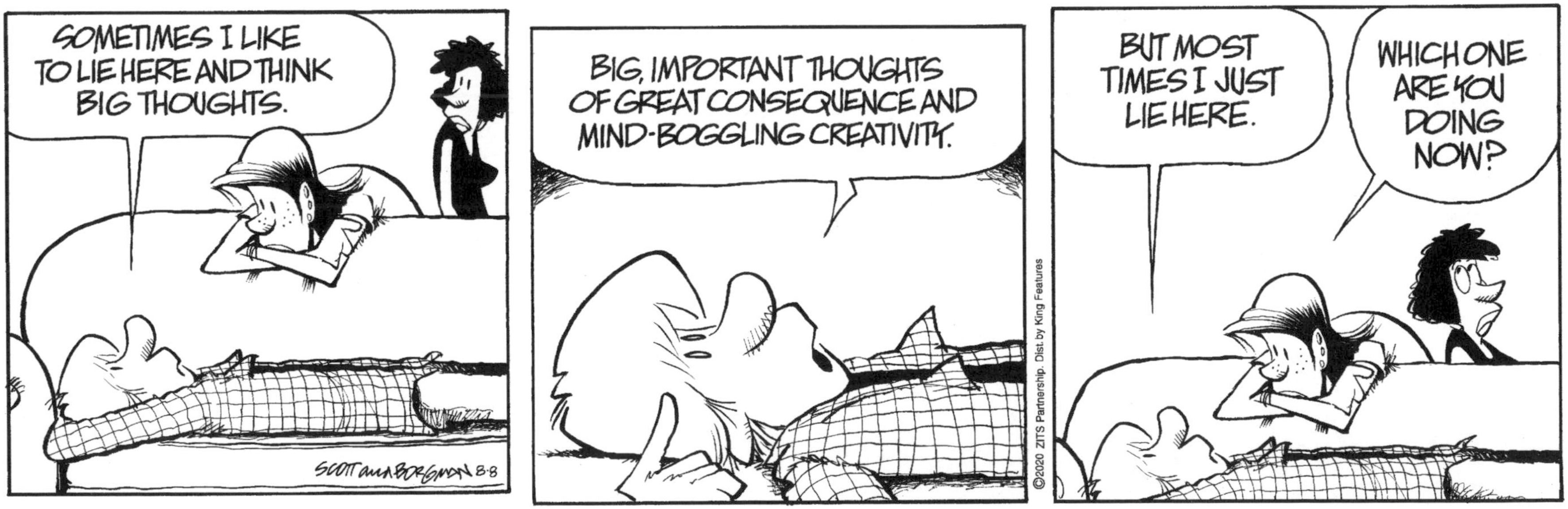
SOMETIMES I LIKE TO LIE HERE AND THINK BIG THOUGHTS.
SCOTT and BORGMAN 8·8
BIG, IMPORTANT THOUGHTS OF GREAT CONSEQUENCE AND MIND-BOGGLING CREATIVITY.
©2020 ZITS Partnership. Dist. by King Features
BUT MOST TIMES I JUST LIE HERE.
WHICH ONE ARE YOU DOING NOW?

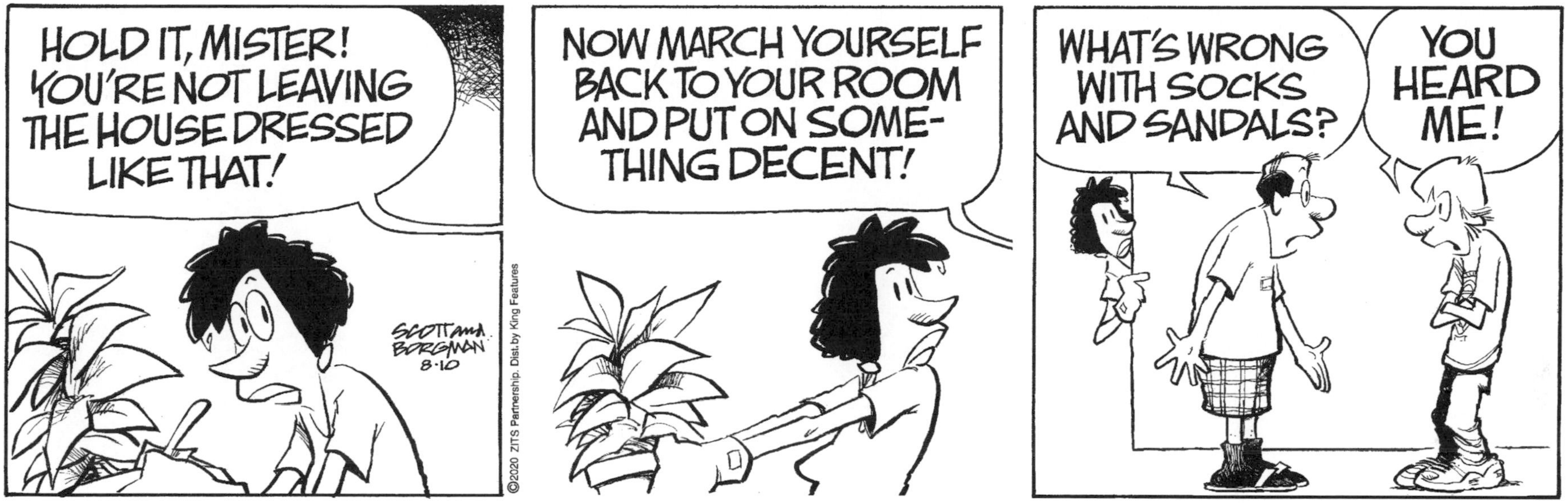
HOLD IT, MISTER! YOU'RE NOT LEAVING THE HOUSE DRESSED LIKE THAT!
SCOTT AND BORGMAN 8-10
©2020 ZITS Partnership. Dist. by King Features
NOW MARCH YOURSELF BACK TO YOUR ROOM AND PUT ON SOMETHING DECENT!
WHAT'S WRONG WITH SOCKS AND SANDALS?
YOU HEARD ME!

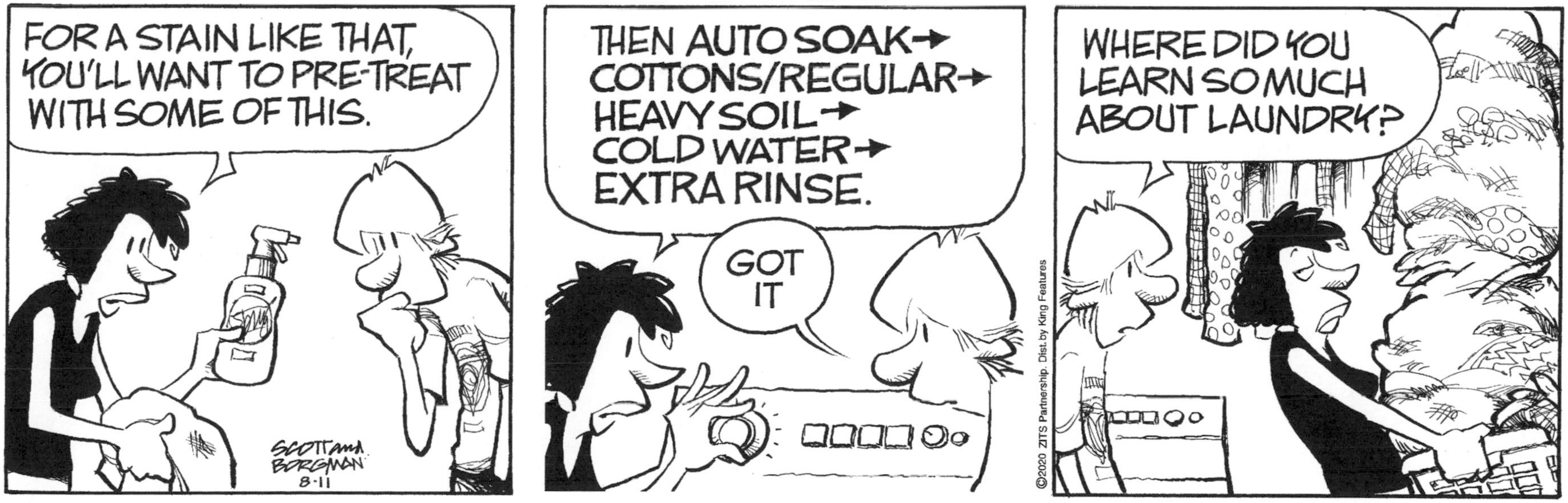
FOR A STAIN LIKE THAT, YOU'LL WANT TO PRE-TREAT WITH SOME OF THIS.
SCOTT AND BORGMAN 8-11
THEN AUTO SOAK→ COTTONS/REGULAR→ HEAVY SOIL→ COLD WATER→ EXTRA RINSE.
GOT IT
©2020 ZITS Partnership. Dist. by King Features
WHERE DID YOU LEARN SO MUCH ABOUT LAUNDRY?

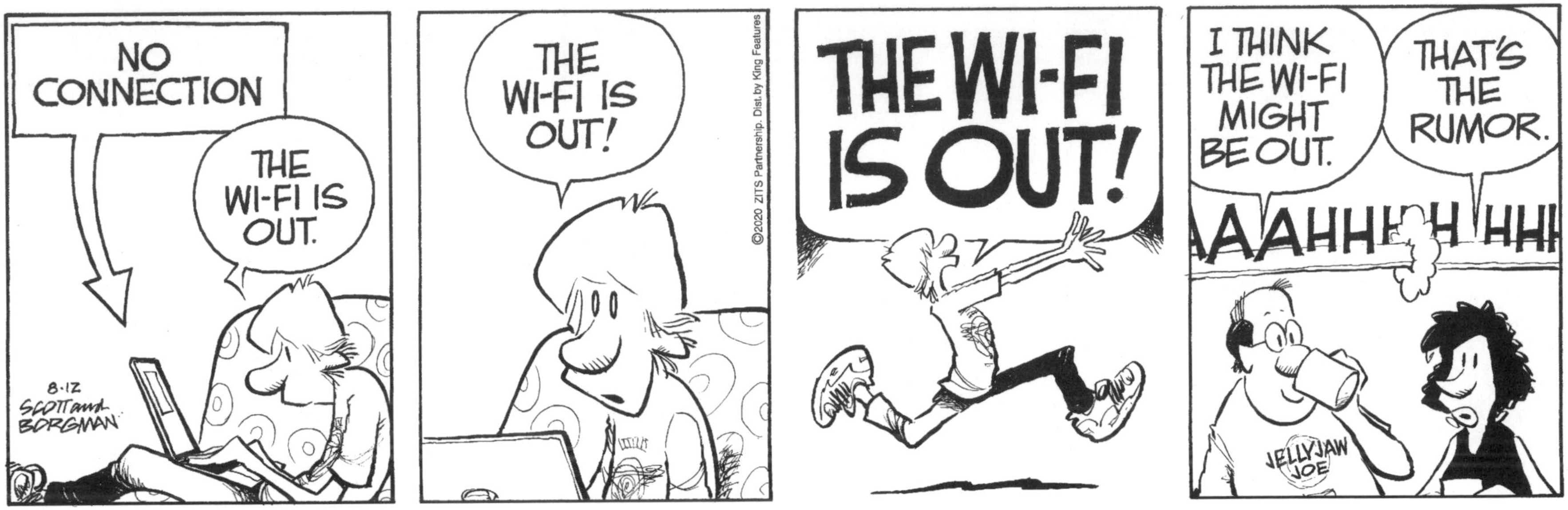
NO CONNECTION
THE WI-FI IS OUT.
8·12 SCOTT and BORGMAN
THE WI-FI IS OUT!
©2020 ZITS Partnership. Dist. by King Features
THE WI-FI IS OUT!
I THINK THE WI-FI MIGHT BE OUT.
THAT'S THE RUMOR.
JELLY JAW JOE

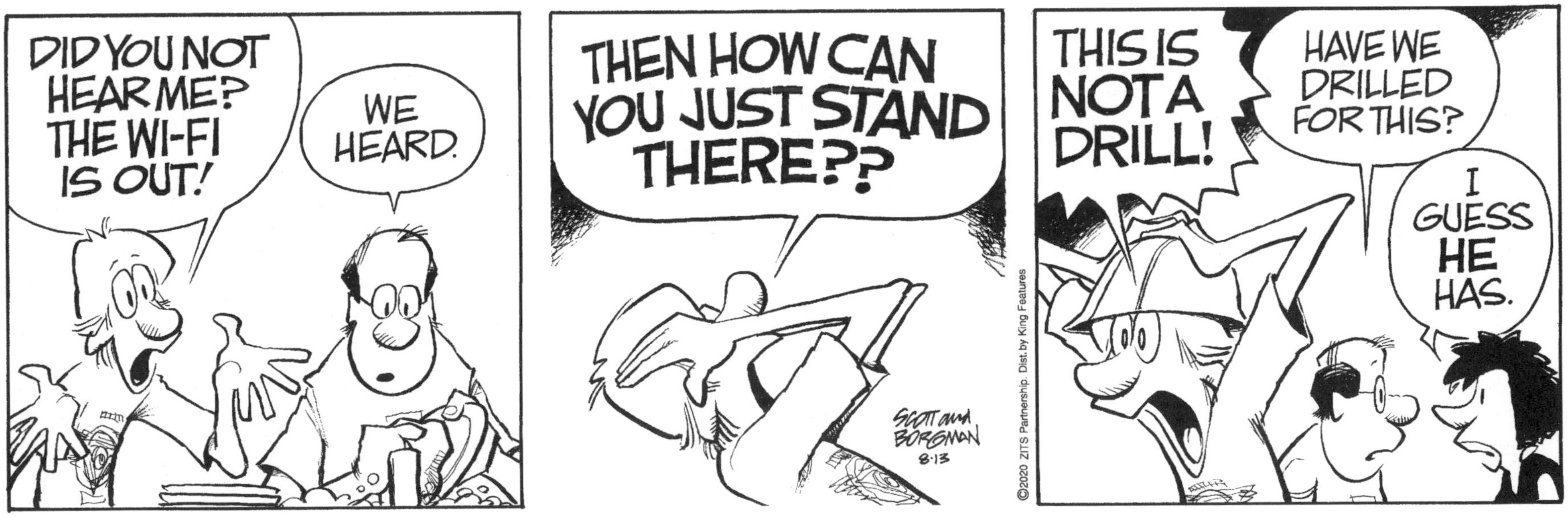
DID YOU NOT HEAR ME? THE WI-FI IS OUT!
WE HEARD.
THEN HOW CAN YOU JUST STAND THERE??
SCOTT and BORGMAN 8·13
©2020 ZITS Partnership. Dist. by King Features
THIS IS NOT A DRILL!
HAVE WE DRILLED FOR THIS?
I GUESS HE HAS.

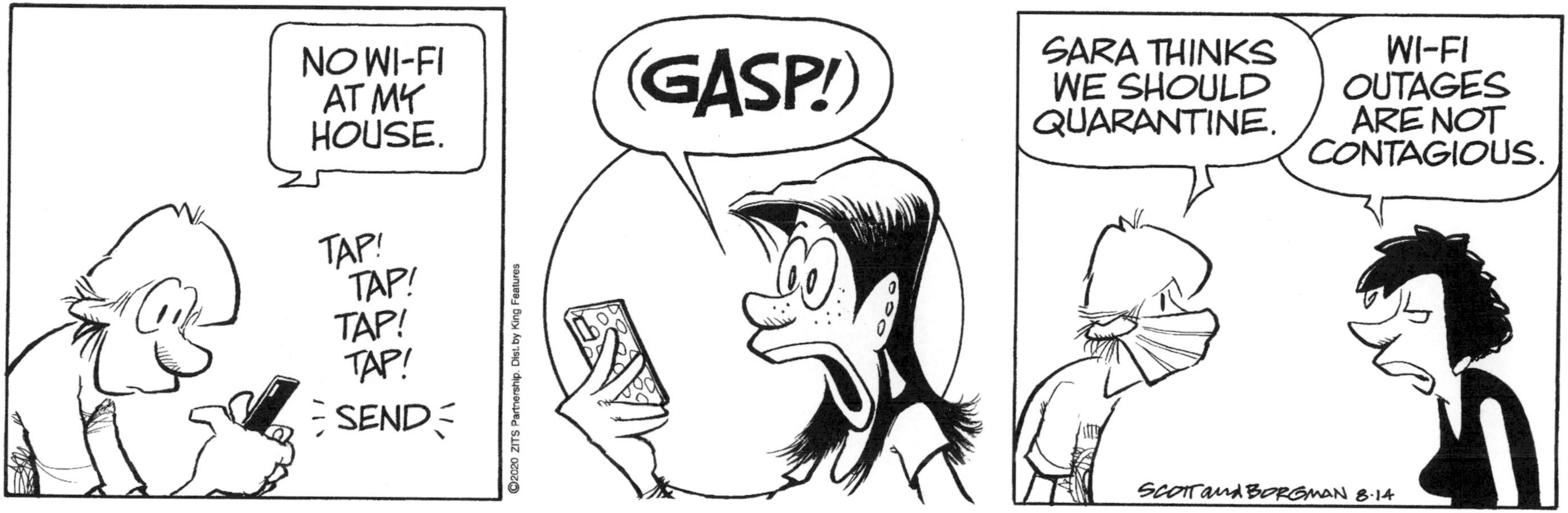
NO WI-FI AT MY HOUSE.
TAP! TAP! TAP! TAP!
SEND
©2020 ZITS Partnership. Dist. by King Features
(GASP!)
SARA THINKS WE SHOULD QUARANTINE.
WI-FI OUTAGES ARE NOT CONTAGIOUS.
SCOTT and BORGMAN 8·14

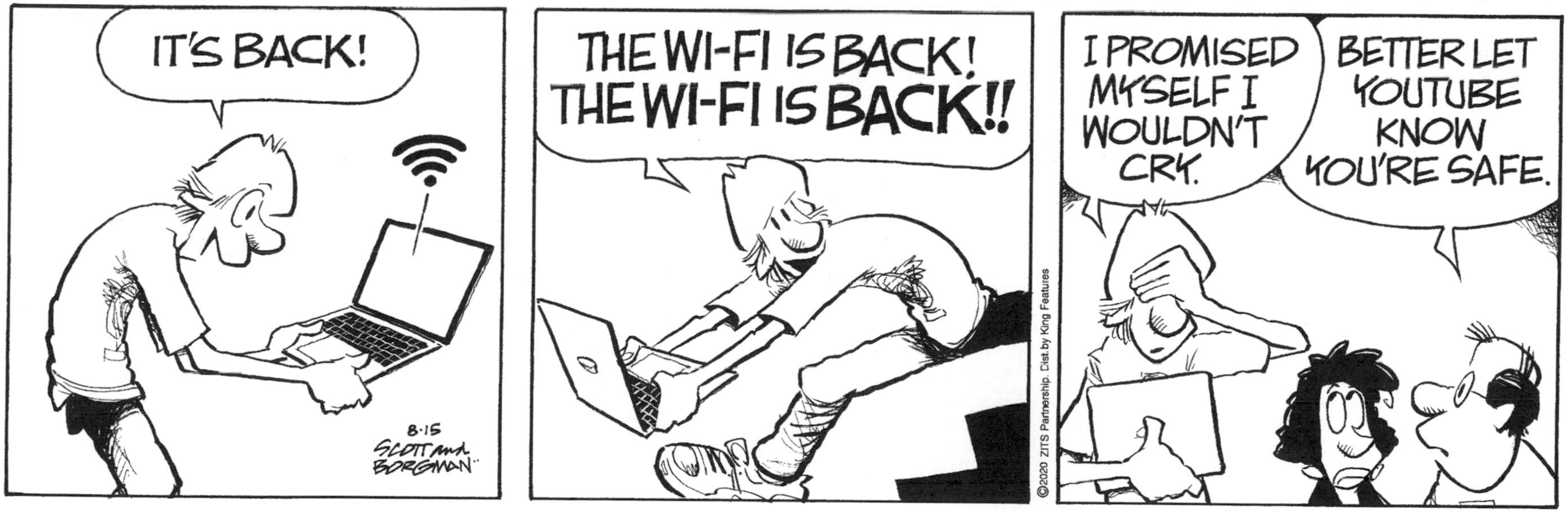
IT'S BACK!
8·15 SCOTT and BORGMAN
THE WI-FI IS BACK! THE WI-FI IS BACK!!
©2020 ZITS Partnership. Dist. by King Features
I PROMISED MYSELF I WOULDN'T CRY.
BETTER LET YOUTUBE KNOW YOU'RE SAFE.

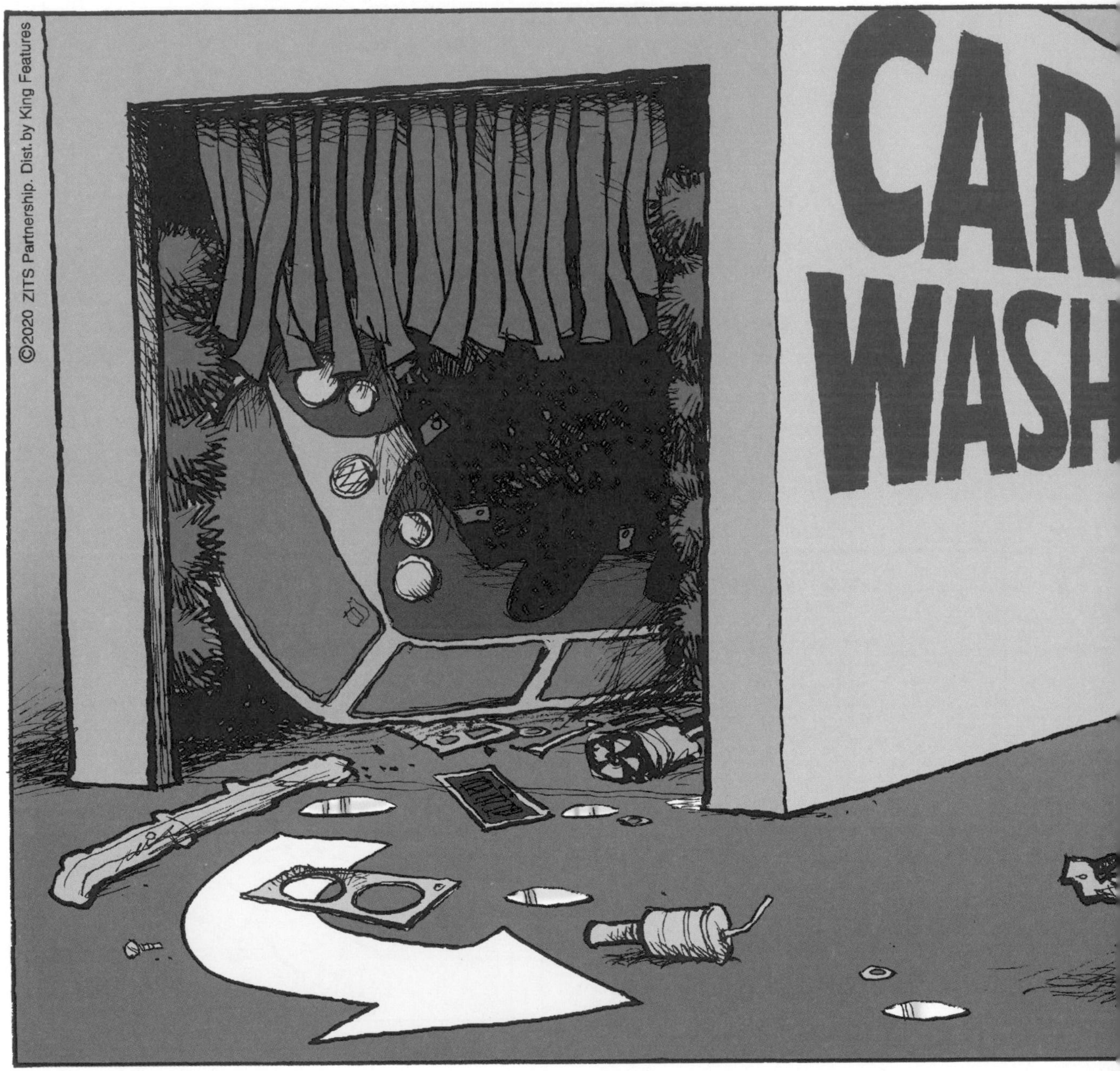
©2020 ZITS Partnership. Dist. by King Features
CAR
WASH

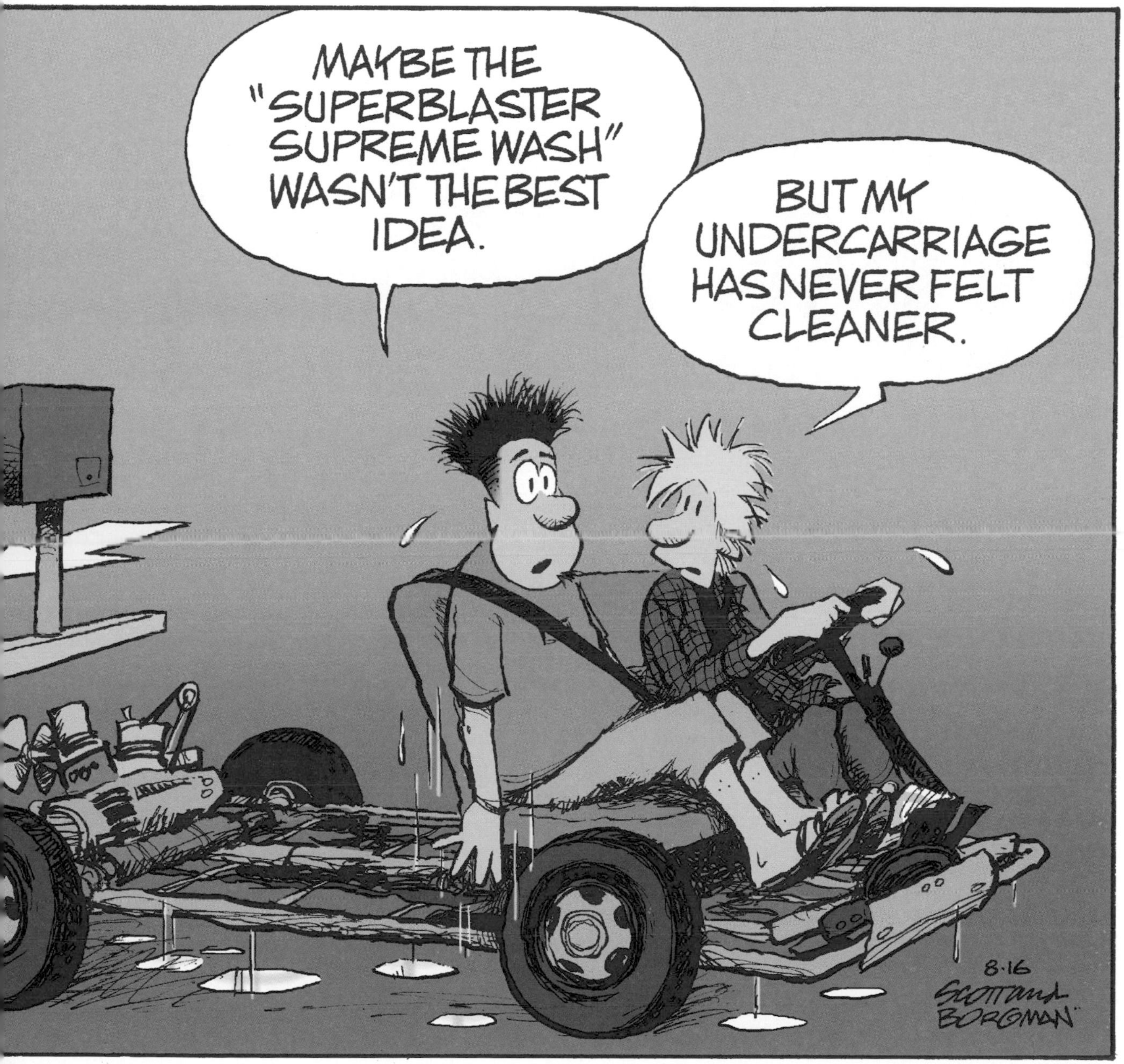
MAYBE THE "SUPERBLASTER SUPREME WASH" WASN'T THE BEST IDEA.
BUT MY UNDERCARRIAGE HAS NEVER FELT CLEANER.
8·16
SCOTT and BORGMAN

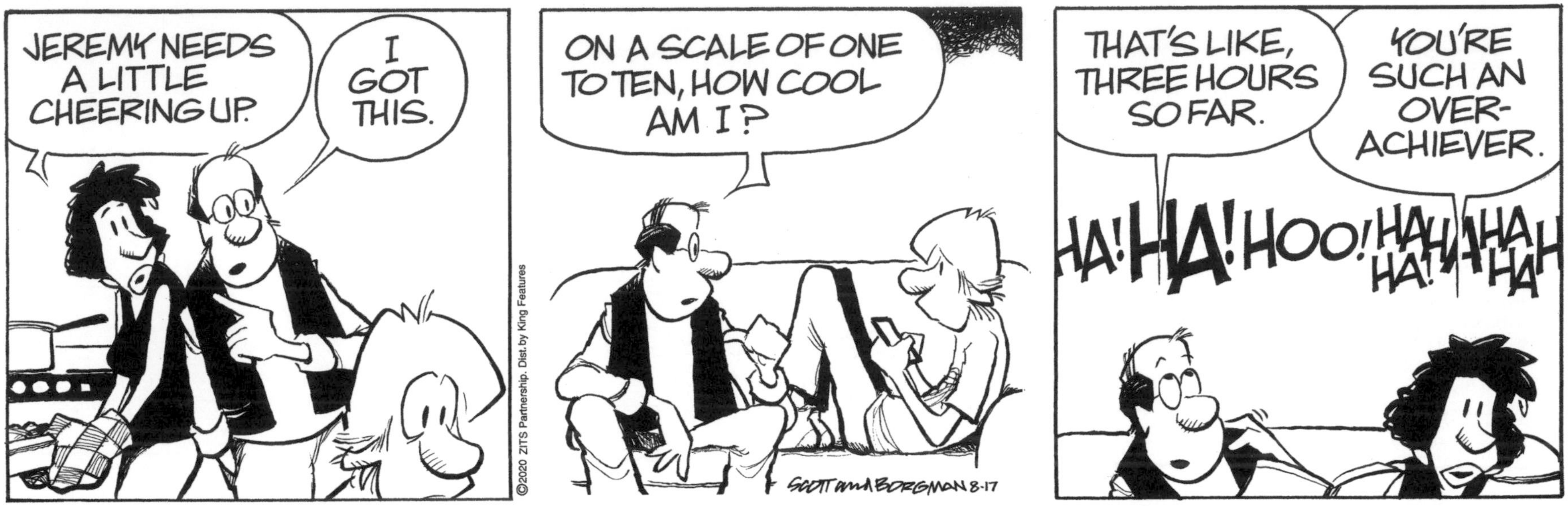
JEREMY NEEDS A LITTLE CHEERING UP.
I GOT THIS.
©2020 ZITS Partnership. Dist. by King Features
ON A SCALE OF ONE TO TEN, HOW COOL AM I?
SCOTT and BORGMAN 8-17
THAT'S LIKE, THREE HOURS SO FAR.
YOU'RE SUCH AN OVER-ACHIEVER.
HA! HA! HOO! HA HA HA!

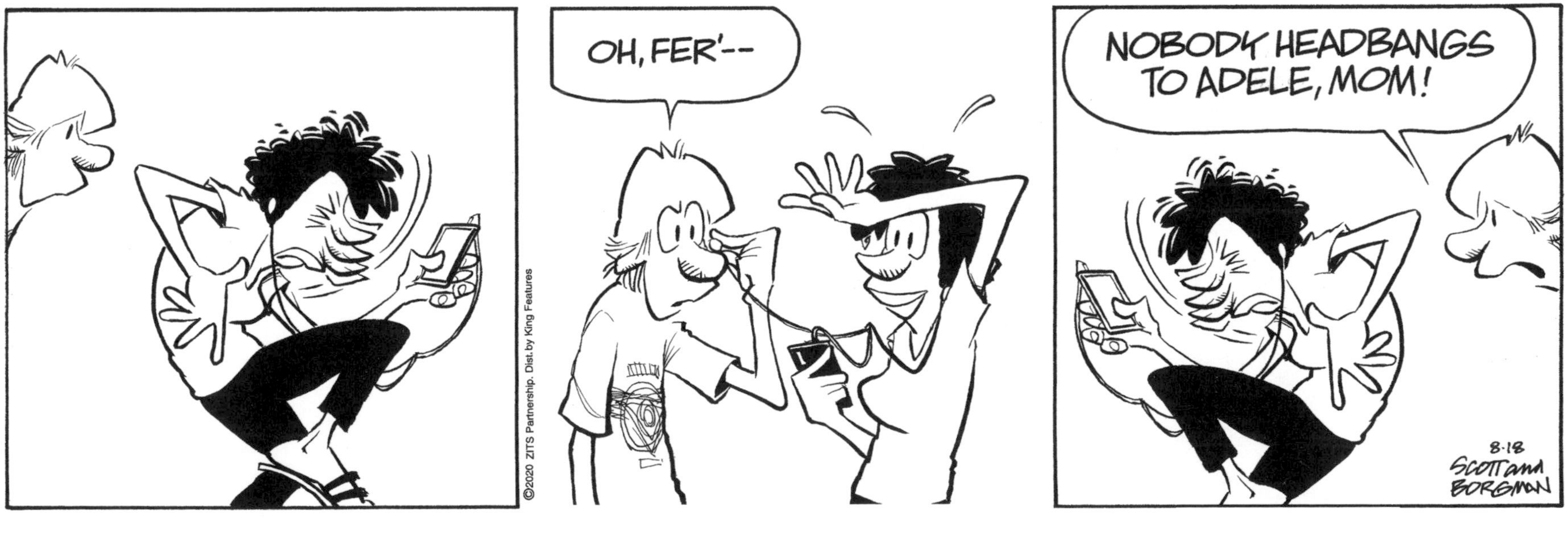
©2020 ZITS Partnership. Dist. by King Features
OH, FER'--
NOBODY HEADBANGS TO ADELE, MOM!
8-18 SCOTT and BORGMAN

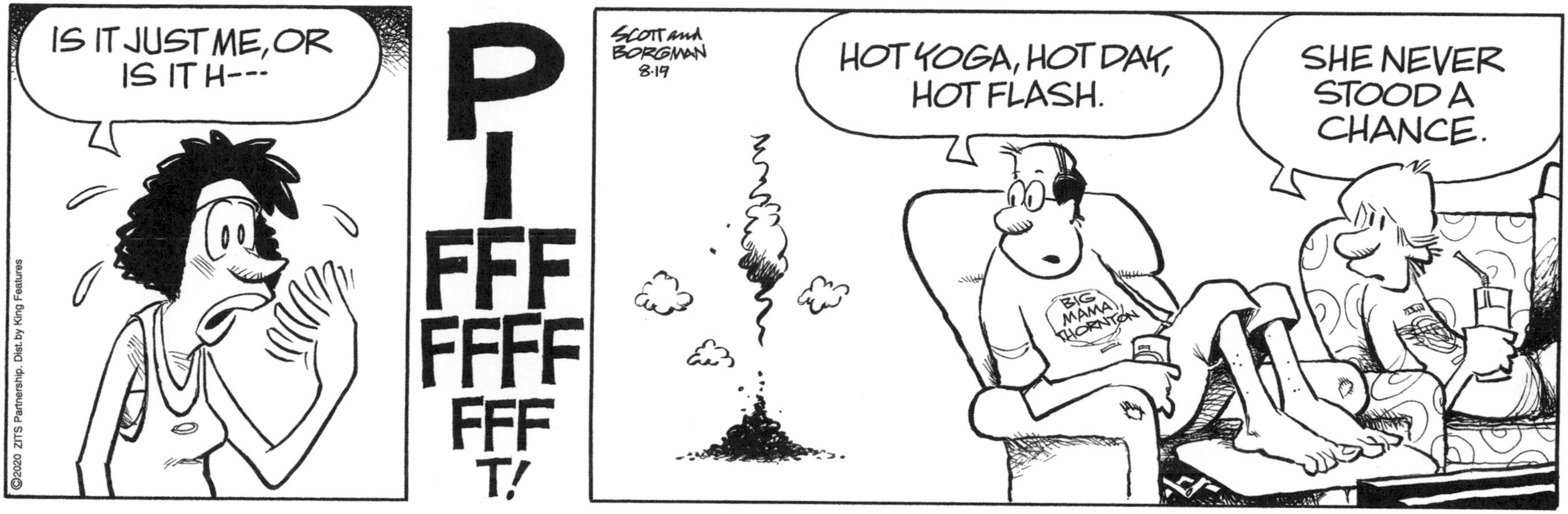
IS IT JUST ME, OR IS IT H---
©2020 ZITS Partnership. Dist. by King Features
P I FFF FFFF FFF T!
SCOTT AND BORGMAN 8-19
HOT YOGA, HOT DAY, HOT FLASH.
BIG MAMA THORNTON
SHE NEVER STOOD A CHANCE.

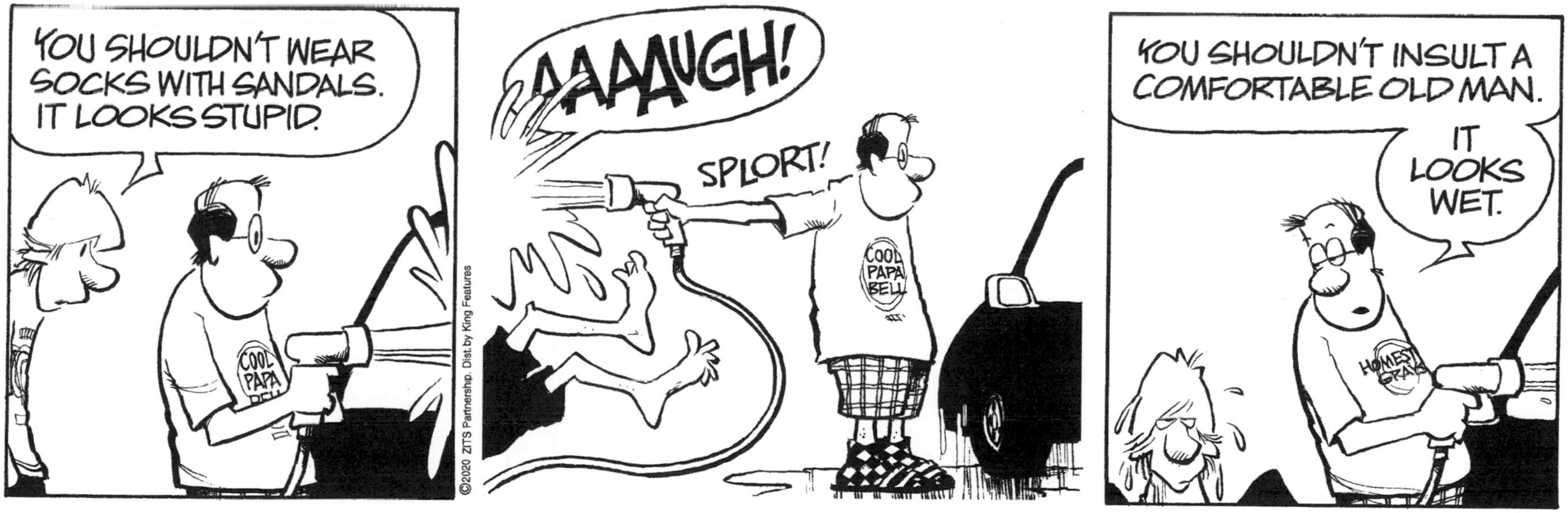
YOU SHOULDN'T WEAR SOCKS WITH SANDALS. IT LOOKS STUPID.
COOL PAPA BELL
©2020 ZITS Partnership. Dist. by King Features
AAAAUGH!
SPLORT!
COOL PAPA BELL
YOU SHOULDN'T INSULT A COMFORTABLE OLD MAN.
IT LOOKS WET.

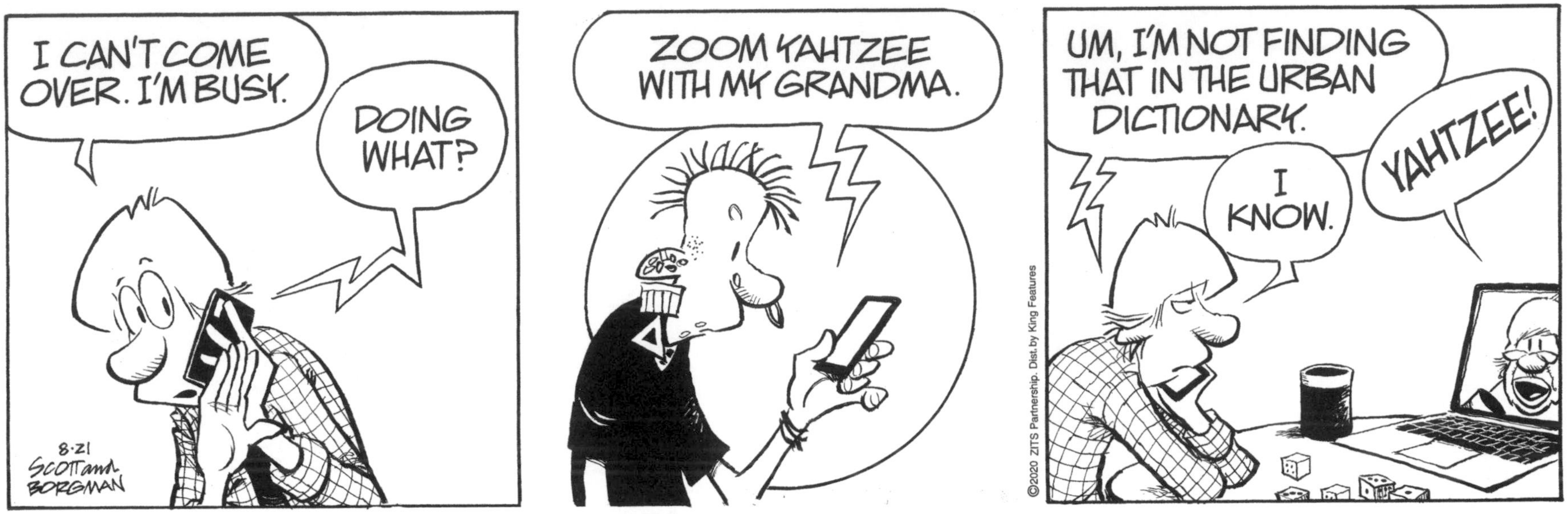
I CAN'T COME OVER. I'M BUSY.
DOING WHAT?
8·21 SCOTT and BORGMAN
ZOOM YAHTZEE WITH MY GRANDMA.
UM, I'M NOT FINDING THAT IN THE URBAN DICTIONARY.
I KNOW.
YAHTZEE!
©2020 ZITS Partnership. Dist. by King Features

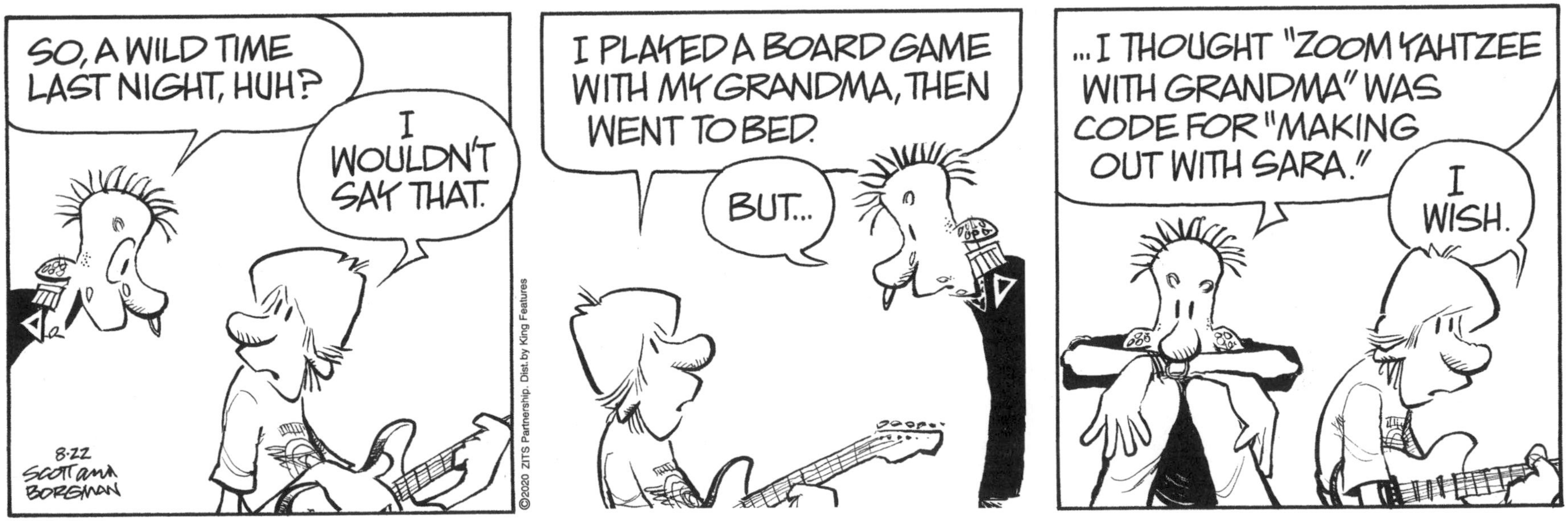
SO, A WILD TIME LAST NIGHT, HUH?
I WOULDN'T SAY THAT.
8·22 SCOTT and BORGMAN
©2020 ZITS Partnership. Dist. by King Features
I PLAYED A BOARD GAME WITH MY GRANDMA, THEN WENT TO BED.
BUT...
...I THOUGHT "ZOOM YAHTZEE WITH GRANDMA" WAS CODE FOR "MAKING OUT WITH SARA."
I WISH.

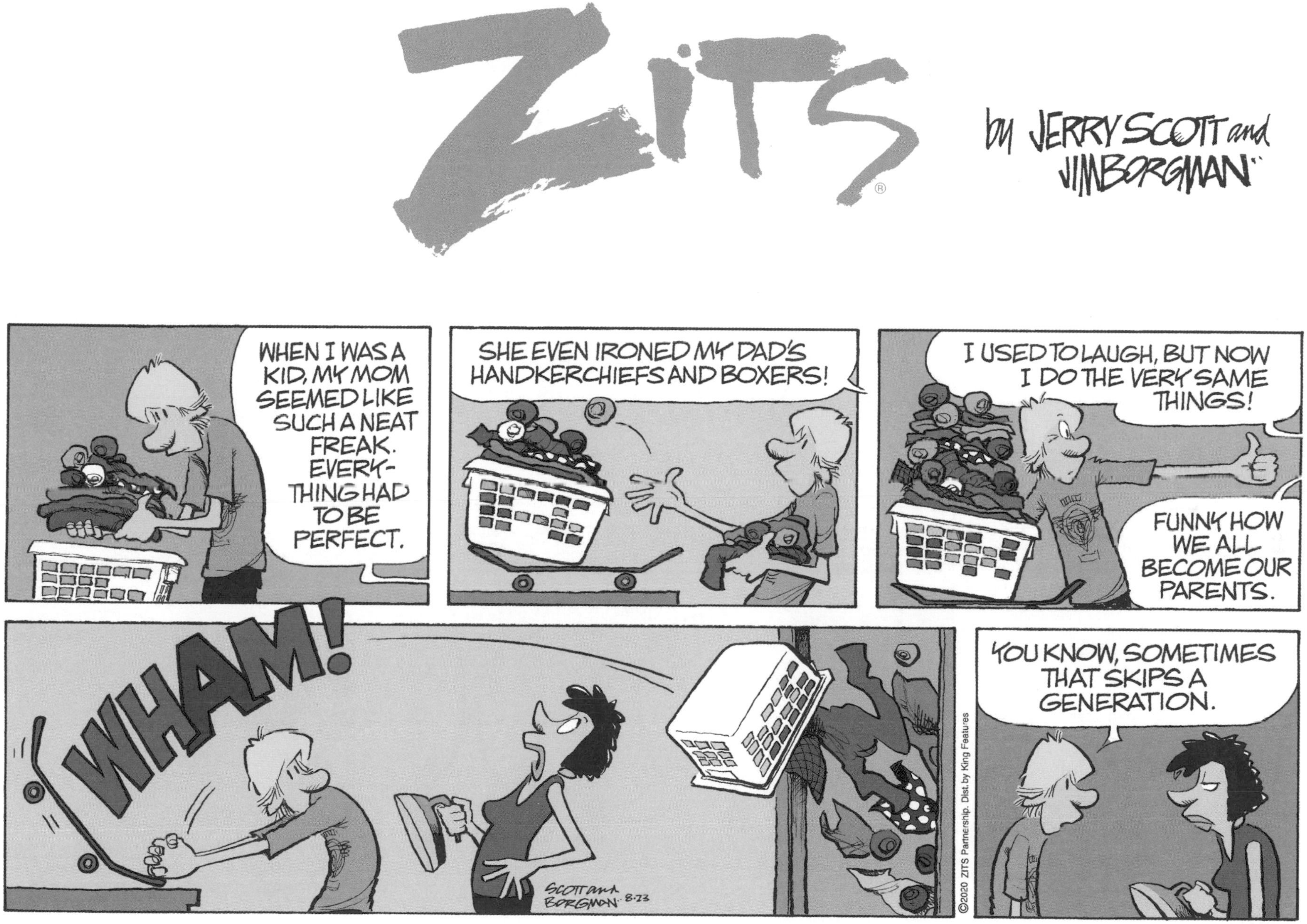
ZITS®
by JERRY SCOTT and JIM BORGMAN
WHEN I WAS A KID, MY MOM SEEMED LIKE SUCH A NEAT FREAK. EVERY-THING HAD TO BE PERFECT.
SHE EVEN IRONED MY DAD'S HANDKERCHIEFS AND BOXERS!
I USED TO LAUGH, BUT NOW I DO THE VERY SAME THINGS!
FUNNY HOW WE ALL BECOME OUR PARENTS.
WHAM!
SCOTT and BORGMAN 8-23
©2020 ZITS Partnership. Dist. by King Features
YOU KNOW, SOMETIMES THAT SKIPS A GENERATION.

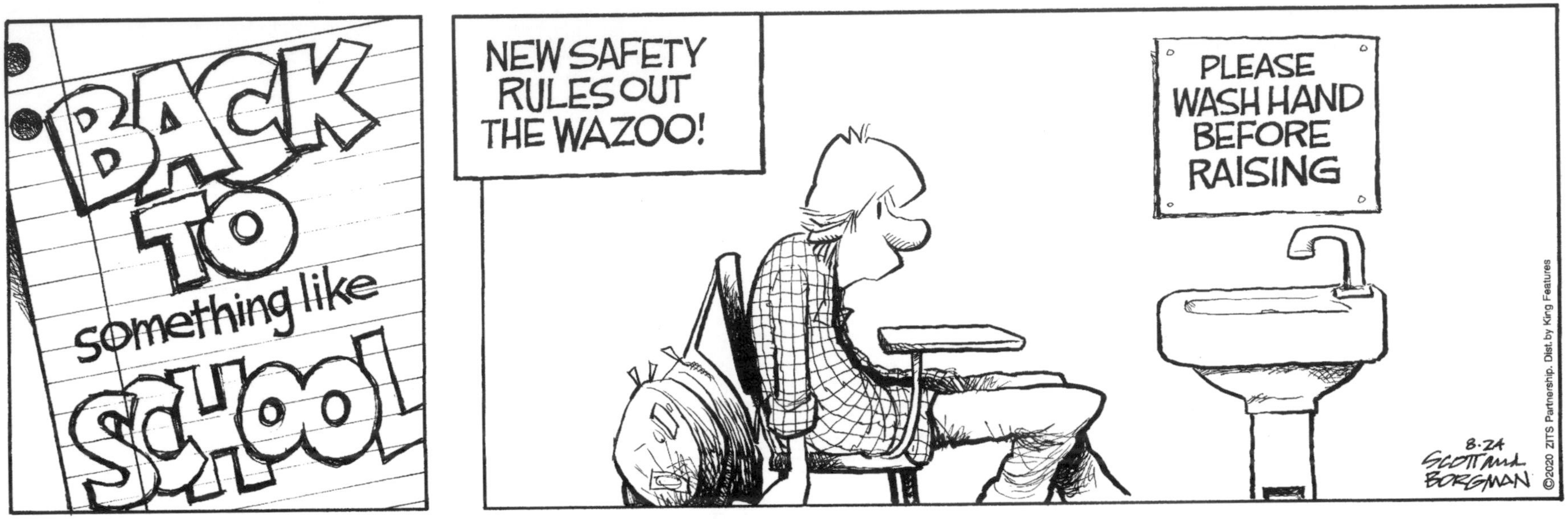
BACK TO something like SCHOOL
NEW SAFETY RULES OUT THE WAZOO!
PLEASE WASH HAND BEFORE RAISING
8·24 SCOTT and BORGMAN
©2020 ZITS Partnership. Dist. by King Features

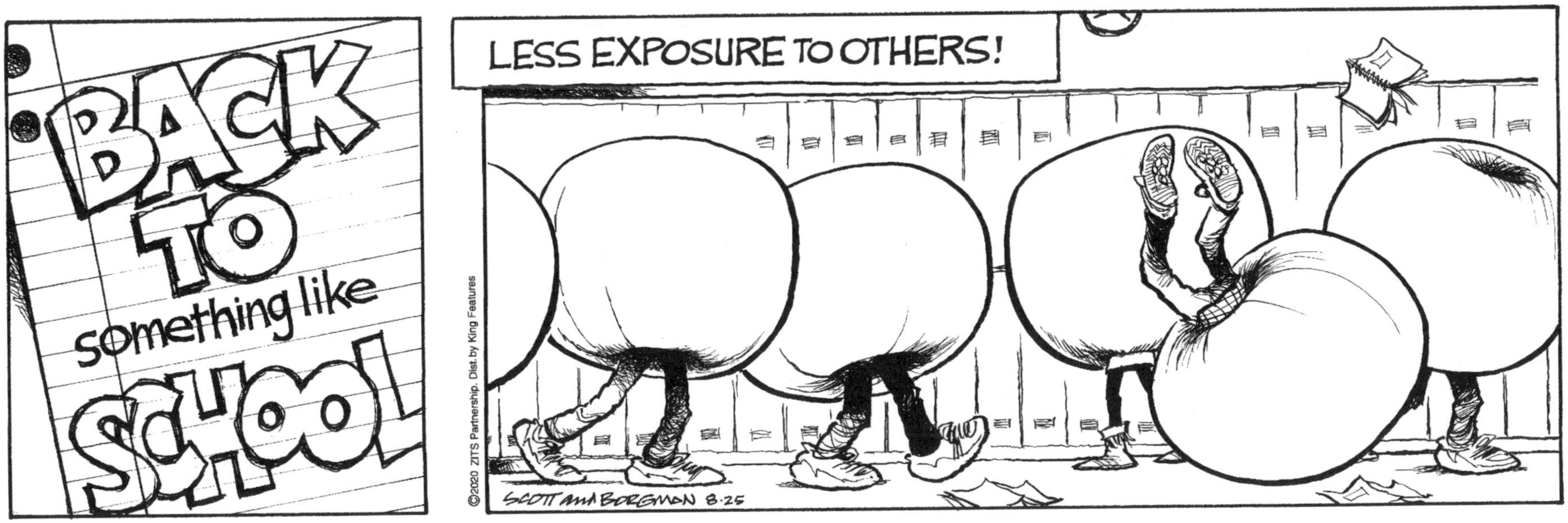
BACK TO something like SCHOOL
LESS EXPOSURE TO OTHERS!
©2020 ZITS Partnership. Dist. by King Features
SCOTT and BORGMAN 8·25

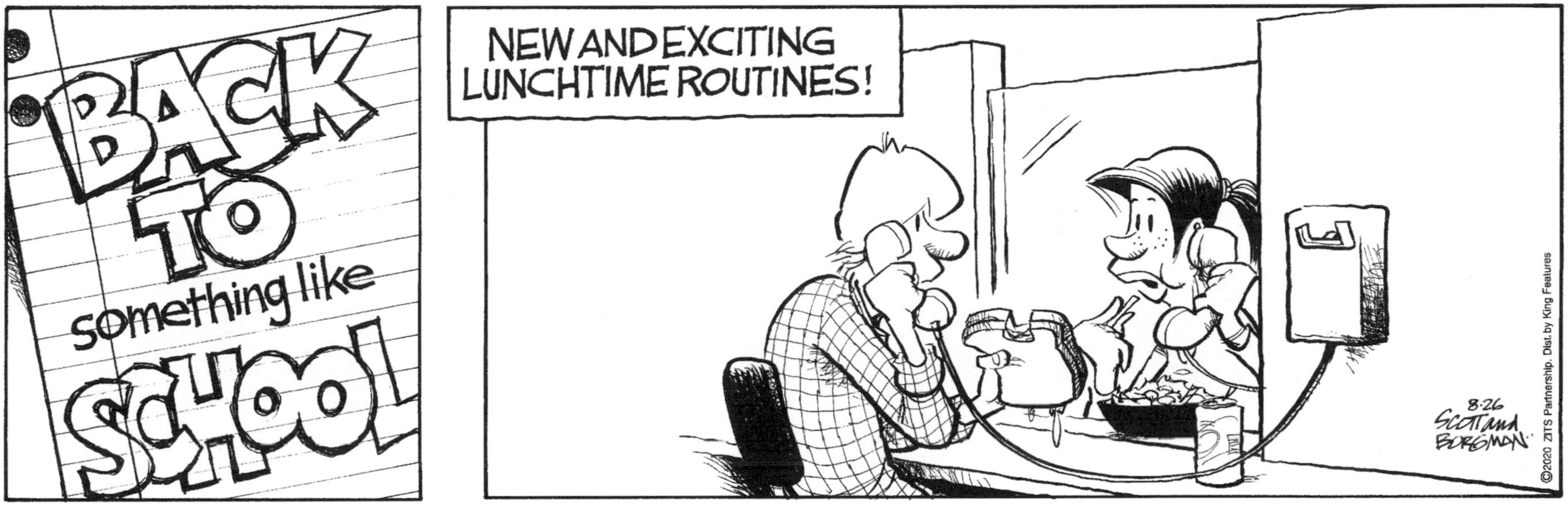
BACK TO something like SCHOOL
NEW AND EXCITING LUNCHTIME ROUTINES!
8·26 SCOTT and BORGMAN
©2020 ZITS Partnership. Dist. by King Features

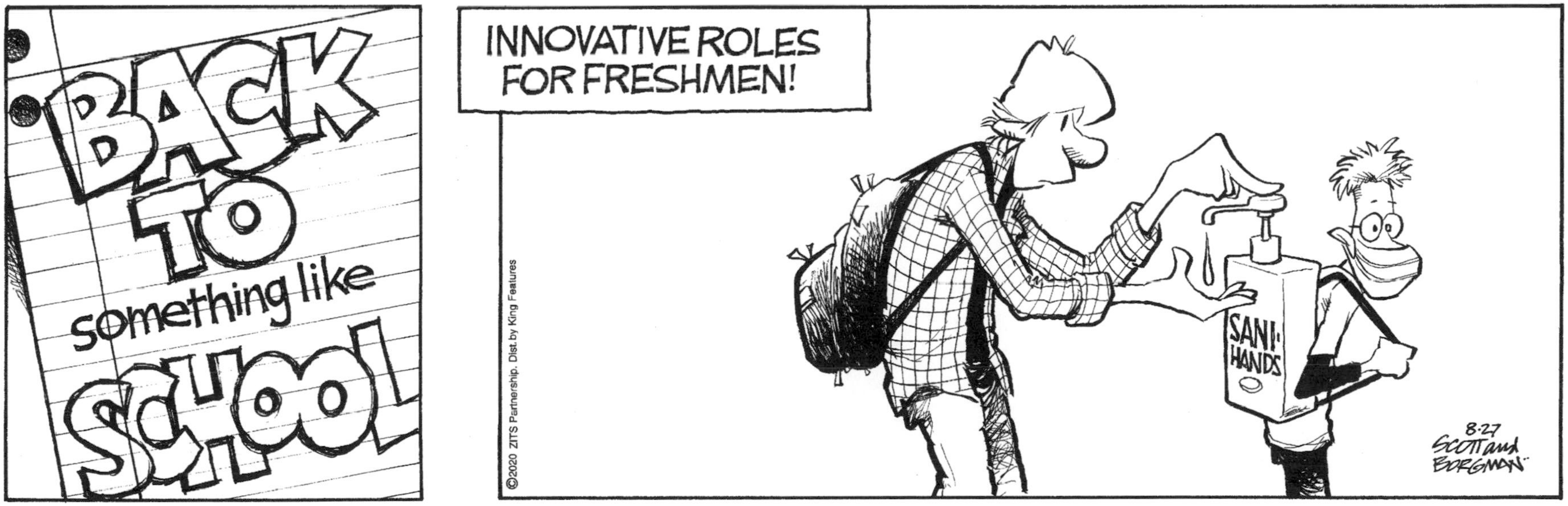
BACK TO something like SCHOOL
INNOVATIVE ROLES FOR FRESHMEN!
SANI-HANDS
8·27 SCOTT and BORGMAN
©2020 ZITS Partnership. Dist. by King Features

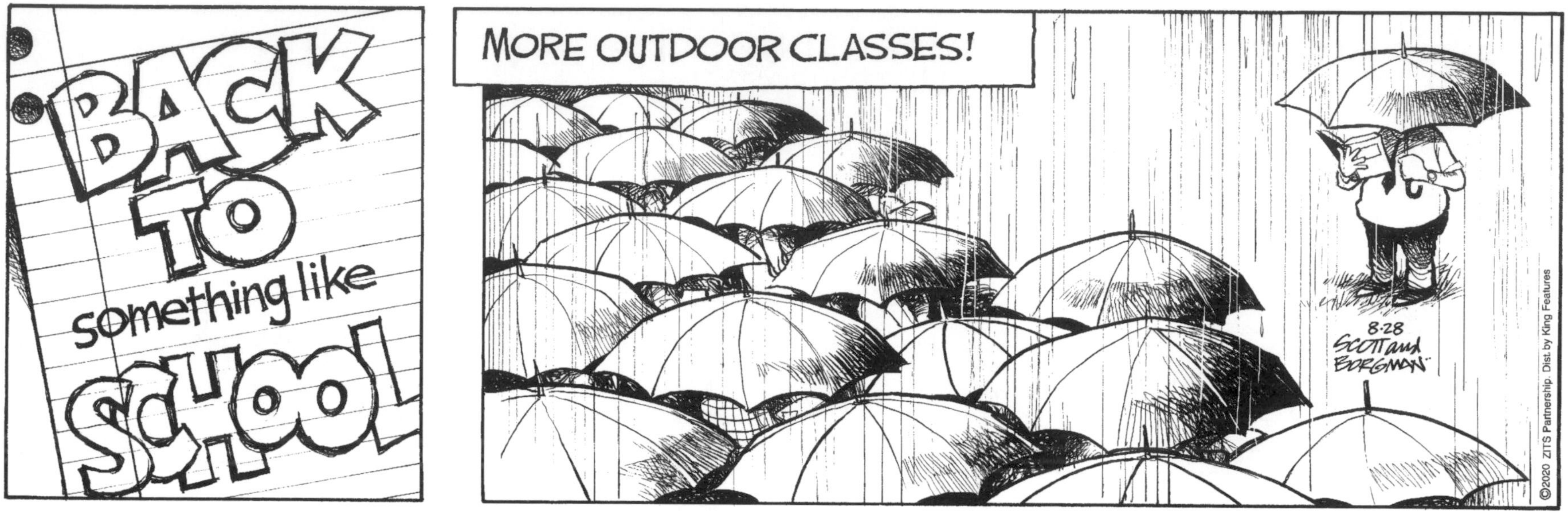
BACK TO something like SCHOOL
MORE OUTDOOR CLASSES!
8·28 SCOTT AND BORGMAN
©2020 ZITS Partnership. Dist. by King Features

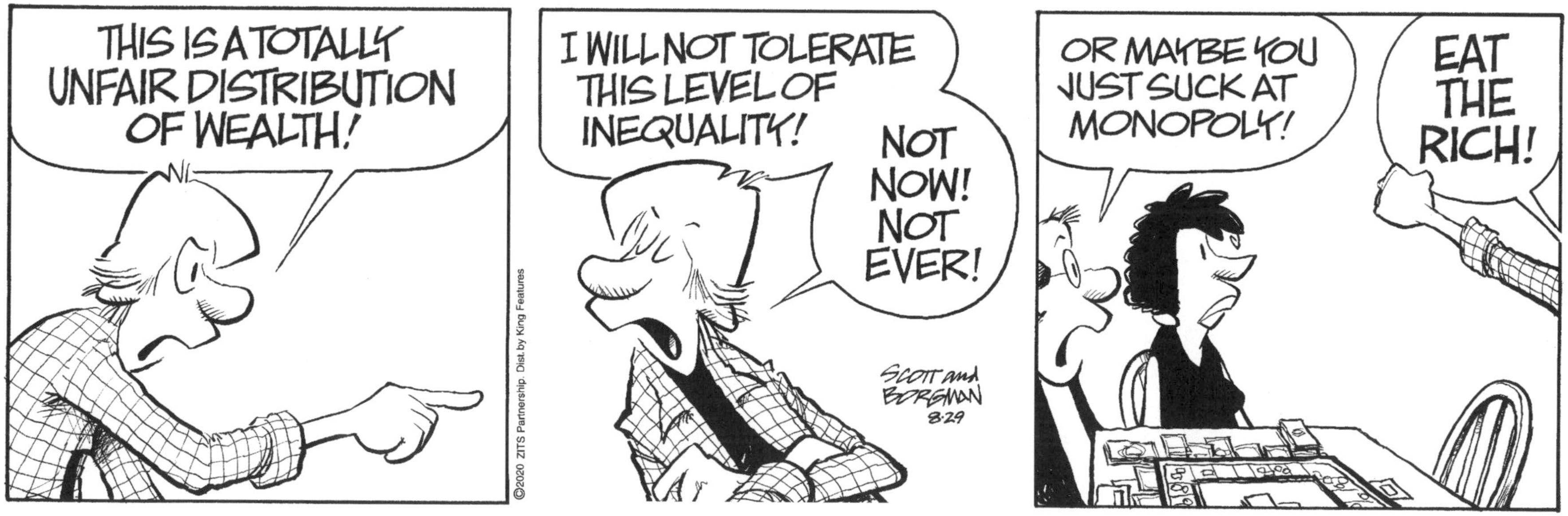
THIS IS A TOTALLY UNFAIR DISTRIBUTION OF WEALTH!
©2020 ZITS Partnership. Dist. by King Features
I WILL NOT TOLERATE THIS LEVEL OF INEQUALITY!
NOT NOW! NOT EVER!
SCOTT AND BORGMAN 8·29
OR MAYBE YOU JUST SUCK AT MONOPOLY!
EAT THE RICH!

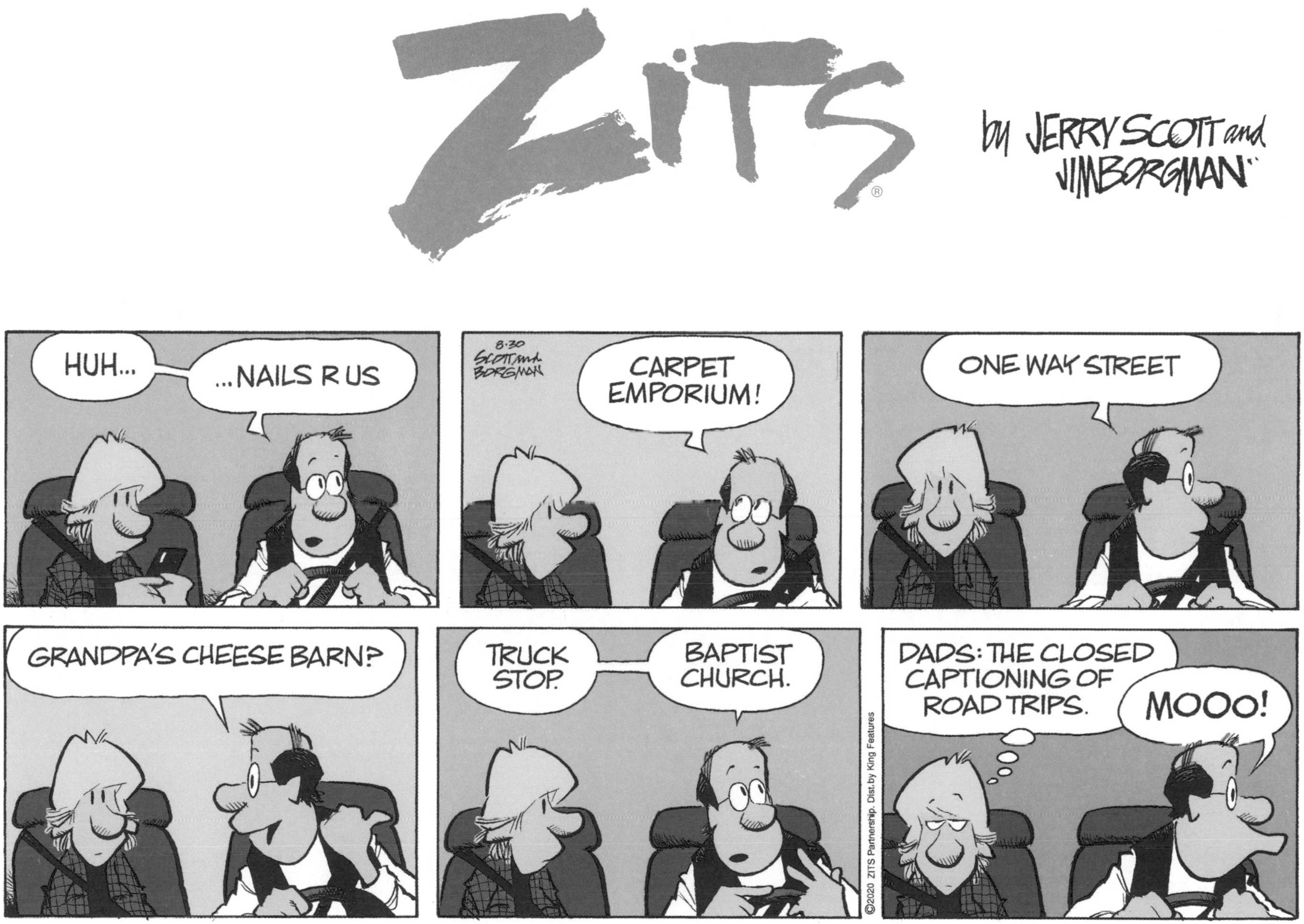
ZITS
by JERRY SCOTT and JIM BORGMAN
HUH...
...NAILS R US
8·30 SCOTT and BORGMAN
CARPET EMPORIUM!
ONE WAY STREET
GRANDPA'S CHEESE BARN?
TRUCK STOP.
BAPTIST CHURCH.
©2020 ZITS Partnership. Dist. by King Features
DADS: THE CLOSED CAPTIONING OF ROAD TRIPS.
MOOO!

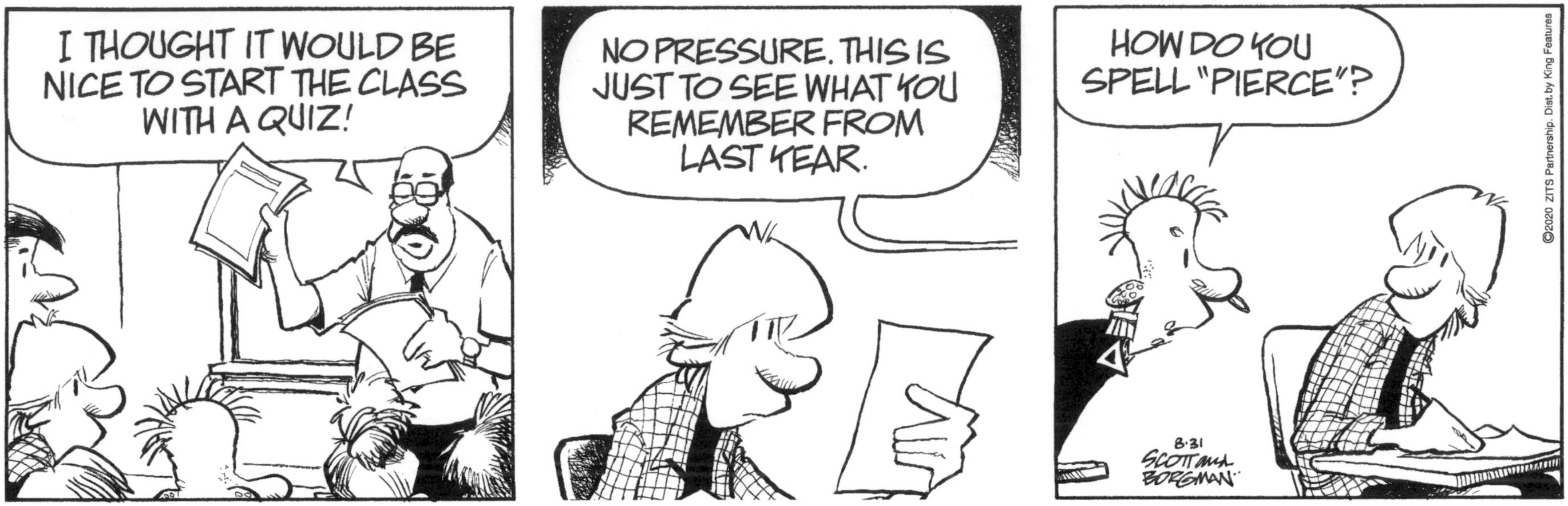
I THOUGHT IT WOULD BE NICE TO START THE CLASS WITH A QUIZ!
NO PRESSURE. THIS IS JUST TO SEE WHAT YOU REMEMBER FROM LAST YEAR.
HOW DO YOU SPELL "PIERCE"?
8·31 SCOTT and BORGMAN
©2020 ZITS Partnership. Dist. by King Features

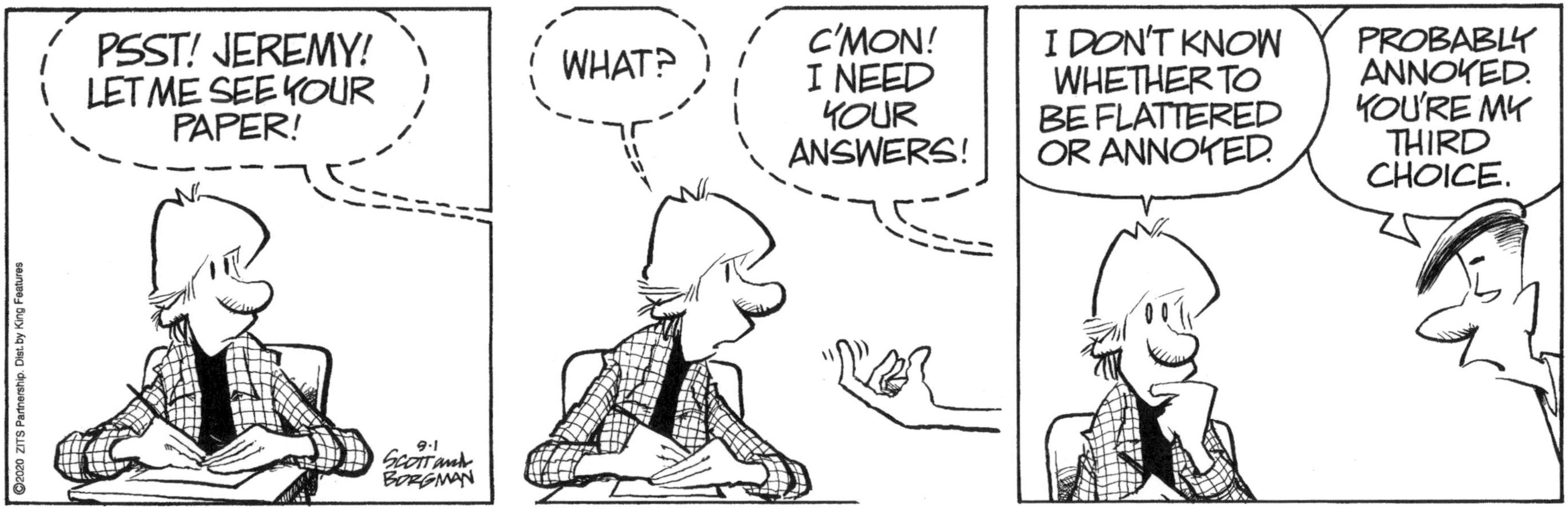
PSST! JEREMY! LET ME SEE YOUR PAPER!
©2020 ZITS Partnership. Dist. by King Features
9·1 SCOTT and BORGMAN
WHAT?
C'MON! I NEED YOUR ANSWERS!
I DON'T KNOW WHETHER TO BE FLATTERED OR ANNOYED.
PROBABLY ANNOYED. YOU'RE MY THIRD CHOICE.

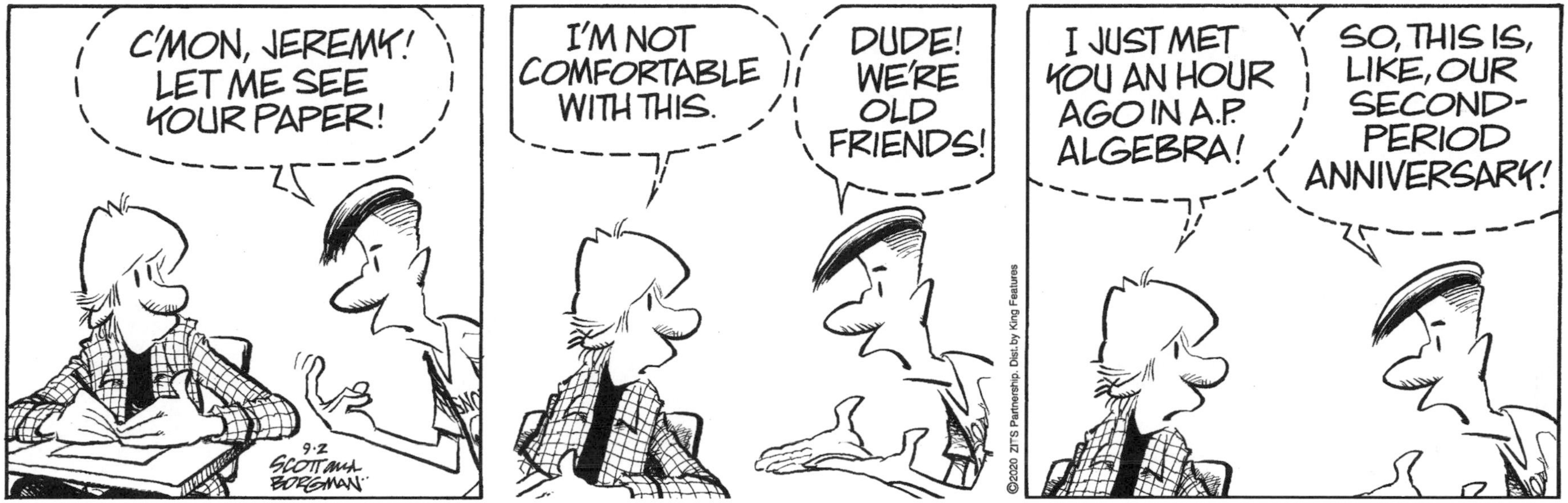
C'MON, JEREMY! LET ME SEE YOUR PAPER!
9·2 SCOTT and BORGMAN
I'M NOT COMFORTABLE WITH THIS.
DUDE! WE'RE OLD FRIENDS!
©2020 ZIT'S Partnership. Dist. by King Features
I JUST MET YOU AN HOUR AGO IN A.P. ALGEBRA!
SO, THIS IS, LIKE, OUR SECOND-PERIOD ANNIVERSARY!

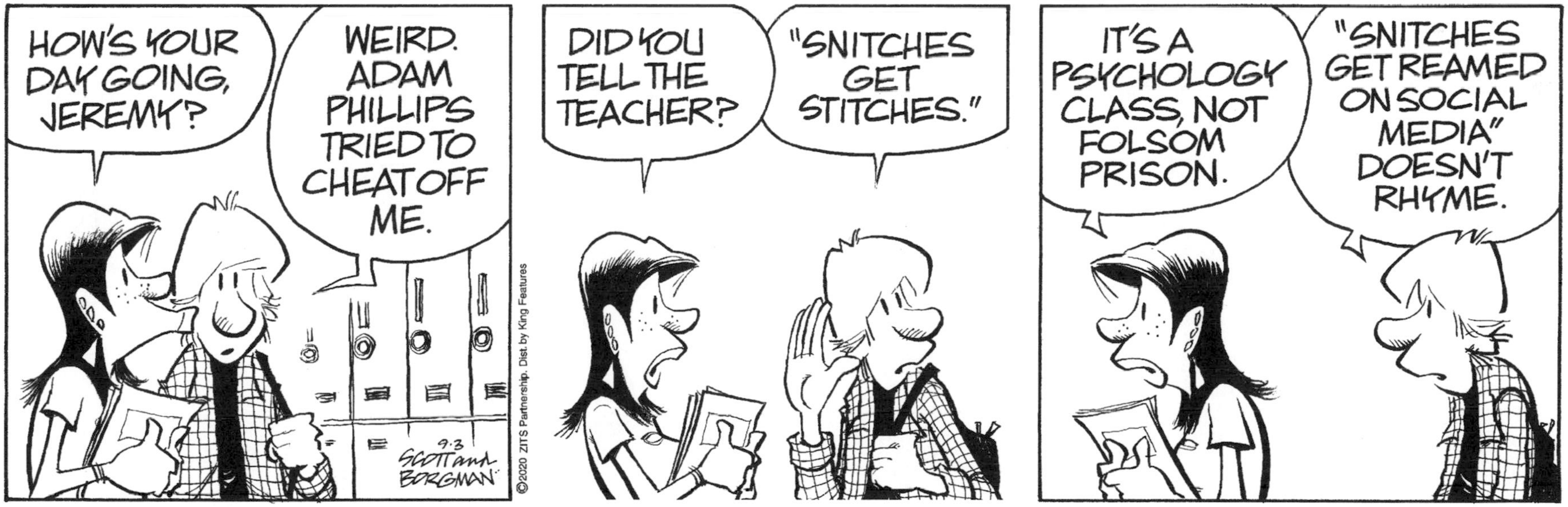
HOW'S YOUR DAY GOING, JEREMY?
WEIRD. ADAM PHILLIPS TRIED TO CHEAT OFF ME.
9·3 SCOTT and BORGMAN
©2020 ZIT'S Partnership. Dist. by King Features
DID YOU TELL THE TEACHER?
"SNITCHES GET STITCHES."
IT'S A PSYCHOLOGY CLASS, NOT FOLSOM PRISON.
"SNITCHES GET REAMED ON SOCIAL MEDIA" DOESN'T RHYME.

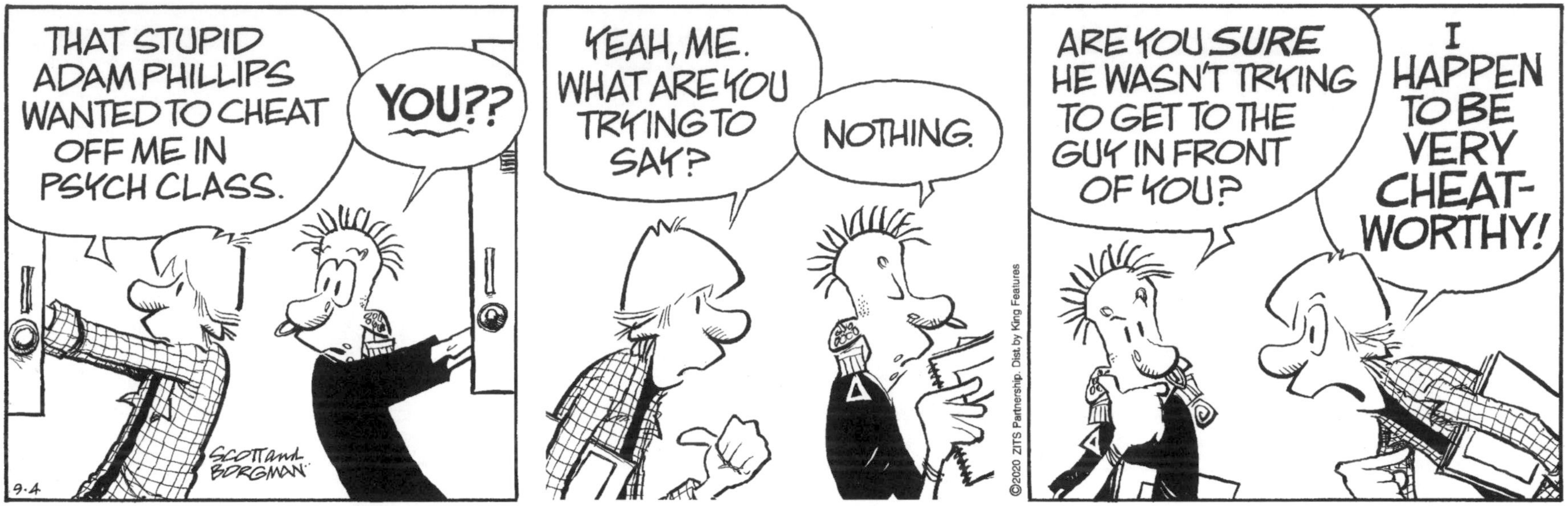
THAT STUPID ADAM PHILLIPS WANTED TO CHEAT OFF ME IN PSYCH CLASS.
YOU??
SCOTT and BORGMAN
9·4
YEAH, ME. WHAT ARE YOU TRYING TO SAY?
NOTHING.
©2020 ZITS Partnership. Dist. by King Features
ARE YOU SURE HE WASN'T TRYING TO GET TO THE GUY IN FRONT OF YOU?
I HAPPEN TO BE VERY CHEAT-WORTHY!

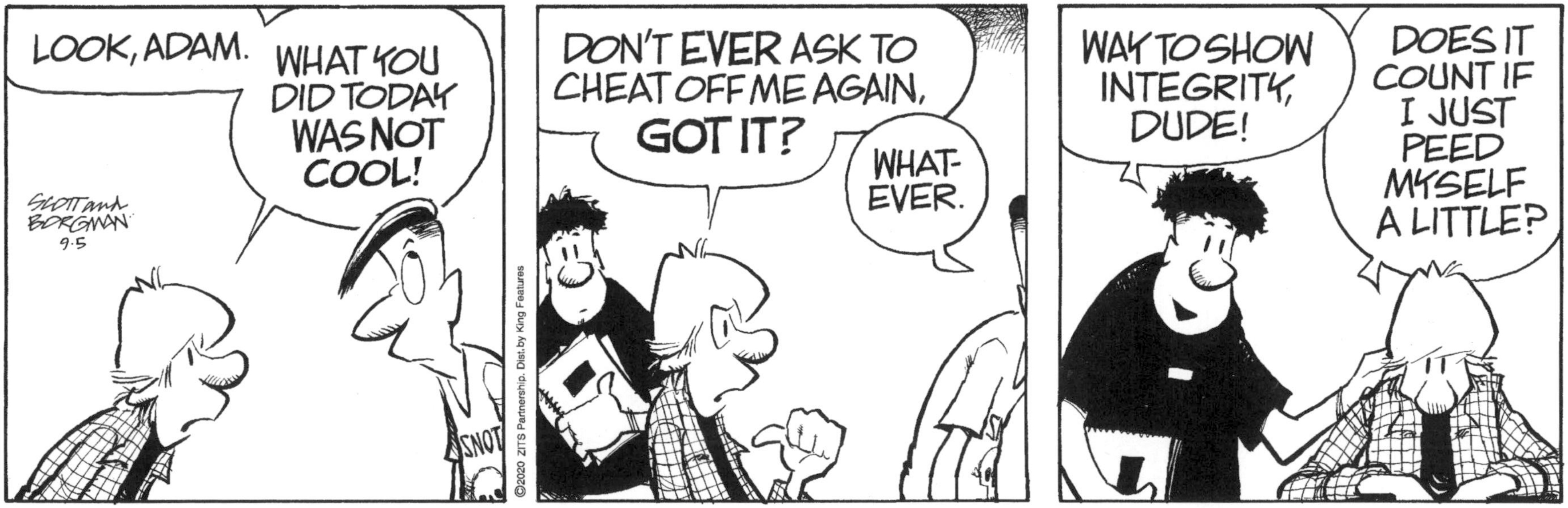
LOOK, ADAM.
WHAT YOU DID TODAY WAS NOT COOL!
SCOTT and BORGMAN
9·5
SNOT
©2020 ZITS Partnership. Dist. by King Features
DON'T EVER ASK TO CHEAT OFF ME AGAIN, GOT IT?
WHAT-EVER.
WAY TO SHOW INTEGRITY, DUDE!
DOES IT COUNT IF I JUST PEED MYSELF A LITTLE?

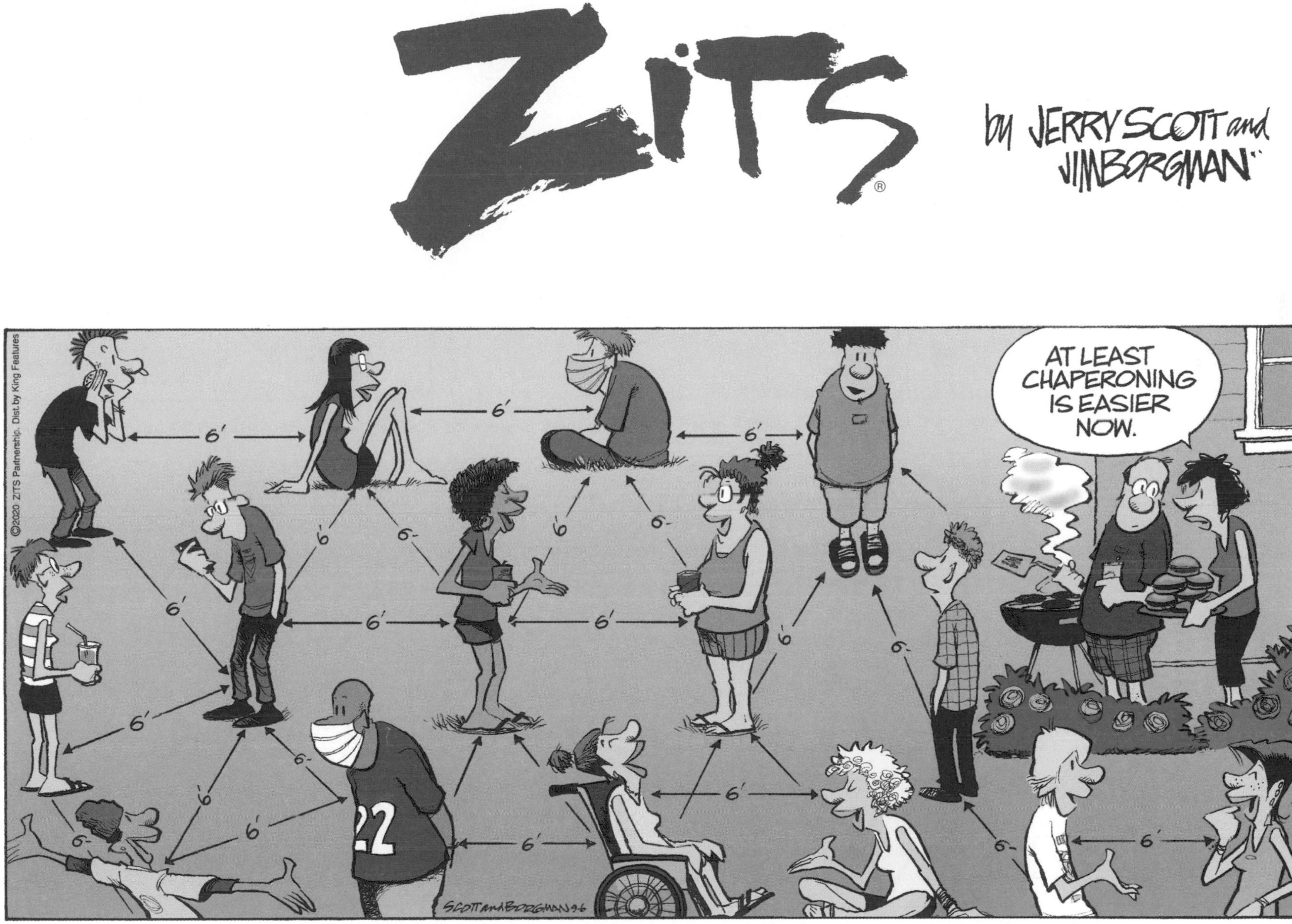
ZITS
by JERRY SCOTT and JIM BORGMAN
©2020 ZITS Partnership. Dist. by King Features
AT LEAST CHAPERONING IS EASIER NOW.
SCOTT and BORGMAN 9-6

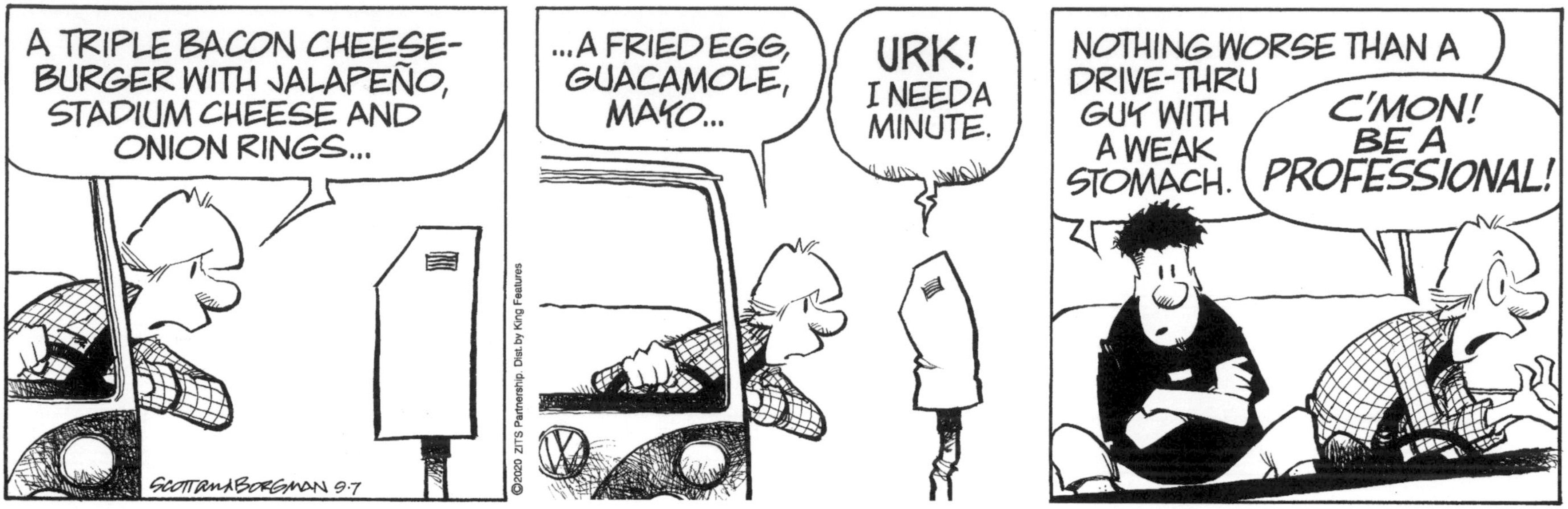
A TRIPLE BACON CHEESE-BURGER WITH JALAPEÑO, STADIUM CHEESE AND ONION RINGS...
SCOTT and BORGMAN 9-7
©2020 ZITS Partnership. Dist. by King Features
...A FRIED EGG, GUACAMOLE, MAYO...
URK! I NEEDA MINUTE.
NOTHING WORSE THAN A DRIVE-THRU GUY WITH A WEAK STOMACH.
C'MON! BE A PROFESSIONAL!

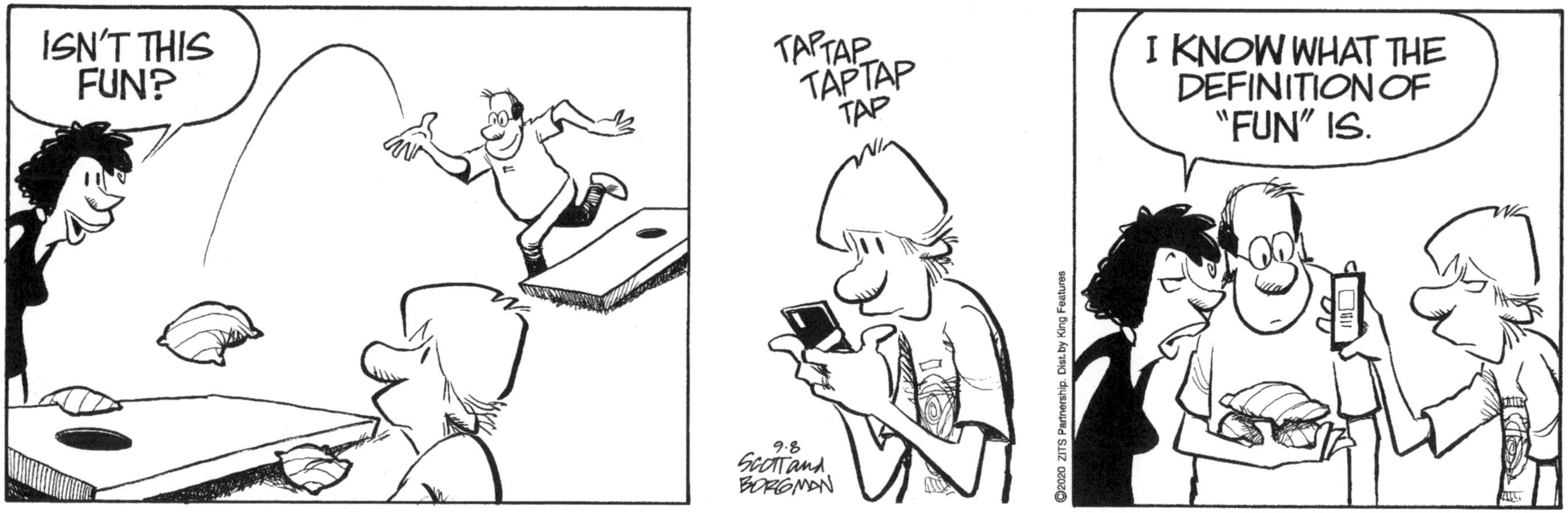
ISN'T THIS FUN?
TAP TAP TAP TAP TAP
9-8 SCOTT and BORGMAN
©2020 ZITS Partnership. Dist. by King Features
I KNOW WHAT THE DEFINITION OF "FUN" IS.

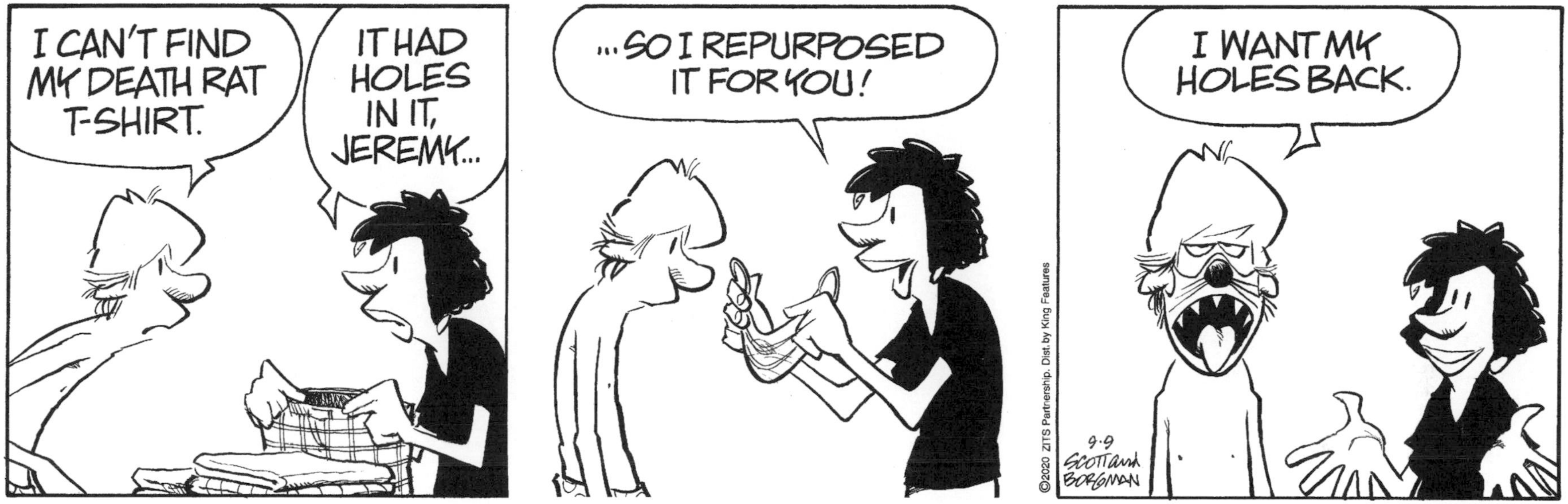
I CAN'T FIND MY DEATH RAT T-SHIRT.
IT HAD HOLES IN IT, JEREMY...
...SO I REPURPOSED IT FOR YOU!
I WANT MY HOLES BACK.
9·9 SCOTT and BORGMAN
©2020 ZITS Partnership. Dist. by King Features

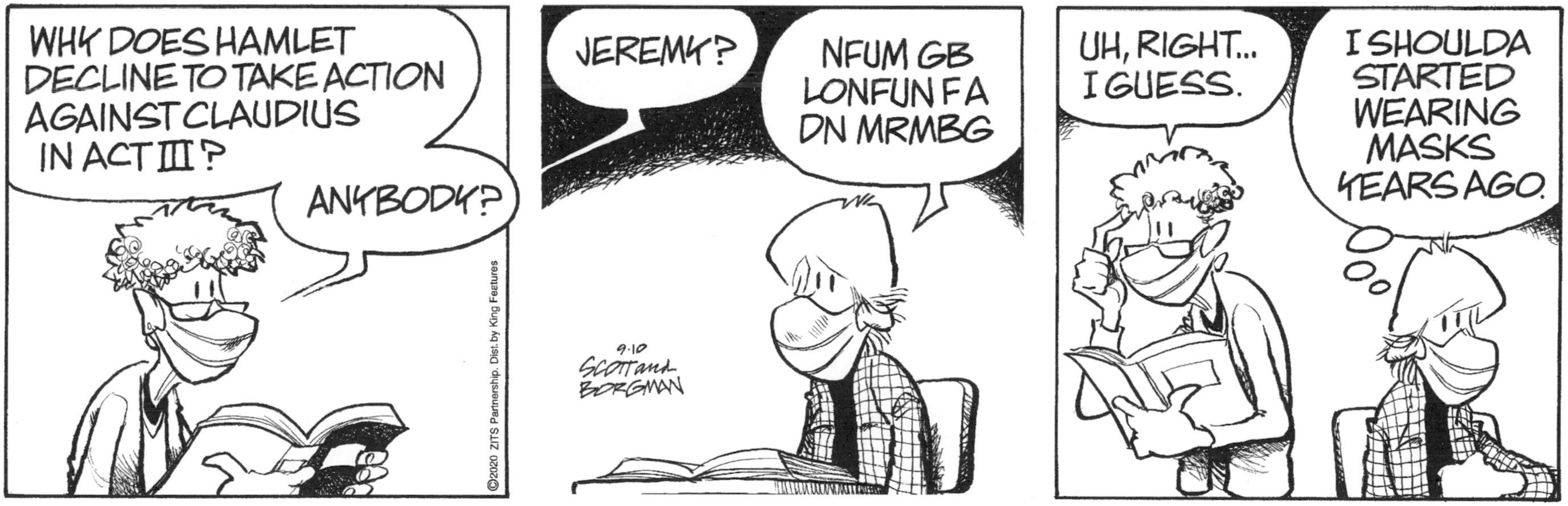
WHY DOES HAMLET DECLINE TO TAKE ACTION AGAINST CLAUDIUS IN ACT III?
ANYBODY?
©2020 ZITS Partnership. Dist. by King Features
JEREMY?
NFUM GB LONFUN FA DN MRMBG
9·10 SCOTT and BORGMAN
UH, RIGHT... I GUESS.
I SHOULDA STARTED WEARING MASKS YEARS AGO.

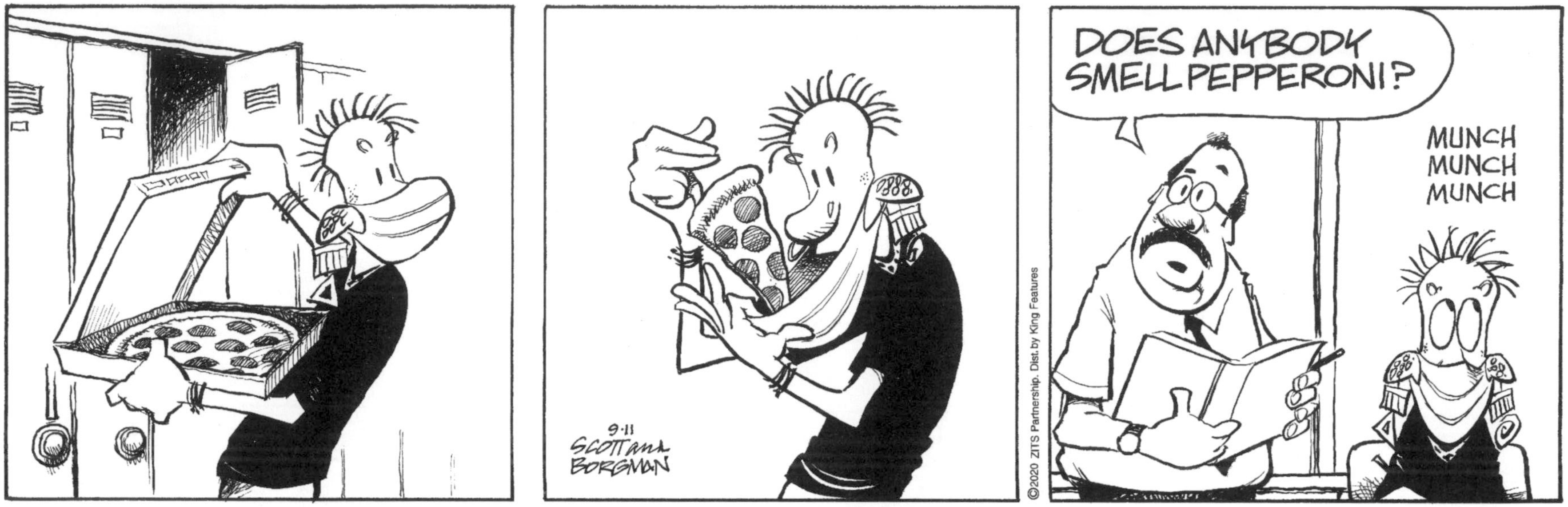
DOES ANYBODY SMELL PEPPERONI?
MUNCH MUNCH MUNCH

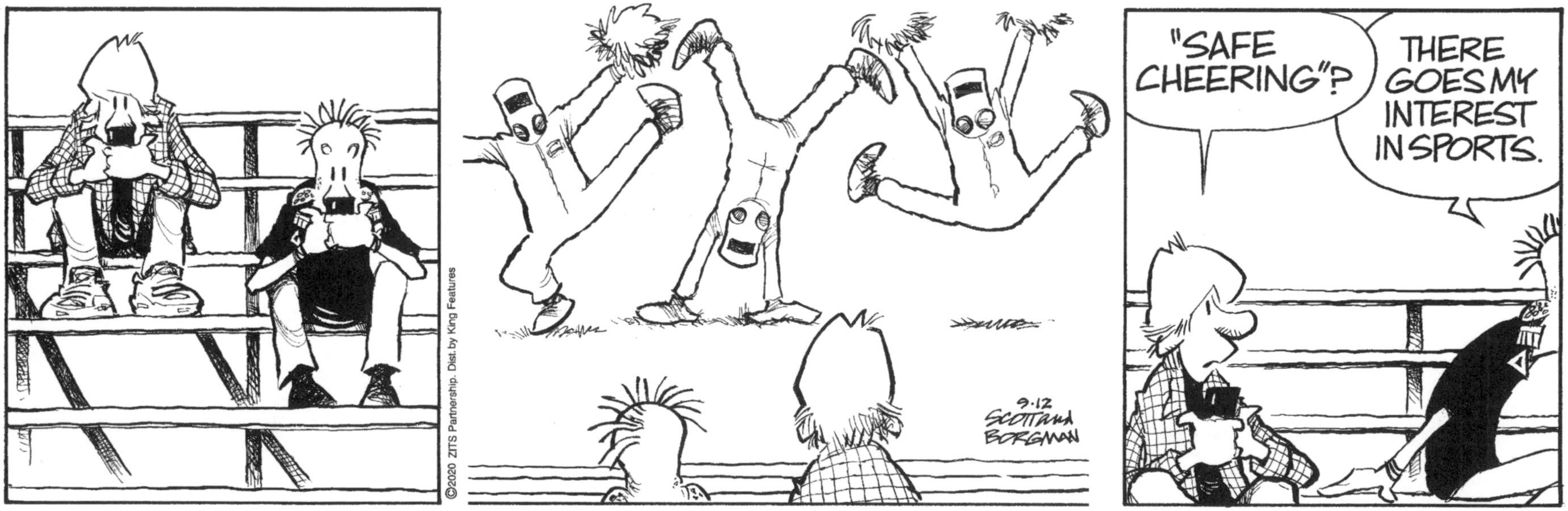
"SAFE CHEERING"?
THERE GOES MY INTEREST IN SPORTS.

ZITS®

by JERRY SCOTT and JIM BORGMAN

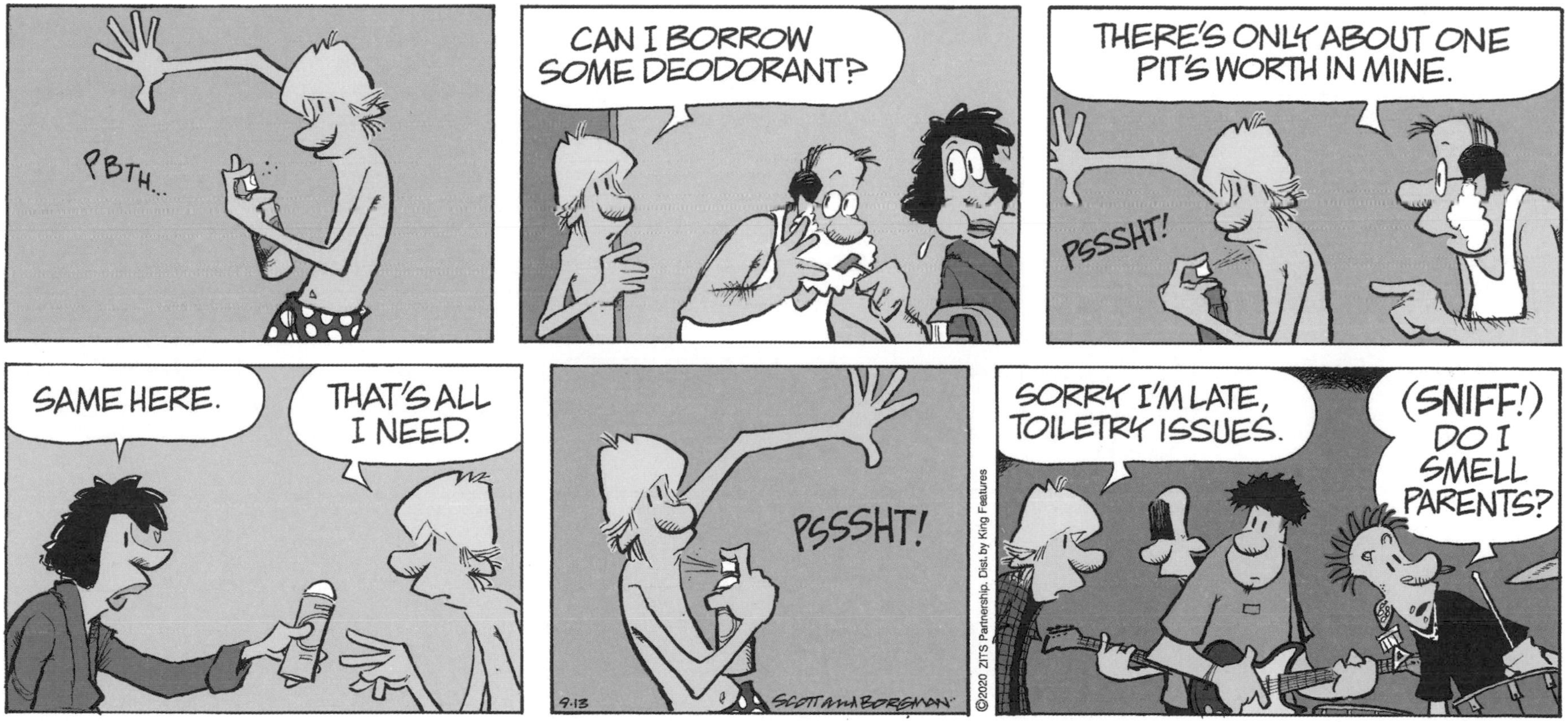

PBTH...
CAN I BORROW SOME DEODORANT?
THERE'S ONLY ABOUT ONE PIT'S WORTH IN MINE.
PSSSHT!
SAME HERE.
THAT'S ALL I NEED.
PSSSHT!
9.13
SCOTT AND BORGMAN
©2020 ZITS Partnership. Dist. by King Features
SORRY I'M LATE, TOILETRY ISSUES.
(SNIFF!) DO I SMELL PARENTS?

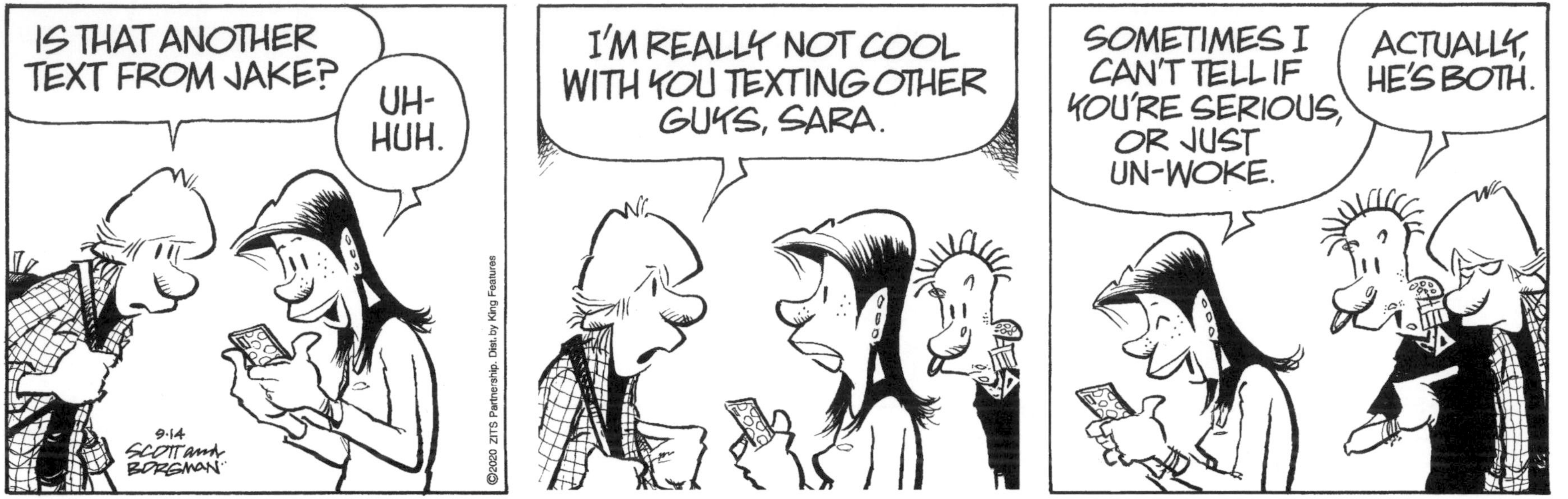
IS THAT ANOTHER TEXT FROM JAKE?
UH-HUH.
9·14
SCOTT and BORGMAN
©2020 ZITS Partnership. Dist. by King Features
I'M REALLY NOT COOL WITH YOU TEXTING OTHER GUYS, SARA.
SOMETIMES I CAN'T TELL IF YOU'RE SERIOUS, OR JUST UN-WOKE.
ACTUALLY, HE'S BOTH.

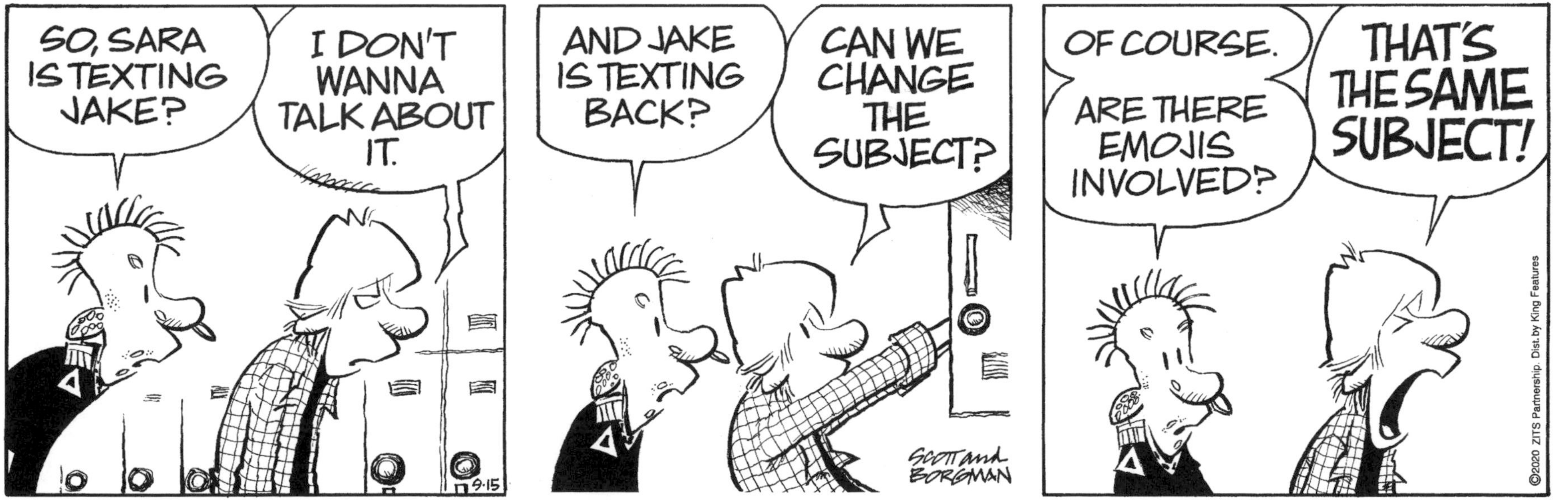
SO, SARA IS TEXTING JAKE?
I DON'T WANNA TALK ABOUT IT.
9·15
AND JAKE IS TEXTING BACK?
CAN WE CHANGE THE SUBJECT?
SCOTT and BORGMAN
OF COURSE.
ARE THERE EMOJIS INVOLVED?
THAT'S THE SAME SUBJECT!
©2020 ZITS Partnership. Dist. by King Features

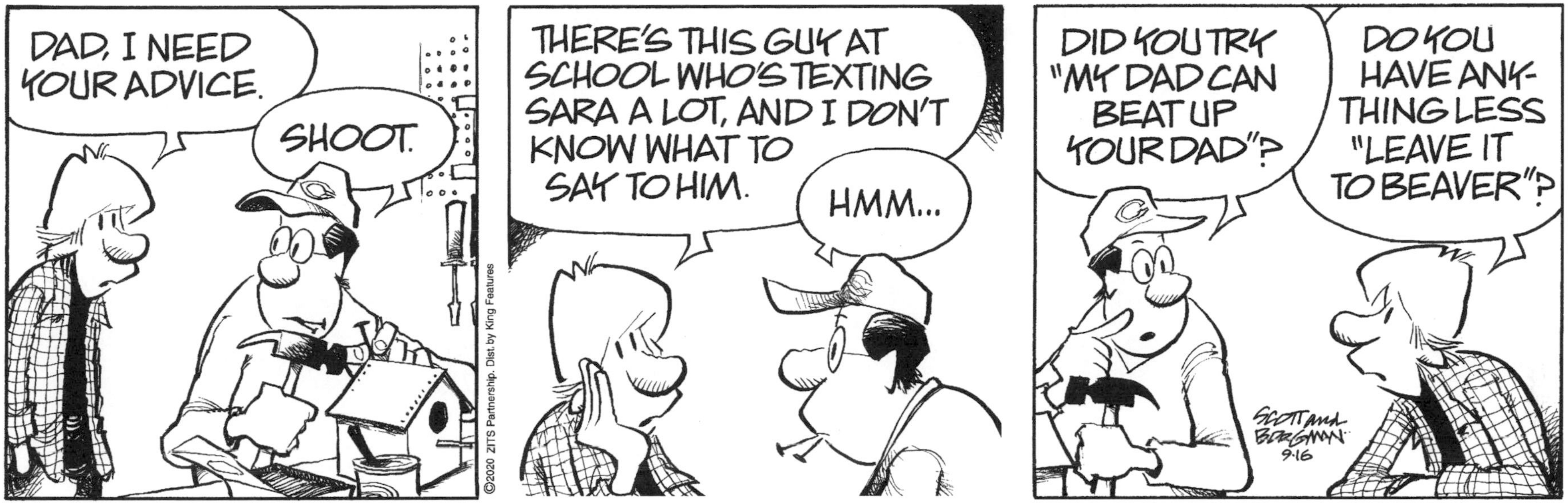
DAD, I NEED YOUR ADVICE.
SHOOT.
©2020 ZITS Partnership. Dist. by King Features
THERE'S THIS GUY AT SCHOOL WHO'S TEXTING SARA A LOT, AND I DON'T KNOW WHAT TO SAY TO HIM.
HMM...
DID YOU TRY "MY DAD CAN BEAT UP YOUR DAD"?
DO YOU HAVE ANYTHING LESS "LEAVE IT TO BEAVER"?
SCOTT and BORGMAN 9·16

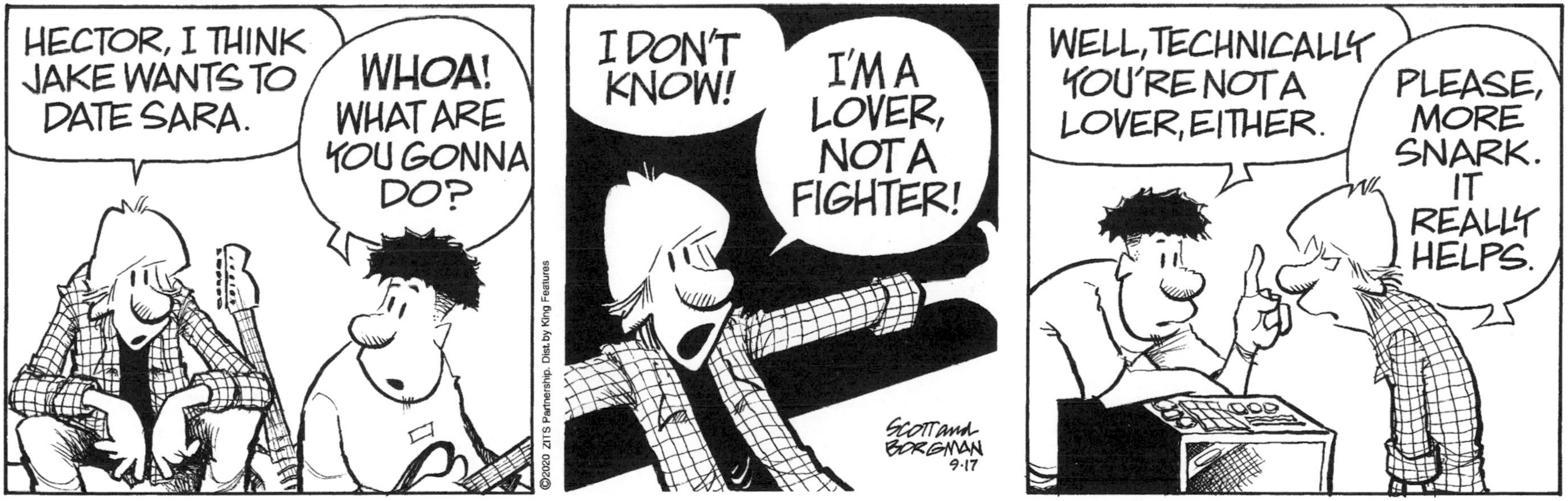
HECTOR, I THINK JAKE WANTS TO DATE SARA.
WHOA! WHAT ARE YOU GONNA DO?
©2020 ZITS Partnership. Dist. by King Features
I DON'T KNOW!
I'M A LOVER, NOT A FIGHTER!
SCOTT and BORGMAN 9·17
WELL, TECHNICALLY YOU'RE NOT A LOVER, EITHER.
PLEASE, MORE SNARK. IT REALLY HELPS.

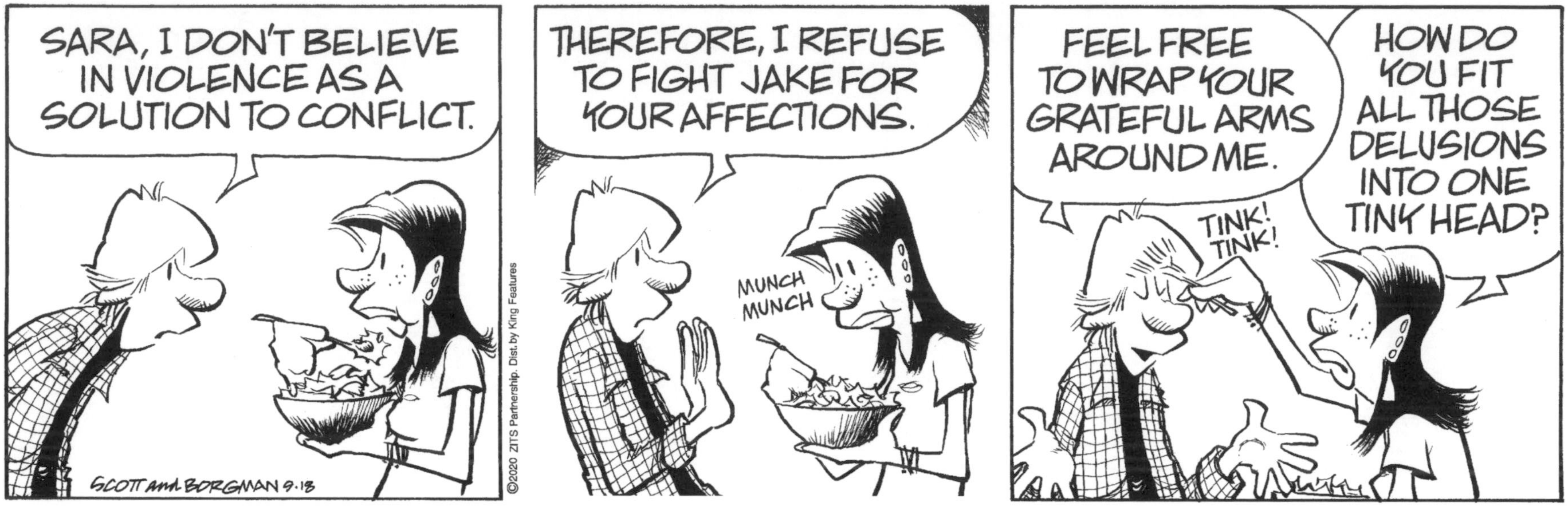
SARA, I DON'T BELIEVE IN VIOLENCE AS A SOLUTION TO CONFLICT.
SCOTT AND BORGMAN 9·18
©2020 ZITS Partnership. Dist. by King Features
THEREFORE, I REFUSE TO FIGHT JAKE FOR YOUR AFFECTIONS.
MUNCH MUNCH
FEEL FREE TO WRAP YOUR GRATEFUL ARMS AROUND ME.
HOW DO YOU FIT ALL THOSE DELUSIONS INTO ONE TINY HEAD?
TINK! TINK!

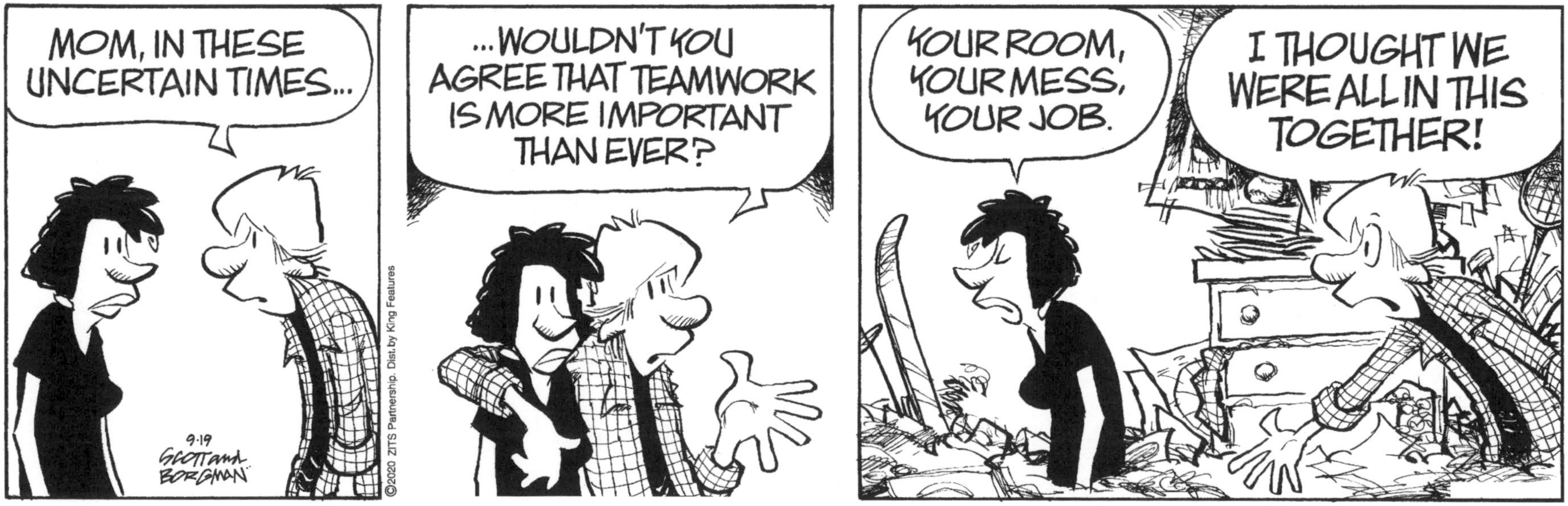
MOM, IN THESE UNCERTAIN TIMES...
9·19 SCOTT AND BORGMAN
©2020 ZITS Partnership. Dist. by King Features
...WOULDN'T YOU AGREE THAT TEAMWORK IS MORE IMPORTANT THAN EVER?
YOUR ROOM, YOUR MESS, YOUR JOB.
I THOUGHT WE WERE ALL IN THIS TOGETHER!

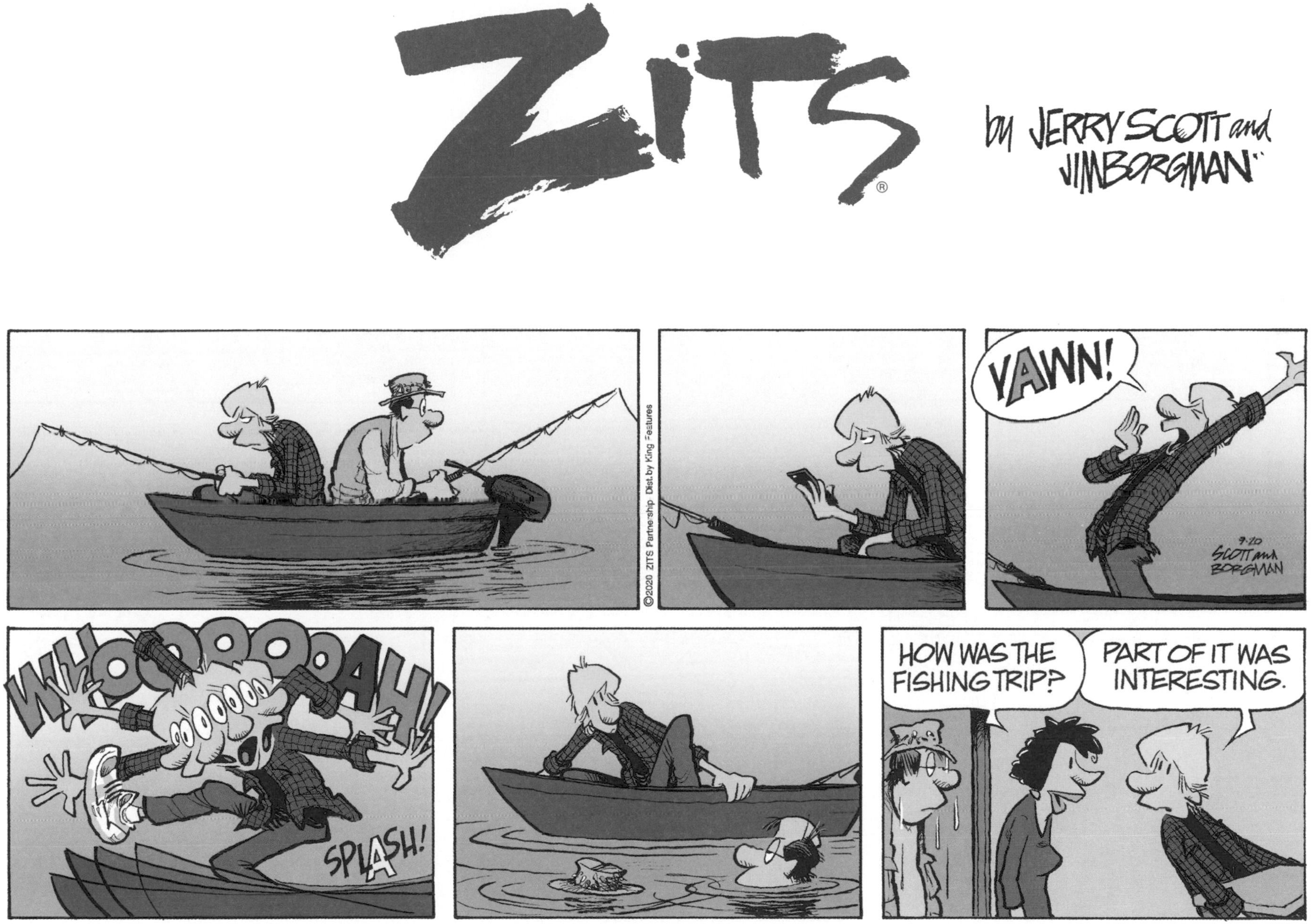
ZITS
by JERRY SCOTT and JIM BORGMAN
©2020 ZITS Partnership Dist. by King Features
YAWN!
SCOTT and BORGMAN
WHOOOOOOOAH!
SPLASH!
HOW WAS THE FISHING TRIP?
PART OF IT WAS INTERESTING.

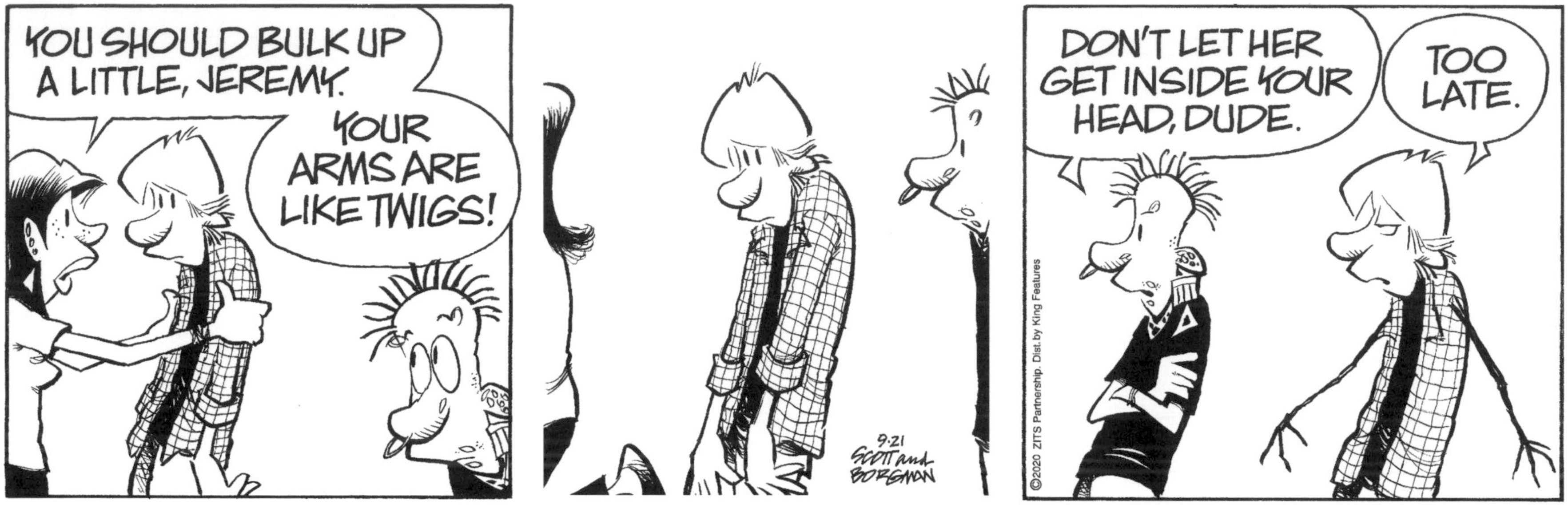
YOU SHOULD BULK UP A LITTLE, JEREMY.
YOUR ARMS ARE LIKE TWIGS!
9·21 SCOTT and BORGMAN
DON'T LET HER GET INSIDE YOUR HEAD, DUDE.
TOO LATE.
©2020 ZITS Partnership. Dist. by King Features

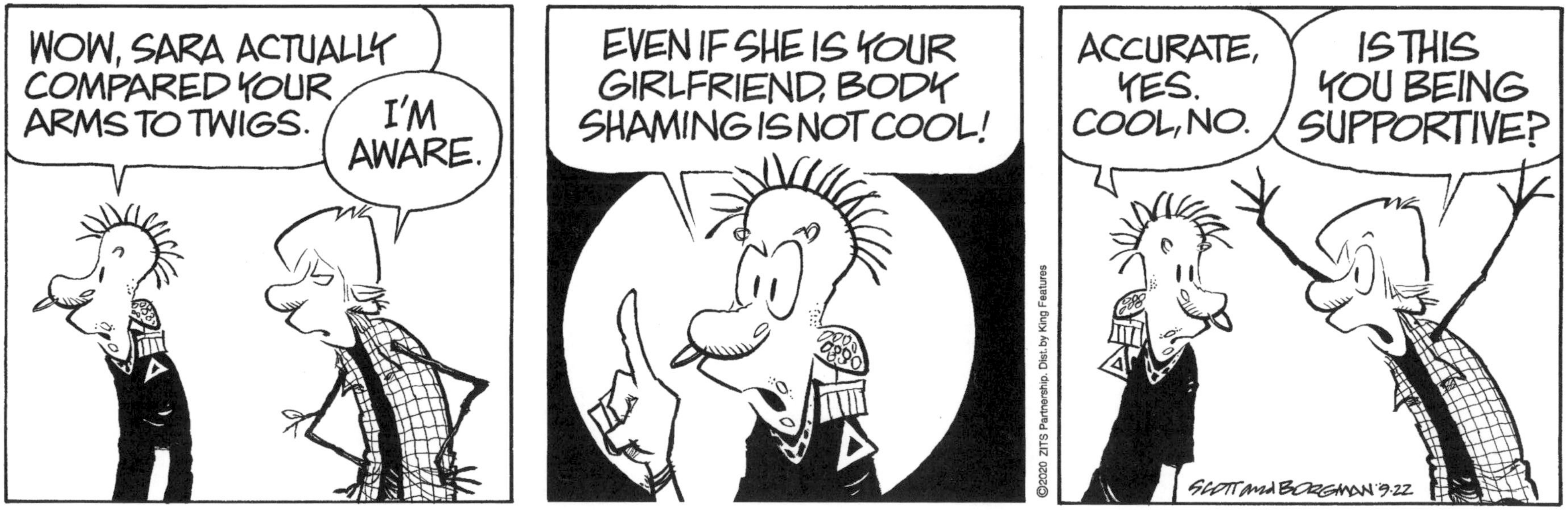
WOW, SARA ACTUALLY COMPARED YOUR ARMS TO TWIGS.
I'M AWARE.
EVEN IF SHE IS YOUR GIRLFRIEND, BODY SHAMING IS NOT COOL!
©2020 ZITS Partnership. Dist. by King Features
ACCURATE, YES. COOL, NO.
IS THIS YOU BEING SUPPORTIVE?
SCOTT and BORGMAN 9·22

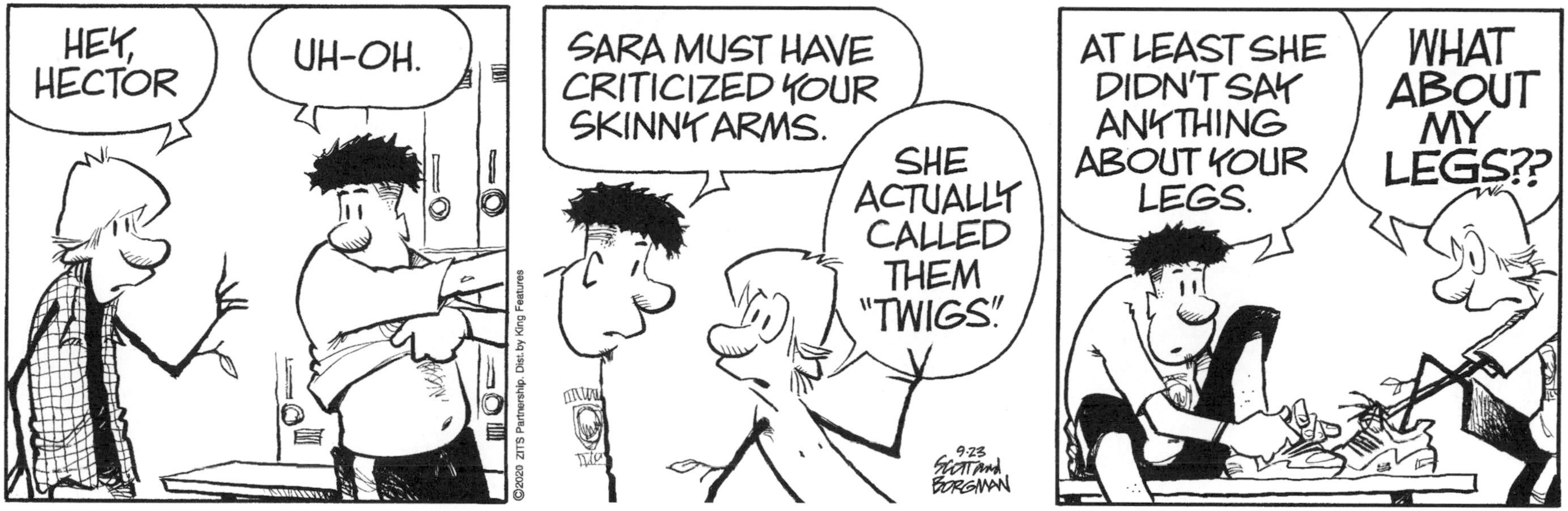
HEY, HECTOR
UH-OH.
©2020 ZITS Partnership. Dist. by King Features
SARA MUST HAVE CRITICIZED YOUR SKINNY ARMS.
SHE ACTUALLY CALLED THEM "TWIGS."
9·23
SCOTT AND BORGMAN
AT LEAST SHE DIDN'T SAY ANYTHING ABOUT YOUR LEGS.
WHAT ABOUT MY LEGS??

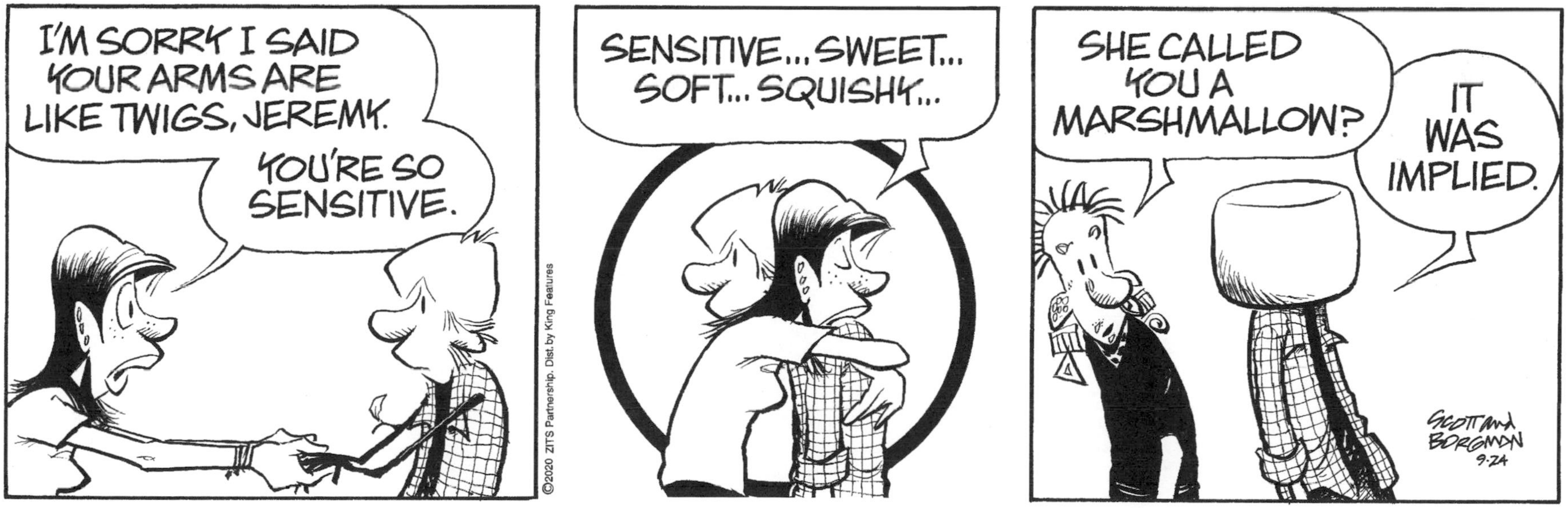
I'M SORRY I SAID YOUR ARMS ARE LIKE TWIGS, JEREMY.
YOU'RE SO SENSITIVE.
©2020 ZITS Partnership. Dist. by King Features
SENSITIVE... SWEET... SOFT... SQUISHY...
SHE CALLED YOU A MARSHMALLOW?
IT WAS IMPLIED.
SCOTT AND BORGMAN
9·24

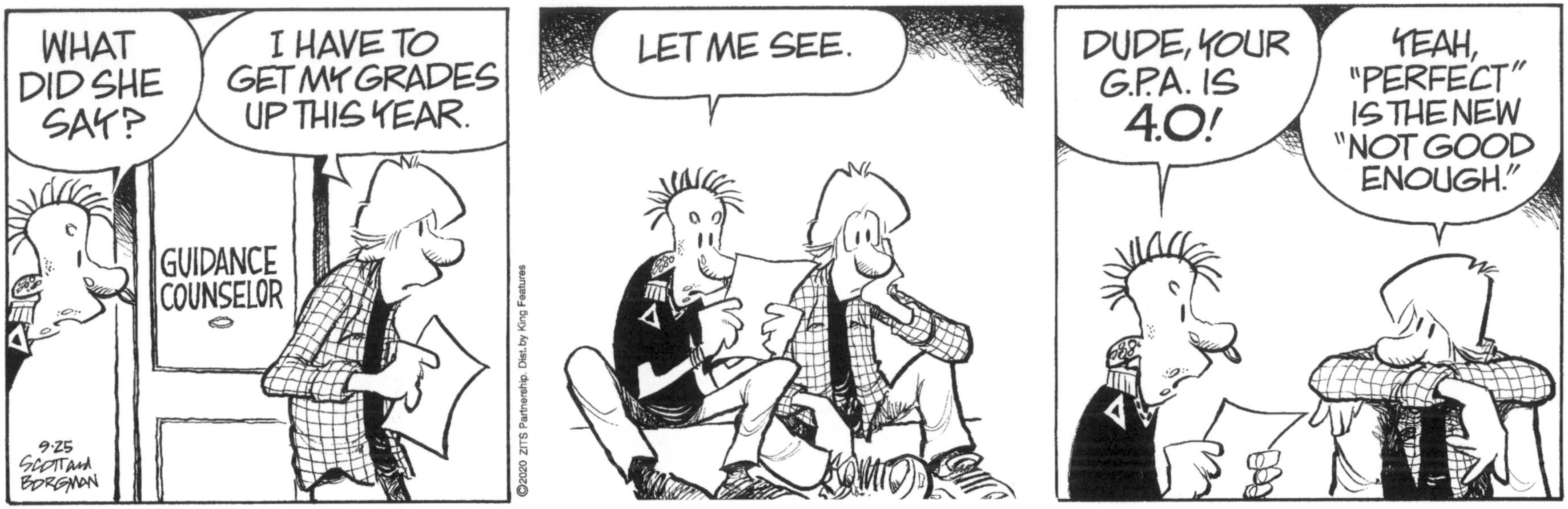
WHAT DID SHE SAY?
I HAVE TO GET MY GRADES UP THIS YEAR.
GUIDANCE COUNSELOR
9·25 SCOTT AND BORGMAN
©2020 ZITS Partnership. Dist. by King Features
LET ME SEE.
DUDE, YOUR G.P.A. IS 4.0!
YEAH, "PERFECT" IS THE NEW "NOT GOOD ENOUGH."

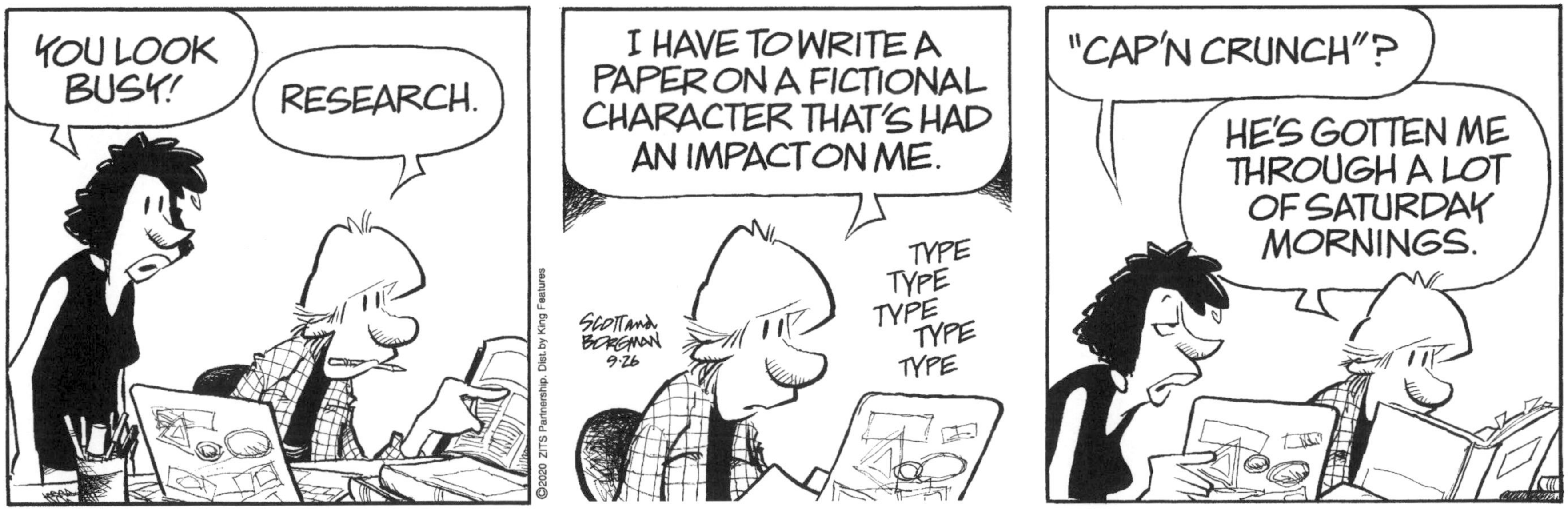
YOU LOOK BUSY!
RESEARCH.
©2020 ZITS Partnership. Dist. by King Features
I HAVE TO WRITE A PAPER ON A FICTIONAL CHARACTER THAT'S HAD AN IMPACT ON ME.
SCOTT AND BORGMAN 9·26
TYPE TYPE TYPE TYPE TYPE
"CAP'N CRUNCH"?
HE'S GOTTEN ME THROUGH A LOT OF SATURDAY MORNINGS.

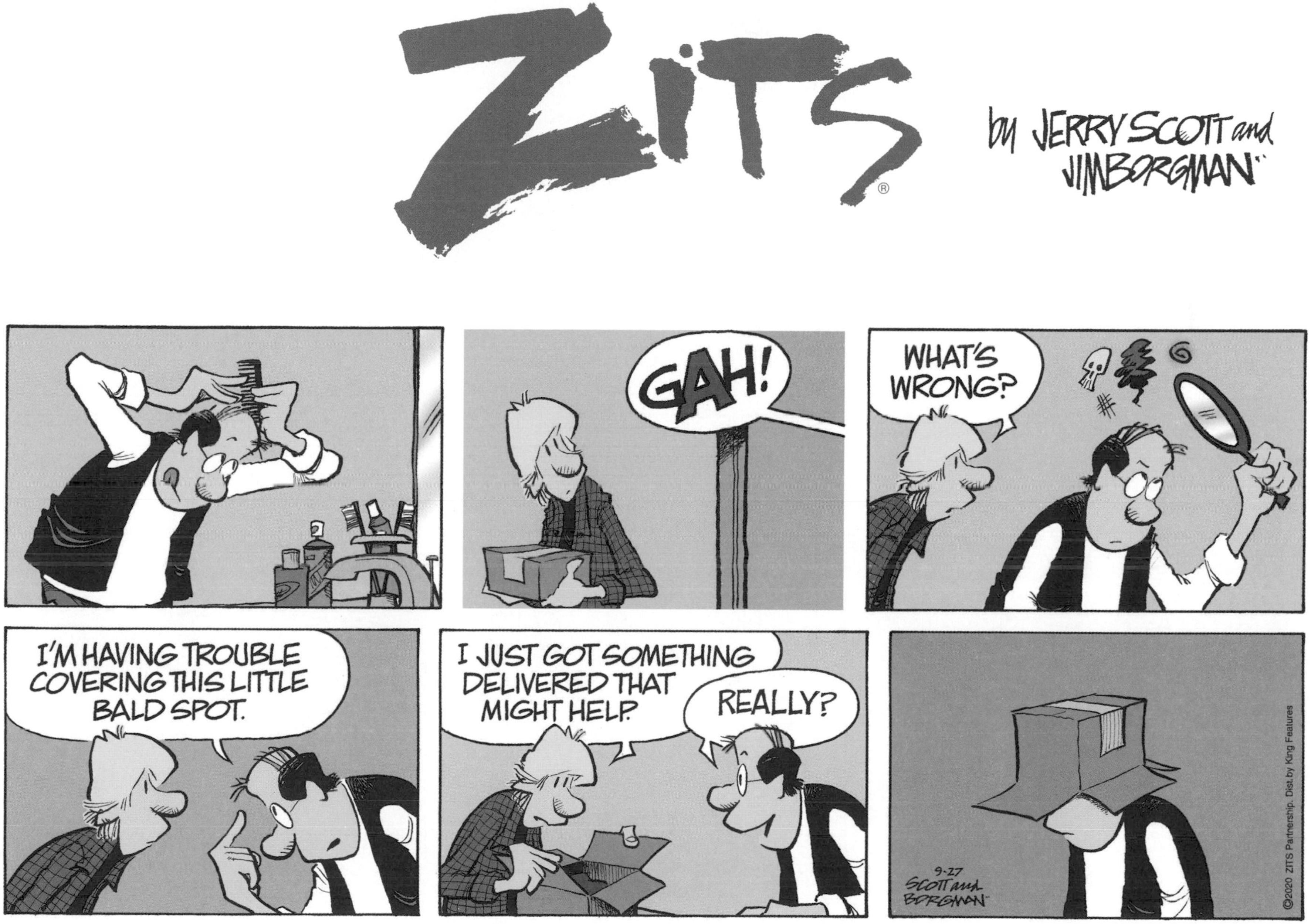
ZITS®
by JERRY SCOTT and JIM BORGMAN
GAH!
WHAT'S WRONG?
I'M HAVING TROUBLE COVERING THIS LITTLE BALD SPOT.
I JUST GOT SOMETHING DELIVERED THAT MIGHT HELP.
REALLY?
9-27 SCOTT and BORGMAN
©2020 ZITS Partnership. Dist. by King Features

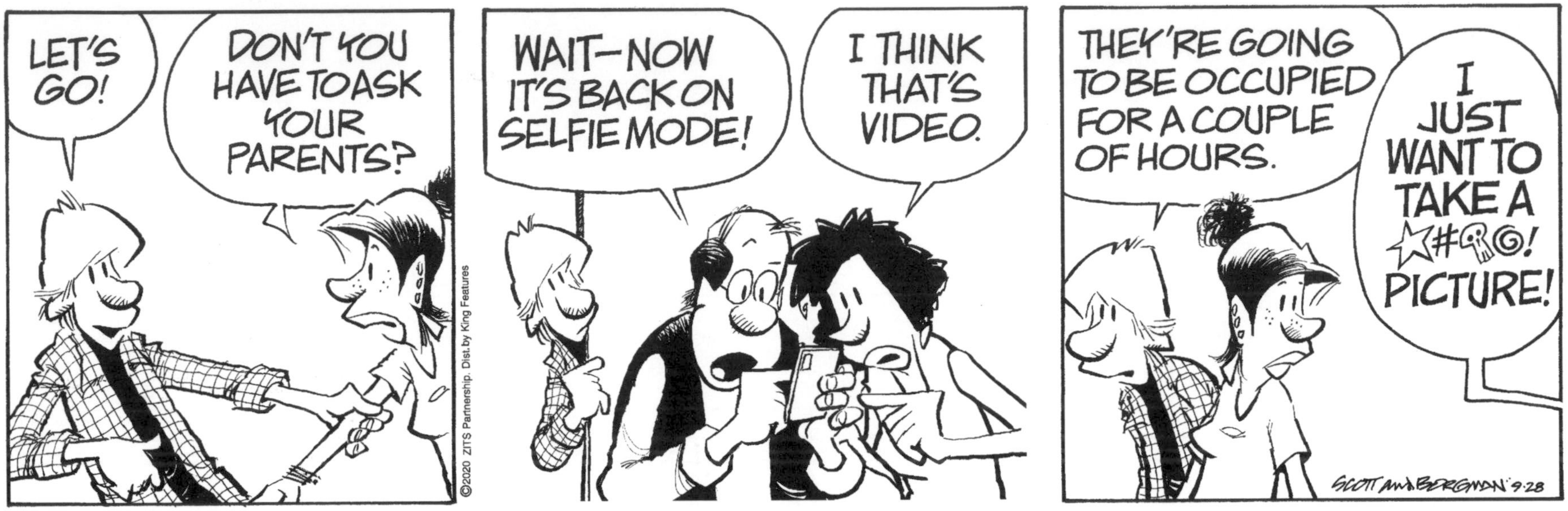
LET'S GO!
DON'T YOU HAVE TO ASK YOUR PARENTS?
©2020 ZITS Partnership. Dist. by King Features
WAIT—NOW IT'S BACK ON SELFIE MODE!
I THINK THAT'S VIDEO.
THEY'RE GOING TO BE OCCUPIED FOR A COUPLE OF HOURS.
I JUST WANT TO TAKE A
PICTURE!
SCOTT AND BORGMAN 9·28

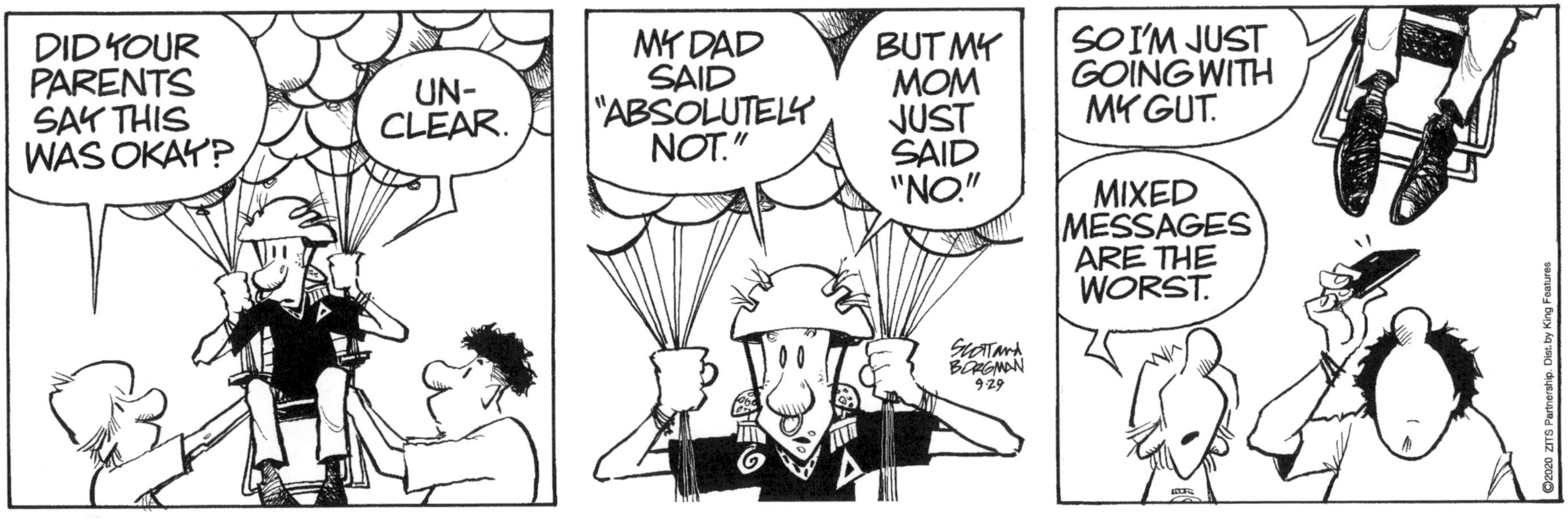
DID YOUR PARENTS SAY THIS WAS OKAY?
UN-CLEAR.
MY DAD SAID "ABSOLUTELY NOT."
BUT MY MOM JUST SAID "NO."
SCOTT AND BORGMAN 9·29
SO I'M JUST GOING WITH MY GUT.
MIXED MESSAGES ARE THE WORST.
©2020 ZITS Partnership. Dist. by King Features

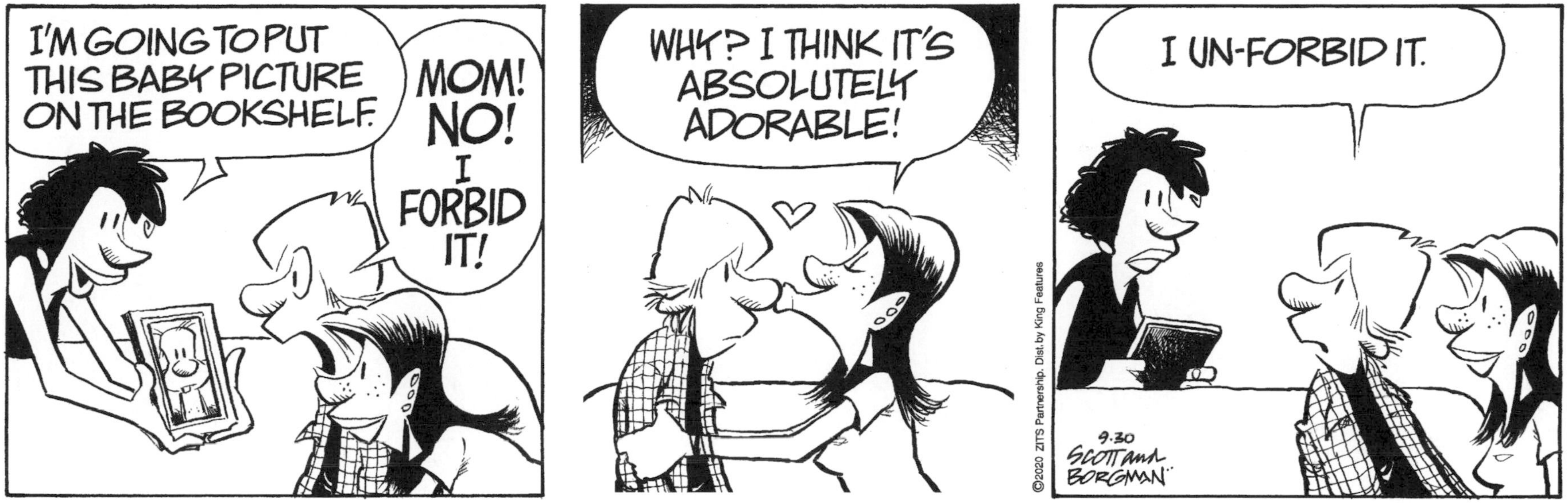
I'M GOING TO PUT THIS BABY PICTURE ON THE BOOKSHELF.
MOM! NO! I FORBID IT!
WHY? I THINK IT'S ABSOLUTELY ADORABLE!
I UN-FORBID IT.
9-30
SCOTT AND BORGMAN
©2020 ZITS Partnership. Dist. by King Features

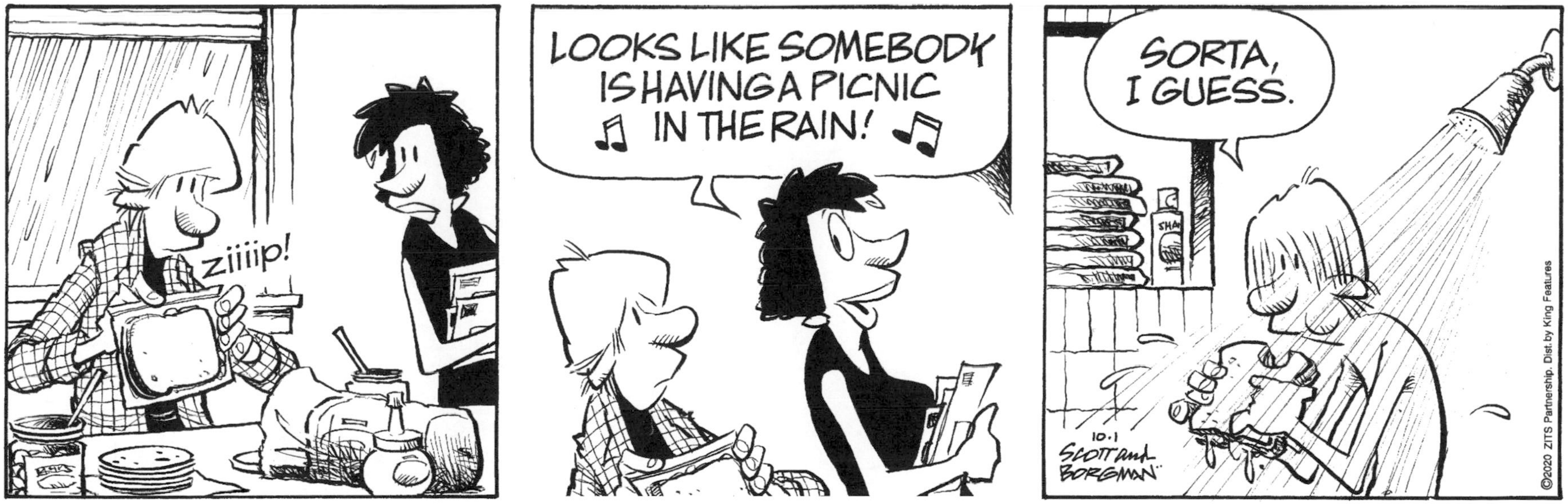
ziiiip!
LOOKS LIKE SOMEBODY IS HAVING A PICNIC ♫ IN THE RAIN! ♫
SORTA, I GUESS.
10-1
SCOTT AND BORGMAN
©2020 ZITS Partnership. Dist. by King Features

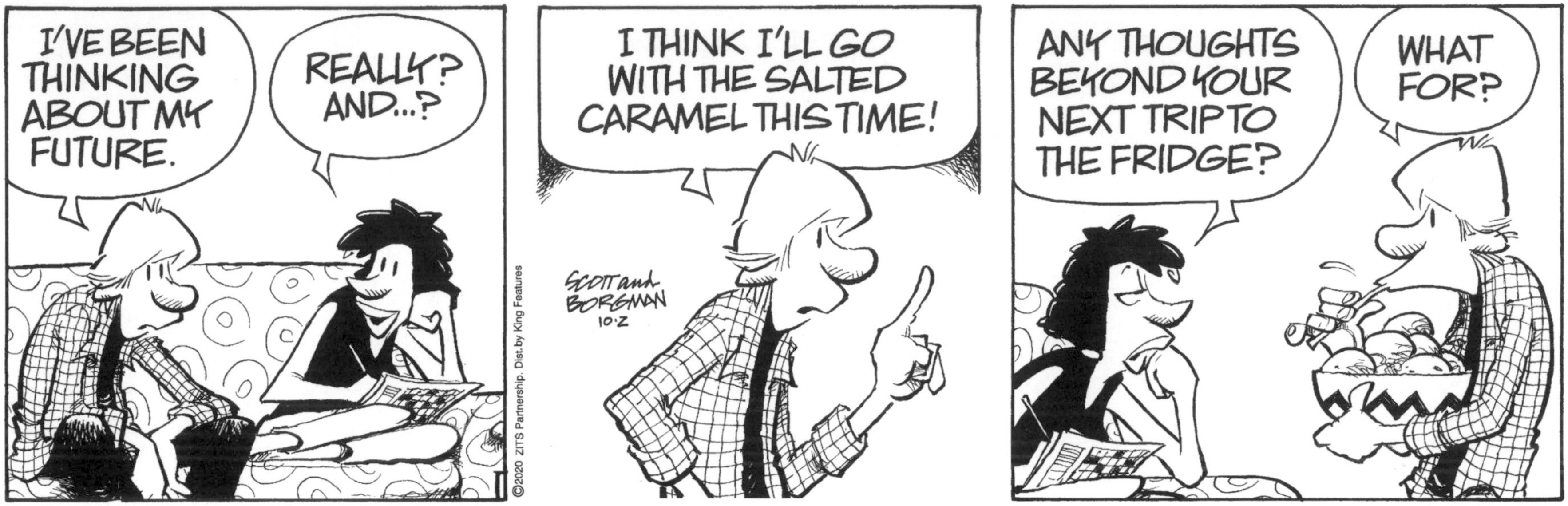
I'VE BEEN THINKING ABOUT MY FUTURE.
REALLY? AND...?
I THINK I'LL GO WITH THE SALTED CARAMEL THIS TIME!
SCOTT and BORGMAN 10·2
©2020 ZITS Partnership. Dist. by King Features
ANY THOUGHTS BEYOND YOUR NEXT TRIP TO THE FRIDGE?
WHAT FOR?

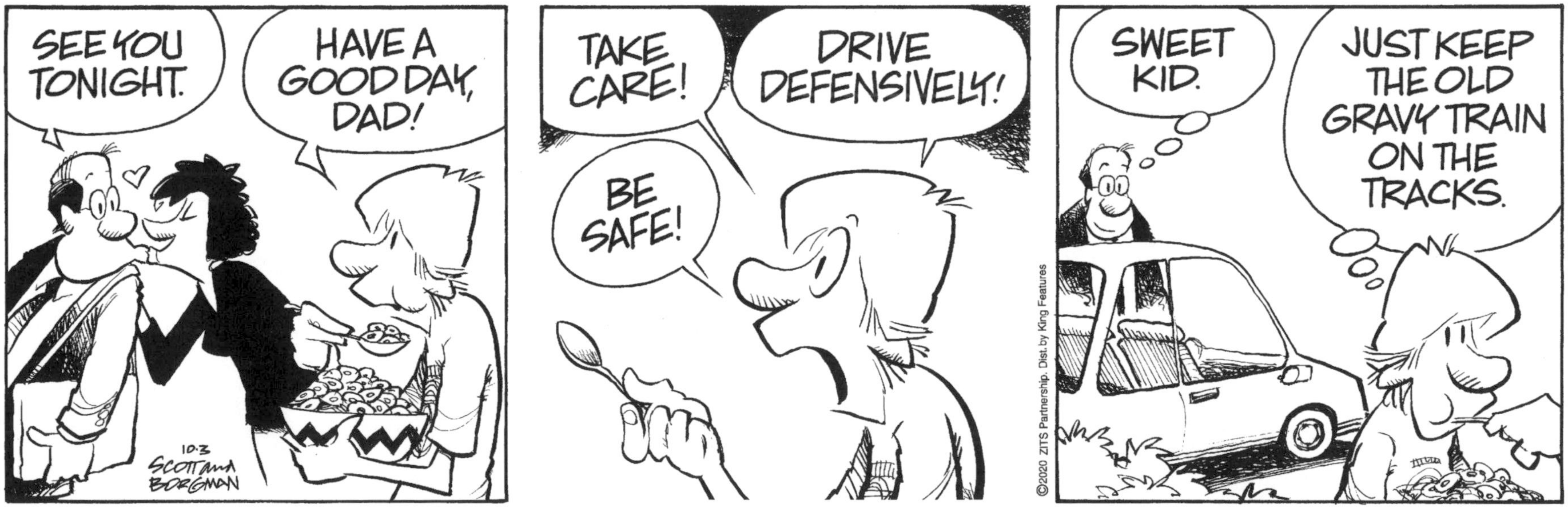
SEE YOU TONIGHT.
HAVE A GOOD DAY, DAD!
10·3 SCOTT and BORGMAN
TAKE CARE!
DRIVE DEFENSIVELY!
BE SAFE!
SWEET KID.
JUST KEEP THE OLD GRAVY TRAIN ON THE TRACKS.
©2020 ZITS Partnership. Dist. by King Features

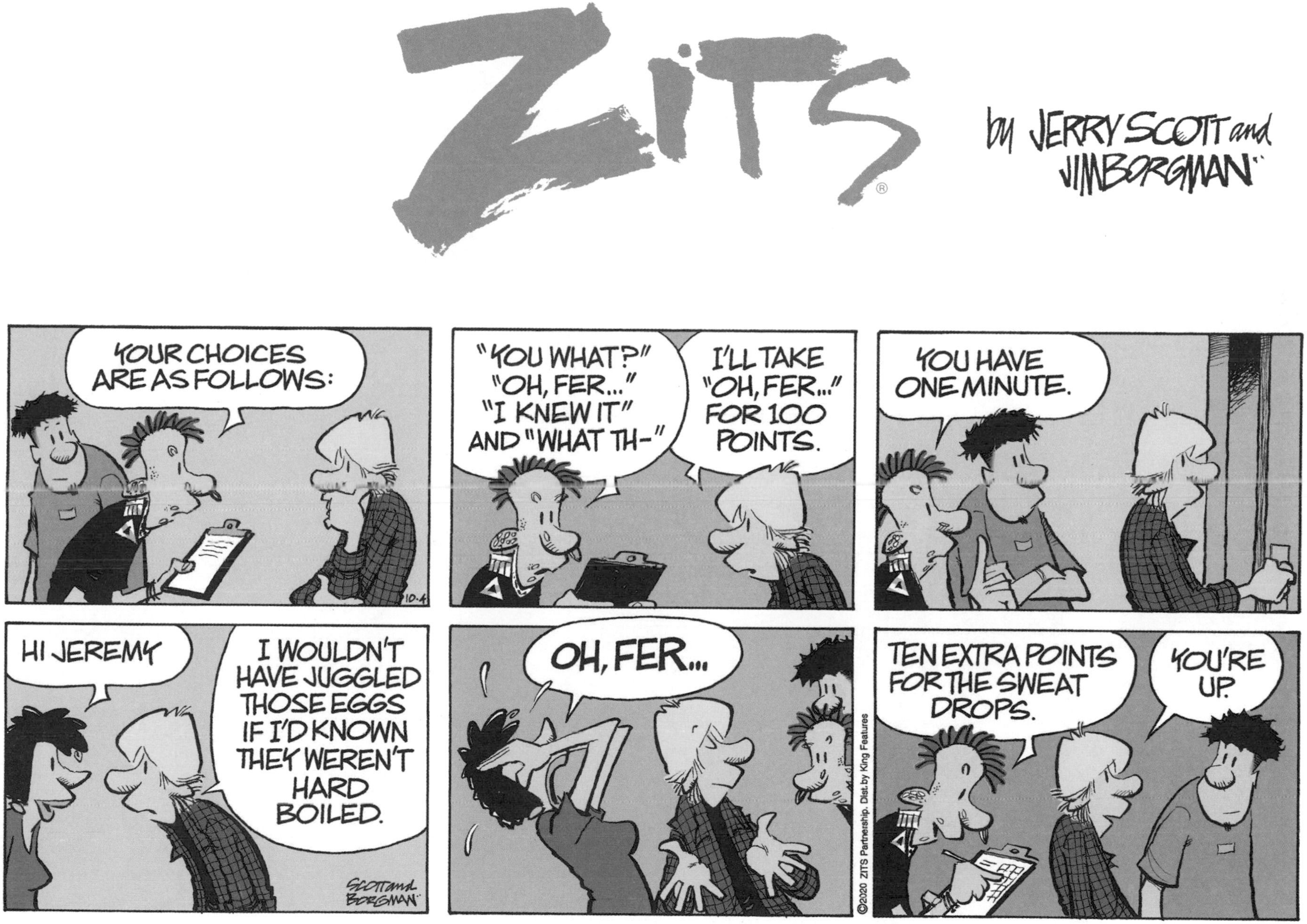
ZITS
by JERRY SCOTT and JIM BORGMAN
YOUR CHOICES ARE AS FOLLOWS:
"YOU WHAT?" "OH, FER..." "I KNEW IT" AND "WHAT TH-"
I'LL TAKE "OH, FER..." FOR 100 POINTS.
YOU HAVE ONE MINUTE.
HI JEREMY
I WOULDN'T HAVE JUGGLED THOSE EGGS IF I'D KNOWN THEY WEREN'T HARD BOILED.
SCOTT and BORGMAN
OH, FER...
©2020 ZITS Partnership. Dist. by King Features
TEN EXTRA POINTS FOR THE SWEAT DROPS.
YOU'RE UP.

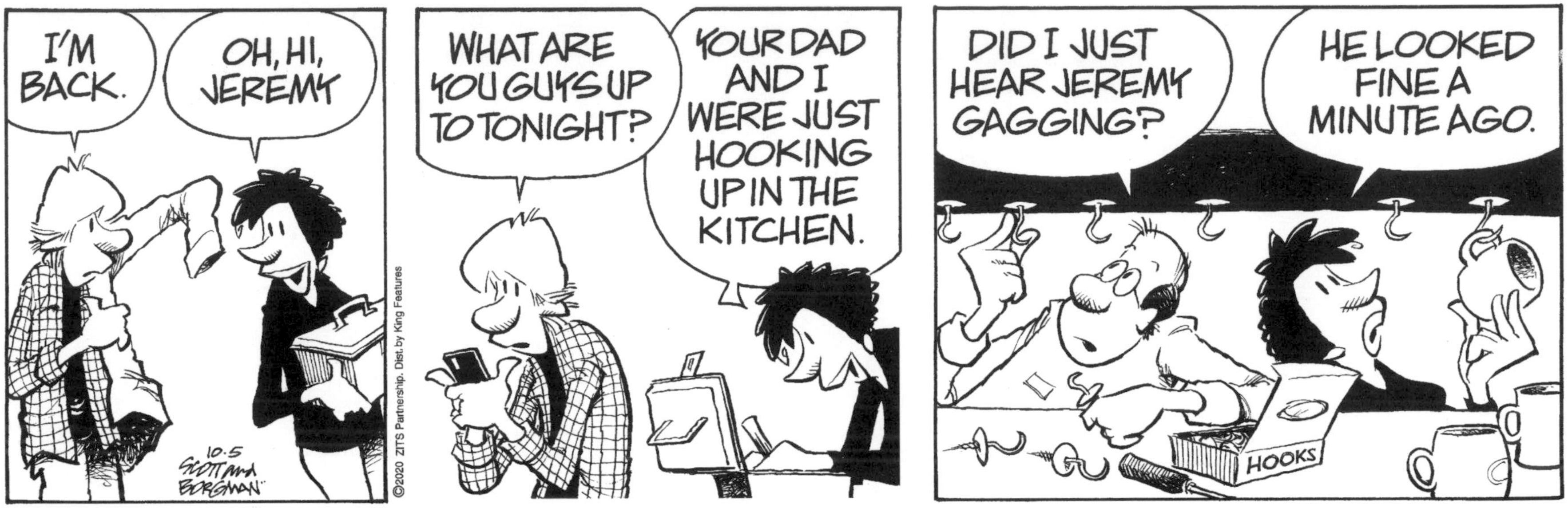
I'M BACK.
OH, HI, JEREMY
10·5
SCOTT AND BORGMAN
©2020 ZITS Partnership. Dist. by King Features
WHAT ARE YOU GUYS UP TO TONIGHT?
YOUR DAD AND I WERE JUST HOOKING UP IN THE KITCHEN.
DID I JUST HEAR JEREMY GAGGING?
HE LOOKED FINE A MINUTE AGO.
HOOKS

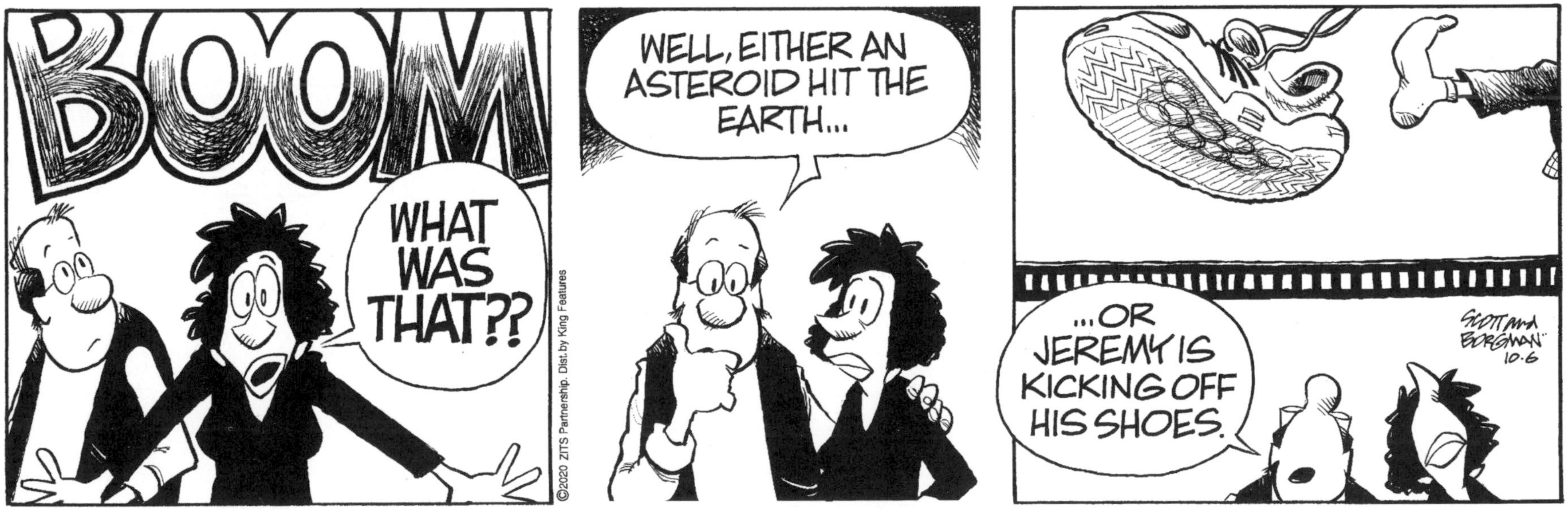
BOOM
WHAT WAS THAT??
©2020 ZITS Partnership. Dist. by King Features
WELL, EITHER AN ASTEROID HIT THE EARTH...
...OR JEREMY IS KICKING OFF HIS SHOES.
SCOTT AND BORGMAN
10·6

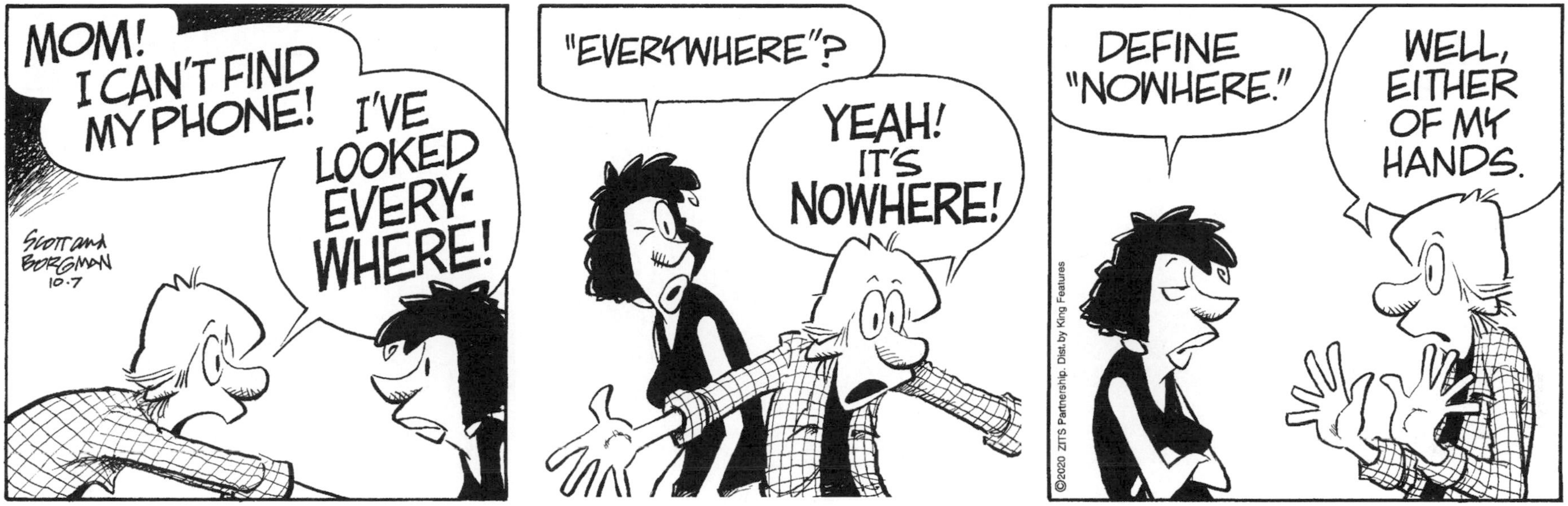
MOM! I CAN'T FIND MY PHONE!
I'VE LOOKED EVERY-WHERE!
SCOTT and BORGMAN 10·7
"EVERYWHERE"?
YEAH! IT'S NOWHERE!
DEFINE "NOWHERE."
WELL, EITHER OF MY HANDS.
©2020 ZITS Partnership. Dist. by King Features

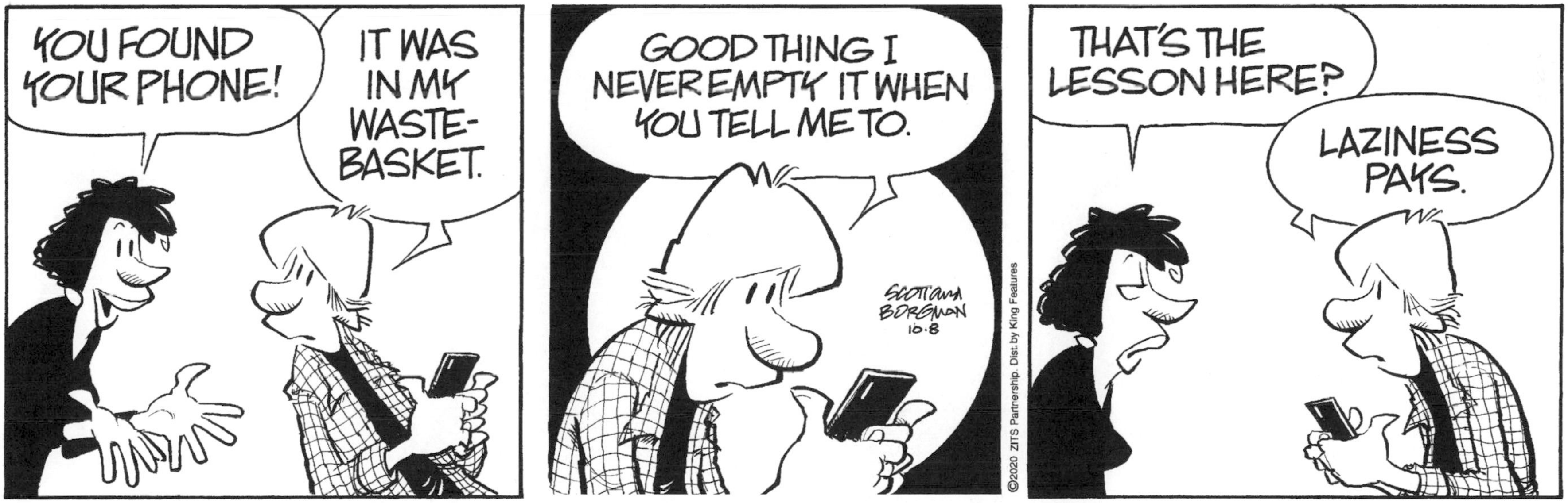
YOU FOUND YOUR PHONE!
IT WAS IN MY WASTE-BASKET.
GOOD THING I NEVER EMPTY IT WHEN YOU TELL ME TO.
SCOTT and BORGMAN 10·8
©2020 ZITS Partnership. Dist. by King Features
THAT'S THE LESSON HERE?
LAZINESS PAYS.

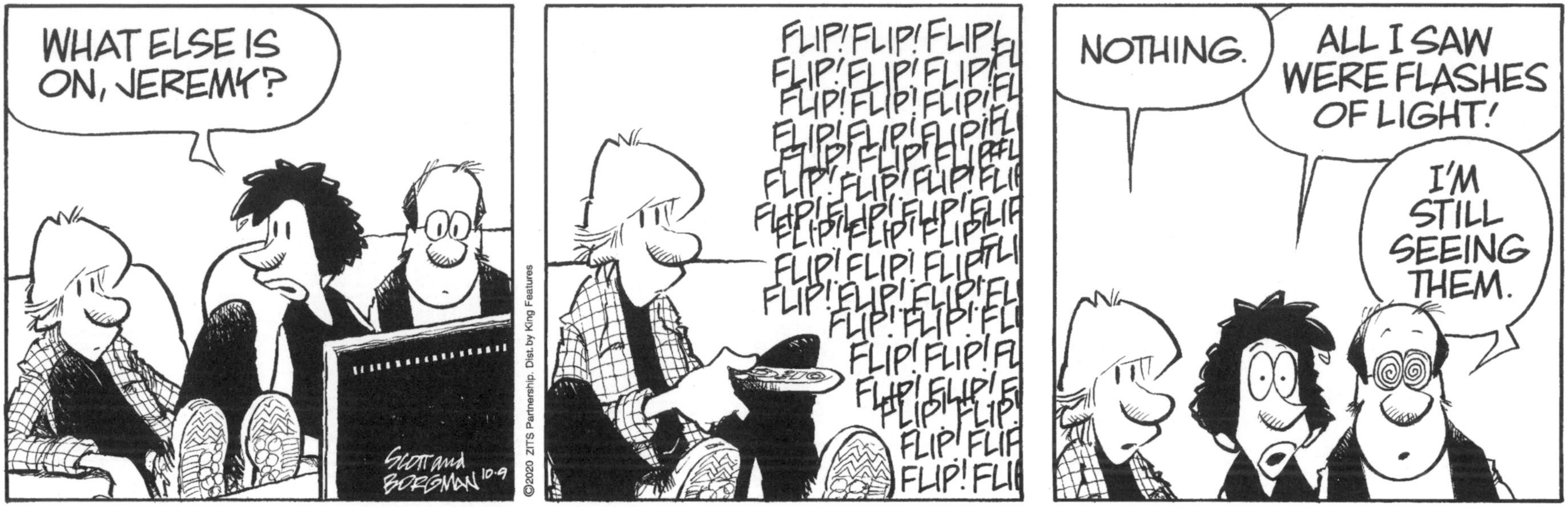
WHAT ELSE IS ON, JEREMY?
FLIP! FLIP! FLIP! FLIP! FLIP! FLIP! FLIP! FLIP!
NOTHING.
ALL I SAW WERE FLASHES OF LIGHT!
I'M STILL SEEING THEM.
©2020 ZITS Partnership. Dist. by King Features

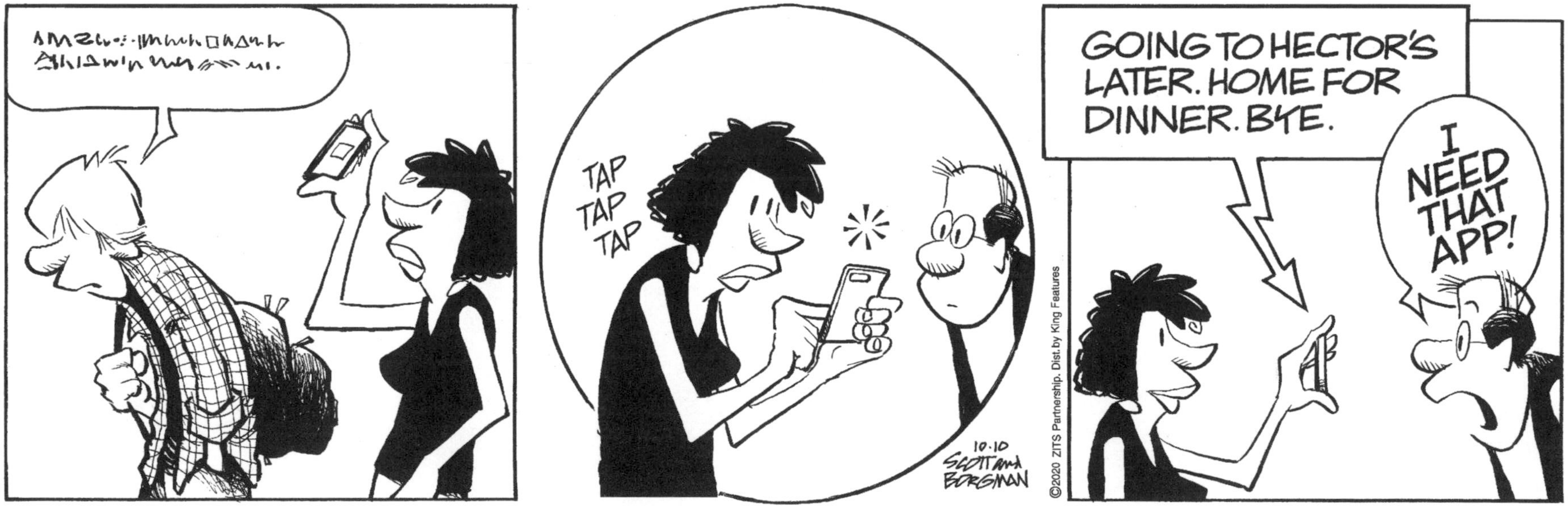
TAP TAP TAP
GOING TO HECTOR'S LATER. HOME FOR DINNER. BYE.
I NEED THAT APP!
©2020 ZITS Partnership. Dist. by King Features

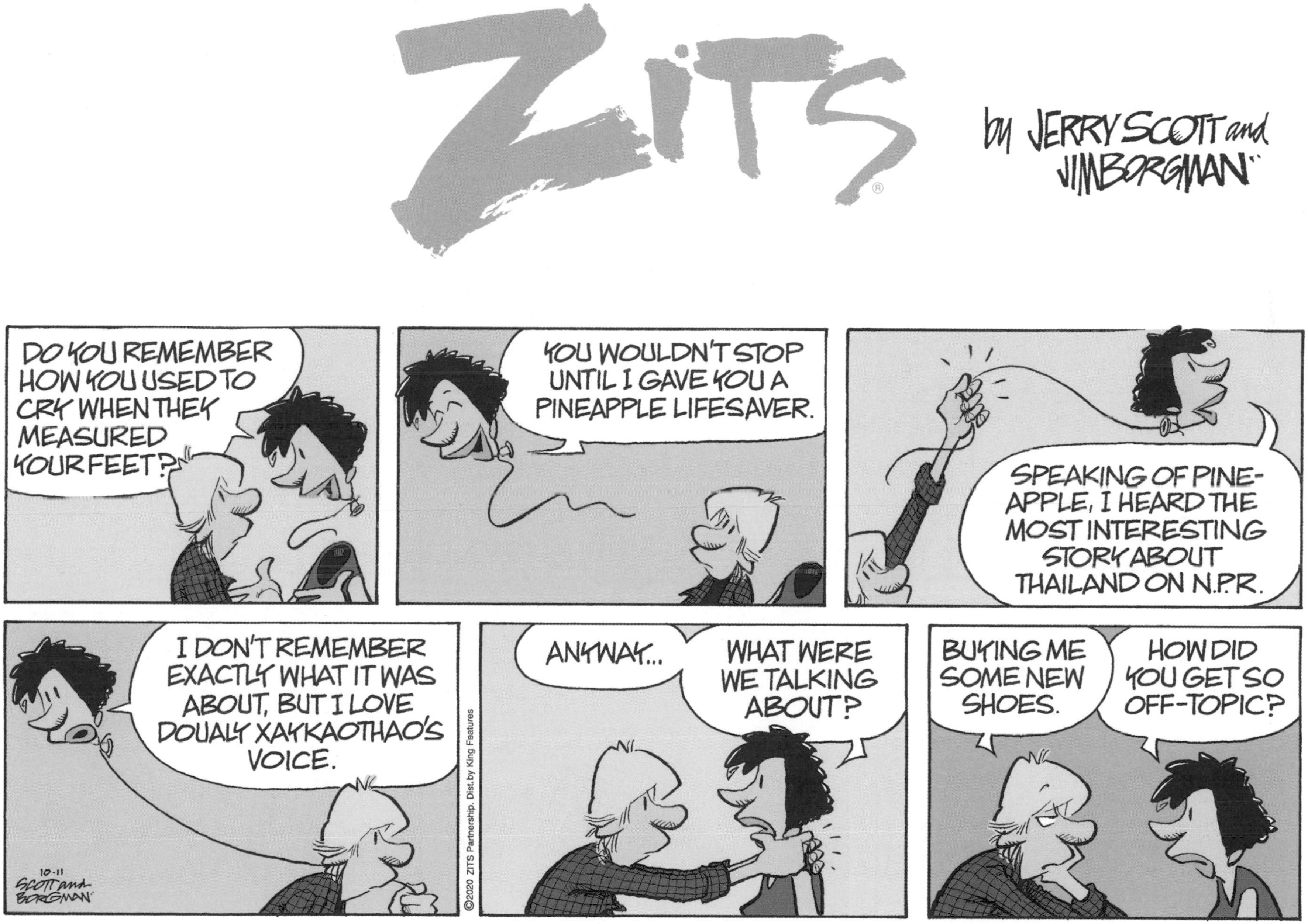
ZITS®
by JERRY SCOTT and JIM BORGMAN
DO YOU REMEMBER HOW YOU USED TO CRY WHEN THEY MEASURED YOUR FEET?
YOU WOULDN'T STOP UNTIL I GAVE YOU A PINEAPPLE LIFESAVER.
SPEAKING OF PINE-APPLE, I HEARD THE MOST INTERESTING STORY ABOUT THAILAND ON N.P.R.
I DON'T REMEMBER EXACTLY WHAT IT WAS ABOUT, BUT I LOVE DOUALY XAYKAOTHAO'S VOICE.
10-11 SCOTT and BORGMAN
©2020 ZITS Partnership. Dist. by King Features
ANYWAY...
WHAT WERE WE TALKING ABOUT?
BUYING ME SOME NEW SHOES.
HOW DID YOU GET SO OFF-TOPIC?

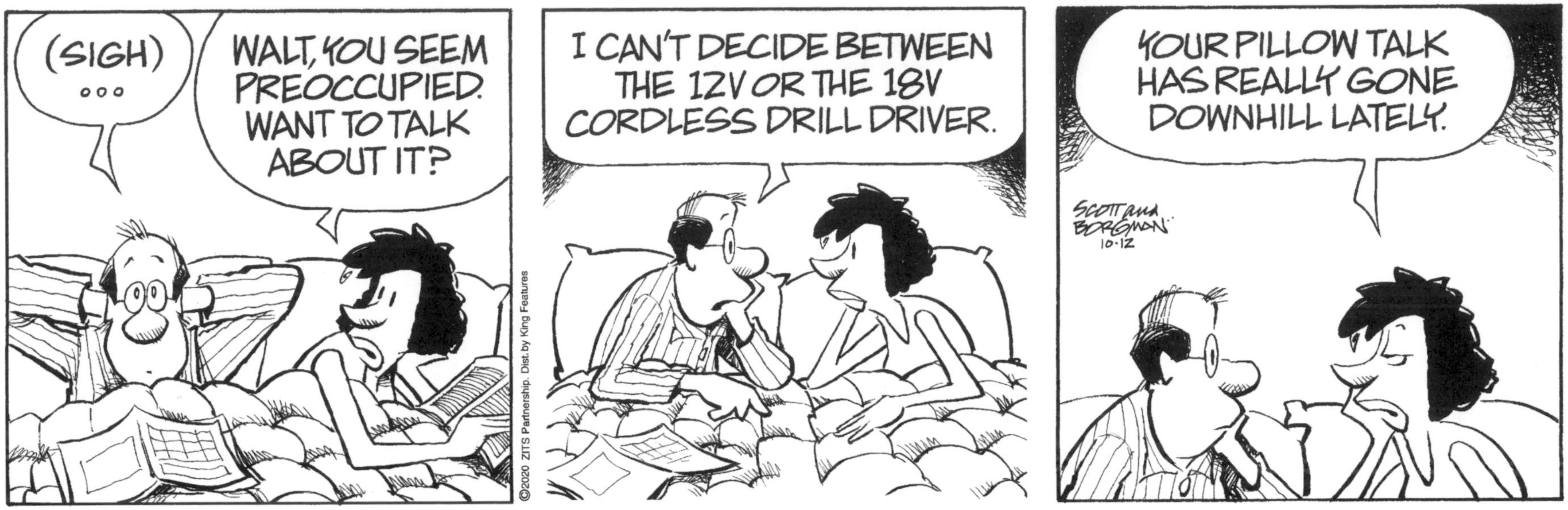
(SIGH) ...
WALT, YOU SEEM PREOCCUPIED. WANT TO TALK ABOUT IT?
©2020 ZITS Partnership. Dist. by King Features
I CAN'T DECIDE BETWEEN THE 12V OR THE 18V CORDLESS DRILL DRIVER.
YOUR PILLOW TALK HAS REALLY GONE DOWNHILL LATELY.
SCOTT AND BORGMAN
10·12

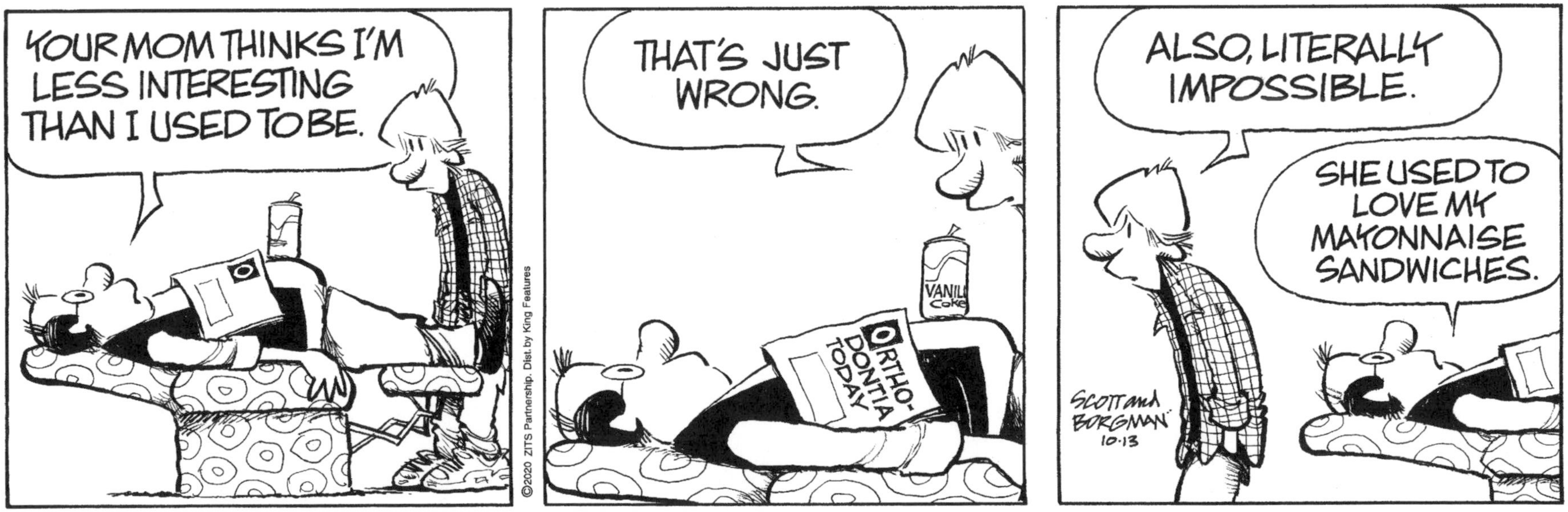
YOUR MOM THINKS I'M LESS INTERESTING THAN I USED TO BE.
©2020 ZITS Partnership. Dist. by King Features
THAT'S JUST WRONG.
ORTHO-DONTIA TODAY
VANILL Coke
ALSO, LITERALLY IMPOSSIBLE.
SHE USED TO LOVE MY MAYONNAISE SANDWICHES.
SCOTT AND BORGMAN
10·13

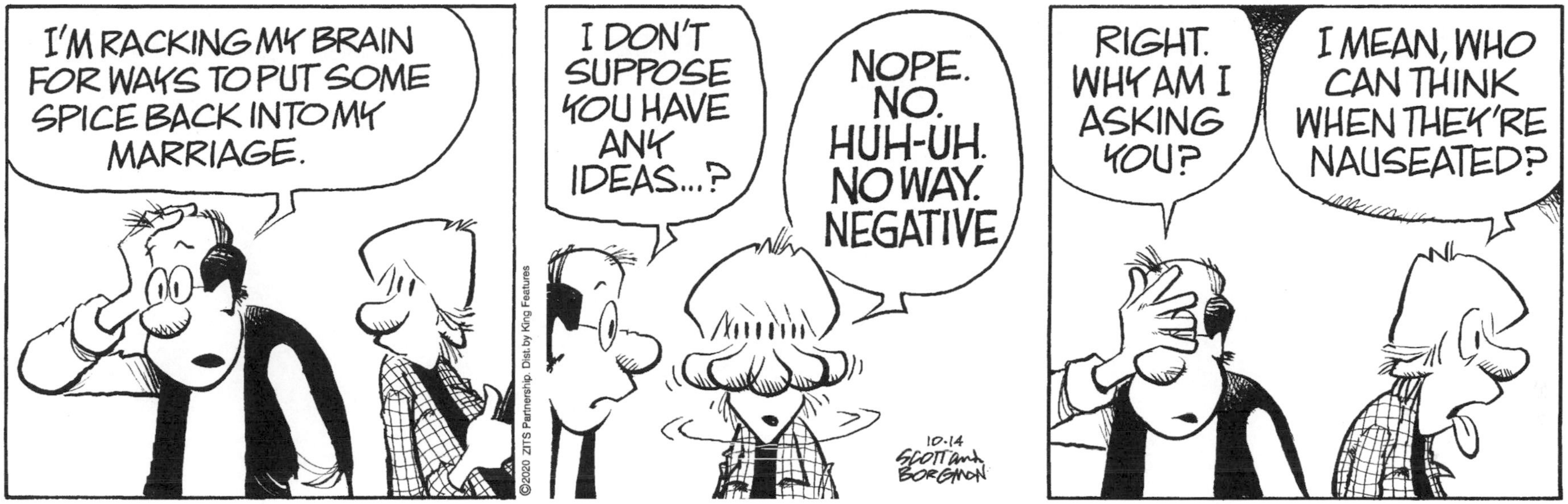
I'M RACKING MY BRAIN FOR WAYS TO PUT SOME SPICE BACK INTO MY MARRIAGE.
I DON'T SUPPOSE YOU HAVE ANY IDEAS...?
NOPE. NO. HUH-UH. NO WAY. NEGATIVE
RIGHT. WHY AM I ASKING YOU?
I MEAN, WHO CAN THINK WHEN THEY'RE NAUSEATED?
©2020 ZITS Partnership. Dist. by King Features
10-14 SCOTT and BORGMAN

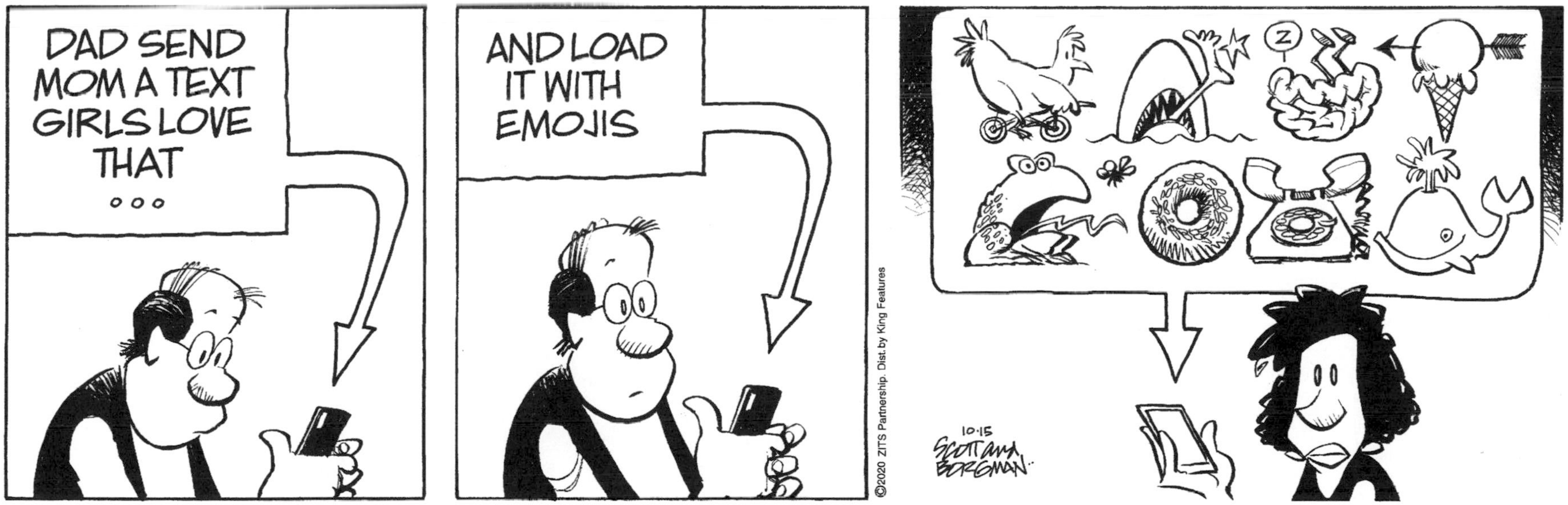
DAD SEND MOM A TEXT GIRLS LOVE THAT ...
AND LOAD IT WITH EMOJIS
Z
©2020 ZITS Partnership. Dist. by King Features
10-15 SCOTT and BORGMAN

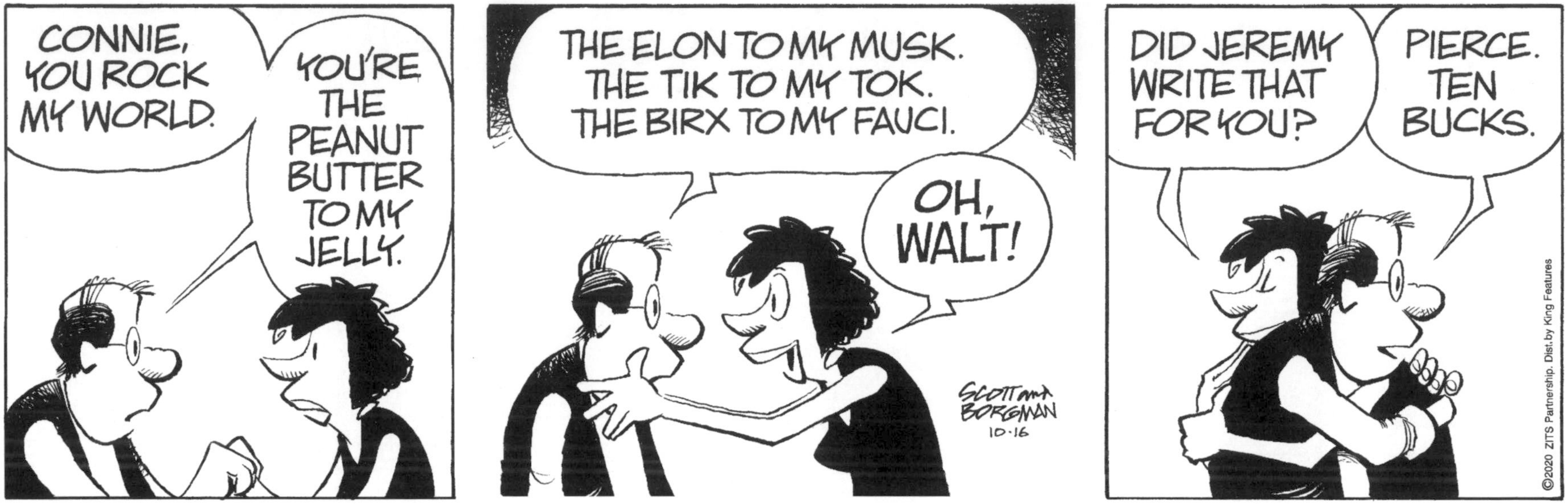
CONNIE, YOU ROCK MY WORLD.
YOU'RE THE PEANUT BUTTER TO MY JELLY.
THE ELON TO MY MUSK. THE TIK TO MY TOK. THE BIRX TO MY FAUCI.
OH, WALT!
SCOTT and BORGMAN 10·16
DID JEREMY WRITE THAT FOR YOU?
PIERCE. TEN BUCKS.
©2020 ZITS Partnership. Dist. by King Features

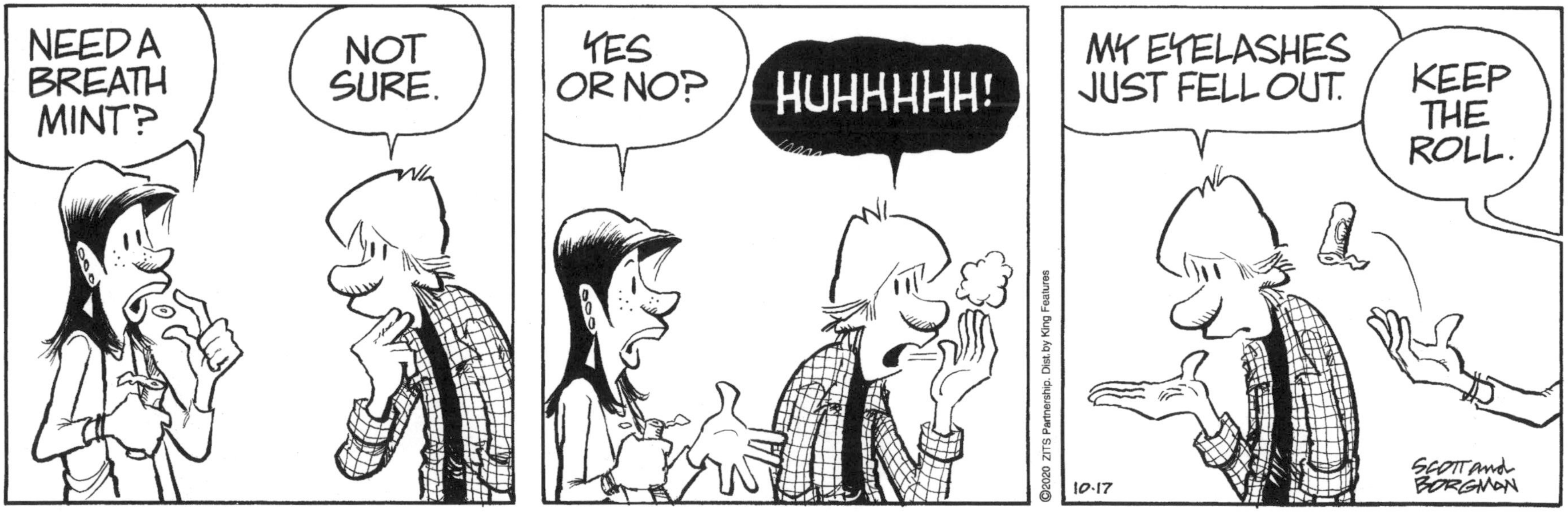
NEED A BREATH MINT?
NOT SURE.
YES OR NO?
HUHHHHH!
©2020 ZITS Partnership. Dist. by King Features
10·17
MY EYELASHES JUST FELL OUT.
KEEP THE ROLL.
SCOTT and BORGMAN

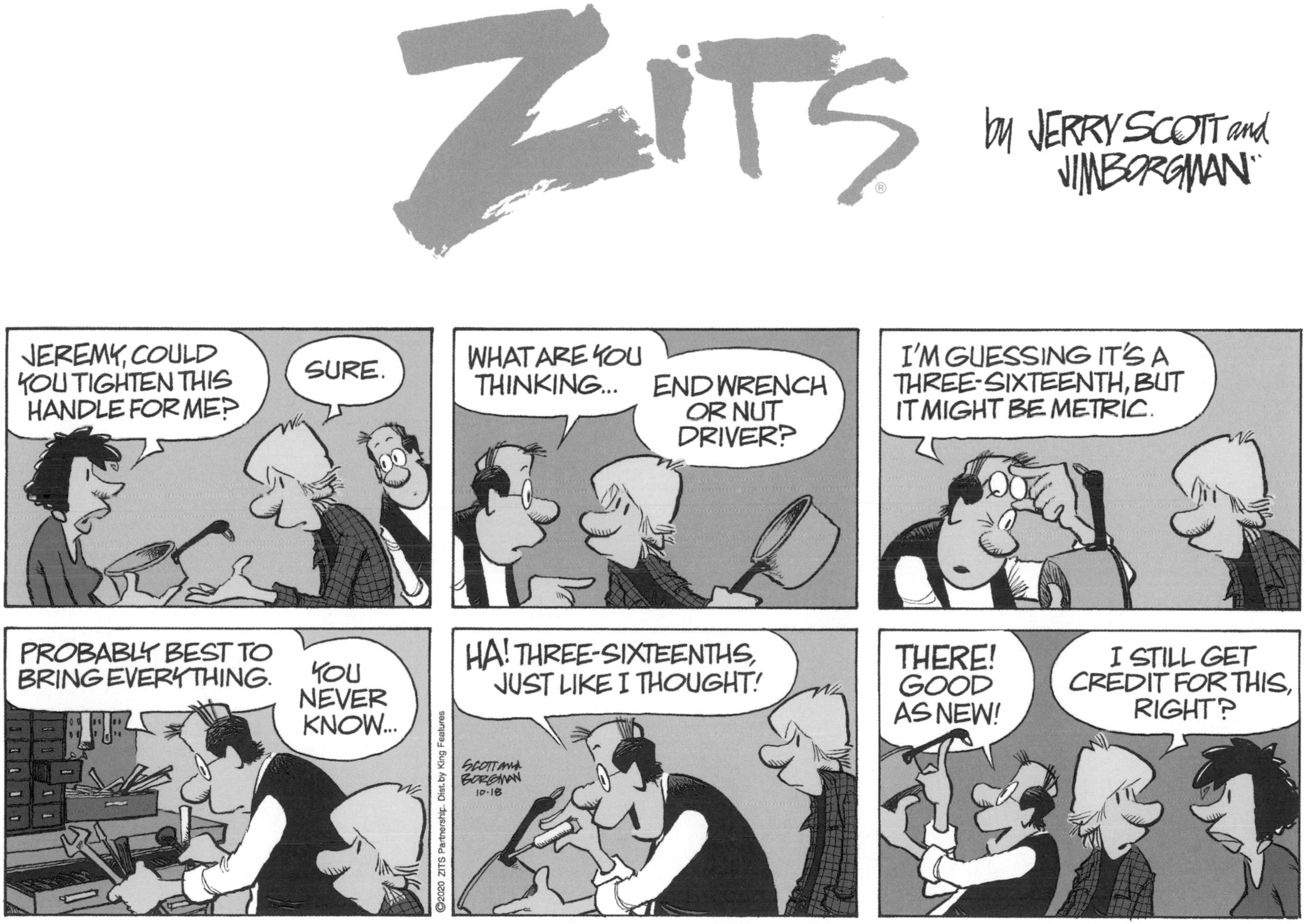
ZITS
by JERRY SCOTT and JIM BORGMAN
JEREMY, COULD YOU TIGHTEN THIS HANDLE FOR ME?
SURE.
WHAT ARE YOU THINKING...
END WRENCH OR NUT DRIVER?
I'M GUESSING IT'S A THREE-SIXTEENTH, BUT IT MIGHT BE METRIC.
PROBABLY BEST TO BRING EVERYTHING.
YOU NEVER KNOW...
©2020 ZITS Partnership. Dist. by King Features
HA! THREE-SIXTEENTHS, JUST LIKE I THOUGHT!
SCOTT and BORGMAN 10·18
THERE! GOOD AS NEW!
I STILL GET CREDIT FOR THIS, RIGHT?

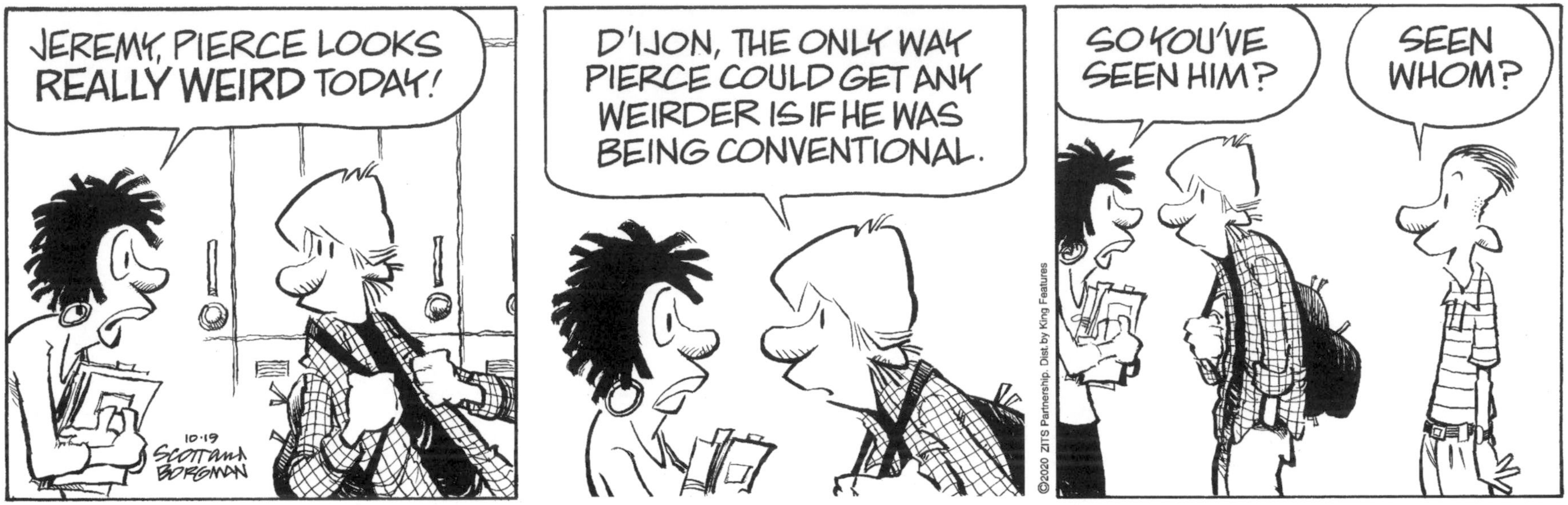
JEREMY, PIERCE LOOKS REALLY WEIRD TODAY!
10·19 SCOTT and BORGMAN
D'IJON, THE ONLY WAY PIERCE COULD GET ANY WEIRDER IS IF HE WAS BEING CONVENTIONAL.
SO YOU'VE SEEN HIM?
SEEN WHOM?
©2020 ZITS Partnership. Dist. by King Features

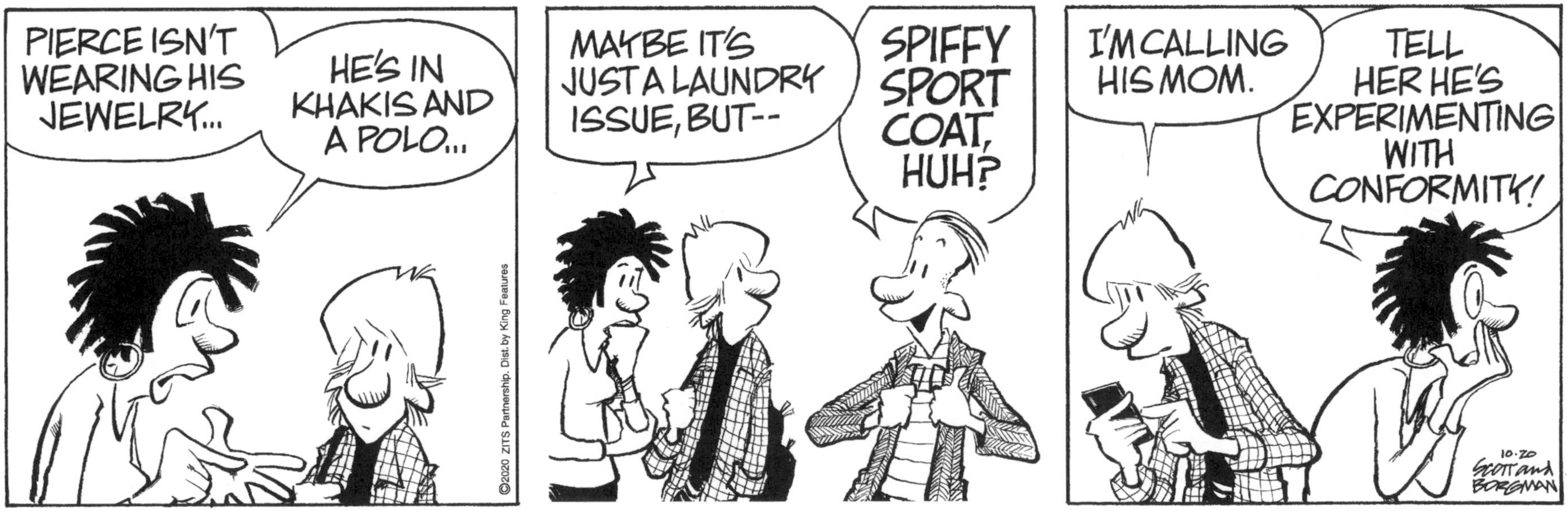
PIERCE ISN'T WEARING HIS JEWELRY...
HE'S IN KHAKIS AND A POLO...
©2020 ZITS Partnership. Dist. by King Features
MAYBE IT'S JUST A LAUNDRY ISSUE, BUT--
SPIFFY SPORT COAT, HUH?
I'M CALLING HIS MOM.
TELL HER HE'S EXPERIMENTING WITH CONFORMITY!
10·20 SCOTT and BORGMAN

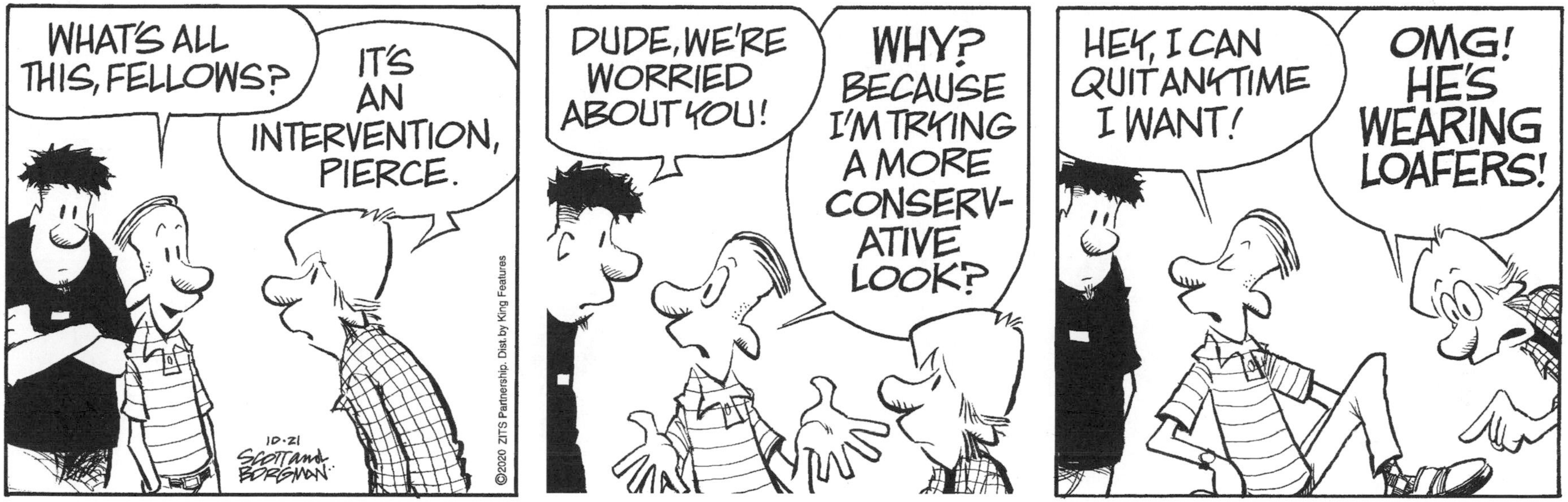
WHAT'S ALL THIS, FELLOWS?
IT'S AN INTERVENTION, PIERCE.
10·21 SCOTT AND BORGMAN
©2020 ZITS Partnership. Dist. by King Features
DUDE, WE'RE WORRIED ABOUT YOU!
WHY? BECAUSE I'M TRYING A MORE CONSERV-ATIVE LOOK?
HEY, I CAN QUIT ANYTIME I WANT!
OMG! HE'S WEARING LOAFERS!

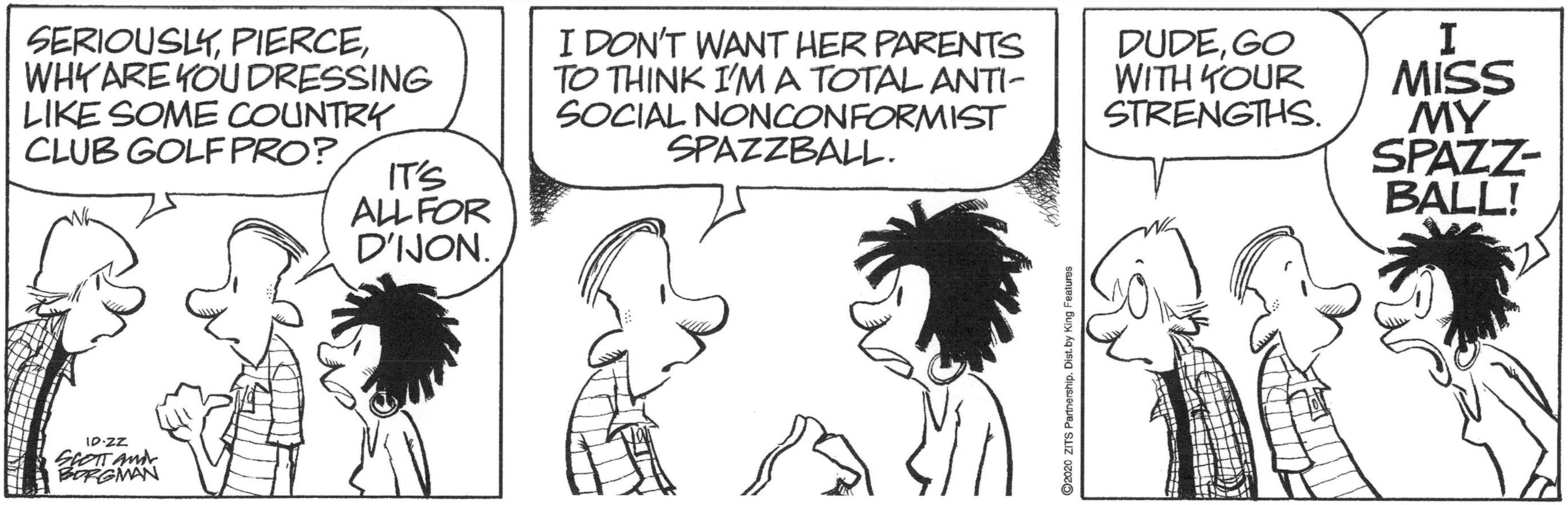
SERIOUSLY, PIERCE, WHY ARE YOU DRESSING LIKE SOME COUNTRY CLUB GOLF PRO?
IT'S ALL FOR D'JON.
10·22 SCOTT AND BORGMAN
I DON'T WANT HER PARENTS TO THINK I'M A TOTAL ANTI-SOCIAL NONCONFORMIST SPAZZBALL.
©2020 ZITS Partnership. Dist. by King Features
DUDE, GO WITH YOUR STRENGTHS.
I MISS MY SPAZZ-BALL!

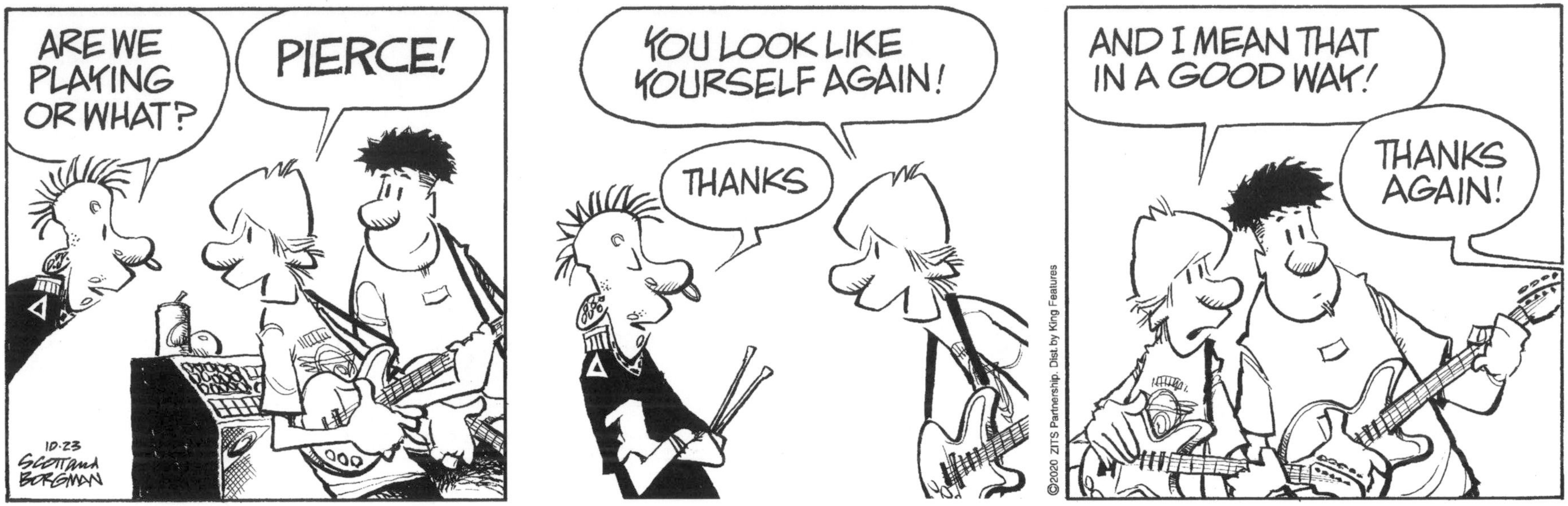
ARE WE PLAYING OR WHAT?
PIERCE!
10-23 SCOTT and BORGMAN
YOU LOOK LIKE YOURSELF AGAIN!
THANKS
©2020 ZITS Partnership. Dist. by King Features
AND I MEAN THAT IN A GOOD WAY!
THANKS AGAIN!

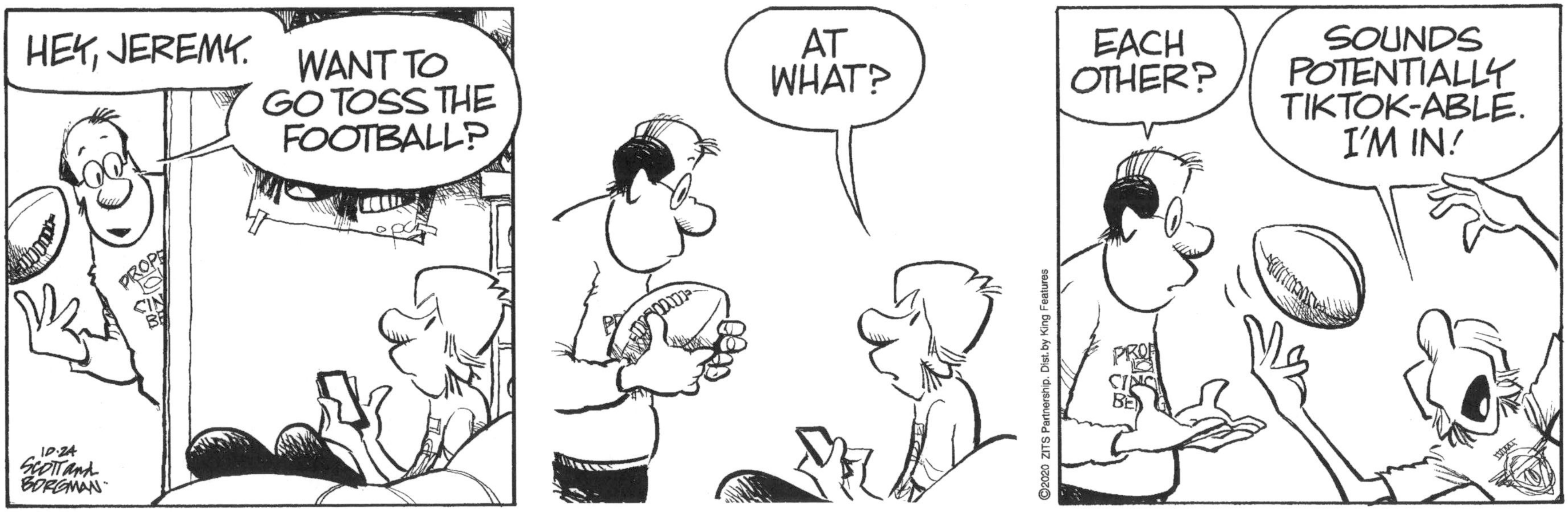
HEY, JEREMY.
WANT TO GO TOSS THE FOOTBALL?
10-24 SCOTT and BORGMAN
AT WHAT?
©2020 ZITS Partnership. Dist. by King Features
EACH OTHER?
SOUNDS POTENTIALLY TIKTOK-ABLE. I'M IN!

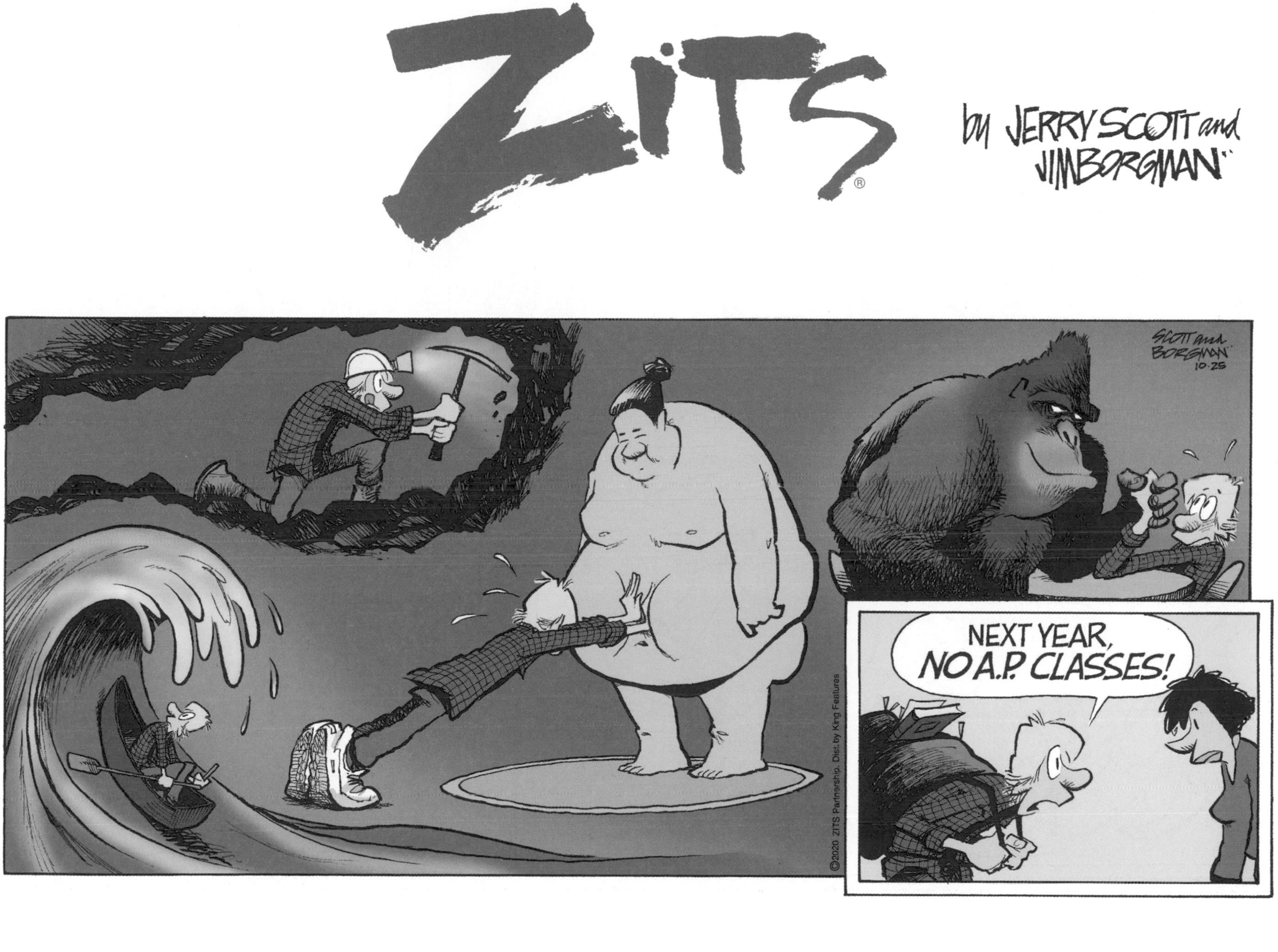
ZITS
by JERRY SCOTT and JIM BORGMAN
SCOTT and BORGMAN 10-25
©2020 ZITS Partnership. Dist. by King Features
NEXT YEAR, NO A.P. CLASSES!

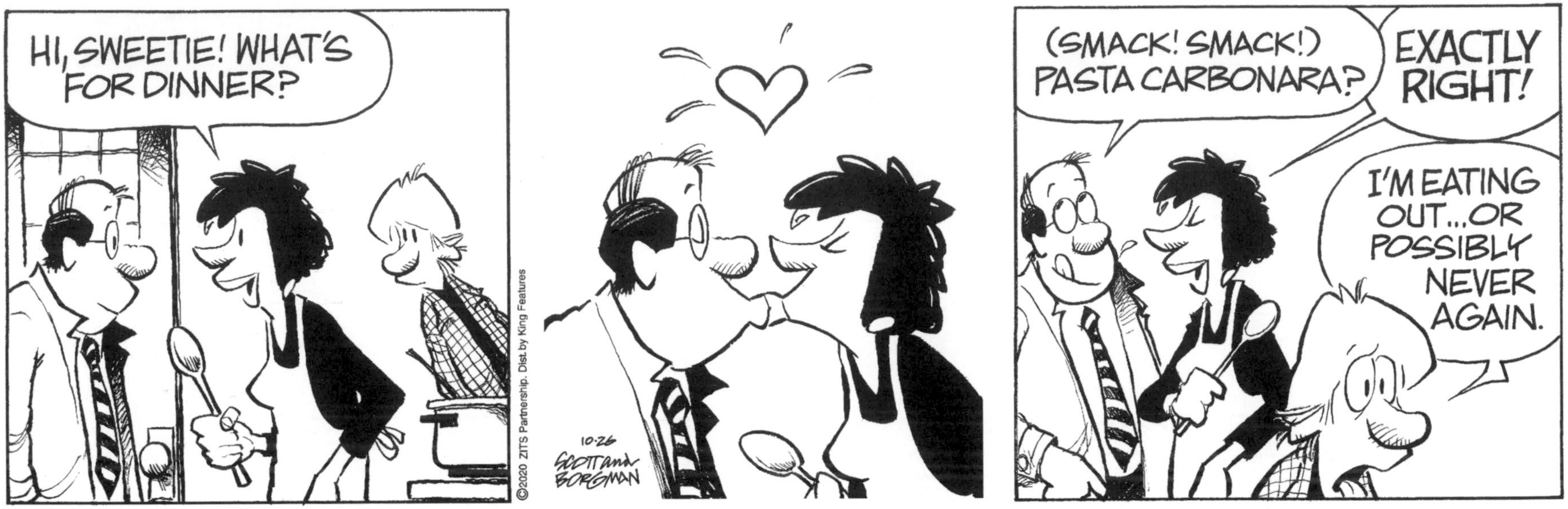
HI, SWEETIE! WHAT'S FOR DINNER?
(SMACK! SMACK!) PASTA CARBONARA?
EXACTLY RIGHT!
I'M EATING OUT...OR POSSIBLY NEVER AGAIN.
©2020 ZITS Partnership. Dist. by King Features

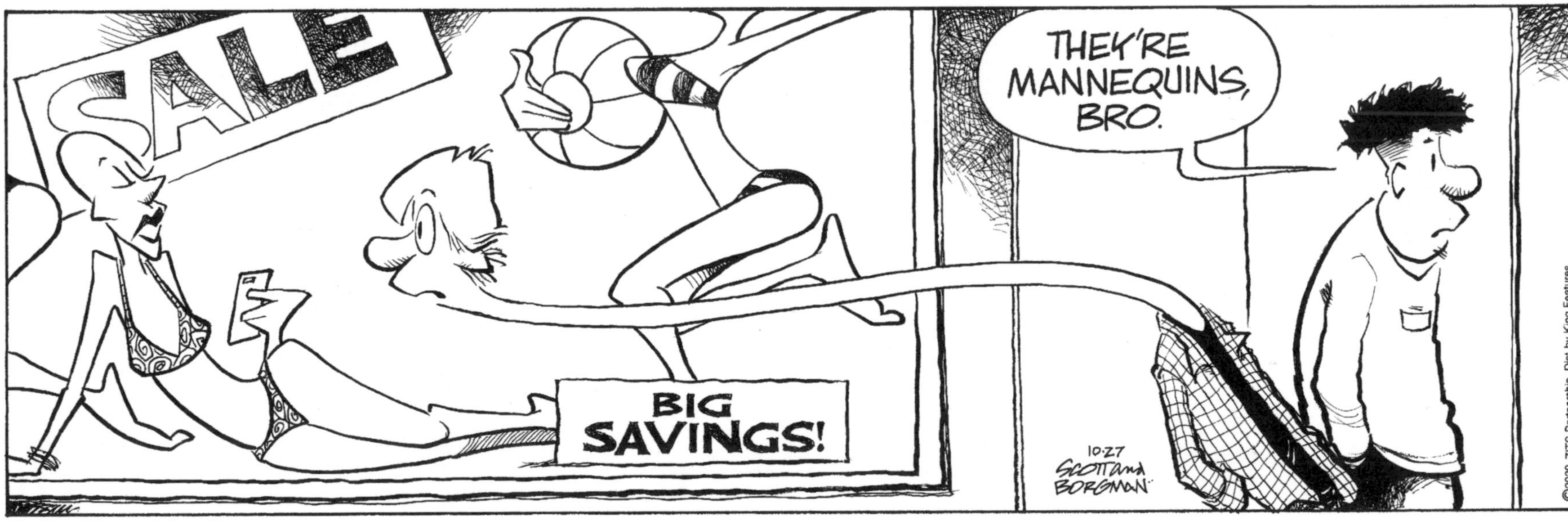
SALE
BIG SAVINGS!
THEY'RE MANNEQUINS, BRO.
©2020 ZITS Partnership. Dist. by King Features

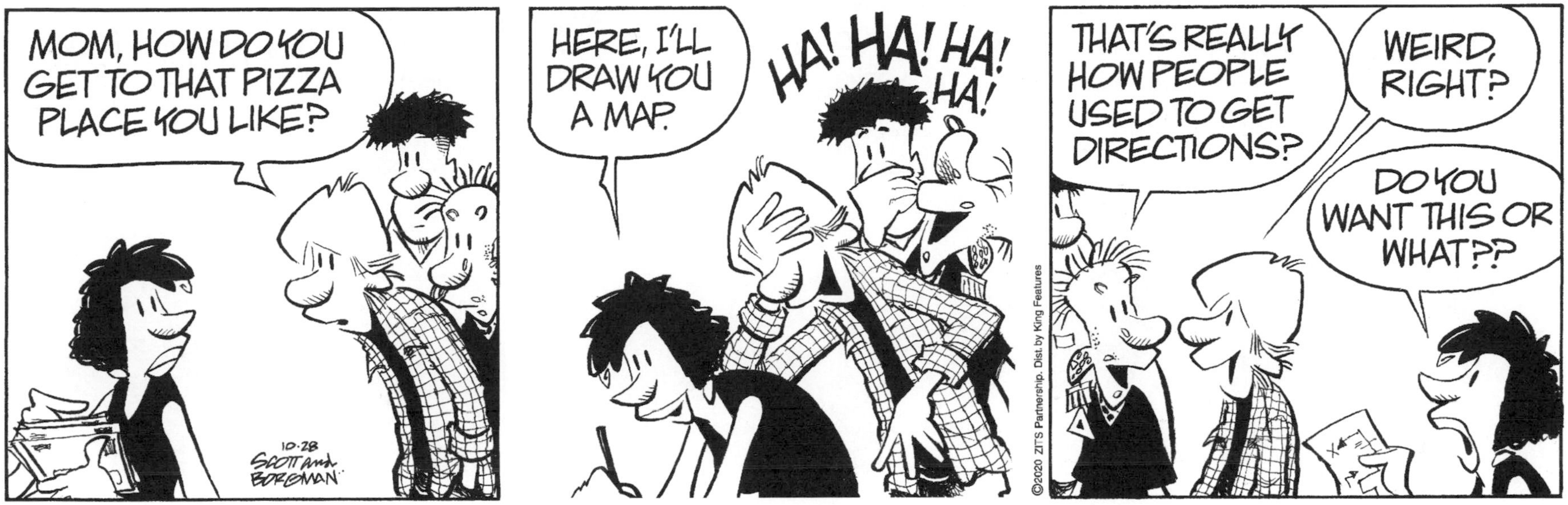
MOM, HOW DO YOU GET TO THAT PIZZA PLACE YOU LIKE?
10·28 SCOTT and BORGMAN
HERE, I'LL DRAW YOU A MAP.
HA! HA! HA! HA!
©2020 ZITS Partnership. Dist. by King Features
THAT'S REALLY HOW PEOPLE USED TO GET DIRECTIONS?
WEIRD, RIGHT?
DO YOU WANT THIS OR WHAT??

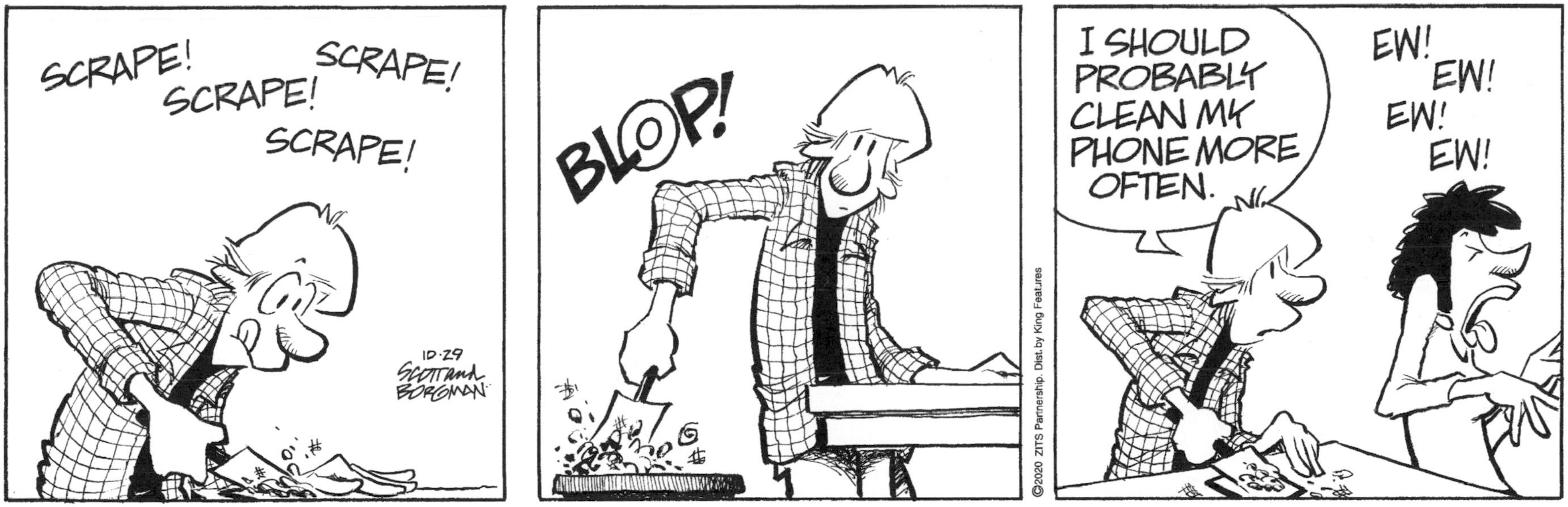
SCRAPE! SCRAPE! SCRAPE! SCRAPE!
10·29 SCOTT and BORGMAN
BLOP!
©2020 ZITS Partnership. Dist. by King Features
I SHOULD PROBABLY CLEAN MY PHONE MORE OFTEN.
EW! EW! EW! EW!

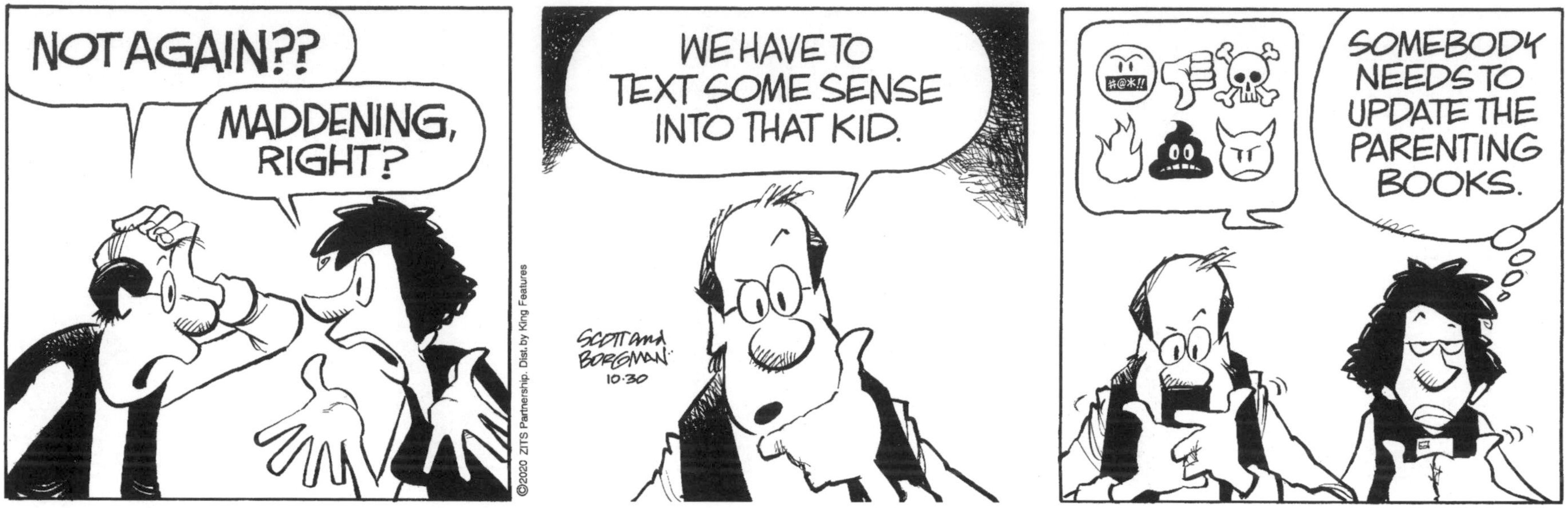
NOT AGAIN??
MADDENING, RIGHT?
WE HAVE TO TEXT SOME SENSE INTO THAT KID.
#@*!!
SOMEBODY NEEDS TO UPDATE THE PARENTING BOOKS.
©2020 ZITS Partnership. Dist. by King Features

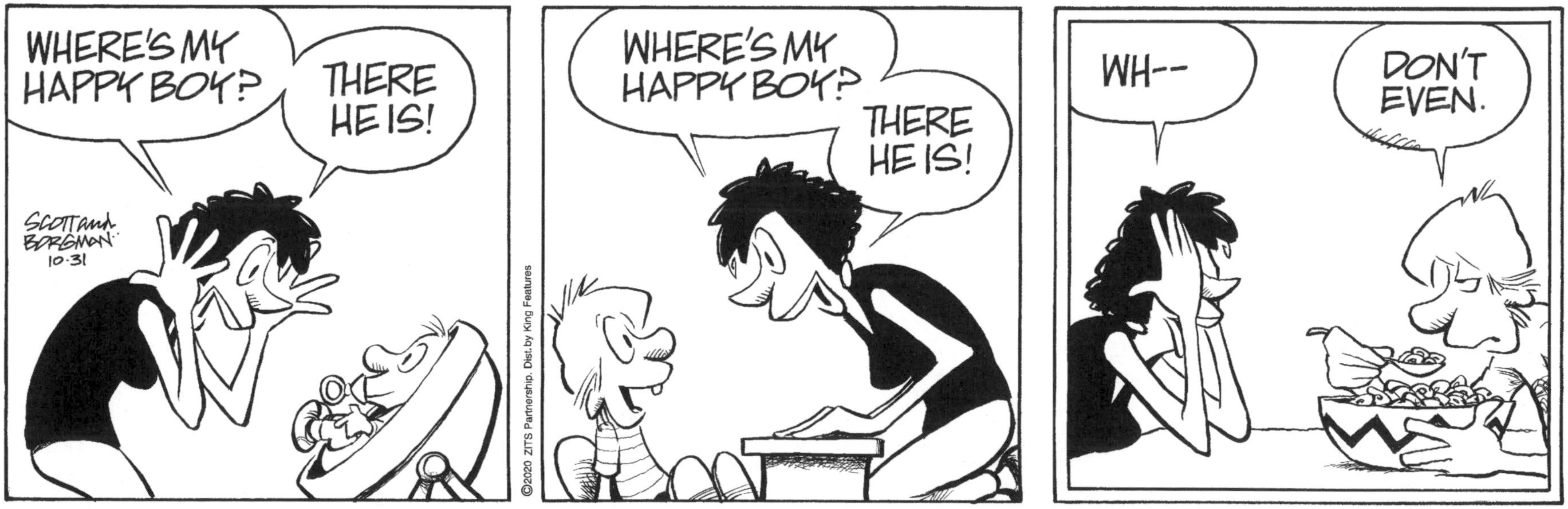
WHERE'S MY HAPPY BOY?
THERE HE IS!
WHERE'S MY HAPPY BOY?
THERE HE IS!
WH--
DON'T EVEN.
©2020 ZITS Partnership. Dist. by King Features

ZITS®

by JERRY SCOTT and JIM BORGMAN

JEREMY, I NEED YOUR UNDIVIDED ATTENTION.
A.P. ENGLISH READING LIST
NOTES
CURRENT PLAYLIST
SPOTIFY
YOUTUBE INSTAGRAM TIKTOK TEXT
ZOOM
BAND STUFF
ASSIGNMENTS
SUSTENANCE
NEW SONG
GIRLFRIEND DRAMA
HOMEWORK
CAFFEINE
IS THAT EVEN A THING?
11-1 SCOTT and BORGMAN
©2020 ZITS Partnership. Dist. by King Features

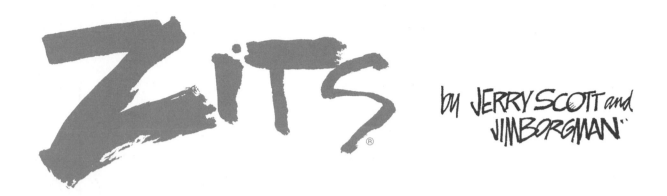

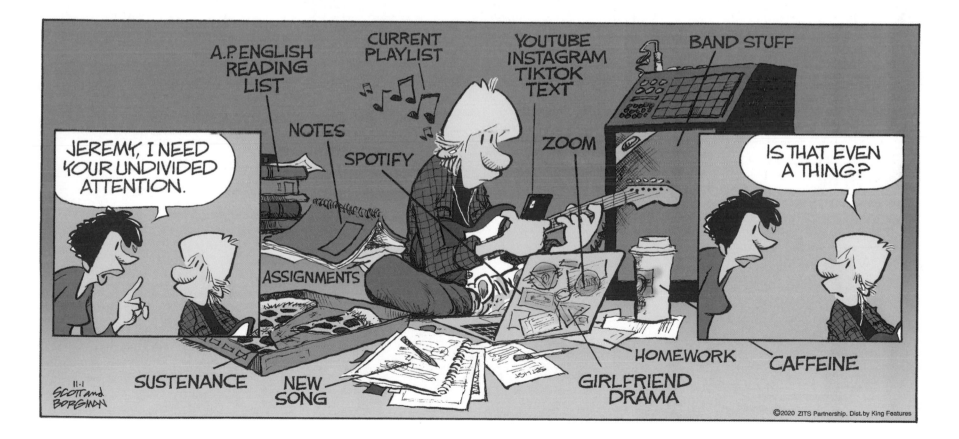

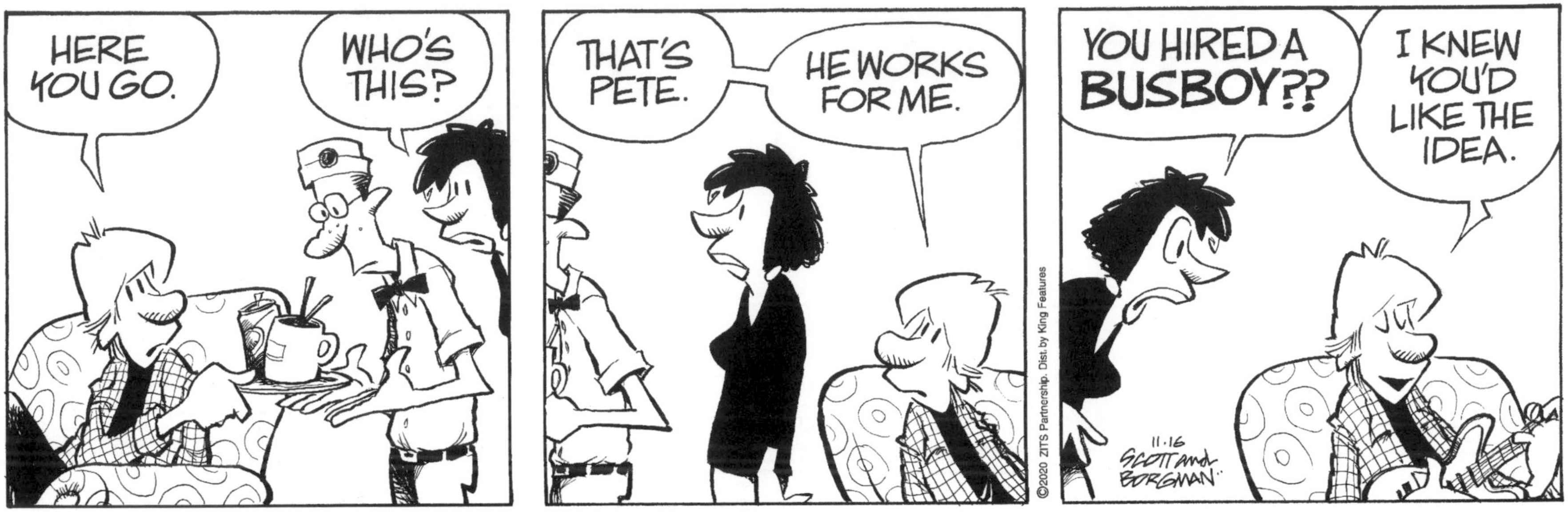
HERE YOU GO.
WHO'S THIS?
THAT'S PETE.
HE WORKS FOR ME.
©2020 ZITS Partnership. Dist. by King Features
YOU HIRED A **BUSBOY**??
I KNEW YOU'D LIKE THE IDEA.
11-16 SCOTT and BORGMAN

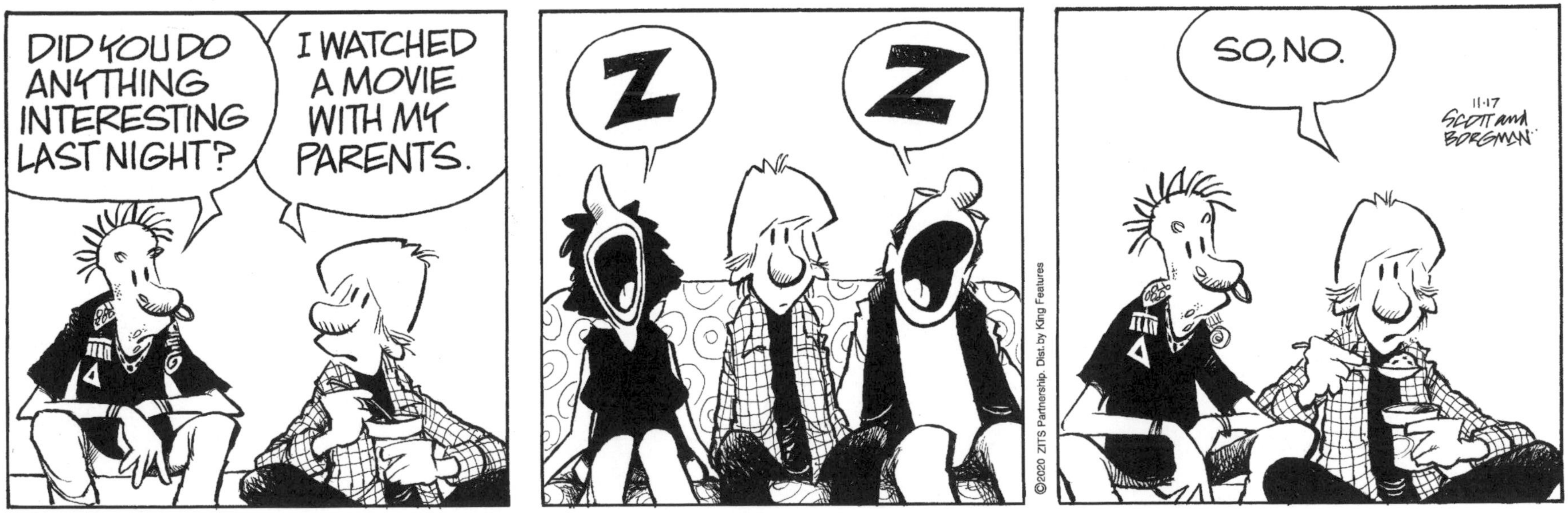
DID YOU DO ANYTHING INTERESTING LAST NIGHT?
I WATCHED A MOVIE WITH MY PARENTS.
Z
Z
©2020 ZITS Partnership. Dist. by King Features
SO, NO.
11-17 SCOTT and BORGMAN

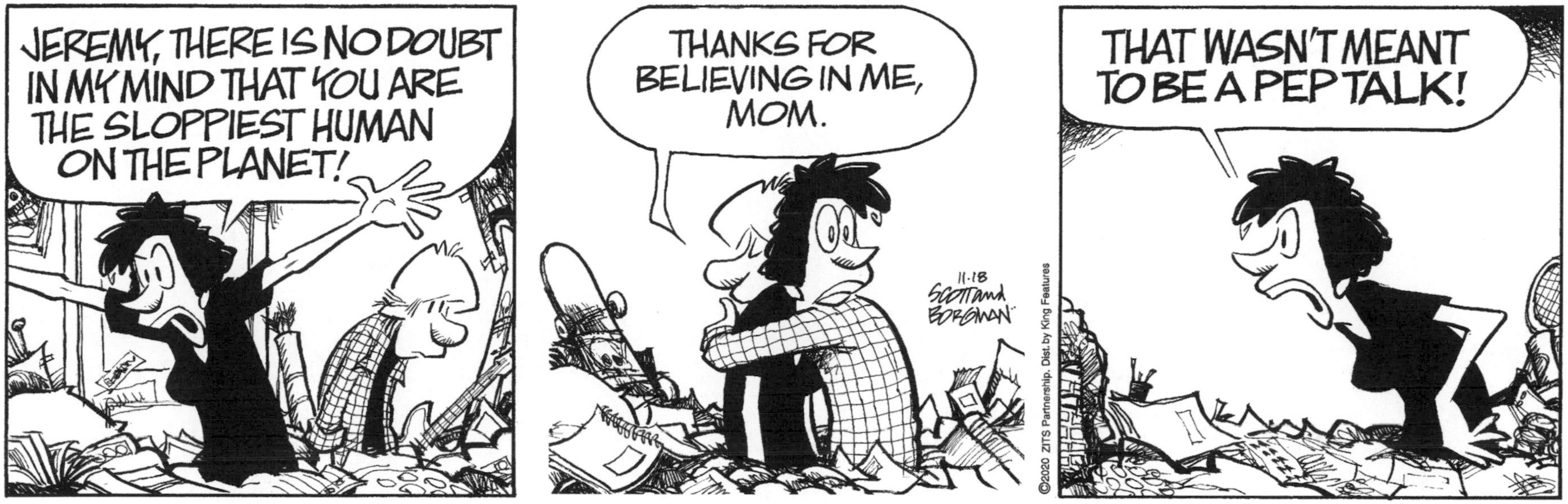
JEREMY, THERE IS NO DOUBT IN MY MIND THAT YOU ARE THE SLOPPIEST HUMAN ON THE PLANET!
THANKS FOR BELIEVING IN ME, MOM.
11-18 SCOTT and BORGMAN
©2020 ZITS Partnership. Dist. by King Features
THAT WASN'T MEANT TO BE A PEP TALK!

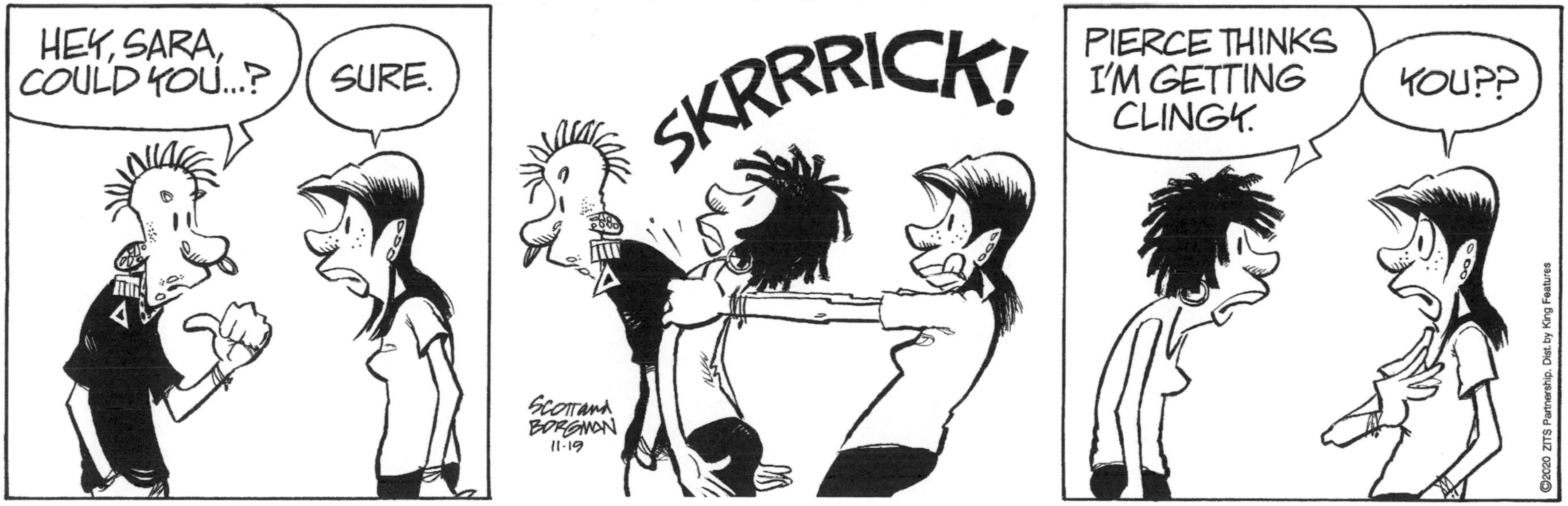
HEY, SARA, COULD YOU...?
SURE.
SKRRRICK!
SCOTT and BORGMAN 11-19
PIERCE THINKS I'M GETTING CLINGY.
YOU??
©2020 ZITS Partnership. Dist. by King Features

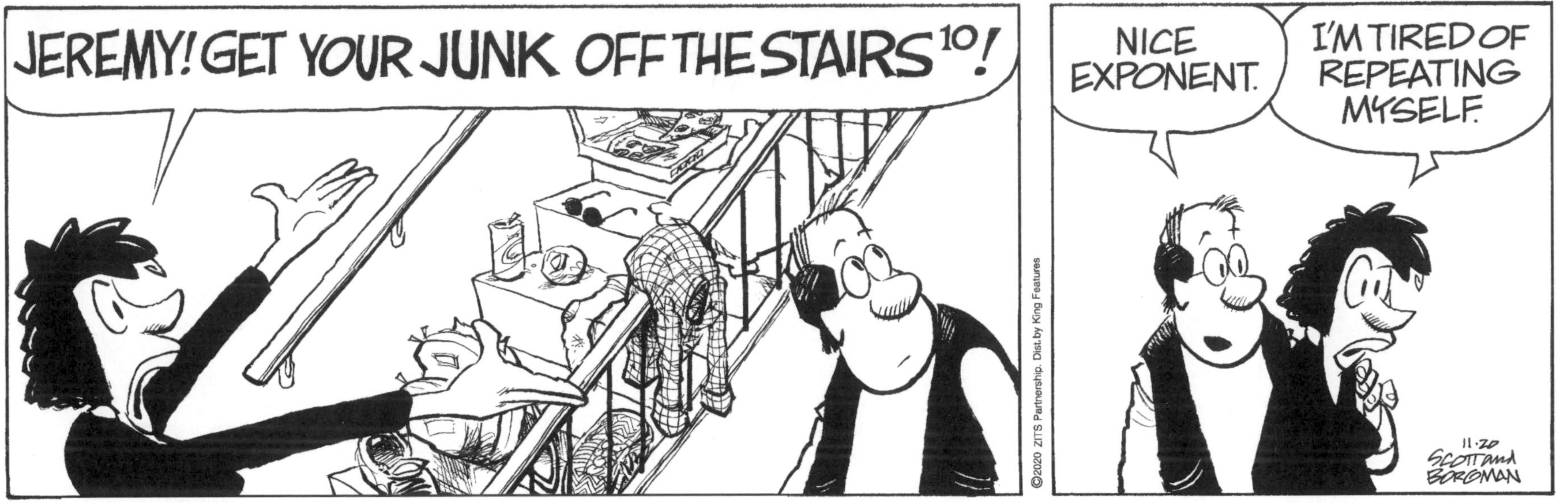
JEREMY! GET YOUR JUNK OFF THE STAIRS^{10}!
NICE EXPONENT.
I'M TIRED OF REPEATING MYSELF.
©2020 ZITS Partnership. Dist. by King Features
11·20 SCOTT and BORGMAN

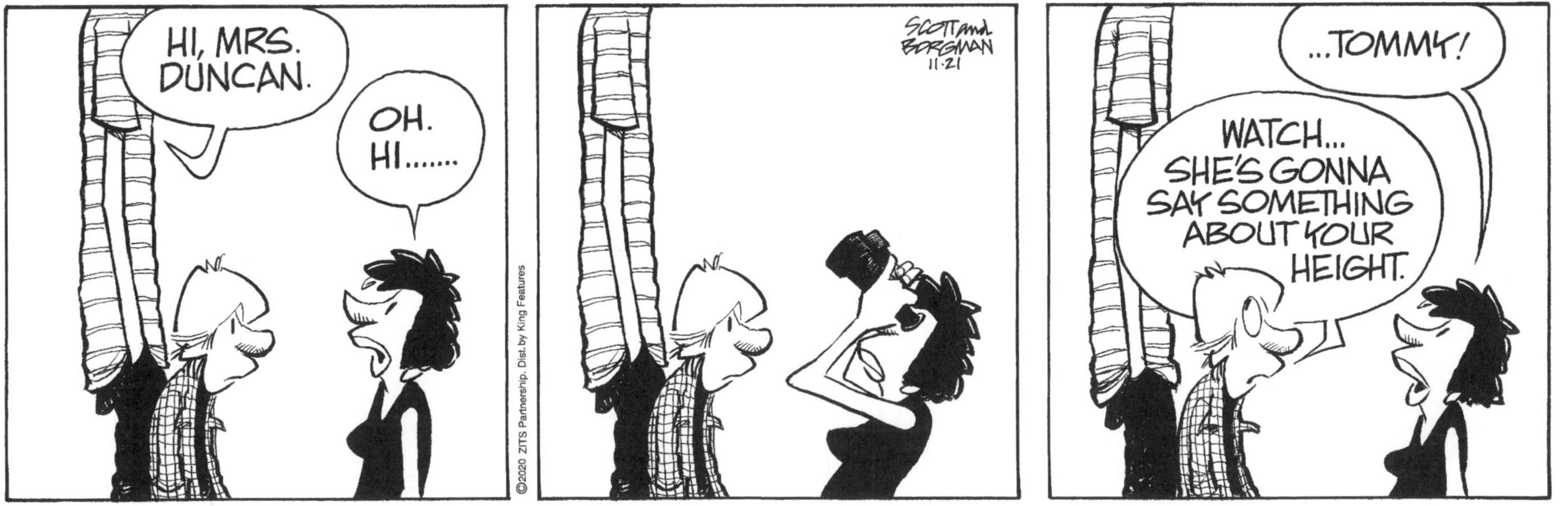
HI, MRS. DUNCAN.
OH. HI.......
©2020 ZITS Partnership. Dist. by King Features
SCOTT and BORGMAN 11·21
...TOMMY!
WATCH... SHE'S GONNA SAY SOMETHING ABOUT YOUR HEIGHT.

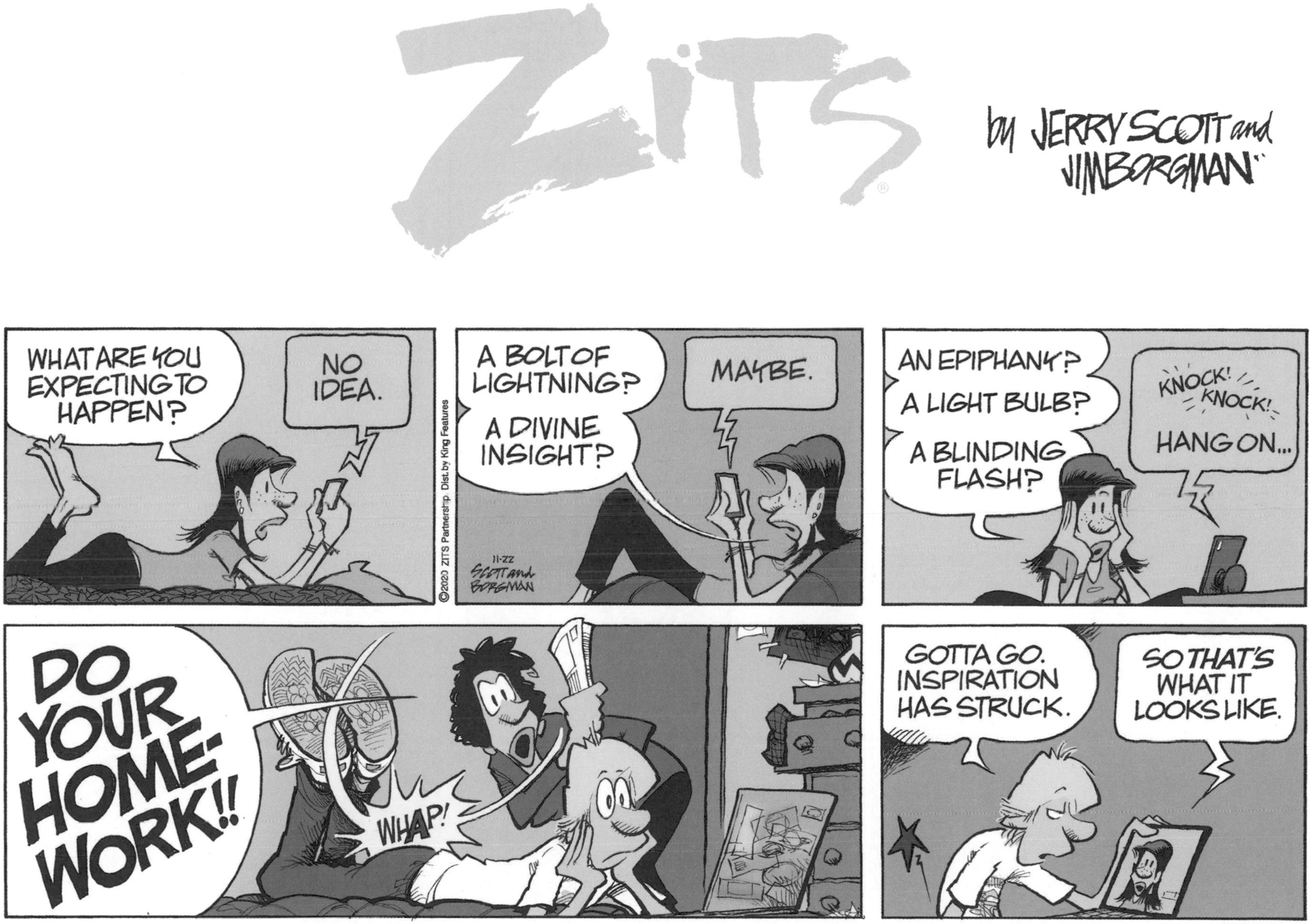
ZITS
by JERRY SCOTT and JIM BORGMAN
WHAT ARE YOU EXPECTING TO HAPPEN?
NO IDEA.
©2020 ZITS Partnership. Dist. by King Features
11-22 SCOTT and BORGMAN
A BOLT OF LIGHTNING?
A DIVINE INSIGHT?
MAYBE.
AN EPIPHANY?
A LIGHT BULB?
A BLINDING FLASH?
KNOCK! KNOCK!
HANG ON...
DO YOUR HOME-WORK!!
WHAP!
GOTTA GO. INSPIRATION HAS STRUCK.
SO THAT'S WHAT IT LOOKS LIKE.

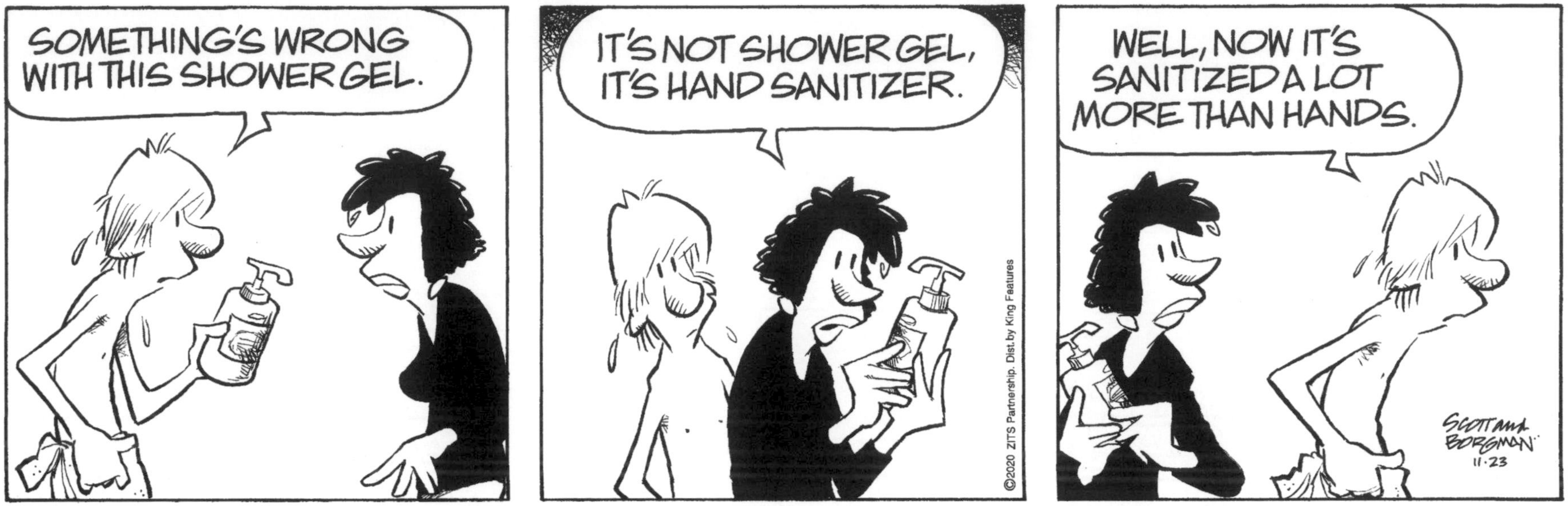
SOMETHING'S WRONG WITH THIS SHOWER GEL.
IT'S NOT SHOWER GEL, IT'S HAND SANITIZER.
©2020 ZITS Partnership. Dist. by King Features
WELL, NOW IT'S SANITIZED A LOT MORE THAN HANDS.
SCOTT AND BORGMAN 11·23

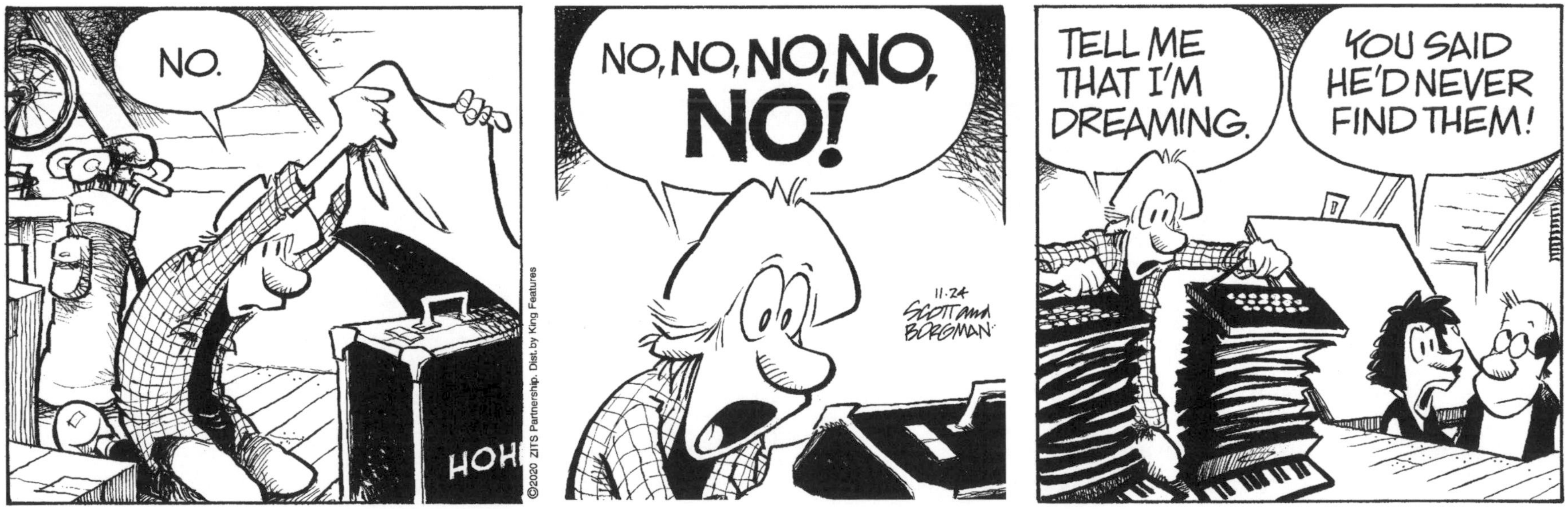
NO.
HOH
©2020 ZITS Partnership. Dist. by King Features
NO, NO, NO, NO, NO!
11·24 SCOTT AND BORGMAN
TELL ME THAT I'M DREAMING.
YOU SAID HE'D NEVER FIND THEM!

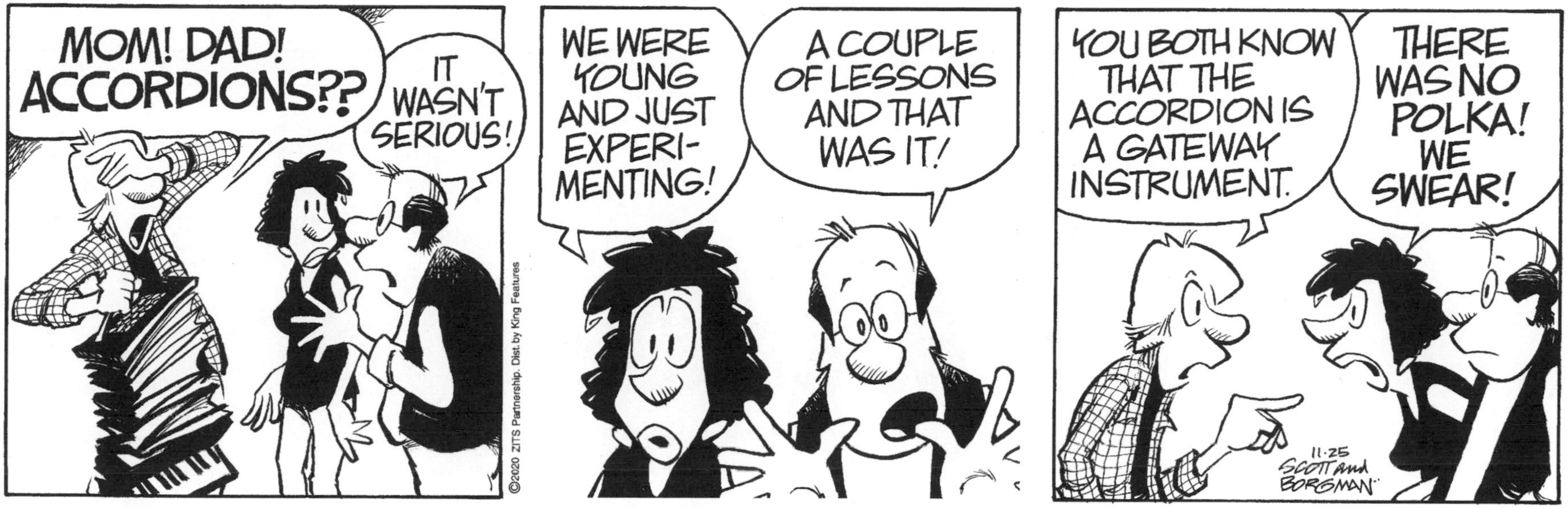
MOM! DAD! ACCORDIONS??
IT WASN'T SERIOUS!
©2020 ZITS Partnership. Dist. by King Features
WE WERE YOUNG AND JUST EXPERI-MENTING!
A COUPLE OF LESSONS AND THAT WAS IT!
YOU BOTH KNOW THAT THE ACCORDION IS A GATEWAY INSTRUMENT.
THERE WAS NO POLKA! WE SWEAR!
11·25
SCOTT AND BORGMAN

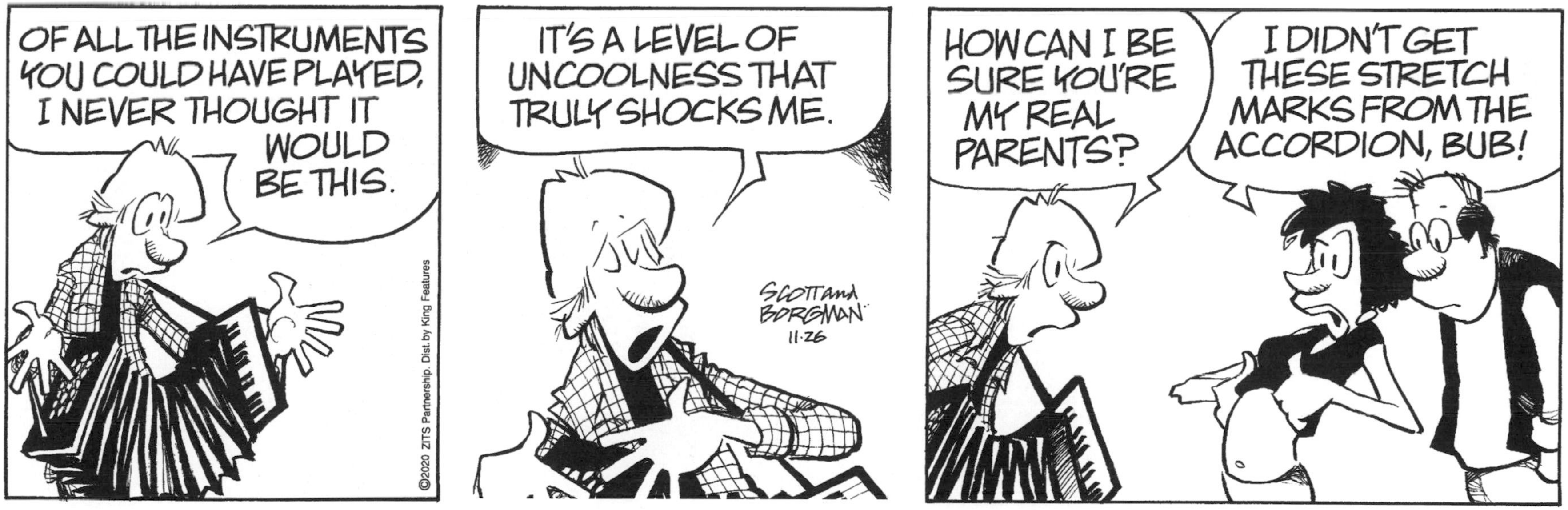
OF ALL THE INSTRUMENTS YOU COULD HAVE PLAYED, I NEVER THOUGHT IT WOULD BE THIS.
©2020 ZITS Partnership. Dist. by King Features
IT'S A LEVEL OF UNCOOLNESS THAT TRULY SHOCKS ME.
SCOTT AND BORGMAN
11·26
HOW CAN I BE SURE YOU'RE MY REAL PARENTS?
I DIDN'T GET THESE STRETCH MARKS FROM THE ACCORDION, BUB!

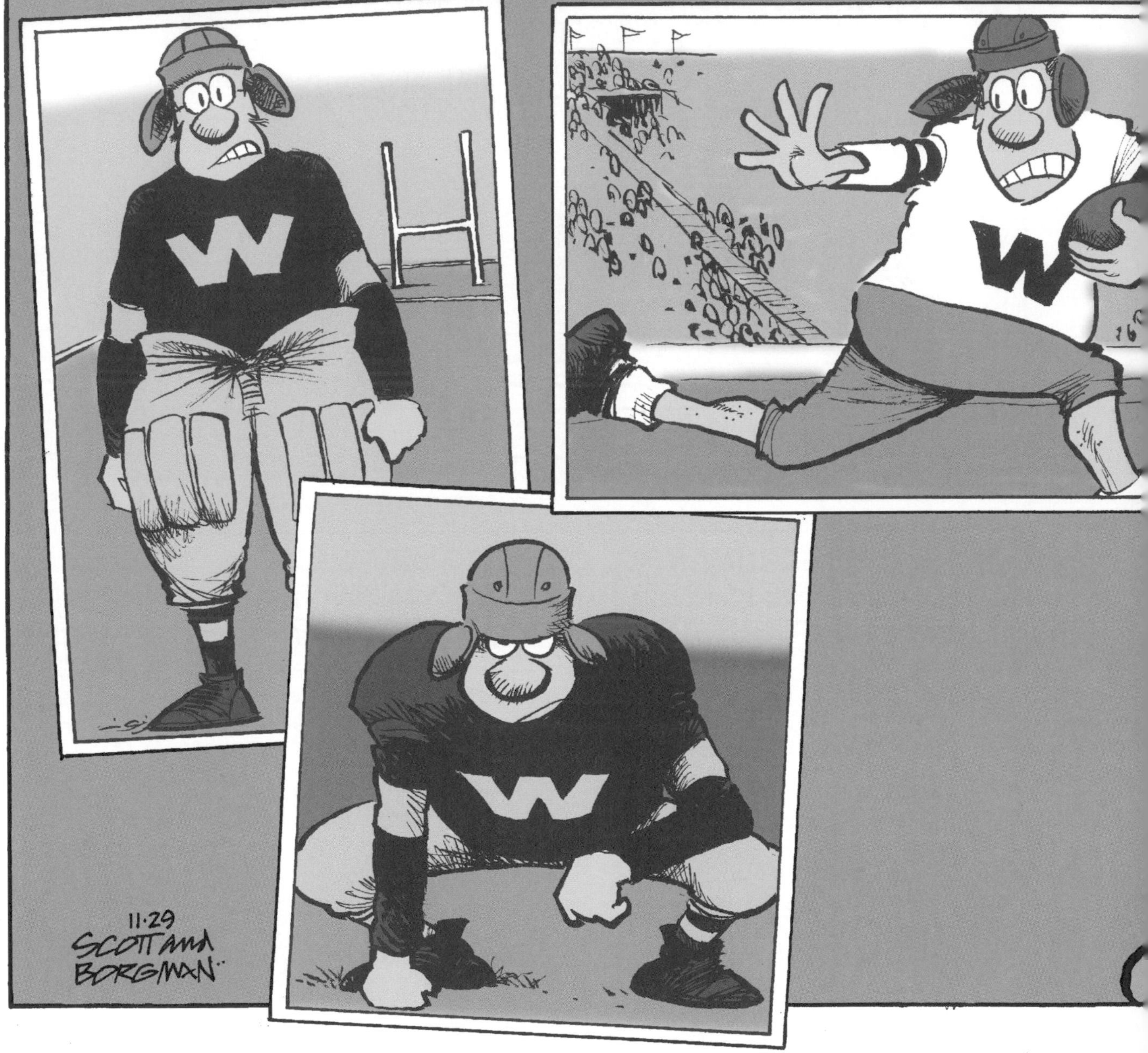
11·29
SCOTT AND
BORGMAN

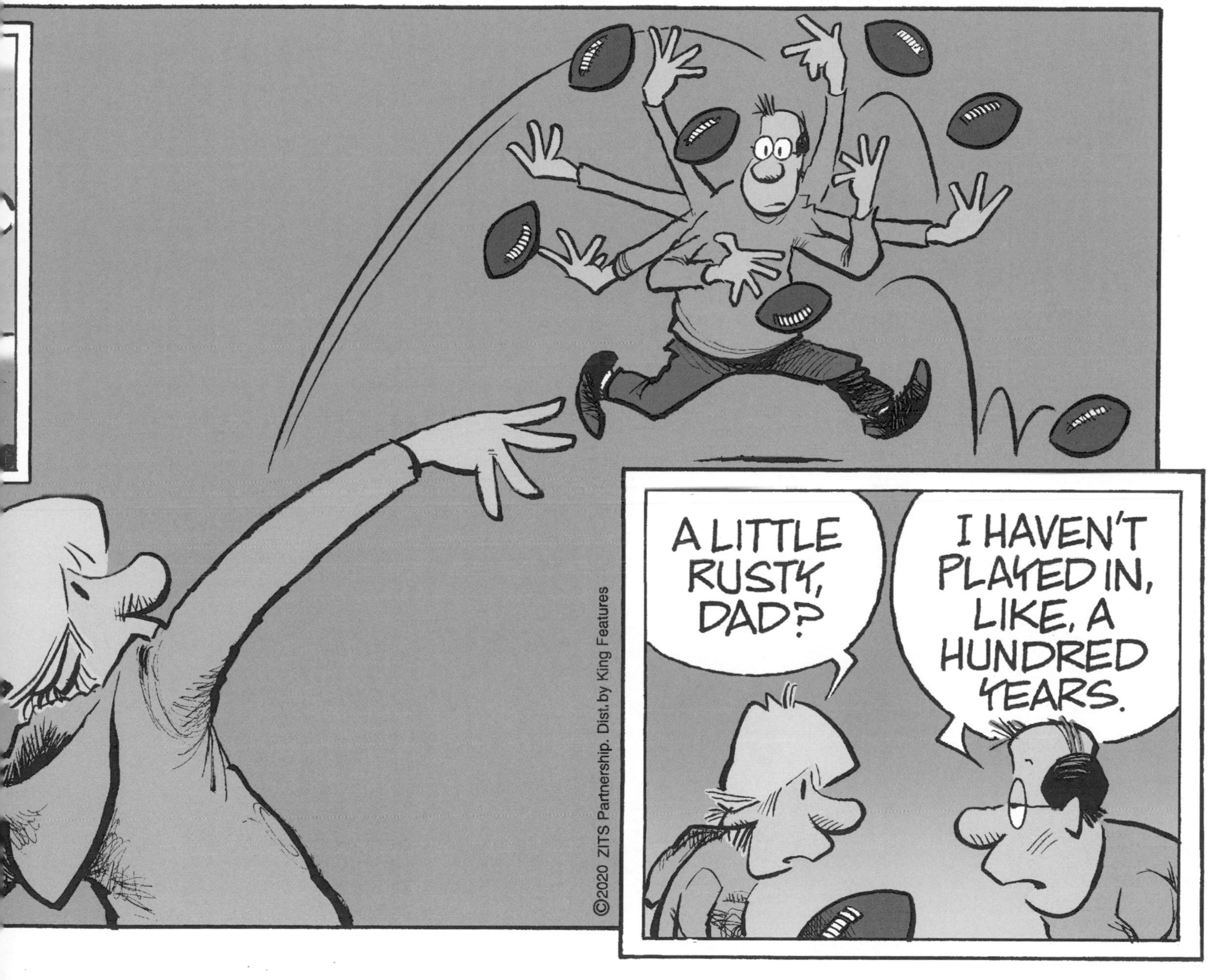
A LITTLE RUSTY, DAD?
I HAVEN'T PLAYED IN, LIKE, A HUNDRED YEARS.

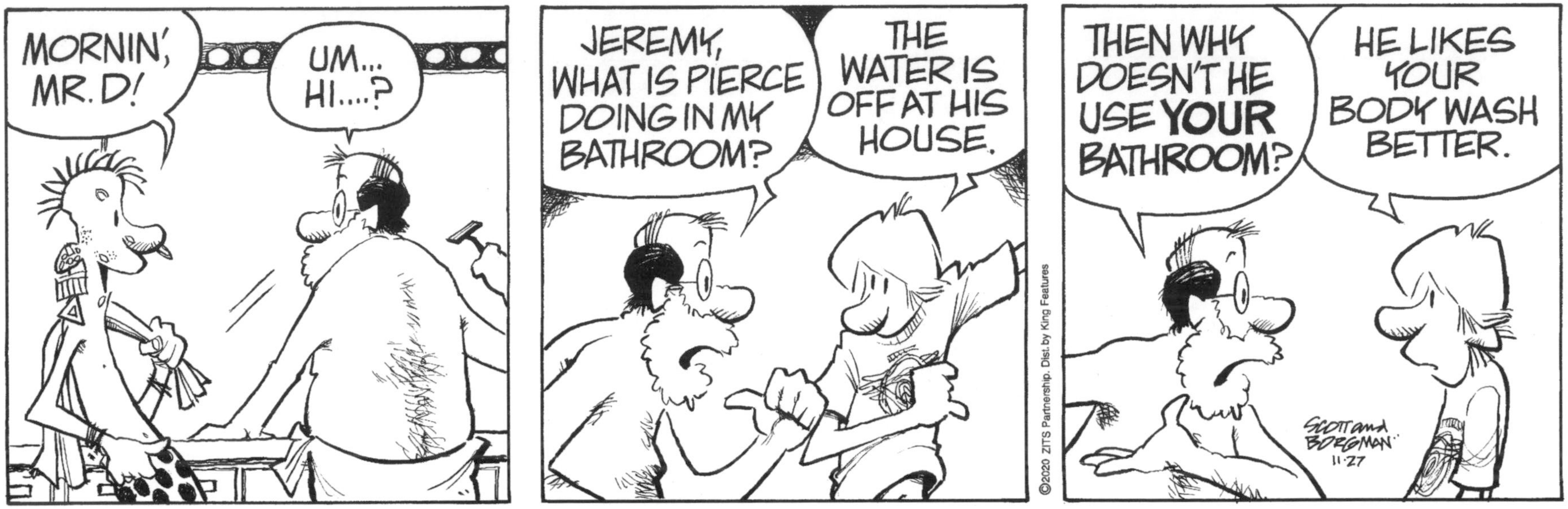
MORNIN', MR. D!
UM... HI....?
JEREMY, WHAT IS PIERCE DOING IN MY BATHROOM?
THE WATER IS OFF AT HIS HOUSE.
THEN WHY DOESN'T HE USE **YOUR** BATHROOM?
HE LIKES YOUR BODY WASH BETTER.
©2020 ZITS Partnership. Dist. by King Features
SCOTT and BORGMAN 11·27

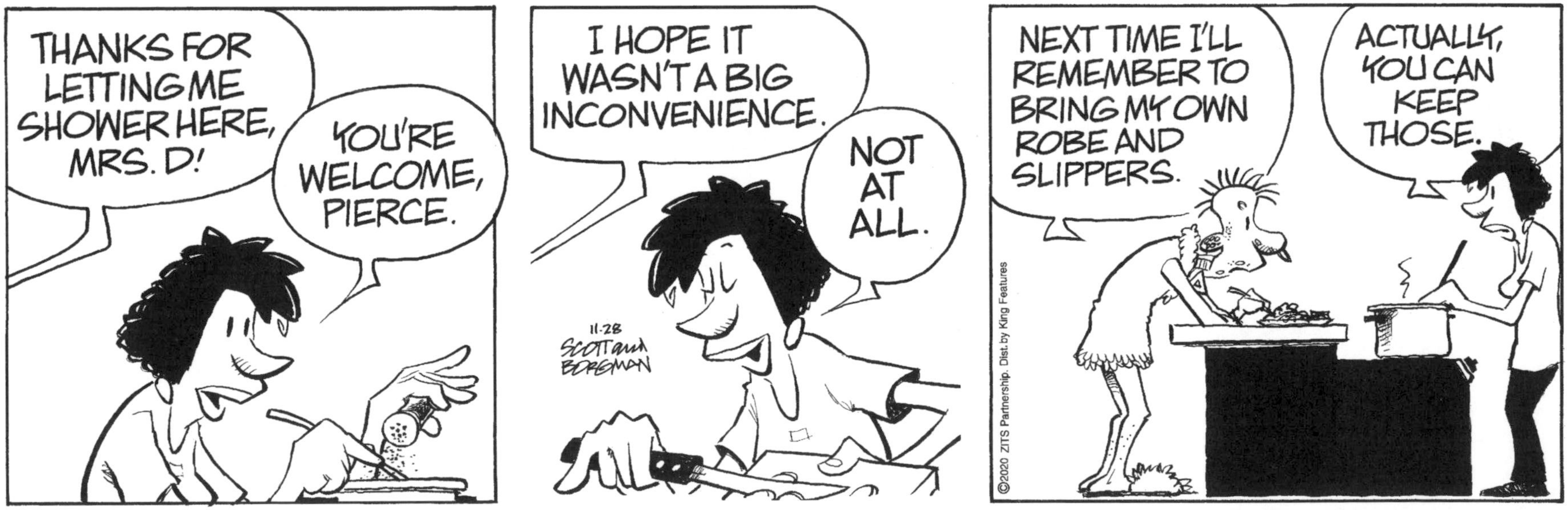
THANKS FOR LETTING ME SHOWER HERE, MRS. D!
YOU'RE WELCOME, PIERCE.
I HOPE IT WASN'T A BIG INCONVENIENCE.
NOT AT ALL.
11·28 SCOTT and BORGMAN
NEXT TIME I'LL REMEMBER TO BRING MY OWN ROBE AND SLIPPERS.
ACTUALLY, YOU CAN KEEP THOSE.
©2020 ZITS Partnership. Dist. by King Features

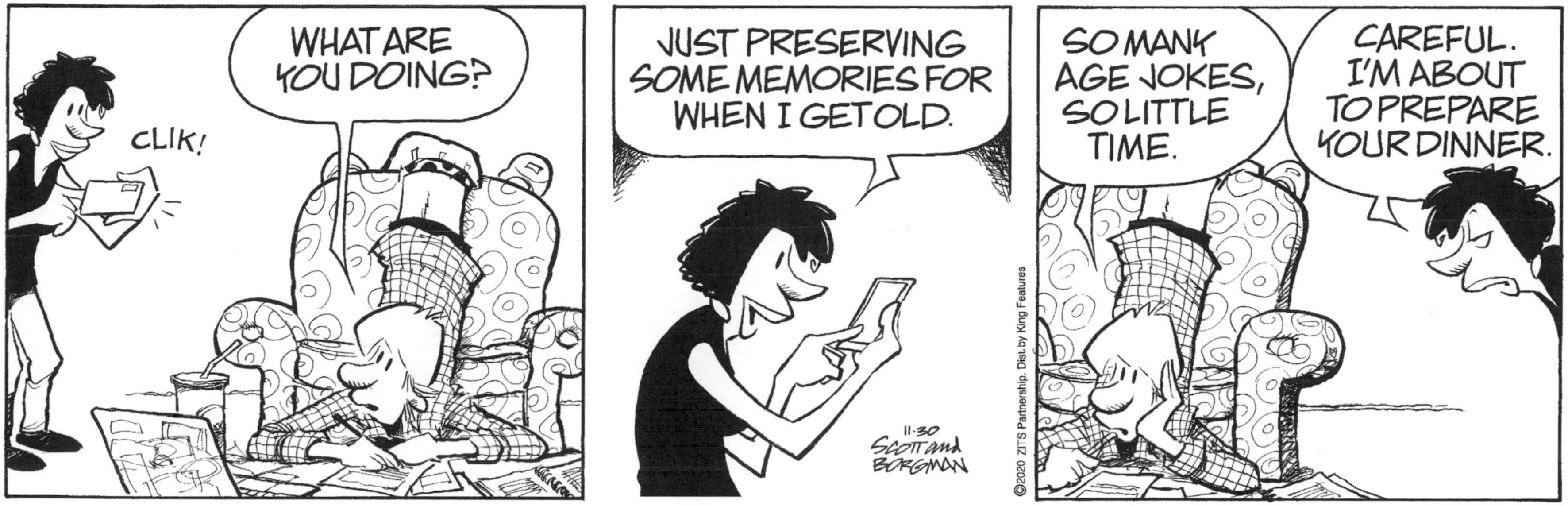
CLIK!
WHAT ARE YOU DOING?
JUST PRESERVING SOME MEMORIES FOR WHEN I GET OLD.
11-30 SCOTT and BORGMAN
©2020 ZITS Partnership. Dist. by King Features
SO MANY AGE JOKES, SO LITTLE TIME.
CAREFUL. I'M ABOUT TO PREPARE YOUR DINNER.

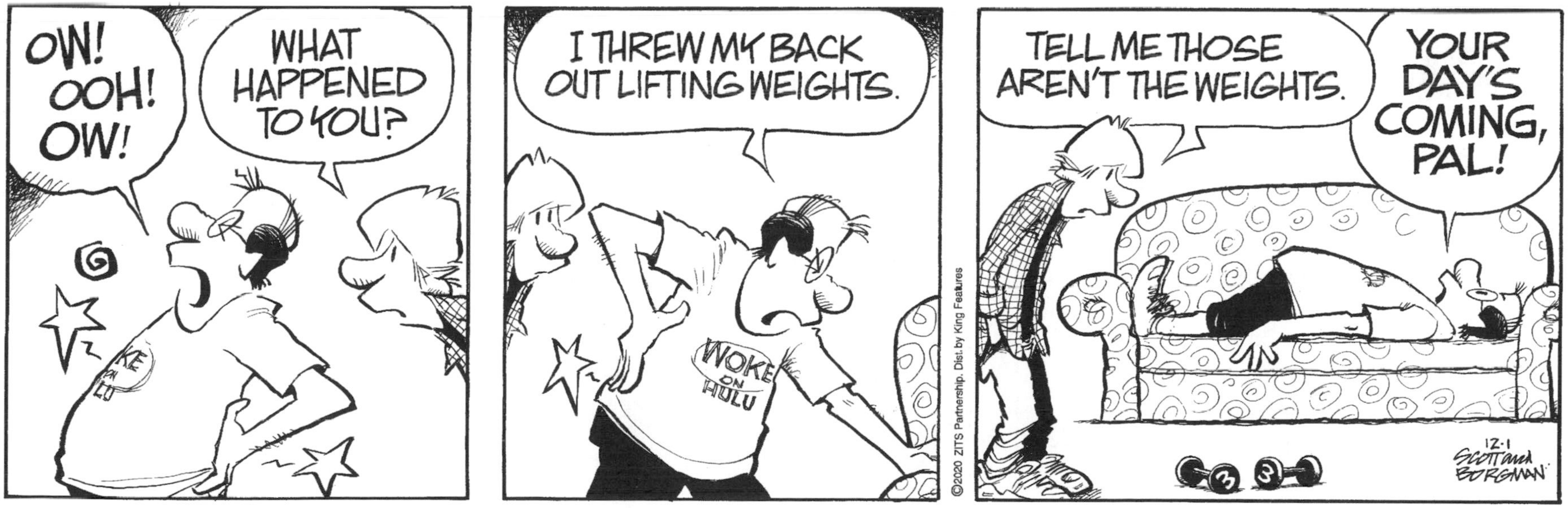
OW! OOH! OW!
WHAT HAPPENED TO YOU?
I THREW MY BACK OUT LIFTING WEIGHTS.
WOKE ON HULU
©2020 ZITS Partnership. Dist. by King Features
TELL ME THOSE AREN'T THE WEIGHTS.
YOUR DAY'S COMING, PAL!
12-1 SCOTT and BORGMAN

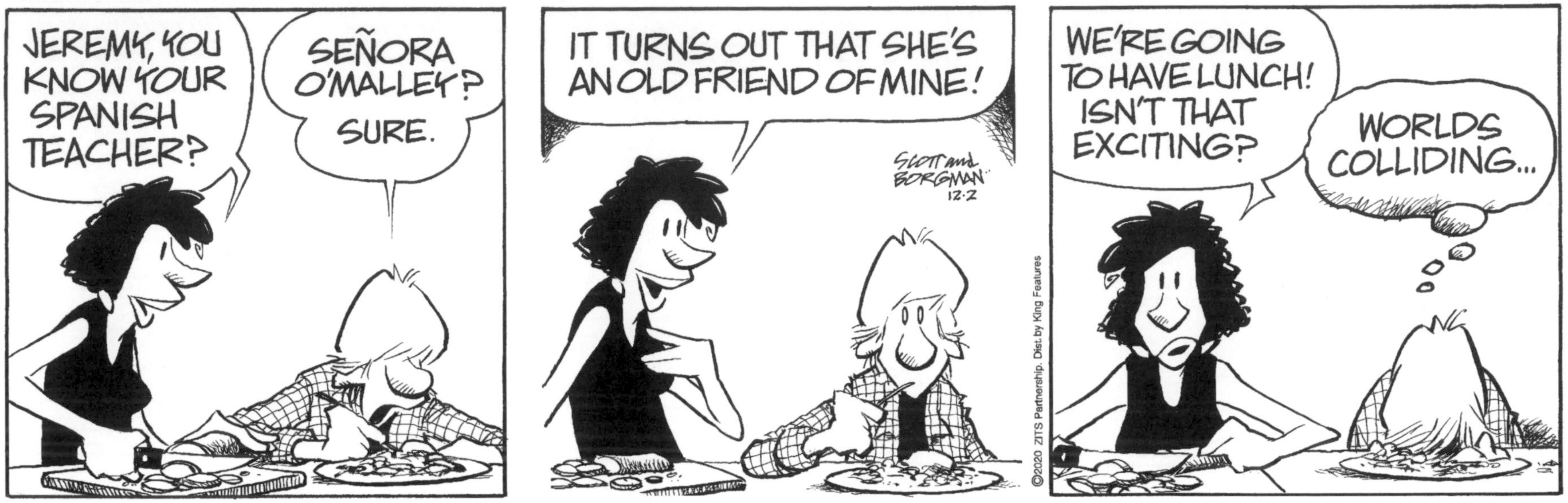
JEREMY, YOU KNOW YOUR SPANISH TEACHER?
SEÑORA O'MALLEY? SURE.
IT TURNS OUT THAT SHE'S AN OLD FRIEND OF MINE!
SCOTT and BORGMAN 12·2
©2020 ZITS Partnership. Dist. by King Features
WE'RE GOING TO HAVE LUNCH! ISN'T THAT EXCITING?
WORLDS COLLIDING...

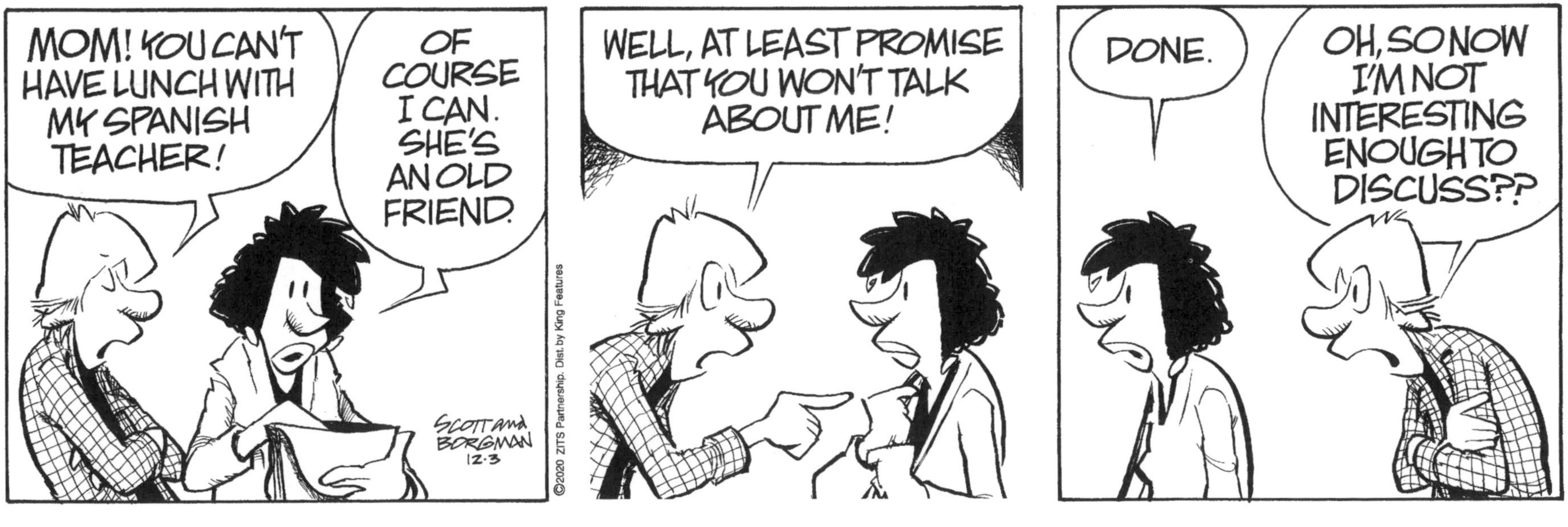
MOM! YOU CAN'T HAVE LUNCH WITH MY SPANISH TEACHER!
OF COURSE I CAN. SHE'S AN OLD FRIEND.
SCOTT and BORGMAN 12·3
©2020 ZITS Partnership. Dist. by King Features
WELL, AT LEAST PROMISE THAT YOU WON'T TALK ABOUT ME!
DONE.
OH, SO NOW I'M NOT INTERESTING ENOUGH TO DISCUSS??

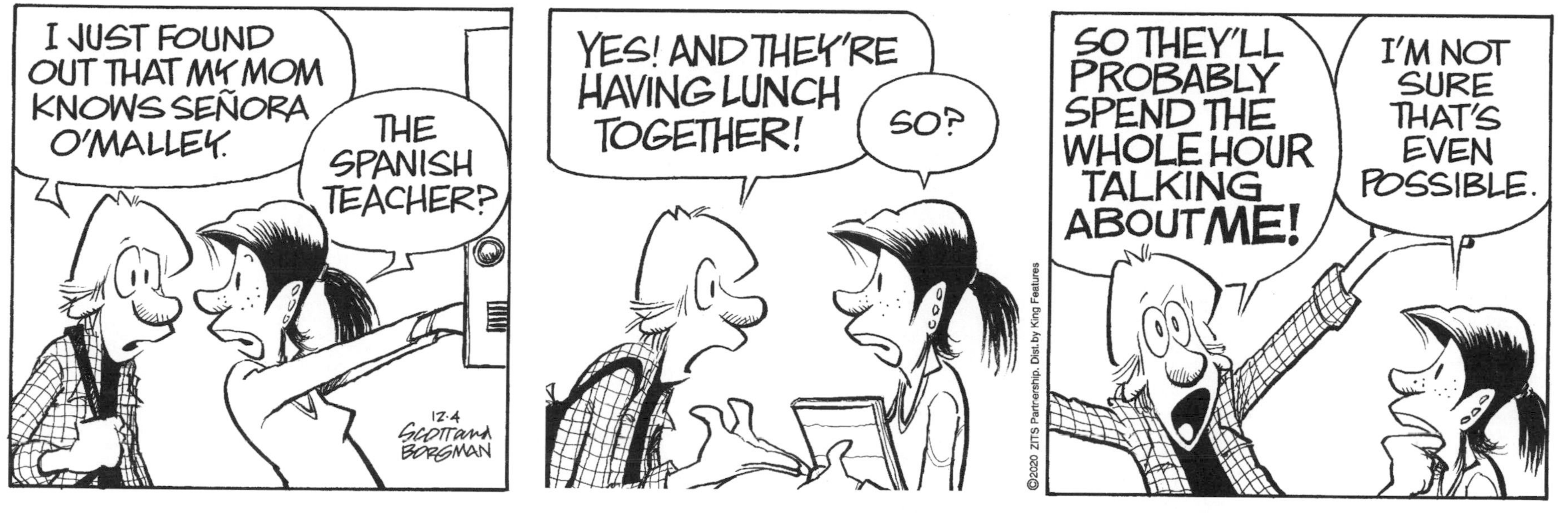
I JUST FOUND OUT THAT MY MOM KNOWS SEÑORA O'MALLEY.
THE SPANISH TEACHER?
12·4 SCOTT AND BORGMAN
YES! AND THEY'RE HAVING LUNCH TOGETHER!
SO?
©2020 ZITS Partnership. Dist. by King Features
SO THEY'LL PROBABLY SPEND THE WHOLE HOUR TALKING ABOUT **ME!**
I'M NOT SURE THAT'S EVEN POSSIBLE.

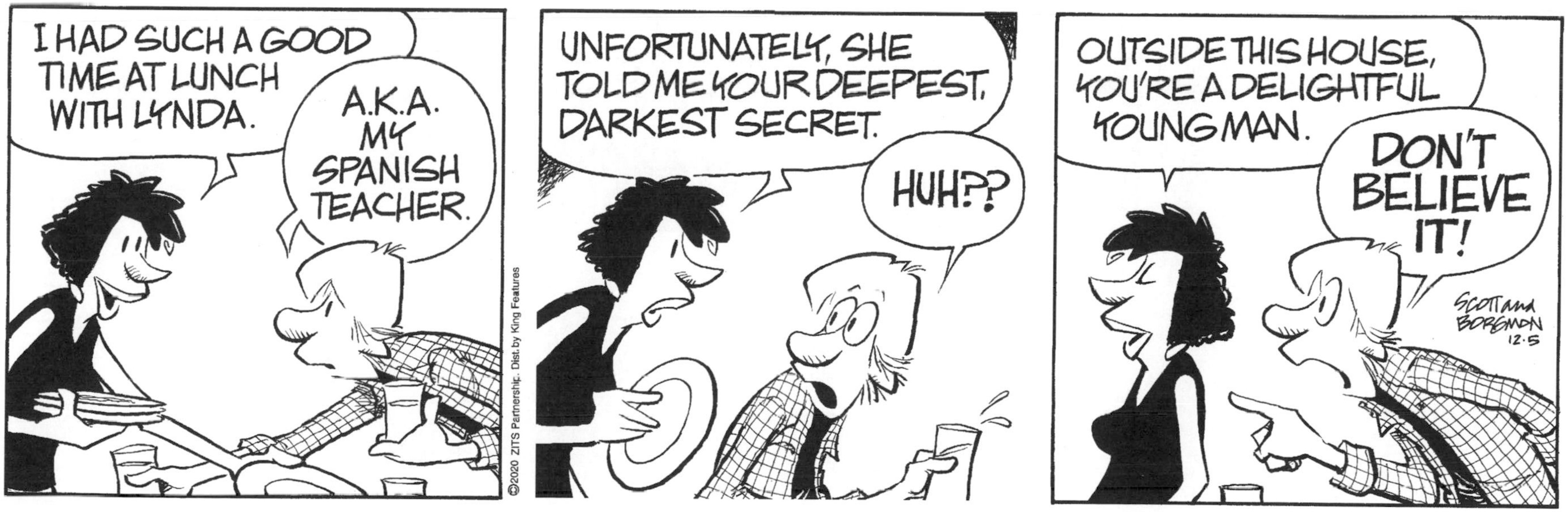
I HAD SUCH A GOOD TIME AT LUNCH WITH LYNDA.
A.K.A. MY SPANISH TEACHER.
©2020 ZITS Partnership. Dist. by King Features
UNFORTUNATELY, SHE TOLD ME YOUR DEEPEST, DARKEST SECRET.
HUH??
OUTSIDE THIS HOUSE, YOU'RE A DELIGHTFUL YOUNG MAN.
DON'T BELIEVE IT!
SCOTT AND BORGMAN 12·5

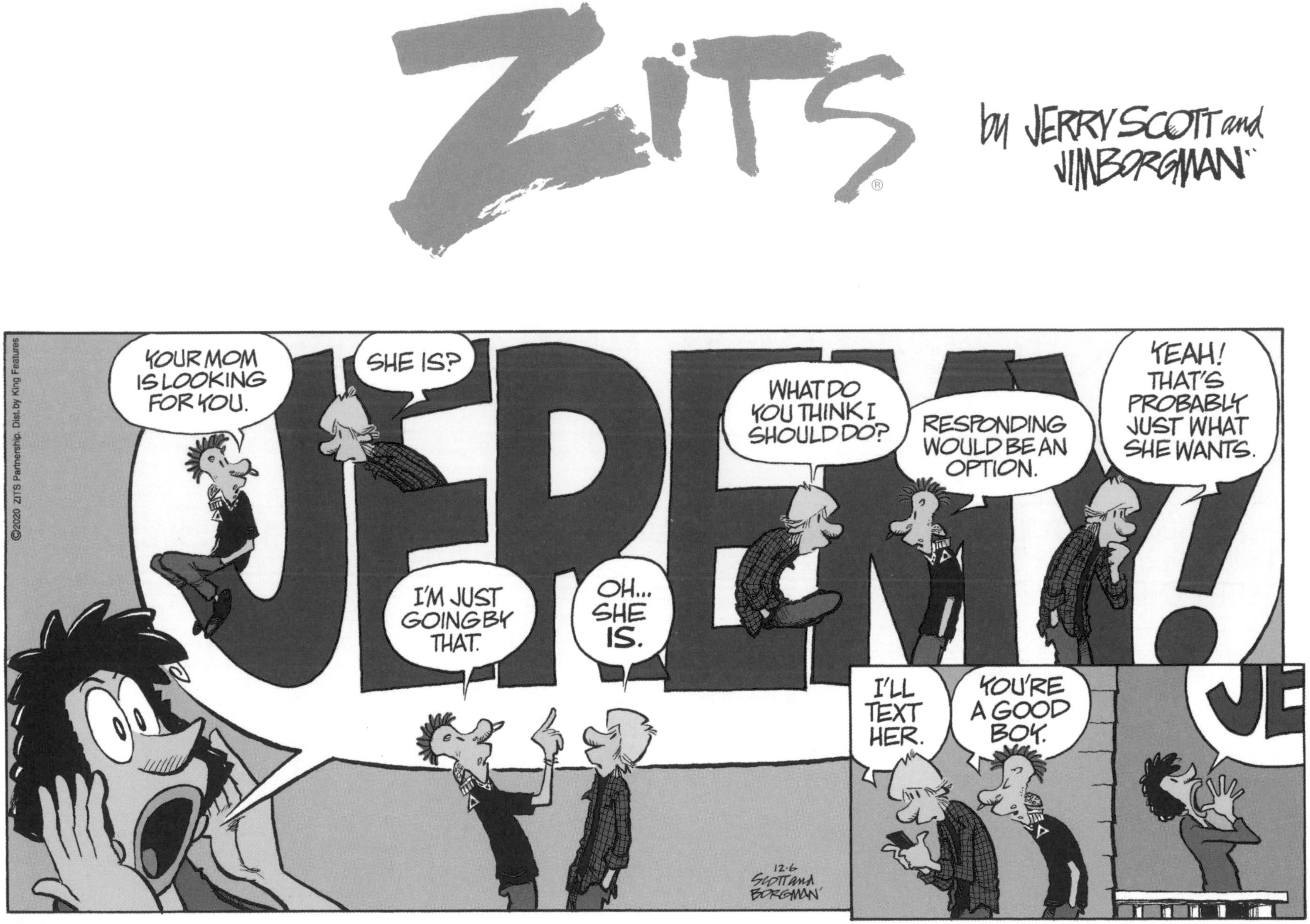
ZITS®
by JERRY SCOTT and JIM BORGMAN
©2020 ZITS Partnership. Dist. by King Features
YOUR MOM IS LOOKING FOR YOU.
SHE IS?
I'M JUST GOING BY THAT.
OH... SHE IS.
JEREMY?
WHAT DO YOU THINK I SHOULD DO?
RESPONDING WOULD BE AN OPTION.
YEAH! THAT'S PROBABLY JUST WHAT SHE WANTS.
12·6 SCOTT and BORGMAN
I'LL TEXT HER.
YOU'RE A GOOD BOY.
JE

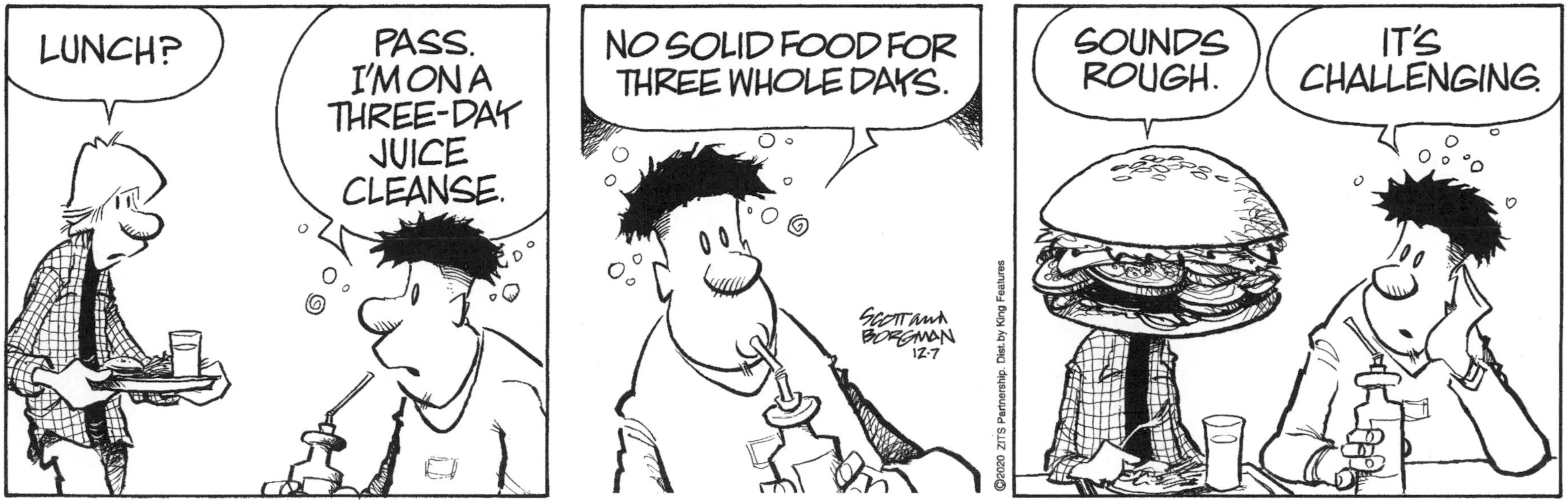
LUNCH?
PASS. I'M ON A THREE-DAY JUICE CLEANSE.
NO SOLID FOOD FOR THREE WHOLE DAYS.
SOUNDS ROUGH.
IT'S CHALLENGING.
©2020 ZITS Partnership. Dist. by King Features

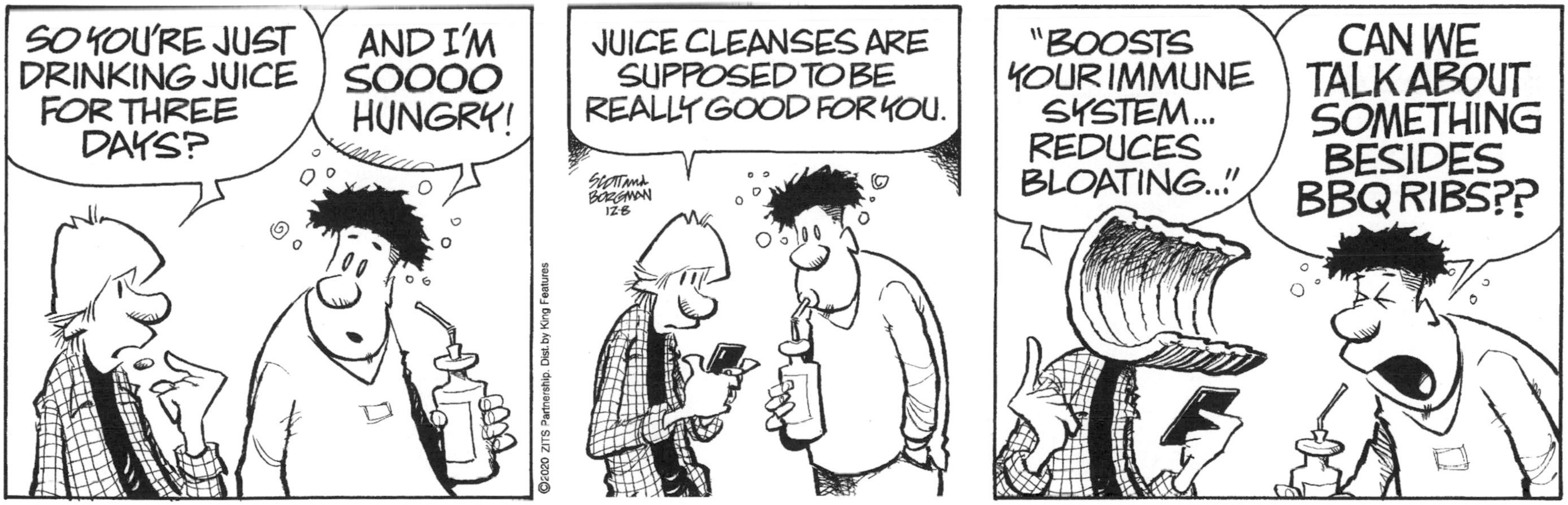
SO YOU'RE JUST DRINKING JUICE FOR THREE DAYS?
AND I'M SOOOO HUNGRY!
JUICE CLEANSES ARE SUPPOSED TO BE REALLY GOOD FOR YOU.
"BOOSTS YOUR IMMUNE SYSTEM... REDUCES BLOATING..."
CAN WE TALK ABOUT SOMETHING BESIDES BBQ RIBS??
©2020 ZITS Partnership. Dist. by King Features

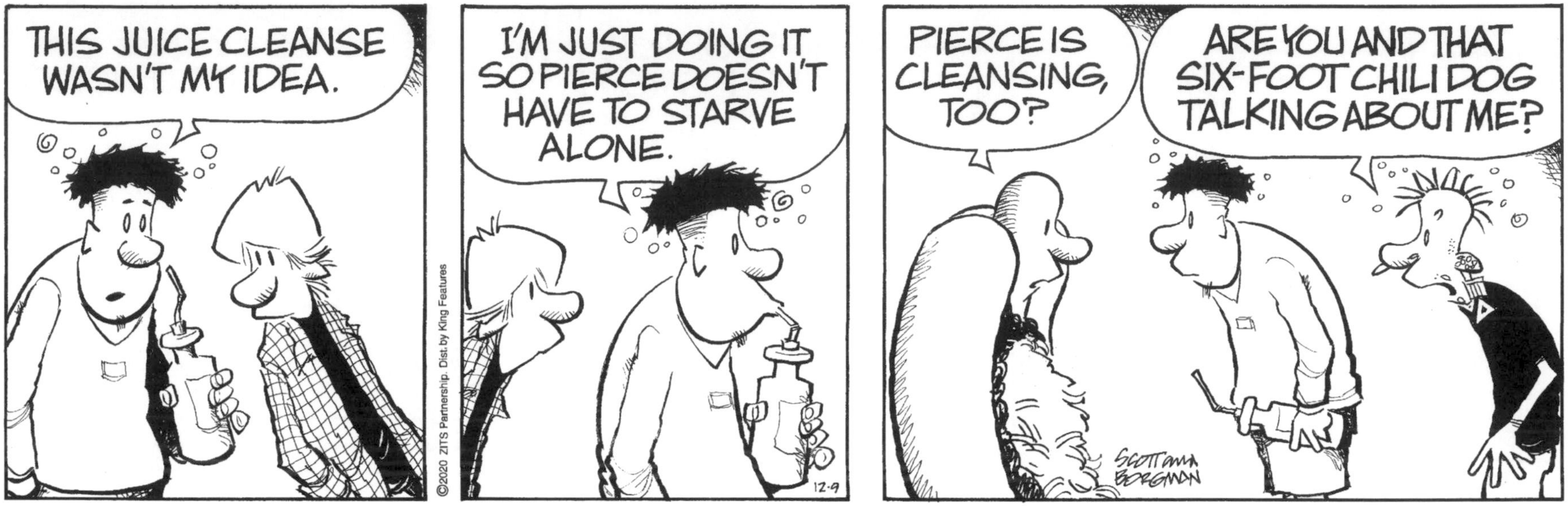
THIS JUICE CLEANSE WASN'T MY IDEA.
I'M JUST DOING IT SO PIERCE DOESN'T HAVE TO STARVE ALONE.
©2020 ZITS Partnership. Dist. by King Features
12-9
PIERCE IS CLEANSING, TOO?
ARE YOU AND THAT SIX-FOOT CHILI DOG TALKING ABOUT ME?
SCOTT and BORGMAN

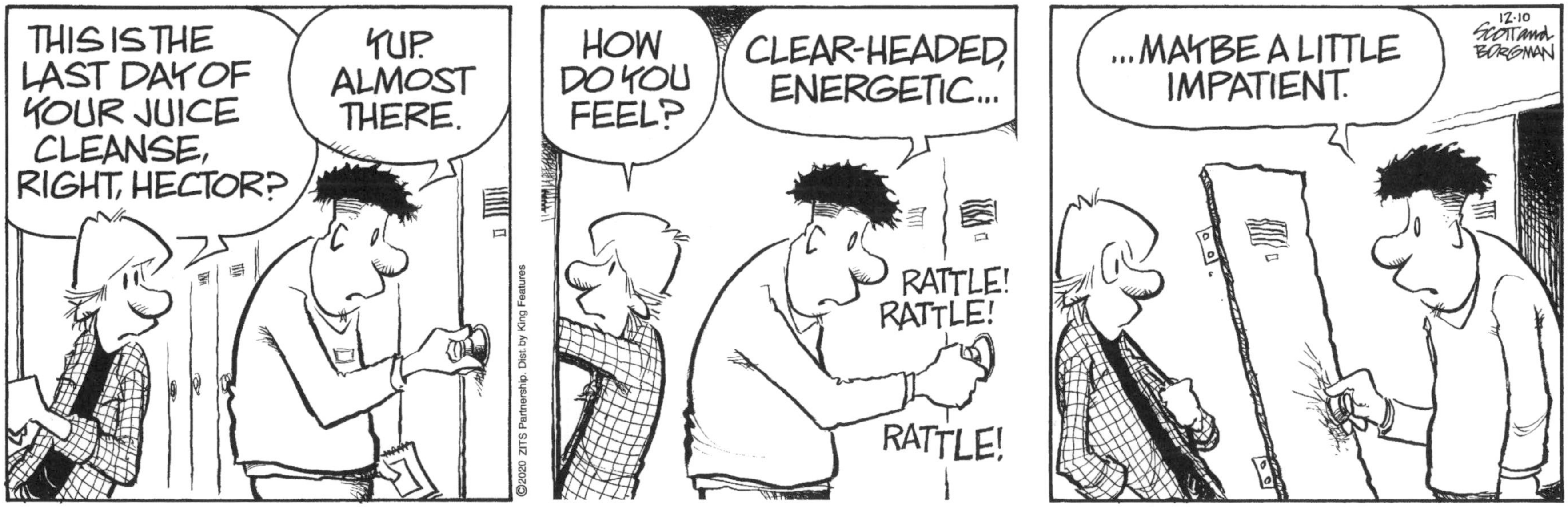
THIS IS THE LAST DAY OF YOUR JUICE CLEANSE, RIGHT, HECTOR?
YUP. ALMOST THERE.
©2020 ZITS Partnership. Dist. by King Features
HOW DO YOU FEEL?
CLEAR-HEADED, ENERGETIC...
RATTLE! RATTLE!
RATTLE!
...MAYBE A LITTLE IMPATIENT.
12-10
SCOTT and BORGMAN

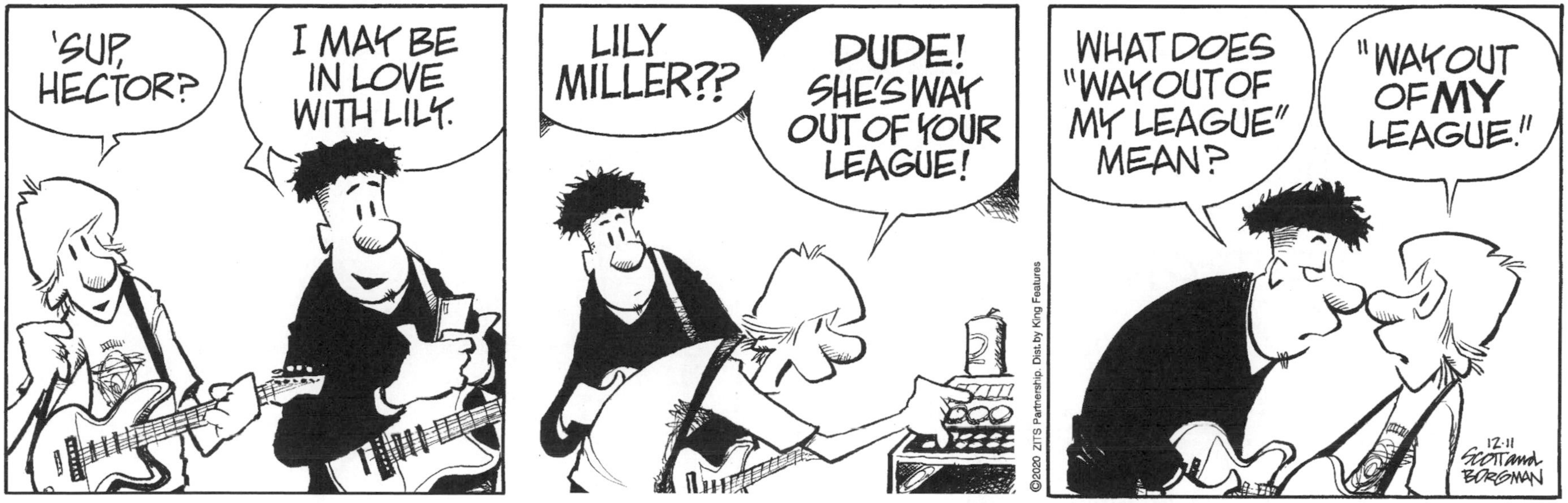
'SUP, HECTOR?
I MAY BE IN LOVE WITH LILY.
LILY MILLER??
DUDE! SHE'S WAY OUT OF YOUR LEAGUE!
WHAT DOES "WAY OUT OF MY LEAGUE" MEAN?
"WAY OUT OF **MY** LEAGUE."
©2020 ZITS Partnership. Dist. by King Features
12-11
SCOTT AND BORGMAN

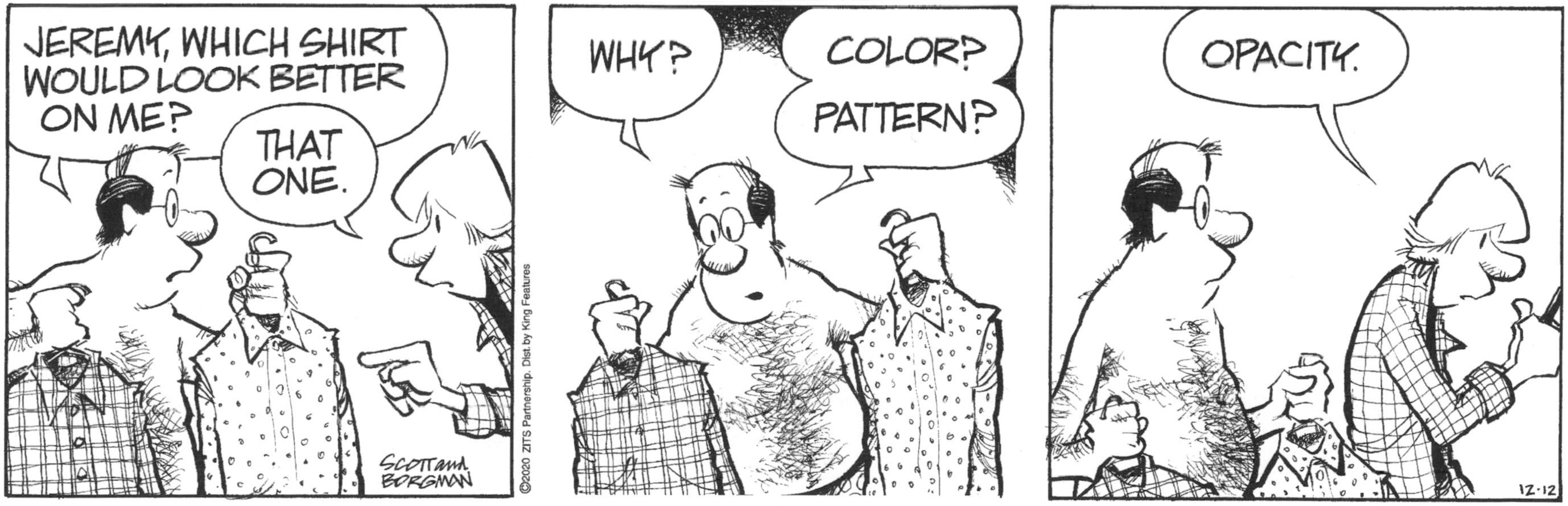
JEREMY, WHICH SHIRT WOULD LOOK BETTER ON ME?
THAT ONE.
SCOTT AND BORGMAN
©2020 ZITS Partnership. Dist. by King Features
WHY?
COLOR?
PATTERN?
OPACITY.
12-12

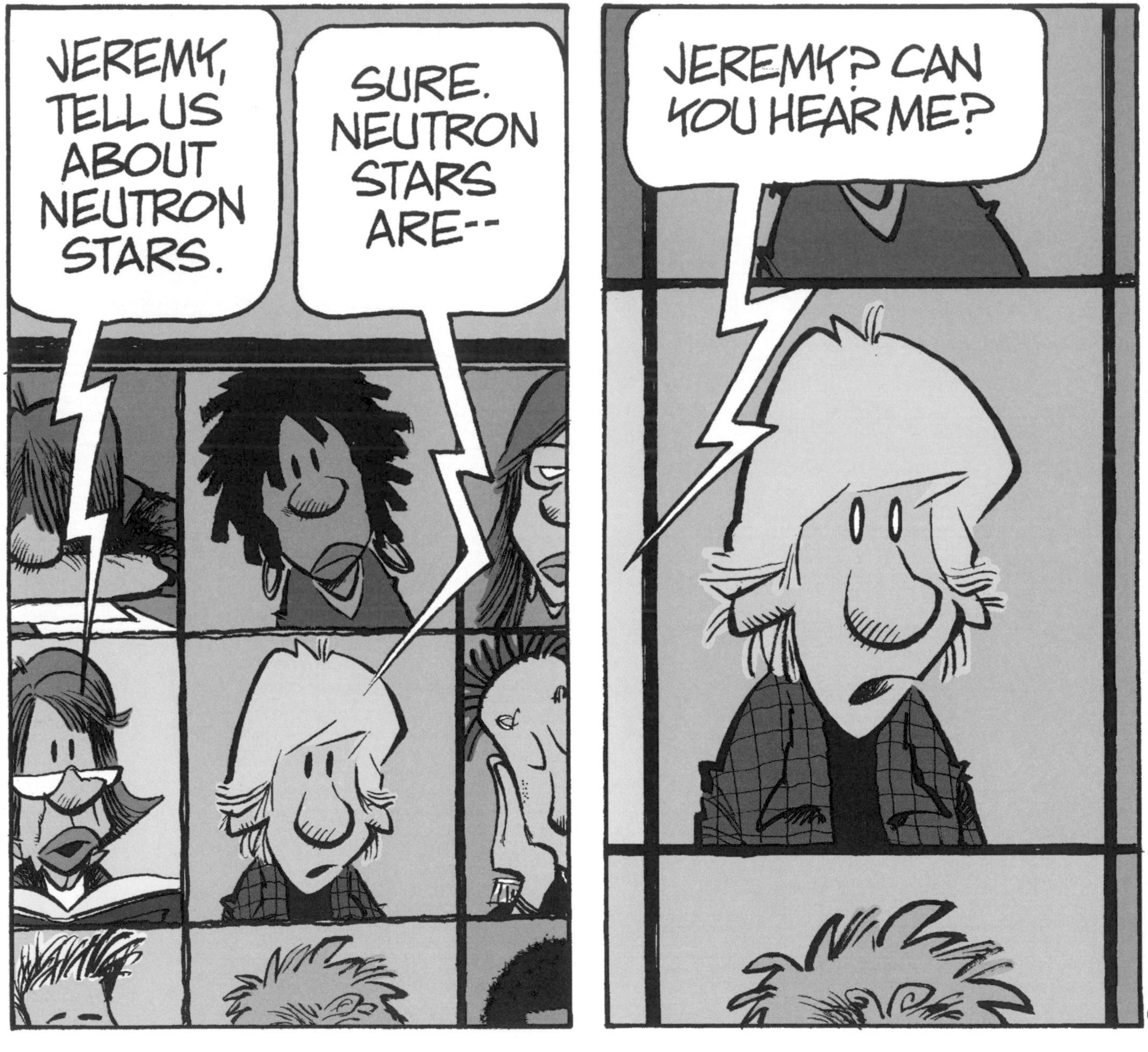
JEREMY, TELL US ABOUT NEUTRON STARS.
SURE. NEUTRON STARS ARE--
JEREMY? CAN YOU HEAR ME?

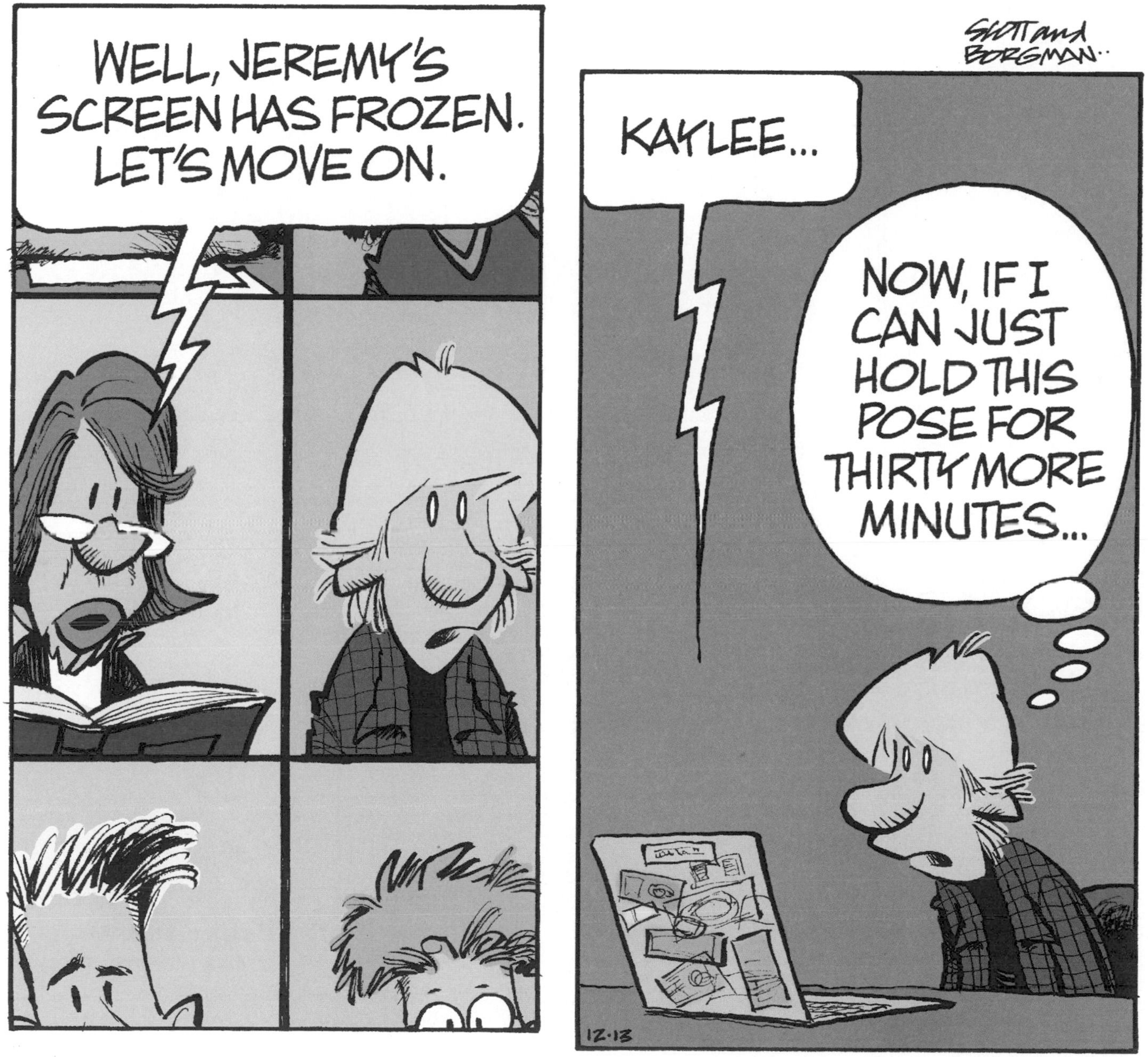
WELL, JEREMY'S SCREEN HAS FROZEN. LET'S MOVE ON.
SCOTT and BORGMAN
KAYLEE...
NOW, IF I CAN JUST HOLD THIS POSE FOR THIRTY MORE MINUTES...
12·13

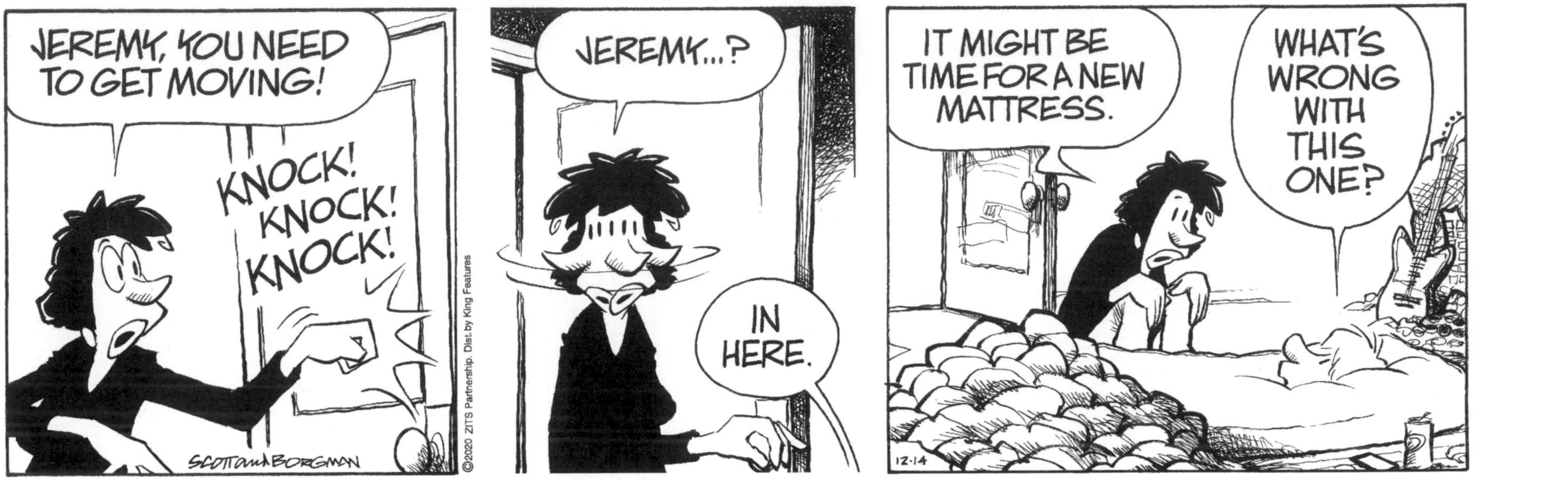
JEREMY, YOU NEED TO GET MOVING!
KNOCK! KNOCK! KNOCK!
SCOTT and BORGMAN
©2020 ZITS Partnership. Dist. by King Features
JEREMY...?
IN HERE.
IT MIGHT BE TIME FOR A NEW MATTRESS.
WHAT'S WRONG WITH THIS ONE?
12·14

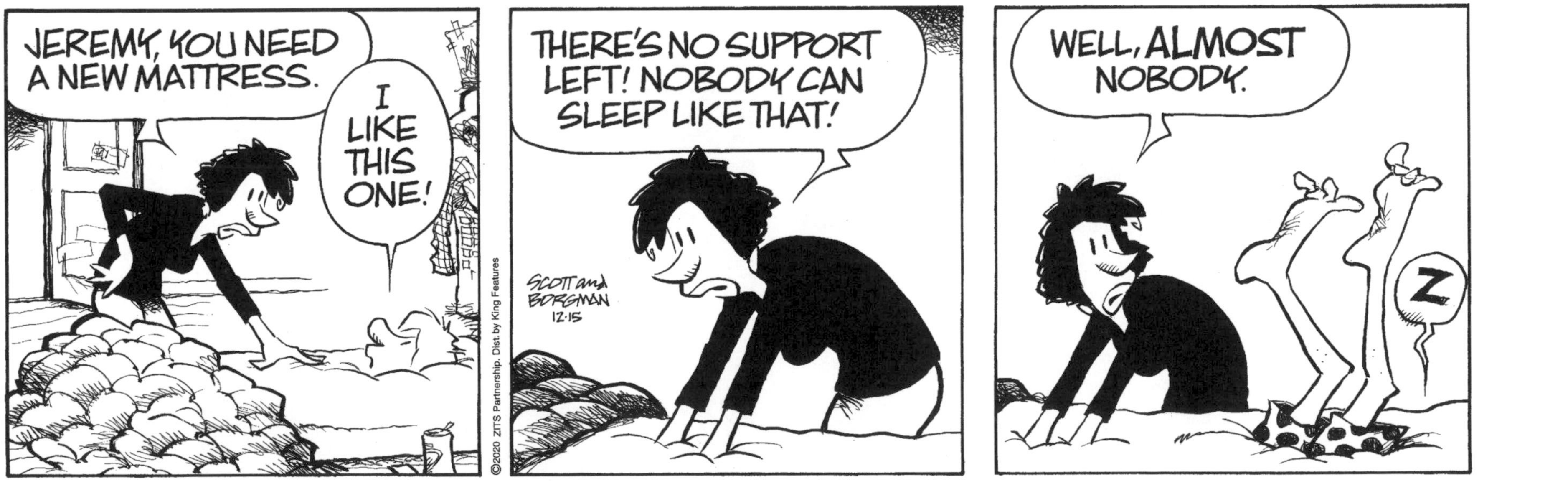
JEREMY, YOU NEED A NEW MATTRESS.
I LIKE THIS ONE!
©2020 ZITS Partnership. Dist. by King Features
SCOTT and BORGMAN 12·15
THERE'S NO SUPPORT LEFT! NOBODY CAN SLEEP LIKE THAT!
WELL, ALMOST NOBODY.
Z

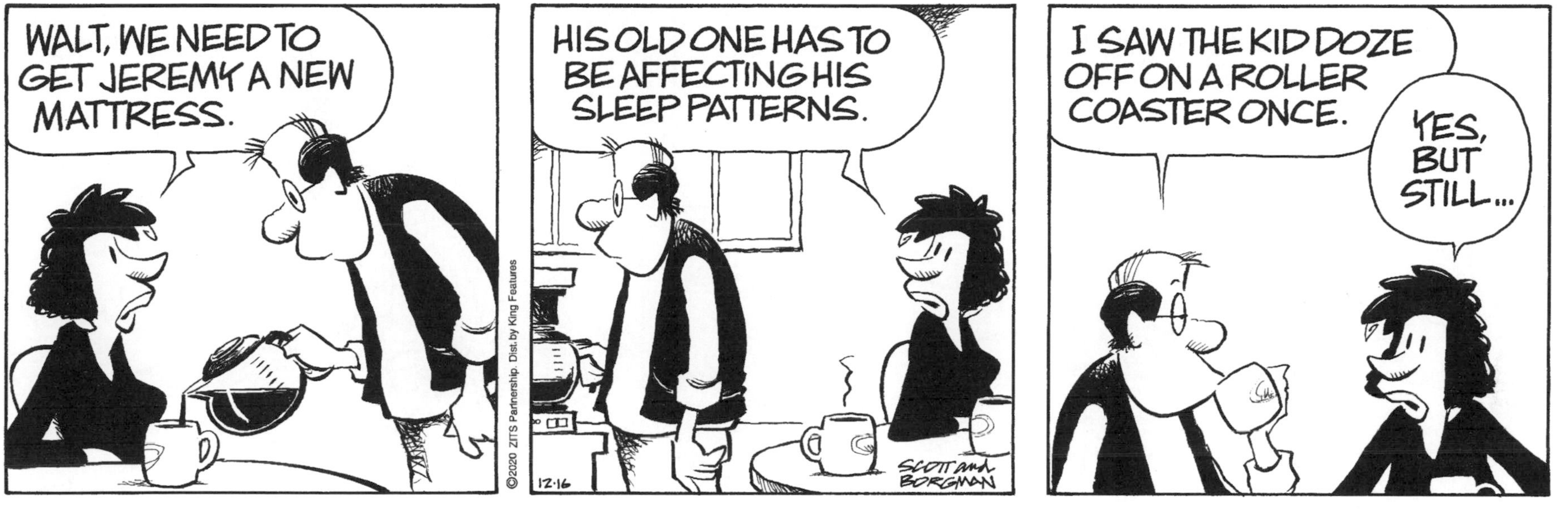
WALT, WE NEED TO GET JEREMY A NEW MATTRESS.
HIS OLD ONE HAS TO BE AFFECTING HIS SLEEP PATTERNS.
©2020 ZITS Partnership. Dist. by King Features
12·16
SCOTT and BORGMAN
I SAW THE KID DOZE OFF ON A ROLLER COASTER ONCE.
YES, BUT STILL...

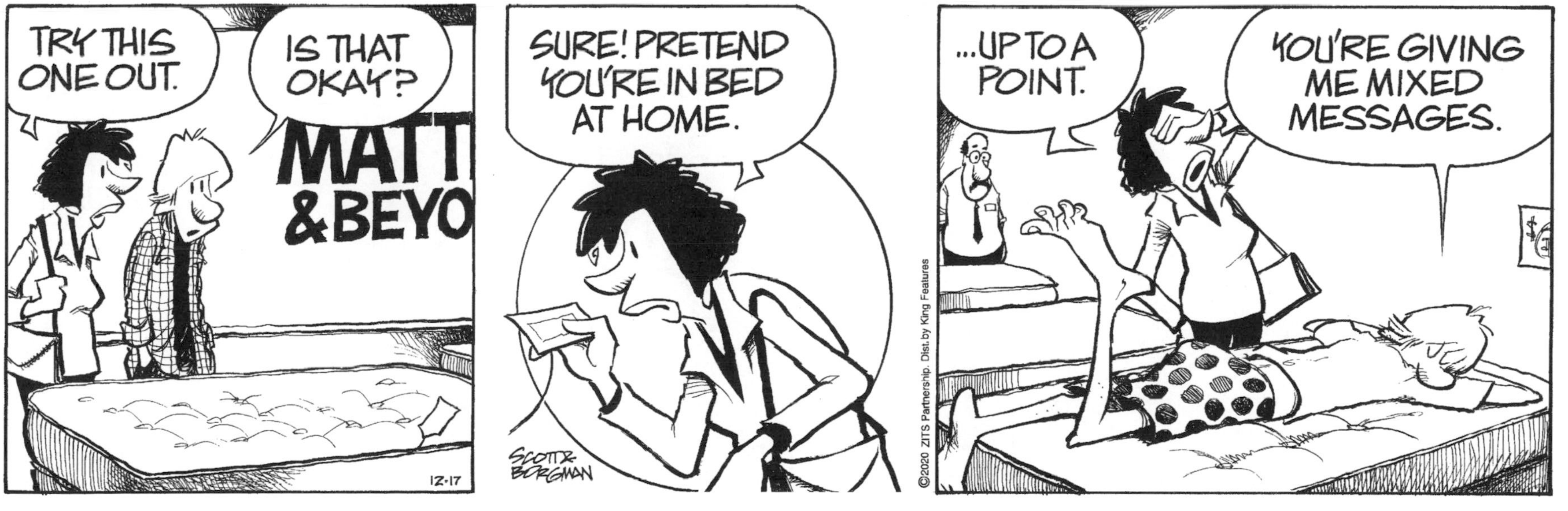
TRY THIS ONE OUT.
IS THAT OKAY?
MATT
&BEYO
12·17
SURE! PRETEND YOU'RE IN BED AT HOME.
SCOTT & BORGMAN
©2020 ZITS Partnership. Dist. by King Features
...UP TO A POINT.
YOU'RE GIVING ME MIXED MESSAGES.

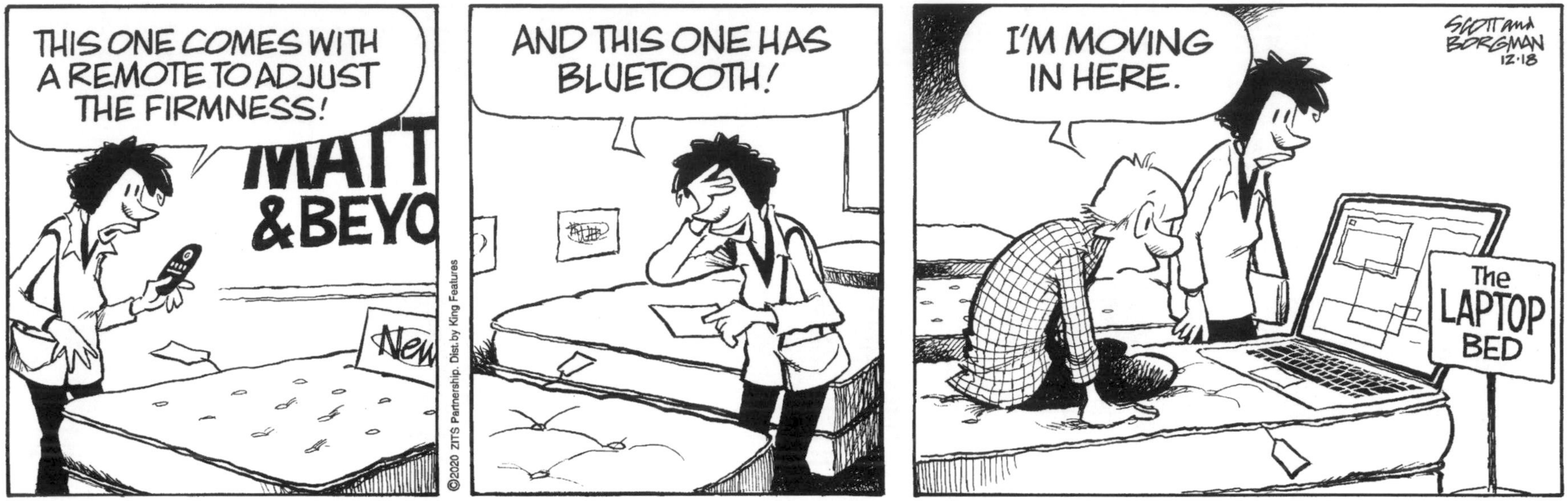
THIS ONE COMES WITH A REMOTE TO ADJUST THE FIRMNESS!
MATT & BEYO
New
©2020 ZITS Partnership. Dist. by King Features
AND THIS ONE HAS BLUETOOTH!
I'M MOVING IN HERE.
SCOTT and BORGMAN 12·18
The LAPTOP BED

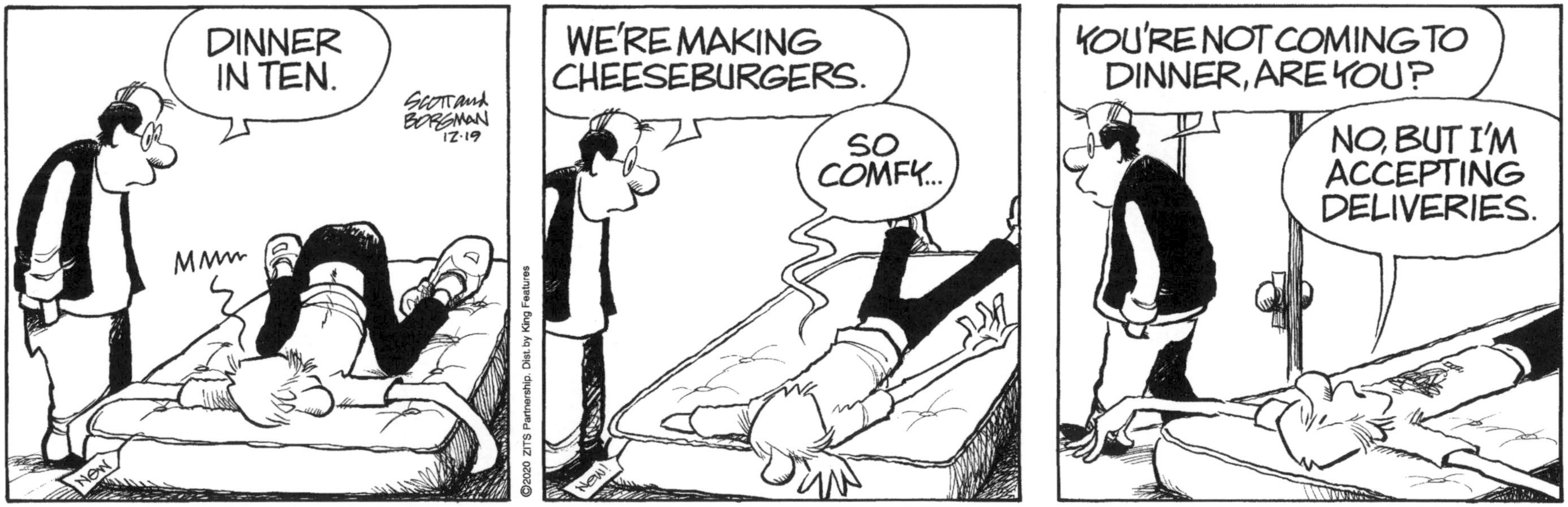
DINNER IN TEN.
SCOTT and BORGMAN 12·19
MMM
NEW
©2020 ZITS Partnership. Dist. by King Features
WE'RE MAKING CHEESEBURGERS.
SO COMFY...
NEW!
YOU'RE NOT COMING TO DINNER, ARE YOU?
NO, BUT I'M ACCEPTING DELIVERIES.

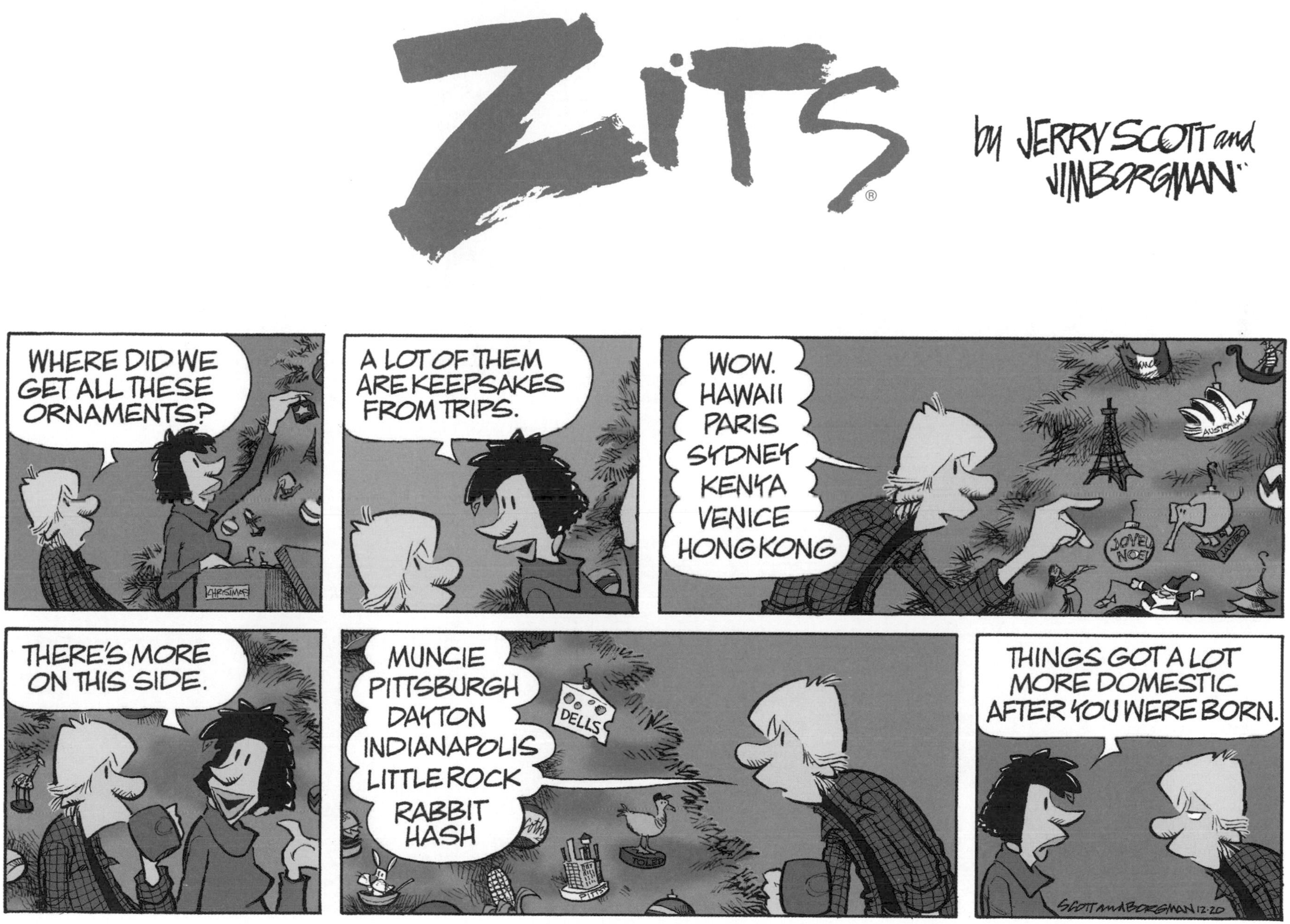
ZITS®
by JERRY SCOTT and JIM BORGMAN
WHERE DID WE GET ALL THESE ORNAMENTS?
A LOT OF THEM ARE KEEPSAKES FROM TRIPS.
WOW. HAWAII PARIS SYDNEY KENYA VENICE HONG KONG
THERE'S MORE ON THIS SIDE.
MUNCIE PITTSBURGH DAYTON INDIANAPOLIS LITTLE ROCK RABBIT HASH
DELLS
THINGS GOT A LOT MORE DOMESTIC AFTER YOU WERE BORN.
SCOTT AND BORGMAN 12-20

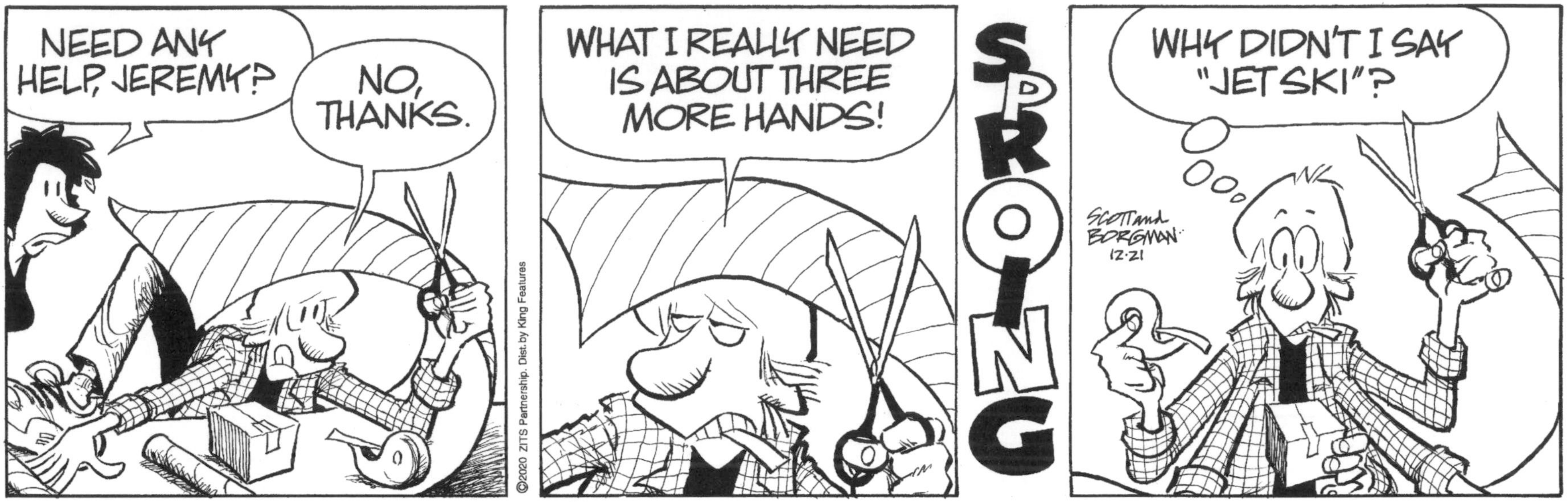
NEED ANY HELP, JEREMY?
NO, THANKS.
©2020 ZITS Partnership. Dist. by King Features
WHAT I REALLY NEED IS ABOUT THREE MORE HANDS!
SPROING
SCOTT and BORGMAN 12·21
WHY DIDN'T I SAY "JET SKI"?

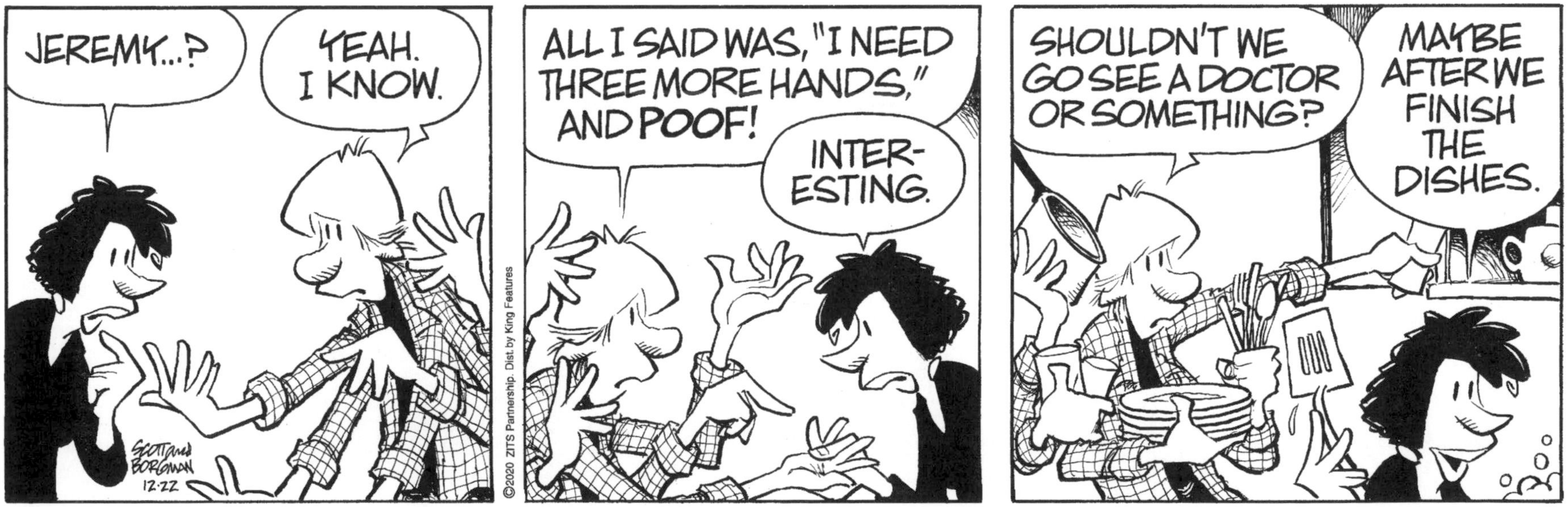
JEREMY...?
YEAH. I KNOW.
SCOTT and BORGMAN 12·22
©2020 ZITS Partnership. Dist. by King Features
ALL I SAID WAS, "I NEED THREE MORE HANDS," AND POOF!
INTER-ESTING.
SHOULDN'T WE GO SEE A DOCTOR OR SOMETHING?
MAYBE AFTER WE FINISH THE DISHES.

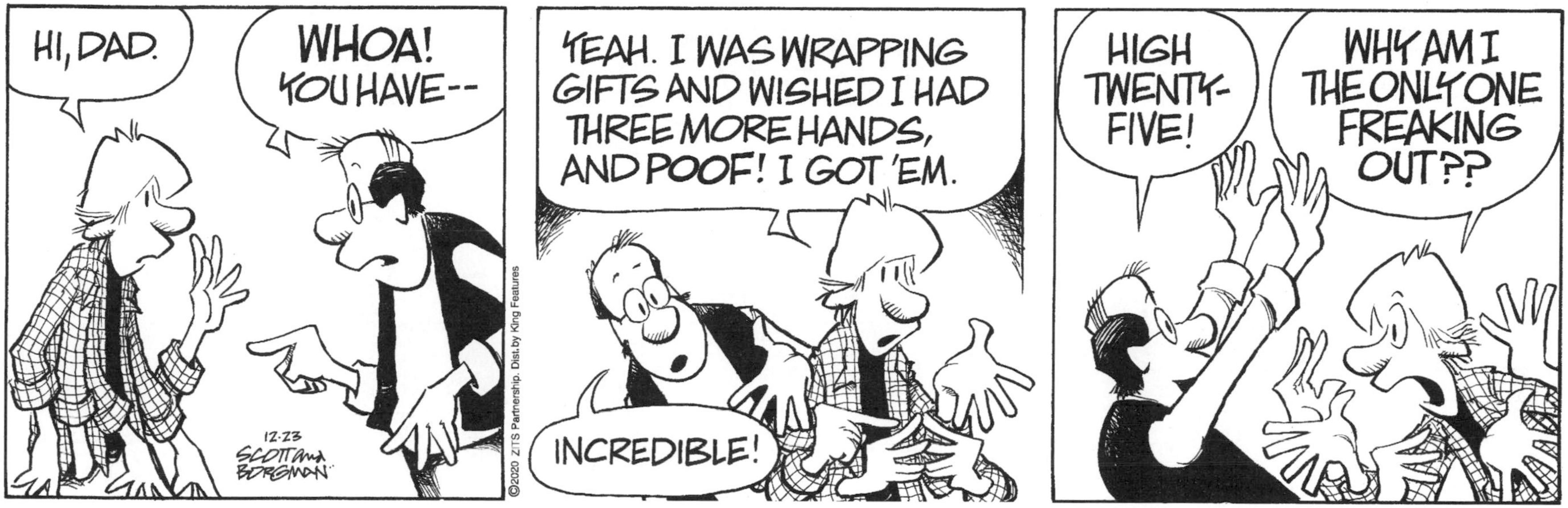
HI, DAD.
WHOA! YOU HAVE--
12·23
SCOTT and BORGMAN
YEAH. I WAS WRAPPING GIFTS AND WISHED I HAD THREE MORE HANDS, AND POOF! I GOT 'EM.
INCREDIBLE!
HIGH TWENTY-FIVE!
WHY AM I THE ONLY ONE FREAKING OUT??

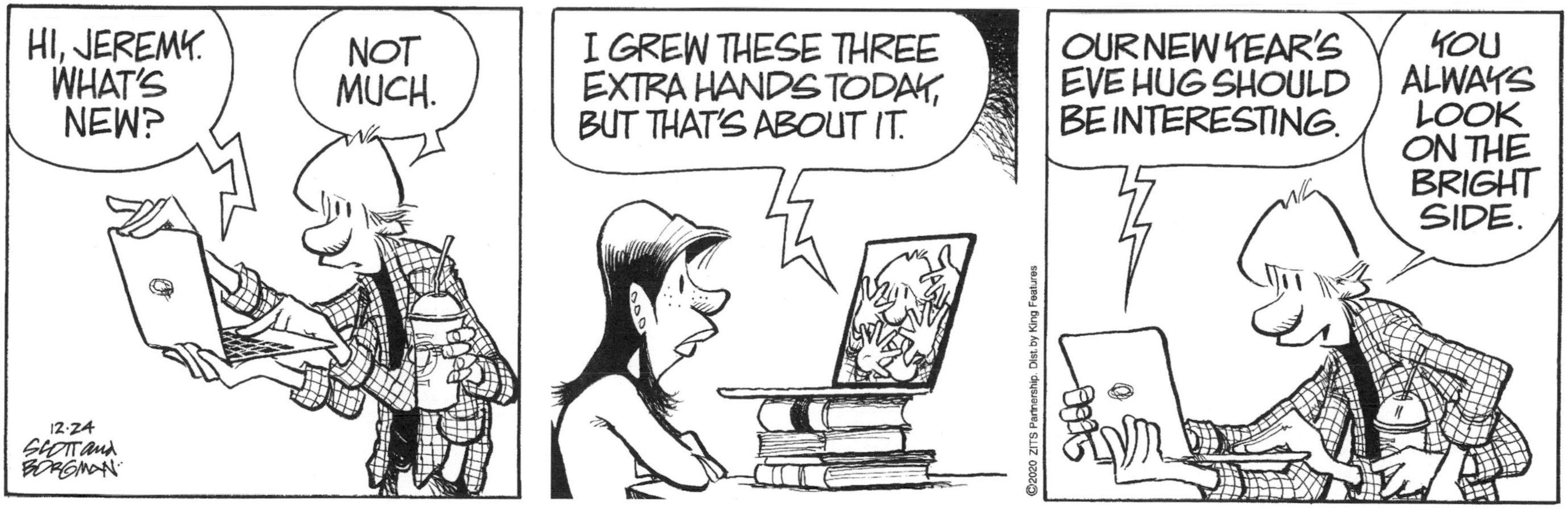
HI, JEREMY. WHAT'S NEW?
NOT MUCH.
12·24
SCOTT and BORGMAN
I GREW THESE THREE EXTRA HANDS TODAY, BUT THAT'S ABOUT IT.
OUR NEW YEAR'S EVE HUG SHOULD BE INTERESTING.
YOU ALWAYS LOOK ON THE BRIGHT SIDE.

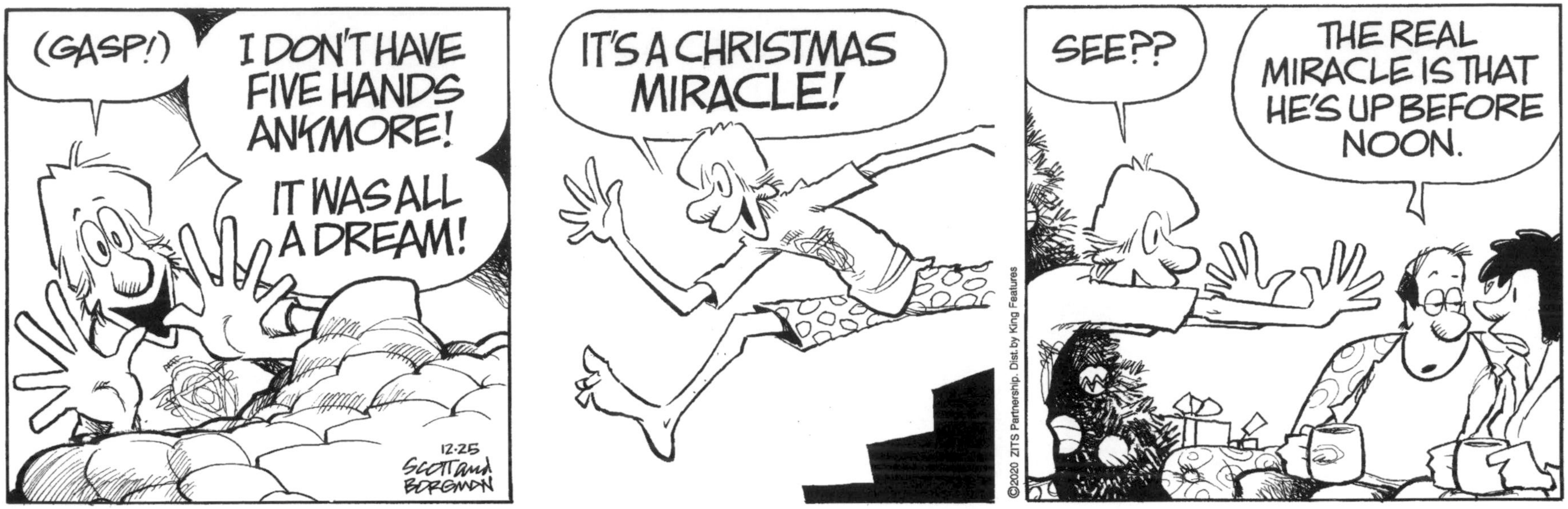
(GASP!)
I DON'T HAVE FIVE HANDS ANYMORE!
IT WAS ALL A DREAM!
12-25
SCOTT and BORGMAN
IT'S A CHRISTMAS MIRACLE!
©2020 ZITS Partnership. Dist. by King Features
SEE??
THE REAL MIRACLE IS THAT HE'S UP BEFORE NOON.

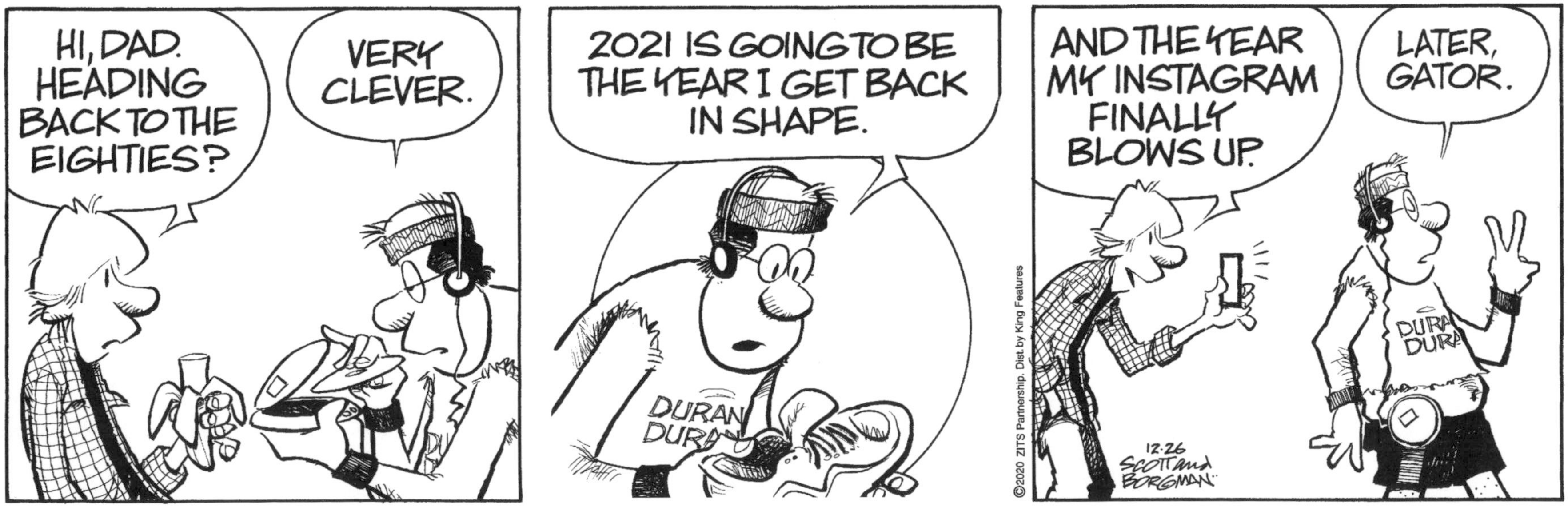
HI, DAD. HEADING BACK TO THE EIGHTIES?
VERY CLEVER.
2021 IS GOING TO BE THE YEAR I GET BACK IN SHAPE.
DURAN DURA
©2020 ZITS Partnership. Dist. by King Features
AND THE YEAR MY INSTAGRAM FINALLY BLOWS UP.
LATER, GATOR.
12-26
SCOTT and BORGMAN

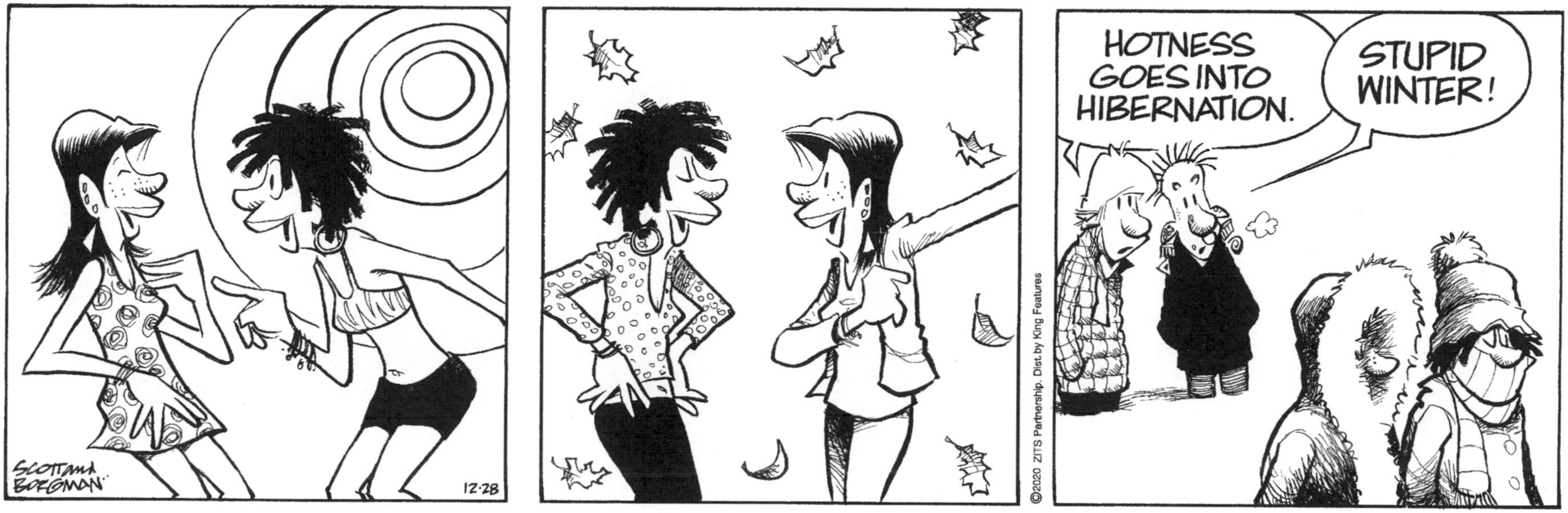
SCOTT and BORGMAN
12·28
HOTNESS GOES INTO HIBERNATION.
STUPID WINTER!
©2020 ZITS Partnership. Dist.by King Features

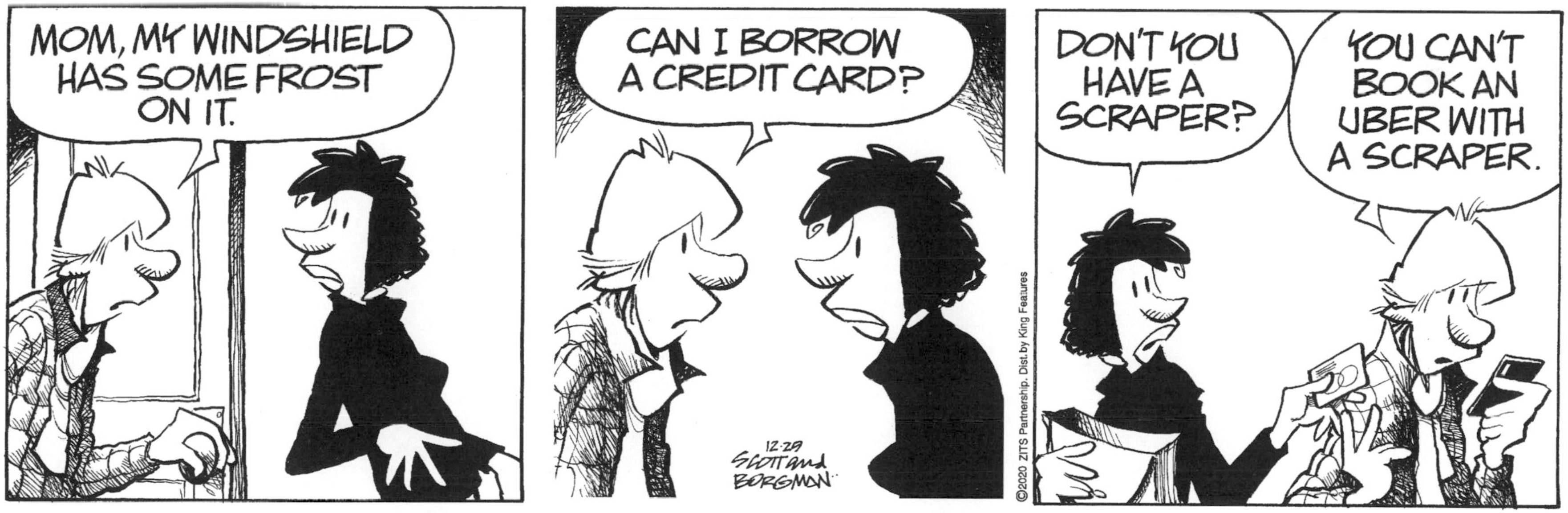
MOM, MY WINDSHIELD HAS SOME FROST ON IT.
CAN I BORROW A CREDIT CARD?
12·29
SCOTT and BORGMAN
DON'T YOU HAVE A SCRAPER?
YOU CAN'T BOOK AN UBER WITH A SCRAPER.
©2020 ZITS Partnership. Dist.by King Features

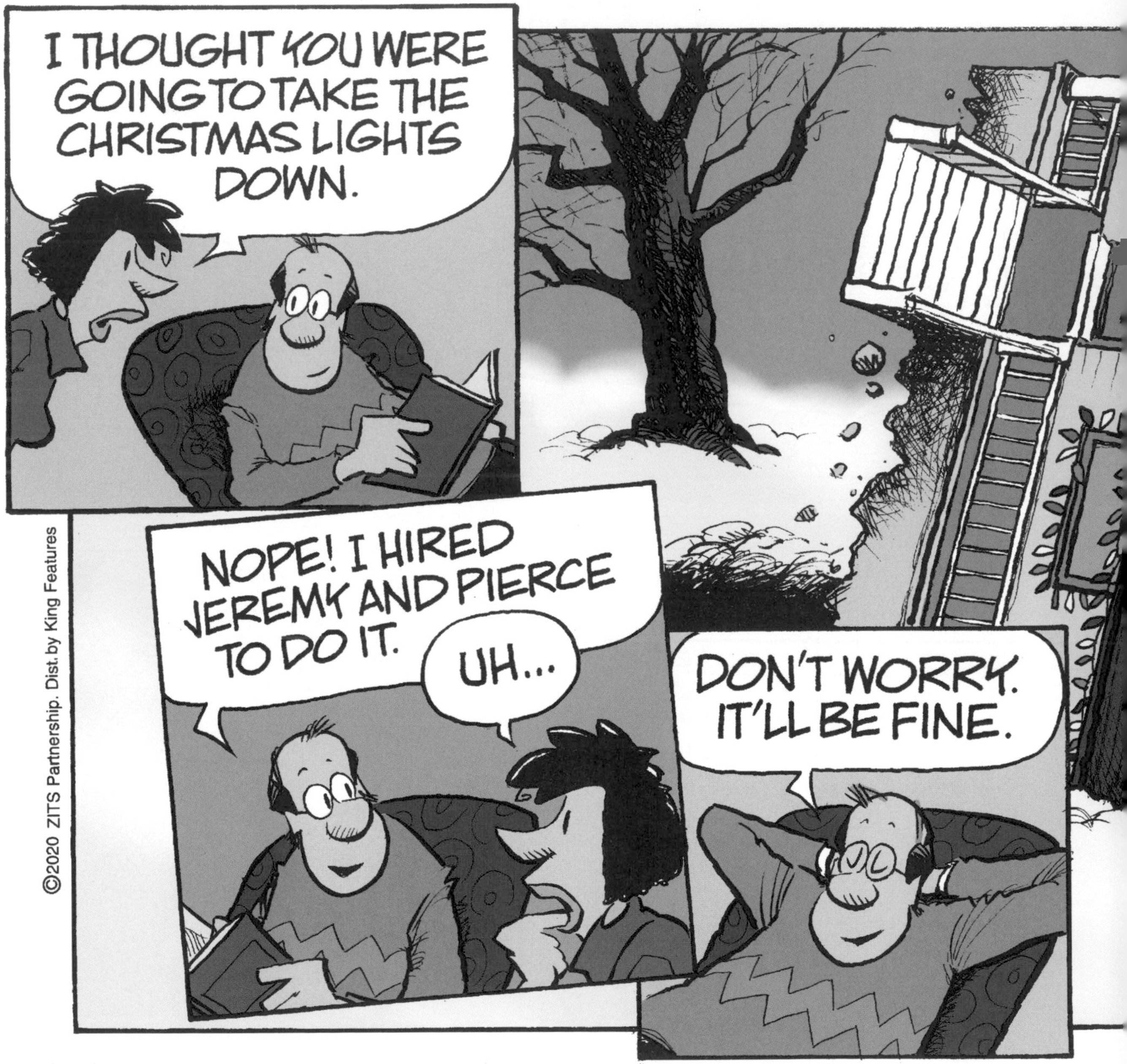
I THOUGHT YOU WERE GOING TO TAKE THE CHRISTMAS LIGHTS DOWN.
NOPE! I HIRED JEREMY AND PIERCE TO DO IT.
UH...
DON'T WORRY. IT'LL BE FINE.
©2020 ZITS Partnership. Dist. by King Features

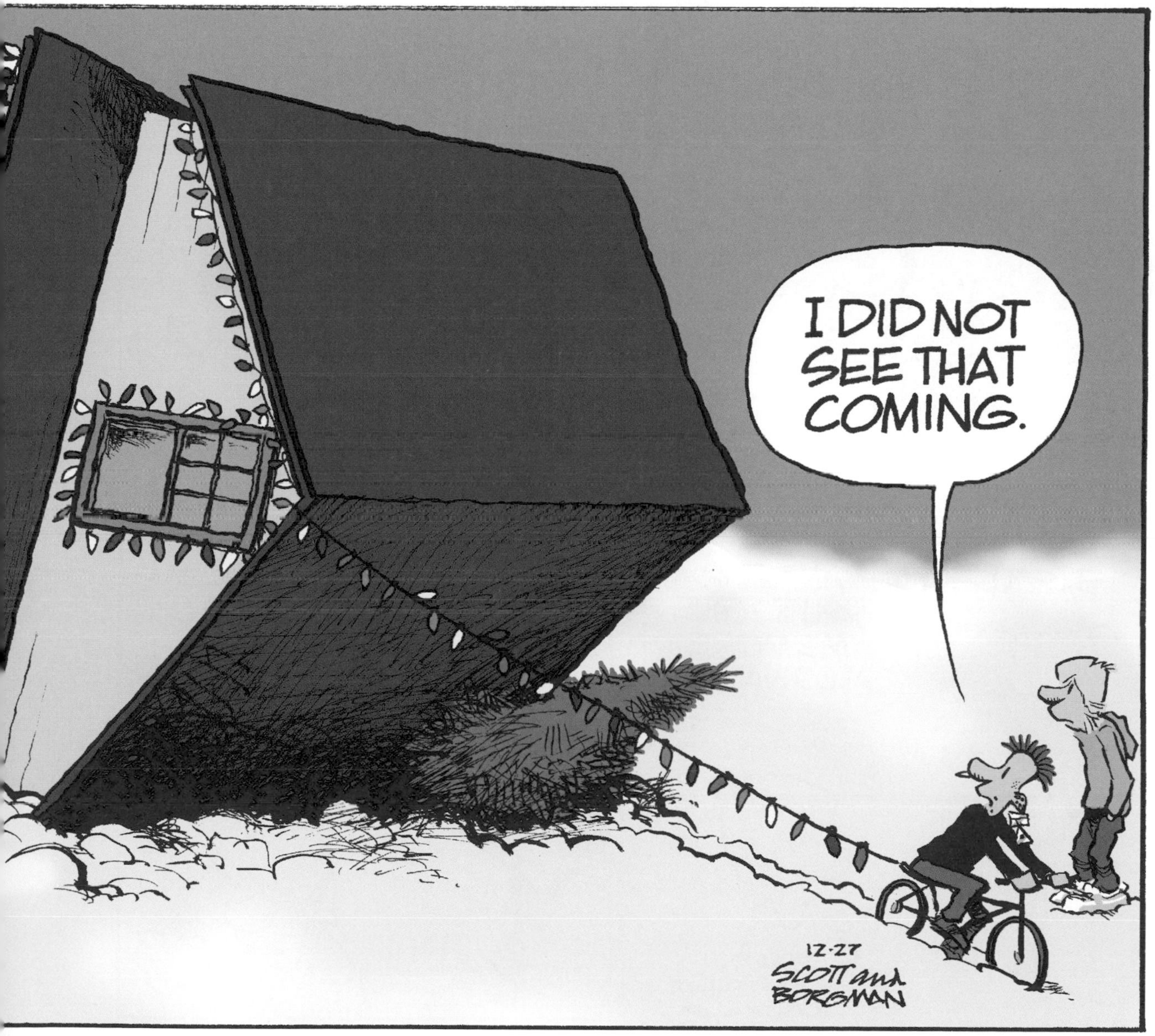
I DID NOT SEE THAT COMING.
12-27
SCOTT and BORGMAN

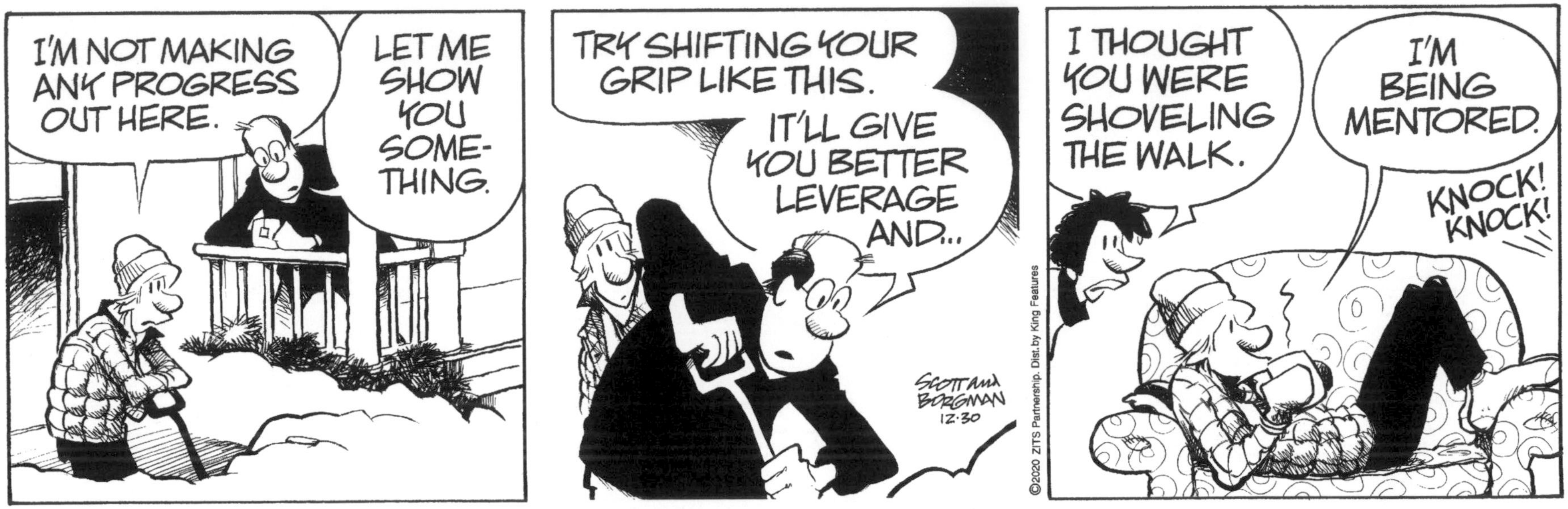
I'M NOT MAKING ANY PROGRESS OUT HERE.
LET ME SHOW YOU SOME-THING.
TRY SHIFTING YOUR GRIP LIKE THIS.
IT'LL GIVE YOU BETTER LEVERAGE AND...
SCOTT AND BORGMAN 12·30
©2020 ZITS Partnership. Dist. by King Features
I THOUGHT YOU WERE SHOVELING THE WALK.
I'M BEING MENTORED.
KNOCK! KNOCK!

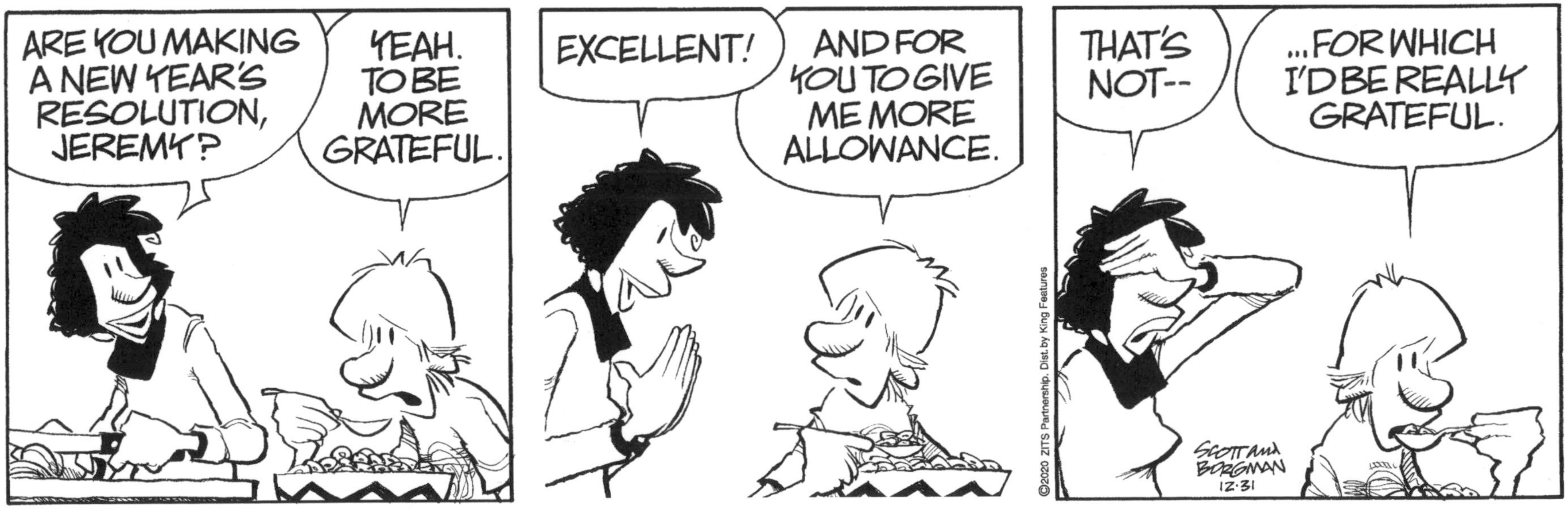
ARE YOU MAKING A NEW YEAR'S RESOLUTION, JEREMY?
YEAH. TO BE MORE GRATEFUL.
EXCELLENT!
AND FOR YOU TO GIVE ME MORE ALLOWANCE.
©2020 ZITS Partnership. Dist. by King Features
THAT'S NOT--
...FOR WHICH I'D BE REALLY GRATEFUL.
SCOTT AND BORGMAN 12·31

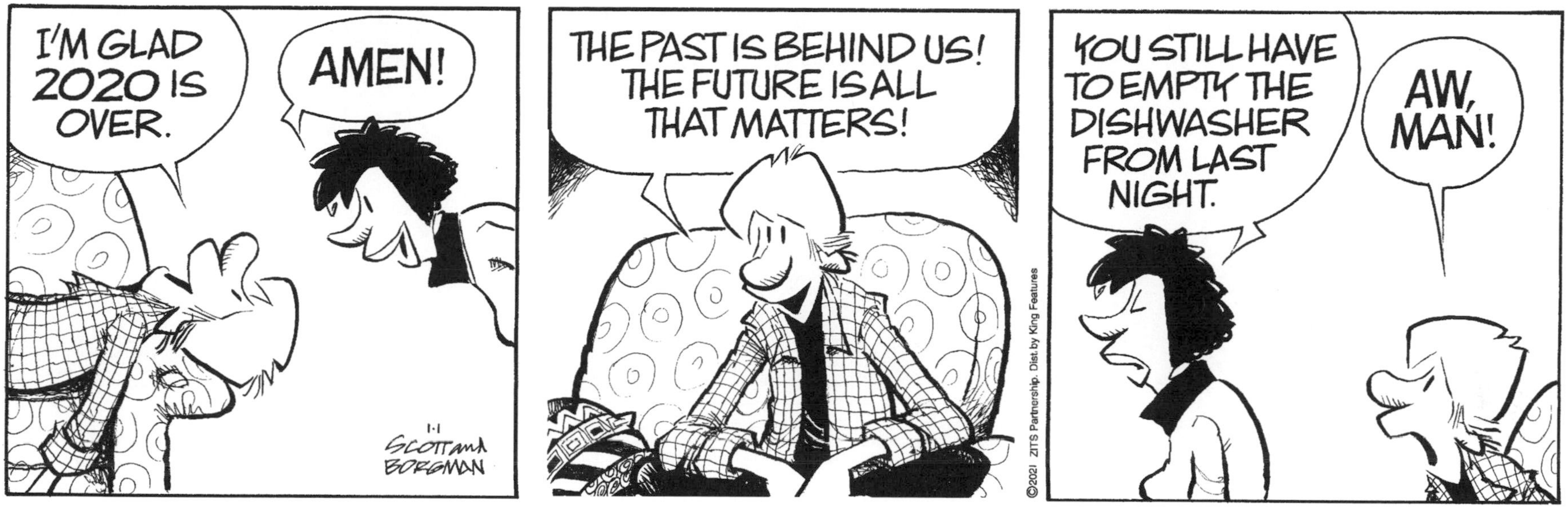
I'M GLAD 2020 IS OVER.
AMEN!
1·1
SCOTT and BORGMAN
THE PAST IS BEHIND US! THE FUTURE IS ALL THAT MATTERS!
©2021 ZITS Partnership. Dist. by King Features
YOU STILL HAVE TO EMPTY THE DISHWASHER FROM LAST NIGHT.
AW, MAN!

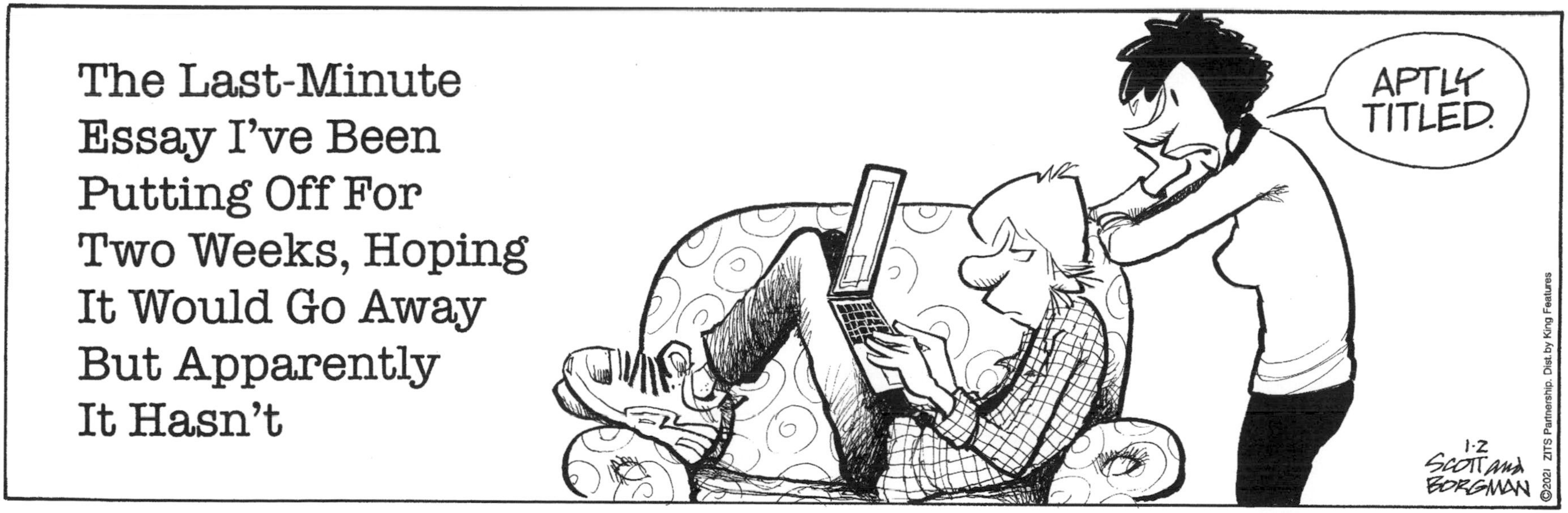
The Last-Minute Essay I've Been Putting Off For Two Weeks, Hoping It Would Go Away But Apparently It Hasn't
APTLY TITLED.
1·2
SCOTT and BORGMAN
©2021 ZITS Partnership. Dist. by King Features

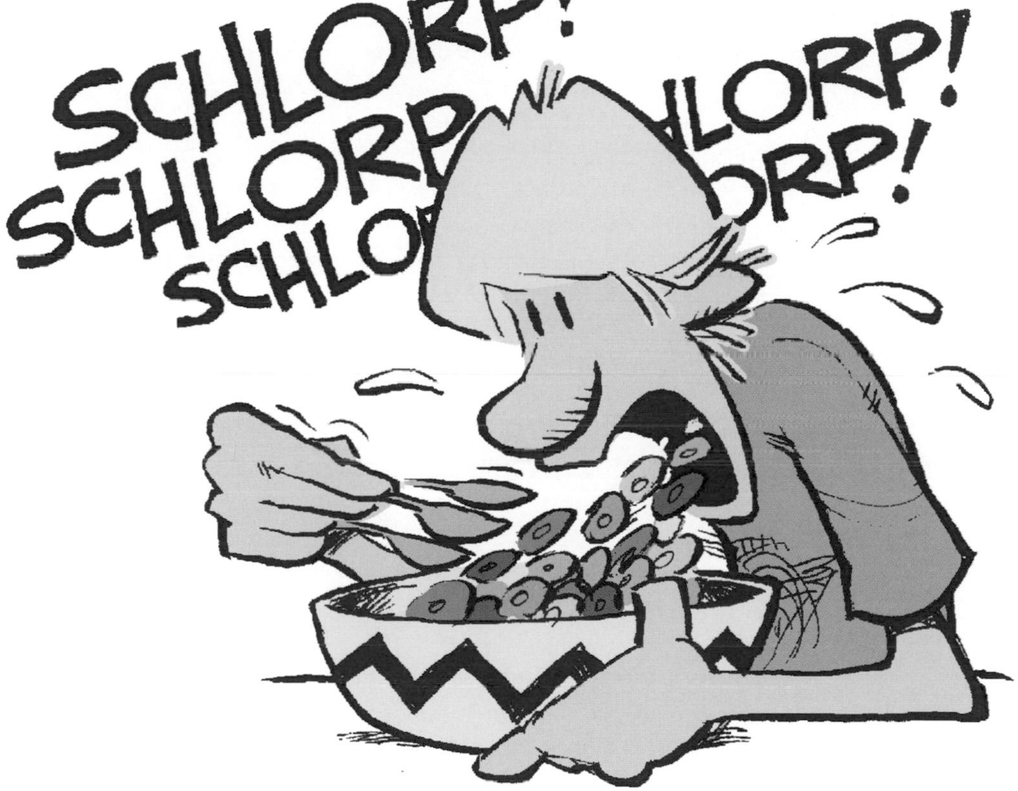
SCHLORP!
SCHLORP
SCHLO
LORP!
ORP!

Zits® is syndicated internationally by King Features Syndicate, Inc.
For information, write King Features Syndicate, Inc., 300 West Fifty-Seventh Street, New York, New York 10019.

Andrews McMeel Publishing
a division of Andrews McMeel Universal
1130 Walnut Street, Kansas City, Missouri 64106
www.andrewsmcmeel.com

22 23 24 25 26 SDB 10 9 8 7 6 5 4 3 2 1

ISBN: 978-1-5248-7564-0

Library of Congress Control Number: 2022933528

Editor: Lucas Wetzel
Art Director: Holly Swayne
Production Manager: Chuck Harper
Production Editor: Julie Railsback

ATTENTION: SCHOOLS AND BUSINESSES

Andrews McMeel books are available at quantity discounts with bulk purchase for educational, business, or sales promotional use
For information, please e-mail the Andrews McMeel Publishing Special Sales Department: specialsales@amuniversal.com.

zitscomics.com • facebook.com/zitscomics • instagram.com/zitsguys